SPORTS LAW

SPORTS LAW
Cases, Documents, and Materials

Walter T. Champion, Jr.
Texas Southern University School of Law

ASPEN
PUBLISHERS

111 Eighth Avenue, New York, NY 10011
www.aspenpublishers.com

ISBN 0-7355-3659-7

2 3 4 5 6 7 8 9 0

Library of Congress Cataloguing-in-Publication Data
Champion, Walter T.
    Sports law: cases, documents, and materials / Walter T. Champion, Jr.
        p. cm
    Includes index.
    ISBN 0-7355-3659-7 (alk. paper)
    1. Sports—Law and legislation—United States. 2. Athletes—Legal status, laws, etc.—United States. I. Title.

KF3989.C474 2005
344 73′099—dc22

2004057396

About Aspen Publishers

Aspen Publishers, headquartered in New York City, is a leading information provider for attorneys, business professionals, and law students. Written by preeminent authorities, our products consist of analytical and practical information covering both U.S. and international topics. We publish in the full range of formats, including updated manuals, books, periodicals, CDs, and online products.

Our proprietary content is complemented by 2,500 legal databases, containing over 11 million documents, available through our Loislaw division. Aspen Publishers also offers a wide range of topical legal and business databases linked to Loislaw's primary material. Our mission is to provide accurate, timely, and authoritative content in easily accessible formats, supported by unmatched customer care.

To order any Aspen Publishers title, go to *www.aspenpublishers.com* or call 1-800-638-8437.

To reinstate your manual update service, call 1-800-638-8437.

For more information on Loislaw products, go to *www.loislaw.com* or call 1-800-364-2512.

For Customer Care issues, e-mail CustomerCare@aspenpublishers.com; call 1-800-234-1660; or fax 1-800-901-9075.

Aspen Publishers
A Wolters Kluwer Company

To Wally and Chuck

SUMMARY OF CONTENTS

CONTENTS

PREFACE

Sports law, a relatively new discipline, is a hodgepodge of already established, clearly defined legal areas, such as contracts, torts, labor law, antitrust, tax, financial planning, and constitutional law. How does one make coherent this somewhat shapeless batch of legal principles, joined together solely by their relationship to a sporting event that then triggers a specific legal discussion? I look at it from the perspective of the hypothetical sports law practitioner, who usually needs general guidance in *all* areas that can be arguably called "sports law." Thus, I have sought to write a true survey of sports law that weaves the disparate principles into an integrated whole.

To that end, in addition to the major cases, this book provides excerpts from real-world documents, including contracts, collective bargaining agreements, waivers, and statutes, within the discussion of the appropriate topics. Questions and Discussion sections also help tie together the material and motivate students to analyze it.

This overview of sports law introduces future practitioners to the various legal concepts and documents that they will encounter in their professional careers as NCAA Compliance Officers, agents, professionals, personal injury attorneys, athletic directors, and sports administrators. I hope that students will find it useful—even after the course—as a guide to the applicable law that tracks sports.

Walter T. Champion, Jr.

November 2004

ACKNOWLEDGMENTS

I owe thanks to people from several periods of my life who encouraged me to become involved in sports and sports law.

My journey in sports law began in 1957, when my late father, "Ace" Champion, urged me as a six-year-old to dive under the turnstiles at Philadelphia's Connie Mack Stadium to avoid paying the fifty-cent entrance fee. Little did I know that that game would see the much-lamented, late Hall of Fame icon Richie Ashburn distribute foul balls at an alarming rate, with one knocking out an elderly, white-haired woman, necessitating stretcher assistance. But, unfortunately, Richie struck her again while she was on the stretcher. Even as a youngster, I realized that she assumed the first battery but did not assume the second.

My dad, of course, continued to be key in my development, and my mother arranged holiday celebrations around baseball games. As a law school student, I was privileged to help sports agent Steve Kauffman develop a disciplinary appeal of one of his athletes; I met Howard "Hoot" Gibson, editor of the *Pennsylvania Law Reporter*, who hired me as a sports law columnist; and I took a sports law course at Temple University Law School under the tutelage of H. Patrick Swygert, now President of Howard University.

I first taught sports law in 1985, at Texas Southern University, and from the beginning I benefited from the collegial insights of a hard-charging group of sports lawyers who guest-lectured in my classes and later spoke at my continuing education seminars. These attorneys include Randy Hendricks, Oliver Luck, Steve Patterson, Carl Poston, Patrick Thornton, and Steve Underwood.

Additionally, other than my dad, no one triggered my passion for sports law more than John Weistart and Cym Lowell, authors of *The Law of Sports*. Recognition is also due to the Hon. Bernie Snyder, the Philadelphia judge I clerked for, and to Mike Cozzillio and Mark Levinstein, authors of *Sports Law: Cases and Materials*.

From the law school ranks, I'd like to acknowledge James Nafziger (international law) and McKen Carrington (taxes and financial planning). Among my former students, I'd like to mention Rey Ramirez and Maj. Gregory "Scrap"

Simmons. Special thanks go to Carmela Tillman, my secretary; Kary Wilson, my research assistant; and Karim Rand, my reference librarian.

I would like to give special recognition to Nick C. Nichols, who represents the father of sports torts to me. The case he won for Rudy Tomjanovich in that player's lawsuit against the Los Angeles Lakers basketball team launched a sea of change in the legal perception of recreational injuries.

John Eichstadt, lawyer, librarian, and friend, applied his editorial hand to the draft, improving its readability.

On an even more personal note, I receive succor and support from my family, including my sons, Walter III and Charles; Charles's godfather, Ricky Anderson, and the extended Anderson clan; my sister, Deb, and her family; and, of course, my mother, Elizabeth.

INTRODUCTION

When you hear "sports law," what comes to mind? A-Rod's 2004 trade to the New York Yankees? The May 2004 two-year suspension of U.S. sprinter and Olympic hopeful Kelli White for using performance-enhancing drugs? The 1987 NFL players' strike?

Sports law involves these issues and many others, in both professional and amateur sports. And although the differences between these two categories of sports — professional and amateur — seem clear enough at first glance, they are increasingly difficult to discern. Typically, athletes who are "paid to play" are professionals. Shaquille O'Neal is a professional; so is Tiger Woods. Their remuneration (excepting endorsements) is tied directly to their participation in a particular sport — a direct pay-for-play system.

Amateur athletes then, it stands to reason, are those who are not paid to play or compete. However, the 2000 Olympics, the American women's soccer team was composed of many professionals. Likewise, America's so-called Dream Team in Olympic basketball was not only composed of NBA professionals but also was the best basketball team ever put together. In the recent past, the hazy area between amateur and professional sports was best exemplified by the world class track athlete Carl Lewis who, although an amateur, still made millions of dollars. He maintained his amateur standing (that is, he was not deemed to be a "professional") because the organizational body that controlled his sport defined what an amateur was for that particular sport and for that particular athlete.

A. PROFESSIONAL SPORTS: AN OVERVIEW

For years the professional sport that defined American culture was baseball. The professional athletes of baseball became household names because of their exemplary achievements. The resulting dynasty created a sports idyll of sorts that elevated professional athletes to a near immortal status.[1] The

---

[1] *See generally* Davis, *What Is Sports Law?*, 11 Marq. Sports L.J. 211 (2001).

mystical baseball movie *Field of Dreams* creates a fertile loam where reality and dreams are indistinct:

> Ray, people will come, Ray. They'll come to Iowa for reasons they can't even fathom. They'll turn up your driveway not knowing for sure why they're doing it. They'll arrive at your door as innocent as children longing for the past. Of course, "we won't mind if you look around," you'll say, "it's only twenty dollars per person." They'll pass over the money without thinking about it, for it's money they have, and peace they lack. Then they'll walk out to the bleachers and sit in their shirt sleeves on a perfect afternoon. They'll find they have reserved seats somewhere along one of the baselines where they sat when they were children, and cheered their heroes and they'll watch the game and it will be as if they dipped themselves in magic waters. The memories will be so thick that they'll have to brush them away from their faces. People will come, Ray. The one constant through all the years, Ray, has been baseball. America has rolled by like an army of steamrollers; it's been erased like a blackboard, rebuilt and erased again. But baseball has marked the time. This field, this game, is a part of our past, Ray. It reminds us of all that once was good and could be again. Oh, people will come, Ray, people will most definitely come.[2]

These sorts of beliefs have created an almost mythic relationship between sports and the ethos of America. They have also contributed to certain present-day attitudes about professional athletes. Each athlete is considered unique, and because of that the law that binds and controls athletes' professional relationships are similarly unique.

When an athlete enters into an employment relationship for pay, he or she signs an employment contract that describes the duties and obligations of each signee. The more closely the athlete suits the needs of the team, the better his ability to negotiate the specific terms of the contract. The contract itself is usually sacrosanct and is not subject to much alteration. The athlete's ability to negotiate is reflected primarily in the amount of money that is stipulated in the contract and the addendums—such as signing bonuses, guaranteed contracts, and attendance clauses—that are added on to the back of the agreement. In the 1980s the best example was Jim Kelly, quarterback for the United States Football League's Houston Gamblers. Kelly had added to his contract two special clauses: one that provided him with a new sports car every month and another, the so-called escalator clause, that automatically increased his salary if a higher-paid quarterback entered the league.

Many clauses are quite unique and show the distinctiveness of the athlete-team relationship. For example, many sports contracts include a morality clause or, in the case of one sport, the "best interest of baseball" clause. These clauses stipulate that the players must conform to certain standards of behavior. In basketball contracts, dangerous sports such as hang gliding are forbidden. An especially important clause to management is one that allows a team to gain an injunction to enjoin a player from jumping to

---

[2] James Earl Jones as Terrance Mann in *Field of Dreams*, a Phil Alden Robinson film (Universal City Studios, Inc.; a Gordon Co. Production; written for the screen and directed by Phil Alden Robinson; 1989).

another team.[3] Collateral documents such as the collective bargaining agreement and the league's constitution and bylaws are also subsumed into the agreement by way of an incorporation clause.

Employment contracts for professional team sports created the necessity for sports agents. The agent has a fiduciary relationship with the athlete and must negotiate the athlete's team employment contract in good faith.[4] The agent must also make a full and complete disclosure of all areas of potential conflicts of interest and must receive prior consent from the athlete if representation is continued after this disclosure.[5] The contract that solidifies the relationship between agent and athlete is called the Standard Representation Contract. This contract and relationship is governed to a certain extent by state regulation and the professional sports unions in the major team sports (baseball, football, hockey, and basketball).

In professional sports, although the team-athlete relationship is controlled by the employment contract, the league-union relationship is controlled by the collective bargaining agreement, which espouses another parallel relationship that falls under the auspices of the National Labor Relations Act.[6] Collective bargaining is the process under the act where both parties participate in the give-and-take of collective negotiations. Their obligation is to bargain in good faith; failure to do so is an unfair labor practice. Under certain circumstances, the parties in this process can resort to concerted actions: strikes for the players, lockouts for the owners. The fuel that drives the collective bargaining process is those procedures in the agreement that stipulate arbitration and mediation as the only remedy to solve problems that arise over grievances. In professional baseball, arbitration is even available to solve differences in salaries.[7]

The process that polices the professional team sports is federal antitrust law. The Sherman Antitrust Act[8] makes illegal every combination in the form of a conspiracy that restrains interstate commerce. When there are alleged conflicts in any of the various documents that control the many relationships in sports, antitrust is the remedy of choice in attempting to curb the alleged imbalance. It is necessary because sports itself is honestly described by the oxymoron of "competitive cohesion." Organized sports must have honest competition to be attractive, but then again, to be organized they must also promulgate rules so as to assure fair play, arrange schedules, punish wrongdoers, and the like. It is this inherent need to be cohesive and organized that has prompted sports organizations and associations to often run afoul of the antitrust laws.[9]

However, a variety of exemptions for sports has nearly swallowed the antitrust laws. The most notable exemption is the so-called nonstatutory

---

[3] *Philadelphia Ball Club v. Lajoie,* 51 A.973 (Pa. 1902).
[4] *Zinn v. Parrish,* 461 F. Supp. 11 (N.D. Ill. 1977), *revd.* 582 F.2d 1282 (7th Cir. 1978), *app. after rem.,* 644 F.2d (7th Cir. 1981).
[5] *Detroit Lions, Inc. v. Argovitz,* 580 F. Supp. 542 (E.D. Mich. 1984).
[6] 29 U.S.C §§151-166.
[7] Champion, *Sports Law in a Nutshell* 44-51 (2d ed. 2000).
[8] 15 U.S.C. §§1 *et seq.*
[9] Champion, *Fundamentals of Sports Law* §26.1 at 456 *et seq.* (1990).

labor exemption, which is a spillover from the statutory exemptions of the Clayton Act[10] and the Norris-LaGuardia Act,[11] which allow unions to enter into agreements to eliminate competition. The nonstatutory labor exemption allows an exemption for agreements that are the product of good-faith and arm's-length negotiation between the union and the employer on the mandatory subjects of collective bargaining.[12] The protection of this exemption continues after the expiration of the collective bargaining agreement and even continues after the parties have reached impasse.[13]

Finally, a constant reality of professional sports is the possibility of injury. Yet injury cannot always be taken for granted. During a professional football game in 1973, when the roles of the tailback and cornerback changed after an interception, the appeals court found that the principles of law governing the infliction of injuries must not be disregarded merely because an individual's injury occurs during a professional football game.[14] The court held that the tailback

> acted impulsively and in the heat of combat in intentionally striking an opposing player on the back of the head during a professional football game and that the appropriate standard was recklessness, rather than assault and battery, since it could be said that [he] . . . intended the act and that he did intend to inflict the serious injury which resulted from the blow.[15]

This opinion brought professional football back into the standard orbit of recovery for tortious injuries and is similarly useful if the injured participant is involved in amateur sports.

B. AMATEUR SPORTS: AN OVERVIEW

Because amateur sports does not involve the use of employment contracts, many of the legal issues discussed above do not appear in amateur settings. This is not to say, however, that amateur sports is without its share of interesting legal entanglements. In fact, it shares one important legal concept with professional sports: Tort law forms the basis of actionable suits for injuries.

In negligence, one needs a duty, a breach of that duty, causation, and damages to be successful. Historically, not only have teams, leagues, other athletic participants, colleges, and the like been able to use powerful defenses to thwart actions for injuries, there has also existed an all-pervasive attitude that in amateur sports one had by definition assumed and essentially volunteered for whatever results occurred whether they were reasonably anticipated or not. As it was succinctly opined by Justice Cardozo, "the timorous may stay at home."[16] In short, "the law did not want to place an

---

[10] 15 U.S.C. §§12 *et seq.*
[11] 29 U.S.C. §§101-115.
[12] Champion, *Fundamentals of Sports Law* §26.2 at 259-260 (1990).
[13] *Powell v. National Football League*, 888 F.2d 559 (8th Cir. 1989).
[14] *Hackbart v. Cincinnati Bengals*, 601 F.2d 516 (10th Cir. 1979).
[15] Champion, *Fundamentals of Sports Law* §7.2 at 133.34 (1990).
[16] *Murphy v. Steeplechase Amusement Co.*, 166 N.E. 173 (N.Y. 1929).

unreasonable burden on active participation in sports. One was assumed to voluntarily embrace any danger that might occur in sporting activity."[17] But, just like the *Hackbart* case for professional football, some cases have not followed Cardozo's maxim and instead have loosened the standards for recovery for injuries in amateur sports. Eventually, courts realized that athletic competition does not exist in a vacuum: "some other restraints of civilization must accompany every athlete on the playing field."[18] Still, injuries to participants as a result of contact with other participants must be based on something more than mere negligence. Gross misconduct must be alleged, and the injury must be the result of unsportsmanlike conduct[19] or a violation of a safety rule.[20]

Another aspect of negligence in amateur sports is the possibility of injury to a spectator. The courts, for example, have taken judicial notice of the fact that injuries from foul balls in baseball are impliedly assumed as a normal and incidental risk to attendance at a baseball game.[21] This no-duty rule applies only to common, frequent, and expected risks; the facility must still protect spectators from foreseeably dangerous conditions not inherent to the activity. Injuries that result from the negligence of schools and their employees may also be actionable. The key element in ascertaining the school district's liability is the determination of whether a duty exists. Coaches can also be liable in their own right for actions or inactions that cause injury. Like coaches, referees can also be, but very rarely are, held accountable for injuries that occur to participants under their supervision.

Many times injured athletes cannot recover because of the doctrine of assumption of risk. It is a voluntary assumption, either expressed or implied, of a known and appreciated risk. "A participant or spectator who assumes the risk created by the conduct of another cannot recover when harm in fact occurs."[22] One form of expressed assumption of risk is the waiver, or release from liability, that many times participants are obligated to sign before participation in an event or program (for example, a health club waiver, pit crew waiver, or release from liability for renting skis). Generally courts favor warnings but disfavor waivers. However, under certain circumstances, the courts do find them valid: they "must be nonambiguous, particular as to the wording . . . [of] liability, not against public policy, not intimate condemnation of gross negligence, and not allow results that . . . indicate a large disparity in bargaining power."[23]

Finally, the key to pure amateur sports is the question of eligibility. There are various organizations such as high school athletic associations, the National Collegiate Athletic Association, and the United States Olympic Committee that police and regulate either groups of athletes or individual athletes who participate in particular sports.

---

[17] Champion, *Sports Law in a Nutshell* 71-72 (2d ed. 2000).
[18] *Nabozny v. Barnhill*, 334 N.E.2d 258 (Ill. App. 1975).
[19] *Bourque v. Duplechin*, 331 So. 2d 40 (La. App. 1976).
[20] *Nabozny v. Barnhill*, 334 N.E.2d 258 (Ill. App. 1975).
[21] *Schentzel v. Philadelphia National League Club*, 96 A.2d 181 (Pa. Super. 1953).
[22] Champion, *Sports Law in a Nutshell* 156 (2d ed. 2000).
[23] *Id.* at 172.

Eligibility is the decision by the athletic governing body of whether a particular athlete or team is eligible to participate in a specific sport or a specific event. Establishing eligibility under a particular rule or by law is the province of the applicable governing association. The question is whether a denial of eligibility is a violation of that participant's constitutional or civil rights. An athlete's right to participate may be protected by the constitutional guarantees of due process and equal protection.[24]

Two other ways that the eligibility to participate is restricted is through the Amateur Sports Act of 1978 and by the Americans with Disabilities Act. The latter was promulgated to prohibit employment discrimination against individuals with real or perceived disabilities and covers professional sports and (probably) college teams.

Perhaps the most obvious way of restricting eligibility is based on sex. In an attempt to give females the same athletic opportunities as men in college, a "gender-equity" movement began in the 1980s: "equal money for both male and female collegiate sports."[25]

---

[24] *Id.* at 207.
[25] *Id.* at 275.

2
CONTRACTS

The legal glue that holds the employment relationship together between athlete and team is contracts. A valid contract is formed when both parties intend the act of signing to be the last act in the formation of a valid contract. Contracts in sports define the rights and responsibilities of the various participants in the business of professional sports.

Sports Contracts Are Different because the money is typically staggering, the terms are unusual and are often offered on a take-it-or-leave-it basis, the length of time is usually relatively short, the maintenance of excellent physical condition is emphasized and the participants are being paid as entertainers who are playing a game.

Contract **Formation** in sports is determined by the same principles as in more standard contracts. In evaluating the validity of a contract, there must be an offer and offeree, consideration, and a proper acceptance.

The **Standard Player's Contract** (SPK) is the standardized agreement between athlete and team. It is an employment contract that specifies the player's rights. The SPK states that the player has unique skills and that the team controls the activities of the player. The SPK is used in the major team sports and is usually a part of the collective bargaining agreement. There is little flexibility in its terms, and its signing is a prerequisite to compliance.

Specialty Clauses are added to a SPK if the player has the relative bargaining strength to demand them. These clauses include signing bonuses, option clauses, no-cut clauses, and various incentive bonuses. Collateral agreements also modify contracts through their inclusion by way of an incorporation clause; examples are collective bargaining agreements and the league constitution and bylaws.

Terminations, Assignments, and Remedies are methods to end, change, or satisfy potential contract disputes. A club must act within its rights when it terminates a contract; if it does not, the termination represents a breach of contract. An assignment of a player's contract occurs when the athlete is traded to another team. Remedies for a breach of contract include money damages, restitution, or specific performance.

Contract **Defenses** are posited when there is an alleged breach of contract; typical defenses for sports contracts include unclean hands, unconscionability, and mutuality.

Negotiating the Contract is usually the prerogative of agents who use their talents to maximize the remunerations for their clients. Although the SPK as a document is inflexible, there are still many ways to flesh out the contract in an attempt to make the best deals for clients.

Contracts for **Coaches** are similar to players contracts, but, at least in the college ranks, there are the added caveats of no job security, no standardized contracts, no unions, and compensation packages.

A. WHY SPORTS CONTRACTS ARE DIFFERENT

Sports contracts are different from other contracts. The preeminent contract in sports is the employment contract. Team A hires Ballplayer to play baseball for a period of three years. The contract contains clauses that appear incongruous. For example, when the athlete signs his contract, he might agree to abide by a morality clause or a clause that forbids his participation in certain sports (for example, hang gliding, scuba diving, bungee jumping, or motocross). This strikes the ordinary fan as unconstitutional and a violation of some basic freedoms. When John Rocker signed his employment contract, there was a rather obscure clause that purported to uphold the "best interests of baseball." Unbeknownst to Rocker, he violated that clause when, in an off-season interview, he disparaged gays, immigrants, New York City, and anyone who looked like a punk rocker. This clause allowed the league to punish him for his verbal assault.

These clauses are allowed because every athlete is deemed to be unique. Unlike widgets or a brand new Chevy truck, each contract stipulates that the athlete, no matter how average he may be, possesses unique and irreplaceable skills. Every athlete then must swear that his skills are one of a kind. A reason for this, at least in team sports, is that the courts recognize the fact that there is a certain indefinable, nearly mystical chemistry that exists between teammates. You take one element from the equation, no matter how unremarkable, and the entire team is changed. Sports contracts recognize this synergy of athletics.

In sports employment contracts, another unique feature is the concept of "juice." Juice is the ability to write your own ticket based on unique skills or rampant popularity. The more juice a player possesses, the greater his ability to modify his employment contract by attaching standard modifications (for example, no-cut, no-trade, or attendance clauses) or not-so-standard modifications (for example, Jim Kelly's contract clauses, discussed in Chapter 1). A clear example of an athlete with juice was Napolean Lajoie, America's premier baseball player during the early 1900s.

PHILADELPHIA BALL CLUB V. LAJOIE

51 A. 973 (Pa. 1902)

The defendant in this case contracted to serve the plaintiff as a baseball player for a stipulated time. During that period he was not to play for any other club. He violated his agreement, however, during the term of his engagement, and, in disregard of his contract, arranged to play for another and a rival organization. The plaintiff . . . sought to restrain him during the period covered by the contract. The court below refused an injunction, holding that to warrant the interference prayed for the defendant's services must be unique, extraordinary, and of such a character as to render it impossible to replace him; so that his breach of contract would result in irreparable loss to the plaintiff. In the view of the court, the defendant's qualifications did not measure up to this high standard. The trial court was also of the opinion that the contract was lacking in mutuality, for the reason that it gave plaintiff an option to discharge defendant on 10 days notice, without a reciprocal right on the part of the defendant.

[However], [w]e have not found any case going to the length of requiring, as a condition of relief, proof of the impossibility of obtaining equivalent service. . . . The Court below finds from the testimony that "the defendant is an expert baseball player in any position; that he has a great reputation as a second baseman; that his place would be hard to fill with as good a player; that his withdrawal from the team would weaken it, as would a withdrawal of any good player, and would probably make a difference in the size of the audiences attending the game." [Lajoie] has become thoroughly familiar with the action and methods of the other players in the club, and his own work is peculiarly meritorious as an integral part of the team work which is so essential. . . . Lajoie is [also] well known, and has great reputation among the patrons of the sport, . . . and was thus a most attractive card for the public. He may not be the sun in the baseball firmament, but he is certainly a bright particular star. . . . [T]he evidence . . . justices the conclusion that [his] . . . services . . . are of such a unique character, and display such a special knowledge, skill, and ability, as renders them of peculiar value . . . , and so difficult of substitution that their loss will produce "irreparable injury." . . . The court cannot compel the defendant to play for the plaintiff, but it can restrain him from playing for another club in violation of his agreement.

Upon careful consideration of the whole case, we are of opinion that the provisions of the contract are reasonable, and that the consideration is fully adequate. The evidence shows no indications of any attempt at overreaching or unfairness. Substantial justice between the parties requires that the court should restrain the defendant from playing for any other club during the term of his contract with the plaintiff. . . . The specifications of error are sustained, and the decree of the court below is reversed, and the bill is reinstated; and it is ordered that the record be remitted to the court below for further proceedings in accordance with this opinion.

The contract of Nap Lajoie, a future Hall of Famer, prohibited him from playing professional baseball with any club other than his current one. This was a part of the consideration for the employer's agreement to pay Lajoie's salary. The injunction was issued since his services were of a unique character, which rendered them of peculiar value to the baseball club. In short, it would be difficult to find a substitute for the services of Napolean Lajoie. (However, the injunction ultimately proved futile since Lajoie was traded to another club in another state and the courts there refused to enforce the injunction.)

The following is an example of a contract from a second-tier professional league. Note how one-sided toward management many of the clauses appear.

SOUTHWEST BASKETBALL LEAGUE CONTRACT

Southwest Basketball League

Agreement . . . between . . . "Club" and . . . the "Player."

NOW THEREFORE, in consideration of the mutual promises hereinafter contained and intending to be legally bound, the parties hereto promise and agree as follows:

1. Term.

The Club hires the Player as a skilled basketball player for a term of ____ years. The Player's employment during any year covered by this contract shall include attendance at any training camp, playing the games scheduled for the Club's team during any schedule season of the League, playing all exhibition games scheduled by the Club during and prior to any schedule season, playing (if invited to participate) in any of the League's All-Star games and attending every event conducted in association with such All-Star games, and playing the playoff games subsequent to any schedule season.

2. Compensation. . . .
3. Assignment.

The Club may sell, exchange, or assign this contract to any other basketball Club and the Player will perform this contract as if he had entered into it with the other Club. . . .

5. League and Club Rules.

The League or the Club may fine or suspend the Player for violating the by-laws, rules or regulations of the League or any Club. The League or the Club may deduct any fine from payments due or to become due to the Player from the League, the Club or any other professional basketball League or Club.

6. Gambling. . . .
7. Medical Policies.

The Player must report in good physical condition at the time and place fixed by the Club, and keep himself in good physical condition the entire season. If the Club's physician judges that the Player is not in good physical condition or unfit to play basketball, before or during the season, the Player may be suspended. Payment during this suspension may also be suspended. Participation in other sports, or basketball out of season, may harm or destroy the Player's ability and skill as a basketball player or result in injury. Accordingly, the Player will not box, wrestle, ride a motorcycle, race autos, sky dive, hang glide, play football, hockey, lacrosse, soccer, or other athletic sport out of season without the Club's written permission. If the Player is injured as a result of participating in a practice or game played for the Club, the Club will pay the Player's hospitalization and medical expenses.

In the event of such suspension, the salary payable to the Player shall be proportionately reduced by the length of the period of suspension, during which, in the sole judgment of the Club physician . . .

8. Use; Possession. Distribution of Marijuana, Cocaine, Crack Cocaine or Heroin. . . .
9. Termination of Contract.

If the Player alleges that the Club has defaulted on any payment of compensation or that the Club has failed to perform any material obligation, the Player must notify in writing, the League and Club, of the facts surrounding his claim. If neither the Club [nor] the League remedies the situation within 15 days after receiving the notification, the Player may request to terminate this contract. The Club may terminate this contract by giving the Player written notice if at any time the Player fails, refuses or neglects to conform his personal conduct to standards of good citizenship, good moral character and good sportsmanship, to keep himself in good physical condition or to obey the training rules or fails to continue to qualify as a member of the Club. Upon termination, Club will have no further obligation to Player. . . . If at any time during the term of this contract, in the sole opinion of Club, Player's skill, performance, or conduct is not sufficient to enable him to stay on Club's active roster . . . , Club shall have the right to terminate this agreement. Upon such termination, Club shall be liable to Player only for that part of the compensation due him hereunder for the number of days in which he is a member of the Club.

If because of any condition, event or occurrence beyond the control of the League or of the Club, it shall be deemed advisable by the League or Club to suspend or cease or reduce operations, then:

(a) In the event of suspension of operations, the Player shall be entitled only to the proportion of salary due at the date of League or Club suspension.

(b) In the event of cessation of operations, the Player's salary shall be automatically canceled on the date of cessation. The Player will be compensated up to the date of cessation.

(c) Irrespective of whether the Club itself encounters events beyond the control of the League or the Club, if a substantial number of teams in the League reduce, suspend or cease operations so the League is unable to go forward with its schedule, Player's salary and this contract shall be automatically canceled on the date the League became unable to go forward with its schedule, [and] the Player will be compensated up to the date of cancellation.

10. Rights of Publicity and Privacy.

11. Uniforms. . . .

12. Player's Warranties.

The Player warrants and represents and agrees that he is not obligated to play basketball for any other team during this contract's term. The Player agrees not to play basketball for any other team during the term of this contract and during any renewal term of this contract. The Player will indemnify and hold harmless the Club and the League for any claims, actions, demands, losses, costs, expenses, liabilities, penalties and damages, with respect to any other contract the Player has signed to play basketball during this contract's term. The Player will be neatly and fully attired in public and conduct himself on and off the court according to the highest standards of honesty, morality, fair play and sportsmanship. The Player will not do anything detrimental to the best interest of the League or any Club.

Player has represented to the Club and agrees that he has unique skill, experience, knowledge and ability, all of which contribute to his being an exceptional basketball player. Player acknowledges that the services he will perform under this contract cannot be replaced or duplicated by the services of any other Player. In addition, he acknowledges that should the Club lose his services, by any breach or threatened breach of this agreement or any other agreement with the Player, Club cannot and properly or adequately be compensated for this loss by the mere payment of money. [I]n addition to any other remedies that may be available to them judicially or by way of arbitration, [the Club], shall have the right to obtain from any court or arbitrator having jurisdiction, such equitable relief as may be appropriate, including a decree enjoining any further breach of this contract, and enjoining Player from playing basketball for any other person, firm, corporation, team or organization during the term of this agreement. Without limiting the generality of the foregoing, it is agreed the Player shall not be entitled to play for any other team without compensation being paid to the Club in any amount to be agreed between Club and the Player's new team. . . .

21. Approval.

This contract is valid only after it has been signed by the Player and the Club and approved by the League. Within 48 hours of signing this contract, the Player must return it to the Club, who must then forward it to the League office. A contract is approved 10 days after it is received in the League office unless the League disapproves it within the 10-day period. If the League disapproves this contract, it is of no force or effect and the Player and the Club are relieved of the rights and obligations in the document. The Player should call the League office if he does not receive a copy within 20 days after he signed it.

22. Option to Renew.

Upon expiration of this agreement, Club may exercise its option to renew this agreement for an additional season under the same terms set forth herein. To renew this agreement, Club must notify Player of its intention to renew on or before October 1, by mailing written notice to Player at his last known address.

IN WITNESS WHEREOF, the parties have hereunto set their hands and seals, the day and year [as] above written.

QUESTIONS AND DISCUSSION

1. Napoleon Lajoie (3,251 career hits and a .339 lifetime batting average) clearly was not fungible (any one of a million widgets), but other athletes may not possess this Napoleonesque stature. What arguments could you formulate for an average athlete who has a chance to play at a higher salary with another league but is saddled with a contract similar to that of the Southwestern Basketball League?
2. Many sports employment contracts are contracts of adhesion. And although an athlete is not forced to sign a contract, should society draw a line through those clauses that are so unconscionable, objectionable, reprehensible, and unconstitutional that they insult polite society?
3. In *Connecticut Professional Sports Corp. v. Heyman*, 276 F. Supp. 618 (S.D.N.Y. 1967) (excerpted in section F.2), the court held that the contract was too harsh and one-sided to permit equitable enforcement. This is the opposite conclusion that the Pennsylvania Supreme Court found in *Lajoie*. What parts of the contract in *Lajoie* appear too harsh and one sided? *Lajoie* was decided in 1902; *Heyman* in 1967. Would there be a different result with Napolean Lajoie if the same facts were adjudicated in 1970? 2000?
4. In the Southwest Basketball League contract under "21. Approval," it appears that failure to obtain approval within ten days will not in itself void the contract. How could you improve this language so as to make the act of approval a condition precedent to the creation of a binding contract?
5. In earlier versions of the standard player's contract in football, the wording was such that the commissioner's signature signifying approval of the agreement was a condition precedent to the formation of a binding contract. Without the commissioner's approval, the player's signature was merely a counteroffer. Players courting offers from competing leagues would use the lack of the commissioner's signature as a means to relinquish their obligations with the NFL team and pursue a more lucrative contract with another team in another football league. The NFL has tightened up the language so that the failure to obtain the commissioner's signature can no longer be used as a loophole to avoid a player's original contractual obligations.
6. In those older contracts, the failure to obtain the commissioner's signature was deemed a material breach of the agreement pursuant to its contractual language. *See Los Angeles Rams v. Cannon*, 185 F. Supp. 717 (S.D. Cal. 1960) (excerpted in section B). Without the commissioner's signature, the player's agreement was merely a revocable offer. *See Detroit Football Co. v. Robinson*, 186 F. Supp. 993 (E.D. La. 1960) (excerpted in section B).

B. FORMATION

A valid contract is formed only if both the team and the athlete intends the signing of the contract as the last and final act in the creation of a binding agreement. There must be a real and genuine meeting of the minds that culminates in the act of signing. The parties of the contract must be identified. The team, the entity that offers the contract, is the offerer, and the athlete, the one who is offered the contract, the offeree.

Once the parties are identified, the next step is to determine if the athlete has properly accepted the team's offer. If the athlete's response is different from what was offered, then it is a variance and a counteroffer to the team's original offer.

The major contractual vehicle is the standard player's contract (SPK), which is the employment agreement between team and player in the major team sports. This document has evolved through the years and is close to "bullet-proof" status as it stands today. However, in earlier versions, the requirement of the league commissioner's signature for approving the contract was worded in such a way as to be a condition precedent to a binding contract. Therefore, without the commissioner's signed approval, the contract was merely a counteroffer. The lack of this signature was a material breach; therefore, the player's signing was merely a revocable offer.

The *Cannon* and *Robinson* cases are early examples of how contracts were interpreted before the National Football League changed its SPK to reflect a lessened importance to the commissioner's signature approving the contract. Both cases came at a time of interleague rivalry between the National Football League and the American Football League in which there was a fierce competition to sign the best collegiate players.

Los Angeles Rams v. Cannon

185 F. Supp. 717 (S.D. Cal. 1960)

... [P]laintiff prays for an injunction to restrain defendant from playing football for anyone other than plaintiff without the plaintiff's consent during the term of a contract or contracts allegedly entered into by the parties on November 30, 1959.

Defendant denies he ever entered into a contract and further claims fourteen affirmative defenses. The first six allege that defendant merely made an offer which was not accepted prior to revocation. The others, allege fraud and deceit on the part of plaintiff, acting through Pete Rozelle, then the General Manager of the Rams. . . .

The defendant, Billy Cannon, is a remarkable football player who has just finished his collegiate career with Louisiana State University. The last intercollegiate game he participated in was the Sugar Bowl game on January 1, 1960. Prior to that time, he was contacted by telephone by Pete Rozelle, now Commissioner of the National Football League, but who was then General Manager for the Los Angeles Rams. . . .

There is no question about the call being made, but there is serious dispute as to the conversation had. However, we can safely assume that it had to do with football. . . .

The telephone call . . . occurred less that 36 hours before the annual [— NFL draft] in Philadelphia. . . .

The Rams . . . concluded that Billy Cannon was the player . . . they would most like to see on their team. The Rams, by virtue of ten losses and only two wins . . . [were] . . . tied . . . for the first draft choice, . . . the tie was . . . broken by [a coin toss, which they won].

[To the Rams, the first pick] . . . is so valuable that careful steps are undertaken . . . [so] that it is not wasted on a player not willing to play for that team. . . .

Following the press interview Cannon and Rozelle went to Rozelle's hotel room where Cannon signed three sets of National Football Player Contract forms covering the years 1960, 1961 and 1962, and took possession of two checks, one for $10,000 and the other for $500. . . .

Mr. Rozelle . . . left one set of . . . [completed] forms . . . [for] the 1960 season—with then acting Commissioner Mr. Gunsel.

Some two weeks later, Billy Cannon was contacted on behalf of a Mr. K. S. "Bud" Adams, Jr., . . . owner of the Houston Oilers, a football club in the recently formed American Football League (AFL). . . . Cannon met with Mr. Adams and . . . negotiat[ed] . . . a so called personal service contract including the playing of football.

On December 30, 1959, Billy Cannon sent to the Rams a letter . . . announc[ing] that he no longer desired to play for the Rams, purportedly revok[ing] any offer he may have made . . . and returned the two checks . . . uncashed and unendorsed.

Prior thereto, however, it is contended that Mr. Gunsel approved the contract for the 1960 season. . . . [P]laintiff tak[es] the position that [the Commissioner's signature] . . . is an unimportant ministerial act concerning only the League and the Club, while [to] the defendant . . . it is an act absolutely essential to the formation of a contract.

. . . [T]his court [holds that his] . . . [a]pproval is essential to the formation of a contract . . . and . . . is so because the terms of the document make it so. [T]hese forms were furnished by the Rams . . . [and stipulated that] "this agreement shall become valid and binding upon each party hereto only when, as and if it shall be approved by the Commissioner." . . .

This clause is too definite to be ignored. It jumps out at you. The words employed are too strong to permit of ambiguity. Their selection was obviously made with great care so that there would be no dispute about their meaning, and this court attaches to them the only meaning it can—that is, that the agreement shall only become valid and binding if, as and when approved by the Commissioner. . . .

Judgment will be for defendant, with costs. . . .

DETROIT FOOTBALL CO. V. ROBINSON

186 F. Supp. 993 (E.D. La. 1960)

SKELLY WRIGHT, District Judge.

This case is but another round in the sordid fight for football players, a fight which begins before these athletes enter college and follows them through their professional careers. It is a fight characterized by decep-tion, double dealing, campus jumping, secret alumni subsidization, semi-professionalism and professionalism. It is a fight which has produced as part of its harvest this current rash of contract jumping suits. It is a fight which so conditions the minds and heart of these athletes that one day they can agree to play football for a stated amount for one group, only to repudiate that agreement the following day or whenever a better offer comes along. So it was with Johnny Robinson. . . .

On December 2, 1959, Robinson was approached in Baton Rouge by the president of the Detroit Football Company and solicited to join the Lions for the 1960 season. He was offered a salary of $14,500, of which $2,500 would be advanced then and there and $1,000 would be paid on January 1. After some discussion, Robinson executed the tendered form, a "Standard Players Contract," and accepted the tendered advance, in currency. It was understood that in view of the forthcoming Sugar Bowl game, no public mention of the arrangement would be made until after New Year's. Later in December, how-ever, Robinson was contacted by a representative of the "Dallas Texans," a club in the new American Football League. A trip to Dallas followed swiftly and Robinson was persuaded to change his mind and sign up with the new team. On December 29, he so notified the Detroit Lions. He did not then return the cash advance he had received, and about the first of the year, the remaining $1,000 was sent to him. Robinson's "contract" with the Detroit club was pre-sented to the Commissioner of the National Football League on January 6, 1960, and approved by him on January 12 or thereabouts. Subsequently, on January 13, Robinson returned plaintiff's money. The club refused the tender and filed this proceeding to enforce what it says was Robinson's binding under-taking to play for the Lions and no one else.

The initial question is whether the instrument executed by Robinson on December 2 was, from that date, a binding contract, or merely an offer, revoc-able until approved by the League Commissioner. Commissioner's approval might be deemed a mere condition precedent to execution of the con-tract . . . , [or] the transaction can be viewed as an offer by Robinson to which the club responded by conditioning its acceptance on securing the Commissioner's approval, in which event no contract was formed on December 2. In other words, securing the Commissioner's signature might be considered a condition precedent to he very existence of a contract.

To determine which was intended, we . . . look to . . . paragraph 13: "This agreement shall become valid and binding upon each party hereto only when, as and if it shall be approved by the Commissioner."

It is difficult to devise clearer language indicating that no valid or binding contract existed until after the required approval was secured. We must conclude, as have others, interpreting the same clause, that all Robinson executed was an offer which had not yet been unconditionally accepted by the Detroit Football Company when he withdrew it on December 29.

It is of course elementary law that an offer may normally be revoked at any time before it is effectively accepted by communicating notice of such a change of mind to the offeree. The exceptions relating to situations in which the other party has been misled into "changing position" in reliance on a promise are not applicable here. Robinson's failure to return the advance as promptly as he might cannot have prejudiced the Lions in view of his unequivocal communication indicating the revocation of his offer to play for that club. Nor did his initial acceptance of the money prevent his subsequent withdrawal, unless of course, the advance be deemed consideration for an option granted. . . . The $3,500 was not an additional bonus for holding an offer open. As the "contract" makes plain, it was an advance on his anticipated salary, and it must be viewed as given conditionally, on the contingency that a binding contract would later come into existence.

The conclusion then, is that despite its efforts to "sign up" this player, and "bait" him with twenty-five one-hundred dollar bills, Detroit failed to land their fish. His struggle to wriggle off the hook has proved successful. But it might not be amiss to remind Robinson of what Judge Rogers said to Sam Etcheverry in a similar case:

> . . . in four or five, six or eight years, some day your passes are going to wobble in the air, you are not going to find that receiver. If you keep playing around here, with these professionals, and others, and jumping your contracts—you are all right this time, . . . but . . . some day your abilities will be such that (your club) won't even send a twice disbarred attorney from Dogpatch to help you. They sent some dandy ones this time. . . .

Judgment accordingly.

1. Offer

The initial contact comes from the team. The team prepares the original offer, seeks out the services of the athlete, and writes the employment contract. The player shows acceptance by signing the contract. But if the signing is not accompanied by consideration and a withdrawal is forwarded to the team before an acceptance, then the player's signature is merely an authentication of a revocable offer as opposed to the formation of a binding contract. The validity of the offer is solely determined by the intent of the parties.

2. Acceptance

The initial question to be determined when considering if there was a valid acceptance is that of timeliness. That is, was the athlete's acceptance of the contract proffered in a timely manner. Acceptance is not a particularly delineated concept. Acceptance is manifested or indicated by any showing that expresses the athlete's willingness to be bound by the exact terms of the offer.

3. Interpretation

There are many contract terms in sports that are almost inherently ambiguous, or even oxymoronic. These terms should be predefined; otherwise they may be misinterpreted by those folks who do not inherently understand the dynamics of the sport. To determine the meaning of a term, the language must be read in light of all the surrounding circumstances. The precontroversy interpretation that parties place on the contract term is given great weight in the process of deciphering the intent and understanding of the now conflicting parties.

In contract interpretation, earlier contracts between the two parties may be useful. Or, as in the case of Mickey Owen, where the breach occurs after partial performance of the contract, it is useful to look at how the parties actually functioned under the contract.

PASQUEL V. OWEN

186 F.2d 263 (8th Cir. 1950)

This was an action brought . . . to recover damages for the alleged breach of a contract to play baseball in Mexico. Appellee, a professional baseball player, . . . admit[ted] the execution of the contract, . . . but denied that he had breached the contract and affirmatively alleged . . . that appellant had broken the contract by discharging him as manager. . . .

The contract . . . was in writing . . . as follows: "This Agreement, made and entered into this 2nd day of April, 1946, between Jorge Pasquel, President, Mexican Baseball League, . . . and Arnold (Mickey) Malcolm Owen, . . . in return for Mr. Owens's signature [he] will become player-manager of the Torreon Club, . . . in return, . . . he agrees to perform . . . as player-manager . . ."

Following the execution of this contract, defendant, having received $12,500 as a bonus and $15,000 for his fifth year's salary, departed for Mexico . . . where he reported not to the Torreon Club but by mutual consent to the Vera Cruz Club. Without protest or objection he played with the Vera Cruz Club for five or six weeks simply as a player and was then made manager. About July 5, 1946, after being manager for about five weeks, he was relieved as manager. He, however, remained as a player for approximately another month, receiving the compensation provided for in his contract. Late in the afternoon of August 5, 1946, he and his wife suddenly decided to leave Mexico and drove by automobile all the way to the border. . . . Defendant testified that he left Mexico since he was unable to see plaintiff after his removal and he was embarrassed and hurt. . . . [He signed a notice memorializing his removal as manager.] . . .

Did the relieving of defendant of his duties as manager as a matter of law constitute a breach of the contract, warranting defendant in abandoning it? Plaintiff at no time repudiated the contract but on the contrary continued to pay defendant his compensation as provided therein. The contract uses the term "player-manager." It does not, however, indicate whether he was to function as player at all times, or whether the employer might designate when he should act as manager or when he should act as player, or whether he should act in both capacities simultaneously. . . . The contract was susceptible of the construction that it was optional with the employer to designate from time to time in what capacity the defendant should act, whether as player or manager. . . .

The contract is specific in compensation but not specific as to the obligations of the parties with reference to the defendant's duties. The parties apparently by their subsequent action indicated that the mere designation as player-manager was not a vital provision. So far as plaintiff was concerned, there was at most, only a partial breach of the contract as he at no time failed to pay the full consideration agreed upon, and following the alleged breach, defendant made no demand of performance upon him but so far as plaintiff knew, defendant accepted plaintiff's performance of the contract. . . .

But there is still a further reason why we think it could not be said as a matter of law that the defendant upon being relieved of his duties as manager had the right to abandon his contract. The evidence is without dispute not only that defendant had under this contract acted as manager only for a period of some five or six weeks, but it is equally without dispute that after he was relieved from his duties as manager he continued to perform his duties as a player and to receive his compensation as such for a period of four or five weeks. He did not communicate with the plaintiff as he might have done. He registered no complaint so far as the plaintiff knew and he gave no intimation to plaintiff that he was dissatisfied or intended to abandon the contract because of its alleged breach. Certainly strict and full performance of a contract may be waived by either of the parties and where one party entitled to strict performance waives such performance there can be no right to damages for the failure to perform strictly; neither can there be a right in the party so waiving strict performance to abandon the contract. . . . As a matter of law, he waived the alleged breach and hence had no right to abandon it. . . .

We pretermit consideration of other contentions urged by the plaintiff. The judgment appealed from is reversed and the cause remanded with directions to grant a new trial and for further proceedings not inconsistent with this opinion.

QUESTIONS AND DISCUSSION

1. What is the purpose of a secondary approval by another entity? What is more important, the intent of the parties or the specific wording?
2. The relative importance of the commissioner's approval clause has decreased in significance since *Cannon* and *Robinson*. In both those cases, a fledgling league was attempting to steal contracts from a more established league (a bidding war). The players used the language in the approval clause to jump contracts and acquire a better deal; essentially the language was a tool to secure better contracts. What language could be used to thwart this practice, especially when it is a recognized fact that a bidding war is brewing?
3. Note that Pete Rozelle dirtied his hands by attempting to sign Billy Cannon before the Sugar Bowl and the termination of his NCAA eligibility.

4. Contracts once frequently contained specific language requiring the approval of the commissioner or the approval of some other third-party entity. Identifying the exact offerer and offeree thus became difficult and abtruse. *See Cannon* and *Robinson. See also International Filter Co. v. Conroe Gin, Ice & Light Co.,* 277 S.W. 631 (Tex. Commn. App. 1925).
5. The Rams argued unsuccessfully that the bonus check paid to Billy Cannon was sufficient consideration to secure an option. The Court rejected this argument on the basis that the money was paid conditionally and did not complete the option.
6. Was the judge in *Pasquel v. Owen* an expert in baseball, or was he naive? Should there be a special sports court? Should knowledge of the sport and the "real" intent of the parties be the deciding element in interpreting the niceties of ambiguous terms in sports contracts? Mickey Owen was an established major league ballplayer who was nearing the end of a storied career and wanted to shift to the managerial side; the Pasquel brothers and their Mexican Baseball League was a fledgling league ensconced in a bidding war. Perhaps Owen would not have played in Mexico without the additional lure of acquiring managerial experience. What additional contractual language would have secured that option? Rewrite the pertinent language of the contract to ensure that Owen's desire to continue as a manager would be protected.

C. STANDARD PLAYER'S CONTRACT

1. Each Player Is Unique

The key link between players and their teams in professional sports is the standard player's contract (SPK). It is the only employment agreement that is allowed in professional sports such as baseball, basketball, football, and hockey. It is a contract of adhesion that has been shaped and reshaped by successful court challenges and the collective bargaining process. The larger goal of a sports contract is to define the rights and responsibilities of the various participants in the business of professional sports. More particularly, the SPK is an employment contract that specifies the player's rights and states that this player, no matter how average she appears to be, possesses unique skills.

Because no person is exactly the same as another person, it follows that no athlete is the same as another player. They might be mirror images of each other, but they are different, if for no other reason than sports has a synergistic element in which all players make subtle contributions (or deletions) to the chemistry of the ensemble (e.g., "good locker room presence" or "a whining malcontent who made everyone miserable while on the bench").

The following case involved a very early version of the National Football League's SPK. The court found for player Clyde Johnson, interpreting the term "season contract" by looking to the sport's customs and its typical business usage of the term to supply a meaning.

Johnson v. Green Bay Packers

74 N.W.2d 784 (Wis. 1956)

Plaintiff's complaint ... prayed for reformation of the [June 30, 1948] contract and for recovery of damages for breach of contract as reformed. ...

Johnson, a professional football player, had a contract with the Los Angeles Rams for the 1947 season. This was a "season" contract under which Johnson could not be released during the season at the option of the Rams. The contract also provided that the Rams had the right to renew the contract for the 1948 season. At the end of the 1947 season the Rams informed Johnson that they would employ him for the 1948 season, but not on the basis of a season contract. This was not satisfactory to Johnson and the parties failed to agree on terms. The Rams then traded Johnson to the defendant Packers.

About June first, Lambeau, in behalf of the defendant Packers, contacted Johnson by phone and arranged an appointment for Johnson and his wife to meet Lambeau at the latter's home at Malibu. ... At the first meeting, ... contract terms were discussed for the employment of Johnson by the Packers. Johnson testified that he insisted on a "season" contract like he had with the Rams and that Lambeau agree. This Lambeau denied.

Later, Lambeau and Johnson met at the Hotel Roosevelt in Hollywood on or about June 30, 1948. Lambeau produced a printed form of contract in blank which was in triplicate (one for the player, one for the Packers and one for the NFL Commissioner). Lambeau wrote in longhand the figure "$7,000" on the face of the contract. Johnson then brought up the fact that a "season" contract had been agreed on, whereupon Lambeau turned over the contract and wrote in longhand on the back: "$7,000 season 1948 (minimum $7,000 1949) Season contracts E.L.L." Both Johnson and Lambeau signed the contract in triplicate and Lambeau retained all copies for the purpose of sending them in to the Packers to be typed and made to conform to the verbal understanding of the parties, after which one of the three would be returned to Johnson.

Johnson testified that ... he asked Lambeau to strike out paragraph 6 on the printed forms of the contract, covering the power to release the player, to which Lambeau replied that he would have them "fixed" as agreed.

Several weeks later Johnson received his copy of the contract which bore the aforementioned notations in ink on the back made by Lambeau, but he noted that paragraph 6 had not been stricken. ...

As soon as Johnson received his copy, he called Lambeau and protested that the printed portion of the contract which gave the Packers the right to release Johnson during the season (paragraph 6) had not been stricken as agreed. Lambeau replied that Johnson should not worry, that the commissioner did not like the contracts to be cut up or have portions crossed out, that his (Lambeau's) word was as good as gold, and that Johnson had a two year "season" contract. ... "Well as closely as I can remember, I took him at his word, plus the notation on the back of the contract that it was a two year seasonal."

Johnson later came to Green Bay, went into training and played two exhibition games. On or about September 17, 1948, the defendant Packers then terminated Johnson's employment by written notice sent by mail. ...

The only compensation Johnson received from the Packers was $100 travel money for the trip to Green Bay. Johnson played the remainder of the 1948 season with the Los Angeles Dons and his earnings were $6,000. Early in the spring of 1949 Johnson wrote to the Packers and informed them that he was ready, willing and able to play for them in 1949, but received no answer. . . .

The following issue is raised on this appeal:

(1) Whether reformation may delete a provision where it was left with the consent of the aggrieved party, even though consent was obtained in reliance upon a contemporaneous [unkept] oral promise. . . .

Judgment affirmed.

The next case emphasizes the importance of decisions made about a player's fitness to play by both the team physician and the coach. Joseph Tillman was injured during a preseason drill, and his damaged knee was operated on and repaired. After sufficient recuperation, he was instructed to return to camp to begin an exercise program and was subsequently cleared by the team physician to resume full duty. He was later released under paragraph 6 of the then-existing SPK.

TILLMAN V. NEW ORLEANS SAINTS

265 So. 2d 284 (La. Ct. App. 4th Cir. 1972)

This appeal is from a judgment dismissing plaintiff's claim for $7,499.99 allegedly due on a written contract entered into between plaintiff and defendant on June 14, 1967. This was a National Football League Standard Player's Contract. Under its terms, the defendant was to pay plaintiff, a football player, $12,000 for the 1967 football season, subject however to right of prior termination by the Saints as specified upon the giving of written notice.

Paragraph 6 of the contract reads:

The Player represents and warrants that he is and will continue to be sufficiently highly skilled in all types of football team play, to play professional football of the caliber required by the League and by the Club, and that he is and will continue to be in excellent physical condition, and agrees to perform his services hereunder to the complete satisfaction of the Club and its Head Coach. If in the opinion of the Head Coach the Player does not maintain himself in excellent physical condition or fails at any time during the football seasons included in the term of this contract to demonstrate sufficient skill and capacity to play professional football of the caliber required by the League and by the Club, or if in the opinion of the Head Coach the Player's work or conduct in the performance of this contract is unsatisfactory as compared with the work and conduct of other members of the Club's squad of players, the Club shall have the right to terminate this contract upon written notice to the Player of such termination.

During practice drill, before the commencement of the regular season, Tillman suffered a torn ligament of the knee.

Plaintiff was waived by the Saints on November 1, 1967, was paid $4,500.01, and his salary was terminated. On April 23, 1969, he filed this action for unpaid wages alleging that under the contract the Saints had no right to waive him, because he was injured at the time.

Turning now to the question of whether plaintiff was physically able to play at the time his contract was terminated, the record reflects the team physician, Dr. Kenneth Saer, performed an operation on July 10, 1967, to repair the injury. Plaintiff's leg was placed in and remained in a cast until August 3, 1967.

Tillman was instructed to return to the Saints' training camp to begin regaining muscle strength through exercises. . . . The doctor testified that at this time plaintiff "was doing quite well, his wound was well-healed. . . . " It was on October 24, 1967 that Dr. Saer felt plaintiff was able to return to full play. . . .

The trial judge accepted the opinion of the club physician and concluded plaintiff was physically able to play professional football at the time the contract was terminated. We find no error in this conclusion.

Finally, we find no merit to plaintiff's contention that because defendant failed to notify him in writing of his termination as required by the contract, there was in effect no notice given, and therefore, the contract was not terminated. It is uncontroverted that Tillman had actual knowledge on November 1, 1967, that he was waived. When Tillman left the Saints' camp in November 1967, his actions indicated he had knowledge of his release. . . .

Accordingly, the judgment of the trial court is affirmed.

———————————

Tillman was cut from the squad on the grounds that he did not possess the requisite skills to make the team. He disputed the physician's conclusion as to his physical condition and contended that he was still suffering from the injury that occurred while he was under contract. The court apparently gave deference to the team physician's finding of fitness.

In the Minor League Uniform Player Contract that follows, note the very specific and detailed language about the physical condition of the player. In fact, this contract strongly favors management throughout, which makes it closer to an adhesion contract than major league contracts, even though the salary remuneration for playing is minimal. This is because minor league players have no union to bargain for less one-sided language through the collective bargaining process.

MINOR LEAGUE UNIFORM PLAYER CONTRACT

VI. Duration and conditions of employment

   A. Club hereby employs Player to render, and Player agrees to render skilled services as a Minor League Player. Unless this Minor League Uniform Player Contract is terminated pursuant to Paragraph XIX, the term of employment shall extend until Player has performed services for Club as a Minor League Player in the requisite total of separate championship playing seasons. . . .

B. This Minor League Uniform Player Contract obligates Player to perform professional services on a calendar year basis, regardless of the fact that salary payments are to be made only during the actual championship playing season. . . .

C. Player's physical condition is important to the safety and welfare of Player and to the success of Club. Thus, to enable Player to fit himself properly for his duties under this Minor League Uniform Player Contract, Club may require Player to maintain his playing condition and weight during the off-season and to report for practice and conditioning at such times and places as Club may determine and may require Player to participate in such exhibition games prior to the championship playing season as Club may arrange. . . . In the event Player fails to report for practice and conditioning as required, or fails to participate in exhibition games, Club may impose a reasonable fine upon Player in accordance with Paragraph XX and also require Player to fit himself for his duties to the satisfaction of Club at Player's own expense.

VII. Payment

A. For the performance of all the skilled services by Player and for Player's other promises herein contained, Club will pay Player at the monthly rate. . . .

VIII. Loyalty

Player agrees to serve Club diligently and faithfully, to keep himself in first-class condition, and to observe and comply with all rules and regulations of Club. Furthermore, Player agrees to conform to high standards of personal conduct (before, during and after working hours), fair play and good sportsmanship.

IX. Promotion of Baseball

Player agrees . . . to cooperate with Club and to participate in any and all promotional activities of Club which, in the sole opinion of Club, will promote the welfare of Club or of professional baseball. . . .

X. Player's Representations

As a further inducement to Club to enter into this Minor League Uniform Player Contract, Player represents to Club as follows:

A. Player has no physical or mental defects which would prevent or impair the performance of Player's skilled services as a professional baseball player for Club. Player is capable of and will perform his services . . . with expertness, diligence and fidelity.

B. Player does not own, directly or indirectly, stock or have any financial interest in the ownership or earnings of any Minor League Club or

Major League Club and covenants that he will not hereafter, while under this Contract, acquire or hold any such stock or interest.

C. Player has exceptional and unique skill and ability as a baseball player, and Player's services to be rendered to Club are of a special and extraordinary character which gives Player his peculiar value which cannot be reasonably or adequately compensated for in damages at law. Therefore, Player agrees that Player's breach of this Contract will cause Club great and irreparable injury and damage. Accordingly, Player agrees that, in addition to other remedies, Club shall be entitled to injunctive and other equitable relief to prevent a breach of the Contract by Player, including the right to enjoin Player from playing professional baseball for any other organization during the term of this Contract. . . .

XI. Termination

A. If Club is in arrears to Player for any payments due Player under this Contract for more than fifteen days . . . Player shall be entitled to apply to the Commissioner to terminate this Contract. Thereafter, if Club fails to remedy the default as to the payment or other obligation within such time as the Commissioner may fix, the Commissioner shall terminate this Contract by a declaration of Player's free agency. . . .

B. Club may terminate this Contract upon the delivery of written or telegraphic notice to Player if Player at any time shall:

1. Fail, refuse or neglect to confirm Player's personal conduct to high standards of good citizenship and good sportsmanship;
2. Fail, refuse or neglect to keep himself in first-class physical condition;
3. Fail, refuse or neglect to obey Club's requirements respecting Player's conduct and service;
4. Fail in the judgment of Club to exhibit sufficient skill or competitive ability to qualify or to continue as a professional baseball player as a member of Club's team; or
5. Fail, refuse or neglect to render Player's services hereunder, or in any other manner to materially breach this Contract.

XII. Disputes

A. For the violation by Player of any of the obligations or duties of Player as set forth in this Contract, or for the violation by Player of any of Club's rules or regulations, Player agrees that Club may impose a reasonable fine upon Player and deduct the amount from Player's compensation, or may suspend Player without compensation, or both. Player also agrees that Club may place him on any disciplinary list.

B. In the event of any dispute or claim between Player and Club arising under any of the provisions of this Contract, the decision of Club regarding the dispute or claim always shall be subject to Player's rights of appeal which Player may exercise by filing a written, itemized and detailed appeal *form with* Commissioner within 120 days of the maturity of the claim. The decision of the Commissioner shall be final and the Player agrees and understands that the decision of the Commissioner may not be challenged in any federal or state court or any other tribunal.

C. Player specifically consents that either Club or the Commissioner may make known to the public the findings, decisions or record of any inquiry, investigation or hearing, including all evidence, information or testimony given, received, obtained or elicited as the result of any such inquiry, investigation or hearing. . . .

This Contract must be received at the Commissioner's Office within 20 days from the date SIGNED by Player. Player must sign NAME, including all INITIALS, and must DATE in OWN HANDWRITING. . . .

QUESTIONS AND DISCUSSION

1. The SPK itself is sacrosanct, but a highly prized player can add addendums to his contract that can make the entire package more attractive. This ability of clubs and players to negotiate individual terms is controlled by the collective bargaining agreement.

2. There is usually an incorporation clause, which modifies the SPK by incorporating into the document other documents, most notably the collective bargaining agreement and the league's bylaws and constitution.

3. The parol evidence rule is also written into the contract. If an agreement is written and represents the parties' final expression, under this rule, the contract as it stands cannot be modified by other agreements or promises.

4. While interpreting ambiguous terms, the agreement is interpreted against its author. Also, handwritten provisions trump typed clauses, which in turn prevail over printed provisions. *See Johnson v. Green Bay Packers, Inc.*, 74 N.W.2d 784 (Wis. 1956). *See also Tollefson v. Green Bay Packers*, 41 N.W.2d 201 (Wis. 1950)

5. Because each player is unique, the SPK includes a clause that gives the team the equitable ability to obtain injunctive relief so as to thwart the player from breaching his contract and jumping to another team (usually in another league). *See Philadelphia Ball Club v. Lajoie*, 51 A. 973 (Pa. 1902).

6. The SPK calls for annual physical examinations. If a player passes the exam, the club cannot later claim that a current, under-contract injury was a result of a previous injury that was not under contract. *See Schultz v. Los Angeles Dons, Inc.*, 238 P.2d 73 (Cal. Ct. App. 1951).

7. Note in the Minor League Uniform Contract that the terms are quite Draconian. This is the classic example of the adhesion contract — take it or leave it. What's most ironic is that the amount of dollars bandied about for the player's monthly salary is minimal. Many contracts provide for less than $1,000 per month. Of course, many of the drafted picks receive generous signing bonuses; however, even those preteen millionaires have to "ride the bus" and make close to a minimum wage salary. But for this less than generous salary, he must give away a plethora of rights. These contracts are legally bullet-proof, but one wonders about the possibility of using the doctrine of unconscionability against such a one-sided contract.

See Connecticut Professional Sports Corp. v. Heyman, 276 F. Supp. 618 (S.D.N.Y. 1967) (excerpted in section F.2). Some of these clauses attempt to control the moral and behavioral attitudes and adjustments of these young potential superstars. Look at the "loyalty" and "promotion of baseball" clauses.

SPK : "Standard Players Contract"

D. SPECIALTY CLAUSES

The SPK leaves little room for negotiating or sweetening the pot. It is the so-called specialty clauses, however, where the astute agent is able to add incentives or bonuses. The more bargaining power an athlete has, the more specialty clauses he can add to the SPK, thus making the entire agreement more attractive. The limit of the specialty clause is delineated only by the player's juice and the agent's imagination (or lack thereof). Specialty clauses include signing bonuses, options, releases, no-cuts, and collateral agreements.

1. Signing Bonus

The signing bonus is the most sought-after goal in the contract negotiation process. As a maxim, the agent wants as much money up front as possible. A signing bonus is up-front money in that all the player has to do, at a minimum, is appear in training camp ready to play. It is not considered salary since the athlete receives it for the mere act of signing, not for actually playing. In fact, if he is "cut" later on, he still keeps all the bonus money received.

The case below goes beyond that and allows the athlete to keep the signing bonus even though the team is no longer in existence.

ALABAMA FOOTBALL, INC. v. STABLER

319 So. 2d 678 (Ala. 1975)

. . . Stabler . . . contend[ed] that defendant breached his contract by failing to pay the balance due in 1974 under the contract, that the contract prohibited him from negotiating with any other professional football club, and that irreparable damage would result if the contract was not held to be null and void. . . .

[Kenny the Snake] Stabler is a professional football player. In April 1974, he signed an agreement with Alabama Football, Inc, effective immediately, . . . [for them to] pay him $50,000 upon signing and an additional $50,000 in the year 1974. . . . Stabler would play football for Alabama Football, Inc. for seven years after the expiration of his existing contract with the Oakland Raiders for a total consideration of $875,000, $100,000 of which was the bonus for signing and payable in 1974, $100,000 payable in 1975, and $135,000 per year thereafter through 1980.

The contract also prohibited Stabler from executing any other contract with any other football franchise or team in any football league.

The $50,000 was paid upon execution of the contract. . . . He received $10,000 of the balance on May 20. In June, he was told that there was no money available to pay the balance; but on June 28, an agreement was entered into which set up a schedule of payments for the $40,000 remaining unpaid. $10,000 remained due at that time. On October 29, Alabama Football, Inc. delivered a note to Stabler for the $30,000 payable on November 29, 1974. When this note was not paid, Stabler filed this suit seeking cancellation of the contract, and also asked the court to issue a temporary restraining order prohibiting the use of his name by Alabama Football, Inc. This was granted and was finally made permanent.

. . . Stabler contended that he was entitled to rescind the contract between him and Alabama Football, Inc., on the grounds that it had breached the contract between them; that it prohibited him from negotiating with any other professional football team; that repeated demands had been made on Alabama Football, Inc., for the payment of the amounts promised him in 1974; that Alabama Football, Inc., had used the fact of Stabler's signing with it to promote ticket sales and to recruit other professional football players; and that it was having financial problems which prevented its ability to live up to the contract between them. At the time of the hearing, the team had no money on deposit in a bank. . . . Stabler argues, and the trial court was of the opinion that, under the facts of this case, Stabler was under no obligation to restore the money paid to him. We agree. . . . The evidence indicates that Alabama, Inc., benefited from the fact that Stabler had signed a contract to play football with it beginning in 1976. It exploited his notoriety as a successful quarterback with the Oakland Raiders to sell tickets to ball games played in 1974; he appeared at press conferences to publicize Alabama Football, Inc., and the World Football League. Finding no error to reverse, the decree appealed from is, therefore, affirmed.

2. Option

The option clause allows the team to unilaterally bind the player for another year at a stated percent (usually 10 percent less) of the prior year's salary. This might be thought to be anticompetitive since even after the contract is over, management still retains some control over the employee. However, the onerous aspects of the option year are usually ameliorated through the collective bargaining process.

In the following case, the court had to answer the question of whether Charles Hennigan was entitled to be paid for the option year when his option was exercised after he was injured.

HENNIGAN v. CHARGER FOOTBALL CO.

431 F.2d 308 (5th Cir. 1970)

. . . [W]e must determine whether a former professional football player is entitled to compensation from his Club for the 1967 season of the American Football League (AFL). The player was sent home when he reported for the team's 1967 training camp too injured to play. Terminated without pay, he seeks redress under the terms of the contract establishing the various rights and obligations of the player and his Club during the so-called option year to which every AFL player commits himself when he signs a standard contract to play football in the League. . . . The issues with which we deal are (1) whether the team's "renewal" of the player's 1964-1966 contract obligated the Club to pay the player salary in 1967 under the injury clause and (2) whether this "renewal" required the Club to pay the player under the "no-cut" clause of the 1964-1966 contract. . . .

On March 19, 1964, Charles T. Hennigan signed an AFL Standard Players Contract (AFL Contract) for three years with the Houston Oilers, Inc., a member club of the AFL. A "no-cut" clause was made a part of that contract. Both the Standard Players Contract form and the "no-cut" clause form used by the parties are among the standard forms the League requires its member clubs to use. . . .

Hennigan claims that the Chargers broke the promises made in paragraph 3 (compensation provision) and paragraph 10 (option provision) with respect to the 1967 football season. He makes this claim under the following circumstances, which the parties do not dispute: (1) Hennigan engaged in professional football as a player for the Houston Oilers through the 1966 football season. (2) While in the performance of his services, Hennigan sustained injuries to his right knee during both the 1965 and 1966 football seasons. (3) In March 1967, the Oilers exercised the Club's right and assigned the contract to the San Diego Chargers. (4) In April 1967, the Chargers, as the assignee of Hennigan's AFL Contract, exercised the "renewal" option by means of a letter. . . . (5) In July 1967, Hennigan reported as directed to the Chargers for the beginning of the training season. Upon reporting, he was examined by the Chargers' physician. The physician determined that Hennigan's right knee, which had been operated upon in February 1967, would not at this time "stand up to the stress and strain of professional football." Accordingly, the physician recommended that Hennigan be rejected for service as a player. . . . (7) On the basis of the physician's report, the Chargers claimed the right under paragraph 6 to terminate its contractual relations with Hennigan because of Hennigan's physical incapacity to perform services as a professional football player, and a wire was mailed to the AFL President. . . . (8) Hennigan returned home and performed no services for the Chargers during the 1967 football season.

This suit was subsequently commenced by Hennigan against the Chargers to recover the salary that would have otherwise been payable for the 1967 season, had the Chargers not acted to terminate this contract. Hennigan . . . contended that because he had sustained the disabling injury to his right knee while performing services under the AFL Contract the Oilers had assigned to the Chargers, paragraph 15 of that contract (the injury clause) obligated the Chargers, by virtue of the latter's exercise of the "renewal" option, to pay him his salary for the 1967 season, and in any event, he contended that the "no-cut" clause added to paragraph 6 was applicable and operative during the 1967 season and expressly precluded the Chargers from terminating the "renewed" contract because of Hennigan's lack of capacity to play professional football. . . .

In paragraph 15 (the injury clause) of the AFL Contract, the words "In the event that Player is injured in the performance of his services under this contract" set forth a condition precedent, the occurrence of which must take place before the Club's duty to perform the promises it makes in that paragraph arises. It is undisputed that Hennigan was injured while performing services for the Houston Oilers. . . . By accepting the assignment, the Chargers assumed the Oilers' obligations to Hennigan under paragraph 15 and the "no-cut" clause added to paragraph 6 of the 1964 contract. Hennigan contends that the Chargers, by exercising the "renewal" option in paragraph 10, became obligated to pay him his salary for the 1967 football season, notwithstanding that he was sent home after failing the Club's physical examination, because the contract under which he was injured in 1965 and 1966 and the "renewed" contract under which he reported to the Chargers in 1967 were one and the same. Therefore, he claims the Chargers Club was not relieved of the obligation to pay him for the 1967 season (the "further term" of the "renewed" contract) because he was physically incapable of passing the Club's physical examination at the beginning of the 1967 training season. The Club does not dispute the fact of Hennigan's injuries or when they occurred. . . .

[The Chargers] contend instead that its exercise of the "renewal" option had the effect of creating a new contract with Hennigan. Because Hennigan's disabling injuries occurred in 1965 and 1966, before the 1967 contract was made, the Club contends that the condition precedent to its duty to pay Hennigan for the 1967 season never took place, that is, Hennigan was not injured while in the performance of any services required of him by the option year contract. . . .

This case turns upon the meaning to the term "renewal" in the AFL Contract with the Houston Oilers. . . . The option to "renew" for a "further term" may mean as the Chargers and the AFL contend, that the Club has the right to hold the player to a new one-year contract as distinguished from the then existing, possibly multi-year contract. On the other hand, the option to "renew" may mean, as Hennigan contends, that the Club has the right to keep the then existing, possibly multi-year contract in force for one more year, with the respective rights and obligations of the Club and the player in the last year as specified in paragraph 10. . . .

Our analysis of the AFL Contract leads us to the conclusion that, when the Chargers exercise the "renewal" option, . . . in essence, a new contract was established.

Our reading of the AFL Contract finds support in the clear purpose and effect of paragraph 10. The paragraph grants the Club an option on the player's services as a professional football player. . . . Unless the player signs a new AFL Contract, itself with a fixed term and an option provision, the Club is entitled in the option year to fix the player's salary, certainly an important consideration to the professional athlete, at an amount 10 per cent less than the player was receiving previously. Moreover, the player is not entitled to whatever bonus or other payments he may have been receiving previously unless such payments are specifically agreed upon by the Club and the player. . . . If a player under contract with an AFL Club is injured while performing services required by that contract, and the player is thereafter unable to perform services because of that injury, the Club is obligated under paragraph 15 to pay him his salary for the balance of the contract term, notwithstanding that the player is no longer able to fulfill the warranty he makes in paragraph 6. . . .

[W]e do not find that the option to "renew" was meant to have the effect upon its exercise of carrying forward injuries suffered during the previous term as occurrences giving rise to the Club's duty to compensate the player in the option year under paragraph 15. If this were the effect, then a retired player attempting to return to professional football as a player could require the Club holding the option on his services to decide at its peril whether to exercise that option. Should the option be exercised, the Club would assume the risk that it might have to pay salary to a person unable to perform any services because of injuries sustained prior to his retirement. . . .

From our conclusion that the exercise of its option on Hennigan's services by the Chargers had the effect of making a new contract with the player for a term of one year, it follows that Hennigan was not entitled to compensation for the 1967 football season from the Chargers. . . . He was terminated for his inability to pass the physical examination. . . . [T]he "no-cut" clause did not protect Hennigan from termination, and the proviso in this clause was inapplicable. Moreover, the "no-cut" clause, by its terms, expired on May 1, 1967. Therefore, summary judgment should have been granted in favor of the Chargers on the issue of their liability to Hennigan.

Reversed.

3. Reserve

The reserve clause is primarily of historical interest these days, but there certainly could be vestiges of it in some contracts. It is infamous and is undoubtedly the most extreme example of baseball management's attempt to control the careers of their minions. It was essentially a perpetual option year, in that each year had an option year, which in turn had another option year. In baseball's old reserve system, a player belonged to a team for life. If the team did not want to request a trade, his only option was to retire or die. The team, however, could release a player or trade him to another team without his consent. In baseball, this most-hated clause was eliminated in 1976 through a bargained-for grievance procedure.

4. No-Cut

A no-cut clause assures the player that he will not be cut during the life of the contract. This is very desirable for the player. Management can terminate a player for many reasons: skill, physical condition, off-season injuries, or suspension, for instance. As a result, there are a variety of no-cut clauses that protect a player from certain types of termination.

The contract for basketball player Billy Cunningham used the following language: "Anything hereinto the contrary notwithstanding Club and Player agree that this shall be deemed a 'no-cut' contract and Player shall not be traded to any other Club without Player's consent."

MUNCHAK CORP. v. CUNNINGHAM

457 F.2d 721 (4th Cir. 1972)

Plaintiffs, the owners of "The Carolina Cougars," sued to enjoin defendant, William John ("Billy") Cunningham, a professional basketball player, from performing services for any club other than the Cougars in violation of a contract between the Cougars and Cunningham. . . .

In this appeal, we conclude that plaintiffs did not have unclean hands, that any breach of contract on the part of plaintiffs was too insubstantial to justify the denial of injunctive relief, and that Cunningham's additional argument that his contract was not assignable is lacking in merit. Accordingly, we reverse and remand the case for entry of an injunction restraining Cunningham from playing for any team other than the Cougars, for the duration of his contract with that club. . . .

Cunningham is a basketball player of special, exceptional, and unique knowledge, skill and ability. For the period October 1, 1969, until October 1, 1970, as well as for four earlier seasons, he had contracted to play professional basketball for the Philadelphia 76ers. For the period October 1, 1969, to October 1, 1970, Cunningham received $40,000.00 compensation under the contract, together with a bonus of $15,000.00, a total of $55,000.00. The contract contained a "reserve clause," which gave that club the right, on or before September 1, 1970, to tender a contract to Cunningham to play the next season. If Cunningham failed, neglected or omitted to sign the tendered contract and to return it by October 1, 1970, the existing contract would be continued for another year, but . . . fixed at not less than 75% of his compensation. . . .

During May or early June of 1969, the Cougars, with knowledge that Cunningham was under contract with the Philadelphia 76ers, and that club had an option . . . , entered into contract negotiations with Cunningham. On August 5, 1969, the negotiations ripened into a three-year contract commencing on the 2nd day of October 1971. . . . The bonus was payable $45,000.00 on August 5, 1969, and the balance of $80,000.00 was evidenced by a promissory note. The contract contained a provision . . . that [allowed] the Cougars to enjoin him from playing basketball for another team during the term of this contract. . . .

It is undisputed that the note would be canceled if Cunningham elected to play for the 76ers during his option year for an amount in excess of a certain sum. . . . If he agreed to play for less than $80,000.00, the note was payable to the extent necessary to make up the difference between the salary with the Philadelphia 76ers and $100,000.00. If he decided not to play with the Philadelphia 76ers during his option year, then the note was to be paid in full. Thus, if we accept the testimony that the note was cancelable if the 76ers paid Cunningham at least $80,000.00, the note provided an incentive for Cunningham to the maximum extent of $20,000.00 to play for the 76ers if they paid him less than $80,000.00; and if we accept the testimony that the note was cancelable if the 76ers paid him at least $100,000.00, then the note provided an even greater incentive for Cunningham to play. . . .

Cunningham testified that the election was by signing a formal contract, but the Cougars' representative testified that if Cunningham reached an agreement to play for the Philadelphia 76ers and earned more than $80,000.00 the note was to be marked canceled and returned to the Cougars. In fact, Cunningham orally agreed, prior to May 15, 1970, to play for the 76ers for the 1970-71 season at a salary of $225,000.00, but this agreement was not reduced to a formal contract because of some difficulty about the 76ers providing for disability insurance. It was later supplanted, after May 15, 1970, by a formal contract . . . at the same salary, but for a three-year period. . . .

Cunningham demanded payment of the note on May 15, 1970, but the Cougars resisted, claiming that the amount due on the note could only be determined after Cunningham decided whether or not he would play for the 76ers during the 1970-71 basketball season and, if so, the amount of his compensation. At trial Cunningham testified, by deposition, that if the $80,000.00 had been paid on May 15, 1970, it was his intention not to play for the 76ers during the 1970-71 season.

When payment was not forthcoming on May 15, Cunningham advised the Cougars that his contract had been breached and he considered it void and no longer binding. . . .

He returned $45,000.00 which had been paid him the previous August. The Cougars refused the tender and asserted that the contracts were in full force. . . . On July 15, 1970, Cunningham entered into contracts with the Philadelphia 76ers covering the basketball seasons of 1970-71, 1971-72, 1972-73, 1973-74 and 1974-75. For the 1970-71 season, Cunningham was to be paid a salary of $225,000.00 and a like amount for each successive season, together with a bonus of $50,000.00 for the first year. . . .

We think that there was neither illegality nor unclean hands in the Cougars' contracting or Cunningham's services to be rendered after the term of his contract with the 76ers had expired, notwithstanding that the negotiations took place while his contract with the 76ers was still in full force and effect.

Nor do we think that there was illegal inducement or unclean hands in the agreement to pay $80,000.00. The note was to be canceled only if the 76ers agreed to pay Cunningham more than a certain sum ($80,000.00), testified to by Cunningham's representative and $100,000.00, according to a Cougar representative. But unless the 76ers agreed to pay at least that sum, the note was payable in whole or in part to the extent necessary to enlarge Cunningham's total compensation to $100,000.00. Thus, the giving of the note was an incentive to Cunningham to perform his contract with the 76ers, not a tortuous interference with the performance of his contract. Of course, the note was payable in full if Cunningham "sat out" his option year with the 76ers, but Cunningham already had this right since he could not be required to render personal services against his will. The incentive the note provided, to a maximum of $20,000.00 over the amount payable if he did not play, substantially diminished the likelihood that he would exercise this right. . . .

It is undisputed that the note was not payable in all events; nor did the Cougars refuse payment in all events. The conclusion is inescapable that the note was payable in whole or in part dependent upon what salary agreement was made between Cunningham and the 76ers for the 1970-71 basketball season. On July 15, 1970, Cunningham made a contract for the option year at a salary in excess of $100,000.00, the largest amount that any witness stated was the sum which would effect cancellation of the note. When it became public knowledge that Cunningham freely conceded that . . . the Cougars had paid the note on May 15, 1970, he would have been obliged to refund that sum after July 15, 1970. We do not think that the Cougars should be penalized for acting in response to reality. . . . Reversed and remanded.

5. Collateral Agreements

Each contract contains an incorporation clause that incorporates into the contract collateral agreements such as the union-management collective bargaining agreement and the league's bylaws and constitution. In essence, the SPK is modified or extended by these collateral agreements. These documents are incorporated into the contract as if they were a part of the contract. Less standard addendums can also be incorporated; once again, only the imagination of the parties limits the list of additives. Examples of less standard collateral agreements are drug usage guidelines and players-agent standards.

QUESTIONS AND DISCUSSION

1. The signing bonus, at least in the NFL can, by mutual agreement, be prorated so that each yearly part of the bonus is paid out annually if it's a long-term contract. This is done as a means to assist management in plotting how to squeeze in all the contract dollars under each year's salary cap.
2. To secure the signing bonus, the player must at least try to perform. However, in the case of *Stabler* and *Alabama Football, Inc. v. Greenwood*, 452 F. Supp. 1191 (W.D. Pa. 1978) (involving Pittsburgh Steeler's defensive standout, L.C.), the court inferred the players' willingness to play by their allowing the team to use their names and likenesses for publicity purposes. Because, in the Alabama Football cases, the team folded before camp, the courts were trying to fashion a compromise, since the players were stopped from any attempt to perform at camp.

    Can you imagine other situations where the court might intervene if the players did or didn't do something else that might be a symbol of their willingness to perform at camp?
3. The option clause is usually now bargained for, and sometimes the player can even opt for it. The rationale behind the option year is that the team has paid money, invested time, and provided instruction that cannot be reasonably quantified in a time-specific contract. The option was invented to pay back management for their intangible investment.
4. The reserve clause, baseball's dirty little secret, was integral to baseball's monopsony prior to the clause's repeal. Baseball is a subtle sport where team chemistry and long stints in the minor leagues develop necessary

skills and karma. The owners, in return for their investment, believed themselves entitled to reserve a player for life. For case descriptions of the reserve system, usually in the context of players trying to breach contracts and jump to other teams or leagues, see *Flood v. Kuhn*, 407 U.S. 258 (1972) (baseball's antitrust exemption protects reserve clause); *Kansas City Royals Baseball Corp. v. Major League Baseball Players Ass.*, 532 F.2d 615 (8th Cir. 1976) (court ruled in favor of players who broke reserve clause through arbitration); and *Philadelphia Ball Club v. Lajoie*, 51 A. 973 (Pa. 1902) (baseball players are unique).

5. There are three models of no-cut contracts. In the Cunningham model, the clause protects the player from a cut based on a lack of skill but not from one based on poor physical or mental condition, inability to perform as result of off-field injuries, or suspension without pay for disciplinary reasons. Another paradigm is the standard NFL no-cut clause, which is comparable to Cunningham except it is more specific as to the necessity of maintaining a superior physical condition. The Hudson model (from *Minnesota Muskies, Inc. v. Hudson*; see section F.1) states that "salary payable in any event." However, even that does not waive the team's right to suspend the player or protect him if he fails to show a good-faith effort. Can you think of other situations where the *Hudson* model would not protect a player? A no-cut clause guarantees only payment; it does not guarantee an automatic spot on the roster. What type of contractual language could you suggest for a "roster clause"? In what situations would it apply?

6. The incorporation clause can make the SPK (, which is envelope size,) into book size. What other collateral agreements might union, management, or both want to add to "flesh out" the contract?

E. TERMINATIONS, ASSIGNMENTS, AND REMEDIES

The majority of rights that foster the drafting and redrafting of a sports contract appear to be most closely associated with management's rights. As a general proposition, the termination of an athlete's employment contract is deemed to be a breach of contract if the termination is not justified. However, justification is interpreted broadly. An employer can terminate a contract if the athlete is physically unable to perform. But, if a team terminates an employee on the basis of an injury, such an action usually is covered by a provision in the union-management collective bargaining agreement.

A club must act within its rights when it terminates an athlete's employment contract. The club can rightfully terminate a player's contract if the athlete is out of shape, lacks skill, or defies club and league rules, or for a material breach of the standard player's contract. But, in the reality of the business of the major team sports, a player with unique, proven, and marketable skills is rarely released, but a player with marginal skills is more often released due to a lack of skills, as judged solely by the team.

Another reality of a professional athlete's life, at least in a major team sport, is the possibility of being traded, that is, the assignment or reassignment of the player's contract from one team to another team. Each standard player's contract contains a clause that allows the team to trade players at will. Of course, if the player has enough bargaining power, he can often negotiate a no-trade clause. Some collective bargaining agreements also provide no-trade provisions in certain situations. These clauses are generally based on time spent in that league and tenure on a specific team.

As in most traditional contracts, there are parts of the contract that stipulate remedies upon material breach of either party. A contract breach usually is remedied by money damages, restitution, or specific performance. Usually, a party will seek the benefit of the bargain — that which was promised in relation to what was actually received. After that, if the legal remedy is inadequate, the aggrieved party may seek specific performance if the services are unique. That's where the inherent uniqueness of an athlete in a team sport comes into play. A court will not force an athlete to play against her will. But, because of the athelete's uniqueness, the court will allow the prevailing party to enjoin the athlete from playing with any team or league other than the one that he is currently under contract with.

Injunctions as a means to force allegiance to a particular team have been enforced as a legal and viable remedy in professional team sports since the 1900s. As noted earlier, the Pennsylvania Supreme Court in *Lajoie* allowed a ball club to enjoin a highly skilled and preeminent baseball player, Napoleon "Nap" Lajoie, when he attempted to "jump" to another team in a newly formed rival league. The injunction was issued to stop him from providing services to the second team on the basis that his services and skills were unique and one-of-a-kind; Nap's special skills (remember, he was a Hall of Famer) were of a peculiar and extraordinary nature to his original team. Because of that, it would be difficult, if not impossible, to find a substitute for the services of this unique athlete.

But an athlete's need not be of Lajoie's caliber. His basic uniqueness, not only as it relates to his individual skills but also to the relationship and comingling of his skills, attitude, personality, and character with the rest of his teammates, allows the first team to enjoin the athlete from playing for another team during the life of the contract (including option years). The courts have viewed contractual provisions that prohibit athletes from jumping to another team as a part, and a fair return for, the consideration of the employer to pay the athlete's salary. Additionally, courts have held that these promises do not lack mutuality or remedy, or that they are so unreasonable so as to prevent the use of injunctive relief. Another rationale for issuing injunctions is that the fact that the contract is already partially performed and that the employer is desirous that the performance of the contract is continued.

Contracts cannot be terminated for illegal purposes, as shown next in *Houston Oilers, Inc. v. Floyd*. But alleged false representations regarding the effective date of a contract and a promise that the matter would be kept secret was insufficient to rescind the contract on fraud in the inducement in *Houston Oilers, Inc. v. Neely*, which follows *Floyd*.

HOUSTON OILERS, INC. V. FLOYD

518 S.W.2d 836 (Tex. Civ. App. 1975)

EVANS, Justice.

This action was brought by Donald Wayne Floyd, a professional football player, against Houston Oilers, Inc. to recover the sum of $14,240.00 which he asserted was the balance of his salary due under his player's contract. Floyd alleged that he had suffered an injury to his right ankle on August 23, 1968 which prevented his performing further service as a football player under his contract; that after being examined by the team physician he was carried on the club's injured reserve list until September 30, 1968, when he was returned to the active player list by the team trainer; that about two days later, October 2, 1968, he was notified that his contract was being terminated and that he would receive no further salary, and that such actions constituted a breach of his player's contract. Houston Oilers, Inc. generally denied these allegations and specially alleged that Floyd had failed to comply with a contractual provision whereby he was to submit himself for examination to a physician of his choice within 72 hours after the decision of the club physician that he was physically able to return to the active player list, and also that he was barred from recovery by reason of a general release of liability which he and his attorney had signed in connection with the settlement of his claim for workman's compensation.

In response to special issues, the jury found that as a result of the injury on August 23, 1968 Floyd was physically disabled from playing football from that date through December 16, 1968 (the end of the regular football season). The jury failed to find that Floyd had intended to release the Houston Oilers from their obligations arising out of their salary contract with him. The court found, among other facts, that Floyd had been restored to the active player roster on September 30, 1968 and terminated on October 2, 1968; that he had fully performed the terms of the salary contract and that the Houston Oilers had breached the contract in failing to pay his salary. The court further found that the contract called for a total salary of $19,000.00 payable at the end of the football season on December 15, 1968; that Floyd had been paid $6,178.00, and the Houston Oilers should be given credit for the $1400.00 workman's compensation payment he had received. It awarded judgment to Floyd in the amount of $11,422.00 with interest at the legal rate from date of judgment.

In its first three points of error, the Houston Oilers assert that the trial court erred in allowing parol evidence of Floyd's intent in signing the release, in submitting an issue to the jury on such matter, and in failing to enforce the release as a bar to Floyd's cause of action.

The agreed judgment entered in Floyd's prior action against the workman's compensation carrier, Standard Insurance Company, awarded Floyd $1120.00 for his injuries and disability, including medical expenses to the date of judgment and $280.00 for medical aid, hospital services, nursing, chiropractic services, medicines, doctor bills and prosthetic appliance expenses which might be incurred by him in the future. The judgment clearly shows that Floyd's suit was to recover workman's compensation benefits for the injury sustained by him on August 23, 1968. The Houston Oilers were not a named party to the suit although they are named in the judgment as Floyd's employer at the time of the injury. The day prior to the date of the judgment, Floyd and his attorney executed a general release whereby they acknowledged receipt of the payment of the sum of $1400.00 and, reciting a consideration of the insurance company's agreement to the entry of said judgment, released and discharged National Standard Insurance Company and Houston Oilers, Inc. . . .

In order to ascertain and give effect to the true intention of the parties to the release, it is appropriate that we construe the release in the light of the facts and surrounding circumstances as shown by the record. . . . When the language of the release is considered together with the recitations showing the nature of the settlement and the payments made under the agreed judgment in the workman's compensation case, it is clear that the release was given to cover the subject matter of that litigation. The release purports only to release those claims and causes of action which Floyd might have had "arising out of and resulting from" his injury and accident of August 23, 1968. The fact that Floyd's injury may have preceded and perhaps have influenced the Houston Oilers' decision to terminate his services under the contract, does not require the conclusion that his claim for salary benefits under the contract is an integral part of his claim to workman's compensation benefits due to his physical injury. . . .

We hold, as a matter of law, that the release does not constitute a bar to this action. We further hold that in the event there is any ambiguity in the terms of the release, that question has been determined against the Houston Oilers' contention by the jury's failure to find that Floyd intended to release the Oilers from their obligations arising out of the contract. Although the Houston Oilers argue that the issue was not submitted in proper form and failed to inquire as to the ultimate issue in the case, it failed to properly apprise the court of that objection. We overrule Houston Oilers' first three points of error.

In its remaining four points of error, Houston Oilers, Inc. asserts that the trial court erred in entering judgment for Floyd because the record conclusively establishes that Floyd failed to comply with a condition precedent to his recovery as found in paragraph 14 of his player's contract.

[Paragraph 14 of the player's contract stipulates the procedures that must occur when a player is injured, including notice to the club physician.]

Under this provision, the parties agreed the contract would remain in effect and the player would be entitled to his stipulated salary for the contract term despite his inability to perform active service by reason of physical injury. If the club's physician certified the injured player able to perform active service, the player might, within 72 hours after such determination, have an examination made by his own physician. In the event of disagreement between the two physicians, a third, disinterested physician was to be selected by the two, and if they were unable to agree, selection was to be made by the Commissioner.

The evidence does not establish whether the club doctor was of the opinion that Floyd was physically able to perform services under the contract. The record shows only that Floyd was advised by the club trainer that he had been placed on the active player list. Floyd testified that the only reason given him by the club trainer for being reactivated was "that he had no choice other than to put me back on, because it was from higher up to reactivate me." It further appears from the evidence and the trial court's finding, against which no attack has been made, that Floyd's services were terminated less than seventy-two hours after he was restored to the active player roster. The evidence does not show that he was given the period of time specified in the contract to have an examination made by a physician of his own choice, even if he had decided to take that course of action.

We hold that the evidence does not establish as a matter of law that Floyd failed to comply with the provisions of the contract, as contended by the Houston Oilers, and we overrule appellant's points of error four through seven.

The judgment of the trial court is affirmed.

HOUSTON OILERS, INC. V. NEELY

361 F.2d 36 (10th Cir. 1966)

PICKETT, Circuit Judge.

This appeal concerns the validity of a professional football contract signed by Ralph Neely, a University of Oklahoma football player, and Houston Oilers, Inc., a Texas corporation which owns and operates a professional football team in the American Football League. Neely, a high school athlete of great promise, graduated from the Farmington, New Mexico high school in 1961, and found his way to the University of Oklahoma at Norman, Oklahoma. There his proficiency in football continued to develop, and in his senior year he became one of the nation's outstanding collegiate football players. He intended to play professional football and desired to take full advantage of the financial benefits arising from the rapidly growing popularity of professional football and the rivalry existing between the two major professional football leagues. Upon completion of the regular football schedule at the University of Oklahoma on November 28, 1964, the right to contract for Neely's services was awarded under a draft process to the Houston Oilers in the American Football League and to the Baltimore Colts in the National Football League. On December 1, 1964, Neely signed American Football League Standard Players Contracts with Houston, each containing a "no-cut" clause, for the seasons 1965 through 1968, and received therefor a $25,000 bonus check. Thereafter Neely signed contracts with the Dallas Cowboys of the National Football League, which had acquired Baltimore's draft rights of Neely, and returned the Houston contracts and the $25,000 bonus check.

Houston thereupon brought this action for a judgment, declaring its contract with Neely to be valid and enforceable, and for an injunction restraining him from playing professional football with any team other than Houston. The trial court, in denying the relief sought, found that the contract was tainted with fraud and violative of the Texas Statute of Frauds. We hold that the undisputed facts in the record disclose a valid and enforceable contract.

Immediately after the draft on November 28, 1964, both Baltimore and Houston had set in motion their contract machinery to acquire the services of

Neely. On that date Neely, while enroute to New York City to accept honors awarded him as an All-American choice and to participate in the Ed Sullivan television show, discussed his plans with representatives of the Baltimore team and was given a firm offer to sign a contract. On the same day, Breen, the personnel director of the Houston team, went to New York for the sole purpose of obtaining a commitment from Neely. Neely was accompanied by his father-in-law, Robert Forte, an Oklahoma City businessman, who participated in all the negotiations as advisor to Neely. In New York City, Neely advised Breen of the Baltimore offer, but indicated that he preferred to play in the southwest. Neely told Breen that in any contract negotiations he wanted to discuss an arrangement for off-season work. Breen assured Neely and Forte that such an arrangement could be worked out, but only K.S. Adams, Jr., President of the Houston Club, could discuss such proposals. For the purpose of continuing contract discussions, the three traveled to Houston, arriving there on November 30th. At a meeting attended by Neely, Forte, Adams and Martin, the club's General Manager, a four-year contract with a "no-cut" clause was offered to Neely. The offer provided for a $25,000 bonus and a salary of $16,000 per year. In addition, Adams agreed to secure employment for Neely with a local real estate firm at a guaranteed annual income of not less than $5,000. Adams also agreed that an oil company which he owned and controlled would construct a "conventional Phillips '66 Service Station" on a suitable location in Harris County, Texas. . . .

From the beginning of the discussions, Neely, for tax reasons, had insisted that the bonus money must be paid in 1964, and further, that the signing of the contract and the acceptance of the bonus money be kept secret to prevent him being declared ineligible to participate in the post-season Gator Bowl game on January 2, 1965, to which the University of Oklahoma had accepted an invitation. . . .

Immediately upon his return to Oklahoma, Neely was advised that the Dallas Cowboys, another team in the N.F.L., had obtained Baltimore's draft rights and desired contract discussions with him. . . . Neely signed letters dated December 29, 1964, prepared by attorneys for Dallas, addressed to Houston and Adams, advising that he did not consider himself bound by the contracts and was withdrawing therefrom. . . . At about midnight on December 31st, Neely was notified that there had been some publicity concerning his signing with Houston. On January 1, 1965, Neely was advised that he had been declared ineligible to participate in the Gator Bowl game. . . . That evening Neely signed a contract to play with Dallas for the 1965 through 1968 seasons. He played for Dallas during the 1965 season and will continue to do so unless enjoined therefrom. . . .

Disagreement over the validity of these contracts does not arise out of the provisions contained therein, but from an extrinsic oral understanding that their existence was to be kept secret until after the post-season game. The essence of Neely's contentions before the trial court and here is that the contracts are unenforceable because Houston falsely represented that the effective date of the agreement would be January 2, 1965, and that Houston's filing of the contract copies with the Commissioner was a violation of its promise to keep the matter secret. . . . The record is too clear for any misunderstanding that the purpose of secrecy surrounding the execution of the contracts was not to preserve Neely's eligibility, but rather to prevent his ineligibility from becoming known; otherwise there was no need for secrecy. . . .

The trial court, in denying the relief sought, apparently applied the equitable maxim that "he who comes into equity must come with clean hands." . . . But the doctrine does not exclude all wrongdoers from a court of equity nor should it be applied in every case where the conduct of a party may be considered unconscionable or inequitable. . . . It is neither unlawful nor inequitable for college football players to surrender their amateur status and turn professional at any time. Neely was free to bind himself to such a contract on December 1, 1964 as he would have been after January 2, 1965. Nor was Houston under any legal duty to publicize the contract or to keep it secret. Its agreement to keep secret that which it had a legal right to keep secret cannot be considered inequitable or unconscionable as those terms are ordinarily used in contract negotiations. . . .

Reversed and remanded with instructions to grant the injunction.

Boxing contracts include boxer-manager, boxer-trainer, boxer-attorney, and boxer-promoter. Usually one side claims tortious interference of a business relationship. In *Madison Square Garden Boxing, Inc. v. Ali*, the court held that the parties mutually abandoned the contract.

MADISON SQUARE GARDEN BOXING, INC. V. ALI

430 F. Supp. 679 (N.D. Ill. 1977)

CROWLEY, District Judge.

Madison Square Garden Boxing, Inc. (MSGB) brought this action against Muhammad Ali (Ali), the heavyweight boxing champion of the world, for breach of contract to fight Duane Bobick (Bobick) in Madison Square Garden. MSGB seeks damages and injunctive relief. The document sued upon was executed on November 25, 1976 and called for Ali to fight Bobick on a date during the period from February 1, 1977 through February 28, 1977. Ali defended on essentially four separate grounds: (1) the document sued upon did not constitute a binding contract because Ali lacked the capacity to enter into a contract without the approval of his manager, Herbert Muhammad (Muhammad), (2) there was no breach, (3) MSGB was unable to perform, and (4) if a contract existed it was mutually abandoned.

Ali, as heavyweight champion of the world, successfully defended his championship in September of 1976, in a contest with Ken Norton. That contest was promoted by MSGB and held at Yankee Stadium in New York, New York, pursuant to a Fighters' Agreement executed on May 13, 1976 between MSGB and Ali, not signed by Ali but signed by his manager, Muhammad.

Shortly after the conclusion of that contest, Ali, while in Istanbul, Turkey, held a press conference and, as he had on several past occasions and would again, announced his retirement from boxing.

Teddy Brenner, president and matchmaker of MSGB, continued contracts with Herbert Muhammad (Muhammad) even after Ali's announced retirement. Brenner attempted to find out if Ali was going to box again. . . .

On November 16, 1976, when negotiations for the Norton-Bobick fight reached an impasse, Brenner told Bobick's manager that he thought he could arrange a fight between Ali and Bobick. . . .

Brenner then called Muhammad and told him he was coming to Chicago, Illinois. Muhammad agreed to meet him. When Brenner arrived in Chicago, he . . . [met with] Charles Lomax. Lomax was Muhammad's attorney and held Muhammad's power of attorney.

Lomax said to Brenner, "I have spoken to Herbert. What are you prepared to offer Ali to fight Bobick?" Brenner replied that he would pay $2,225,000.00. Lomax had a telephone conference with Muhammad, and then told Brenner, "Two and a half million dollars and you have yourself a deal." [The parties ultimately agreed on $2.5 million.] . . .

The next morning, Brenner met Lomax in his law offices. Lomax had another telephone conversation with Muhammad. After that conversation, Lomax caused a letter to be prepared for Ali's signature. Throughout the trial this letter was referred to as a letter of intent. There was no claim that it constituted a binding contract.

Brenner, at Muhammad's direction, flew to Houston, Texas, where Ali was working on a movie. Brenner gave Ali the letter of intent and said, "I have those papers for you to sign that Herbert talked to you about." Ali signed.

Brenner returned to New York and delivered the signed letter of intent. . . .

Brenner, . . . then flew to California to make the final arrangements with Biron concerning Norton. Biron, in addition to his prior demand for the first fight with Bobick, also demanded and ultimately received on November 24, 1976, commitments that Norton would fight Ron Lyle as a part of a double-header with Ali-Bobick and Norton would be paid $100,000.00 more than he would have received from the Norton-Bobick contest.

Simultaneously negotiations were being conducted with Lyle's representatives, and they agreed to the Norton-Lyle contest. Brenner filled in a form contract and mailed it to Lyle on November 24th. This contract was executed by Lyle and mailed to Madison Square Garden.

Brenner called Muhammad in the late evening hours of November 24 and told him that everything was arranged. . . .

Armed with the document which is the subject matter of this suit, Brenner, in joyful anticipation, flew to Houston and arrived in the early morning of November 25th. He met with Ali and Ali signed the agreement. Exhausted from what one of counsel has called his "Odyssey," Brenner mistakenly inserted the date of November 24th on the agreement. . . .

Unbeknownst to Brenner, another promoter Don King, had arrived in Houston shortly after Brenner left. King secured Ali's signature on an agreement for Ali to fight a man named Schutte, who was the South African champion. Before Ali signed he told King of the agreement with Brenner and that he would fight both Bobick and Schutte. King allegedly penciled in on his agreement a legend that it wasn't valid without Muhammad's signature.

King flew to Chicago and had Lomax come to his law office on Thanksgiving and he and Lomax caused several pages of the Ali-Schutte agreement to be retyped. Lomax then signed the agreement with Muhammad's name. Although Lomax denied having seen or been aware of the details of the Ali-Bobick agreement until late December, the revised Ali-Schutte agreement was dated November 24, 1976 and it recognized the existence of the Ali-Bobick agreement and its changed payment date of November 29, 1976. . . .

On November 29th, Brenner heard from Lyle's manager that rumors were circulating that Ali would not fight. The next day he saw a newspaper article that indicated that Ali would retire. The publicity director of Madison Square Garden then told him that he had received official word that Ali was not going to fight. . . .

Ali, at the request of the Garden's publicity director, telephonically participated in a press conference where he simultaneously announced his retirement and helped to promote the Norton-Bobick contest. . . .

However, this complex story did not end here. On or about December 16, 1976, Muhammad wrote to Burke and Brenner and advised them that Ali was prepared to fight Bobick in accordance with the terms of the November 18th letter of intent. He also stated that if MSGB was committed to the Norton-Bobick contest Ali would fight Bobick within four months after that contest. Muhammad stated that if an agreement wasn't signed by December 24th, the payment of the $125,000.00 would be returned. MSGB never responded to this letter, and on January 25, 1977, the $125,000.00 was returned to and accepted by MSGB. . . .

The document signed on November 25th clearly established a mutuality of obligation and was supported by adequate consideration. . . . It is also clear that Muhammad approved of and was aware of all of the contract's provisions. . . .

MSGB, after receiving notice of Ali's then intent to retire, took no action to enforce this contract. On the contrary, the Norton-Bobick contest was reinstated and Ali's aid was solicited and accepted to promote that contest. Brenner felt the matter was "over and done with". This sentiment of Brenner was reinforced by the MSGB's subsequent conduct by accepting the return of the $125,000.00, and its failure to respond to Muhammad's letter of December 16, and its failure to bring this action until after the time for performance expired. Considering all of the circumstances and the conduct of the parties, there was mutual abandonment of the contract. . . .

Accordingly, the defendant has established his defense of abandonment and judgment shall enter for the defendant and against the plaintiff.

In the next case, plaintiff sought an injunction on the basis that the benefit of the bargain was the baseball team's promise to play its home games at the publicly funded and operated stadium.

METROPOLITAN SPORTS FACILITIES COMMISSION V. MINNESOTA TWINS PARTNERSHIP

638 N.W.2d 214 (Minn. Ct. App. 2002)

TOUSSAINT, Chief Judge.

Appellants Minnesota Twins Partnership and Major League Baseball challenge the temporary injunction (1) requiring the Twins to play their 2002 home schedule at the Hubert H. Humphrey Metrodome stadium; (2) enjoining Major League Baseball from interfering with the contract; (3) enjoining the Twins from taking action that would prevent them from playing their 2002 home schedule at the Metrodome; and (4) enjoining the sale of the Twins unless the new owner agrees to comply with the lease terms requiring the Twins to play their 2002 home schedule at the Metrodome. Because the district court did not abuse its discretion in issuing the temporary injunction against the Twins and Major League Baseball to maintain the status quo pending resolution of the merits, we affirm.

Facts

The Minnesota Twins (Twins), a privately owned and operated baseball team, are a member of Major League Baseball. Major League Baseball is an unincorporated association of 30 major-league baseball teams. The Metropolitan Sports Facilities Commission (the commission) is a Minnesota governmental entity that was created in 1977 to construct and operate the Hubert H. Humphrey Metrodome in Minneapolis.

The use agreement between the Twins and the commission has been amended over the years and is governed by both legislation and the parties' agreements. As originally enacted, the legislation required that the use agreement be no longer than 30 years and no shorter than the term of the bonds used to finance the stadium. Minn. Stat. 473.581, subd. 3(a) (1978). In 1979, the legislature amended the act so that the agreement could provide for termination upon conditions related and limited to the bankruptcy, insolvency, or financial capability of the organization. 1979 Minn. Laws ch. 203, 8. . . .

The 1998 use agreement provided the Twins with a fixed-term agreement for the years 1998-2000, with the option of exercising three one-year extensions following the fixed-term period. In September 2001, the Twins exercised their lease option for the 2002 season.

Under the terms of the agreement, . . . [r]ent may be charged only in very limited circumstances. . . .

Therefore, with no rent being collected, the major benefit that the commission receives under the use agreement is the Twins' promise to play baseball at the Metrodome. The Twins are excused from this obligation only if the *force majeure* clause applies and they are unable to play a home game for a reason beyond the Team's and the Commission's control, including strikes, an act of God, a natural casualty, or a court order. If the Twins cease playing games at the Metrodome as required, or if they cease playing major-league professional baseball for any reason, they are in default of the agreement. The remedies available to the commission under the contract include, but are not limited to, injunctive relief and orders for specific performance requiring the Team to play its Home Games at the Stadium during the Term hereof. The agreement is binding on the Twins' successors and assigns as well.

The commission became concerned that the Twins would not comply with their one-year agreement after reports that Major League Baseball intended to eliminate or contract two franchises, including the Minnesota Twins. On November 6, 2001, the commission brought a declaratory-judgment action seeking, in relevant part, specific performance of the use agreement and an injunction preventing Major League Baseball from interfering with the commission's contractual relationship with the Twins. The commission alleged that the Twins sought to circumvent their contractual obligations by selling their franchise to Major League Baseball for $250 million and that the league would then terminate the franchise. . . .

Issue

Did the district court abuse its discretion in temporarily enjoining the Twins from breaching their one-year use agreement with the commission and enjoining Major League Baseball from interfering with the commissions contractual relationship with the Twins?

Analysis . . .

We now turn to the main issue on appeal, in which we review the injunction for an abuse of discretion. . . .

1. Nature and Background of the Relationship

A temporary injunction is issued to maintain the status quo pending a decision on the merits. . . .

2. Balancing Harms

The district court concluded that the commission, the state, citizens, and fans would suffer irreparable harm if the Twins failed to play their 2002 home games at the Metrodome. The court (1) cited the role of baseball as a tradition and as a national pastime, the history of the Twins in Minnesota for some 40 years, including two World Series championships, the role of Twins legends who have bettered the community by their volunteer work with children, and the availability of Twins games as affordable family entertainment; (2) noted that private buildings had been condemned to build the Metrodome; (3) found that the welfare, recreation, prestige, prosperity, trade, and commerce of the people of the community are at stake; and (4) ruled that the vital public trust outweighs any private interest.

a. Harm to Be Suffered by the Commission If the Temporary Injunction Is Denied

The party seeking an injunction must establish that legal remedies are inadequate and that an injunction must issue to prevent great and irreparable injury. . . .

. . . We address appellants' arguments in turn. . . .

Appellants first claim that a landlord may not obtain specific performance requiring a tenant to stay in business. . . . They argue that under the hard and fast rule, specific performance is not available in commercial-lease cases. . . .

Caselaw, however, does not preclude equitable relief as a matter of law in all commercial-lease cases. . . .

Upon examination, the district court may ultimately conclude that the use agreement at issue here is not a typical commercial lease. Under the agreement, the Twins pay no rent for their use of the Metrodome for the 2002 home games or for their year-round use of locker and office space. Generally, in a commercial lease, the tenant pays the landlord rent as consideration for the use and occupancy of the property. . . .

Next, appellants contend that if the Twins breach the use agreement, the only harm the commission will suffer is lost revenue from concession sales and advertising, in the amount of some $500,000, as well as the loss of the potential for rent from postseason play. . . . They assert that money damages will compensate the commission for its injuries and that injunctive relief is, therefore, unavailable.

The availability of money damages to efforts to stop the relocation of the Milwaukee Braves, Selig told Congress that he believed that the professional sports league and Major League Baseball should vigilantly enforce strong policies prohibiting clubs from abandoning local communities which have supported them. . . . He further stated that franchise relocation should be prohibited except in the most dire circumstances where the local community has, over a sustained period, demonstrated that it cannot or will not support the franchise. . . .

b. Harm to Be Suffered by Appellants If Injunction Is Granted

The district court found that the public interest outweighs any private interests, but otherwise made no specific findings on the potential harm that appellants claim. The Twins contend that the harm they will suffer if forced to stay in business is financial. They (1) cite the commission's admission on its website that the Metrodome is unsuitable for professional baseball and its reference to the Twins' inability to generate sufficient stadium revenues; (2) rely on material in the commissions appendix referring to losses the Twins have suffered; and (3) assert that when interest payments are considered, the Twins lost almost $4 million last season. . . .

The commission also contends that the irreparable harm attributable to contraction and the league's voluntary decision to approve its members' contracts and do business in Minnesota justifies an injunction with an impact outside Minnesota. The commission notes that Major League Baseball has not contested personal jurisdiction in the district court and argues that it voluntarily availed itself of the forum offered by Minnesota courts. . . .

On the record before this court, viewed most favorably to the prevailing party, we conclude that the district court did not abuse its discretion in concluding that the possibility of irreparable harm to the commission and the public outweighed the potential harm shown by the Twins and Major League Baseball.

3. Likelihood That Commission Will Prevail on the Merits

If a plaintiff can show no likelihood of prevailing on the merits, the district court errs as a matter of law in granting a temporary injunction. . . .

a. Whether the Use Agreement Explicitly Authorizes Specific
Performance as a Remedy for Breach

The Twins first challenge the district court's determination that the use agreement entitles the commission to specific performance requiring the Twins to play [their] home games at the [Metrodome]. . . . We agree with the parties that the plain language of the use agreement authorizes any remedy allowed by law or equity, including but not limited to injunctive relief and specific performance in the event of a breach.

b. Whether the Commission Has Established a substantial
Likelihood of Success on the Merits . . .

Appellants argue that specific performance is not available to enforce a commercial lease. . . .

Finally, Major League Baseball contends that the district court injunction impermissibly regulates interstate commerce in violation of the Commerce Clause. . . .

4. Consideration of Public Policy

The district court found that a temporary injunction would further public policy because local professional sports franchises are an important community asset and should fulfill their contractual obligations. . . .

Decision

The district court did not abuse its discretion in issuing a temporary injunction in favor of the Metropolitan Sports Facilities Commission pending trial on the merits.

Affirmed.

QUESTIONS AND DISCUSSION

1. A club can rightfully terminate a contract for material breach. What are some potential breaches that a club might argue are sufficiently material if it wants to terminate the player's contract? What are some potential breaches that a player might argue are material enough to void the contract?

2. The ability to trade players from team to team as if they were chattel has been a cherished and sacrosanct prerogative of management. Some players, however, are local heroes (e.g., Nolan Ryan in Texas, for whom a major state highway, the Nolan Ryan Expressway, is named) and have substantial business interests in the particular community. Is this right to reassign fair? Should seniority affect the team's unbridled right to trade? Collective bargaining agreements in some sports have established a right of first refusal for veterans. Should this clause be mandatory in all sports?

3. Injunctions are allowed since the other option, forcing the athlete to specifically perform, is considered unacceptable as well as impractical,

since the athlete might not perform to his utmost capability. However, the most fundmental truism of sports is that the glow of youth is fleeting and an athlete's career is a limited few years. Another truism is that you can't play a team sport alone. Considering these truisms, is it fair to allow injunctions, especially if the remuneration is low, when one result might be the effective ending of that athlete's playing career due to an irrevocable erosion of skills because of a halt in his playing days? *See Connecticut Professional Sports Corp. v. Heyman*, 276 F. Supp. 618 (S.D.N.Y. 1967) (excerpted in section F.2).

4. Earlier forms of player employment contracts allowed the team to simply terminate the contract after a brief period following notice. *See American League Baseball Club of Chicago v. Chase*, N.Y. App. Div. 146 N.Y.S. 6, 14 (1914); *Metropolitan Exhibition Co. v. Ward*, 9 N.Y.S. 779, 782-84 (1890). With this type of language, the club had the right to release the player at any time with or without cause. *See Tollefson v. Green Bay Packers, Inc.*, 41 N.W.2d 201, 203 (Wis. 1950).

5. In some professional contracts, the question of whether the athlete exhibits sufficient ability is determined solely by the head coach or manager. Team physicians also are empowered with the discretion to make decisions that could trigger termination since they must decide whether the player is physically fit to play. *See* Weistart & Lowell, *The Law of Sports* §3.08 at 239-240 (1979).

6. Donald Floyd's contract stipulated that the team physician had the discretion to decide whether Floyd was physically able to perform. However, "[t]he evidence does not establish whether the club doctor was of the opinion that Floyd was physically able to perform services under the contract." Floyd was merely advised by the club trainer that he was placed back on the active list. Also, Floyd's services were terminated less than 72 hours after he was reactivated, thus negating his contractual right to secure a second opinion from a doctor of his own choice. Would the court have decided differently if the team terminated his contract exactly at 72 hours?

7. In *New York Football Giants, Inc. v. Los Angeles Chargers Football Club, Inc.*, 291 F.2d 471 (5th Cir. 1961), Charles Flowers, an outstanding University of Mississippi football player, was induced by the owner of the Giants to sign a professional contract before the Sugar Bowl. A part of the contract was that "[t]his agreement shall become valid and binding upon each party hereto only when, as and if it shall be approved by the Commissioner." Contrary to their understanding, the Giants filed and the contract was approved by the commissioner two weeks before the Sugar Bowl; however, the commissioner agreed to withhold the announcement of his approval until after the game on January 1. On December 29, Flowers had negotiations with the Los Angeles Chargers of the rival American Football League (AFL) and agreed to a better contract, which was not formally executed until after the game. Flowers wrote to the Giants on December 29 withdrawing his agreement and returning the uncashed bonus checks. The court held against the Giants' attempt to secure an injunction prohibiting Flowers from playing with the Chargers on the basis that the Giants were deceitful: "We think no party has the right thus

to create problems by its devious and deceitful conduct and approach a court of equity with a plea that the pretended status which it has foisted on the public be ignored and its rights be declared as if it had acted in good faith throughout."

8. An injunction was denied in the case of Charles Flowers (see preceding question) but granted in the case of Ralph Neely. Why? Is there a difference between the two cases?

9. Oscar Chavez, a former star pitcher for the Cuban National Team, defected and then played for the Miami Mavericks, a professional baseball team. He became an instant celebrity and local hero to the town that is known as "Little Havana." He defected in Mexico but then choose to emigrate from Honduras so he could be a free agent and negotiate the best contract for the highest purse.

   Unfortunately, his family was still in Cuba. He had two great years where he won 45 games and lost only twelve (45-12) and was a source of local pride; but the team routinely finished last. When he pitched at home, the team would draw 60,000 fans; without him, the average home attendance was around 10,000. Because of his concerns about his family and the lousy record of his team (he was 150-20 with the Cuban National Team and hated losing), he announced his retirement; he was in the third year of a $32 million four-year contract. His contract contained the typical injunctive language that he would not play baseball "or engage in related activities . . . except with the prior written consent of the Club." He also received a $4 million signing bonus upon signing the contract; its purpose was to dissuade Chavez from signing with a team in the newly formed, now defunct, Greater Florida Baseball Association. Chavez announced that he would pursue a broadcasting career and host the "Chavez Pachanga" every weeknight with baseball clips, pitching hints, scouting reports and some singing, salsa, and so on. He signed a three-year, $10 million contract. The Mavericks attendance continued to plummet while Chavez' show rocked. The Mavericks sued Chavez for breach of contract and sought an affirmative injunction requiring him to report back to the Mavericks immediately, an injunction precluding him from "performing" for the TV network, and damages. Chavez also had a negative convenant in his contract with the TV network. Discuss the merits of the Mavericks' lawsuit. See Cozzillio & Levinstein, *Sports Law: Cases and Materials* 249-250 (1997).

10. In *Metropolitan Sports Facilities Comm. v. Minnesota Twins Partnership*, 638 N.W.2d 214 (Minn. Ct. App. 2002), the local sports facilities commission successfully sought a temporary injunction that forced the Minnesota Twins, which was subject to "contraction" by the professional baseball association, to play its season 2002 in a public stadium pursuant to the use agreement between team and commission. (The Twins made it into the playoffs that year.) So, contraction by commissioner's fiat was stopped, at least for the time being. Another way might be to use the labor laws to halt contraction on the basis that it is a unilateral league procedure that affects wages, hours, and conditions of employment, and thus must be decided through the give-and-take of union-management

negotiations. Like in *Lajoie* and those cases that discuss remedies for breach when a player contemplates jumping to a new team, *Metropolitan Sports Facilities Commission* emphasizes the fact that in a use agreement between a governmental sports authority and a professional sports team, money damages cannot fully compensate the nonbreaching party when the agreement provided that the benefit of the bargain is the team's promise to play its home games at the publicly funded and operated stadium.

F. DEFENSES

When either party alleges a breach of contract, several defenses are available. In team sports, the collective bargaining agreement might come into play, for example, when a team terminates the contract due to an injury. In that case, the diagnosis of the team doctor is submitted to arbitration after a review by a neutral physician. Some of the club's defenses that can be raised in arbitration are failure to pass the preseason medical exam, failure to make complete disclosure of a physical or mental condition, an injury that occurred prior to the physical examination, a nonsport injury, no new sports related injury after exam, and no aggravation of a prior injury after the physical.

1. Unclean Hands

A party cannot request the court to grant an equitable remedy if the party enters court with unclean hands. Athletes have successfully used this doctrine to defend against teams that have attempted to enjoin a player from playing with another team.

MINNESOTA MUSKIES V. HUDSON
_____

294 F. Supp. 979 (M.D.N.C. 1969)

. . . The plaintiffs seek to enjoin the defendant, Louis C. Hudson, from playing professional basketball for any professional basketball team other than the plaintiff for the term of an alleged contract he signed with plaintiff, Minnesota Muskies, Inc., on May 3, 1967. . . .

[Plaintiff Minnesota Muskies was a professional basketball team in the American Basketball Association (ABA); the team was subsequently transferred to Florida Professional Sports. Defendant is Louis C. Hudson, basketball player and University of Minnesota alumnus. The Atlanta Hawks is a National Basketball Association (NBA) franchise that was previously in St. Louis. Hudson signed a standard contract with the Hawks, which contained a reserve clause (basically a one-year option clause). He was a highly skilled player who was named Rookie of the Year. The ABA was just formed, and the Muskies wanted players with Minnesota connections; thus the team offered Hudson a three-year contract even though he was still under contract with the Hawks. Hudson had a change of heart and signed a five-year contract with the Hawks less than a month after he signed the Muskies contract.]

The sole question is whether the plaintiffs are entitled to an injunction restraining Hudson from playing professional basketball with any team other than Miami for the term he signed with the Muskies on May 3, 1967. . . .

It is generally held that where a person agrees to render personal services to another, which require special and unique knowledge, skill and ability, so that in default the same services cannot easily be obtained from others, a court of equity is empowered to negatively enforce performance of the agreement by enjoining its breach. While acknowledging this principle of law, the defendants correctly assert that equitable relief should be denied to a suitor who comes into court with unclean hands. . . .

[T]he conclusion is inescapable that the Muskies, in its dealings with Hudson, soiled its hands to such an extent that the negative injunctive relief sought should be denied. This is not to say that Hudson was an innocent bystander, or that he was an unwilling participant in his dealings with the Muskies. On the contrary, viewed strictly from the standpoint of business morality, his position in this litigation, like that of the Muskies, is not an enviable one.

On May 17, 1966, Hudson, an adult with four years of university education, freely and voluntarily executed a contract to play professional basketball with St. Louis for one year, with the provision that St. Louis might renew the contract for successive basketball seasons under certain prescribed conditions. A sizeable bonus for executing the contract was paid by St. Louis and received by Hudson.

Beyond question, both Hudson and St. Louis anticipated that the contract would be renewed for subsequent years. A short time before his initial contact with the Muskies, Hudson had borrowed $4,000.00 from St. Louis with the specific provision that it was to be repaid by deductions from his 1967-68 contract with St. Louis. Additionally, by his leading his team in scoring, and his being named Rookie of the Year in the NBA, Hudson's skill and ability as a professional basketball player had been well established during his first year with St. Louis.

. . . [T]he Court is convinced that the Muskies, admittedly desirous of acquiring a winning basketball team as quickly as possible, contacted Hudson while he was still actively engaged in play-off games with St. Louis. Without this unwarranted interference on the part of the Muskies, it is very likely that Hudson would have fulfilled his contractual and moral obligations with St. Louis. . . .

Even if the "reserve clause" in the St. Louis contract is of doubtful validity, the fact remains that the Muskies, knowing that Hudson was under a moral, if not legal, obligation to furnish his services to St. Louis for the 1967-68 and subsequent seasons, if St. Louis chose to exercise its option, sent for Hudson and induced him to repudiate his obligation to St. Louis. Such conduct, even if strictly within the law because of the St. Louis contract being unenforceable, was so tainted with unfairness and injustice as to justify a court of equity in withholding relief. . . .

Finally, plaintiffs insist that they are entitled to relief, notwithstanding their unfair and unjust conduct, because St. Louis was also guilty of inequitable and unlawful conduct in signing Hudson to a second contract on June 5,

1967, when it knew that Hudson had signed a valid contract with the Muskies on May 3, 1967. This argument is also lacking in merit. . . . It is irrelevant that the conduct of St. Louis may have been more reprehensible than that of the Muskies, since it is the devious conduct of the Muskies that created the problems presented in this litigation. Consequently, a determination of the validity of the "reserve clause" in the St. Louis contract is immaterial to a resolution of this controversy. No effort was made to avoid the contract in an honest way, but instead the Muskies consciously attempted to nullify and ignore it to the manifest injury of St. Louis. In so doing, it foreclosed its right to seek the aid of a court of equity. . . . [A] judgment will be entered dismissing the complaint with prejudice.

2. Unconscionability

Either side, although most likely the plaintiff, might attempt to void a sports contract on the basis that it is illegal or unfair. A court will not permit equitable enforcement if the contract's terms are too harsh or one-sided. Contractual provisions of this sort are deemed to be unconscionable.

CONNECTICUT PROFESSIONAL SPORTS CORP. v. HEYMAN

276 F. Supp. 618 (S.D.N.Y. 1967)

. . . [P]laintiff . . . has moved for an injunction to prevent defendant Arthur Heyman from playing professional basketball with the New Jersey Americans or with any professional basketball team other than the Hartford Capitols of the Eastern Professional Basketball League.

Heyman, an All-American while at Duke University, was elected as one of the top 50 college basketball players of the century. Following his inability to succeed with two National Basketball Association teams, plaintiff purchased Heyman's contract from the Wilmington Blue Bombers of the Eastern League for $1500. On October 20, 1966, [Heyman] entered into a contract with plaintiff in which he agreed to furnish his services as a basketball player exclusively to the Club for the one-year period ending August 31, 1967, engaging in "as many games as requested by the club" and giving "his best and most skillful performance at all times," for which he was to be paid $125, plus $50 expenses, for each regular season and play-off game "actually played." The agreement acknowledged that Heyman possessed "special knowledge, skill and ability to play professional basketball, and (that) the services of the player are of unique character and require a high degree of efficiency which must be maintained at all times in order to meet the requirements of competition within the league." The Club was given the option of renewing the contract with all of the terms, provisions and conditions for a one-year period, provided that the new salary should be agreed upon by the parties, or in default of agreement, should be fixed by the Club. In order to exercise its option, the Club was required to serve Heyman with written notice prior to August 31, 1967. . . .

At any time, the Club could give written notice terminating all of its liabilities and obligations under the contract and able "to negotiate a new contract for himself with any other club in the league." . . .

Heyman also agreed that, if he played professional basketball for another club or organization during the option period, without the Hartford Capitols' written consent, the Club would be entitled to commence proceedings to obtain injunctive relief. . . .

During the 1966-67 season, Heyman played in every one of the 28 games that the Hartford Capitols played. His sharpshooting ability (an average of 33 points per game) made him the League's highest scorer, the star of the Capitols and Hartford's darling; he was awarded a trophy as the most popular player on the team. In March 1967, the fickle hero learned that the American Basketball League was being formed, and a short time later, Heyman signed a contract to play for the New Jersey Americans during the 1967-68 season at a salary of $15,000. Upon becoming aware of these events, on May 23, 1967, the Club, intending to give the written notice required to exercise its option, mailed Heyman a document identical to the former contract except that the salary provision was increased to $150 per game and the renewal option was not inserted. Heyman did not sign the document. On the same date, the Club wrote to Messrs. Arthur Brown and Mark Bimstein, partners doing business as the New Jersey Americans, informing them of its renewal rights under the original contract with Heyman, and indicating a willingness to settle the matter on an amicable basis. . . . [T]his court believes that the terms and provisions of this contract are too harsh and one-sided to permit equitable enforcement.

Injunctive relief that has the effect of precluding an athlete from appearing before the public is an extraordinary remedy, to be granted only where the equities favor the plaintiff, and the injury that will be suffered by the plaintiff upon denial of relief is irreparable and outweighs the harm to the defendant that will be caused by the granting of relief. . . .

The primary reason for denying relief is the fact that plaintiff seeks to enforce a contract that purports to bind defendant for a one-year period and at the same time permit plaintiff to terminate at will. The existence of a provision entitling plaintiff to end the contract whenever it chooses, is an important factor in determining whether injunctive relief is appropriate. Furthermore, Heyman is entitled as a matter of right to engage only in those games where his services are "requested by the Club." Since he is compensable under the contract only for "each game actually played," it is questionable whether he would be entitled to compensation for games in which he did not "actually" play, or at least dress. For instance, if he were injured (a distinct occupational hazard) or became ill, he would not be entitled to any compensation, although he would be obliged to play with the Club when he recovered. In addition, although the Hartford Capitols played 28 games during the 1966-67 season, there is no provision in the contract requiring that a minimum number of games be played. . . .

We recognize that plaintiff did not, during Heyman's one year with it, invoke any of the foregoing one-sided provisions to his harm, and that plaintiff contemplated another harmonious season in which, if all went well, the basketball player would continue as a star, possibly receiving as much as

$6550 for the 1966-67 season and up to $8500 if the Capitols qualified for an eight-game playoff. Plaintiff also enabled defendant to supplement his income by finding for him a job as an insurance agent in Hartford. These considerations, however, are insufficient to justify giving plaintiff the right to equitable enforcement of a contract which could be used by it to prevent defendant from earning a living wage from his basketball court activities. . . . Motion denied, so ordered.

3. Mutuality

The player can also defend against an injunction by claiming a lack of mutuality. This inequality could be exemplified by the difference between the athlete's obligation of many years and the team's obligation for a minimal amount of time, or, the difference between the availability of specific performance for the team as opposed to the fact that it is not available for the athlete.

QUESTIONS AND DISCUSSION

1. As regards the doctrine of unclean hands, a court of equity will not grant injunctive relief if the plaintiff has acted in bad faith concerning the problem under litigation. *See New York Football Giants, Inc. v. Los Angeles Chargers Football Club, Inc.*, 291 F.2d 471 (5th Cir. 1961). What are some examples of "bad faith" that might be sufficient to dirty plaintiff's hands?
2. How did the plaintiff in *Hudson* dirty its hands, thus denying equitable relief? Remember, the essence of equitable intervention is at best problematic; therefore, what may be tolerable actions under the analysis of one court may be sufficiently intolerable when viewed by another court so as to deny injunctive relief based on similar conduct. The *Hudson* court determined "that the Muskies, in its dealings with Hudson, soiled its hands to such an extent that the negative injunctive relief sought should be denied." Hudson anticipated the continuation of his original contract; in fact, he received a bonus for the signing thereof, and borrowed money with the understanding that it would be repaid from next year's contract. The court viewed the Muskies' interference as "unwarranted." "[T]he fact remains that the Muskies [knew] that Hudson was under a moral, if not legal, obligation [to] St. Louis." The court saw this as a sufficient injustice to warrant denying equitable relief: The contract "was so tainted with unfairness and injustice as to justify . . . withholding relief."
3. Historically, some form of the reserve clause might well have been unconscionable and thus unenforceable. Many of the player retention and player restriction systems have been ameliorated through collective bargaining. In *Heyman*, plaintiff was on a team in a nonmajor league. What were the real reasons behind the judge's decision to allow *Heyman* to skip his original contract, even though the judge did not appear to be unduly sympathetic to his cause (the judge called him a "fickle hero")?
4. The nonstatutory labor exemption (covered more fully later) allows an exemption for anticompetitive practices if they are a result of (allegedly)

bona fide, arm's-length negotiation on mandatory subjects of collective bargaining (hours, wages, and conditions of employment). The contract is a part of the collective bargaining agreement and thus is protected from antitrust attack even if some clauses are facially unconscionable. Is this fair?

5. In *Philadelphia Ball Club v. Lajoie*, 51 A. 973 (Pa. 1902), the court disallowed Napoleon Lajoie's claim that he was free to abandon his contract because it lacked consideration, that is, the appearance of object one-sidedness. Lajoie averred that when seeking mutuality of obligation, the court does not have to find that the duties of each party must be identical; the seminal concern is that there must be some form of mutuality of consideration, that is, some type of bargained-for exchange in which each party has suffered tangible legal loss. *See* Cozzillio & Levinstein, *Sports Law: Cases and Materials* 129 (1997). *See also Erving v. Virginia Squires Basketball Club*, 468 F.2d 1064 (2d Cir. 1972); *Nassau Sports v. Peters*, 352 F. Supp. 870, 876 (E.D.N.Y. 1972).

6. Notwithstanding the above line of cases evolving from *Lajoie*, Heyman came to an opposite conclusion. With the *Lajoie*-type cases, there was competition between two season contracts. However, in *Heyman*, the party seeking injunctive relief offered remuneration on a game-by-game basis only, as opposed to Heyman's new contract, which was seasonally based. His contract with the Hartford Capitals allowed compensation only for games "actually played." It also included an option year, which is most unusual since the original contract was on a per-game basis. Was this the straw that made the agreement unconscionable? The indices appear to be entirely on the side of Hartford. The original contract also allowed for injunctive relief if Heyman played for another team. The *Heyman* court based its decision on the fact that "the terms and provisions of this contract are too harsh and one-sided to permit equitable enforcement."

G. NEGOTIATING THE CONTRACT

Suppose an athlete chooses you as his agent. What does your job description include? To begin with, although agents are not required to be attorneys, the first document an agent must be familiar with, the collective bargaining agreement, is written by lawyers for lawyers. It is a difficult document to understand, even for those who are legally trained. Most sports agents, then, are lawyers or have some legal training. (Chapter 3, Agents, explores some of the regulations, that control the activities and education of would-be athlete representatives.)

The document that you, the agent, negotiate about with the representative of management is the standard player's contract (SPK). This agreement is a part of the collective bargaining agreement, which is the agreement that controls the union-management relationship in that sport. Some sports currently have salary caps. The salary cap information is found in the collective bargaining agreement. You must know the "cap status" of the team you are negotiating with. Other materials that you must be familiar with are the league constitution and bylaws and the team's biographical information as expressed in the league's annual yearbook (or guide or register or whatever the source of the biographical information is called in each particular league).

Know the parties involved. Know yourself. Know the athlete thoroughly. Know the team. Know each entity's strengths and weaknesses. Know your opposite number in the team's negotiation team. Leverage your contacts. Who do you know who knows the team's negotiator? Also, keep close track of that team's cap salary and its projected cap status as the "negotiation season" wears on.

Generally, the art of negotiation in sports is similar to negotiating in more standard venues. Although the SPK is relatively fixed, there are still ways to flesh it out and maximize the benefits for your client. As an axiom, the more money up front, the better. The more money in the signing bonus, the better. Longer contracts are good. Longer guaranteed contracts are better. Some of these goals are almost impossible because of collective bargaining and salary cap considerations, but occasionally inroads may be made. Although the SPK is a monolith, management will usually not object to incentive clauses, for example, bonuses for making the "all-rookie" team, attendance clauses, and so on.

Currently, one of the easiest things about negotiation is the wealth of comparative statistics and information that are available from the particular union. In prior times, agents seeking information about the contract value of similarly situated draft choices from earlier drafts had to scour yellowed copies of *The Sporting News* or call up the agent for a comparable athlete from an earlier draft (and hope that the agent wasn't exaggerating too much). The unions, and to some extent the Internet (but again, watch out for puffery, and the information is somewhat piecemeal) can provide by draft pick, or team, or position, or physical measurements, a complete statistical file of the relative worth of each potential professional athlete. All this leads to an understanding of the type and worth of contracts that similarly positioned athletes were able to obtain. Also, it is important to work with the unions since they are in essence the athlete's cofiduciary in negotiating the contract. Remember, the athlete may be a client, but he's also a union member. The unions, with their comparable statistical data, take the guesswork out of creating a bottom-line figure for establishing the relative worth of your client's contract.

As is discussed in Chapter 4, Labor Law, much of the athlete's potential negotiation strengths are defined by the collective bargaining agreement. Again, it is imperative that an agent immerse herself in this document before attempting to negotiate a professional athlete's contract. The SPK and collective bargaining agreement contain many rules and benefits that automatically accrue to the athlete; however, there are still certain issues that reside completely within the domain of the athlete's negotiation representative. Some examples are amount of signing bonus, time of payment of the signing bonus, desirability of a loan, insurance, length of contract, injury or skill guarantees, various bonuses and incentives, deciding the appropriate mix of initial year salary and annual installments, option clauses, salary adjustment, roster bonuses, and individual and team incentives generally.

The *Sample* case can be used by an astute agent as an example of understanding the needs of a client and then negotiating so that those requirements are satisfied. The question ripe for interpretation because of ambiguous contractual language was whether the simultaneous execution of several instruments resulted in one contract or in several separate agreements.

SAMPLE v. GOTHAM FOOTBALL CLUB, INC.

59 F.R.D. 160 (S.D.N.Y. 1973)

EDELSTEIN, Chief Judge.

Defendant has moved, pursuant to Fed. R. Civ. P. 56(b) for summary judgment on the three causes of action alleged in plaintiff's complaint. These causes of action charge respectively: (1) a breach of plaintiff's 1969 personal services contract; (2) a breach of plaintiff's 1970 personal services contract; and (3) injury to plaintiff's good name, reputation, and career as a result of his allegedly wrongful dismissal. . . .

As to the first cause of action both motions must be denied because there exist genuine issues of material fact. Fed. R. Civ. P. 56(c). Defendant is the owner and operator of a professional football team popularly known as the "New York Jets." On September 1, 1968, it entered into three separately executed written agreements with plaintiff under which plaintiff was required to render services as a professional football player for the 1968, 1969 and 1970 football seasons. Each document represents the agreement between plaintiff and defendant for a different year. The current dispute only pertains to the contracts covering the 1969 and 1970 football seasons.

The first cause of action is predicated on the alleged wrongful termination of plaintiff's contract for the 1969 season. The termination of plaintiff's contract arose from a series of events related to an injury he allegedly sustained while performing in a pre-season exhibition football game on August 1, 1969, and a subsequent dispute concerning his physical ability to resume normal player activities for defendant.

With regard to the first cause of action, defendant argues that any claim is barred because plaintiff failed to comply with the grievance procedures set forth in paragraph 14 of their contract [the injury-benefits clause], i.e., plaintiff has not met the three pre-requisites of paragraph 14,[2] which limit defendant's unqualified right to terminate plaintiff's contract, salary, or both. Whether plaintiff has met these requirements appears to raise genuine issues of material fact. Additionally, it seems clear that factual questions likewise exist with respect to defendant's compliance with both paragraph 14 and other contractual provisions. [Paragraph 14 describes the procedures available to the injured athlete upon notice to the club physician.] . . .

Plaintiff argues that his dismissal was arbitrary since it came only after the defendant unsuccessfully sought to obtain "waivers"[4] and trade him to

---

[2] Briefly stated the three pre-requisites are as follows: (1) there must be an injury sustained during the performance of services pursuant to the contract; (2) written notice of such injury must be given to the team physician within thirty-six (36) hours of its occurrence; and (3) once the team physician certifies a player as physically fit to resume normal player activities the player must submit within the next seventy-two (72) hours to a physical examination by a physician of his choice in order to dispute such finding.

[4] "Waivers" is the process whereby a team informs the league office that it is terminating a player's contract. Before a player is let go, however, each team gets an opportunity to claim the

another professional football team. The defendant denies this allegation, and justifies the dismissal on plaintiff's alleged failure to comply with paragraph 14. The points and counterpoints made by both parties need not be detailed. It is sufficient that these matters arguably raise genuine issues of fact. . . .

Turning to an examination of the second cause of action the court is confronted with the allegation that plaintiff's dismissal in 1969 entitles him to recovery of his 1970 salary under the injury-benefits clause of his contract. This allegation is grounded on plaintiff's contention that both parties intended to enter into one three-year contract covering the 1968, 1969 and 1970 football seasons, notwithstanding the existence of three separately executed documents. Accordingly, plaintiff argues that since his alleged injury was sustained during the performance of a three-year contract he is entitled to his salary for the remaining term of the contract. . . .

To the contrary, defendant contends that the three separately executed documents were intended to represent three one-year contracts. Thus, if obligated to pay at all, it would be liable only for the salary provided under the contract pertaining to the season in which the injury was sustained. After a careful and thorough independent review of the record the court finds that the parties entered into three one-year contracts, rather than a single three-year contract. Accordingly, defendant is granted summary judgment with respect to plaintiff's second cause of action. . . .

Having determined that the parties entered into three separate contracts, it is necessary to evaluate plaintiff's second claim in light of this conclusion.

Paragraph 14 of the 1970 contract makes it unequivocally clear that the injury-benefits provision[9] is operative only during the relevant contract period. In this instance only during the 1970 football season. In pertinent part, paragraph 14 provides that if a

> Player is injured in the performance of his services *under this contract* . . . the Club will . . . continue, *during the term of this contract*, to pay Player his salary . . . if and so long as it is the opinion of the Club Physician that Player, because of such injury, is unable to perform the services required of him *by this contract* (emphasis added.)

Since the injury alleged by plaintiff occurred during the term of his 1969 contract, and since the 1970 contract is a separate agreement, plaintiff cannot prevail on his second cause of action. Only if plaintiff had sustained a disabling injury during the term of the 1970 contract would he be entitled to invoke the injury-benefits clause of that contract. Hence, defendant is entitled to summary judgment as a matter of law with respect to plaintiff's second claim. . . .

Reviewing the dispositions, the court denies plaintiff's cross-motion for summary judgment on both its first and second causes of action. Plaintiff's motion in the alternative for an order under Rule 12(f) striking defendant's

---

player. The team with the worst record during the previous season gets first crack at claiming the player. If no team selects the player after all teams in inverse order of their league standing have had an opportunity to claim the player, the player is deemed waived.

[9] The injury-benefits provision, which is contained in paragraph 14, . . . allows a player to collect his entire salary under the contract if he is injured and unable to play during the term of the contract.

third affirmative defense is likewise denied. Defendant's motion for summary judgment is denied with respect to plaintiff's first cause of action but granted with respect to plaintiff's second cause of action. As to the last branch of defendant's motion, a continuance is granted until such time as plaintiff can obtain sufficient discovery to further perfect his third claim.

So ordered.

The next case, *Eckles v. Sharman*, involved a coach's contract, but the same negotiation skills that one would use with an athlete are similarly meritorious here. In *Eckles*, the court held that the record did not permit a determination that, as a matter of law, the option and pension clauses were unessential and could be severed. Accordingly, the court could not find that the coach had agreed to the assignment of his contract from a defunct team to plaintiff's basketball team. In negotiations, the coach's agent should have reinforced the contractual language so as to indicate his client's desire to maintain and continue both the option and pension clauses in case his contract was assigned.

ECKLES V. SHARMAN

548 F.2d 905 (10th Cir. 1977)

BREITENSTEIN, Circuit Judge.

This is an action by the owner of a professional basketball team for breach of contract by a former coach and for the inducement of that breach by the owner of another professional basketball team. Judgment was entered on a jury verdict for $250,000 against the coach and for $175,000 against the inducing owner. We reverse and remand with directions.

After these appeals were filed, the plaintiff-appellee Mountain States Sports, Inc., became bankrupt and R. T. Eckles, trustee in bankruptcy, was substituted as the appellee in each case. References herein will be to Mountain States rather than to the trustee.

Defendant-appellant Sharman was the coach of the San Francisco Warriors, a professional basketball team of the National Basketball Association, NBA. In 1968 he was persuaded to leave the San Francisco team and to coach the Los Angeles Stars of the newly formed American Basketball Association, ABA. The contract between Sharman and the Los Angeles team was for seven years and called for a starting salary of $55,000 with yearly increases of 5%. Provisions of the contract pertinent to these cases are:

(1) Sharman was given an "option to purchase 5% ownership of the Club" at a price to be agreed upon between him and the owner.
(2) Sharman was to participate in a "pension plan" of an undefined nature.
(3) The parties agreed that: "In the event any one paragraph of this Agreement is invalid, this Agreement will not fail by reason thereof but will be interpreted as if the invalid portion were omitted."
(4) California law governs the agreement.

In 1970 the Los Angeles Stars were sold for $345,000 to plaintiff Mountain States Sports, Inc., a Colorado corporation, of which Bill Daniels was the president and principal stockholder. An addendum to the sale agreement provided:

> Buyer shall not be obligated to assume the Sharman contract unless he shall have confirmed his willingness to transfer to the city selected by Buyer for operation of the team. Seller states that Sharman has orally expressed his willingness to do so.

The team was moved to Salt Lake City, Utah, and became the Utah Stars. Without anything in writing pertaining to his participation in the move, Sharman went to Salt Lake City with the team. Sharman coached the Utah Stars during the 1970-1971 season and the team won the ABA championship.

During the two years that the team was in Los Angeles with Sharman as coach nothing was done with regard to the option and pension provisions of the contract. Boryla, the general manager of the Utah Stars, told Sharman that the pension provision would be worked out. Later Sharman and Daniels, the president of Mountain States, had numerous communications, both oral and written, concerning Sharman's pension rights. No final agreement was reached. In June, 1971, Sharman resigned as coach of the Utah Stars and, in July, signed a contract to coach the Los Angeles Lakers of the NBA.

Mountain States brought suit in Utah state court charging Sharman with breach of contract. The complaint was amended to assert a claim against defendant-appellant California Sports, Inc., the owner of the Los Angeles Lakers, and two individuals for the tortious inducement of Sharman's breach of contract. Service was obtained on California Sports under the Utah long-arm statute. . . . The case was removed to the United States District Court for the District of Utah and fell before Judge Anderson.

California Sports contends that the court erred in assuming in personam jurisdiction over it on the basis of service under the long-arm statute. . . .

The court acknowledged that the contracts of California Sports in Utah were unrelated to the alleged inducement and then referred to Utah contracts "resulting from exhibition and scouting ventures and nationwide telecasts." The court noted that the complaint charged injury to the Utah business of Mountain States.

Judge Anderson conducted extensive pre-trial proceedings and entered a comprehensive pre-trial order. [He ruled that the parties' intent regarding the severability and pension clauses are fact question. Judge Anderson ruled a mistrial and the case was assigned to Judge Ritter.] At the conclusion of all the evidence, Judge Ritter directed a verdict against Sharman on the question of liability.

The case went to the jury on the questions of damages recoverable from Sharman, liability of the other defendants charged with inducement of contract breach and, if there was inducement, the damages resulting therefrom. The jury returned verdicts (1) in favor of the individual sued for inducement, (2) against Sharman in the amount of $250,000, and (3) against California Sports in the amount of $175,000.

Implicit in the direction of a verdict against Sharman on the question of liability is a ruling that as a matter of law (1) the contract between Sharman and the Los Angeles Stars was valid and enforceable, (2) the contract was validly assigned to Mountain States Sports, and (3) the option and pension provisions of the contract were severable from the remainder thereof.

The option clause was unenforceable because it was nothing more than an agreement to agree. The pension clause did not state (1) the amount of pension, (2) the manner in which it would be funded, and (3) the age at which the pension would begin. The plaintiff does not seriously contest the defense claim that the pension clause is ambiguous.

Plaintiff relies on the severance clause which says that "[i]n the event any one paragraph of this Agreement is invalid," the agreement will not fail but will be interpreted as if the invalid portion was omitted. We have a failure of two paragraphs. Sharman and representatives of the plaintiff negotiated for about 15 months over the two mentioned clauses, principally that pertaining to the pension.

Good faith negotiations over various terms of an agreement do not make a fatally ambiguous contract valid and enforceable. The controlling California law is that for there to be an enforceable contract the parties must agree on the essential and material terms. . . . If a contract has been agreed upon and all that remains is good faith negotiations or elaboration of nonessential terms, the contract will be held legally cognizable despite the uncertainties. . . . The question is not whether good faith negotiations had taken place but whether the option and pension were so essential to the contract that failure to agree on the pertinent terms made the contract unenforceable. . . .

The crucial question is whether the clauses to be severed are essential to the contract. Essentiality depends on the intent of the parties. . . .

The intent evidence is not all one way. Sharman testified that without the option and pension provisions he would not have left the well-established NBA for the newly-established ABA. His testimony was corroborated by other witnesses. On the other hand, the record reveals that Sharman never made any serious efforts to clarify or enforce the option clause. Nothing was done about the pension clause during the two years that Sharman and the team were in Los Angeles. During the fifteen months that Sharman was with the Utah Stars many communications, both written and verbal, passed between Sharman and representatives of the team owners. Nothing was accomplished. From the evidence in the record a reasonable man could have drawn an inference one way or the other on the question of intent.

We have repeatedly held that a verdict may not be directed unless the evidence all points one way and is susceptible of no reasonable inferences which sustain the position of the party against whom the motion is made. . . . On the record presented it may not be said, as a matter of law, that the option and pension clauses were unessential and hence severable. Neither can it be said, as a matter of law, that without the resolution of the controversy over those clauses Sharman agreed to the assignment of the contract to the owners of the Utah Stars. The pertinent intent questions required factual determination by the jury under proper instructions. The court erred in directing a verdict against Sharman and in favor of Mountain States on the liability issue.

The liability of California Sports depends on whether the contract between Sharman and the owner of the Los Angeles Stars was valid and whether the contract was enforceable by the owner of the Utah Stars against Sharman. If the contract was not valid, and if the contract was not enforceable by the Utah Stars, California Sports is not liable under the claim of tortious inducement of breach. The error of the court in directing a verdict on the question of Sharman's liability requires the reversal of the judgment against California Sports.

In the circumstances, it is not necessary for us to discuss the defendants' claims of many errors based on admission and rejection of evidence and on restriction of cross-examination. It is enough to say that the trial was not conducted in an impartial manner. In a new trial, judicial conduct similar to that appearing in the record before us, hopefully, will not be repeated.

The potential of a new trial impels us to discuss one matter in which the parties are in disagreement. The problem is the measure of damages and the instructions relating thereto. The defendants say that they are not liable for lost profits and that the measure of damages is either the increased replacement expense or, if the employee is unique or irreplaceable, the increased remuneration which the employee would receive in the open market. Defendants point out that Sharman's replacements were obtained at lower salaries than that paid Sharman and that the Los Angeles Lakers paid Sharman basically what he received from the Utah Stars.

Damages for breach of contract should be sufficient "to place the plaintiff in the position he would be in if the contract had been fulfilled." . . . Lost profits may be recovered in an employee breach of contract case if the employer can show that the parties had reason to believe that losses would result from the breach. . . .

Consequential damages such as lost profits may be recovered in an appropriate case for breach of an employment contract. In the case here, they can be justified only on a finding that Sharman, as a coach, was unique or irreplaceable. The evidence in this regard was conflicting. The jury should have been told that the plaintiff could not recover damages for lost profits or diminished franchise value without a finding that Sharman was irreplaceable as a coach.

Additionally, the recovery of consequential damages may be had in a suit for breach of an employment contract only if those damages were reasonably foreseeable when the contract was made. The court instructed the jury that it could presume that all damages which were the natural result of the breach were were reasonably foreseeable. Natural result and foreseeability do not equate in a breach of employment case. Consequential damages for breach of an employment contract may only be those that the employee had reason to believe at the time of contract making would occur if he breached the contract. . . . The failure of the court to instruct the jury that to award consequential damages the jury must find that the claimed losses were reasonably foreseeable at the time when the contract was made may explain how the jury awarded $250,000 in damages against Sharman. The entire franchise of the Los Angeles Stars had been sold to the plaintiff a little more than a year before the breach for $345,000. The sale contract included the players and attributed no value to the services of Sharman.

The jury verdicts awarded a recovery of $250,000 from Sharman and $175,000 from California Sports. The judgment of the court reads that the plaintiff "recover against defendants, William Sharman and California Sports, Inc., jointly and severally, the sum of $250,000" and against California Sports individually $175,000. The judgment is inconsistent with the verdicts and cannot stand. It may be that damages for inducement may not be less than damages for breach. We know of no law which permits the pyramiding of losses for inducement on top of damages for breach. The pyramiding action of the court is indicative of the atmosphere in which the trial was conducted.

In Nos. 75-1434 and 75-1435, the judgments are severally reversed and the case is remanded for a new trial in accordance with this opinion.

Upon consideration of the entire record we conclude that the interests of justice require that the retrial of this case should be by a judge from without the District of Utah. Judge Anderson recused because of the incident which resulted in the mistrial. The conduct of the trial by Judge Ritter indicates that he has a strong personal bias and prejudice incompatiable "with the impartiality that litigants have a right to expect in a United States district court." See *United States v. Ritter*, 10 Cir., 540 F.2d 459, 464.

The panel is authorized to say that the other members of court, except for Judge Hill who did not participate, agree that the retrial of this case should be by a judge from without the District of Utah.

QUESTIONS AND DISCUSSION

1. Each sport has its own issues, but there are some general truisms. Professors Berry and Wong cite the following as key considerations negotiators should be aware of before attempting to negotiate:

   a. Length of the contract (including options)
   b. Basic salary per year (or season)
   c. Signing bonus (perhaps reporting bonus as well)
   d. Incentive or performance bonuses
   e. Guarantees
   f. Trade provisions (contract assignments)
   g. Additional injury protection
   h. Fringes and special benefits
   i. Personal conduct provisions

   Berry & Wong, 1 *Law and Business of the Sports Industries* §422 at 232 (1986). Can you think of other considerations? See also Falk, *The Art of Contract Negotiation*, 3 Marq. Sports L.J. 101 (1992); Lindgren, *Sport and the Law: The Player's Contract*, 4 J. Cont. L. 135 (1991); and Zucker, *Sports Negotiations: The Art of the Contract*, 7 DePaul-LCA J. Art & Ent. L. & Poly. 194 (1997).

2. Each sport has its own special considerations. Probably the most individualistic is the National Football League because of its hard (dollar-for-dollar) cap. There is almost a pseudoscience of "capology" that accompanies the sport these days. Even incentives, if they are likely to be

achieved in that year, must be counted against that year's cap. Some pundits have stated that you can best serve your client by negotiating first (and fast and friendly) while there are still cap pie pieces left. Is that sage advice?

The current NFL collective bargaining agreement's duration is 1993-2003, so the following articles are more background in nature: Steinberg, *Negotiating Contracts in the National Football League*, 5 Sports Law. 1 (1987). Roberts, *Interpreting the NFL Player Contract*, 3 Marq. Sports L.J. 29 (1992); For hockey contracts, see Weiler, *Legal Analysis of the NHL Player's Contract*, 3 Marq. Sports L.J. 59 (1992).

3. *See generally* Fisher & Ury, *Getting to Yes: Negotiating Agreement without Giving In* (2d ed. 1991). *See also* Chapman, *NHL Contract Negotiation*, in *Law of Professional and Amateur Sports* ch. 8 (Uberstine ed., 1988); Faber, *The Evolution of Techniques for Negotiation of Sports Employment Contracts in the Era of the Agent*, 10 U. Miami Ent. & Sports L.J. 165 (1993); Fishof & Shapiro, *Putting It on the Line: The Negotiating Secrets, Tactics, and Techniques of a Top Sports and Entertainment Agent* (1983); Greenberg & Gray, *Sports Law Practice* §§3.01-5.25 (2d ed. 1998); Moorad, *Negotiating for the Professional Baseball Player*, in *Law of Professional and Amateur Sports* ch. 5 (Uberstine ed., 1988); Simon, *The Game Behind the Game: Negotiating in the Big Leagues* (1993); Steinberg, *Negotiating NBA Contracts*, in *Law of Professional and Amateur Sports* ch. 7 (Uberstine ed., 1988); Steinberg, *Representing the Professional Football Player*, in *Law of Professional and Amateur Sports* ch. 6 (Uberstine ed., 1988); Yasser et al., *Sports Law: Cases and Materials* ch. 9, at 607-647 (4th ed. 2000).

4. The question in *Sample* was whether the simultaneous execution of several instruments resulted in one contract or in several separate agreements. A good negotiator will anticipate the potential problems that might arise from a seemingly ambiguous clause. If there is a possible concern, a representative should negotiate a change in the language so that it will be in her client's favor if a problem does indeed occur. In *Sample*, plaintiff would want the three contracts to be viewed as one instrument instead of separate agreements; he would also want some of the terms to continue from instrument to instrument. If that is his goal, he should have negotiated the inclusion of such language (e.g., "notwithstanding the usual practice, the execution of several instruments will be deemed to be one separate and unitary agreement with all terms of each instrument continuing throughout the life of the contractual relationship").

H. COACHES

The amount that NBA and NFL coaches receive as salaries are nearly as staggering as some of their players' salaries. Added to this sticker shock are the salaries that collegiate basketball and football coaches can receive in some premier sports programs. However, other than the amount, another unique aspect of coaches' contracts is the absolute lack of job security.

Coaches have no real union or standardized contract.[1] Martin Greenberg explains the many hats that a college coach must wear these days:

> The coach of the 1990's [and later] is not only required to be an instructor, but also a fund raiser, recruiter, academic coordinator, public figure, budget director, television and radio personality, alumni glad hander, and whatever else the university's athletic director or president may direct the coach to do in the best interest of the university's athletic program.[2]

Apparently, each duty, if not performed to the desires of the university's administration, can result in immediate termination.

Another part of a college coach's responsibility is to assist in achieving high graduation rates and, correspondingly, to monitor their athletes' grade point averages so as to maintain and continue their ongoing National Collegiate Athletic Association (NCAA) eligibility. But remember, if the team does not win, the coach probably will be fired, regardless of stellar graduation rates.

Many of these programs have the capacity to generate great sums of money, funds that are needed to pay for other athletic programs in that university and money that is used for that school's general fund. The less tangible benefits include the heightened prestige a winning program can bring to the university and to its status vis-à-vis attracting better (and more affluent) students.

1. Contract Formation

A collegiate coach's contract offers not only a salary with institutional fringe benefits but also additional compensation packages, which might include shoe, apparel, and equipment endorsements; television and radio shows; speaking engagements; personal appearances; and summer camps. The job may also provide housing, insurance premiums, country club memberships, business opportunities, and use of automobiles.[3]

Most coaches, because of the variety of their tasks, have "historically been able to leave their employment virtually at will despite their prior contractual commitments."[4] However, as in SPKs, a university can include a clause within the coach's contract that allows an injunction to prohibit a coach from "jumping" his contract and working with another entity.[5]

Upon termination by the school prior to contract expiration, the courts usually allow the coach to recover monetary damages. However, the coach's right to be compensated may be reduced if there is a mitigation of damages clause, which offsets the relief if she obtains other employment. The question of severance pay usually involves the amount of money earned in related contracts (perquisites) such as shoe endorsements.

---

[1] See generally The Coaching Game: Turnovers Tell the Story How Long They Stay, USA Today, Mar. 26, 1990, at 10C; Dodd, Job Security Remains Elusive in Pro Sports, USA Today, Feb. 20, 1992, at 9C.

[2] Greenberg, 1 Sports Law Practice §6.01(2) at 447 (1993). See also Greenberg, Representation of College Coaches in Contract Negotiations, 3 Marq. Sports L.J. 101 (1992); Greenberg, College Coaching Contracts Revisited: A Practical Perspective, 12 Marq. Sports L. Rev. 127 (2001).

[3] Greenberg, 1 Sports Law Practice §6.01(6) at 454 (1993).

[4] Graves, Coaches in the Courtroom, 12 J.C. & U.L. 545, 549 (1986).

[5] New England Patriots Football Club, Inc. v. University of Colorado, 592 F.2d 1196 (1st Cir. 1979).

The court in the case that involved Georgia Tech's football coach "Pepper" Rodgers held that most of his perquisites should be deemed to be a part of his compensation and must be included in the severance package.

RODGERS v. GEORGIA TECH ATHLETIC ASSOCIATION

303 S.E.2d 467 (Ga. Ct. App. 1983)

Franklin C. "Pepper" Rodgers brought this breach of contract action against the Georgia Tech Athletic Association to recover the value of certain perquisites which had been made available to him as the head coach of football at the Georgia Institute of Technology. . . . The issue presented for resolution by this appeal is whether Rodgers is entitled to recover the value of certain perquisites or "fringe benefits" of his position as head coach of football under the terms of his contract of employment with the Association.

Rodgers was removed from his coaching position by vote of the Association's Board of Trustees on Dec. 18, 1979, notwithstanding a written contract . . . [to] December 31, 1981. In addition to an annual salary, the contract provided that Rodgers, as an employee of the Association, would be entitled "to various insurance and pension benefits and perquisites" as he became eligible . . . which were provided voluntarily by the Association through December 31, 1981, . . . the expiration date claims entitlement under this employment contract.

Rodgers lists some 29 separate items as such perquisites. . . . The subject contract was in the form of a letter from the Association dated April 20, 1997 offering Rodgers the position of head coach of football for three years at an annual salary plus certain benefits and perquisites. This contract provided that Rodgers could be terminated for illness or other incapacity continuing for three months, death, or "any conduct or activity involving moral turpitude or would constitute an embarrassment to the school." Rodgers accepted this contract on April 25, 1977. This contract was extended until January 1, 1982 by a subsequent letter agreement between the parties. At its December 18, 1979 meeting, the Association's Board of Trustees determined that a change should be made in the position of head coach of football. . . . [T]he evidence of record supports the Association's view that Rodgers was merely relieved of his duties as the head coach of football yet remained an employee of the Association. . . . [T]his disassociation of Rodgers from his position and duties was not "for cause" pursuant to the terms of the contract. Therefore, the Association was obligated to pay Rodgers that part of the amount set forth in the contract "which he himself was entitled to receive as compensation for his services. . . ."

[Rodgers, as an employee of the Association and as head football coach, was entitled to "perquisites."]

The evidence was in dispute as to the remaining items — profits from his television and radio shows and from his summer football camp plus the loss of use of a new automobile and tickets to professional sporting events — i.e., whether such items were contemplated by the parties at the time the contract was executed as perquisites or fringe benefits to which Rodgers would be entitled as the result of his position as head coach of football at Georgia

Tech. These items are of the same evidence that the Association knew that Rodgers would receive (and, in fact, did receive) as the result of his head coaching position and that his removal from that position would result in the loss of these benefits. Finding no error to reverse, the decree appealed from is therefore, affirmed.

2. Salaries, Benefits, Clauses, and Breaches

There is no standard form of a coach's employment contract. There is no union that represents coaches. The crux of the contract is whether the coach agrees to perform all duties and responsibilities that accompany the position. The coach must also agree to comply with all pertinent NCAA regulations. Collegiate coaching contracts are usually three to five years in length. Many contracts contain a "rollover" provision, which extends the contract for an additional year. That is, if a coach had a five-year contract with a rollover, the university, at the end of each season and with the coach's consent, has a right to extend it for an additional year.

A coach's contract may also contain a reassignment clause that allows the university to remove a person as a head coach, without per se ending his contract by assigning him to a new title or new responsibilities. This clause may contain a caveat that stipulates that this job reassignment will not be inconsistent with the coach's education and experience. If the coach refuses to accept this reassignment, the school may dissolve the employment contract pursuant to the contract's termination provisions.

As regards compensation, every coaching contract contains a guaranteed base salary. For example,

> The guaranteed based salary paid by the University to the coach for services and satisfactory performance under the terms and conditions of this Employment Agreement shall be at the rate of $_____ per year, payable in _____ installments by the University to the Coach on the _____ day of each calendar month during the term of this Agreement.[6]

Since the contract is usually long term, there usually are stipulated periodic increases to the guaranteed base salary during the length of the contract.

The contract also contains a provision for fringe benefits, which may include life and health insurance, paid vacation, retirement plans, travel or out-of-pocket expenses, use of an automobile, auto insurance, gas credit card, car maintenance expenses, tuition waivers for family members, complimentary tickets, country club and health club memberships, and possibly living accommodations. There also are bonus clauses: They may be in the form of a set amount or a percentage of either base salary or net revenues. The bonuses may be in the form of a signing bonus or based on postseason tournament participation, win-loss record, home attendance, graduation rates, length of service, and so on. All contracts provide the coach with outside or supplemental income sources common to many major sport coaching contracts, for

---

[6] Stoner & Nogay, *The Model University Coaching Contract (MCC): A Better Starting Point for Your Next Negotiation*, 16 J.C. & U.L. 43, 63-64 (1989).

example, the added benefit of payment for radio and TV talk show programs. Perhaps the most consistent money maker is the caveat that the coach will supervise summer athletic camps and clinics.

Although there is no standard contract, most coaching contracts follow a basic pattern, as exemplified by the following form.

PRO FORMA COLLEGE CONTRACT

EMPLOYMENT AGREEMENT

THIS   AGREEMENT   made   and   entered   into   at   _____ City, _____, this _____ day of _____, 19___, by and between the   _____   (hereinafter   referred   to   as   "University") and _____ (hereinafter referred to as "Employee").

WITNESSETH:

WHEREAS, the University desires to formalize the terms and conditions under which the Employee shall serve as the University's Head Coach Varsity Basketball Coach; and

WHEREAS, Employee is willing to devote his best efforts and ability to the furtherance of the University's Varsity Basketball program.

NOW, THEREFORE, in consideration of the premises and of the mutual promises hereinafter set forth, University and Employee agree as follows:

1. Employment. The University hereby employs Employee as the Head Coach for the Men's Varsity Basketball Program. . . . It is hereby acknowledged by the University that the position for which the Employee is hired is unique and requires special talents. . . . Difference of opinion, complaints, or misunderstandings which Employee may have arising out of this Agreement, shall be resolved in accordance with the procedures contained in the University's "Handbook for Full Time Staff."

Employee agrees to be a loyal Employee of the University. . . . Employee further agrees to abide by and comply with the constitution, bylaws, interpretations and policies of the National Collegiate Athletic Association ("NCAA") . . . including recruiting rules, as now constituted or as may be amended. . . . If Employee is found to be in violation of NCAA rules and regulations, whether while employed by the University or during prior employment at another NCAA member institution, Employee shall cooperate fully and completely with any investigation of any alleged violation of [these] . . . or any . . . regulations of the NCAA. . . .

2. Term of Employment. The term of this Agreement shall be for a period of five (5) years. . . . [T]he University shall have the right to extend the term of this Agreement with the prior written approval of the Employee for one (1) additional year following the completion of each Men's Varsity Basketball season. . . .

3. Compensation:

    A. An Annual Salary of: $_____
    B. T.V. and radio compensation of: $_____

C. Annual supplement from private
   donations of: $_____

              TOTAL Base Salary: $_____

4. Bonus Compensation. . . .

c. [Attendance bonus]
d. [Win bonus—20 or more games]
e. ["Coach of Year" bonus]
f. [Graduation rate bonus]

5. Guaranteed Contract. Notwithstanding anything to the con-
trary, . . . [this] compensation [is] deemed to be a Guaranteed Base Salary. . . .
10. Outside Employment. . . .
11. Restrictive Covenant. . . .
12. Termination by the University for Cause. The University shall have the
right to terminate this Employment Agreement for just cause at any time
during the term of this Agreement. . . . [Just clause includes:]

f. continuing series or pattern of violations of any laws, rules, regulations,
   constitutional provisions, by laws or interpretations of the
   University . . . or the NCAA which may, in the sole judgment of the
   University, reflect adversely upon the University or its athletic program;
g. Conduct of the Employee seriously prejudicial to the best interest of the
   University or its athletic program or which violates the University's
   mission. . . .

13. Termination Without Cause. . . .
14. Voluntary Termination by Employee. . . .

IN WITNESS WHEREOF, the parties hereto have executed this Agreement
as of the day and year first written.
BY: _____   _____
    UNIVERSITY   EMPLOYEE

3. Endorsements

Coaches are intrinsically high profile. Because of that coaches often attract
endorsement offers. The type of product endorsements for these local heros
run the gamut from car dealerships to sporting goods to restaurants to health
clubs. Shoe contracts (also apparel and equipment contracts) are especially
common and usually negotiated between the coach and the shoe company.
The shoe company (for example, L.A. Gear, Converse, Nike, or Adidas) pays
the coach a certain sum of money to act as a consultant and provides shoes,
warmups, gym bags, and so on, in exchange for the coach wearing or using the
company's products.

QUESTIONS AND DISCUSSION

1. One court has ruled that a university may remove a basketball head coach
   and offer reassignment as golf coach or basketball rules compliance

coordinator on the grounds that the coach's contract incorporated a statute that allowed the university to reassign personnel according to staff need. *See Munson v. State of Oregon*, 901 P.2d 904 (Or. Ct. App. 1995).

2. As regards the term of employment for a coaching contract, see *Roberts v. Wake Forest University*, 286 S.E.2d 119 (N.C. Ct. App. 1982); *Lindsey v. University of Arizona*, 754 P.2d 1152 (Ariz. Ct. App. 1987). A coach should define the length of term of the contract in writing and not let custom, usage, or the intentions of the parties dictate the length of employment. In different sports, the custom and usage of that sport may imply a longer term. For example, golf coaches traditionally have very long tenures, at least six years.

3. What contract terms can you imagine that would provide more security for the coach? How about more flexibility for the university?

4. Should coaching contracts be standardized? Alternatively, should college coaches be unionized? Should professional coaches be unionized?

5. Martin Greenberg points out the unique concerns of college coaching including "the added pressures of the public concern involving student eligibility, academic progress and, most recently, the posting and disclosure of grades and graduation rates of student athletes." Greenberg, 1 *Sports Law Practice* 448 (1993).

6. "College sports has become a big business with high financial stakes. If the coach is not bringing in enough revenue, or is not perceived positively by the alumni or public a university may be forced to terminate his employment for fear of losing large amounts of money." Martin Greenberg, 1 *Sports Law Practice* 450 (1993). If you are the coach's attorney, what contractual language would you use to block termination on "whim" if the coach has achieved certain tangible milestones such as victories, NCAA compliance, and acceptable graduation rates?

7. Alternatively, if termination by whim is allowed, what language would you use as a coach's attorney in the liquidated damages clause that would assure a just, favorable, and comprehensive severance package?

CHAPTER 3

AGENTS

The **Concept of Agents** is a relatively new phenomenon in sports. The field of sports agency has flourished because of the increased salaries and complexity of the collective bargaining agreements along with the many options that are available in structuring the athlete's renumeration.

As a response to alleged abuse, the unions initiated **Standard Representation Contracts** in the major team sports as a means to standardize the terms and the agents' fee percentages. This contract establishes the rights and responsibilities between the parties. Its use is mandatory as part of the union-agent certification process.

The **Duties and Responsibilities** that are a part of the athlete-agent relationship are varied and include contract negotiation, tax and financial investments, and public relations. The preeminent nexus in this relationship is the negotiation of the employment contract. A good-faith effort on the part of the agent is required.

Agent Regulation is a piecemeal attempt by the states, unions, and the National Collegiate Athletic Association (NCAA) to help control perceived agent excesses. For example, the National Football League Players' Association (NFLPA) established that all agents must first be certified as contract advisors before they negotiate an employment contract, even if the athlete is a rookie.

A. THE CONCEPT OF AGENTS

It is the very rare professional athlete these days who negotiates her own contract. Most athletes hire an agent to represent their interests. This relatively recent phenomenon is a direct result of the negotiation milieu (multiyear contracts, bonuses, salary caps, collective bargaining agreements, deferred compensation, and so on), as well as the huge amounts in total salary (for example, baseball player Alex Rodriquez's ten-year, $252 million contract). Representation includes many functions, but the key chore is the negotiation of a personal services contract with a professional sports team. Agents and athletes have a fiduciary relationship. As a result, agents are obligated to exercise the utmost care, good faith, honesty, and loyalty in all of their relations with the athlete.

The player-agent relationship is spelled out in the standard representation contract. Like the standard player's contract between the player and the team, the standard representation contract establishes the rights and responsibilities between player and agent. A representation contract calls only for a good-faith effort on the part of the agent; the agent's efforts do not necessarily have to be successful. But the agent is obligated to make a full disclosure of possible conflicting commitments and must receive prior consent from the athlete if potential conflicting interests exist.

The *Pickens* case is an example of what occurs when an athlete changes his mind regarding the selection of an agent. Bruce Pickens signed a representation agreement and then decided to sign with another agent who ultimately negotiated an employment contract with the National Football League. The original agent successfully sued Pickens for anticipatory breach of contract.

Total Economic Athletic Management of America, Inc. v. Pickens

898 S.W.2d 98 (Mo. Ct. App. 1995)

Ulrich, Presiding Judge.

This anticipatory breach of contract case arose from a representation agreement signed by Bruce Evon Pickens and Total Economic Athletic Management of America, Inc., d/b/a Team America, a Nebraska Corporation. That representation agreement was to allow Team America to act as Mr. Pickens' contract advisor in negotiating his National Football League player contract. However, before negotiations, Mr. Pickens engaged another contract advisor who actually negotiated the NFL player contract. The ensuing litigation resulted in a $20,000 judgment entered on a jury verdict for Team America and against Mr. Pickens.

Both parties appeal. In its appeal, Team America claims that the trial court erred in restricting argument on damages, in denying its motion for additur, and in overruling its motion for a new trial on damages only. In his cross-appeal, Mr. Pickens contends that the trial court erred in giving and refusing instructions. The judgment is affirmed.

Mr. Pickens' Cross-Appeal

. . . While a student at the University of Nebraska, Bruce Evon Pickens played football for the University's football team, a perennial National Collegiate Athletic Association (NCAA) Division I football power. Howard Misle is the president and owner of Total Economic Athletic Management of America, Inc., a corporation incorporated in Nebraska, d/b/a Team America. Mr. Misle apparently owns other businesses, including an automobile dealership in Lincoln, Nebraska. In behalf of Team America, Mr. Misle negotiates player contracts for athletes with professional football teams. Mr. Misle is a certified contract advisor by the National Football League Players' Association (NFLPA).

Trial evidence discloses that Mr. Misle and Mr. Pickens met when Mr. Pickens was a student at the University of Nebraska. On January 3,

1991, Mr. Pickens encountered Mr. Misle at Mr. Misle's automobile dealership. Mr. Pickens purchased a vehicle from the dealership, and Mr. Misle, in behalf of the dealership, advanced Mr. Pickens credit on a "house note." Mr. Pickens paid nothing for the automobile. Mr. Misle told Mr. Pickens that Mr. Pickens would be approached by many agents seeking to represent him in negotiations with a National Football League (NFL) professional football team to obtain a professional football player contract.

According to Mr. Misle's testimony, an agreement was signed by Mr. Pickens and Mr. Misle on January 18, 1991. The agreement bears the date January 20, 1991. Except for the deletion of paragraph 7, the agreement was a standard form entitled "Standard Representation Agreement Between NFLPA Contract Advisor and Player." Mr. Pickens was not given a copy of the document when it was signed. . . .

Team America had representation agreements with other football players. Mr. Misle had sent those agreements to the NFLPA office as provided by paragraph 7 in the NFLPA form contract. . . .

Mr. Pickens' testimony about signing the representation agreement differed from Mr. Misle's. . . .

Sometime in early 1991, after Mr. Pickens and Mr. Misle signed the document at the automobile dealership, Mr. Pickens played in the East-West Shrine game. According to Mr. Pickens, sometime after the game a coach at Nebraska asked him if he had an agent, and when he replied that he did not, the coach suggested Tom Condon, a former Kansas City Chief professional football player and agent of numerous professional football players. Mr. Pickens met with Mr. Condon several times in Kansas City and in Lincoln. Mr. Pickens then signed a standard NFLPA representation agreement making Mr. Condon his contract advisor to negotiate a professional football player contract with an NFL team.

Mr. Pickens testified that he spoke to Mr. Misle after he signed the agreement with Mr. Condon. He informed Mr. Misle that he had signed the agreement with Mr. Condon and that he had decided that Mr. Condon would be his agent. Mr. Pickens informed Mr. Misle that he would return the Audi automobile, and would reimburse Mr. Misle for the money he periodically extended to him after January 18, 1991. The money consisted of numerous checks and goods totaling more than $2,900. The money and the automobile were provided to Mr. Pickens when he was a student at the University of Nebraska in 1991.

NCAA rules preclude giving things of value to athletes when they are undergraduates. Additionally, the NFLPA precludes giving athletes anything of value to induce them to sign an NFLPA representation agreement.

The Atlanta Falcons professional football team drafted Mr. Pickens. He was the number three selection in the first-round draft selections. Tom Condon conducted the negotiations. The Atlanta Falcons initially offered $2,700,000 in three one-year player contracts. Mr. Condon eventually negotiated five one-year contracts which Mr. Pickens signed on October 5, 1991. Those NFL player contracts for the 1991, 1992, 1993, 1994, and 1995 football seasons provided for total compensation and work-out bonuses of $4,100,000 and other incentive bonuses. Mr. Pickens' entitlement to compensation under each player contract depended on his making the Atlanta Falcons team for that year. The NFL player contracts also provided for a guaranteed signing bonus of $2,492,000 payable over five years.

Issues

Mr. Pickens' six points on cross-appeal relate to giving or refusing instructions. . . .

Mr. Pickens' Points II, III, and VI concern the refusal of his proposed, alternative affirmative converse instructions. . . .

[Jury Instructions: . . .]

Instruction H

Your verdict must be for defendant if you believe plaintiff and defendant agreed to be governed by the NFLPA code of conduct and that the written agreement was thereafter not sent to the NFLPA. . . .

Mr. Pickens' claimed entitlement to a damage instruction based on quantum meruit is unfounded. . . .

No error resulted from submitting the damage instruction based on breach of contract. In its amended petition, Team America, as a wrongfully-terminated agent, pleaded anticipatory breach of contract and sought damages based on the provisions of the representation agreement with Mr. Pickens. Team America proceeded on a breach of contract theory. The trial court submitted to the jury a verdict director and a damage instruction modeled in part on the breach of contract pattern instructions. . . . The damage instruction submitted, therefore, was consistent with the cause of action pleaded and proved. . . .

Points IV and V are denied.

Team America's Appeal

Team America's appeal asserts the inadequacy of the $20,000 damage award for the anticipatory breach of the representation agreement. . . . The following facts are pertinent to damages:

In engaging a contract advisor, Mr. Pickens first signed an agreement with Howard Misle of Team America; Mr. Pickens then signed an agreement with Tom Condon. Mr. Misle and Mr. Condon had different backgrounds and experiences with negotiating NFL player contracts. Mr. Misle worked as an automobile dealer and a sports advisor. While working with another sports advisor, Mr. Misle negotiated for four or five NFL players in 1989. After obtaining certification as an NFLPA contract advisor and incorporating Team America, Mr. Misle negotiated contracts for eight to ten players. On the other hand, Mr. Condon had played football for the Kansas City Chiefs for eleven years. He was a licensed attorney. He served as president of the NFLPA for three years. As a certified NFLPA contract advisor, Mr. Condon had represented in contract negotiations with NFL teams over 200 NFL football players and numerous first-round draft selections. . . .

To prove damages Team America offered evidence of the NFL contracts that Tom Condon had actually negotiated for Mr. Pickens. Those NFL player contracts guaranteed Mr. Pickens signing bonuses of $2,492,000 and compensation for each season that he made the team. Mr. Pickens was required to qualify for the Atlanta Falcons team each year to receive compensation for that year. . . .

At the time of trial in 1993, Mr. Pickens had played football for the Atlanta Falcons during the 1991 and 1992 seasons and had been compensated for those seasons. At trial, Mr. Condon testified that Mr. Pickens would become a team member of the Atlanta Falcons Football Team in the 1993 season.

Restricting Argument on Damages

In Point II D, Team America contends that the trial court erred by not allowing it to claim damages based on Mr. Pickens' compensation for the 1994 and 1995 football seasons. . . .

Because no evidence established with reasonable certainty that Mr. Pickens would qualify and become a member of the Atlanta Falcons Football Team in 1994 and 1995, his fulfillment of the contracts for those years was uncertain and speculative. . . .

Alternative Motion for Additur . . .

Alternative Motion for a New Trial on Damages Only . . .

Arguing error from the denial of a new trial on damages, Team America asserts that the jury either made a mistake in calculating damages or disregarded the instruction on damages. Team America insists that its damages were determinable by the formula in the representation agreement entitling it to four percent of all money received by Mr. Pickens under his NFL player contracts. Team America sets Mr. Pickens' minimum receipts at $2,700,000, which represents the opening offer made by the Atlanta Falcons in negotiating the NFL player contract with Tom Condon. Team America also notes that under the contract actually negotiated, Mr. Pickens was guaranteed to receive $4,392,000, which represents his signing bonus of $2,492,000 plus compensation of $1,900,000 for the 1991, 1992, and 1993 seasons. According to Team America's calculations, the jury should have awarded damages of $108,000 ($2,700,000 × 4%) or $175,680 ($4,392,000 × 4%).

Countering, Mr. Pickens contends that the $20,000 damage award was within the range of the evidence presented to the jury. He contends that Team America's damages were not solely determinable by mathematical formula. He maintains that the damage evidence included matters other than the amounts actually negotiated by Tom Condon under the NFL player contracts. Stressing that Team America did not negotiate the NFL player contracts, Mr. Pickens contends that Team America was required to establish what it would have negotiated. Mr. Pickens asserts that the disparity between the experience of Mr. Misle and Mr. Condon demonstrated that Mr. Misle would not have been as successful as Mr. Condon in negotiating the contracts.

In reply, Team America asserts that it proved it would have negotiated NFL player contracts as favorable as those negotiated by Mr. Condon. In support, Team America points to Mr. Pickens' selection as number three in the first-round draft. As additional support, Team America points to evidence that Mr. Pickens' average annual compensation fell between those of the number two and the number four first-round draft choices. Team America emphasizes that, to award only $20,000 in damages, the jury would have had to determine that Mr. Misle would have negotiated a NFL player contract of only $500,000. . . .

In the context of professional sports, the player's breach of an agency agreement does not necessarily entitle the agent to commission. . . . Technically, the agent is only entitled to damages for breach of contract, *i.e.*, the value of the promised performance reduced by any expenses saved. . . . In addition, the agent is entitled to his commission only if he can show that, had he been permitted to continue performance, he would have been able to consummate the contracts upon which he claims commission. . . .

Contrary to Team America's assertions, it was not entitled to commissions based solely on the contracts negotiated by others. Although required to show what it would have negotiated, Team America points to no evidence showing its own past achievements in negotiating NFL player contracts. . . . Here, the $20,000 damage award appears to be within the range of the evidence, and is not unwarranted. The trial court's denial of a new trial on damages was not a clear abuse of discretion. Team America's Point II is denied.

Conclusion

Team America's appeal and Mr. Pickens' cross-appeal present no grounds for reversing the trial court's judgment. The judgment is affirmed.

All concur.

The real issue in *Pickens* is the calculation of damages. The jury decided on an amount, which defendant thought was too small, reasoning that the calculation should have been based on anticipatory damages. But the contract that was actually signed was not negotiated by the relatively inexperienced Howard Misle but by the extremely experienced Tom Condon. "Mr. Pickens asserts that the disparity between the experience of Mr. Misle and Mr. Condon demonstrated that Mr. Misle would not have been as successful as Mr. Condon in negotiating the contracts." The jury apparently agreed with this summation.

In *Brown v. Woolf*, the athlete sought punitive damages on the grounds that the agent violated his fiduciary obligation by not thoroughly investigating the financial stability of a certain sports franchise.

BROWN V. WOOLF

554 F. Supp. 1206 (S.D. Ind. 1983)

STECKLER, District Judge.

This matter comes before the Court on the motions of defendant, Robert G. Woolf, for partial summary judgment and for summary judgment. Fed. R. Civ. P. 56.

The complaint in this diversity action seeks compensatory and punitive damages and the imposition of a trust on a fee defendant allegedly received, all stemming from defendant's alleged constructive fraud and breach of fiduciary duty in the negotiation of a contract for the 1974-75 hockey season for plaintiff who was a professional hockey player. Plaintiff alleges that prior to the 1973-74 season he had engaged the services of defendant, a well known sports attorney and agent, who represents many professional athletes, has authored a book, and has appeared in the media in connection with such representation, to negotiate a contract for him with the Pittsburgh Penguins of the National Hockey League. Plaintiff had a professionally successful season that year under the contract defendant negotiated for him and accordingly again engaged defendant's services prior to the 1974-75 season. During the negotiations in July 1974, the Penguins offered plaintiff a two-year contract at $80,000.00 per year but plaintiff rejected the offer allegedly because defendant asserted that he could obtain a better, long-term, no-cut contract with a deferred compensation feature with the Indianapolis Racers, which at the time was a new team in a new league. On July 31, 1974, plaintiff signed a five-year contract with the Racers. Thereafter, it is alleged the Racers began having financial difficulties. Plaintiff avers that Woolf continued to represent plaintiff and negotiated two reductions in plaintiff's compensation including the loss of a retirement fund at the same time defendant was attempting to get his own fee payment from the Racers. Ultimately the Racers' assets were seized and the organizers defaulted on their obligations to plaintiff. He avers that he received only $185,000.00 of the total $800,000.00 compensation under the Racer contract but that defendant received his full $40,000.00 fee (5% of the contract) from the Racers.

Plaintiff alleges that defendant made numerous material misrepresentations upon which he relied both during the negotiation of the Racer contract and at the time of the subsequent modifications. Plaintiff further avers that defendant breached his fiduciary duty to plaintiff by failing to conduct any investigation into the financial stability of the Racers, failing to investigate possible consequences of the deferred compensation package in the Racers' contract, failing to obtain guarantees or collateral, and by negotiating reductions in plaintiff's compensation from the Racers while insisting on receiving all of his own. Plaintiff theorizes that such conduct amounts to a prima facie case of constructive fraud for which he should receive compensatory and punitive damages and have a trust impressed on the $40,000.00 fee defendant received from the Racers.

Defendant's motion for partial summary judgment attacks plaintiff's claim for punitive damages, contending that plaintiff has no evidence to support such an award and should not be allowed to rest on the allegations of his complaint. Further, he claims that punitive damages are unavailable as a matter of law in a constructive fraud case because no proof of fraudulent intent is required. By his motion for summary judgment, defendant attacks several aspects of plaintiff's claims against him. He argues (1) that plaintiff cannot recover on a breach of contract theory because Robert G. Woolf, the individual, was acting merely as the agent and employee of Robert Woolf Associates, Inc. (RWA), (2) that defendant's conduct could not amount to constructive fraud because (a) plaintiff alleges only negligent acts, (b) there is no evidence defendant deceived plaintiff or violated a position of trust, (c) there is no showing of harm to the public interest, and (d) there is no evidence that defendant obtained an unconscionable advantage at plaintiff's expense.

Turning first to the questions raised in the motion for partial summary judgment, the Court could find no Indiana case specifically discussing the availability of punitive damages in an action based upon the theory of constructive fraud. Cases from other jurisdictions reflect a division of authority. The Court concludes that Indiana courts would not adopt a per se rule prohibiting such damages in a constructive fraud action, but would rather consider the facts and circumstances of each case. If elements of recklessness, or oppressive conduct are demonstrated, punitive damages could be awarded. . . .

Indiana cases contain several formulizations of the tort of constructive fraud. Generally it is characterized as acts or a course of conduct from which an unconscionable advantage is or may be derived. . . .

Defendant argues that despite the customary existence of such fact questions in a constructive fraud case, judgment is appropriate in this instance because plaintiff has produced nothing to demonstrate the existence of fact questions. He makes a similar argument in the motion for partial summary judgment on the punitive damages issue. . . .

In this case, defendant has offered affidavits, excerpts of depositions, and photocopies of various documents to support his motions. He contends that such materials demonstrate that reasonable minds could not conclude that defendant did the acts with which the complaint charges him. In response, plaintiff rather belatedly offered portions of plaintiff's depositions as well as arguing that issues such as those raised by a complaint based on constructive fraud are inherently unsuited to resolution on a motion for summary judgment.

Having carefully considered the motions and briefs and having examined the evidentiary materials submitted, the Court concludes that summary judgment would not be appropriate in this action. The Court is not persuaded that there are no fact questions remaining unresolved in this controversy such that defendant is entitled to judgment as a matter of law. As movant for summary judgment, defendant bears the "heavy burden" of clearly demonstrating the absence of any genuine issue of a material fact. . . .

By reason of the foregoing, defendant's motions for partial summary judgment and for summary judgment are hereby Denied.

It is so ordered.

The question here is what, if anything, did Bob Woolf do wrong? That is, what duty as an agent did Woolf breach? Plaintiff claims that Woolf breached his fiduciary duty by failing to investigate the Racers' financial stability. Plaintiff further alleges that this failure to investigate amounts to constructive fraud. This opinion only addresses Woolf's motion for summary judgment, which is denied.

QUESTIONS AND DISCUSSION

1. In *Pickens*, the agent sought an anticipatory breach of contract after the athlete retained a new agent. In professional sports, the player's breach of an agent agreement does not in itself entitle the agent to commission. So then how should the agent be compensated if the agreement is terminated before the employment contract is negotiated? The agent is entitled only to damages for breach of contract, the value of the promised performance reduced by any expenses saved. The agent is entitled to commission only if he can prove that, if allowed to continue to perform, he would have been able to complete the contract. In *Pickens*, the court awarded the agent $20,000, although he had asked for either $108,000 or $175,680. How did the court arrive at $20,000?

2. In *Brown v. Woolf*, the athlete brought a suit in constructive fraud and breach of fiduciary duty against the late, pioneering agent Bob Woolf. The key element in the concept of an agent is the fiduciary duty toward the client, the athlete. At the core of this obligation is the fiduciary's duty to act for the benefit of the beneficiary and not for the fiduciary's own interests. Plaintiff claimed that the agent breached his fiduciary duty by not investigating the financial stability of the Indianapolis Racers and "failing to investigate possible consequences of the referred compensation package . . . [and] obtain guarantees . . . and by negotiating reductions in plaintiff's compensation . . . while insisting on receiving all of his own." Plaintiff wants punitive damages. Punitive damages is a sum in excess of any compensatory damages and are available only when the tortfeasor, here, the agent, commits quite serious misconduct with a bad intent. Punitive damages could be awarded here if plaintiff Brown can prove recklessness or oppressive conduct on the party of the agent. Are punitive damages warranted here?

3. Constructive fraud is found if the court finds that the fiduciary breached a duty to another that induces a justifiable reliance to his or her prejudice. *Brown v. Woolf* involved the agent's motions for partial summary judgment and for summary judgment, both of which were denied on the basis that substantial fact issues existed as to the existence of a fiduciary relationship as regards the agent's allegedly false representations. What additional facts would the court need to answer the question of whether constructive fraud occurred?

4. The question is whether Woolf breached the representation contract with Andrew Brown or committed fraud. A typical representation contract calls for an agent's good-faith effort and no potential conflicts of interest. Is there anything in the facts that show that Woolf violated these two obligations?

5. Are agents necessary? Should they be regulated? If so, what should be the requirements, and who should be the regulating entity? Agents are only a very recent phenomenon, and as Steve Patterson, currently President of the Portland Trailblazers, opined about the "good ol' days" (pre-1970), "[o]nce a contract was agreed to, there was as much a chance that it would be written on a restaurant placemat as anything else since there was no Uniform Player Contract." Champion, *Sports Law in a Nutshell* × (2d ed. 2000).

See generally Faber, *The Evolution of Techniques for Negotiation of Sports Employment Contracts in the Era of the Agent*, 10 U. Miami Ent. & Sports L. Rev. 117 (1993); Garbarino, *So You Want to Be a Sports Lawyer, or Is It a Player's Agent, Player's Representative, Sports Agent, Contract Advisor, Family Advisor, or Contract Representative?* 1 VILL. Sports & Ent. L. J. 11 (1994); Muleherji, *The Role of Sports Agents*, 2 Vand. J. Ent. L. & Prac. 108 (2000); Wahl, *Representation of an Athlete: The Team Approach*, 11 Ent. & Sports Law. 1 (1993); Weiss, *Professions and Businesses: Athlete Agent*, 10 Ga. St. U.L. Rev. 189 (1993).

6. Oliver Luck, former quarterback with the Houston Oilers, negotiated his own contract, but then again, he was a lawyer. Should all agents be lawyers since all the pertinent forms and materials that must be mastered are legal documents (the standard player's contract, the collective bargaining agreement, the league's constitution and bylaws, and so on)? How about former coaches with degrees in sports administration who want to negotiate contracts? Should there be some definitive line of demarcation — perhaps a course in sports law and then a "certification of successful completion and mastery"? See Nahrwald, *'Are Professional Athletes Better Served by a Lawyer Representative than an Agent? Ask Grant Hill*, 9 Seton Hall J. Sport L. 431 (1999).

B. STANDARD REPRESENTATION CONTRACTS

Like the standard player's contract (SPK), there is the standard representation contract (SRK). This contract between the athlete and the agent establishes the rights and responsibility of both parties in the major team sports. The SRK is usually provided by the union. It calls for an agent's good-faith effort in the negotiation of the player's employment contract and for a full and complete disclosure of all areas of potential conflicts of interest.

There are at least four essential clauses within as SRK: notice in writing of potential conflicts, a negotiation in good-faith clause, an arbitration provision, and a provision that stipulates which state's law will govern if interpretation of the contract becomes necessary. An agent's basic responsibility is to exercise good faith overall and to act as a trustee for the client's money when investing it.

The following is an example of a form player-agent representation agreement.

STANDARD REPRESENTATION AGREEMENT

Champion, Fundamentals of Sports Law 712-714 (2d ed. 2004)

Representation Agreement

AGREEMENT made this _____ day of _____ 19____,
by_____ (herein called the Representative)
and _____ (herein called the Player).

Witnesseth

In consideration of the mutual promises made in this agreement, the parties agree as follows:

2. Representative Services

During the term of this Agreement, Representative shall have the exclusive right to represent, advise, counsel, and assist Player as follows:

(a) Negotiation of any and all professional athletic contracts on behalf of the Player;
(b) Consultation and advice with respect to finances, taxes and tax planning;
(c) Preparation of income tax returns due during the term of this agreement;
(d) Collection of income due to Player and maintenance of commercial and other bank accounts under Player's name at such bank or banks as Player may designate;
(e) Payment of Player's accounts due the term of this agreement;
(f) Engagement of services of an investment advisor to provide investment advice to Player at no additional cost. . . .

4. Compensation

Player shall pay to representative for services rendered pursuant to this Agreement a sum equal to the greater of either (a) the sum of standard hourly rate charged by Representative for such services up to a maximum of $___per hour multiplied by the hours spent on those services by Representative, or (b)____ percent (____%) of the gross amount of all monies received by Player. . . .

5. Expenses

Player agrees to reimburse Representative for travel expenses actually incurred by Representative in the performances of his services. . . .

[The agent agrees to be ethical and that any disputes will be arbitrated.]

9. Entire Agreement

This document sets forth the entire agreement between the parties and replaces or supersedes all prior agreements between the parties relating to the same subject matter. This Agreement cannot be changed orally. . . .

11. Governing Law

This agreement shall be construed, interpreted and enforced according to the laws of the state of _____.

12. Severability

In the event any provision of this agreement shall be for any reason rendered illegal or unenforceable, the same shall not affect the validity or enforceability of the remaining provisions. . . .

In *Bias v. Advantage International, Inc.*, the court held that Bias's estate failed to prove whether agent could possibly have fulfilled contractual commitment (in SRK) to procure life insurance policy given Bias's history of cocaine abuse. The court further held that the estate failed to prove whether agent could have possibly obtained Reebok endorsement during the two days between the selection of Len Bias by the Boston Celtics in the first round of the NBA draft and his death from cocaine poisoning.

BIAS v. ADVANTAGE INTERNATIONAL, INC.,

905 F.2d 1558 (D.C. Cir. 1990)

SENTELLE, Circuit Judge:

This case arises out of the tragic death from cocaine intoxication of University of Maryland basketball star Leonard K. Bias ("Bias"). James Bias, as Personal Representative of the Estate of Leonard K. Bias, deceased ("the Estate"), appeals an order of the District Court for the District of Columbia which granted summary judgment to defendants Advantage International, Inc. ("Advantage") and A. Lee Fentress on the Estate's claims arising out of a representation agreement between Bias and Advantage. . . . For the reasons which follow, we affirm the order of the District Court granting to the defendants' summary judgment with respect to the Estate's claims. . . .

I. Background

On April 7, 1986, after the close of his college basketball career, Bias entered into a representation agreement with Advantage whereby Advantage agreed to advise and represent Bias in his affairs. Fentress was the particular Advantage representative servicing the Bias account. On June 17 of that year Bias was picked by the Boston Celtics in the first round of the National Basketball Association draft. On the morning of June 19, 1986, Bias died of cocaine intoxication. The Estate sued Advantage and Fentress for two separate injuries allegedly arising out of the representation arrangement between Bias and the defendants.

First, the Estate alleges that, prior to Bias's death, Bias and his parents directed Fentress to obtain a one-million dollar life insurance policy on Bias's life, that Fentress represented to Bias and Bias's parents that he had secured such a policy, and that in reliance on Fentress's assurances, Bias's parents did not independently seek to buy an insurance policy on Bias's life. Although the defendants did obtain increased disability coverage for Bias, in a one-million dollar disability insurance policy with an accidental death rider, they did not secure any life insurance coverage for Bias prior to his death.

Second, on June 18, 1986, the day after he was drafted by the Boston Celtics, Bias, through and with Fentress, entered into negotiations with Reebok International, Ltd. ("Reebok") concerning a potential endorsement contract. The Estate alleges that after several hours of negotiations Fentress requested that Bias and his father leave so that Fentress could continue negotiating with Reebok representatives in private. The Estate alleges that Fentress then began negotiating a proposed package deal with Reebok on behalf of not just Bias, but also other players represented by Advantage. The Estate contends that Fentress breached a duty to Bias by negotiating on behalf of other players, and that because Fentress opened up these broader negotiations he was unable to complete the negotiations for Bias on June 18. The Estate claims that as a result of Fentress's actions, on June 19, when Bias died, Bias had no contract with Reebok. The Estate alleges that the contract that Bias would have obtained would have provided for an unconditional lump sum payment which Bias would have received up front.

The District Court awarded the defendants summary judgment on both of these claims. With respect to the first claim, the District Court held, in effect, that the Estate did not suffer any damage from the defendants' alleged failure to obtain life insurance for Bias because, even if the defendants had tried to obtain a one-million dollar policy on Bias's life, they would not have been able to do so. The District Court based this conclusion on the facts, about which it found no genuine issue, that Bias was a cocaine user and that no insurer in 1986 would have issued a one-million dollar life insurance policy, or "jumbo" policy, to a cocaine user unless the applicant made a misrepresentation regarding the applicant's use of drugs, thereby rendering the insurance policy void.

With respect to the Estate's second claim, the District Court concluded that the defendants could not be held liable for failing to produce a finished endorsement contract with Reebok before Bias's death because the defendants had no independent reason to expedite the signing of the endorsement contract to the extent argued by the Estate, and because the defendants could not have obtained a signed contract before Bias's death even if they had tried to do so.

The Estate appeals both of the District Court's conclusions, arguing that there is a genuine issue as to Bias's insurability and regarding the defendants' failure to sign a Reebok contract on Bias's behalf prior to Bias's death. . . .

V. Conclusion

In order to withstand a summary judgment motion once the moving party has made a prima facie showing to support its claims, the nonmoving party must come forward with specific facts showing that there is a genuine issue for trial. Fed. R. Civ. P. 56(e). The Estate has failed to come forward with such facts in this case, relying instead on bare arguments and allegations or on evidence which does not actually create a genuine issue for trial. For this reason, we affirm the District Court's award of summary judgment to the defendants in this case.

QUESTIONS AND DISCUSSION

1. Other than the four essential clauses that must be included in a standard representation (disclosure of conflicts, good faith, arbitration, and indication of prevailing law), can you think of any other "essential" clauses that should be included?
2. Unions these days stipulate the form of agreement and the percent of renumeration that is allowable. For example, the National Football League

Players' Association (NFLPA) stipulates that before an individual can be an agent for a union member in contract negotiations, he must first be certified as a contract advisor. Once certified, the agreement that must be used between agent and athlete is the "Standard Representation Agreement Between NFLPA Contract Advisor and Player." "Contract advisor" must pay money, submit an application, pass a test, and attend continuing education seminars. Should there be more? *See generally* Grosse & Warren, *The Regulation, Control, and Protection of Athlete Agents*, 19 N. Ky. L. Rev. 49 (1991).

3. *In Bias v. Advantage International, Inc.*, the estate failed to recover for alleged negligent performance of agent's duties based on his failure to execute insurance policy and endorsement contracts prior to the death of basketball player Len Bias. Do you find the court's rationale convincing for holding against the estate on these questions? If Advantage actually sought a package deal (including other Advantage clients) with Reebok, instead of an individual endorsement contract for Len Bias, would that action amount to a breach of a fiduciary duty? A conflict of interest? Both?

4. The draft in which Len Bias was selected in the first round by the Boston Celtics was on June 17, 1996. He died of cocaine poisoning on June 19, 1996. The court held that no duty was breached by defendant for "failing to push to obtain a signed [endorsement] contract on June 18, 1996." Defendants argued that "an endorsement contract cannot be negotiated, drafted, and signed in a single day." The court stressed that plaintiff did not refute defendants' assertions that an insurance policy could not be obtained for a drug user and that an endorsement contract could not be executed in one day. The estate alleged that defendants tried to negotiate with Nike about several of their clients at one time, which precluded the successful conclusion of the Bias endorsement contract on June 18, 1996. Is this case an example of a losing cause from the beginning, or does it show that the estate failed in its attempts to specifically refute defendants' contentions?

5. In *Zinn v. Parrish*, 644 F.2d 360 (7th Cir. 1981), (*infra*) the court emphasized that the representation agreeement calls for good faith in negotiating the employment contract. In *Detroit Lions v. Argovitz*, 580 F. Supp. 542 (E.D. Mich. 1984), (*infra*), the court emphasized that all conflicts of interest must be completely known and understood. In *Bias*, is the failure to obtain insurance comparable to the *Zinn v. Parish* obligation of good-faith negotiation? In *Bias*, the contract could not have been negotiated since he died two days after he was drafted. Should the failure to provide insurance be sufficient to create an actionable breach of contract?

6. In *Jones v. Childers*, 18 F.3d 899 (11th Cir. 1994), an agent was held liable for knowingly recommending problematic tax shelters in violation of his fiduciary duties in the representation agreement. Could one argue under *Zinn v. Parrish* that securing tax shelters is not essential to the goal of negotiating the representation agreement?

7. In *Mandich v. Watters*, 970 F.2d 462 (8th Cir. 1992), a former hockey player sued an agent for secretly negotiating an illegal side agreement that deprived the player of some postretirement salary. Apparently these side agreements were common although technically illegal. The court of

appeals affirmed the district court's holding that the player's claim was collaterally estopped by a National Hockey League arbitrator's resolution of Mandich's prior contract claim against the North Stars. In both *Bias* and *Mandich*, the agents were sued on the basis that the results were less than the athlete had anticipated. However, the standard is the reasonably prudent agent using good-faith efforts overall. Both efforts showed good faith, although it is easier to see it in *Bias* where the athlete had a drug addiction. But, good faith was also evident in *Mandich*, where side deals were common and the agent secured the best contract possible for a client whose health was seriously suspect. Should the standard change from case to case? Should the reasonably prudent agent in *Mandich*, as a fiduciary, at least inform Mandich that he might enter into side deals that negatively affect some future renumeration?

C. DUTIES AND RESPONSIBILITIES

An agent's raison d' etre is to negotiate the employment contract for the athlete-client. To do this, an agent must possess the necessary background, skills, experiences, and expertise to perform this task in such a manner that it will correspond with the skills and knowledge that are standard to the profession—in effect, the ordinarily prudent and skilled athlete agent for that particular sport. The goal is not the best contract humanly attainable; but the obligation is merely to negotiate the contract in good faith using one's best abilities. The standard responsibilities of the agent usually include contract negotiation, investments, taxes, and public relations. But the number of functions that an agent can agree to perform can cover many other areas. A possible list of jobs includes

1. contracts,
2. taxes,
3. financial planning,
4. money management,
5. investments,
6. income tax preparations,
7. incorporation,
8. estate planning,
9. endorsement,
10. sports medicine consultations,
11. health and physical training consultation,
12. career and personal development counseling,
13. postcareer development,
14. insurance, and
15. legal consultations.

To achieve these goals, there are a variety of steps that must be accomplished:

1. contract negotiation, including tax planning;
2. medical needs and assessment;

3. postcareer planning, including job evaluation, etc.
4. short-term monthly budgets and long-term financial planning;
5. off-the-field opportunities, including endorsements, commercials, developing musical or broadcasting talents, education and job consulting, continued educational and job counseling, and public appearances; and
6. self-improvement plans, including drug and alcohol counseling (if necessary), continued educational or career preparation, speech and acting lessons, and advice relating to grooming, relationships with the media, and improved self-image and confidence.

Zinn v. Parrish is an iconic case that stands for the principle that a good-faith effort overall in the negotiation of the contract is called for when an agent represents an athlete. *Detroit Lions v. Argovitz*, on the other hand, which follows *Zinn*, can be used to emphasize the importance of fully explaining any potential conflicts of interest between the agent and the athlete.

1. Good Faith

ZINN V. PARRISH

644 F.2d 360 (7th Cir. 1981)

BARTELS, Senior District Judge.

This is an appeal in a diversity action by Leo Zinn from a judgment of the District Court for the Northern District of Illinois, Eastern Division, wherein he sought to recover agent fees due him under a personal management contract between him and the defendant Lamar Parrish. In an earlier posture of the case, Parrish prevailed against Zinn on a motion for summary judgment on the ground that the contract was unenforceable because of Zinn's failure to obtain a license under the Illinois Private Employment Agency Act, Ill. Rev. Stat., ch. 48, §§197a et seq. ("the Employment Agency Act"). Zinn v. Parrish, 461 F. Supp. 11 (N.D. Ill. 1977). This court reversed and remanded, concluding that certain unresolved issues of fact precluded an award of summary judgment. 582 F.2d 1282 (7th Cir. 1978).

On remand, the district court rendered a verdict in Parrish's favor following a bench trial, on the grounds that the contract was void for Zinn's failure to register under the Investment Advisers Act of 1940, 15 U.S.C. §§80b-1 et seq. ("the 1940 Act"), and that Zinn had failed to perform his own obligations under the contract. In this appeal Parrish renews his contention, rejected by the trial court, that the contract was unenforceable under the Employment Agency Act.

Facts

For over two decades the appellant Zinn had been engaged in the business of managing professional athletes. He stated that he was a pioneer in bringing to the attention of various pro-football teams the availability of talented players at small black colleges in the South. In the Spring of 1970, Parrish's coach at Lincoln University approached Zinn and informed him that Parrish had been picked by the Cincinnati Bengals in the annual National Football League draft of college seniors, and asked him if he would help Parrish in negotiating the contract. After Zinn contacted Parrish, the latter signed a one-year "Professional Management Contract" with Zinn in the Spring of 1970, pursuant to which Zinn helped Parrish negotiate the terms of his rookie contract with the Bengals, receiving as his commission 10% of Parrish's $16,500 salary. . . .

Under the 1971 contract, Zinn obligated himself to use "reasonable efforts" to procure pro-football employment for Parrish, and, at Parrish's request, to "act" in furtherance of Parrish's interest by: a) negotiating job contracts; b) furnishing advice on business investments; c) securing professional tax advice at no added cost; and d) obtaining endorsement contracts. It was further provided that Zinn's services would include, "at my request efforts to secure for me gainful off-season employment," for which Zinn would receive no additional compensation, "unless such employment (was) in the line of endorsements, marketing and the like," in which case Zinn would receive a 10% commission on the gross amount. . . .

The 1974-77 contracts with the Bengals were signed at a time when efforts were being made by the newly-formed World Football League to persuade players in the NFL to "jump" to the WFL to play on one of its teams. By the end of 1973 season Parrish had become recognized as one of the more valuable players in the NFL. . . .

Shortly after signing the 1974 series of contracts, Parrish informed Zinn by telephone that he "no longer needed his services." . . .

In addition to negotiating the Bengals contracts, Zinn performed a number of other services at Parrish's request. In 1972 he assisted him in purchasing a residence as well as a four-unit apartment building to be used for rental income; he also helped to manage the apartment building. That same year Zinn negotiated an endorsement contract for Parrish with All-Pro Graphics, Inc., under which Parrish received a percentage from the sales of "Lemar Parrish" t-shirts, sweat-shirts, beach towels, key chains, etc. The record shows that Zinn made a number of unsuccessful efforts at obtaining similar endorsement income from stores with which Parrish did business in Ohio. He also tried, unsuccessfully, to obtain an appearance for Parrish on the Mike Douglas Show. Zinn arranged for Parrish's taxes to be prepared each year by H & R Block. . . .

Discussion

I

We turn, first, to the district court's decision that Zinn's contract was void under the 1940 Act. The Act makes void any contract for investment advice made by an unregistered adviser. 15 U.S.C. §80b-15(b). The issue thus presented is whether Zinn was engaged by reason of the terms of his contract and all his activities thereunder in the business of advising others as to security transactions. If so, he was required to register as an investment adviser. 15 U.S.C. §80b-3(a). . . .

Zinn was not a dealer or trader in securities and there was no evidence to indicate that he was financially interested in the securities recommendations he passed along. Therefore the conflict of interest at which the Act was aimed was not present here. . . .

II

From these findings the court concluded that Zinn "was unable to and did not provide the services which he was obligated to provide by the contract under which he sues." We address the findings seriatim.

Employment Procurement

Zinn's obligation under the 1971 Management Contract to procure employment for Parrish as a profootball player was limited to the use of "reasonable efforts." . . .

We conclude that up to that point it is impossible to fault Zinn in the performance of his contract, nor can we find any basis for Parrish to complain of Zinn's efforts in 1974 with respect to procuring employment for him as a pro-football player. . . .

Other Obligations

We focus next on the other obligations, all incidental to the main purpose of the contract. . . .

Zinn was further obligated to act in Parrish's professional interest by providing advice on tax and business matters, by "seek(ing) . . . endorsement contracts," and by making "efforts" to obtain for Parrish gainful off-season employment. Each of these obligations was subject to an implied promise to make "good faith" efforts to obtain what he sought. . . .

Parrish fully accepted Zinn's performance for the years 1970, 1971, 1972, and 1973 by remitting the 10% due Zinn under the contract. Parrish was at all times free to discharge Zinn as his agent before a new season began. Instead, he waited until Zinn had negotiated a series of contracts worth a quarter of a million dollars for him before letting Zinn know over the phone that his services were no longer required. That call, coupled with Parrish's failure to make the 10% commission payments as they came due, was a breach of the 1971 contract. . . .

We must disagree with the district court's interpretation of the terms of the contract, and Zinn's obligations thereunder, and also with its findings and conclusions concerning Zinn's performance. Insofar as the district court made any findings of fact which are inconsistent with the foregoing, we find them to be clearly erroneous. Consequently, judgment should be entered for Zinn. The decision of the district court is Reversed, and the case Remanded for further proceedings consistent with this opinion, including the calculation of damages and interest, if any, due Zinn.

2. Conflicts of Interest

DETROIT LIONS V. ARGOVITZ

580 F. Supp. 542 (E.D. Mich. 1984)

DeMascio, District Judge.

The plot for this Saturday afternoon serial began when Billy Sims, having signed a contract with the Houston Gamblers on July 1, 1983, signed a second contract with the Detroit Lions on December 16, 1983. On December 18, 1983, the Detroit Lions, Inc. (Lions) and Billy R. Sims filed a complaint in the Oakland County Circuit Court seeking a judicial determination that the July 1, 1983, contract between Sims and the Houston Gamblers, Inc. (Gamblers) is invalid because the defendant Jerry Argovitz (Argovitz) breached his fiduciary duty when negotiating the Gamblers' contract and because the contract was otherwise tainted by fraud and misrepresentation. Defendants promptly removed the action to this court based on our diversity of citizenship jurisdiction.

For the reasons that follow, we have concluded that Argovitz's breach of his fiduciary duty during negotiations for the Gamblers' contract was so pronounced, so egregious, that to deny recision would be unconscionable.

Sometime in February or March 1983, Argovitz told Sims that he had applied for a Houston franchise in the newly formed United States Football League (USFL). In May 1983, Sims attended a press conference in Houston at which Argovitz announced that his application for a franchise had been approved. The evidence persuades us that Sims did not know the extent of Argovitz's interest in the Gamblers. He did not know the amount of Argovitz's original investment, or that Argovitz was obligated for 29 percent of a $1.5 million letter of credit, or that Argovitz was the president of the Gamblers' Corporation at an annual salary of $275,000 and 5 percent the yearly cash flow. The defendants could not justifiably expect Sims to comprehend the ramifications of Argovitz's interest in the Gamblers or the manner in which that interest would create an untenable conflict of interest, a conflict that would inevitably breach Argovitz's fiduciary duty to Sims. Argovitz knew, or should have known, that he could not act as Sims' agent under any circumstances when dealing with the Gamblers. Even the USFL Constitution itself prohibits a holder of any interest in a member club from acting "as the contracting agent or representative for any player."

Pending the approval of his application for a USFL franchise in Houston, Argovitz continued his negotiations with the Lions on behalf of Sims. On April 5, 1983, Argovitz offered Sims' services to the Lions for $6 million over a four-year period. The offer included a demand for a $1 million interest-free loan to be repaid over 10 years, and for skill and injury guarantees for three years. The Lions quickly responded with a counter offer on April 7, 1983, in the face amount of $1.5 million over a five-year period with additional incentives not relevant here. The negotiating process was working. The Lions were trying to determine what Argovitz really believed the market value for Sims really was. On May 3, 1983, with his Gamblers franchise assured, Argovitz significantly reduced his offer to the Lions. He now offered Sims to the Lions for $3 million over a four-year period, one-half of the amount of his April 5, 1983, offer. Argovitz's May 3rd offer included a demand for $50,000 to permit Sims to purchase an annuity. Argovitz also dropped his previous demand for skill guarantees. The May 10, 1983 offer submitted by the Lions brought the parties much closer.

On May 30, 1983, Argovitz asked for $3.5 million over a five-year period. This offer included an interest-free loan and injury protection insurance but made no demand for skill guarantees. The May 30 offer now requested $400,000 to allow Sims to purchase an annuity. On June 1, 1983, Argovitz and the Lions were only $500,000 apart. We find that the negotiations between the Lions and Argovitz were progressing normally, not laterally as Argovitz represented to Sims. The Lions were not "dragging their feet." Throughout the entire month of June 1983, Mr. Frederick Nash, the Lions' skilled negotiator and a fastidious lawyer, was involved in investigating the possibility of providing an attractive annuity for Sims and at the same time doing his best to avoid the granting of either skill or injury guarantees. The evidence establishes that on June 22, 1983, the Lions and Argovitz were very close to reaching an agreement on the value of Sims' services.

Apparently, in the midst of his negotiations with the Lions and with his Gamblers franchise in hand, Argovitz decided that he would seek an offer from the Gamblers. . . .

. . . When Sims arrived in Houston, he believed that the Lions organization was not negotiating in good faith; that it was not really interested in his services. His ego was bruised and his emotional outlook toward the Lions was visible to Burrough and Argovitz. Clearly, virtually all the information that Sims had up to that date came from Argovitz. . . .

During these negotiations at the Gamblers' office, Mr. Nash of the Lions telephoned Argovitz, but even though Argovitz was at his office, he declined to accept the telephone call. . . . Although it is generally true that an agent is not liable for losses occurring as a result of following his principal's instructions, the rule of law is not applicable when the agent has placed himself in a position adverse to that of his principal. . . .

Argovitz's conflict of interest and self dealing put him in the position where he would not even use the wedge he now had to negotiate with the Lions, a wedge that is the dream of every agent [the Gamblers' offer]. . . .

On November 12, 1983, when Sims was in Houston for the Lions game with the Houston Oilers, Argovitz asked Sims to come to his home and sign certain papers. . . . Included among those papers . . . was a waiver of any claim that Sims might have against Argovitz for his blatant breach of his fiduciary duty brought on by his glaring conflict of interest. . . . In spite of his fiduciary relationship he had Sims sign a waiver without advising him to obtain independent counseling. . . .

We are mindful that Sims was less than forthright when testifying before the court. However, we agree with plaintiff's counsel that the facts as presented through the testimony of other witnesses are so unappealing that we can disregard Sims' testimony entirely. We remain persuaded that on balance, Argovitz's breach of his fiduciary duty was so egregious that a court of equity cannot permit him to benefit by his own wrongful breach. We conclude that Argovitz's conduct in negotiating Sims' contract with the Gamblers rendered it invalid.

Conclusions of Law . . .

5. In light of the express agency agreement, and the relationship between Sims and Argovitz, Argovitz clearly owed Sims the fiduciary duties of an agent at all times relevant to this lawsuit.

6. An agent's duty of loyalty requires that he not have a personal stake that conflicts with the principal's interest in a transaction in which he represents his principal. . . .

7. A fiduciary violates the prohibition against self-dealing not only by dealing with himself on his principal's behalf, but also by dealing on his principal's behalf with a third party in which he has an interest, such as a partnership in which he is a member. . . .

12. Argovitz clearly had a personal interest in signing Sims with the Gamblers that was adverse to Sims' interest—he had an ownership interest in the Gamblers and thus would profit if the Gamblers were profitable, and would incur substantial personal liabilities should the Gamblers not be financially successful. Since this showing has been made, fraud on Argovitz's part is presumed, and the Gamblers' contract must be rescinded unless Argovitz has shown by a preponderance of the evidence that he informed Sims of every material fact that might have influenced Sims' decision whether or not to sign the Gamblers' contract. . . .

Judgment will be entered for the plaintiffs rescinding the Gamblers' contract with Sims.

It is so ordered.

3. Miscellaneous Duties

a. Financial Planning

The basic tenet for money management and financial planning from the prospective of the agent should be the athlete's financial security at the time of his retirement.

The first steps are to evaluate assets, outline objectives, and implement a plan to achieve these objectives. There should be three fundamental financial principles for the professional athlete, namely preservation of capital (an athlete receives a large amount of money in a short period of time), tax reduction, and liquidity (money when one needs it). While the athlete might make a large amount of money in a short span of time (for example, 5 years), afterwards he still has 40 or so years to contend with before retirement. The agent then must adopt a strategy to maximize the appreciation of the athlete's investment portfolio. There are many ways and methods to achieve these goals; the alternatives range from conservative investments with no risk (for example, certificates of deposit) to those which are more speculative (for example, common stock). The dilemma is palpable: The money is limited, so it is unwise to lose money. Perhaps one should be conservative in financial strategies. On the other hand, the athlete's savings may be insufficient to stretch to retirement unless the process is more speculative, so perhaps one should choose investments with higher risk but greater yield.

b. Taxation Strategies

Because of the nature of the athlete's existence—a lot of money in a short span of time while young and that's it—it is imperative that taxes be minimized. The money is limited, so it is necessary to reduce tax liability during those few money-making years. One strategy is to defer some of the income to nonplaying (and nonearning) years so that the amount taxed during the playing years is a lesser amount. The purpose of this planning is to maximize the benefit from those years in which a high income is recognized by spreading the tax liability to those years of lower income. There are many different ways in which an agent can arrange a financial strategy that includes tax awareness. These arrangements include deferred compensation plans, tax-sheltered investments, assignment of income, incorporation, and other contractual arrangements that spread out the receipt of income over a longer period than the period in which the athlete actively participated in her sport.

c. Public Relations

Another function of the agent can be to control the athlete's public relations. Bad press can destroy an already truncated career. A good relationship with the media might guarantee a positive public persona. If the fans like the athlete, then the other part of public relations — the marketing side — can come into play. An astute agent can manipulate popular sentiment into a marketing bonanza: magazine covers, car dealerships ads, beer pitches, a Wheaties box appearance, shoe endorsements, TV and motion pictures careers, trade shows, and so on. Agents have a fiduciary relationship with their athletes and must maintain a high ethical standard. This is especially true when the agent is also a lawyer.

d. Ethical Concerns

IN RE HENLEY

478 S.E.2d 134 (Ga. 1996)

PER CURIAM. This disciplinary matter concerns the appropriate sanction for violations of Standard 30 of Bar Rule 4-102(d), involving an attorney's representation of a client where the attorney has a financial or personal interest which may reasonably affect his professional judgment, where the client is a close friend of the attorney and does not object to the attorney's conduct. We hold that the client's relationship to the attorney and lack of objection to the attorney's conduct are not mitigating factors, and that, under the circumstances of this case, including the attorney's violation of Standard 40, by accepting compensation for legal services from one other than his client, a suspension of 90 days is the appropriate sanction.

The underlying facts are undisputed. From the fall of 1992 until early 1993, respondent, Fredrick J. Henley, Jr., represented Todd Kelly, a 1992 member of the University of Tennessee football team and a 1993 first round draft choice for a National Football League team. In this same time period, Henley entered into an agreement with Bienstock Sports in New York whereby Henley would assist Bienstock in recruiting Kelly as its client. Under the agreement, if Kelly became a client of Bienstock Henley would receive one-third of any commissions paid by Kelly to Bienstock. Bienstock gave Henley $5,000 in expenses and loaned him an additional $25,000. Following Henley's successful recruitment of Kelly, Bienstock sent Henley a statement crediting him for the kickback on Kelly's commission payment and deducting the amount Henley owed Bienstock in loans.

Based on the foregoing, the State Bar filed a formal complaint against Henley charging him with violations of various professional standards under Bar Rule 4-102(d), including Standard 30 (representing a client where the attorney has a financial interest, without fully disclosing that interest, and obtaining written consent or giving written notice), and Standard 40 (accepting compensation for legal service from one other than the client without the client's consent after full disclosure). In addition, the State Bar alleged Henley violated Standards 33, 35, 36, and 37, involving an attorney's business transactions with a client and representation of multiple clients by an attorney. . . .

We agree with the Review Panel that this disciplinary matter concerns Henley's violations of Standards 30 and 40. We disagree, however, with the Review Panel's assessment of the severity of Henley's conduct in this case, and of the mitigating and aggravating factors involved, as well as its recommendation of the appropriate sanction.

The record shows Henley violated Standard 30 by failing to give Kelly written notice of the full extent of Henley's own financial interest in Bienstock Sports' obtaining Kelly as its client, or obtaining Kelly's written consent to Henley's representation notwithstanding Henley's financial interests. . . . There is no evidence that Henley disclosed the kickback arrangement between him and Bienstock Sports which is the very essence of Henley's conflict in this case. . . . A lawyer's representation of a client where the lawyer has a financial or personal interest which will or reasonably may affect the lawyer's professional judgment illustrates one of the most blatant appearances of impropriety. . . .

We next turn to the appropriate discipline to impose, and in doing so we are guided by the American Bar Association Standards for Imposing Lawyer Sanctions (1991). . . . In light of Henley's violations in this matter, and having considered the mitigating and aggravating factors above, a 90-day suspension from the practice of law is appropriate. Accordingly, Henley is hereby suspended from the practice of law in this state for 90 days, and reminded of his duties under Bar Rule 4-219(c), to notify all clients of his inability to represent them, to take all actions necessary to protect the interest of his clients, and to certify to this Court that he has satisfied the requirements of this rule. . . .

All the Justices concur.

In *Speakers of Sport, Inc., v. ProServ, Inc.*, an agent sued competitor for tortious interference with a business relationship. Plaintiff alleged that defendant lured client away with fraudulent promises of obtaining endorsements, inducing him to terminate contract. Plaintiff wanted the agent's fee for the contract, which was ultimately negotiated for the player, Ivan Rodriguez, by a third agent.

SPEAKERS OF SPORT, INC. V. PROSERV, INC.

178 F.3d 862 (7th Cir. 1999)

POSNER, Chief Judge.

The plaintiff, Speakers of Sport, appeals from the grant of summary judgment to the defendant, ProServ, in a diversity suit in which one sports agency has charged another with tortious interference with a business relationship and related violations of Illinois law. The essential facts, construed as favorably to the plaintiff as the record will permit, are as follows. Ivan Rodriguez, a highly successful catcher with the Texas Rangers baseball team, in 1991 signed the first of several one-year contracts making Speakers his agent. ProServ wanted to expand its representation of baseball players and to this end invited Rodriguez to its office in Washington and there promised that it would get him between $2 and $4 million in endorsements if he signed with ProServ — which he did, terminating his contract (which was terminable at will) with Speakers. This was in 1995. ProServ failed to obtain significant endorsement for Rodriguez and after just one year he switched to another agent who the following year landed him a five-year $42 million contract with the Rangers. Speakers brought this suit a few months later, charging that the promise of endorsements that ProServ had made to Rodriguez was fraudulent and had induced him to terminate his contract with Speakers. . . .

Speakers could not sue Rodriguez for breach of contract, because he had not broken their contract, which was, as we said, terminable at will. Nor, therefore, could it accuse ProServ of inducing a breach of contract, as in *J.D. Edwards & Co. v. Podany*, 168 F.3d 1020, 1022 (7th Cir. 1999). But Speakers did have a contract with Rodriguez, and inducing the termination of a contract, even when the termination is not a breach because the contract is terminable at will, can still be actionable under the tort law of Illinois, . . . as an interference with prospective economic advantage. . . .

There is in general nothing wrong with one sports agent trying to take a client from another if this can be done without precipitating a breach of contract. That is the process known as competition, which though painful, fierce, frequently ruthless, sometimes Darwinian in its pitilessness, is the cornerstone of our highly successful economic system. . . .

Criticized for vagueness . . . the Illinois rule yet makes sense in a case like this, if only as a filter against efforts to use the legal process to stifle competition. Consider in this connection the characterization by Speakers' own chairman of ProServ's promise to Rodriguez as "pure fantasy and gross exaggeration" in other words, as puffing. Puffing in the usual sense signifies meaningless superlatives that no reasonable person would take seriously, and so it is not actionable as fraud. . . .

Rodriguez thus could not have sued ProServ (and has not attempted to) in respect of the promise of $2-$4 million in endorsements. If Rodriguez thus was not wronged, we do not understand on what theory Speakers can complain that ProServ competed with it unfairly.

The promise of endorsements was puffing not in the most common sense of a cascade of extravagant adjectives but in the equally valid sense of a sales pitch that is intended, and that a reasonable person in the position of the "promisee" would understand, to be aspirational rather than enforceable — an expression of hope rather than a commitment. It is not as if ProServ proposed to employ Rodriguez and pay him $2 million a year. That would be the kind of promise that could found an enforceable obligation. ProServ proposed merely to get him endorsements of at least that amount. They would of course be paid by the companies whose products Rodriguez endorsed, rather than by ProServ.

ProServ could not force them to pay Rodriguez, and it is not contended that he understood ProServ to be warranting a minimum level of endorsements in the sense that if they were not forthcoming ProServ would be legally obligated to make up the difference to him.

It is possible to make a binding promise of something over which one has no control; such a promise is called a warranty. . . . But it is not plausible that this is what ProServ was doing — that it was guaranteeing Rodriguez a minimum of $2 million a year in outside earnings if he signed with it. The only reasonable meaning to attach to ProServ's so-called promise is that ProServ would try to get as many endorsements as possible for Rodriguez and that it was optimistic that it could get him at least $2 million worth of them. So understood, the "promise" was not a promise at all. But even if it was a promise (or a warranty), it cannot be the basis for a finding of fraud because it was not part of a scheme to defraud evidenced by more than the allegedly fraudulent promise itself. . . .

We add that even if Speakers could establish liability under either the common law of torts or the deceptive practices act, its suit would fail because it cannot possibly establish, as it seeks to do, a damages entitlement (the only relief it seeks) to the agent's fee on Rodriguez's $42 million contract. That contract was negotiated years after he left Speakers, and by another agent. Since Rodriguez had only a year-to-year contract with Speakers — terminable at will, moreover — and since obviously he was dissatisfied with Speakers at least to the extent of switching to ProServ and then when he became disillusioned with ProServ of *not* returning to Speakers' fold, the likelihood that Speakers would have retained him had ProServ not lured him away is too slight to ground an award of such damages. . . .

Such an award would be the best example yet of puffing in the pie in the sky sense.

Affirmed.

It is unethical for agents and attorneys *qua* agents to purposefully and fraudulently interfere with a business relationship. Speakers of Sports wanted their contract fee, but the ultimate employment contract was negotiated not by ProServ but with yet another third party.

QUESTIONS AND DISCUSSION

1. In *Zinn*, the agent's assistance in financial planning was deemed to be "isolated advice" about securities. What type of advice and planning would be necessary to advance beyond "isolated advice"?
2. In *Zinn*, the agent sent his athlete to H&R Block for tax assistance; that type of lackluster performance was found insufficient to defeat Zinn's suit to recover his fees due under the SRK. Is this fair? Should there be some standard to regulate the agent's duties in the field of tax planning?
3. In *Argovitz*, the conflict of interest was real and permeated the very existence of the relationship between agent-owner and athlete. This an

egregious situation; other conflict-type scenarios are less blatant and may involve, for example, an agent's attempts to represent a player and a coach from the same club or her attempt to represent two competing quarterbacks. Would *Argovitz* have been decided differently if the conflict of interest was less blatant, mean spirited, and odious? See Brown, *The Battle the Fans Never See: Conflicts of Interest for Sports Lawyers*, 7 Geo. J. Legal Ethics 813 (1994).

4. Agents should err on the side of a complete and detailed disclosure of any possible conflict of interest that might occur between agent and client.

5. Does the existence of a hard salary cap create the possibility of a conflict of interst when an agent has more than one player on any particular team?

6. The *Argovitz* case showed a breach of an agent's fiduciary duty as shown by the fact that Argovitz give Jim Kelly a much better contract even though Kelly was an uncontested rookie. There were conflicting interests. *Argovitz* should have demanded the same clauses for his client, Billy Sims, for example, Kelly's escalator clause where he would always be paid in the top three at his position of USFL players. Argovitz was wearing two hats; he violated his duty of loyalty to his client. His personal interests conflicted with the principal's interests. His behavior was "egregious conduct" — "no man can faithfully serve two masters whose interests are in conflict." Does Jim Kelly have a case against Argovitz too?

7. See Champion, *Attorneys Qua Sports Agents: An Ethical Conundrum*, 7 Marq. Sports L.J. 349 (1997). *See also Cuyahoga County Bar Ass. v. Glenn*, 649 N.E.2d 1213 (Ohio 1995); like in *Henley*, an attorney-agent was disciplined for misconduct that emanated from the agent-athlete relationship. But, *Glenn* dealt with some very typical forms of attorney misconduct, comingling of funds and misrepresentation of a claim. The *Henley* case discusses the responsibility of an attorney to inform his client of possible conflicts of interests; in this case, the fact that the attorney received a kickback for securing the athlete as a client was sufficient to initiate disciplinary procedures.

D. AGENT REGULATION

An agent's responsibilities are many and diverse, but these responsibilities have not always been regulated. If these functions were done by other professionals who were already certified (for example attorneys, certified public accountants, and certified financial planners), then very particular sets of rules and regulations would control their activities.

In an attempt to fill in these loopholes and to correct perceived abuses, two major regulatory schemes were developed. One is public and is usually in the form of state regulation, for example, the California Athletic Agencies Act. The other regulatory arrangement is private and is usually in the form of a union certification program of individuals who might be an agent for members of that union, for example the National Football League Players' Association (NFLPA) Contract Advisor Program.

The Uniform Athlete Agents Act, an except of which follows, represents one attempt to standardize state regulations for agents.

1. State Regulations

UNIFORM ATHLETE AGENTS ACT

July 2000 Draft

Prefatory Note

A high percentage of athlete agents provide valuable services which are greatly needed by student-athletes who are qualified to seek professional sports services contracts. The services usually include negotiations with professional sports organizations and securing endorsement contracts. The services may also include financial and investment management, tax planning, legal counseling and a variety of other career management services.

Unfortunately, there are other athlete agents, or would be agents, who are motivated solely by a desire to obtain a "cut" of a student-athlete's future income. These unscrupulous individuals are willing to use any means to obtain an agency contract with any student-athlete who has any possibility of a professional career. The multi-million dollar contracts now being offered to many student-athletes have provided additional impetus to this minority.

The damage done by improper and illegal enticements to student-athletes is far greater than the casual observer might believe. The student-athlete who enters into an agency contract loses any remaining eligibility and may diminish his or her value in the professional sports market. Additionally, in some States, the student-athlete may be subject to civil and criminal sanctions. The educational institution (usually a college or university) attended by the student-athlete may be subject to severe financial penalties. Penalties can result either from loss of eligibility to participate in post-season events or from the effect of programs weakened by sanctions on ticket sales. Perhaps even more damaging is the impact of a "scandal" on the integrity and credibility of educational institutions and on intercollegiate sports in general.

Since 1981 at least 28 States have enacted statutes regulating athlete agents. Those statutes are not uniform and do not provide for reciprocal registration and enforcement. Several major universities and the NCAA have asked the Conference to draft this Uniform Act and have pledged their support in securing adoption in the 50 states. The NCAA agreed to finance the drafting project.

Section 1. Short Title.

This [Act] may be cited as the Uniform Athlete Agents Act. . . .

Section 3. Administration; Service of Process; Subpoenas. . . .

Section 4. Athlete Agents: Registration Required. . . .

Section 5. Registration as Athlete Agent; Form; Requirements. . . .

Section 6. Certificate of Registration; Issuance or Denial; Renewal. . . .

Section 7. Suspension, Revocation, or Refusal to Renew Registration. . . .

Section 8. Temporary Registration. . . .

Section 9. Registration and Renewal Fee. . . .

Section 10. Form of Contract. . . .

(c) An agency contract must contain, in close proximity to the signature of the student-athlete, a conspicuous notice in boldface type in capital letters stating:

WARNING TO STUDENT-ATHLETE IF YOU SIGN THIS CONTRACT, YOU WILL LOSE YOUR ELIGIBILITY TO COMPETE IN YOUR SPORT. BOTH YOU AND YOUR ATHLETE AGENT ARE REQUIRED TO TELL YOUR ATHLETIC DIRECTOR, IF YOU HAVE ONE, IF YOU SIGN THIS CONTRACT. IF YOU SIGN, YOU MAY CANCEL THIS CONTRACT WITHIN 14 DAYS AFTER SIGNING IT. CANCELLATION OF THE CONTRACT MAY NOT REINSTATE YOUR ELIGIBIITY.

(d) An agency contract that does not conform to this section is voidable by the student-athlete.

(e) The athlete agent shall give a copy of a completed contract to the student-athlete at the time of signing. . . .

Section 11. Notice to Educational Institution. . . .

Section 12. Student-Athlete's Right to Cancel. . . .

Section 13. Required Records. . . .

Section 14. Prohibited Acts. . . .

Section 15. Criminal Penalties.

The knowing commission of any act prohibited by Section 14 by an athlete agent is a [misdemeanor] [felony] punishable by [ ] and revocation of the license of the athlete agent.

Section 16. Civil Remedies.

(a) And educational institution has a right of action against an athlete agent or a student-athlete, or both, for damages caused by a violation of this [Act]. In a successful action under this section, an educational institution may also recover costs and reasonable attorney's fees. . . .

Section 17. Administrative Penalty.

The [Secretary of State] may assess a civil penalty not to exceed [$25,000] for a violation of this [Act]. . . .

Section 19. Severability.

If any provision of this [Act] or its application to any person or circumstance is held invalid, the invalidity does not affect other provisions or applications of this [Act] which can be given effect without the invalid provision or application, and to this end the provisions of this [Act] are severable. . . .

People violating the law can be punished criminally; this is true for sports agents also. They can be prosecuted under laws such as the Racketeer Influenced and Corrupt Organizations (RICO) Act, larceny, and mail fraud. Likewise, some of the state statutes that regulate the conduct of professional sports agents impose criminal penalties for violations. For example, in Alabama an agent can be prosecuted under a statute that prohibits tampering with sporting events. Ala. Code §§8-26-1 to 8-26-41 (Supp. 1989). These penalty provisions mandate that all offenses under the act are felony violations. These offenses range from failure to properly register to failure to provide a ten-point type on the face of the representation agreement warning that the athlete's amateur standing might be jeopardized by entering into the contract.

An important exemption to the California Athletic Agencies Act is that California attorneys do not have to register when they act as attorneys. In *Wright v. Bonds*, Wright the attorney never registered. The court held the exemption was inapplicable since he acted as an agent and not as an attorney.

a. Criminal Liability

WRIGHT V. BONDS

117 F.3d 1427 (9th Cir. 1997)

Section 1510 of the California Labor Code requires all athlete agents to register with the Labor Commissioner. Wright, who never registered, claims he was exempt because he was a lawyer. *See* Cal. Lab. Code §1500(b) (defining "athlete agent" not to include California Bar members "when acting as legal counsel"). However, Wright was not acting as Bonds' legal counsel. Not only would some provisions of the Wright-Bonds contract have been illegal if entered into between a lawyer and client, but the contract specifically excluded legal work. Wright also used the stationery of his sports management firm — as opposed to his law firm — in corresponding with Bonds. Wright's argument that lawyers need never register renders the "when acting as legal counsel" language in section 1500 meaningless. The contract is void, see Cal. Lab. Code §1546, and this defeats Wright's breach of contract and tortious interference with contract claims.

To prove interference with prospective economic advantage, Wright must show that Borris, Gilbert or BHSC (collectively BHSC) engaged in some wrongful conduct beyond mere interference. *Della Penna v. Toyota Motor Sales, U.S.A., Inc.*, 902 P.2d 740, 751 (Cal. 1995)

BHSC moved for summary judgment claiming no wrongful conduct occurred. Wright tried to meet his burden under *Celotex Corp. v. Catrett*, 477 U.S. 317 (1986), by showing that BHSC contacted Bonds and then tried to hide the fact; that Bonds made false claims against Wright soon after talking to BHSC; and that BHSC had a history of contacting athletes under contract to other agents. This comes nowhere near proving that BHSC acted wrongfully; if introduced at trial, this evidence could not support a verdict for interference with prospective economic advantage. While the District Court granted summary judgment on other grounds, we can affirm on any basis fairly supported by the record. . . .

Affirmed.

2. Union Regulations

APPLICATION FOR CERTIFICATION AS AN MLBPA PLAYER AGENT

VERIFIED APPLICATION FOR CERTIFICATION AND
CERTIFICATION STATEMENT

**Part 1: APPLICATION FOR CERTIFICATION AS AN
MLBPA PLAYER AGENT**

I, _____   Soc. Sec. No. _____

_____
(Business address and affiliation, if any)   (Zip Code)

_____
(Home address)   (Zip Code)

_____
(Business telephone)   (Home telephone)

hereby apply for certification as an MLBPA Player Agent pursuant to the MLBPA Regulations Governing Player Agents, effective June 17, 1988 [hereinafter "Regulations"], a copy of which has been provided to me and which I have read prior to completing and executing this Application for Certification and accompanying Certification Statement [collectively the "Application"].

In submitting the Application, I affirm that I understand and agree.

1. That only persons certified by the Major League Baseball Players Association ("Association" or "MLBPA") will be permitted to engage in any of the activities set forth in Section 1(A) of the Regulations, entitled Scope of Regulations;

2. That I will completely and accurately fill out the "MLBPA Player Agent Certification Statement." . . .

3. That I will comply with and be bound by the MLBPA Regulations Governing Player Agents . . . and that my failure to comply in any material respect with . . . the Regulations shall constitute grounds for the revocation or suspension of my certification, or other disciplinary action;

4. That the making of any material misrepresentation . . . in my Application shall constitute grounds for denial of certification. . . .

7. That I must enter into a written Player-Player Agent contract with any Player I seek to represent, which contract shall be in plain, understandable language and shall specify the services to be provided and the fees to be charged; that no such contract shall be deemed executed until a completed copy has been provided to the Player; that a copy of each such contract shall be provided to the Association within thirty (30) days of execution. . . .

10. That no Player-Player Agent contract entered into before the time a Player first becomes a member of the 40-man roster of a Major League Club shall be recognized or enforceable once the Player is on the roster of a Major League Club, unless such contract is reexecuted by the Player in accordance with the provisions of the Regulations. . . .

15. That, upon the request . . . I will permit [an] audit [of] all relevant books. . . .

16. That I will not engage in any activity which . . . creates an actual or potential conflict of interest. . . .

17. That, by certifying me as a Player Agent, the MLBPA does not endorse or recommend me as a Player Agent. . . .

Part II. MLBPA PLAYER AGENT
CERTIFICATION STATEMENT

This Certification Statement, filled out accurately and completely, must accompany and is part of the Application to the MLBPA for certification as a Player Agent. Within thirty (30) days of each anniversary date of your Application, you must file a verified update of this Part of the Application. . . .

I. PERSONAL INFORMATION

General . . .

Education . . .

II. BUSINESS INFORMATION . . .

III. RELATIONSHIPS WITH PLAYERS . . .

IV. RELATIONSHIPS WITH OWNERS

(A) Do you or anyone else in your firm or organization have a proprietary interest in any professional sport team? . . .

V. MISCELLANEOUS

(A) Have you ever been convicted of or pled guilty to a criminal charge, other than minor traffic violations? If so, state the nature of the offense, date of conviction, criminal authority involved and disposition of case.

(B) Have you ever been adjudicated insane or legally incompetent by any court? If yes, provide details.

Part III: VERIFICATION

City of: _____

State of: _____

I, _____, being first duly sworn, say that I have read the foregoing MLBPA Player Agent Application and understand and agree to the terms and conditions set forth therein, and that I have read the foregoing Certification Statement, which is Part II of the Application, have personally answered the questions in it, and the answers to those questions are true to my knowledge.

_____

Signature of Applicant

_____

It is well established that the individual unions are empowered to provide agent certification regulations for agents who wish to negotiate individual employment contracts for those athletes that are included within the appropriate bargaining unit. These regulations, with corresponding punishment clauses that provide for penalties including decertification, are contained within the collective bargaining agreement and thus protected from antitrust attack by the nonstatutory labor exemption. In *Collins v. NBPA*, the Court confirmed the legality of the basketball union's agent certification process.

COLLINS V. NATIONAL BASKETBALL PLAYERS ASSOCIATION

976 F.2d 740 (10th Cir. 1992)

TACHA, Circuit Judge. . . .

Plaintiff-appellant Thomas Collins appeals a summary judgment order in favor of defendants-appellees National Basketball Players Association (NBPA) and Charles Grantham. On appeal, Collins contends that the district court misapplied the labor exemption to the antitrust laws. Collins further contends that the district court erred by granting summary judgment while there remain genuine disputes of material fact relating to the issues of waiver and estoppel. After reviewing the district court's opinion and the parties' briefs, we affirm. . . .

The underlying material facts in this case are not in dispute and are set out in the district court's opinion. In summary, the NBPA is a labor union that the National Basketball Association (NBA) has recognized for over thirty years as the exclusive bargaining representative for all NBA players, pursuant to section nine of the National Labor Relations Act, 29 U.S.C. §159. For over twenty years, the NBPA and the NBA have entered into collective bargaining agreements establishing the minimum salary an individual player must be paid, the maximum aggregate salary a team may pay all of its players, and other issues unique to professional sports. The NBPA, however, has always authorized the players or their individually selected agents to negotiate their individual compensation packages within the framework established by the collective bargaining agreements.

Player agents were unregulated before 1986. But in that year, in response to a growing number of player complaints about agent abuses — including violations of various fiduciary duties — the NBPA established the Regulations, a comprehensive system of agent certification. The Regulations permit only certified agents to represent NBPA members. The Regulations also establish the Committee, which is authorized to issue or deny certification of prospective player agents. The Committee may deny certification if it determines that the prospective agent has made a false statement of material fact in his application or that he has engaged in any conduct that significantly impacts on his credibility, integrity, or competence to serve in a fiduciary capacity. Any prospective agent whose application for certification is denied may appeal by filing a timely demand for final and binding arbitration.

Collins had been a player agent representing NBPA members since 1974. The Committee certified Collins as a player agent in 1986, the year the Regulations first took effect. However, Collins voluntarily suspended his activities as an agent during the pendency of a lawsuit filed by one of his clients, Kareem Abdul-Jabbar, and a corporation Abdul-Jabbar had established, Ain Jeem, Inc. Abdul-Jabbar alleged that Collins had breached a number of fiduciary duties when Collins mishandled Abdul-Jabbar's income tax returns, improvidently invested his money, mishandled his assets, and transferred funds from his accounts to the accounts of other players represented by Collins. The *Ain Jeem* lawsuit was settled in 1989, but in the interim the Committee had decertified Collins for violations of other regulations.

Collins reapplied for certification in 1990, and the Committee commenced an informal investigation into Collins' application. The Committee took testimony from both Collins and Abdul-Jabbar, and was provided with nonconfidential discovery material from the *Ain Jeem* suit. The Committee denied Collins' application because it found that Collins was unfit to serve in a fiduciary capacity on behalf of NBA players and that he had made false or misleading statements to the Committee during the investigation. It reached this conclusion after it found substantially all of Abdul-Jabbar's allegations to be true. The Committee informed Collins of his right to final and binding arbitration, but Collins did not demand arbitration and instead filed this lawsuit.

Before the district court, Collins claimed that the NBPA certification process violates the antitrust laws because it amounts to a group boycott. We agree with the district court's analysis of the labor and antitrust statutes and its conclusion that the statutory labor exemption from the Sherman Act permits the NBPA to establish a certification procedure for player agents. . . .

On appeal, Collins now acknowledges that the NBPA has the statutory authority to establish player agent regulations. But he maintains his attack on the Committee's decision to deny his certification because it was based in part on its finding that he had breached his fiduciary duty as an investment agent and money manager. He argues that his conduct outside of negotiations between players and their teams is not a legitimate interest of the union because it has no bearing on the union's interest in the wage scale and working conditions of its members.

The district court properly rejected this argument. The NBPA established the Regulations to deal with agent abuses, including agents' violations of their fiduciary duties as labor negotiators. It was entirely fair for the Committee to conclude that a man who had neglected his fiduciary duties as an investment agent and money manager could not be trusted to fulfill his fiduciary duties as a negotiator. The integrity of a prospective negotiating agent is well within the NBPA's legitimate interest in maintaining the wage scale and working conditions of its members.

Collins next contends that the district court erred in granting summary judgment because there still exists a genuine dispute over whether the NBPA intended to waive its statutory right to act as the exclusive bargaining agent of the NBA players. He argues that the fact that the NBPA permitted agents to negotiate individual salaries for over twenty years reasonably implies that the union intended to waive its exclusive right to bargain, and thereby waived its statutory exemption to the Sherman Act. . . .

Finally, Collins contends that the district court erred in granting summary judgment because there still exists a genuine dispute over whether the NBPA estopped itself from failing to certify Collins as an agent. Collins argues that a reasonable jury could conclude that the NBPA's failure either to regulate agents for over twenty years or to inform him that it might someday regulate agents induced him to believe that it would never regulate agents.

The district court properly granted summary judgment because there is no genuine dispute over the factual elements of estoppel. . . .

For these reasons, we affirm the district courts order granting summary judgment. The mandate shall issue forthwith.

As in *Collins*, the court in *Black v. NFLPA* acknowledged the legality of the pertinent union establishing a regulatory program of agent certification.

BLACK V. NATIONAL FOOTBALL LEAGUE PLAYERS ASSOCIATION

87 F. Supp. 2d 1 (D.D.C. 2000)

ROBERTSON, District Judge.

William Black claims that the National Football League Players Association (NFLPA) unlawfully initiated disciplinary proceedings against him, affecting his livelihood as a player agent. NFLPA moves for summary judgment. Plaintiff opposes that motion and moves for leave to amend. Plaintiff will be permitted to take discovery on his claim of discrimination under 42 U.S.C. §1981, but defendant is entitled to judgment as a matter of law on the claims of tortious interference and violation of the Federal Arbitration Act. Leave to file new claims of defamation and trade disparagement will de denied. The reasons for those rulings are set forth below.

Background . . .

NFLPA is the exclusive collective bargaining representative of NFL players pursuant to Section 9(a) of the National Labor Relations Act, 29 U.S.C. §159(a). NFLPA nevertheless permits individual agents, or "contract advisors," to represent individual players in negotiations with NFL Clubs. NFLPA "certifies" contract advisors pursuant to a set of regulations. Those regulations set forth a code of conduct for contract advisors, and require that issues regarding the activities of contract advisors be resolved by arbitration.

Mr. Black was first certified as a NFLPA contract advisor in March 1995. He submitted a sworn application to continue his certification on September 9, 1998. . . .

In May 1999, Mr. Black received a disciplinary complaint from NFLPA's Disciplinary Committee.[2] He commenced this action a month later, asserting

---

[2] The disciplinary complaint alleged, *inter alia*, that, in violation of the regulations: (1) at various times in 1997 and 1998 Mr. Black provided cash payments to several college players before their eligibility had expired; (2) in late December 1998 Mr. Black arranged the purchase of a Mercedes-Benz automobile for a University of Florida player who was still competing at the college level; (3) in December 1998 Mr. Black met with an assistant coach at Louisiana State University and admitted to purchasing the Mercedes-Benz for the University of Florida football player; (4) in December 1998 an agent identifying himself as Mr. Black's representative offered a bribe to an assistant coach at LSU to encourage an LSU player to enlist Mr. Black as his agent; (5) at various

that the disciplinary complaint was the product of an antitrust conspiracy and a secondary boycott, in violation of the Sherman Antitrust Act and the National Labor Relations Act, and that the arbitration system established by the regulations violates the Federal Arbitration Act. Mr. Black's motion for a temporary restraining order was denied on June 22, 1999 by Judge Hogan, and Mr. Black filed an answer to the disciplinary complaint on July 6, 1999.

On July 27, 1999, the Disciplinary Committee issued a proposed ruling revoking Mr. Black's contract advisor certification for a minimum of three years. The regulations provide that Mr. Black may challenge the proposed ruling only by taking the matter to arbitration before an arbitrator selected by NFLPA—in this case, Roger P. Kaplan, Esq.

On July 29, 1999, Mr. Black filed an amended complaint. This first amended complaint jettisons the antitrust and secondary boycott claims and adds two new claims: that NFLPA's initiation of the disciplinary proceedings was based on race discrimination in violation of Section 1981; and that NFLPA tortiously interfered with Mr. Black's business relations (and those of his corporate entity Professional Management, Inc.) by invoking disciplinary action. Mr. Black continues to claim that the arbitration process established by the regulations is illegal under the FAA.

Now before the Court are NFLPA's motion to dismiss or, in the alternative, for summary judgment on all three counts in plaintiffs' first amended complaint, and plaintiffs' motion for leave to file a second amended complaint that would add claims of defamation and trade disparagement.

Analysis

A. Section 1981 Claim

Mr. Black asserts that NFLPA deprived him and his company of full enjoyment of their contractual relationship with NFLPA in violation of 42 U.S.C. §1981. He asserts that three white agents subjected to disciplinary action by the NFLPA—Joel Segal, Jeffrey Irwin and James Ferraro—were treated more favorably than he.

To establish a prima facie case of discrimination under Section 1981, Mr. Black must demonstrate that his non African-American comparators were similarly situated to him in all material respects. . . . This standard makes it questionable whether Mr. Black's claim can succeed. The timing and gravity of the charges against Mr. Segal appear to be quite different from those against Mr. Black. Mr. Black has not yet had an opportunity for discovery, however, and he has asked in his LCvR 7.1(h) statement for "a chance to obtain affidavits and take depositions and other discovery" pursuant to Fed. R. Civ. P. 56(f). Because Rule 56(f) requests should be "liberally construed," . . . Mr. Black will have a "reasonable opportunity" to justify his opposition. . . . The same ruling

times in 1996 Mr. Black sold stock in a publicly-traded company to several players; (6) over the past three years Mr. Black has provided a bill paying service for his clients whereby they deposit funds in accounts which Mr. Black's firm jointly controls; (7) on his application for certification as a contract advisor, Mr. Black untruthfully answered "NO" when asked: "Do you manage, invest, or in any other manner handle funds for NFL players?"; and (8) in May 1997 Mr. Black filed suit in South Carolina state court against Brantley Evans, Jr., in contravention of exclusive arbitration procedures in the regulations.

will apply with respect to the other alleged comparators, Messrs. Irwin and Ferraro, as to whom the NFLPA has made no factual response to Mr. Black's section 1981 claims.

B. Tortious Interference

Mr. Black and PMI allege that NFLPA, by means of its racially discriminatory actions and by making defamatory statements, tortiously interfered with their existing and prospective business and contractual relations. NFLPA's motion argues that these state law based claims are preempted by Section 301 of the Labor Management Relations Act. It is undisputed that NFLPA is a labor union and that the NFLPA contract advisor regulations were formulated in accordance with the collective bargaining agreement.

In *Allis-Chalmers Corp. v. Lueck*, 471 U.S. 202, 213, 105 S. Ct. 1904, 85 L. Ed. 2d 206 (1985), the Supreme Court applied the rule that a tort claim "inextricably intertwined with consideration of the terms of the labor contract" is preempted under Section 301. Mr. Black and PMI are not parties to the labor contract, but, as contract advisors, they have agreed to be bound by the regulations promulgated under the collective bargaining agreement. Their license to act as agents for NFL players comes by delegation from the NFLPA, which is a party to the collective bargaining agreement.

State law based claims that depend on construction and application of terms in a collective bargaining agreement are preempted. Those that have a basis wholly independent of the labor contract are not. . . .

The gravamen of Mr. Black's tortious interference claim is that NFLPA engaged in "discriminatory treatment . . . under the pretext of a disciplinary proceeding" and thereby deliberately interfered with his contractual relationships with NFL players. . . . He does not assert a violation of a right to contract "owed to every person in society," *Rawson*, 495 U.S. at 370, 110 S. Ct. 1904 or any other generalized statutory right. Mr. Black's complaint is about the way in which NFLPA has conducted and will conduct his disciplinary proceeding. That complaint turns upon the proper application of the regulations to Mr. Black's alleged illegal activities as a contract advisor. Thus, . . . Mr. Black's state law claim "cannot be described as independent of the collective-bargaining agreement." *Id.* at 370.[4]

The validity of PMI's contracts with "various football players relating to certain marketing, promotional and public relations services that PMI was to render for players," . . . and PMI's expectancy that those contracts would continue in effect are derivative of Mr. Black's position. Thus, even though PMI's tortious interference claim is in some sense further removed from the regulations than Mr. Black's individual claim, its very existence depends upon interpretation and application of the regulations.

---

[4] The District of Columbia law of tortious interference confirms that Mr. Black's claim is "inextricably intertwined" with the regulations. To make out a prima facie case of tortious interference, a plaintiff must show: (1) "the existence of a valid business relationship and expectancy, (2) knowledge of the relationship or expectancy on the part of the interferer, (3) intentional interference inducing or causing a breach or termination of the relationship or expectancy, and (4) resultant damage." *Bennett Enterprises, Inc. v. Domino's Pizza, Inc.*, 45 F.3d 493, 498 (D.C. Cir. 1995). The NFLPA's regulations in this case establish the parameters of Mr. Black's *expectancy* that his business relationship would continue, in view of his actions.

C. Federal Arbitration Act

Mr. Black attacks NFLPA's arbitration system as inherently biased, asserts that Arbitrator Kaplan, who is scheduled to hear the appeal of his disciplinary complaint, is not "neutral" under the terms of the regulations, and demands that Mr. Kaplan be removed. As authority for his demand, Mr. Black invokes Section 10 of the FAA, which empowers a federal court to vacate an arbitration award in limited and specified circumstances, one of which is evident partiality or corruption of the arbitrator.

Mr. Black consented to be bound by NFLPA's contract advisor regulations and agreed that, if his certification should be "suspended or revoked, the exclusive method for challenging any such action is through the arbitration procedure set forth in the Regulations." Section 5.D of the regulations provides: "NFLPA shall select a skilled and experienced person to serve as the outside impartial Arbitrator for all cases arising hereunder."

A written agreement to arbitrate a dispute is "valid, irrevocable, and enforceable" except on grounds that would exist at law or in equity for the revocation of contract. 9 U.S.C. §2. The Supreme Court has observed that "Section 2 is a congressional declaration of a liberal federal policy favoring arbitration agreements." . . .

Mr. Black's legal proposition is that a federal court may step in to preempt agreed-upon arbitration methods and appoint a "neutral" arbitrator where "the potential bias of a named arbitrator makes arbitration proceedings a prelude to later judicial proceedings challenging the arbitration award." . . .

Mr. Black admits that he was aware of and freely agreed to the arbitration terms contained in the regulations, and he makes no allegation about infirmities in the drafting of the regulations. As *Aviall* [*Inc., v. Ryder System, Inc.*, 110 F.3d 892 (2d Cir. 1997)] makes clear, it is of no moment that Mr. Black did not have a hand in the structuring of the arbitration process. *See Aviall*, 110 F.3d at 896. An NFL selected arbitrator may have an incentive to appease his or her employer, but "[t]he parties to an arbitration choose their method of dispute resolution, and can ask no more impartiality than inheres in the method they have chosen." . . . Mr. Black's peremptory challenge to the neutrality of the NFLPA arbitrator must accordingly be rejected. . . .

D. Second Amended Complaint

Mr. Black's proposed second amended complaint sets forth new claims of defamation and trade disparagement. It is well settled that "a liberal, pro-amendment ethos dominates the intent and judicial construction of Rule 15(a)." . . . It is also true, however, that "[a] motion to amend the [c]omplaint should be denied as 'futile' if the complaint as amended could not survive a motion to dismiss." . . .

Defamation claims are subject to a "heightened pleading standard." . . .

In his second amended complaint, Mr. Black does not set forth his defamation claims with the specificity required to withstand a motion to dismiss. . . . Rather, he makes generalized and conclusory allegations about statements made "by NFLPA representatives at [ ] NFLPA Players Representatives meeting[s] . . . to the effect that" Mr. Black was a "bad and corrupt agent" who had engaged in "illegal activities." . . . Mr. Black presents no "factual allegations" that defamatory statements were actually made, let alone what they were and who made them. . . .

Mr. Black's one reference to a specific publication does not withstand even modest scrutiny. The charge is that "the NFLPA," in a February 8-14, 1999, edition of *Street & Smith's Sports Business Journal*, stated that "Black tried to bribe an LSU assistant football coach." In fact, the article states that the "Union President . . . wouldn't comment on the Black investigation." . . . No reasonable juror could determine that "no comment" is defamatory. Because none of Mr. Black's defamation claims could survive a motion to dismiss, they are "futile" for the purpose of a second Rule 15(a) amendment.

The trade disparagement claim in plaintiffs' proposed second amended complaint, . . . depends for its legal sufficiency on the presence of defamatory statements, so it, too, is futile.

An appropriate order accompanies this memorandum.

Order

For the reasons set forth in the accompanying memorandum, it is this 1st day of February 2000, ordered that defendant's motion to dismiss or for summary [# 23] is granted in part and denied in part. And it is further ordered that plaintiffs' motion for leave to file a second amended complaint [# 25] is denied.

White v. National Football League is yet another problem-based case penned by Judge Doty, the special master who brokered the stipulation and settlement agreement (SSA) that settled an earlier lawsuit between the National Football League (NFL) and the National Football League Players' Association (NFLPA). This particular version of *White v. NFL* was an attempt to punish one team and three prominent agents (who were also NFLPA certified contract advisors) who entered into an undisclosed (to the NFL) compensation agreement with players in violation of the pertinent collective bargaining agreement and the SSA.

WHITE V. NATIONAL FOOTBALL LEAQUE

92 F. Supp. 2d 918 (D. Minn. 2000)

DOTY, District Judge.

This matter is before the court on the cross-objections of the parties to the decision of the special master dated February 18, 2000. Based on a review of the file, record, and proceedings herein, the court reverses in part and affirms in part the decision of the special master.

Background

This appeal arises out of a special master proceeding commenced by the National Football League Management Council ("NFLMC") in June 1999. The NFLMC alleges that the San Francisco 49ers and certain player agents entered into undisclosed agreements concerning player compensation, in violation of the NFL Collective Bargaining Agreement ("CBA") and the stipulation and settlement agreement in this case ("SSA"). In the underlying proceeding, the NFLMC has pursued discovery against player agents Leigh Steinberg, Jeffrey Moorad, and Gary Wichard. These agents have opposed discovery on the ground that they were not signatories to the CBA and SSA and are not subject to any penalty scheme provided in those agreements. Because of this dispute, discovery of player agents has been stayed since January 3, 2000.

On February 18, 2000, after extensive briefing and oral argument on the status of player agents under the CBA and SSA, the special master issued a decision dismissing the player agents from the underlying proceeding. . . . However, the special master also conditionally ruled that, if this court were to find that player agents were bound by the CBA and SSA, then player agents could be subject to penalties under Article XXIX, Section 3 of the CBA and Section XVI, Paragraph 3 of the SSA.

The NFLMC and the National Football League Players Association ("NFLPA") have filed objections to that portion of the special master's decision dismissing the player agents from the underlying proceeding. Steinberg, Moorad, and Wichard have filed objections to the special master's conditional ruling that player agents are subject to the penalty provision contained in Article XXIX, Section 3 of the CBA and Section XVI, Paragraph 3 of the SSA.

Discussion

A. Standard of Review

In reviewing the special master's decision, the court must separately address the two fundamental issues raised by this dispute: (1) whether the contracting parties intended to bind player agents to the CBA and SSA and (2) whether, under the applicable legal rules, player agents have in fact been bound. The first issue involves a purely legal question of contractual interpretation. *See White v. NFL*, 899 F. Supp. 410, 413 (D. Minn. 1995) (interpreting the unambiguous terms of a contract is a question of law). The second issue involves a primarily factual question of consent. Thus, the court's review of the special master's rulings on the first issue will be de novo, while its review of the special master's ruling on the second issue will be conducted under the clearly erroneous standard. (under the CBA and SSA, the special master's conclusions of law are reviewed de novo and his factual findings are reviewed for clear error).

B. Did the Parties Intend to Bind Player Agents to the CBA and SSA?

The court will first address whether the CBA and SSA purport to bind player agents to their terms. The interpretation of the CBA and SSA is governed by New York law. . . . Further the court must give effect and meaning to every term of the contract, making every reasonable effort to harmonize all of its terms. . . . The contract must also be interpreted so as to effectuate, not nullify, its primary purpose. . . .

The CBA and SSA contain a pair of provisions that, on their face, would appear to manifest the contracting parties' intent to bind player agents to the agreements. The first provision states:

> Binding Effect. This agreement *shall be binding upon* and shall inure to the benefit of the Parties hereto and their heirs, executors, administrators,

> *representatives, agents*, successors and assigns and any corporation into or with
> which any corporate party hereto may merge or consolidate.

CBA Art. LV. §14; SSA §XXX, ¶2 (emphasis added). Notwithstanding the
clarity of this provision, the special master concluded that it should be
discounted on the ground that it is "mere boilerplate." However, while it is
true that language of this kind commonly appears in contractual agreements,
this fact alone does not render the provision inoperative. As the special master
himself recognized, this provision is "utilized throughout the law to ensure
continuity of obligation against those who stand in the shoes of a party."
Further, "a court may not rewrite into a contract conditions the parties did
not insert or, under the guise of construction, add or excise terms." *White v.
NFL*, 899 F. Supp. at 415 (citation omitted). Boilerplate or not, then, the
court must take seriously the parties' broad declaration of "binding effect" in
evaluating whether they intended to subject player agents to the CBA and SSA.

Moreover, a second provision, addressing contract "certifications," makes
it abundantly clear that the parties intended to bind player agents to the agreements. *See* CBA Art. XXXIX; SSA §XVI. This provision sets forth the procedure
by which the persons negotiating a player contract must certify the integrity of
the contract under the CBA and SSA, and specifically instructs that "any player
representative who negotiated the contract on behalf of the player" must
execute the certification. CBA Art. XXIX, §1(a); SSA §XVI, ¶1. It then provides:

> Any person who knowingly files a false certification required [above] shall be
> subject to a fine of up to $250,000, upon a finding of such violation by the
> Special Master. The amount of such fine as to a Club or non-player Club
> employee shall be determined by the Commissioner.

CBA Art XXIX, §3 SSA §XVI, ¶1. As the special master stated, "the only sensible
interpretation of [the penalty provision] is that it was intended to apply to any
person who executes such a false certification with the intent the Player
Contract involved will become effective." The special master thus found,
and the court agrees, that the false certification provision empowers him to
impose a fine on a player agent who executes a false certification.

Notwithstanding this finding, however, the special master concluded that
his power to penalize player agents is negated by a separate provision in the
CBA addressing the regulation of player agents. . . .

The special master concluded that this provision vests in the NFLPA exclusive regulatory authority over player agents, thereby depriving him of
jurisdiction to fine a player agent for submitting a false certification.

In reaching this conclusion, however, the special master made several interpretive errors. First, he read the word "exclusively" into the first sentence of this
provision, thereby disregarding the principle that a court shall neither add nor
remove terms in the service of construction. *See White v. NFL*, 899 F. Supp. at
415. Second, he interpreted the agent regulation provision so as to create a
direct conflict with the false certification provision, thereby disregarding the
principle that a court shall make every reasonable effort to harmonize the terms
of a contract. . . . Third, he improperly downplayed the fact that, in a sentence
appearing toward the end of the provision, the parties clearly demonstrate that
they know how to assign "exclusive" authority to the NFLPA when they want

to: "The NFLPA shall have *sole and exclusive* authority to determine the number of agents to be certified, and the grounds for withdrawing or denying certification of an agent." CBA Art. VI, §1 (emphasis added).

The special master justified this departure from the plain language of the text on the ground that he was correcting an obvious instance of "imprecise drafting." In fact, however, this provision appears to offer an example of very careful drafting, whereby the contracting parties achieve three important results: (1) they explicitly "recognize" that the NFLPA has direct regulatory authority over player agents; (2) they implicitly "recognize" that the NFLMC and the Clubs do not have direct regulatory authority over player agents; and (3) they leave open the possibility of some other regulatory arrangement by separate agreement of the parties, so long as the subject matter of that special arrangement does not involve determining "the number of agents to be certified, and the grounds for withdrawing or denying certification." In other words, this provision fully anticipates, and is wholly consistent with, the parties' decision in Article XXIX of the CBA to vest the special master with regulatory authority over player agents with respect to the issue of false certification.

In sum, after conducting a de novo interpretation of the relevant contractual provisions, the court concludes that the parties to the CBA and SSA clearly intended to bind player agents to those agreements.

C. Have the Player Agents Consented to Be Bound by the CBA and SSA?

This conclusion, however, does not end the court's analysis. As the special master aptly observed, "under basic common law contract doctrine, borne by simple justice, a [third party] cannot be bound to a contract without his or her consent in some form." The Supreme Court has directly addressed the issue of third-party consent in two cases relevant to the present dispute. . . .

Under common law contract doctrine, a third party may consent to the terms of a contract expressly through words or tacitly by conduct. . . . Although silence does not ordinarily manifest assent, where the relationship between the parties is such that even a non-signatory would be expected to reply, silence can create a binding contract. . . .

In light of this precedent, the court concludes that the player agents have consented to be bound by the terms of the CBA and SSA. Several factors dictate this conclusion. First, player agents and the NFLPA are engaged in precisely the kind of special relationship that gives rise to principles of implied consent. Under federal labor law, the NFLPA has exclusive authority to negotiate with NFL clubs on behalf of NFL players. *See* National Labor Relations Act §9(a) (codified at 29 U.S.C. §159(a)). Player agents are permitted to negotiate player contracts in the NFL only because the NFLPA has delegated a portion of its exclusive representational authority to them. *See Collins v. NBA*, 850 F. Supp. 1468, 1475 (D. Colo. 1991) ("A union may delegate some of its exclusive representational authority on terms that serve union purposes, as the NBPA has done here. The decision whether, to what extent and to whom to delegate that authority lies solely with the union."). In *H.A. Artists & Associates v. Actors' Equity Association*, the Supreme Court concluded that a closely analogous representational scheme — one involving theatrical agents who individually negotiated contracts for the members of an actors' union — demonstrated an "economic interrelationship" such that the agents must be defined as a "labor group" under federal labor law. 451 U.S. 704, 721-22, 101 S. Ct. 2102, 68 L. Ed. 2d 558. *See also id.* at 721, 101 S. Ct. 2102 ("Agents perform a function — the representation of union members in the sale of their labor — that in most nonentertainment industries is performed exclusively by unions."); *Collins*, 850 F. Supp. at 1477-78 (analogizing agents for professional basketball players to the theatrical agents in *H.A. Artists*). Because an almost identical "interrelationship" exists here, it is not legally tenable for player agents to claim that they are strangers to the core legal agreements entered into by the NFLPA and the players.

Second, player agents enjoy significant and ongoing economic benefits because of their relationship with the NFLPA and the players, benefits that flow directly from the CBA and SSA. For example, Article VI of the CBA specifically bars NFL clubs from negotiating with anyone other than an agent certified by the NFLPA, thereby granting certified agents a powerful competitive advantage in the market for player-clients. And because player agents are compensated under percentage-fee arrangements, the CBA and SSA directly benefit them by mandating guaranteed league-wide salaries and minimum club salaries. *See* CBA Art. XXIV; SSA §X. The legal consequence of this arrangement is clear: When third parties like the player agents silently reap the benefits of contractual agreements like the CBA and SSA, they cannot later disclaim the obligations these agreements impose on them.

Third, apart from manifesting consent through their conduct, certified player agents have expressly agreed to be bound by NFLPA agent regulations, which include specific provisions (1) requiring each certified player agent to become familiar with "applicable Collective Bargaining Agreements and other governing documents" and (2) prohibiting certified agents from "negotiating and/or agreeing to any provision in any agreement involving a player which directly or indirectly violates any stated policies or rules established by the NFLPA." NFLPA Regs. §§3.A(15); 3.B(10). There is no question that the CBA and SSA are among the "Collective Bargaining Agreements and other governing documents" and "policies or rules" referenced in these regulations. Thus, by expressly agreeing to represent players under these provisions of the NFLPA regulations, player agents have necessarily agreed to comply with the relevant terms of the CBA and SSA.

Despite the fact that they would appear to support a finding of consent, the NFLPA regulations played a central role in the special master's decision to dismiss the player agents from the underlying proceeding. The special master concluded that player agents are not subject to a false certification penalty under the CBA and SSA because the NFLPA did not specifically provide for this penalty in its regulations. However, this conclusion is based on the faulty premise that the CBA vests exclusive regulatory authority in the NFLPA. . . . [T]he CBA clearly provides for concurrent regulatory jurisdiction, whereby the NFLPA generally regulates agent conduct while the special master specifically regulates agent conduct relating to false certifications. *See* CBA Art. VI, §1; CBA Art. XXIX, §3. The NFLPA regulations are entirely consistent with the contractual scheme, focusing on the agents' obligations to the players, not on the agents' specific obligations under the CBA and SSA. . . . Nothing in the NFLPA regulations forecloses the possibility that a player agent will be subject to a penalty under the CBA and SSA if he submits a false certification. To the contrary, and as just discussed, the NFLPA regulations specifically direct the player agent to learn about and comply with any other obligation he might have under the CBA and SSA. . . .

Finally, even if the NFLPA regulations did not expressly charge player agents with knowledge of the contents of CBA and SSA, no player agent can credibly argue that he is surprised by the penalty for false certification. The CBA and SSA govern the economics of professional football just as surely as the official NFL rulebook governs the game of professional football. To successfully negotiate with NFL clubs, player agents must be intimately familiar with many aspects of the CBA and SSA, including their detailed rules about free agency, franchise player designation, guaranteed minimum salary, and salary cap operation. Further, to execute a valid player contract, agents must carefully follow the contract certification rules set out in Article XXIX of the CBA and Section XVI of the SSA. Indeed, the standard player contract, which must be used in each negotiation, and which the negotiating player agent himself must sign, directly quotes the contract certification provision. . . . And it is precisely here, in the contract certification provision, that the player agent is warned that "[a]ny person who knowingly files a false certification . . . shall be subject to a fine of up to $250,000, upon a finding of such violation by the Special Master." . . .

The agent's act of player contract certification thus places in bold relief the issue of consent presented by this dispute: It represents both the moment at which the player agent most clearly stands to reap the benefits of the CBA and SSA and the moment at which he is made most acutely aware of his obligations, and his potential liability, under those agreements. When the agent signs his name to the contract certification, fully informed of the rewards and obligations attaching to this act, he has manifested a consent to be bound by the CBA and SSA just as clearly as if he had signed the CBA and SSA themselves.

For all these reasons, the court concludes that the player agents are bound by the terms of the CBA and SSA. The special master's finding to the contrary was clearly erroneous. As a legal matter, the special master incorrectly assumed that the NFLPA has sole regulatory authority over player agents. As a factual matter, the special master failed to consider uncontradicted evidence demonstrating that the player agents have consented to be bound by the CBA and SSA. Accordingly, the court must reverse the special master's decision insofar as it dismisses the player agents from the underlying proceeding.

D. Applicable Penalty Provisions

Steinberg, Moorad, and Wichard have objected to the special master's conditional ruling that he has the power to penalize player agents for false certification. As discussed in Part B above, however, the court wholly concurs with this aspect of the special master's decision. The court also disagrees with any suggestion by the NFLMC that player agents may be subject to penalties under the CBA and SSA other than by Article XXIX, Section 3 of the CBA and Section XVI, Paragraph 3 of the SSA. As the court's analysis in Part B demonstrates, when the contracting parties intended to subject player agents to a penalty, they expressly provided for it. Finally, because the special master has declined to rule on the scope of his civil contempt powers, the court will not address the issue here, except to note its agreement with his observation that, under the clear terms of the CBA and SSA, "those powers are strictly limited." . . .

Conclusion

For the foregoing reasons, it is hereby ordered that:

1. The portion of the special master's decision dismissing player agents from the underlying proceeding is reversed.
2. The portion of the special master's decision finding that player agents are subject to the penalty provision contained in Article XXIX, Section 3 of the CBA and Section XVI, Paragraph 3 of the SSA is affirmed.

3. NCAA-Based Regulations

Another entity that has a stake in the protection of athletes against abusive or overly aggressive agents is the National Collegiate Athletic Association (NCAA). The NCAA is an unincorporated association of individual schools that is the primary regulator of intercollegiate athletics. Some of these regulations attempt to police agents. In 1984 the NCAA established a voluntary Player Agent Registration Plan, which urges agents to register with the NCAA. If the agent registers, she must provide information on employment and educational background; additionally, she must notify the coach or athletic director (AD) before contacting the athlete. The agent's name is then placed on a list that is provided to member schools. The agent is removed if he provides gifts or fails to notify the AD before contacting either athlete or coach. Many states have designed their agent regulation schemes to dovetail with the NCAA rules. Although they differ greatly, most SRKs, at a minimum, possess a written notice regarding the possibility of losing eligibility upon signing and a cooling-off period that allows the athlete an opportunity to rescind the contract. Usually, an SRK that violates the statute is void. Also, an agent must notify the school of a potential contract. Some statutes require that notice be given to the university prior to the proposed signing. Other statutes simply prohibit the signing of an athlete before the expiration of his NCAA eligibility.

In *Walters v. Fullwood*, the agent-athlete agreement, especially the loan security agreement, violated NCAA rules since it was signed at a time when the athlete still possessed NCAA eligibility to continue playing collegiate football.

WALTERS V. FULLWOOD

675 F. Supp. 155 (S.D.N.Y. 1987)

BRIEANT, Chief Judge.

By motion fully submitted on October 5, 1987 in this diversity action, defendants Brent Fullwood and George Kickliter move (1) under 9 U.S.C.

sec. 3, to stay, pending arbitration sought to be compelled by this Court pursuant to 9 U.S.C. sec. 4, the claims against Fullwood asserted by plaintiffs Norby Walters and Lloyd Bloom, doing business as World Sports and Entertainment, Inc. ("W.S. & E."). . . .

The following facts are uncontroverted.

Defendant Brent Fullwood, a Florida resident, was an outstanding running back with the University of Auburn football team in Alabama. His success in the highly competitive Southeastern Athletic Conference marked him as a top professional prospect. At an unspecified time during his senior year at Auburn, Fullwood entered into an agreement with W.S. & E., a New York corporation ("the W.S. & E. agreement"). The agreement was dated January 2, 1987, the day after the last game of Fullwood's college football career, and the first day he could sign such a contract without forfeiting his amateur status under sec. 3-1-(c) of the N.C.A.A. Constitution, quoted *infra*. The contract was arranged and signed for the corporation by plaintiff Bloom, and granted W.S. & E. the exclusive right to represent Fullwood as agent to negotiate with professional football teams after the spring draft of the National Football League ("N.F.L."). Walters and Bloom were the corporate officers and sole shareholders of W.S. & E. As a provisionally certified N.F.L. Players' Association ("N.F.L.P.A.") contract advisor, Bloom was subject to the regulations of that body governing agents ("N.F.L.P.A. Agents' Regulations"), which require the arbitration of most disputes between players and contract advisors.

On August 20, 1986, W.S. & E. paid $4,000 to Fullwood, who then executed a promissory note in plaintiffs' favor for that amount. . . . At various times throughout the 1986 season, plaintiffs sent to Fullwood or his family further payments that totaled $4,038. . . .

While neither plaintiffs nor defendants have specifically admitted that the W.S. & E. agency agreement was post dated, they have conspicuously avoided identifying the actual date it was signed. There is a powerful inference that the agreement was actually signed before or during the college football season, perhaps contemporaneously with the August 20 promissory note, and unethically postdated as in other cases involving these plaintiffs. No argument or evidence has been presented to dispel this inference, and the Court believes the parties deliberately postdated the contract January 2. Even if this likelihood is not accepted, it is conceded by all parties and proven by documentary evidence that a security interest was granted on Fullwood's future earnings from professional football, by the express terms of the promissory note of August 20, 1986.

At some point prior to the N.F.L. spring 1987 draft, Fullwood repudiated his agreement with W.S. & E. and chose to be represented by defendant George Kickliter, an attorney in Auburn, Alabama. As anticipated, Fullwood was taken early in the N.F.L. draft. The Green Bay Packers selected him as the fourth player in the first round; he signed a contract with them, and currently is playing in his rookie season in the N.F.L.

In March, 1987, Walters and Bloom brought suit, since removed from New York State Supreme Court, alleging (1) that Fullwood breached the W.S. & E. agency agreement, (2) that Fullwood owed them $8,038 as repayment for the funds he received during the autumn of 1986, which are now characterized as loans, (3) that Kickliter tortiously induced Fullwood's breach of the 1986 agreement, and (4) that Fullwood and Kickliter tortiously interfered with plaintiffs' contractual relations with other players by breaching or inducing the breach of the W.S. & E. agency agreement by Fullwood. . . .

Plaintiffs' Claim for "Interference with Business Relations"

The fourth claim asserted by Walters and Bloom alleges that, by breaching or inducing the breach of the W.S. & E. agency agreement, Fullwood and Kickliter caused W.S. & E. to lose other clients, and damaged their business reputation. . . .

Treatment of defendants' motion to compel arbitration, and plaintiffs' surviving claims "We are living in a time when college athletics are honeycombed with false-hood, and when the professions of amateurism are usually hypocrisy. No college team ever meets another today with actual faith in the other's eligibility."

—President William Faunce of Brown University, in a speech before the National Education Association, 1904. *Quoted in* J. Betts, *America's Sporting Heritage 1850-1950,* 216 (1974).

The N.C.A.A. was organized in 1906 largely to combat such evils. Its constitution provides in relevant part that:

Any individual who contracts or who has ever contracted orally or in writing to be represented by an agent in the marketing of the individual's athletic ability or reputation in a sport no longer shall be eligible for intercollegiate athletics in that sport.

N.C.A.A. Constitution, sec. 3-1-(c). Section 3-1-(a) prohibits any player from accepting pay in any form for participation in his college sport, with an exception for a player seeking, directly without the assistance of a third party, a loan from an accredited commercial lending institution against future earnings potential solely in order to purchase insurance against disabling injury.

This Court concludes that the August 1986 loan security agreement and the W.S. & E. agency agreement between Fullwood and the plaintiffs violated sections 3-1-(a) and 3-1-(c) of the N.C.A.A. Constitution, the observance of which is in the public interest of the citizens of New York State, and that the parties to those agreements knowingly betrayed an important, if perhaps naive, public trust. Viewing the parties as *in pari delicto,* we decline to serve as "paymaster of the wages of crime, or referee between thieves". . . . We consider both defendant Fullwood's arbitration rights under the N.F.L.P.A. Agents' Regulations, and plaintiffs' rights on their contract and promissory note with Fullwood, unenforceable as contrary to the public policy of New York. . . .

Absent these overriding policy concerns, the parties would be subject to the arbitration provisions set forth in section seven of the N.F.L.P.A. Agents' Regulations and plaintiffs' rights under the contract and promissory note with Fullwood also would be arbitrable. . . .

However, under the "public policy" exception to the duty to enforce otherwise-valid agreements, we should and do leave the parties where we find them.

It is well settled that a court should not enforce rights that arise under an illegal contract. . . .

An agreement may be unenforceable in New York as contrary to public policy even in the absence of a direct violation of a criminal statute, if the sovereign has expressed a concern for the values underlying the policy implicated. . . .

Even in the context of a non-criminal contract, "a prime and long-settled public policy closes the doors of our courts to those who sue to collect the rewards of corruption." . . .

The principles requiring non-enforcement of contracts on public policy grounds apply equally to arbitration agreements. . . .

The New York State legislature has spoken on the public policies involved in this case, by expressing a concern for the integrity of sporting events in general, and a particular concern for the status of amateur athletics. . . .

Even were we not convinced of the legislative concern for the values underlying sec. 3-1-(c) of the N.C.A.A. Constitution, New York case law prevents judicial enforcement of contracts the performance of which would provoke conduct established as wrongful by independent commitments undertaken by either party. . . .

All parties to this action should recognize that they are the beneficiaries of a system built on the trust of millions of people who, with stubborn innocence, adhere to the Olympic ideal, viewing amateur sports as a commitment to competition for its own sake. Historically, amateur athletes have been perceived as pursuing excellence and perfection of their sport as a form of self-realization, indeed, originally, as a form of religious worship, with the ancient games presented as offerings to the gods. . . .

There also is a modern, secular purpose served by secs. 3-1-(a) and 3-1- (c) of the N.C.A.A. Constitution. Since the advent of intercollegiate sports in the late 19th century, American colleges have struggled, with varying degrees of vigor, to protect the integrity of higher education from sports-related evils such as gambling, recruitment violations, and the employment of mercenaries whose presence in college athletic programs will tend to preclude the participation of legitimate scholar-athletes.

Sections 3-1-(a) and 3-1-(c) of the N.C.A.A. Constitution were instituted to prevent college athletes from signing professional contracts while they are still playing for their schools. The provisions are rationally related to the commendable objective of protecting the academic integrity of N.C.A.A. member institutions. A college student already receiving payments from his agent, or with a large professional contract signed and ready to take effect upon his graduation, might well be less inclined to observe his academic obligations than a student, athlete or not, with uncertainties about his future career. Indeed, he might not play at his college sport with the same vigor and devotion.

The agreement reached by the parties here, whether or not unusual, represented not only a betrayal of the high ideals that sustain amateur athletic competition as a part of our national educational commitment; it also constituted a calculated fraud on the entire spectator public. Every honest amateur player who took the field with or against Fullwood during the 1986 college football season was cheated by being thrown in with a player who had lost his amateur standing.

In August 1986, Brent Fullwood was one of that select group of college athletes virtually assured of a lucrative professional sports contract immediately upon graduation, absent serious injury during his senior year. The fruits of the system by which amateur players become highly paid professionals, whatever its flaws, were soon to be his. That is precisely why plaintiffs sought him out. Both sides of the transaction knew exactly what they were doing, and they knew it was fraudulent and wrong. This Court and the public need not suffer such wilful conduct to taint a college amateur sports program.

Conclusion

Plaintiffs' claims against defendant Kickliter are dismissed under Rule 12(b)(2), F. R. Civ. P., for lack of personal jurisdiction over that defendant. Plaintiffs' fourth claim is dismissed against defendant Fullwood under Rule 12(b)(6), F. R. Civ. P. for failure to state a claim on which relief can be granted. The first and second claims against Fullwood are dismissed with prejudice, and Fullwood's requests to stay this action and compel arbitration are denied, as the underlying agreements violate the public policy of New York, and the parties are *in pari delicto*. The Clerk shall enter final judgment.

So ordered.

QUESTIONS AND DISCUSSION

1. The link between the agent and the athlete is the union. Some unions are now involved, but there is still no standard regulations. Should there be? See Trandall, *The Agent-Athlete Relationship in Professional and Amateur Sports: The Inherent Potential for Abuse and the Need for Regulation*, 30 Buff. L. Rev. 815 (1981).

2. Norby Walters and Lloyd Bloom gave even sports agents bad names. *See United States v. Walters*, 997 F.2d 1219 (7th Cir. 1993); and Cox, *Targeting Sports Agents with the Mail Fraud Statue*: U.S. v. Walters, 41 Duke L.J. 1157 (1992). One might say that one duty for the agent is staying out of jail. These gentlemen would sign college athletes to secret contracts; they'd also bribe and threaten as the need arose. However, their convictions on racketeering, conspiracy, and mail fraud were reversed. Walters's was reversed on the basis that his actions were based on good faith and on the advise of counsel. Bloom's conviction was reversed for a failure to sever trial. "Walters is by all accounts a nasty and untrustworthy fellow, but the prosection did not prove that his efforts to circumvent the NCAA's rules amounted to mail fraud." Narayanan, *Criminal Liability of Sports Agents: It Is Time to Reline the Playing Field*, 24 Loy. L.A. L. Rev. 273 (1990). *See also People v. Sorkin*, 407 N.Y.S.2d 772 (A.D. 1978), in which an agent was sentenced to prison for misappropriating his athlete's money. This is an example of an agent engaging in blatant criminal activity.

3. An athlete should *sign* with an agent who may have conflicts only after consulation and consent in writing. Although *Detroit Lions v. Argovitz*, 580 F. Supp. 542 (E.D. Mich. 1984), was egregious, it's certainly possible in these days when agents and coaches make as much money as their athletes that an agent would try to represent both a coach and a player (who is perhaps traded to a new team) on the same team. Most unions address this situation, and in some cases prohibit it. What do you think? Is the "consent after consultation" rubric sufficient to protect the players from abuse? If it is not improper per se, does this dual representation present at least an appearance of impropriety? See Brown, *The Battle the Fans Never See: Conflicts of Interest for Sports Lawyers*, 7 Geo. J. Legal Ethics 813 (1994).

4. There are many attempts to regulate professional sports agents, but they are at best piecemeal. The Uniform Athlete Agents Act might solve some problems, but it is a long way from being an established force in the lexicon of agent regulation. Of course, the problem as it stands now, is (1) the agent ignores the state statute, or (2) he "forum shops" for the most lenient venue. It is a sad state. The question is, who should regulate agents? And, once we ascertain the appropriate regulating party, what should we stress? Income-generation? Information-gathering? Maintaining standards? Punishing wrongdoers? This topic has created a beehive of comment. *See, e.g.,* Dunn, *Regulation of Sports Agents: Since at First It Hasn't Succeeded, Try Federal Legislation*, 39 Hastings L.J. 1031 (1988); Ehrhardt & Rogers, *Tightening the Defense Against Offensive Sports Agents*, 16 Fla. St. U. L. Rev. 633 (1988); Fox, *Regulating the Professional Sports Agents: Is California in the Right Ballpark*? 15 Pac. L.J. 1230 (1984); Lefferts, *The NFL Players Association's Agent Certification Plan: Is It Exempt from Antitrust Review*? 26 Ariz. L. Rev. 699 (1984); Ruxin, *Unsportsmanlike Conduct: The Student Athlete, the NCAA, and Agents*, 8 J.C. & U.L. 347 (1981-1982); Weiss, *The Regulation of Sports Agents: Fact or Fiction*? 1 Sports Law. J. 329 (1994).

5. The Uniform Athlete Agents Act has not passed yet. The impetus is to stop "unscrupulous individuals [who] are willing to use any means to obtain an agency contract with any student-athlete who has any possibility of a professional career." Every statute is different, so there is a tendency for an agent to "forum shop" to find the right venue where he might be more able to circumvent the law.

> Since 1981 at least 28 States have enacted statutes regulating athlete agents. Those statutes are not uniform and do not provide for reciprocal registration and enforcement. Several major universities and the NCAA have asked the Conference to draft this Uniform Act and have pledged their support in securing adoption in the 50 states. The NCAA agreed to finance the drafting project.

Note the language in §10(c) of this proposed act that requires contracts to include in a bold, dark font a warning that the student-athlete might lose eligibility by signing. What more could be added to improve this document?

6. Regulating the agent began in the 1980s. Is there any one standard that would be fair for all parties? Is it possible to regulate agents effectively,

while at the same time promulgate a statute that actually polices the agents and provides realistic penalties for noncompliance? *See* Kohn, *Sports Agents Representing Professional Athletes: Being Certified Means Never Having to Say You're Qualified*, 6 Ent. & Sports Law. 1 (1988); Powers, *The Need to Regulate Sports Agents*, 4 Seton Hall J. Sport L. 253 (1994); Remis, *The Art of Being a Sports Agent in More Than One State: An Analysis of Registration and Reporting Requirements and Development of a Model Strategy*, 8 Seton Hall J. Sport L. 419(1998); Ring, *An Analysis of Athlete Agent Certification and Regulation: New Incentives with Old Problems*, 7 Loy. Ent. L.J. 321 (1987); Stiglitz, *A Modest Proposal: Agent Deregulation*, 7 Marq. Sports L.J. 361 (1997); Note, *The NFL Players Association Agent Certification Plan: Is It Exempt from Antitrust Review?* 26 Ariz. L. Rev. 699 (1984).

7. *In Black v. NFLPA*, 87 F.Supp. 2d (D.D.C. 2000), the infamous sports agent William "Tank" Black sued the NFLPA on the grounds that its unlawful disciplinary proceedings against him to suspend him for three years from his status as a contract advisor unlawfully affected his livelihood. Tank brought suit against the NFLPA, claiming, inter alia, that the harsh punishment was racially motivated. The judge allowed Tank's suit to continue on this allegation alone. Tank alleged that the disciplinary proceedings were based on illegal racial discrimination and that the NFLPA tortiously interfered with his business relations by invoking disciplinary action. The legality of the contract advisor program emerges unscathed: "It is undisputed that NFLPA is a labor union and that the NFLPA contract advisor regulations were formulated in accordance with the collective bargaining agreement." Tank avoided complete summary judgment only to allow him an opportunity for discovery to ascertain if three non-African American competitors were "similarly situated to him in all material aspects." The court does not think he can accomplish this: "This standard makes it questionable whether Mr. Black's claim can succeed." What type of evidence must Tank produce to succeed?

In *Collins v. NBPA*, the NBPA established regulations and a committee with the authority "to issue or deny certification of prospective player agents." Collins was decertified by the committee. The court held that the nonstatutory labor exemption to the antitrust laws allowed the union to establish a certification procedure for player agents. Collins is more subtle—he claims that this decertification was based on an alleged breach of fiduciary duty as investment agent and money manager; he argues that this conduct is outside of negotiating the employment contract and thus not a legitimate interest of the union. The court disagreed, noting that an agent who neglected his fiduciary duties with investments could not be trusted to fulfill his fiduciary duties as negotiator. Collins lost his certification because he was "unfit to serve in a fiduciary capacity on behalf of NBA players." What could Collins argue that would place his conduct outside the regulatory ambit of the NBPA?

8. In *Walters v. Fullwood*, the agent signed a prize athlete by the use of deceptive, postdated agreements, in violation of the athlete's collegiate eligibility. Plaintiff sues alleging tortious interference of a business relationship, which induced breach. However, the agent's wrongful

conduct precluded recovery and could not compel arbitration. The court refused to act as a "referee between thieves." Court rejected plaintiff's claims under the doctrine of unclean hands. Should these penalties be state-based or NCAA-based? Should the agent be suspended by the appropriate union for a certain period? Should the states initiate criminal proceedings against agents who jeopardize a state school's successful bowl bid? *See* Arkell, *Agent Interference with College Athletics: What Agents Can and Cannot Do and What Institutions Should Do in Response,* 4 Sports Law. J. 147 (1997); Ruxin, *Unsportsmanlike Conduct: The Student-Athlete, the NCAA, and Agents,* 8 J.C. & U.L. 347 (1981-1982); Wood & Mills, *Tortious Interference with an Athletic Scholarship: A University's Remedy for the Unscrupulous Sports Agent,* 40 Ala. L. Rev. 141 (1988); Comment, *The Offer Sheet: An Attempt to Circumvent NCAA Prohibition of Professional Contracts,* 14 Loy. L.A. L. Rev. 187 (1980). *See also Begley v. Corp. of Mercer Univ.,* 367 F. Supp. 908 (E.D. Tenn. 1973); *Gulf South Conference v. Boyd,* 369 So. 2d 553 (Ala. 1979); *Taylor v. Wake Forest Univ.,* 191 S.E.2d 379 (N.C. Ct. App. 1972).

CHAPTER 4

LABOR LAW

Unions in Professional Sports protect the interests of the athletes in their struggles against management. Once a union is recognized it becomes the exclusive bargaining representative for all members of the unit.

Labor-Management Relations is the system of interaction between employers and employees. In sports, the relationship has been a stormy one characterized by management fiat and unilateral decisions that affected labor.

The National Labor Relations Act (NLRA) controls union-management relations in professional sports. The act is administered by the National Labor Relations Board (NLRB), which has jurisdiction over professional sports labor relations. The NLRB's policy is to promote collective bargaining through protecting employees' rights to organize and choose their own representation.

Collective Bargaining and Collective Bargaining Agreements refers to the process and the document used in union-management negotiation. The NLRA specifics collective bargaining as the method to solve labor discord. It is the process where owners and the players' union participate in a give-and-take process that produces a collective bargaining agreement.

Concerted Actions, strikes and lockouts, are the remedies that players and owners, respectively, can use when negotiation breaks down. Collective bargaining works only because of the threat of concerted actions that each party can legally invoke if negotiation reaches an impasse.

Arbitration is one of the results of the collective bargaining process and is incorporated into the collective bargaining agreement as the preeminent and often exclusive remedy for resolving disputes.

A. UNIONS IN PROFESSIONAL SPORTS

Professional sports unions faced a particularly difficult struggle in organizing. Until 1969, labor groups were insufficiently organized to receive recognition as unions under the NLRA. After the advent of unionism, the relationship between management and unions has been unusually, and in some cases, spectacularly, contentious. The owners historically acted as if the players were their children and the teams their personal and private fiefdoms. The owners' behavior toward the unions often included procrastination and bullying.

The NLRB deemed that coverage of the NLRA was broad enough to include professional sports on the basis that its effect on commerce was not minimal. Then, the NLRB determined that the appropriate bargaining unit (usually) was the league (as opposed to individual teams or particular positions, e.g., a union of only left-handed relief pitchers). Once recognized, under § 9(a) of the NLRA the union becomes the exclusive bargaining representative for all members of the unit. The NLRB's directive is only to select an appropriate unit under the circumstances.

The duty to bargain requires that both sides bargain in good faith. Both parties must meet at reasonable times and confer on mandatory subjects of collective bargaining; the failure to do so is an unfair labor practice (ULP). The duty to bargain in good faith is defined as a willingness to enter in negotiations with an open and fair mind and a sincere desire to find a basis for agreement. This duty is subjective and calls for sincerity, or the appearance thereof, and not results.

The union has the duty to fairly represent all members of the bargaining unit, even those who are not members or those who have showed an anti-union animus or, worse yet, were former replacement players ("scabs"). To prove a violation of this duty, one must show that the union acted arbitrarily or in bad faith. If a union, for example, always defends players who are disciplined for on-field fisticuffs but ignores one particular player who just happens to be a former replacement player, then that would be deemed a violation of the duty of fair representation.

The following case is an attempt to decide the appropriate bargaining unit for the Northern American Soccer League.

NORTH AMERICAN SOCCER LEAGUE V. NATIONAL LABOR RELATIONS BOARD

613 F.2d 1379 (5th Cir. 1980)

The correct collective bargaining unit for the players in the North American Soccer League is at issue in this case. Contrary to our first impression, which was fostered by the knowledge that teams in the League compete against each other on the playing fields and for the hire of the best players, our review of the record reveals sufficient evidence to support the National Labor Relations Board's determination that the League and its member clubs are joint employers, and that a collective bargaining unit comprised of all NASL players on clubs based in the United States is appropriate.

The North American Soccer League is a non-profit association comprised of twenty-four member clubs. The North American Soccer League Players Association, a labor organization, petitioned the NLRB for a representation election among all NASL players. The Board found the League and its clubs to be joint employers and directed an election within a unit comprised of all the soccer players of United States clubs in the League. Excluded from the unit were players for the clubs based in Canada, because the Board concluded its jurisdiction did not extend to those clubs as employers.

Players in the unit voted in favor of representation by the Association. After the League and its clubs refused to bargain, the Board found them in violation of Sections 8(a)(1) and (5) of the National Labor Relations Act, 29 U.S.C. §§158(a)(1) and (5), and ordered collective bargaining. . . . Thus the issues in this case are whether there is a joint employer relationship among the League and its member clubs, and if so, whether the designated bargaining unit of players is appropriate. [The court concludes affirmatively as to both issues.] . . .

The existence of a joint employer relationship depends on the control which one employer exercises, or potentially exercises, over the labor relations policy of the other. In this case, the record supports the Board's finding that the League exercises a significant degree of control over essential aspects of the clubs' labor relations, including but not limited to the selection, retention, and termination of the players, the terms of individual player contracts, dispute resolution and player discipline. Furthermore, each club granted the NASL authority over not only its own labor relations but also . . . over . . . the other member clubs. . . .

[The court found that a joint employer relationship existed because of the control the League had over the labor relations of its players. Examples of this control include Club activities governed by League constitution; the commissioner, who is selected and compensated by the clubs, is the League's chief executive officer; the commissioner conducts an annual collegiate draft; the commissioner is empowered to void trades; the League exercises considerable control over the contractual relationships between the clubs and the players since each player contract must be approved by the commissioner; and the League, through the commissioner, has broad power to discipline players for misconduct either on or off the field.]

The joint employer relationship among the League and its member clubs having been established, the next issue is whether the league-wide unit of players designated by the Board is appropriate. . . .

The Board is not required to choose the most appropriate bargaining unit, only to select a unit appropriate under the circumstances. . . .

Notwithstanding the substantial financial autonomy of the clubs, the Board found they form, through the League, an integrated group with common labor problems and a high degree of centralized control over labor relations. In these circumstances the Board's designation of a league-wide bargaining unit as appropriate is reasonable, not arbitrary or capricious. . . .

Thus the facts successfully refute any notion that because the teams compete on the field and in hiring, only team units are appropriate for collective bargaining purposes. Once a player is hired, his working conditions are significantly controlled by the League. Collective bargaining at that source of control would be the only way to effectively change by agreement many critical conditions of employment. . . .

Petition for review denied. Order enforced.

NATIONAL FOOTBALL LEAGUE PLAYERS ASSOCIATION V. NATIONAL LABOR RELATIONS BOARD

503 F.2d 12 (8th Cir. 1974)

[The act of various club owners and their management council in unilaterally promulgating and implementing a rule providing for an automatic fine to be levied against any player who left the bench area while a fight or altercation was in progress on the football field constituted an "unfair labor practice" within the NLRA.]

HEANEY, Circuit Judge.

The National Football League Player's Association (Union) petitions this Court to review an order of the National Labor Relations Board dismissing a complaint against the Employers, consisting of the National Football League (Owners) and the National Football League Management Council (Council). The complaint alleged that Employers violated § 8(a)(5) and (1) of the National Labor Relations Act, 29 U.S.C. § 151 et seq., by unilaterally establishing a rule that "any player leaving the trench area while a fight is in progress on the field will be fined $200." . . .

On January 22, 1971, the Union was certified by the NLRB as the exclusive bargaining representative for the professional football players employed by the NFL and its member clubs. A collective bargaining agreement was signed by the Union, Council's predecessor and each of the member clubs on June 17, 1971, effective February 1, 1970. The agreement expired on January 31, 1974.

In early 1971, the NFL Commissioner, Pete Rozelle, discussed with his staff the problem of injuries to players through violence on the football field. He directed a member of the NFL staff to discuss this problem with the competition committee (consisting of four Owners or their representatives) to deal with the effect of proposed changes in policy on the competitive aspects of football. The committee recommended that a rule be established to fine players who left the bench during a fight on the field. . . . The Owners then adopted a rule which read: "Any player leaving the bench area while fight is in progress on the field will be fined $200."

Rozelle subsequently fined thirty-four players for leaving the bench while a fight was in progress during the Minnesota-San Diego exhibition game on August 4, 1971, fifty-eight players for doing the same thing during the Atlanta-San Francisco game on August 15th, and fourteen players for identical conduct during the Chicago-New Orleans game on October 10th.

On September 30th, the Union's Executive Director, Edward Garvey, wrote to the Commissioner requesting information with respect to the fines imposed as a result of . . . [these] incident[s] . . . on the grounds . . . that the rule . . . was violative of the Collective Bargaining Agreement, which provided that ". . . any change in current practices affecting employment conditions of the players shall be negotiated in good faith." . . .

The Union filed an unfair labor practice charge with the Board on December 10, 1971, alleging that the Employers' unilateral adoption of the rule was a refusal to bargain. . . . It alleged that the Employers violated § 8(a)(5) of the Act by unilaterally promulgating and implementing a new rule providing for an automatic $200.00 fine against any player leaving the bench area during a fight or altercation on the football field during the game. . . .

We understand the Board to have made the following findings: (1) that the Union conceded that the Commissioner had a right to adopt the bench-fine rule; (2) that the bench-fine rule had in fact been promulgated by the Commissioner rather than the Owners and that the Owners engaged in no meaningful or substantial conduct with respect to its adoption or promulgation; and (3) that, as a matter of law, there is no substantive difference between the Commissioner's imposing individual fines for conduct detrimental to the game after notice and hearing and promulgating the bench-fine rule—thus, promulgation of the rule was within the authority of the Commissioner.

We hold that the Employers, by unilaterally promulgating and implementing a rule providing for an automatic fine to be levied against any player who leaves the bench area while a fight or an altercation is in progress on the football field, have engaged in unfair labor practices within the meaning of the Section 8(a)(5) and (1) of the Act.

We remand to the Board with instructions to it to adopt a remedy consistent with this opinion.

QUESTIONS AND DISCUSSION

1. The choice of bargaining unit is key in determining the dynamics of the collective bargaining relationship. The union wants the largest unit possible, usually the league. Management wants to divide and conquer, so they prefer smaller units, such as unions based on individual teams or even particular positions (something akin to a trade union, e.g., a union for pitchers only). Imagine all the various bargaining units that are reasonably possible in professional team sports. What would be their relative strengths and weakness?

2. The duty to bargain in good faith covers only mandatory subjects of collective bargaining, which are wages, hours, and conditions of employment. *NFLPA v. NLRB* stands for the principle that any unilateral action by either the management or the union on a mandatory subject of collective bargaining can result in an unfair labor practice levied against the offender. In *NFLPA v. NLRB*, the action that resulted in an ULP against management was the league's rule that provided for an automatic and mandatory fine for leaving the bench when there is an on-field brawl. This action affected a mandatory subject of collective bargaining, namely, wages. Can you think of other unilateral actions either by the union or management that would affect a mandatory subject? *See generally* Hale, 'Step Up to the Scale: Wages and Unions in the Sports Industry,' 5 Marq. Sports L.J. 123 (1994).

3. The first step in the collective bargaining process is a request for recognition from the *NLRB*. This typically takes the form of presenting signed "authorization cards" to the employer. Generally, employers refuse to acknowledge the union's request for recognition, and then the union resorts to filing a Petition for Election with the NLRB. If the union can show that at least 30 per cent of the subject employees seek an election,

then the NLRB will entertain the petition. However, in professional sports, most leagues have voluntarily recognized labor organizations. Why? Is management's "paternalism" the sole reason? Or can you think of other reasons behind management's seemingly inconsistent behavior?

4. After the NLRB honors the petition and chooses the appropriate bargaining unit, it directs that an election be held. The union must secure 50 per cent plus one to be certified as the collective bargaining representative. Once a union is certified, management loses its ability to govern athlete-team relations through unilateral managerial fiat if the decision affects wages, hours, or conditions of employment. *See NFLPA v. NLRB*, 503 F.2d 12 (8th Cir. 1974). *See also Silverman v. Major League Baseball Player Relations Comm., Inc.*, 67 F.3d 1054 (2d Cir. 1995) (injunction upheld against the owners who attempted to unilaterally establish a salary cap, impose limitations on free agency, and eliminate salary arbitration). In *Silverman*, the owners argued that negotiations had reached an impasse, which would allow the employer to unilaterally implement terms that have been discussed and were consistent with proposals exchanged between the parties. The *Silverman* court concluded that impasse did not occur.

B. LABOR-MANAGEMENT RELATIONS

As noted above, the history of labor-management relations in professional sports, although relatively short in time, has been unusually contentious. An integral part of management's attempt to treat their player as fiefs were the so-called player restraint mechanisms, which were attempts to thwart athletes from becoming free agents and going to another team that bids for their services. Baseball's reserve system created a never-ending option contract, whereas football's Rozelle Rule made free agency very difficult.

1. Baseball's Reserve System

Under baseball's reserve system, the player was the property of his employer for life. The only alternative available to the dissatisfied player was to either request that his contract be traded or to retire from the sport. On the other side, of course, owners could release or assign a player without consent. Additionally, the Major League Rules had a no-tampering rule that prohibited negotiations between a player and another team. This rule kept a player ignorant of his open market value and of whether any other club was interested in securing his services. The reserve clause was a mandatory requirement of each player's standard contract and completely abrogated any possible freedom of movement that the player ordinarily might possess.

Baseball club owners saw the reserve clause as their sport's defining feature. However, Judge Frank in *Gardella v. Chandler* disagreed:

> Defendant suggests that "organized baseball," which supplies millions of Americans with desirable diversion, will be unable to exist without the reserve clause. Whether that is true, no court can predict. In any event, the answer is that the public's pleasure does not authorize the courts to condone illegality,

and that no court should strive ingeniously to legalize a private (even if benevolent) dictatorship.[1]

Although the 1972 Supreme Court decision of *Flood v. Kuhn* did not eliminate the reserve clause, it allowed its continuance only on the narrow grounds of stare decisis; it also averred that "courts are not the forum in which the tangled web ought to be unsnarled."[2] The implication was clear: Baseball must take steps to straighten its affairs. Accordingly, a neutral grievance procedure was established though collective bargaining. Two ballplayers, Andy Messersmith and Dave McNally, filed a grievance seeking free agency after they played out their option years. In 1975, the arbitrator, Peter Sietz, found that there was no contractual bond between the club and the plaintiffs, and that the clubs had no right to reserve their exclusive services beyond the "renewal year." He concluded that a perpetual employee contract could not be assumed; that is, the arbitrator would not translate the one-year option to mean a one-year perpetually renewable option.[3] With that, the parties were forced to enter collective bargaining:

> Certainly, the parties are in a better position to negotiate their differences than to have them decided in a series of arbitrations and court decisions. We commend them to that process and suggest that the time for obfuscation has passed and that the time for plain talk and clear language has arrived.[4]

In 1976, the owners and the union approved a restructuring of the reserve system in that year's collective bargaining agreement, which eliminated the reserve clause.

Even in 2002, baseball continues its unique status when Major League Baseball attempted contraction from 30 to 28 clubs. In the *Butterworth* case, it was decided that the "business of baseball," included the decision whether to allow contraction and thus exempt from antitrust analysis (under baseball's historical exemption from the antitrust laws).

MAJOR LEAGUE BASEBALL V. BUTTERWORTH

181 F. Supp. 2d. 1316 (N.D. Fla. 2001)

HINKLE, District Judge.

Major League Baseball has announced its intention to contract from 30 clubs to 28 for the 2002 season. The issue in this action is whether the federal and state antitrust laws apply to the proposed contraction. The defendant Attorney General of the State of Florida asserts that the antitrust laws do apply. Pursuant to his statutory authority to investigate possible violations of the federal and state antitrust laws, the Attorney General has issued civil investigative demands to plaintiffs Major League Baseball, its Commissioner, and the two Florida major league baseball clubs. Plaintiffs seek declaratory and

---

[1] *Gardella v. Chandler*, 172 F.2d 402 (2d Cir. 1949).

[2] *Flood v. Kuhn*, 407 U.S. 258, 286 (1972).

[3] *In re Abitration of Messersmith*, 66 Lab. Arb. 101, 106, 117-118 (1975).

[4] *Kansas City Royals Baseball Corp. v. Major League Baseball Players Assn.*, 409 F. Supp. 233 (W.D. Mo.), *aff'd*, 532 F.2d 615, 632 (8th Cir. 1976).

injunctive relief against the Attorney General on the grounds that the "business of baseball," including the decision whether to contract, is exempt from the federal and state antitrust laws. Plaintiffs are correct.

By separate order, a preliminary injunction has been entered. This opinion sets forth the court's findings of fact and conclusions of law in support of the preliminary injunction and establishes a procedure for further consideration of this case.

I. Background

Baseball is an American game that has occupied a unique position in American society. Its history traces to the 19th century and has been described with some wistfulness in the normally pedestrian pages of the United States Reports. *See Flood v. Kuhn,* 407 U.S. 258, 260-64, 92 S. Ct. 2099, 32 L. Ed. 2d 728 (1972). But whatever its history, big league baseball is also big business. Some would say it faces big issues.

Major League Baseball is an unincorporated association of the 30 major league baseball clubs. It is governed by a Constitution adopted in January 2000. The Constitution authorizes contraction on the affirmative vote of three-fourths of the clubs.

On November 6, 2001, the clubs voted 28 to 2 in favor of contracting from 30 clubs to 28 for the 2002 season. The two Florida clubs voted in favor of contraction. On December 13, 2001, Major League Baseball announced that negotiations with the Players Association, an organization representing major league baseball players, had failed and that Major League Baseball was proceeding with the planned contraction. As this opinion is written, it appears that contraction is imminent.

On November 13, 2001, the Attorney General of the State of Florida issued sweeping civil investigative demands ("CIDs") to the plaintiffs in this action: Major League Baseball, Commissioner Allan H. Selig in his official and individual capacities, and the two Florida major league baseball clubs, the Tampa Bay Devil Rays, Ltd., and the Florida Marlins Baseball Club, L.L.C. Each CID said it was "issued pursuant to the Florida Antitrust Act of 1980, Section 542.28, Florida Statutes," identifying no other authority for its issuance. Each CID demanded that the recipient answer broad interrogatories and produce voluminous documents by December 13, 2001. The Attorney General refused to extend the deadline.

On December 10, 2001, plaintiffs filed this action, contending that, as a matter of federal law, the "business of baseball," a concept that plaintiffs assert includes the proposed contraction from 30 teams to 28, is exempt from the federal and state antitrust laws. Plaintiffs' complaint demanded declaratory and injunctive relief. . . .

IV. The Merits

Under an unbroken line of United States Supreme Court decisions, as well as under numerous decisions of lower courts, including the United States Court of Appeals for the Eleventh Circuit, the federal antitrust laws do not apply to the "business of baseball"; the business of baseball is, as it is sometimes phrased, exempt from the antitrust laws. The exemption applies as well to state antitrust laws, which are, to the extent otherwise applicable to baseball, invalid.

The Attorney General asserts the exemption applies only to the "reserve clause," part of the contract between clubs and players reserving each club's right to its players, subject to various terms. The Attorney General's assertion cannot be squared with the plain language and clear import of the many reported cases in this area. Nor can the Attorney General's assertion be squared with the United States Supreme Court's oft repeated rationale for continuing to recognize the exemption of the business of baseball: that any change in this long standing interpretation of the antitrust laws should come from Congress (which has left the decisions intact in relevant respects for now 79 years), not from the courts. . . .

C. Applying the Baseball Exemption to Contraction

The Attorney General asserts that, even if the "business of baseball" is exempt from the antitrust laws, that does not necessarily dispose of this case, because, the Attorney General says, the proposed contraction may not be part of the "business of baseball."

It is difficult to conceive of a decision more integral to the business of major league baseball than the number of clubs that will be allowed to compete. . . . The basic league structure, including the number of teams, remains an essential feature of the business of baseball, exempt from the antitrust laws. . . .

D. Applicability of the Florida Antitrust Act . . .

The Florida Antitrust Act explicitly exempts the same subjects as are exempt under federal law. . . .

E. Applying the Baseball Exemption to the CIDs at Issue

As set forth above, the proposed contraction of Major League Baseball is exempt from the federal or state antitrust laws, and the Attorney General thus has no authority to enforce the antitrust laws against the proposed contraction or to issue CIDs as part of an investigation of whether to file an enforcement action. . . .

Accordingly, it is ordered:

1. The preliminary injunction entered December 21, 2001 (document 27) remains in effect in accordance with its terms.
2. The Attorney General shall file by January 10, 2002, a statement of whether he seeks further proceedings in this court or agrees to entry of a final judgment.

2. Football's Rozelle Rule

The so-called Rozelle Rule, named after the National Football League's commissioner, Pete Rozelle, was the counterpart of baseball's reserve clause. But instead of forcing athletes to play on one team for life it concentrated on eliminating the interest of one team to acquire the free agents of another team. The Rozelle Rule allowed the commissioner to require the club that acquires a free agent to compensate the former club in the form of money, players, and/or valuable draft picks. This rule significantly deterred clubs from negotiating with and successfully signing free agents. The result of the Rozelle Rule was that a club would sign free agents only if it was able to reach a compensation agreement with the player's former team or if it was willing to risk the commissioner's "justice" in his sole discretion by awarding an array of unknown compensation.[5]

QUESTIONS AND DISCUSSION

1. Player restraint mechanisms were historically the most contentious element in the labor-owner relationship. One major goal of all unions is to attain some type of free agency so that its players can seek the highest bidder for their services — capitalism at its best. On the other hand, owners seek to limit players' mobility. Most of the player restraint problems were at least somewhat mollified through collective bargaining. And, as we'll find out in Chapter 5, Antitrust, the nonstatutory labor exemption to the antitrust laws kicks in to protect agreements that are a result of bona fide, arm's-length negotiation on mandatory subjects of collective bargaining. The reserve clause, now dead and buried, was the single most explosive weapon in the owners' arsenal to subjugate and exploit their athletes. *See Flood v. Kuhn*, 407 U.S. 258 (1972). *See also* Devine, '*The Legacy of Albert Spalding, the Holdouts of Ty Cobb, Joe Dimaggio, Sandy Koufax/Don Drysdale, and the 1994-95 Strike: Baseball's Disputes Are as Linear as the Game,*' 31 Akron L. Rev. 1 (1997).
2. Although not as monolithic as the reserve clause, the Rozelle Rule too also effectively curtailed the flow of free agents — this time from the source. The new teams that would have been covetous of securing talent via free agency were frightened away by Commissioner Rozelle's compensation, which in effect were forced trades that were deleterious and ruinous to the acquiring team. See Chalian, *Fourth and Goal: Player Restraints in Professional Sports, a Look, Ahead*, 67 St. John's L. Rev. 593 (1993).
3. Labor-management relations in baseball and football were categorized by the strife that revolved around respectively, the reserve clause and the Rozelle Rule. Both procedures were player restraint mechanisms that were anathema to the interests of the unions. It was the major goal of both unions to eradicate these procedures in the hope of relaxing the control that management had over player movement. Today, both procedures have been ameliorated through litigation and collective bargaining.
4. In *Major League Baseball v. Butterworth*, the court held that contraction was a part of the business of baseball and thus exempted from antitrust. Even though the reserve clause, essentially a perpetual option year, was eliminated through grievance arbitration as stipulated in the collective

---

[5] *Mackey v. NFL*, 543 F.2d 606 (8th Cir. 1976), *modifying info.* 407 F. Supp. 1000 (D. Minn. 1975).

bargaining agreement, *Butterworth* still dealt with the question of whether baseball's antitrust exemption applied solely to the now moribund reserve clause. As a result of the exemption, antitrust laws do not apply to Major League Baseball's conduct as regards the business of baseball. The *Butterworth* court held that determining the number of clubs that were allowed to compete was a decision that was integral to the business of baseball.

5. *Major League Baseball v. Butterworth*, a 2001 case, began when Florida's attorney general issued civil investigative demands (CIDs) seeking injunctive relief regarding the proposed contraction pursuant to state antitrust laws. As in *Minnesota Twins Partnership v. State* (excerpted in Chapter 5), the injunction was denied. Since antitrust was ineffective, contracts was used in *Metropolitan Sports Facilities Commission v. Minnesota* (2002) (excerpted in Chapter 2), as an attempt to defeat contraction; it was successful. Are there any other ways to defeat contraction? Contraction, collusion, salary caps, and luxury tax are management's new ways to control labor. In essence, these four mechanisms have supplanted the reserve clause and the Rozelle Rule as management's primary procedures that are designed to control player movement.

6. Another way to curtail contraction would be if the union alleged that it cannot be promulgated unilaterally by management but must be negotiated through collective bargaining since it affects wages, hours, and conditions of employment, and therefore it is a mandatory subject of collective bargaining. There's no question that the proposed contraction of two teams would, at least, affect the wages of union members. Although the contraction issue is somewhat settled for the time being after *Metropolitan Sports Facilities Commission v. Minnesota*, would it be in labor's best interest to seek declaratory relief that contraction is a mandatory subject of collective bargaining?

7. In *Metropolitan Sports Facilities Commission v. Minnesota*, the Minnesota court of appeals blocked professional baseball's contraction of the Minnesota Twins. The Metropolitan Sports Facilities Commission, which operated the Metrodome in downtown Minneapolis where the Twins played, settled a lawsuit against the Twins and Major League Baseball that allowed the Twins to play there through the 2003 season. That is, the Twins could not be contracted out until then; the Twins also agreed to extend their lease through 2003.

8. "Major League Baseball has announced its intention to contract from 30 clubs to 28 for the 2002 season. The issue is . . . whether the federal and state antitrust laws apply to the proposed contraction." *Butterworth*, 181 F. Supp. 2d at 1318. The thrust of baseball's argument is that baseball's antitrust exemption deals with the business of baseball, which is more than simply the reserve clause. The attorney general's argument was that "the baseball exemption really only applied to the reserve clause." *Id.* at 1325. After the Curt Flood Act of 1998 (15 U.S.C. § 27a), the exemption no longer applied to matters that directly affected the employment of baseball players (including the reserve clause). But the act did not render the antitrust laws applicable to baseball in any other respect (§ 27a(b)); also, the act does not repeal *Flood v. Kuhn*, 407 U.S. 258 (1972) (see Chapter 5).

C. NATIONAL LABOR RELATIONS ACT

A noted above, for many years, organized professional sports was viewed as an anomaly that did not merit consideration from the labor laws promulgated to protect employees. However, from 1969 on, union-management relations have been controlled by the National Labor Relations Act (NLRA), 29 U.S.C. §§151-166. In 1922, the Supreme Court in *Federal Baseball Club, Inc. v. National League of Professional Baseball Clubs*, 259 U.S. 200, excepted baseball and baseball's reserve clause (essentially a perpetual option year) from the antitrust laws; this had a prophylactic effect on attempts at unionization. Professional sports, however, employs many other people than just (allegedly) overpaid athletes; there are, for example, relatively low-paid clubhouse attendants, bat boys, traveling secretaries, physical therapists, ushers, and ticket sellers.

The heart of the NLRA is § 7, which demands that "Employees shall have the right to self-organization, . . . to bargain collectively through representatives of their own choosing, and to engage in other concerted activities for the purpose of collectively bargaining or other mutual aid or protection. . . . " The National Labor Relations Board (NLRB) was formed to police these § 7 rights. The NLRA applies to all employees whose employer's business affects commerce, that is, if the effect is more than minimal. An excerpt of the NLRA follows.

THE NATIONAL LABOR RELATIONS ACT

29 U.S.C. §§151 *et seq.*

29 U.S.C. § 151. Findings and Declaration of Policy

The denial by some employers of the rights of employees to organize and the refusal by some employers to accept the procedure of collective bargaining lead to strikes and other forms of industrial strife or unrest, which have the intent or the necessary effect of burdening or obstructing commerce. . . .

The inequality of bargaining power between employees who do not possess full freedom of association or actual liberty of contract, and employers who are organized in the corporate or other forms of ownership association substantially burdens and affects the flow of commerce, and tends to aggravate recurrent business depressions, by depressing wage rates and the purchasing power of wage earners in industry and by preventing the stabilization of competitive wage rates and working conditions within and between industries.

Experience has proved that protection by law of the right of employees to organize and bargain collectively safeguards commerce from injury, impairment, or interruption, and promotes the flow of commerce by removing certain recognized sources of industrial strife and unrest, by encouraging practices fundamental to the friendly adjustment of industrial disputes arising out of differences as to wages, hours, or other working conditions, and by restoring equality of bargaining power between employers and employees. . . .

29 U.S.C. § 152. Definitions . . .

(3) The term "employee" shall include any employee and shall not be limited to the employees of a particular employer. . . .

(5) The term "labor organization" means any organization of any kind, in which employees participate and which exists for the purpose . . . of dealing with employers concerning grievances, labor disputes, wages, rates of pay, hours of employment, or conditions of work. . . .

(9) The term "labor dispute" includes any controversy concerning terms, tenure or conditions of employment, or concerning the association or representation of persons in negotiating, fixing, maintaining, changing, or seeking to arrange terms or conditions of employment. . . .

29 U.S.C. § 157. Right of Employees as to Organization, Collective Bargaining, Etc.

Employees shall have the right to self-organization, to form, join, or assist labor organizations, to bargain collectively through representatives of their own choosing, and to engage in other concerted activities for the purpose of collective bargaining. . . .

29 U.S.C. § 158. Unfair Labor Practices

(a) Unfair labor practices by employer. It shall be unfair labor practice for an employer—

(1) to interfere with, restrain, or coerce employees in the exercise of the rights guaranteed in section 157 of this title;

(2) to dominate or interfere with the formation or administration of any labor organization or contribute financial or other support to it. . . .

(3) by discrimination in regard to hire or tenure of employment or any term or condition of employment to encourage or discourage membership in any labor organization. . . .

(4) to discharge or otherwise discriminate against an employee because he has filed charges or given testimony under this Act;

(5) to refuse to bargain collectively with the representatives of his employees, subject to the provisions of section 159(a) of this title.

(b) Unfair labor practices by labor organization. It shall be an unfair labor practice for a labor organization or its agents—

(1) to restrain or coerce (A) employees in the exercise of the rights guaranteed in section 157 of this title. . . . or (B) an employer in the selection of his representatives for the purposes of collective bargaining . . . ;

(3) to refuse to bargain collectively with an employer. . . .

(c) Expression of views without threat of reprisal or force or promise of benefit . . .

(d) Obligation to bargain collectively. For the purposes of this section, to bargain collectively is the performance of the mutual obligation of the employer and the representative of the employees to meet at reasonable times and conditions of employment, or the negotiation of an agreement, or any question arising thereunder, and the execution of a written contract incorporating any agreement reached if requested by either party, but such obligation does not compel either party to agree to a proposal or require the making of a concession. . . .

29 U.S.C. § 159. Representatives and Elections . . .

(b) Determination of bargaining unit by Board . . .

29 U.S.C. § 160. Prevention of Unfair Labor Practices . . .

(c) Reduction of testimony to writing; findings and orders of Board . . .

(j) Injunctions. The Board shall have power . . . to petition . . . for appropriate temporary relief or restraining order. . . .

The NLRB saw fit to recognize professional baseball (and by analogy all professional team sports) as subject to NLRA jurisdiction.

In re American League of Professional Baseball Clubs

180 N.L.R.B. 190 (1969)

Upon a petition duly filed under Section 9(c) of the National Labor Relations Act, as amended, a hearing was held before Hearing Officer Francis V. Paone. The Hearing Officer's rulings made at the hearing are free from prejudicial error and are hereby affirmed.

Upon the entire record in this case, including the briefs, the National Labor Relations Board finds:

1. The Petitioner seeks an election in a unit of umpires employed by the American League of Professional Baseball Clubs (hereinafter called the Employer or the League). The Employer while conceding the Board's constitutional and statutory power to exercise jurisdiction herein, nevertheless urges the Board, as a matter of policy, not to assert jurisdiction pursuant to Section 14(c) of the Act.

The Employer is a nonprofit membership association consisting of 12 member clubs located in 10 states and the District of Columbia Operating pursuant to a constitution adopted and executed by the 12 member clubs, the Employer is engaged in the business of staging baseball exhibitions and, with its counterpart the National League of Professional Baseball Clubs, constitutes what is commonly known as "major league baseball." The Employer currently employs, among other persons, the 24 umpires requested herein, and one umpire-in-chief. . . .

[W]e find that professional baseball is an industry in or affecting commerce, and as such is subject to Board jurisdiction under the Act.

Section 14(c)(1) of the National Labor Relations Act. . . . permits the Board to decline jurisdiction over labor disputes . . . where, . . . the effect of such labor dispute on commerce is not sufficiently substantial to warrant the exercise of its jurisdiction. . . ." . . .

We have carefully considered the positions of the parties, and the amicus briefs, and we find that it will best effectuate the mandates of the Act, as well as national labor policy, to assert jurisdiction over this Employer. . . .

We can find, neither in the statute nor in its legislative history, any expression of a Congressional intent that disputes between employers and employees in this industry should be removed from the scheme of the National Labor Relations Act. . . .

Accordingly, we find that the effect on interstate commerce of a labor dispute involving professional baseball is not so insubstantial as to require withholding assertion of the Board's jurisdiction, under Section 14(c) of the Act, over Employers in that industry, as a class. As the annual gross revenues of this Employer are in excess of all of our prevailing monetary standards, we find that the Employer is engaged in an industry affecting commerce, and that it will effectuate the policies of the Act to assert jurisdiction herein. . . .

The record indicates that an umpire's basic responsibility is to insure that each baseball game is played in conformance with the predetermined rules of the game. Thus, the umpire does not discipline except to the extent he may remove a participant from the game for violation of these rules. Testimony shows that after such a removal the umpire merely reports the incident to his superiors, and does not himself fine, suspend, or even recommend such action. As the final arbiter on the field, the umpire necessarily makes decisions which may favor one team over another, and which may determine to some extent the movements of various players, managers, and other personnel on the ball field. The umpire does not, however, direct the work force in the same manner and for the same reasons as a foreman in an industrial setting. As every fan is aware, the umpire does not — through the use of independent judgment — tell a player how to bat, how to field, to work harder or exert more effort, nor can he tell a manager which players to play or where to play them. Thus, the umpire merely sees to it that the game is played in compliance with the rules. It is the manager and not the umpire who directs the employees in their pursuit of victory.

Accordingly, we find that the umpires are not supervisors, and thus the Employer's motion to dismiss on this ground is hereby denied. We further find that the following employees of the Employer constitute a unit appropriate for the purposes of collective bargaining within the meaning of Section 9(b) of the Act:

All persons employed as umpires in the American League of Professional Baseball Clubs, but excluding all other employees, office clerical employees, guards, professional employees and supervisors as defined in the Act. . . .

QUESTIONS AND DISCUSSION

1. Several groups of employees are still not covered by the NLRA (for example, agricultural workers, domestic servants). Do you think that coverage of sports was a correct decision?
2. Independent contractors, such as jockeys, are likewise not protected by the NLRA. *See In re Yonkers Raceway, Inc.*, 196 N.L.R.B. 373 (1972); *In re Centennial Turf Club, Inc.*, 192 N.L.R.B. 698 (1971).
3. In *Radovich v. NFL*, 353 U.S. 931 (1957), football was specifically brought under the coverage of the antitrust laws, yet another precursor to *In re American League of professional Baseball Clubs*. By the early 1970s, all professional sports were deemed to affect interstate commerce and thus come under NLRA protection. *See Haywood v. NBA*, 401 U.S. 1204 (1971) (basketball); *United States v. International Boxing Club*, 348 U.S. 236 (1955) (boxing); *Deeson v. PGA*, 358 F.2d 165 (9th Cir. 1966) (golf); *Nassau Sports v. Peters*, 352 F. Supp. 870 (E.D.N.Y. 1972) (hockey).
4. The NLRA applies to all employers whose business affects commerce, although the NLRB can decline to intervene if the effect on commerce is minimal. All major professional sports are now covered. Can you think of any circumstances where a sport or a league might not initiate NLRA coverage?
5. In *Federal Base Ball Club of Baltimore v. National League of Professional Baseball Clubs*, 250 U.S. 200, (1922), the Supreme Court excepted baseball and the reserve clause from antitrust scrutiny, thus stagnating any attempts by the players to organize as a union. The NLRB took jurisdiction finally in 1969 in baseball in a dispute that involved umpires (*In re American League of Professional Baseball Clubs*). The NLRB decided that baseball is an industry that affects commerce (and not minimally) and is therefore subject to the NLRB's coverage and jurisdiction. The NLRB also specifically took jurisdiction over professional football in *In re National Football League Management Council*, 203 N.L.R.B. 165 (1973).

D. COLLECTIVE BARGAINING AND COLLECTIVE BARGAINING AGREEMENTS

Collective bargaining is the process under the NLRA in which management and employees through their union participate in a give-and-take, which produces a document, the collective bargaining agreement (CBA), that establishes the rules and regulations of the relationship. The parties must bargain in good faith; failure to do is an unfair labor practice (ULP). The CBA specifies the scope of the agreement and prohibits the use of either strikes or lockouts. Although the agreement varies from sport, it usually also covers club discipline, noninjury grievances, commissioner discipline, injury grievance, SPKs, college draft rules, option clauses, waivers, base salaries, access to personnel files, medical rights, retirement benefits, insurance, and the duration of the agreement.

The following is an excerpt from the NFL CBA.

NFL COLLECTIVE BARGAINING AGREEMENT

1993-2003 (As Amended June 6, 1996)

Preamble

This Agreement, which is the product of bona fide, arm's length collective bargaining is made and entered into on the 6th day of May, 1993, in accordance with the provisions of the National Labor Relations Act, as amended, by and between the National Football League Management Council ("Management Council" or "NFLMC"), which is recognized as the sole and exclusive bargaining representative of present and future employer member Clubs of the National Football League ("NFL" or "League"), and the National Football League Players Association ("NFLPA"), which is recognized as the sole and exclusive bargaining representative of present and future employee players in the NFL in a bargaining unit described as follows:

1. All professional football players employed by a member club of the National Football League;
2. All professional football players who have been previously employed by a member club of the National Football League who are seeking employment with an NFL Club;
3. All rookie players once they are selected in the current year's NFL College Draft; and
4. All undrafted rookie players once they commence negotiation with an NFL Club concerning employment as a player.

Article II. Governing Agreement

Section 1. **Conflicts:** The provisions of this Agreement supersede any conflicting provisions in the NFL Player Contract, the NFL Constitution and Bylaws, or any other document affecting terms and conditions of employment of NFL players, and all players, Clubs, the NFLPA, the NFL, and the Management Council will be bound hereby. The provisions of the Stipulation and Settlement Agreement in *White v. NFL*, No. 4-92-906 (D. Minn.) ("Settlement Agreement"), shall supersede any conflicting provisions of this Agreement. . . .

Article III. Scope of Agreement

Section 1. **Scope:** This Agreement represents the complete understanding of the parties on all subjects covered herein, and there will be no change in the terms and conditions of this Agreement without mutual consent. . . . provided, however, that if any proposed change in the NFL Constitution and Bylaws during the term of this Agreement could significantly affect the terms and conditions of employment of NFL players, then the Management Council will give the NFLPA notice of and negotiate the proposed change in good faith.

Section 2. **Arbitration:** The question of whether the parties engaged in good faith negotiations, or whether any proposed change in the NFL Constitution and Bylaws would violate or render meaningless any provision of this Agreement, may be the subject of a non-injury grievance under Article IX (Non-Injury Grievance), which shall be the exclusive method for resolving disputes arising out of this Section 2. If the arbitrator finds that either party did not engage in good faith negotiations, or that the proposed change would violate or render meaningless any provision of this Agreement, he may enter an appropriate order, including to cease and desist from implementing or continuing the practice or proposal in question; provided, however, that the arbitrator may not compel either party to this Agreement to agree to anything or require the making of a concession by either party in negotiations.

Article IV. No Strike/Lockout/Suit

Section 1. **No Strike/Lockout:** Except as otherwise provided in Article V (Union Security), Section 6, or Article LIV (Workers' Compensation), Section 7, neither the NFLPA nor any of its members will engage in any strike, work stoppage, or other concerted action interfering with the operations of the NFL or any Club for the duration of this Agreement, and no Clubs, either individually or in concert with other Clubs, will engage in any lockout for the duration of this Agreement. . . .

Section 2. **No Suit:** The NFLPA agrees that neither it nor any of its members, nor agents acting on its behalf, nor any member of its bargaining unit, will sue, or support financially or administratively, or voluntarily provide testimony or affidavit in, any suit against, the NFL or any Club with respect to any claim relating to any conduct permitted by this Agreement, the Settlement Agreement, or any term of this Agreement or the Settlement Agreement, including, without limitation, the Articles concerning the College Draft, the Compensatory Draft, the Option Clause, the Entering Player Pool, Veterans With Less Than Three Accrued Seasons, Veteran Free Agency, Franchise and Transition Players, the Final Eight Plan, Guaranteed League-wide Salary, Salary cap and Minimum Team Salary, and the Waiver System, and provisions applicable to the trading of players. . . .

Article V. Union Security

Section 1. **Union Security:** Every NFL player has the option of joining or not joining the NFLPA; provided, however, that as a condition of employment commencing with the execution of this Agreement and for the duration of this Agreement and wherever and whenever legal: (a) any active player who is or later becomes a member in good standing of the NFLPA must maintain his membership in good standing in the NFLPA; and (b) any active player (including a player in the future) who is not a member in good standing of the NFLPA must, on the 30th day following the beginning of his employment or the execution of this Agreement, whichever is later, pay, pursuant to Section 2 below or otherwise to the NFLPA, an annual service fee in the same amount as any initiation fee and annual dues required of members of the NFLPA. . . .

Article VI. NFLPA Agent Certification

***Section 1.* Exclusive Representation:** The NFLMC and the Clubs recognize that the NFLPA regulates the conduct of agents who represent players in individual contract negotiations with Clubs. The NFLMC and the Clubs agree that the Clubs are prohibited from engaging in individual contract negotiations with any agent who is not listed by the NFLPA as being duly certified by the NFLPA in accordance with its role as exclusive bargaining agent for NFL players. The NFLPA shall provide and publish a list of agents who are currently certified in accordance with its agent regulation system, and shall notify the NFLMC and the Clubs of any deletions or additions to the list pursuant to its procedures. The NFLPA agrees that it shall not delete any agent from its list until that agent has exhausted the opportunity to appeal the deletion to a neutral arbitrator pursuant to its agent regulation system. The NFLPA shall have sole and exclusive authority to determine the number of agents to be certified, and the grounds for withdrawing or denying certification of an agent. The NFLPA agrees that it will not discipline, dismiss or decertify agents based upon the results they achieve or do not achieve in negotiating terms or conditions of employment with NFL Clubs. . . .

In *Morris*, the court evaluated the status of the arbitration clause in the CBA and the SPK after the expiration of the agreement.

MORRIS v. NEW YORK FOOTBALL GIANTS, INC.

575 N.Y.S.2d 1013 (App. Div. 1991)

Herman CAHN, Justice.

By separate motions, defendants New York Football Giants, Inc. (N.Y. Giants), New York Jets Football Club, Inc. (N.Y. Jets), and Paul Tagliabue (on behalf of the National Football League (NFL), an unincorporated association) seek an order, pursuant to CPLR § 7503 and/or the Federal Arbitration Act, 9 U.S.C. § 1 et seq., staying this action and compelling arbitration of all disputed claims. Plaintiffs Joseph Morris and Michael Shuler cross-move for an order, in the event this court submits the dispute to arbitration, appointing a neutral and unbiased arbitrator.

This action arises out of a dispute between two professional football players and their former football clubs over the amount of compensation owed to the players for their services in 1990 prior to the start of the football season (1990 pre-season).

On or about May 30, 1989, Shuler signed a one year standard players contract with the N.Y. Jets pursuant to which he agreed to play for the Jets for the 1990 NFL season. On or about April 30, 1990, Morris executed a one-year standard players contract with the N.Y. Giants wherein he agreed to play for said team for the 1990 season. Paragraph 20 of each of said contracts expressly provided:

> DISPUTES. Any dispute between Player and Club involving the interpretation or application of any provision of this contract will be submitted to final and binding arbitration in accordance with the procedure called for in any collective bargaining agreement in existence at the time the event giving rise to any such dispute occurs. If no collective bargaining agreement is in existence at such time, the dispute will be submitted within a reasonable time to the League Commissioner for final and binding arbitration by him, except as provided otherwise in Paragraph 13 of this contract.

On September 4, 1990, after providing the pre-season services in accordance with their agreements, each of the players was released by their respective team and their contracts terminated. Thereafter, a dispute arose in connection with the amount due for players' compensation for the 1990 pre-season. The plaintiffs assert that they are entitled to compensation for their preseason services equal to ten per cent of the contract amount which would have been due for the whole season. Defendants assert that they are only liable for a specific per-diem payment, which is only a small fraction of the amount plaintiffs' claim.

Plaintiffs commenced this action alleging that the respective clubs have breached the terms of their individual player contracts with respect to compensation (Count II and III of the complaint); they have also made a derivative claim against Paul Tagliabue and the NFL for tortious interference with their (players) contracts. (Count I of the complaint). Thereafter, defendants brought on the instant motions alleging that the underlying dispute is not one for the courts, but for arbitration.

In support of the motions, defendants allege that the 1982 Collective Bargaining Agreement ("CBA") between the National Football League Players Association ("NFLPA"), which then acted as the players' union, and the National Football League Management Council ("NFLMC"), the collective bargaining representative of the NFL contains a broad arbitration clause that embraces the underlying dispute, despite the CBA's formal expiration in August of 1987. Defendants contend that the players representatives, players and clubs have, to date, continued to utilize the grievance and arbitration machinery established by the CBA. As a result, defendants allege that the CBA governs.

In opposition to defendants' motion, plaintiff relies on, inter alia, *McNeil v. National Football League, et al.,* 764 F. Supp. 1351 (D.C. Minn. 1991), wherein, the court found that the NFLPA continued to represent NFL players in collective bargaining only until November 6, 1989, when the NFLPA notified the NFLMC that it (NFLPA) was relinquishing its role as the players' collective bargaining representative. On December 5, 1989, the NFLPA adopted new by-laws which expressly prohibited it from ever again serving as a collective bargaining representative for NFL players. Upon those facts, the *McNeil* court held "that the plaintiffs (NFL players) are no longer part of an 'ongoing collective bargaining relationship' with the defendants" *Id.* at p. 1358. Thus, as of November 6, 1989, there has been no players' collective bargaining representative relating to the NFL. The CBA, which was negotiated with NFLPA, but which by its own terms expired some time ago, does not have any continuing effect. (See also *Mullin v.*

Los Angeles Rams Football, Case No. CV91-1932 R6, U.S. Dist. Ct. (D.C. Cal. 1991)) wherein the court expressly found that the CBA expired on August 31, 1987, and was not extended or renewed. . . . The court agrees with the holdings of the *McNeil* and *Mullin* courts in those regards. . . . Therefore, plaintiffs are bound by their agreements to resolve any disputes relating to their contracts, by arbitration.

A very serious issue is raised as to who the arbitrator should be. The contracts expressly provide that the disputes be submitted to the Commissioner of the NFL. Plaintiffs allege (in support of their cross-motion) that Tagliabue, the Commissioner of the NFL, has an inherent interest in the outcome of the dispute, and is therefore biased and, consequently, should be replaced by a neutral and impartial arbitrator in advance of arbitration proceedings. . . . [I]t is this court's view that a neutral arbitrator should be substituted for the Commissioner in order to insure a fair and impartial hearing. . . .

Based upon the record now before it, the court finds that plaintiffs have shown evidence of lack of neutrality and "evident partiality" and bias on the part of the Commissioner with respect to this specific matter. . . .

Further, this court's authority to select a neutral arbitrator is "inherent when the potential bias of a designated arbitrator would make arbitration proceedings simply a prelude to later judicial proceedings challenging the arbitration award." . . . Therefore, this court finds that the Commissioner should not serve as arbitrator herein.

Defendants argue that the underlying dispute should be submitted to the CBA labor arbitrators if the Commissioner is disqualified, who are experienced in sports-related disputes. However, the CBA labor arbitrators are potentially biased inasmuch as the viability of these labor arbitrators' employment is dependent on whether the 1982 CBA is found to be in existence, the very position asserted by defendants. Further, the court has found herein that the 1982 CBA is no longer in existence, and is not binding. Thus, an arbitrator will be appointed by the court.

Accordingly, defendants' motion staying this action and compelling arbitration is granted. Plaintiffs' cross-motion for appointment of a neutral and impartial arbitrator is granted.

King v. Detroit Lions, Inc., also looked to the status of the CBA's arbitration clause after expiration of the agreement.

KING V. DETROIT LIONS, INC.

748 F. Supp. 488 (E.D. Mich. 1990)

DUGGAN, District Judge.

This matter is before the Court on defendant Detroit Lions, Inc.'s June 27, 1990 motions to dismiss the lawsuits filed against it by plaintiffs Angelo T. King (case no. 90-CV-71253-DT) and Stanley Edwards (case no. 90-CV-71273-DT). Since these cases involve similar allegations and requests for relief, plaintiffs filed a single response to defendant's motions on August 8, 1990. . . .

Facts

Plaintiffs Angelo T. King ("King") and Stanley Edwards ("Edwards") each filed complaints in this Court alleging that defendant Detroit Lions, Inc., breached the terms of a collective bargaining agreement which was applicable to them as employee football players and that defendant also violated the terms of individual player contracts entered into with each plaintiff by defendant.

King's complaint alleges that on September 30, 1987, he entered into an individual player contract with defendant. This contract provided that King would be employed by defendant for one year at a salary of $135,000. The contract also provided for various benefits to King if he should become injured while performing services under the contract.

Edwards' complaint alleges that in May, 1987, he entered into an individual player contract with defendant which provided that he would be employed by defendant for one year at a salary of $100,000. Edwards' contract provided benefits similar to King's contract if he should become injured while performing services under the contract.

As professional football players under contract with defendant, King and Edwards became members of a collective bargaining unit made up of other professional football players under contract with National Football League teams. The bargaining unit's representative was the National Football League Players Association ("NFPLA"). The NFPLA had negotiated a collective bargaining agreement in 1982 with the National Football League Management Council ("NFLMC") which represented the various National Football League team franchises, including defendant, in collective bargaining and other labor relations matters. The 1982 collective bargaining agreement expired on August 31, 1987. However, both parties to the agreement continued to operate under its terms while efforts were made to negotiate a new collective bargaining agreement.

In early October of 1987, King allegedly suffered an injury while playing in a football game for defendant. Later that same month defendant terminated King's individual player contract. King, via the NFPLA, filed a grievance pursuant to the Injury Grievance procedure of Article IX of the expired collective bargaining agreement in November of 1987. In December of that year the NFPLA filed a notice of appeal on the grievance pursuant to the same Article. Also in that December, defendant denied the allegations contained in King's grievance. In October of 1988, the NFPLA filed another grievance on behalf of King, this time predicated on the Injury Protection terms of Article X of the collective bargaining agreement. In November of 1988, while King's grievances were still pending, the NFPLA renounced its status as collective bargaining representative of National Football League players, including King.

Edwards' allegations are quite similar to King's. . . .

Both plaintiffs allege that since their termination from employment, defendant has refused to pay their salaries or provide them benefits pursuant to their individual player contracts and the collective bargaining agreement. Plaintiffs now seek an order from this Court requiring defendant to compensate them for its alleged breach of contract.

Defendant has filed motions to dismiss plaintiffs' complaints. Defendant contends that plaintiff's claims are required to be submitted to arbitration for resolution under the terms of both the individual player contracts and the collective bargaining agreement.

In their complaints, plaintiffs allege that defendant violated the collective bargaining agreement by terminating their contracts while they were allegedly injured. Had these alleged violations occurred before the expiration of the collective bargaining agreement it is clear that the resulting dispute would have been governed by the arbitration clauses contained in Articles IX [Injury Grievance] and X [Injury Protection] of the agreement. Here, however, plaintiffs claim that since the alleged violations occurred after the expiration of the collective bargaining agreement, arbitration is not required and that this Court may resolve the parties' dispute.

The parties do not dispute the fact that, subsequent to the expiration of the 1982 collective bargaining agreement, the players' bargaining unit, via their representative the NFPLA, agreed with the NFLMC, of which defendant was a member, to continue to operate under the terms of the expired contract. Indeed, this agreement to continue using the expired collective bargaining agreement provides the foundation for plaintiffs' claims against defendant. Despite this fact, plaintiffs contend that the arbitration provisions of the expired agreement do not apply to their claims. This Court disagrees with plaintiffs' selective approach to the applicability of the expired agreement.

Arbitration as a means of resolving labor-management disputes is a well-established and broadly-favored principle of federal labor law. . . .

Following this policy, the Supreme Court has held that the expiration of a collective bargaining agreement does not automatically extinguish a party's duty to arbitrate grievances arising out of the agreement. . . . Also, an agreement to continue operating under the terms of an expired collective bargaining agreement is generally sufficient to require arbitration under agreement provisions that have thus been revived. . . . Further, the Supreme Court has held that an employee's claim arising under a collective bargaining agreement is subject to the agreement's arbitration provisions even though the claim arose *after* the agreement was terminated. . . .

With such considerations in mind, plaintiffs' contention that the expired collective bargaining agreement's arbitration provisions do not apply to their claims, but that other agreement provisions do, fails to recognize the strong federal labor policy favoring arbitration as the means of resolving labor disputes arising out of collective bargaining agreements. Plaintiffs advance no arguments sufficient to overcome this policy as it applies to their claims. . . .

As a result, this Court concludes that the expired collective bargaining agreement's arbitration provisions apply to plaintiffs' claims against defendant.

Accordingly, this Court grants defendant's motions to dismiss both plaintiff King's and plaintiff Edwards' claims against it insofar as they seek redress in this court. *Because they have to use CBA ordered.*

An order consistent with this opinion shall issue forthwith. *arbitration instead.*

NFLPA v. Pro Football, Inc., shows the importance of the venue in which the controversy began. Virginia, as a right-to-work state, was not compelled to enforce the CBA's agency shop provision.

NATIONAL FOOTBALL LEAGUE PLAYERS ASSOCIATION v. PRO-FOOTBALL, INC.

857 F. Supp. 71 (D.D.G 1994)

Thomas F. HOGAN, District Judge.

The history of professional football is dotted with moments where last minute heroics produced stunning victories. For example, on December 28, 1958, with the score tied 17-17 in overtime, Johnny Unitas handed the ball to Alan ("the Horse") Ameche, who burst into the endzone to give the Baltimore Colts a championship victory over the New York Giants. This case presents the Court with the opportunity to address another type of last minute activity: a last minute legal battle that at one point threatened to stop the last game of the Washington Redskins' 1993 football season.

The parties in this suit seek to resolve a dispute arising out of the labor agreement governing the players and teams in the National Football League ("NFL"). The parties normally rely upon an arbitrator to act as a referee when disputes arise, but in this particular case, the Court is forced to don a black and white striped shirt and interpret the rules by which the parties have agreed to be bound. Having carefully considered the parties' cross-motions for summary judgment, the oral arguments of counsel, and the entire record in this case, the Court will grant the defendants' motions for summary judgment and dismiss this case.

Background

The facts in this case are undisputed. The plaintiff, the National Football League Players Association ("NFLPA"), is the union representing NFL players. The defendants are Pro-Football, Inc. d/b/a the Washington Redskins ("the Redskins") and the NFL Management Council ("Management Council"). The NFLPA and the NFL Management Council signed a collective bargaining agreement ("CBA") on May 6, 1993, that governs the employment of professional football players. In executing the CBA, the NFLPA acted as the sole and exclusive representative of the individuals who play football for NFL teams and the Management Council acted as the sole and exclusive representative of the NFL teams that employ these football players. CBA, Preamble.

Article V of the agreement contains a standard agency shop provision that requires NFL players to pay union dues or an equivalent service fee within 30 days of employment. The agreement states that this provision is applicable "wherever and whenever legal." CBA, Art. V, § 1. If, after written notification to the NFL Management Council that a player has not paid the proper fees, the matter is not resolved within seven days, the agreement indicates that the player should be suspended without pay. Additionally, Article V states that "[a]ny dispute over compliance with, or the interpretation, application or administration of this Article" will be resolved through arbitration. CBA, Art. V, § 6. The resulting arbitration decision "will constitute full, final and complete disposition of the dispute, and will be binding on the player(s) and Club(s) involved and the parties to this agreement." *Id.* . . .

On December 17, 1993, the NFLPA sent a written notice to the Management Council which identified the players who had not paid dues or fees to the

NFLPA for 1993. The Management Council then informed the Redskins that the team should suspend any players who failed to pay their fees or dues by December 24, 1993. On December 24, 1993, the NFLPA advised the Redskins that 37 Redskins players should be suspended for failing to pay the required fees. The Redskins refused to suspend the delinquent players, asserting that Virginia's right-to-work law prohibited the club from suspending the players.

Based on the refusal of the Redskins to suspend the players, on December 24, 1993, the NFLPA then filed a grievance pursuant to the CBA and obtained an expedited hearing before an arbitrator, Herbert Fishgold. The arbitrator conducted a six-hour hearing on December 28, 1993. . . . During the hearing, the Redskins argued that the club is a Virginia employer, subject to Virginia's right-to-work laws. Since the club's players spend the vast majority of their working hours at Redskins Park in Loudoun County, Virginia, the Redskins took the position that it would be illegal to enforce the agency shop provision against the Redskins and the team's players. The NFLPA argued that the players' predominant job situs was in the District of Columbia and that Virginia's right-to-work law did not apply to the Redskins. Specifically, the NFLPA pointed out that the Redskins play two preseason and eight regular season games at Robert F. Kennedy Stadium ("RFK Stadium") in the District of Columbia, the club's revenue is predominantly derived from playing football games, and players' salaries are related to the number of games in which they remain on the club's roster.

On December 29, 1993, the arbitrator issued his finding. The arbitrator ordered the Redskins to comply with the agreement and to suspend players who failed to pay their dues or fees. . . . Therefore, the arbitrator issued an award that required the Redskins to suspend any players who failed to pay the proper fees.

On December 27, 1993, prior to the arbitration hearing, Terry Orr, a Redskins player who is not a party to this suit, sought a temporary restraining order ("TRO") in the Circuit Court of Loudoun County, Virginia. Orr sought to enjoin the enforcement of the agency shop provision on the grounds that the provision was illegal under Virginia's right-to-work law. On December 30, 1993, Judge Thomas D. Horne granted the temporary restraining order and enjoined the Redskins from suspending Orr. *Orr v. National Football League Players Ass'n* No. 15460, 1993 WL 604063 (Va. Cir. Ct. December 30, 1993). . . .

Following Judge Horne's action, the NFLPA filed this suit seeking injunctive relief and a TRO ordering the defendants to comply with the arbitration award. The NFLPA sought to have the players suspended prior to the Redskins' December 31 game against the Minnesota Vikings. Judge Joyce Hens Green denied the motion on December 30, 1993. *National Football League Players Ass'n v. Pro-Football, Inc.*, 849 F. Supp. 1, (D.D.C. 1993). Judge Green found that the NFLPA was unable to demonstrate a substantial likelihood of success on the merits. . . .

Discussion

In this case, the Court needs to determine whether the Redskins can make an end run around the arbitrator's decision. In order to make such a determination, the Court needs to address two issues: (1) the standard of review to apply; and (2) whether the arbitrator correctly . . . found [that] the job situs [was] the District of Columbia. The Court finds that it is required to act much like the mysterious individual in the NFL's instant replay booth and review the prior decision *de novo*. . . . Accordingly, the Court finds that the defendants are entitled to summary judgment.

I. The Appropriate Standard for Reviewing the Arbitrator's Decision . . .

II. Determining the Job Situs of Redskins' Players . . .

Conclusion

For the foregoing reasons, the Court finds that this case presents no genuine issue of material fact and that the defendants are entitled to a judgment as a matter of law pursuant to Fed. R. Civ. P. 56. Therefore, the Court will vacate the arbitrator's award and enter a declaratory judgment finding that the award is unenforceable because it is contrary to the laws and public policy of Virginia. Accordingly, the Court will grant the defendants' motions for summary judgment, deny the plaintiff's motion for summary judgment, and dismiss this case.

In *White v. NFL*, 149 F. Supp. 2d 858 (D. Minn. 2001) (one of many decisions under this name), Judge Doty, the special master, interpreted the CBA's definition of an "Accrued Season."

WHITE V. NATIONAL FOOTBALL LEAGUE

149 F. Supp. 2d 858 (D. Minn. 2001)

DOTY, District Judge.

This matter is before the court on the objections of class counsel and the National Football League Players' Association ("NFLPA") to the decision of Special Master Jack H. Friedenthal dated March 15, 2001. Based on a review of the file, record and proceedings herein, the court affirms the special master's decision.

Background

This case arises out of a proceeding commenced by class counsel and the NFLPA regarding the status of Kyle Richardson ("Richardson"), a punter for the Baltimore Ravens last season. Under the Collective Bargaining Agreement and the Stipulation and Settlement Agreement (hereafter collectively referred to as the "CBA"), a NFL player is entitled to become an Unrestricted Free Agent if he has four or more Accrued Seasons. *See* CBA Art. XIX § 1. The CBA further specifies that a player is credited with an Accrued Season if he was on full pay status for six or more regular season games. *See* CBA Art. XVIII, § 1(a). . . .

In the 1997 season, Richardson was on full pay status with two different clubs during five weeks when those clubs engaged in regular season games.

Additionally, he was on full pay status during a sixth week when the club that was paying him had a bye. The special master determined that Richardson was prevented from receiving a fourth Accrued Season, thereby denying him unrestricted free agency, since his team had a bye week during one of his qualifying weeks of full pay status for the six or more regular season games.

The sole question that the special master addressed, now before this court, is whether the bye week, during which Richardson was on full pay status, counts as a "game" for purposes of defining an Accrued Season under the provisions of the CBA. Special Master Friedenthal concluded that the clear language of the CBA provides that a player will only be credited with an Accrued Season if he is on full pay status for a total of six or more regular season games in a given year and that games played by other NFL teams during a week in which a player's team has a bye cannot count toward the calculation of an Accrued Season. For the reasons stated, the court concurs with the special master and affirms his decision. . . .

Discussion

The parties do not dispute the relevant language of the CBA but rather its interpretation. The interpretation of the CBA is governed by New York law. . . .

Class counsel argues that a player should be credited with a "game" under the definition of an Accrued Season when his team is on a bye week so long as he is on full pay status and there are other regular season games being played during that week. In other words, they believe that CBA Art. XXVIII, § 1(a) should be interpreted to read as "six or more *weeks* during the regular season." To support this position, class counsel points out that a player on a team with a bye week is still required to practice and is still entitled to receive 1/17th of his regular season salary. Class counsel also argues that there are other instances in the NFL's constitution and Bylaws where a "week" is treated as a "game."

The court, however, is unpersuaded by this argument. The court acknowledges that there is no explicit guidance as to whether the regular season games referred to in this provision are limited to games played by the player's team or whether this provision should be interpreted to encompass the period of time in which the player is on full pay status and regular season games are being played regardless of whether the player's team has a bye week. However, the court agrees with the special master's conclusion that the language here, in specifying "six or more regular season *games*," contemplates a certain level of participation or readiness to participate. [Emphasis added.] That is, the choice of the word "games" must be construed to denote its plain and obvious meaning. If the parties intended that only the number of *payments* or the number of *weeks* that games were played in the league were to be used to calculate an Accrued Season, it would have been more logical for the parties to simply draft the provision to require "six or more payments" or "full pay status for six or more weeks." This provision does not state "weeks" or "payments," but "games." The court may not rewrite the parties' agreement to substitute the term "weeks" for the term "games" since this would defeat the intent of the parties as indicated by the plain language of the contract. . . .

Moreover, contrary to class counsel's assertions, the court is not convinced that affirming the special master's interpretation of this provision leads to an arbitrary or discriminatory result. The distinction between games and weeks was drawn by the parties in the CBA, not by the special master or this court. The requirement that a player be on full pay status for six or more regular season games is no more arbitrary or discriminatory than any other bright line rule, such as the agreement to require full pay status for six as opposed to five or seven games. The fact that players may be required to perform other services or receive an allotment of compensation during bye weeks does not suggest anything arbitrary or irrational, but instead reflects one of the many compromises reached by the parties during the course of negotiations. . . .

The court thus believes that its interpretation of Article XVIII § 1(a), i.e., construing the definition of an Accrued Season to count only games actually played by a team that is paying a player and not bye weeks in which other NFL teams are playing games, reflects a fair and reasonable interpretation of the CBA since it is consistent with other provisions in the CBA and is in conformance with the purposes of the parties as reflected in the record. . . . Had the parties intended the word "games" to simply means "weeks," they would have explicitly provided, as they did elsewhere, that a bye week counts as a game. . . .

Thus, this court will not read into the CBA under the guise of contract construction a condition that the parties did not insert or intend to add.

Therefore, after a *de novo* review, the court affirms Special Master Friedenthal's conclusion that the intent of the parties is reflected in the unambiguous language providing that "a player shall receive one Accrued Season for each season during which he was on . . . full pay status for a total of six or more regular season games." CBA Art. XVIII § 1(a). And under this provision, a player cannot count toward an Accrued Season a game played by other NFL teams during a week in which the team that pays' him has a bye. Since Kyle Richardson was on full pay status for only five regular season games during the 1997 season, he cannot receive credit for an Accrued Season for that season.

Accordingly, it is hereby ordered that the objections of class counsel are overruled and the decision of the special master is affirmed.

---

1. Salary Caps

The current flash point in labor-management relations is the discussion over the applicability of a salary cap. Management wants it labor usually does not. There are hard caps (dollar for dollar), such as in the NFL, or soft caps, such as in the NBA of the 1990s (a team could sign its own players regardless of cap limitations). A salary cap limits the total amount that each team can pay annually to its players, thus limiting the salary that an individual player can negotiate from the team. But salary caps these days are usually protected from antitrust scrutiny on the basis of the nonstatutory labor exemption, which exempts all procedures that are a result of bona fide, arm's-length negotiation. Unions accept salary caps only under economic pressure. Baseball's union has successfully resisted the cap but reluctantly agreed to a luxury tax, which is imposed on teams that spend over a certain amount on their players' salaries. Many personnel decisions in those sports that possess a hard cap are motivated solely by cap considerations. The salary cap in the NFL forces each team to make tough personnel decisions. Many player retention and assignment decisions are now based solely on the particulars and requirements of that sport's salary cap.

MIKE FREEMAN

SALARY CAP FORCES GIANTS TO JOIN TEAMS MAKING DEEP CUTS*

N.Y. Times, Mar. 1, 2002, at C15

The Giants are going through what a number of N.F.L. teams have endured this week—cutting many players and restructuring multiple contracts to get under the $71.1 million salary cap.

This year's cuts are hitting teams harder than ever, and are expected to lead to one of the slowest free agency periods, which begins today. Teams simply do not have the cash available to spend on free agents, unless those players are their own. The Giants yesterday made official what had long been anticipated, announcing the release of linebacker Jessie Armstead. It was the team's most prominent move to get under the cap by today's deadline. Although Armstead, who has played in the last five Pro Bowls, knew this moment was coming, he was upset. . . . The giants will wait until June to release Glenn Parker, the offensive guard, in order to maximize the salary cap savings.

According to team officials, the Giants will make little, if any, significant foray into free agency, concentrating mainly on signing their own players.

Of the group cut yesterday, the Giants would like to re-sign Garrett for a lower salary and possibly Garnes. The Giants now also have to deal with a second group of players who have become free agents because their contacts have ended. . . .

By releasing Armstead, the Giants saved less than $1 million against the cap, a paltry savings that could have been increased by restructuring his contract.

Brad Blank, an agent who represents dozens of N.F.L. players said: "This is the worst, by far, in terms of salary-cap cuts."

The reason is simple. The salary cap went from $67 million last season to $71 million. While that is not the smallest increase, it is much lower than some teams expected. The league normally puts significant portions of its revenues into the cap but this year much of that money went into player benefits such as healthcare.

The players union is increasing the benefits packages—the rising number of crippled veteran players is frightening—and in the short term the lower salary cap is leading to current players losing their jobs.

"Sometimes you have to release players you wouldn't normally release if there wasn't this kind of system," said Ernie Accorsi, the Giants' general manager.

---

* Reprinted with permission.

QUESTIONS AND DISCUSSION

1. Collective bargaining could be more appropriately termed "NLRA-Monitored Good Faith Negotiation between Unions and Management on Wages, Hours, and Conditions of Employment."
2. CBAs are voluminous, complex, legally prepared, and exhaustive in their coverage. They are usually well prepared and written by labor law experts who explain and describe, in detail, every possible concern that may arise as a result of NLRA-sanctioned, union-management dynamics.
3. Most arbitrators are chosen by agreement of both parties; the court in *Morris v. New York Football Giants* chose a neutral arbitrator in lieu of the commissioner. Is there any situation where a union official or management representative might possibly be neutral?
4. In *King v. Detroit Lions, Inc.,* 748 F. Supp. 488 (E.D. Mich. 1990) football players were terminated because of injuries in violation of the C.B.A. and the individual contracts. The court held that the claims were subject to arbitration under the C.B.A., even though the alleged violations occurred after its expiration. The parties had continued to use the expired agreement; therefore, arbitration was appropriate. What other options did the union have?
5. In *NFLPA v. Pro-Football, Inc.*, the union sought an injunction ordering team to comply with arbitration award requiring them to suspend players who fail to pay union dues. The job situs was where the team's practice facility was located; and in that venue, the arbitrator's decision enforcing the CBA was contrary to public policy. Does this case represent the type of problem that, under a CBA, should be arbitrated?
6. *White v. NFL* is an example of CBA interpretation. As such, should it have been arbitrated under the clause in Kyle Richardson's individual contract?
7. Reread Mike Freeman's *New York Times* article on the salary cap. A salary cap limits player salaries to a certain percent of the league's gross. Football's hardcap is dollar for dollar, that is, every dollar spent on salaries is subtracted from that team's salary cap for that year. Although just a part of their CBA, the continuation of football's 'hard' cap is management's deal breaker. It is the new millennium's 'reserve clause'. Of course, management is able to successfully bargain for a hard cap only if (1) it can withstand economically a strike or a lockout and the players cannot; (2) the owners are relatively strong while the union is not; and (3) the owners are solidly behind their management council while the union members are (relatively) less solid, cohesive, determined (steely-eyed), and unified. Of course, it's not that simple. Unlike baseball, with its antitrust exemption, most of the other sports unions were trying to solve their labor problems through antitrust end-runs. Good luck. The much more successful Major League Baseball Players Association was forced to duke it out in the labor trenches. Also, it appears that baseball players either are better unionists or can better financially withstand the effects of a prolonged concerted action. Football players do not handle prolonged strikes well. After seven games of the 1987 "replacement" season (with some veterans already playing), it appeared as if

the majority of the union rank and file were about to fold, so the union capitulated. However, in defense of the union, a football player's career is very short, and the lost time from a prolonged strike or lockout might terminate his career. Most football players are not eligible for Bert Bell retirement monies; nor are they financially secure or well prepared enough to earn significant income after the end of their careers. For many, their only source of income is to continue their career regardless. See *Wood v. NBA*, 602 F. Supp 525 (S.D.N.Y. 1984), *aff'd,* 809 F.2d 954 (2d Cir 1987) (NBA's first version of salary cap was exempted from antitrust laws under the nonstatutory labor exemption on the basis that it affected only the parties to the CBA (management and players), that it involved only mandatory subjects of collective bargaining, and that it was the result of bona fide, arms'-length negotiations). *See also* Graves, '*Controlling Athletes with the Draft and the Salary Cap: Are Both Necessary?*' 5 Sports Law. J. 185 (1998); Levine, '*Hard Cap or Soft Cap: The Optimal Player Mobility Restrictions for the Professional Sports Leagues*,' 6 Fordham Intell. Prop. Media & Ent. L.J. 243 (1995); McPhee, '*First Down, Goal to Go: Enforcing the NFL's Salary Cap Using the Implied Covenant of Good Faith and Fair Dealing*,' 17 Loy. L.A. Ent. L.J. Rev. 449 (1997).

8. In *Wood v. NBA*, 602 F. Supp. 525 (S.D.N.Y. 1984), *aff'd,* 809 F.2d 954 (2d Cir. 1987), the salary cap limited salaries to 53 percent of the NBA's gross. The question is, what types of earnings are included in the cap figure? *See generally* Graves, 'Controlling Athletes with the Draft and the Salary Cap: Are Both Necessary?' 5 Sports Law. J. 185 (1998); Hertz, '*The NBA and the NBPA Opt to Cap Off the 1988 C.B.A., with a Full Court Press* In re Chris Dudley,' 5 Marq. Sports L.J. 251 (1995); Levine, 'Hard Cap or Soft Cap: The Optimal Player Mobility Restrictions for the Professional Sports Leagues,' 6 Fordham Intell. Prop. Media & Ent. L.J. 243 (1995); Patterson, '*The NBA Salary Cap: Dead or Alive*,' 19 T. Marshall L. Rev. 535 (1994).

E. **CONCERTED ACTIONS**

Concerted actions such as strikes and lockouts are a normal and expected part of the negotiations between labor and management as orchestrated by the NLRA. The collective bargaining process is effective only *because* of the threat of concerted actions, which each party can legally invoke if negotiation reaches an impasse. The threat and the ability of either party to withstand the work stoppage is the key to the NLRA machinery that places some logical parameters to the potentially chaotic and violent relationships between labor and management. This is especially true and poignant in professional sports, where the season is only so long and the athletes' careers (that is, the days of making significant dollars) are very limited in duration (especially in football).

In labor relationships, the initial years are often stormy. But in professional sports, unions faced an unusually tough struggle to organize, as evidenced by their many aborted attempts to unionize. The NLRB finally agreed to put professional sports within its jurisdiction in 1969. Although the history of collective bargaining in sports is not very long, it has been unusually contentious, with an almost annual ritual in the major sports of either concerted actions (strikes or lockouts), the threat of concerted actions, or accusations of ULPs.

1. Unfair Labor Practices

An unfair labor practice (ULP) is the NLRA's method to penalize behavior that violates its stipulations. If either side's actions or inactions merit an ULP, then their behavior can be legally enjoined. Section 8(d) of the NLRA indicates that both parties must meet at reasonable times and confer on mandatory subjects of collective bargaining; failure to do so is an unfair labor practice.

In *Smith v. Houston Oilers*, the players alleged that the team required their participation in an abusive rehabilitation program under threats of black-balling them from further participation in the sport. These claims, if proven, would certainly constitute unfair labor practices. However, in *Smith*, the players' claims were preempted by federal labor law.

SMITH V. HOUSTON OILERS, INC.

87 F.3d 717 (5th Cir. 1996)

Patrick E. HIGGINBOTHAM, Circuit Judge:

Sherman Smith and Tracy Smith sued the Houston Oilers and members of the Oilers' staff, alleging that the defendants required their participation in an abusive rehabilitation program under threats of being dismissed from the Oilers and blackballed from other teams in the National Football League. The district court dismissed the state claims based on the abusive rehabilitation program on the ground that those claims were preempted by federal labor law, but it remanded to state court related state claims of intentional infliction of emotional distress to the extent that those claims arose from the allegations of threatened blackballing. The players appeal the dismissal, and the Oilers cross-appeal the order remanding to state court.

We conclude that all claims are preempted by federal labor law. We affirm the dismissal, vacate the order remanding to state court, and remand with instruction to dismiss those claims as well.

I

Sherman Smith and Tracy Smith alleged the following facts, and we accept them as true in the present posture of the case: Sherman Smith and Tracy Smith each signed a one-year contract to play professional football for the Houston Oilers. During preseason training camp in the summer of 1994, Sherman broke his thumb and Tracy tore a leg muscle. These injuries prevented them from playing, and they were placed in a routine rehabilitation program with other injured players. In the first week of required player cuts, however, the Oilers sought to dismiss Sherman and Tracy. But since the

National Football League prohibits teams from terminating football players while they are recovering from football-related injuries, the Oilers offered to settle Sherman's and Tracy's contracts for a "meager" sum if they left voluntarily. Sherman and Tracy rejected these offers.

According to the Smiths' allegations, Floyd Reese and Steve Watterson of the Oilers responded by compelling Sherman and Tracy to submit to severe abuse in a phony "rehabilitation" program designed to coerce them into leaving the team. The abuse, they allege, included: reduction of rehabilitation treatment previously allowed, such as stretching and ice treatment; sleep deprivation resulting from morning workouts begining at 4:00 a.m. and evening workouts ending at 11:00 p.m.; strenuous exercise that far exceeded previous demands, including humiliating water-barrel-pulling exercises; veiled threats of dismissal for noncompliance with rehabilitation; intentional confusion as to workout schedules; and threats to blackball Sherman and Tracy from playing for other NFL teams in the future.

No other players participated in this abusive program. Three days after Sherman and Tracy began the program, Sherman collapsed during a 4:00 a.m. workout and was taken to the hospital. Later that day, Tracy complained to the NFL Players Association, after which the Oilers ceased the program. . . .

The players do not dispute that the CBA at issue here permits NFL teams to require their players to participate in rehabilitation and conditioning programs. Rather, the players urge that the district court erred because the Oilers' demands in rehabilitation were so egregious that the CBA could not possibly have condoned them. . . .

Here, however, the alleged misconduct cannot be separated from the underlying dispute between the players and the Oilers over the adequacy of the Oilers' offer of termination pay. That dispute is fundamentally a labor dispute; indeed, the abuse complained-of by the players occurred only because they wanted to remain with a team that did not want them. There is no allegation that anyone from the Oilers' management or staff committed a direct act of physical violence against Sherman Smith or Tracy Smith. Rather, the abuse of the two players resulted from their compelled participation in an ostensible rehabilitation program under threats of termination or blackballing. The players could have avoided the abuse by refusing to participate. In sum, the complained of conduct was the Oilers' unreasonable negotiating position regarding termination, not any infliction of violence upon the two players. . . .

We agree with the district court that the Oilers' alleged misconduct was not sufficiently outrageous to defeat preemption . . . That is, since we think it necessary to refer to the CBA to determine the extent to which the Oilers' rehabilitation demands were *permissible*, it is likewise necessary to measure the *outrageousness* of their conduct by reference to what the CBA authorizes. . . .

III

The Oilers argue on cross-appeal that the district court erred in remanding to state court the players' claims of intentional infliction of emotional distress resulting from the Oilers' alleged blackballing threats. The Oilers contend that such claims based on allegations of threatened blackballing are claims of unfair labor practices, and as such are preempted by § 7 and § 8 of the National Labor Relations Act, 29 U.S.C. § 151 *et seq.* . . . .

We agree that NLRA §§7 and 8 preempt the players' claims of intentional infliction of emotional distress based on blackballing threats. . . .

The players do not dispute that blackballing is an unfair labor practice proscribed by § 7 and § 8 of the NLRA; rather, they argue that because they did not engage in any *"concerted* activity" as contemplated by NLRA § 7, the NLRA does not govern the Oilers' blackballing threats, which were directed toward the players' non-concerted activity. This argument lacks merit. . . . We conclude that § 7 and § 8 of the NLRA preempt the emotional-distress claims based on the Oilers' blackballing threats.

IV

We affirm the district court's dismissal of the plaintiffs' claims based on the abusive rehabilitation program. We vacate and remand to the district court its order remanding to state court the claims of intentional infliction of emotional distress based on blackballing threats with instructions to dismiss those claims.

2. Strikes

Unions of professional athletes, as employee representatives under the NLRA, are guaranteed the right to engage in strikes and other concerted activities. After impasse, the union can legally strike. A strike is defined as the failure to report to training camp or to the playing field. It is the union's primary weapon in coercing the owners to adopt the players' demands, compromise, or at least return to the table and continue good-faith negotiations. The "winner" of a strike or lockout is the last party standing (economically).

The right to strike usually cannot be diminished or estopped (by agreement) and receives considerable legal protection. Although there is a right to strike, the union must still bargain in good faith even while the players are striking. Additionally, the union loses its right to strike if (1) it agrees to a no-strike clause in the CBA; (2) it engages in an activity that has an unlawful objective; or (3) it uses improper means such as rendering inoperable company machinery. Also, the owners can impose sanctions on the strikers while they are striking; but these striking athletes are still employees. Since they are still deemed to be employees, they cannot be punished by any ULPs that are committed by management during a strike. In other words, even though collective bargaining has broken down and the employees are forced to strike, the NLRA provides mechanisms of restraint (the issuance of ULPs) that force the "combatants" to treat each other in a "civilized" manner.

3. Lockouts

The owners have their form of concerted activity: the lockout. Here, the owners can lock out the players, that is, not allow the athletes to report to training camp. Comparable to the union's right to strike, the lockout is the owner's primary economic weapon in that it is the power to withhold employment. The lockout is used to economically coerce the players to return to the table or to reignite the players' desire to continue good-faith bargaining. Lockouts are legal if good-faith negotiations continue and the lockout occurs only after impasse.

Employers use lockouts tactically to preclude employees from working and collecting income. Lockouts may entail a shutdown of a team's entire operation or may be just a foreclosure of a work opportunity. Tactically, a lockout may be employed to avoid the consequences of a union work stoppage at an inopportune time (for example, the first game of the season).

> Still, from the owners' perspective, the lockout is an important weapon because it enables them to dictate the timing of a work stoppage or other economic pressure. If baseball owners anticipate a strike being called over Memorial Day or Labor Day weekend, historically high attendance periods, they may seek to seize the initiative and lock out the players in order to force an agreement. At times, owners expecting a strike have locked out players only to characterize the cessation of play as a strike. In 1990, baseball's owners again locked out the players in an attempt to reinforce their bargaining demand that the players accept, among other things, a salary cap and an end to salary arbitration. This lockout ended with the owners withdrawing their demands regarding elimination of arbitration and implementation of a salary cap.[6]

As you can see, lockouts are a tactical ploy on the part of management to manipulate the course and pace of the negotiation process.

QUESTIONS AND DISCUSSION

1. In 1981 was the famous 50-day strike in baseball. Coincidentally, management agreed to essentially the same proposals that the union had offered 50 days before. The reason, of course, was that for the first and last time, Lloyd's of London had insured against strikes for 50 days. *See generally* Cozzillio, *'From the Land of Bondage: The Greening of Major League Baseball Players and the Major League Baseball Players Association,'* 41 Cath. U.L. Rev. 117 (1991).

2. In 1994 was the infamous strike that canceled the World Series, which was unprecedented in any time other than during the world wars. The bad feelings from that debacle continued like a cancer and seriously eroded the popularity and marketability of baseball until the McGuire-Sosa home run derby at the end of that decade. Should the NLRB have stepped in to end this strike?

3. In 1990, a baseball lockout was ended by Commissioner Fay Vincent. Should the commissioner have that much power? Was his action in the "best interest of baseball"?

4. Another famous lockout was in basketball in 2000 when the union capitulated as a result of growing dissension in the rank and file. This successful lockout ushered in a new, harder version of the existing salary cap. *See also* Latimer, *'The NBA Salary Cap: Controlling Labor Costs Through Collective Bargaining,'* 44 Cath. U. L. Rev. 205 (1994); Rothstein, *'The Salary*

---

[6] Cozzillie & Levinson, *Sports Law: Cases and Materials* 681 (1997).

Cap: A Legal Analysis of and Practical Suggestions for Collective Bargaining in Professional Baseball,' 11 Miami Ent. & Sports L. Rev. 251 (1994).
5. The *Smith v. Houston Oilers* court held that termination pay could not be divorced from the team's conduct in forcing players to choose between accepting termination terms and participating in an abusive rehabilitation plan. The court held that the negotiation of claims was too dependant on an analysis of the CBA to escape preemption of the players' state claims. The court also held that claims based on allegations of threatened blackballing were ULPs and preempted by the NLRA. In short, their state claims were preempted by federal labor law. Should this problem have been subject to the arbitration clauses?

F. ARBITRATION

Arbitration procedures are a product of collective bargaining in the team sports. There are two types: grievance and salary. An arbitration clause in most CBAs makes arbitration the exclusive remedy. Courts rarely reverse an arbitrator's decision if the party that seeks arbitration makes a claim that on its face is governed by the CBA's arbitration provisions. The preeminent concern is whether the dispute is arbitrable, that is, within the range of matters intended to be arbitrated through the grievance procedure.

The SPK, part of the CBA, gives each party certain rights; the question is how to enforce these rights. The answer generally is arbitration. The arbitration clause usually stipulates that all disputes will be resolved by nonjudicial means, though the actual wording of the SPK determines exactly which controversies are subject to arbitration. Usually the club retains the right to seek injunctive relief, a judicial remedy, to enforce the player's promise to exclusively play for one team. Arbitration is preferred to judicial remedies since it is more informal, less costly, less time-consuming, and more private. Additionally, the parties may choose an arbitrator who knows the sport.

There are some matters, however, that are not subject to arbitration. They include (1) controversies not covered in the agreement; (2) situations when the breaching party waived its arbitration rights; and (3) matters in which judicial enforcement is preferred for public policy reasons.

Courts set aside arbitrators' awards only in extreme cases. Awards are final because the parties have freely bargained away their rights to seek judicial remedies. Presumably, each party has received something in return; therefore, the parties should be made to keep their bargain. Moreover, arbitration is deemed to be a desirable mechanism for dispute resolution and, therefore, arbitration decisions must be maintained and honored.

1. Grievance

Each SPK contains a standard grievance arbitration clause. This clause usually stipulates that disputes be grievance or contract disputes; but, as in professional baseball, clauses can be formulated to deal with other concerns, such as salary disputes. The typical grievance arbitration procedure as contained within a CBA provides an orderly and expeditious procedure for handling and solving disputes, grievances, and complaints. However, most sports arbitration procedures specifically exclude the benefit plan, union dues check-off, and complaints that involve the integrity of the sport.

The following case affirms the arbitrator's decision that signaled the demise of the reserve clause and allowed the possibility of free agency in professional baseball.

Kansas City Royals Baseball Corp. v. Major League Baseball Players Association

532 F.2d 615 (8th Cir. 1976)

The owners of the twenty-four Major League Baseball Clubs seek reversal of a judgment of the District Court for the Western District of Missouri. The court refused to set aside and ordered enforced an arbitration panel's award rendered in favor of the Major League Baseball Players Association. The arbitration panel was established pursuant to a collective bargaining agreement between the Club Owners and the Players Association. The award relieved pitcher Andy Messersmith of any contractual obligation to the Los Angeles Dodgers, and pitcher Dave McNally of any similar obligation to the Montreal Expos. It directed the Dodgers and Expos to remove Messersmith and McNally, respectively, from their reserve or disqualified lists. It ordered the American and National Leagues to inform and instruct their member clubs that the provisions of Major League Rule 4-A (reserve list rule) and Rule 3(g) (no-tampering rule) do not inhibit, prohibit or prevent such clubs from negotiating or dealing with Messersmith and McNally with respect to employment.

We hold that the arbitration panel had jurisdiction to resolve the dispute, that its award drew its essence from the collective bargaining agreement, and that the relief fashioned by the District Court was appropriate. . . .

I

On February 25, 1973, the Club Owners and the Players Association entered into a collective bargaining agreement to be in effect from January 1, 1973 to December 31, 1975, [which included arbitration for grievances]. . . .

On October 7, 1975, the Players Association filed a grievance on behalf of Andy Messersmith. The grievance alleged that Messersmith played for the Los Angeles Dodgers in 1975 under a renewed 1974 contract, that the renewal year was completed on September 28, 1975, that Messersmith thus became a free agent on that date, and that the Club Owners had denied him his right to deal with other teams for his services in 1976. The Players Association asked that the Club Owners be ordered to treat Messersmith as a free agent and to compensate him for any financial detriment he might incur due to their delay in doing so.

On October 9, 1975, the Players Association filed a companion grievance on behalf of Dave McNally, alleging similar circumstances.

The Club Owners responded to both grievances on October 24, 1975. Their primary contention was that the claims raised fell outside the scope of the agreed upon grievance procedures and were, therefore, not subject to the jurisdiction of the arbitration panel. They argued that Article XV of the 1973 agreement excluded disputes concerning the "core" or "heart" of the reserve system from the grievance procedures set forth in Article X. . . .

With respect to the merits of the dispute, the Club Owners argued that under the Uniform Player's Contract, the Dodgers and the Expos had the right to renew Messersmith's and McNally's contracts from year to year for a reasonable number of years. They alternatively argued that under the Major League Rules, the two clubs could obligate the pitchers to play for them and no other Major League Club, simply by placing their names on the clubs' reserve lists. . . .

On December 23, 1975, the [arbitration] panel rendered its decision, holding that the grievances were within the scope of its jurisdiction and that Messersmith and McNally were free agents. It directed that both parties be removed from the reserve or disqualified lists of their respective clubs, and that the leagues promptly notify their member clubs that they may negotiate with Messersmith and McNally with respect to future employment. . . .

The District Court held that the Messersmith-McNally grievances were within the scope of the arbitration panel's jurisdiction, and that neither the arbitrators' resolution of the merits nor the relief awarded exceeded the bounds of the panel's authority. It ordered enforcement of the arbitration panel's award. . . .

We begin with the proposition that the language of Article X of the 1973 agreement is sufficiently broad to require arbitration of the Messersmith-McNally grievances. We think this clear because the disputes involve the interpretation of the provisions of agreements between a player or the Players Association and a club or the Club Owners. . . .

During the negotiations leading up to the 1970 agreement, the Players Association submitted a number of proposed modifications of the reserve system, including a provision which would give each player the option of becoming a free agent once every three years. The Club Owners rejected these proposals as unacceptable, stating that they went to the heart of the game and the reserve system. In February, 1970, it became apparent that the parties had reached an impasse on the reserve system. . . .

At approximately the same time that the 1970 negotiations were reaching an impasse on the reserve system, Curt Flood, an outfielder traded by the St. Louis Cardinals to the Philadelphia Phillies, filed suit in federal court challenging the validity of the reserve system. Flood's complaint defined the reserve system as a number of provisions designed to bind a player to a particular club for the duration of his career. He claimed that the reserve system violated federal antitrust laws.   *Flood v Kuhn et al*

The Club Owners asserted, as a defense to the Flood action, that the parties had agreed to the reserve system through collective bargaining, and that the system was, therefore, exempt from federal antitrust laws. . . . As a result of the assertion of that defense, Arthur Goldberg, Chief Counsel for Flood, suggested to the Players Association's negotiators that a provision be included in the 1970 agreement which would obviate the Jewel Tea defense [the so-called nonstatutory labor exemption to the antitrust laws]. . . .

The parties finally agreed upon the following language, which became Article XIV of the 1970 agreement:

Reserve System

Regardless of any provision herein to the contrary, this Agreement does not deal with the reserve system. The parties have differing views as to the legality and as to the merits of such system as presently constituted. This Agreement shall in no way prejudice the position or legal rights of the Parties or of any Player regarding the reserve system.

It is agreed that until the final and unappealable adjudication (or voluntary discontinuance) of Flood v. Kuhn et al., . . . neither of the Parties will resort to any form of concerted action with respect to the issue of the reserve system, and there shall be no obligation to negotiate with respect to the reserve system. Upon the final and unappealable adjudication (or voluntary discontinuance) of Flood v. Kuhn et al., either Party shall have the right to reopen negotiations on the issue of the reserve system as follows. . . .

The parties finally agreed to carry over the language of Article XIV of the 1970 agreement into the 1973 agreement with two exceptions. First, the clause "except as adjusted or modified hereby" was substituted as the prefatory language to "this Agreement does not deal with the reserve system." Second, reference to the Flood litigation was deleted. Article XIV of the 1970 agreement, as modified, was incorporated into the 1973 agreement as Article XV. . . .

[I]t may be said that the arbitration panel's decision did not change the reserve system, but merely interpreted various elements thereof under circumstances which had not previously arisen. . . .

We find that the arbitration panel did nothing more than to interpret certain provisions of the Uniform Player's Contract and the Major League Rules. We cannot say that those provisions are not susceptible of the construction given them by the panel. Accordingly, the award must be sustained. . . .

Conclusion

We hold that the arbitration panel had jurisdiction to hear and decide the Messersmith-McNally grievances, that the panel's award drew its essence from the collective bargaining agreement, and that the relief fashioned by the District Court was appropriate. Accordingly, the award of the arbitration panel must be sustained, and the District Court's judgment affirmed. In so holding, we intimate no views on the merits of the reserve system. We note, however, that Club Owners and the Players Association's representatives agree that some form of a reserve system is needed if the integrity of the game is to be preserved and if public confidence in baseball is to be maintained. The disagreement lies over the degree of control necessary if these goals are to be achieved. Certainly, the parties are in a better position to negotiate their differences than to have them decided in a series of arbitrations and court decisions. We commend them to that process and suggest that the time for obfuscation has passed and that the time for plain talk and clear language has arrived. Baseball fans everywhere expect nothing less. . . .

This Court's mandate affirming the judgment of the District Court shall issue seven days from the date this opinion is filed. Our previous order staying enforcement of the District Court's decree shall continue in effect until the issuance of the mandate.

In *Major League Umpires' Association v. American League of Professional Baseball Clubs*, the court once again enforced an arbitrator's award on the basis that the award drew its essence from the CBA.

Major League Umpires' Association v. American League of Professional Baseball Clubs

160 L.R.R.M. (BNA) 2099 (E.D. Pa. 1997)

Ludwig, J.

Plaintiff The Major League Umpires' Association appeals an arbitrator's decision denying the umpires compensation for the unplayed 1994 post-season and allowing a formula apportionment to the umpires who worked the 1994 All-Star Game. ...

[handwritten: Court found in favor of ALPBC]

I. Facts

From January 1, 1991 through December 31, 1994, the parties operated under a collective bargaining agreement, and, during this period, the American League and the National League each employed 32 umpires. On July 12, 1994, six umpires officiated at the 1994 All-Star Game in Pittsburgh. On August 12, 1994, the players engaged in a work stoppage that lasted until March, 1995. As a result, the remainder of the 1994 season, the Division Playoffs, the League Championship Series and the World Series were cancelled. The umpires did not receive "Special Events" compensation for the unplayed 1994 post-season games. Under the Collective Bargaining Agreement, "Special Events" compensation included so-called "pool payments"—a fixed amount related to the umpire's years of service—and "working money"—a fixed amount for each post-season series worked. ... The total "Special Events" compensation claimed to be due is $755,000 for the American League umpires and $685,000 for the National League.

Following denial of its grievance, plaintiff demanded arbitration before the American Arbitration Association pursuant to Article XV of the Collective Bargaining Agreement. On October 7, 1996, the arbitrator returned the following decision: (1) The umpires were not entitled to Special Events "pool payments" or "working payments" for post-season games not played; (2) the umpires were entitled to a portion of "pool payments" for the 1994 All-Star Game; and (3) the apportionment formula established by President Nixon in arbitrating a similar dispute between the parties in 1985 was appropriate for allocating the 1994 All-Star Game "pool payments." Arb. Op. and Award at 34-35. Applying this formula, umpires with up to five years of service were awarded $728.44 and with six years or more, $1,394.44, as "pool" money.

On this appeal, plaintiff's contention is that the arbitrator exceeded his authority by disregarding the specific questions submitted for arbitration. The issue presented was whether the umpires provided services with respect to "Special Events" or, in the alternative, whether Article VII pay is "salary" as that term is used in Article XIV. *Id.* Stip. Record, ex. 10.

II. Discussion

The familiar rule is that "federal policy in favor of settling labor disputes by arbitration requires that courts refrain from reviewing the merits of arbitration awards." . . .

So long as the arbitrator's award is "drawn from the essence" of the collective bargaining agreement, it is enforceable. On appeal, a court should not substitute its views even if it disagrees with the award, or finds the basis for it to be ambiguous. Only a manifest disregard of the parties' agreement or of the law will require a reviewing court to intrude upon the "province of the arbitrator." . . .

Here, plaintiff contends that the arbitrator, by resolving the dispute in a manner not contemplated in the collective bargaining agreement, went beyond his authority. . . .

The arbitrator determined that Article XIV of the Collective Bargaining Agreement, concerning salary in case of a strike or lockout, is controlling because it "fits" the specific facts of the parties' dispute. . . . He also concluded that because there was no provision for additional compensation for post-season games in the event of a player strike or lock-out, there must not have been "a meeting of the minds" as to this issue. He reasoned that compensation due under Article VII does not fall within the category of "salary" under Article XIV. Instead, it is additional compensation. Therefore, the umpires were not entitled to such payment since the post-season games were cancelled. A portion of "pool money" was awarded solely for the All-Star Game at which six umpires had officiated.

Plaintiff complains that the "pool money" formula adopted by the arbitrator was outside the scope of his authority, since it was not part of the agreement — and was derived from another arbitration nine years earlier. This type of resolution, however, can be supported. . . .

Plaintiff refers to several labor arbitration cases for the proposition that where there is no pertinent "meeting of the minds" in a collective bargaining agreement, the dispute is not arbitrable. . . .

Given these precepts, it cannot be said that the arbitrator's interpretation was devoid of a reasoned basis. "If the interpretation can in any rational way be derived from the agreement, viewed in light of its language, its context, and any other indicia of the parties' intention," it will be enforced. *United Transp. Union Local*, 51 F.3d at 379. The arbitrator's decision was founded upon the collective bargaining agreement and the plain meaning of its terms. Accordingly, plaintiff's motion for summary judgment must be denied and defendants granted judgment and as a matter of law — regardless of the arguable desirability of the result.

Order

And now, this 29th day of August, 1997, the summary judgment motion of defendants The American League of Professional Baseball Clubs and The National League of Professional Baseball Clubs is granted, and the cross-motion for summary judgment of the The Major League Umpires' Association is denied. A memorandum accompanies this order.

In *Major League Baseball Players Association v. Garvey*, the U.S. Supreme Court affirmed the arbitrator's decision that denied a former major league baseball player's claim of monetary damages that resulted from the alleged collusion of clubs to thwart free agency.

MAJOR LEAGUE BASEBALL PLAYERS ASSOCIATION V. GARVEY

532 U.S. 1015 (2001)

PER CURIAM.

The Court of Appeals for the Ninth Circuit here rejected an arbitrator's factual findings and then resolved the merits of the parties' dispute instead of remanding the case for further arbitration proceedings. Because the court's determination conflicts with our cases limiting review of an arbitrator's award entered pursuant to an agreement between an employer and a labor organization and prescribing the appropriate remedy where vacation of the award is warranted, we grant the petition for a writ of certiorari and reverse. The motions for leave to file briefs *amicus curiae* of the National Academy of Arbitrators and the Office of the Commissioner of Baseball are granted.

In the late 1980's, petitioner Major League Baseball Players Association (Association) filed grievances against the Major League Baseball Clubs (Clubs), claiming the Clubs had colluded in the market for free-agent services after the 1985, 1986, and 1987 baseball seasons, in violation of the industry's collective-bargaining agreement. A free agent is a player who may contract with any Club, rather than one whose right to contract is restricted to a particular Club. In a series of decisions, arbitrators found collusion by the Clubs and damage to the players. The Association and Clubs subsequently entered into a Global Settlement Agreement (Agreement), pursuant to which the Clubs established a $280 million fund to be distributed to injured players. The Association also designed a "Framework" to evaluate the individual player's claims, and, applying that Framework, recommended distribution plans for claims relating to a particular season or seasons.

The Framework provided that players could seek an arbitrator's review of the distribution plan. The arbitrator would determine " 'only whether the approved Framework and the criteria set forth therein have been properly applied in the proposed Distribution Plan.' " *Garvey v. Roberts*, 203 F.3d 580, 583 (C.A.9 2000) *(Garvey I)*. The Framework set forth factors to be considered in evaluating players' claims, as well as specific requirements for lost contract-extension claims. Such claims were cognizable " 'only in those cases where evidence exists that a specific offer of an extension was made by a club prior to collusion only to thereafter be withdrawn when the collusion scheme was initiated.' " *Id.*, at 584.

Respondent Steve Garvey, a retired, highly regarded first baseman, submitted a claim for damages of approximately $3 million. He alleged that his contract with the San Diego Padres was not extended to the 1988 and 1989 seasons due to collusion. The Association rejected Garvey's claim in February 1996, because he presented no evidence that the Padres actually offered to extend his contract. Garvey objected, and an arbitration hearing was held. He testified that the Padres offered to extend his contract for the 1988 and 1989 seasons and then withdrew the offer after they began colluding with other teams. He presented a June 1996 letter from Ballard Smith, Padres' President and CEO from 1979 to 1987, stating that, before the end of the 1985 season, Smith offered to extend Garvey's contract through the 1989 season, but that the Padres refused to negotiate with Garvey thereafter due to collusion.

The arbitrator denied Garvey's claim, after seeking additional documentation from the parties. In his award, he explained that " '[t]here exists . . . substantial doubt as to the credibility of the statements in the Smith letter.' " *Id.*, at 586. He noted the "stark contradictions" between the 1996 letter and Smith's testimony in the earlier arbitration proceedings regarding collusion, where Smith, like other owners, denied collusion and stated that the Padres simply were not interested in extending Garvey's contract. *Ibid.* The arbitrator determined that, due to these contradictions, he " 'must reject [Smith's] more recent assertion that Garvey did not receive [a contract] extension' " due to collusion, and found that Garvey had not shown a specific offer of extension. . . .

Garvey moved in Federal District Court to vacate the arbitrator's award, alleging that the arbitrator violated the Framework by denying his claim. The District Court denied the motion. The Court of Appeals for the Ninth Circuit reversed by a divided vote. The court acknowledged that judicial review of an arbitrator's decision in a labor dispute is extremely limited. But it held that review of the merits of the arbitrator's award was warranted in this case, because the arbitrator " 'dispensed his own brand of industrial justice.' " *Id.*, at 589. . . .

The District Court then remanded the case to the arbitration panel for further hearings, and Garvey appealed. The Court of Appeals, again by a divided vote, explained that *Garvey I* established that "the conclusion that Smith made Garvey an offer and subsequently withdrew it because of the collusion scheme was the only conclusion that the arbitrator could draw from the record in the proceedings." . . .

The Court of Appeals reversed the District Court and directed that it remand the case to the arbitration panel with instructions to enter an award for Garvey in the amount he claimed. . . .

Judicial review of a labor-arbitration decision pursuant to such an agreement is very limited. Courts are not authorized to review the arbitrator's decision on the merits despite allegations that the decision rests on factual errors or misinterprets the parties' agreement. . . .

In *Garvey II*, the court clarified that *Garvey I* both rejected the arbitrator's findings and went further, resolving the merits of the parties' dispute based on the court's assessment of the record before the arbitrator. For that reason, the court found further arbitration proceedings inappropriate. But again, established law ordinarily precludes a court from resolving the merits of the parties' dispute on the basis of its own factual determinations, no matter how erroneous the arbitrator's decision. . . .

For the foregoing reasons, the Court of Appeals erred in reversing the order of the District Court denying the motion to vacate the arbitrator's award, and it erred further in directing that judgment be entered in Garvey's favor. The petition for a writ of certiorari is granted, the judgment of the Court of Appeals is reversed, and the case is remanded for further proceedings consistent with this opinion.

It is so ordered. . . .

2. Salary

Salary arbitration is the singular achievement of the Major League Baseball Players Association. Players with a certain amount of time (somewhere between two and three years) in the major leagues are eligible for salary arbitration. The technique is "high-low"; both parties must submit proposed salary to the arbitrator, who then chooses one amount without modification. Both sides use statistics to substantiate the dollar amount that they believe reflects the player's relative merit as indicated by their proposed salary.

The following is an excerpt from baseball's collective bargaining agreement, which explains professional baseball's salary arbitration system. Note that it calls for "final and binding arbitration."

MLB Collective Bargaining Agreement

1997-2000

F. Salary Arbitration

The following salary arbitration procedure shall be applicable:

(1) Eligibility. The issue of a Player's salary may be submitted to final and binding arbitration by any Player or his Club, provided the other party to the arbitration consents thereto. Any Club, or any Player with a total of three or more years of Major League service, however accumulated, but with less than six years of Major League service, may submit the issue of the Player's salary to final and binding arbitration without the consent of the other party. . . .

In addition, a Player with at least two but less than three years of Major League service shall be eligible for salary arbitration if: (a) he has accumulated at least 86 days of service during the immediately preceding season; and (b) he ranks in the top seventeen percent . . . in total service in the class of Players who have at least two but less than three years of Major League service. . . .

Within three days after the notice of submission has been given, the Association and the PRC shall exchange salary figures. It shall be the responsibility of the Association during this three-day period to obtain the salary figure from the Player, and the PRC shall have a similar responsibility to obtain the Club's figure. . . .

(6) Form of Submission. The Player and the Club shall exchange with each other in advance of the hearing single salary figures for the coming season. . . .

(12) Criteria.

(a) The criteria will be the quality of the Player's contribution to his Club during the past season (including but not limited to his overall performance, special qualities of leadership and public appeal), the length and consistency of his career contribution, the record of the Player's past compensation, comparative baseball salaries . . . the existence of any physical or mental defects on the part of the player, and the recent performance record of the Club including but not limited to its League standing and attendance as an indication of public acceptance. . . .

QUESTIONS AND DISCUSSION

1. In *Dryer v. Los Angeles Rams*, 709 P.2d 826 (Cal. 1985), Fred Dryer (defensive end turned actor, '*Hunter*') alleged that he was illegally removed from the active roster; since his claims arose from the SPK, they were subject to its arbitration provisions. The fact that the SPK contained a clause that allowed the league commissioner to intervene and remove certain disputes from the arbitration procedures did not invalidate the provision as a whole on the basis of unconscionability or for failing to meet the requisite minimum levels of integrity. *See generally* Gilbert, '*The Use of Contract Interpretation by Professional Sports Arbitrators*,' 3 Marq. Sports L.J. 215 (1993); Pollack, '*Take My Arbitrator, Please: Commissioner "Best Interest" Disciplinary Authority in Professional Sports*,' 67 Fordham L. Rev. 1645 (1999). Another SPK clause dispute, of course, was the John Rocker debacle that tested baseball's 'best interests' provision. *See* Hylton, '*John Rocker: The Historical Origins of Professional Baseball Grievance Arbitration*,' 11 Marq. Sport L.J. 175 (2001).

2. In *Morris v. New York Football Giants, Inc.*, 575 N.Y.S.2d 1013 (App. Div. 1991), a group of football players alleged they were owed 10 per cent of their contracts when they were released in the preseason. The court held that even though the CBA had expired, the grievance arbitration provisions of the SPK were still in effect. However, since the arbitrator was the (undoubtedly) biased commissioner, the court appointed a neutral arbitrator. *See generally* Blackshaw, *Resolving Sports Disputes by ADR*, 142 New L.J. 1753 (1992); Netzle, *The Court of Arbitration for Sport: An Alternative for Dispute Resolution in U.S. Sports*. 10 Ent. & Sports Law. 1 (1992).

3. Another form of arbitration in sports are disputes between agents and athletes. In *Allen v. McCall*, 531 So. 2d 182 (Fla. Ct. App. 1988), an arbitrator was called to resolve a conflict between a football player and his agent as to the amount the agent was entitled to for negotiating the contract. Ultimately, a default judgment was vacated on the grounds that the agent did not receive adequate notice of the arbitration. *See 'The*

NFLPA's Arbitration Procedure: A Forum for Professional Football Players and Their Agents to Resolve Disputes, 6 Ohio St. J. Disp. Resol. 107 (1990).

4. Arbitration for sporting disputes such as allegations of drug use has been a part of the Olympic tradition now for many years; it lacks many of the due process protections that we take for granted. Is that fair? *See* Ansley, *International Athletic Dispute Resolution Tarnishing the Olympic Dream,* 12 Ariz. J. Intl. & Comp. L.Q. 277 (1995); *Arbitration of Disputes for the Olympic Games: A Procedure That Works,* 47 Arb. J. 33 (1992); Bitting, *Mandatory, Binding Arbitration for Olympic Athletes: Is the Process Better or Worse for "Job Security"?* 25 Fla. St. U.L. Rev. 655 (1998); Fitzgerald, *The Court of Arbitration for Sport: Doping and Due Process During the Olympics,* 7 Sports L.J. 213 (2000); Hollis, *The USOC and the Suspension of Athletes: Reforming Grievance Procedure under the Amateur Sports Act of 1978,* 71 Ind. L.J. 183 (1995); Kaufman, *Issues in International Sports Arbitration,* 13 B.U. Intl. L.J. 527 (1995); Nafziger, *International Sports Law as a Process for Resolving Disputes,* 45 Intl. & Comp. L.Q. 130 (1996); Paulsson, *Arbitration of International Sports Disputes,* 11 Ent. & Sports Law. 12 (1994); Polvino, *Arbitration as Preventive Medicine for Olympic Ailments: The International Sporting Disputes,* 8 Emory Intl. L. Rev. 347 (1994); Raber, *Dispute Resolution in Olympic Sport: The Court of Arbitration for Sport,* 8 Seton Hall J. Sport L. 75 (1998); Rejerson, *Out of Bounds? Applicability of Federal Discovery Orders Under 28 U.S.C. § 1782 by International Athletic Governing Bodies for Use in Internal Dispute Resolution Procedures,* 19 Loy. L.A. Ent. L.J. Rev. 631 (1999); Reuben, *And the Winner Is . . . Arbitrators to Resolve Disputes as They Arise at Olympics,* 82 A.B.A.J. 20(1) (1996).

5. Another more basic Olympic arbitration question is, who is going to the Olympics? In *Lindland v. U.S. Wrestling Assn., Inc.,* 227 F.3d 1000 (7th Cir. 2000), an arbitrator directed the U.S. Wrestling Association to rerun a bout in which the grievant won the rematch, which entitled him to be nominated to the U.S. team. See also *Lindland v. U.S. Wrestling Assn.,* 230 F.3d 1036 (7th Cir. 2000); Steedman, Lindland v. U.S. of A. Wrestling Assn.: *The Role of Arbitration and the Federal Courts in the Making of an Olympic Success,* 11 J. Art & Ent. L. 133 (2001).

6. Baseball's salary arbitration was the key that unlocked the box of (allegedly) outlandish salaries. The high-low technique is used; both parties must submit proposed salary figures and the arbitrator must choose only one. Both parties try to sway the arbitrator by using, statistics that cover the player's productivity, longevity, and potential and comparable worth as compared to like-situated players. Even though the arbitrator is chosen by mutual consent of the union and the owners, the major complaint is that the arbitrator lacks the requisite baseball expertise to properly decipher the often confusing statistics. It can get nasty: The team must argue that their prized player is really ineffective in the clutch, that he drives in RBI's only after the sixth inning in losing causes, and the like. See Hopkins, Abrams, *Inside Baseball's Salary Arbitration Process,* 6 U. Chi. L. Sch. Roundtable 55 (1999); Burgess & Marburger, *Do Negotiated and Arbitrated Salaries Differ under Final-Offer Arbitration* 46 Indus. & Lab. Rel. Rev. 548 (1993); Conti, *The Effect of Salary Arbitration on Major League*

Baseball, 5 Sports Law. J. 221 (1998); Dillard, *An Analysis of Salary Arbitration in Baseball: Could a Failure to Change the System Be Strike Three for Small-Market Franchises?"* 3 Sports Law. J. 125 (1996); Donegan, *The Use of Arbitration in Professional Baseball,* 1 Sports Law. J. 183 (1994); Fizel, *Play Ball: Baseball Arbitration After 20 Years,* 49 J. Disp. Resol. 42 (1994); *Arbitration: A Major League Effect on Players' Salaries*, 2 Seton Hall J. Sport L. 301 (1992); Swank, *Arbitration and Salary Inflation in Major League Baseball*, 1992 J. Disp. Resol. 159 (1992).

7. It is accepted policy that labor disputes should be settled by arbitration and that courts should refrain from reviewing the merits of arbitration awards. So long as the arbitrator's award is drawn from the essence of the CBA, it is enforceable. In *Major League Umpires Assn. v. American League of Professional Baseball Clubs,* plaintiff contended that the arbitrator went beyond his authority when he resolved the dispute in a manner not contemplated in the CBA. Plaintiff claimed that there was no meeting of the minds as regards "special events" pay. The court disagreed: "[I]t cannot be said that the arbitrator's interpretation was devoid of a reasoned basis." Are plaintiff's claims sufficient to set aside the award? Do they represent an extreme case? What extreme situation would justify setting aside an arbitrator's award?

8. *Major League Baseball Players Assn. v. Garvey* was a collusion case in which the arbitrator's decision was again vindicated. Courts are simply not authorized to review labor arbitration decisions on their merits despite allegations that the decision rests on factual errors or misinterprets the parties' agreement. What is collusion? Should collusion cases be arbitrated?

5
ANTITRUST

Antitrust in Sports is the analysis of the interaction of antitrust laws and sporting relationships. The antitrust laws assert that every conspiracy that restrains trade is illegal. Antitrust laws have been used by all parties in sports to police what they conceive to be excesses; they are the major mechanism to effectuate change in sports. However, there are exceptions that have decreased antitrust's overall regulatory effectiveness; they are, generally, baseball's exemption, labor's exemption, the nonstatutory labor exemption, the NFL exemptions, the Sports Broadcasting Act of 1961, and the Curt Flood Act of 1998.

Historically, antitrust laws were used to eliminate or ameliorate **Player Restraints** that hindered the athlete from negotiating the highest salary from the highest bidder, thus restricting the player's commerce. However, these restrictions have either been softened by the collective bargaining agreement or protected by an exemption to the antitrust laws. The **Exemptions** have almost swallowed the law itself. Baseball has a unique exemption based on precedence, which still applies (at least to some extent) today. The so-called nonstatutory labor exemption allows all procedures that are a product of good-faith, arm's-length negotiation to be exempted from antitrust analysis; it is by far the dominant claim in antitrust litigation in sports.

Antitrust litigation can develop from many sports relationships, including the competition of **League versus League.** The usual scenario is that the new league sues the established league, alleging unfair competition. As sports have become multibillion dollar industries, the competition between cities for teams and arenas to attract franchises has become an annual ritual. **Franchise Relocation and Arena Financing** is also an area where antitrust litigation is still in evidence, usually as a catalyst in allowing a team to relocate to a more lucrative location.

Even **Amateur Sports** have not escaped the use of antitrust laws to alleviate procedures that allegedly have a negative effect on competition; these lawsuits are against the policies of various athletic associations and allege that these policies violate the antiturst laws.

A. ANTITRUST IN SPORTS

Every combination in the form of a conspiracy that restrains trade is illegal under the Sherman Antitrust Act. As noted above, the antitrust laws have been the primary method to police and change the dynamics in sports. The antitrust laws have been used by various groups, players, owners, colleges, individual teams, and leagues as a means to alleviate an alleged condition that has oppressed them, whether it is low wages, the inability to relocate, low TV revenue, or unfair competition.

Organized sports is summarized by the oxymoron of "competitive cohesion." There must be honest competition to be attractive, but it must also be organized sufficiently so as to establish rules that assure fair play, arrange schedules, punish wrongdoers, and so on. The duality of competition and combination is explained as follows:

> Professional sports leagues present a unique form of economic organization, whose members must compete fiercely in some respects and cooperate in others. The end product of the teams is competition on the playing field. But the demands of producing the best sports competition often require cooperative action rather than competition in the economic sphere. . . . The basic house-keeping arrangements of league sports such as scheduling, limits of team rosters, and uniform playing rules throughout the league are the deviations from a purely competitive model which are most clearly necessitated by the nature of the industry. . . . [I]n addition to these minimum agreements . . . they have adopted many restrictive arrangements, affecting both control of players and ownership of teams, which present more trouble-some antitrust problems.[1]

These restrictive arrangements have attracted intense antitrust scrutiny.

The question is what is the least restrictive alternative in securing the goal of competitive sports. The method to ensure that the restrictive qualities of sports are kept to a minimum is the Sherman Act. Even though there is a dose of unreality and glitter (not to mention the arguably exorbitant salaries) that permeates professional sports, the essential significance of antitrust as the moral and fiscal regulator cannot be diminished.

> The importance of the antitrust laws to every citizen must not be minimalized. They are as important to baseball players as they are to football players, lawyers, doctors, or members of any other class of workers. Baseball players cannot be denied the benefits of competition merely because club owners view other economic interests as being more important. . . .[2]

Both leagues and associations in sports are riddled with monopolies and monopolistic practices, but the question becomes whether these actions run afoul of the antitrust laws.

There are three basic ways to interpret an antitrust controversy: per se analysis, quick-look analysis, or the rule of reason. Professional sports, because of the complexity and nuances of the "competitive cohesion" model usually merit a rule of reason analysis. The per se and quick-look approaches are

---

[1] Note, *The Super Bowl and the Sherman Act: Professional Team Sports and the Antitrust Laws*, 81 Harv. L. Rev. 418, 419-420 (1967).

[2] *Flood v. Kuhn.* 407 U.S. 258, 292, (1972), (Marshall, J., dissenting).

usually reserved for restraints that have a clear and predictable anticompetitive effect. Under the rule of reason, plaintiff must show that any legitimate objectives could be achieved in a substantially less restrictive manner.

All antitrust concerns in sports begin with an analysis of the applicability of the Sherman Act.

SHERMAN ACT

15 U.S.C. §§1 *et seq.*

Section 1 (15 U.S.C. §1). Trusts, etc., in restraint of trade illegal; penalty.

Every contract, combination in the form of trust or otherwise, or conspiracy, in restraint of trade or commerce among the several States, or with foreign nations, is declared to be illegal. . . .

Section 2 (15 U.S.C. §2). Monopolization; penalty.

Every person who shall make any contract or engage in any combination or conspiracy hereby declared illegal shall be deemed guilty of a felony. . . .

The case of *Toscano v. PGA Tour, Inc.*, shows how the antitrust laws might be (unsuccessfully) used in an attempt to challenge the eligibility rules of a professional golf association.

TOSCANO v. PGA TOUR, INC.

(E.D. Cal. 2002 201 F. Supp. 2d 1106)

LEVI, District Judge.

Plaintiff Harry Toscano ("Toscano"), a senior professional golfer, brings this antitrust action against defendants Professional Golfers Association ("PGA") Tour, Inc., the PGA Tour's player-directors, and the PGA Tour's current and past commissioners. Toscano contends that the Tour used its media rights and conflicting events rules to prevent the formation of competing senior professional golf events and tours. Having monopolized the market for senior professional golf, the Tour allegedly adopted restrictive eligibility rules to protect the player directors and other Tour members from competition from other senior golfers. As a result, Toscano alleges that he was: (1) excluded from competing in and winning prize money at Senior Professionals Golfs Tour Association tournaments; (2) denied the opportunity to earn money through endorsements; and (3) denied the opportunity to earn prize money by participating in golf tournaments organized by would-be Tour competitors. Defendants now move for summary judgment on the alternative grounds that: (1) Toscano lacks antitrust standing to challenge the media rights and conflicting events rules; (2) the eligibility rules are not anticompetitive and do not violate antitrust law; (3) Toscano's claim for damages is overly speculative; and (4) the player directors and the current and past commissioners are not proper defendants.

A. *The PGA Tour's Rules and Regulations*

The Senior PGA Tour is a separate division of the PGA that co-sponsors professional golf tournaments for players over the age of 50. Though substantially similar, Senior PGA Tour tournaments differ in several important respects from traditional PGA Tour tournaments. First, Senior Tour tournaments consist of three rounds of play instead of four. Second, Senior Tour tournaments include a field of 78 golfers in contrast to a traditional 144-player field. Third, barring injury or illness, all 78 golfers who start a tournament on Friday are allowed to play through to its completion on Sunday while in traditional PGA Tour events there is a "cut" such that the 144-player field is "pared by fifty percent half-way through the tournament." . . .

As to eligibility, the 78 players in a Senior Tour event are drawn from [certain] categories of golfers. . . . As a result, "[n]o more than approximately 5% of the places in any Tour open event are available to qualified professionals not playing under an exemption."

The Senior PGA Tour Tournament Rules and Regulations restrict the ability of Tour members to participate in non-Tour events. Under the "conflicting events" rule, a player who qualifies to play in a Tour event generally may not enter a non-Tour tournament scheduled on the same date unless he first obtains a written release from the Tour Commissioner. . . .

The Tour contends that the eligibility and media rules are key components to ensuring the commercial viability of the Senior Tour. The Tour relies on the conflicting events rules to guarantee to sponsors and televisers that a significant number of marquee players will play in any scheduled Tour event as opposed to a competing golf event. Where the events do not actually conflict, the media rights rule ensures that the two events are not televised at the same time. The eligibility rules preserve the Senior Tour's no cut format ensuring that marquee players will compete for the whole of the Tournament however well, or poorly, they play in the opening rounds. By attracting marquee players, and hence the public, the rules gain the backing of sponsors who provide most of the money on which the Tour depends. . . .

B. *Harry Toscano*

Harry Toscano entered the world of professional golf in 1962 shortly after he graduated from college. Between 1962 and 1984, Toscano played in several tournaments on the regular PGA Tour and won $53,240.00. Toscano also worked as a steel salesman, operated a go-cart track, ran a golf club repair business, and gave golf lessons at several golf clubs.

Toscano became eligible to play on the Senior PGA Tour in 1992 when he turned fifty years old. At the end of 1992, Toscano participated in the Senior Tour's National Qualifying Tournament and finished high enough that he was a fully exempt player for all Senior Tour Events in 1993. Toscano participated in all Senior Tour events in 1993 but because he did not finish sufficiently high on the yearly money list, he had only conditional exempt status in the following years. Nevertheless, Toscano's conditional exempt status allowed him to participate in 29 of the Senior Tour's 33 events in 1994, 33 of the Tour's 34 events in 1995, and 24 of the Tour's 34 events in 1995.

In 1996, Toscano sustained a shoulder injury that substantially limited his tournament play in 1996 and 1997. He ultimately lost his conditional exempt status for 1997 because he did not finish high enough on the previous year's money list. However, in 1997, Toscano played in ten to twelve tournaments on the Nitro Senior Series, a competing senior professional golf tour, and finished 13th on the money list earning approximately $20,000. Further, Toscano played in the qualifying rounds of several Senior PGA Tour tournaments in 2000 and 2001 though he failed to make it through the qualifying rounds in all but one of the tournaments. Toscano currently ranks 125th on the Senior Tour's alltime money list and has career earnings of $739,029 on the Senior Tour. . . .

II. Antitrust Standing: Media Rights and Conflicting Events Rules

Section 4 of the Clayton Act authorizes a private damages action for violations of the antitrust laws: "any person who shall be injured in his business or property by reason of anything forbidden in the antitrust laws may sue therefor . . . and shall recover threefold the damages by him sustained, and the cost of suit, including a reasonable attorney's fee." 15 U.S.C. §15(a). . . . "The Supreme Court has determined, however, that Congress did not intend §4 to have such an expansive scope. Therefore, courts have constructed the concept of antitrust standing, under which they 'evaluate the plaintiff's harm, the alleged wrongdoing by the defendants, and the relationship between them,' to determine whether a plaintiff is a proper party to bring an antitrust claim."

Antitrust standing is generally determined by reference to five factors: (1) the nature of the plaintiff's alleged injury; that is, whether it was the type the antitrust laws were intended to prevent; (2) the directness of the injury; (3) the speculative measure of the harm; (4) the risk of duplicative recovery; and (5) the complexity in apportioning damages. The plaintiff does not need to prevail on each factor to establish standing, and no single factor is dispositive, although the absence of antitrust injury is fatal. In light of these factors, the court finds that plaintiff Toscano lacks standing to attack the media rights and conflicting events rules.

A. *Nature of the Alleged Injury*

Toscano may only pursue an antitrust action if he demonstrates an "*antitrust* injury, which is to say injury of the type the antitrust laws were intended to prevent and that flows from that which makes defendants' acts unlawful." . . .

[A]s a professional golfer allegedly excluded from the senior professional golf tournament market, Toscano is a market participant and satisfies the antitrust injury requirement. . . .

B. *Directness of the Injury*

The directness inquiry requires the court to analyze "the chain of causation between [Toscano's] injury and the alleged restraint in the market." To prevail on this factor, Toscano's injuries must be close in the chain of causation to the alleged market restraint. . . .

The existence of parties closer in the chain of causation to the market restraint and capable of bringing their own antitrust suit, however, "diminishes the justification for allowing a more remote party" like Toscano to bring a suit of his own. . . .

F. *Conclusion*

Toscano's alleged injuries stemming from the media rights and conflicting events rules are indirect, speculative, and complex. Although Toscano may have pleaded an injury of the sort that is the subject of the federal antitrust laws, the indirectness of the injury and the speculative nature of his damages predominate and preclude a finding of standing. . . .

III. Eligibility Rules

A. *Rule of Reason versus Quick Look Analysis* . . .

Courts rely on three tests to determine whether an agreement constitutes an unreasonable restraint of trade: (1) *per se* analysis; (2) quick-look analysis; and (3) the rule of reason. . . .

At one end of the continuum, *per se* analysis is used for restraints that "have such predictable and pernicious anticompetitive effect, and such limited potential for procompetitive benefit, that they are deemed unlawful *per se*." . . .

At the other end of the spectrum, rule of reason analysis is used "if the reasonableness of a restraint cannot be determined without a thorough analysis of its net effects on competition in the relevant market." Finally, courts use quick look analysis when "the anticompetitive impact of a restraint is clear from a quick look, as in a *per se* case, but procompetitive justifications for it also exist." . . .

The court finds that the eligibility rules withstand analysis under the rule of reason because Toscano has failed to carry his initial burden of demonstrating significant anticompetitive effects. . . .

V

The Senior PGA Tour is an entertainment product presenting athletic competition between mostly well known professional golfers over the age of 50. It uses the eligibility rules to secure the participation of marquee players for the entirety of each tournament. With this business model, it has survived where other tours have failed. Toscano does not show that the eligibility rules are an unreasonable restraint of trade. The reasonableness of the Tour's media rights and conflicting events rules is a question that must be left for another day because Toscano has failed to demonstrate that he is the proper party to challenge these rules. Finally, his claim of damages is only speculative and tenuous. For the foregoing reasons, the defendants' motion for summary judgment is Granted.

It is so ordered.

QUESTIONS AND DISCUSSION

1. Edward Garvey, former executive director of the National Football League Players Association (NFLPA), asserted that the NFL

is a monopoly, and I think that this is an important fact. It's an unregulated monopoly, and I think that's an important fact. It has exclusive control of the product of the labor market. If a talented player decides that he is going to play football for pay in this country, he must do so under rules established by the owners and by their commissioner.

National Academy of Arbitrators, *Proceedings of the 26th Annual Meeting* 120 (1973).

2. The goal of the antitrust acts is to stop monopolies and protect fair competition. But in sports, antitrust is more likely used by former monopolists, e.g., individual teams against the league, a league against a league, universities against the National Collegiate Athletic Association (NCAA), and so on. Does this negate the logic of using the antitrust laws as the cop on the beat to control alleged outrages in sports?

3. Antitrust laws are the major mechanism available to effect change in sports. However, with the rise of the so-called nonstatutory labor exemptions protecting apparently monopolistic practices from antitrust scrutiny, a weak union's only option is to decertify as a union if it hopes to reinvigorate its chances of successfully effectuating change through the antitrust laws. *See* Gould, Brown . . . *To Decertify or Not to Decertify?*, 14 Ent. & Sports Law. 9 (1996).

4. In the past, the typical situation involved players who contended that they were victims of anticompetitive practices. The goal of the Sherman Act is to protect the public interest from these practices. Can the act still be viable in a milieu where the players, or "victims" of anticompetition, are paid many millions of dollars per year to play sports?

5. Monopolies are deemed to be against public interest since they can result in exorbitant prices because they are unchallenged by free competition. Is a fair salary cap, if there is one, a realistic and legal approach to public interest concerns?

6. *Toscano v. PGA Tour, Inc.,* presents a capsule synopsis of the fairly typical elements contained in a sports antitrust law suit. The threshold question is whether the allegedly injured plaintiff has antitrust standing to sue. In *Toscano,* plaintiff's alleged injuries were not sufficiently direct to establish standing to bring claim against the PGA on the basis that their media rights and conflicting events rules are anticompetitive. Who would have standing? If Harry Toscano, a senior professional golfer, does not have standing, who would?

7. Of the three methods used in interpreting an antitrust problem (per se analysis, quick-look analysis, or the rule of reason), what approach is used in *Toscano*? Why? What are the results?

B. PLAYER RESTRAINTS

Antitrust got its beginning in sports as a natural evolution from the goals of the Sherman Act, namely, to vouchsafe fair competition. The evil that antitrust was used against was to protect players' salaries from the effects of unfair competition as exhibited by various player restraints. At least in professional team sports in the major sports, many of these concerns have been eliminated by litigation or exempted out by the nonstatutory labor exemption, as was the NBA salary cap in *Wood v. National Basketball Assn.*[3] Player restraints have historically taken many different forms; but their objective is to either restrict a player's mobility or to restrict the player's ability to negotiate increases in salary. For example, baseball's reserve clause and football's Rozelle Rule were certainly examples of player restraint mechanisms. The Rozelle Rule, which involved compensation to the jilted team in the free agent dance, greatly restricted player movement since the relinquishing of draft choices, or the threat thereof, was a powerful deterrent to signing a free agent. A team rarely signs a free agent when the cost in compensation might be disastrous to the franchise. The team that signs the free agent must also pay him his salary, so they suffer a negative impact twice.

The standard player's contract SPK, which each player had to sign, was also a form of player restraint:

> Before a player can participate in the NFL he must sign a Standard Player Contract. This was part of the 1968 collective bargaining agreement, and appears in Article 15 of the 1971 NFL Constitution. The contract provides that the player becomes bound by "the Constitution and By-laws, the Rules of the League, of the club, and the decisions of the Commissioner of the League." . . . Specific terms such as salary, length of contract, and other matters were incorporated into the Standard Player Contract for each player.[4]

But the SPK is not a restraint of trade per se since it is subject to a modification; some contracts can provide, for example, "no-cut" and "nonrelease" clauses.[5] However, most drafted players and free agents do not possess the relative bargaining strength to modify the contract; so, for those people, the SPK is a player restraint.[6]

The district court in *Mackey v. National Football League*[7] held that the Rozelle Rule was a per se violation of the Sherman Act. Even if the rule of reason standard was applied, this rule would still violate antitrust since it was unreasonably broad, lacked due process and notice, and was unreasonable in duration. The court of appeals in *Mackey* affirmed the decision but preferred a "rule of reason" analysis. However, it noted that their decision "does not mean that every restraint on competition for players services would necessarily violate the antitrust laws. . . . [I]t may be that some reasonable restrictions relating to player transfer are necessary for the successful operation of the NFL."[8]

The annual college draft, when coupled with the Rozelle Rule and the option rule (which theoretically allowed a player to become a free agent after he played out his option year), was yet another player restraint since it decreased player mobility.

> The "draft" rule contained in Article 14 of the NFL Constitution provides that at an annual meeting the members clubs would select prospective players,

---

[3] 602 F. Supp. 525 (S.D.N.Y. 1984), *aff'd*, 809 F.2d 954 (2d Cir. 1987).
[4] *Kapp v. National Football League*, 586 F.2d 644 (9th Cir. 1978).
[5] *Chuy v. Philadelphia Eagles*, 407 F. Supp. 717, 725 (E.D. Pa. 1976).
[6] *Hayes v. National League*, 469 F. Supp. 247, 250 (C.D. Cal. 1979).
[7] 407 F. Supp. 1000 (D. Minn. 1975), *aff'd in part & rev'd in part*, 543 F.2d 606 (8th Cir. 1976).
[8] 543 F.2d at 623.

principally from the ranks of the outstanding college and university graduates. The effect of this rule is to prevent other teams from negotiating with a player, even if selecting club made an unacceptable offer to him.[9]

Once the drafting team chose, it had exclusive rights to that player; he had no recourse since there were no other available markets for college football players.

The AFL and NFL merged in 1977 and held their first common draft; the merger of their two draft systems was specifically excluded from the antitrust laws.[10] But the exemption said nothing about the legality of the draft itself. In *Smith v. Pro Football, Inc.*, All-American Jim "Yazoo" Smith claimed that if he wasn't forced to sign with one club, he would have been able to sign a contract that would have more correctly reflected his free market value. The court found that since the draft rule was thrust upon a weak union, the nonstatutory labor exemption did not come into play. Using the rule of reason test, it found that the draft virtually eliminated competition in securing college football players. The draft "leaves no room whatever for competition among the teams for services of the college players, and utterly strips them of any measure of control over the marketing of their talents."[11] Although the draft was reduced from 17 rounds to 9 rounds to 7 rounds, and although the drafted player's trade is still restricted since he is obliged to negotiate with only one team and cannot seek out the highest bidder, these new draft procedures are undoubtedly exempted since they are a product of bona fide, arm's-length negotiation between management and labor and are mandatory subjects of collective bargaining.

The *Mackey* case held that the Rozelle Rule violated the antitrust laws and that the NFL failed to establish that these practices were protected by the nonstatutory labor exemption.

MACKEY V. NATIONAL FOOTBALL LEAGUE

543 F.2d 606 (8th Cir. 1976)

LAY, Circuit Judge.

This is an appeal by the National Football League (NFL), twenty-six of its member clubs, and its Commissioner, Alvin Ray "Pete" Rozelle, from a district court judgment holding the "Rozelle Rule"[1] to be violative of the Sherman Act, and enjoining its enforcement.

This action was initiated by a group of present and former NFL players, appellees herein, pursuant to §§4 and 16 of the Clayton Act, of the Sherman Act, Their complaint alleged that the defendants' enforcement of the Rozelle

---

[9] *Kapp v. National Football League*, 586 F.2d 644, 646 (9th Cir. 1978).

[10] 15 U.S.C. §1291 (1976).

[11] 420 F. Supp. 738, 746, (D.D.C. 1976), 593 F.2d 1173 (D.C. Cir. 1978).

[1] The Rozelle Rule essentially provides that when a player's contractual obligation to a team expires and he signs with a different club, the signing club must provide compensation to the player's former team. If the two clubs are unable to conclude mutually satisfactory arrangements, the Commissioner may award compensation in the form of one or more players and or draft choices as he deems fair and equitable.

Rule constituted an illegal combination and conspiracy in restraint of trade denying professional football players the right to freely contract for their services. Plaintiffs sought injunctive relief and treble damages.

The court granted the injunctive relief sought by the players and entered judgment in their favor on the issue of liability. This appeal followed.

Trial on the issue of damages was deferred pending the disposition of this appeal.

The district court held that the defendants' enforcement of the Rozelle Rule constituted a concerted refusal to deal and a group boycott, and was therefore a per se violation of the Sherman Act. Alternatively, finding that the evidence offered in support of the clubs' contention that the Rozelle Rule is necessary to the successful operation of the NFL insufficient to justify the restrictive effects of the Rule, the court concluded that the Rozelle Rule was invalid under the Rule of Reason standard. Finally, the court rejected the clubs' argument that the Rozelle Rule was immune from attack under the Sherman Act because it had been the subject of a collective bargaining agreement between the club owners and the National Football League players Association (NFLPA).

The defendants raise two basic issues on this appeal: (1) whether the socalled labor exemption to the antitrust laws immunizes the NFL's enforcement of the Rozelle Rule from antitrust liability; and (2) if not, whether the Rozelle Rule and the manner in which it has been enforced violate the antitrust laws. . . .

The NFL, which began operating in 1920, is an unincorporated association comprised of member clubs which own and operate professional football teams. It presently enjoys a monopoly over major league professional football in the United States. The League performs various administrative functions, including organizing and scheduling games, and promulgating rules. A constitution and bylaws govern its activities and those of its members. Pete Rozelle, Commissioner of the NFL since 1960, is an employee of the League and its chief executive officer. His powers and duties are defined by the NFL Constitution and Bylaws.

Throughout most of its history, the NFL's operations have been unilaterally controlled by the club owners. In 1968, however, the NLRB recognized the NFLPA as a labor organization, and as the exclusive bargaining representative of all NFL players. . . . Since that time, the NFLPA and the clubs have engaged in collective bargaining. . . . Since 1974, the parties have been negotiating; however, they have not concluded a new agreement.

For a number of years, the NFL has operated under a reserve system whereby every player who signs a contract with an NFL club is bound to play for that club, and no other, for the term of the contract plus one additional year at the option of the club. Once a player signs a Standard Player Contract, he is bound to his team for at least two years. He may, however, become a free agent at the end of the option year by playing that season under a renewed contract rather than signing a new one. A player "playing out his option" is subject to a 10% salary cut during the option year. . . .

Prior to 1963, a team which signed a free agent who had previously been under contract to another club was not obligated to compensate the player's former club. In 1963, after R. C. Owens played out his option with the San

Francisco 49ers and signed a contract with the Baltimore Colts, the member clubs of the NFL unilaterally adopted the following provision, now known as the Rozelle Rule, as an amendment to the Leagues Constitution and Bylaws:

> Any player, whose contract with a League club has expired, shall thereupon become a free agent and shall no longer be considered a member of the team of that club following the expiration date of such contract. Whenever a player, becoming a free agent in such manner, thereafter signed a contract with a different club in the League, then, unless mutually satisfactory arrangements have been concluded between the two League clubs, the Commissioner may award to the former club one or more players, from the Active, Reserve, or Selection List (including future selection choices) of the acquiring club as the Commissioner in his sole discretion deems fair and equitable; any such decision by the Commissioner shall be final and conclusive.

This provision, unchanged in form, is currently embodied in §12.1(H) of the NFL Constitution. The ostensible purposes of the rule are to maintain competitive balance among the NFL teams and protect the clubs' investment in scouting, selecting and developing players. . . .

We review first the claim that the labor exemption immunizes the Commissioner and the clubs from liability under the antitrust laws.

History

The concept of a labor exemption from the antitrust laws finds its basic source in §§6 and 20 of the Clayton Act, and the Norris-LaGuardia Act. Those provisions declare that labor unions are not combinations or conspiracies in restraint of trade, and specifically exempt certain union activities such as secondary picketing and group boycotts from the coverage of the antitrust laws. The statutory exemption was created to insulate legitimate collective activity by employees, which is inherently anticompetitive but is favored by federal labor policy, from the proscriptions of the antitrust laws.

The statutory exemption extends to legitimate labor activities unilaterally undertaken by a union in furtherance of its own interests. It does not extend to concerted action or agreements between unions and non-labor groups. The Supreme Court has held, however, that in order to properly accommodate the congressional policy favoring free competition in business markets with the congressional policy favoring collective bargaining under the N.L.R.A., certain union-employer agreements must be accorded a limited nonstatutory exemption from antitrust sanctions.

The players assert that only employee groups are entitled to the labor exemption and that it cannot be asserted by the defendants, an employer group. We must disagree. Since the basis of the nonstatutory exemption is the national policy favoring collective bargaining, and since the exemption extends to agreements, the benefits of the exemption logically extend to both parties to the agreement. Accordingly, under appropriate circumstances, we find that a non-labor group may avail itself of the labor exemption.

The clubs and the Commissioner claim the benefit of the nonstatutory labor exemption here, arguing that the Rozelle Rule was the subject of an agreement with the players union and that the proper accommodation of federal labor and antitrust policies requires that the agreement be deemed immune from antitrust liability. The plaintiffs assert that the Rozelle Rule was the product of unilateral action by the clubs and that the defendants cannot assert a colorable claim of exemption.

The district court found that neither the 1968 nor the 1970 collective bargaining agreement embodied an agreement on the Rozelle Rule, and that the union has never otherwise agreed to the Rule. . . .

Based on the fact that the 1968 agreement incorporated by reference the Rozelle Rule and provided that free agent rules would not be changed, we conclude that the 1968 agreement required that the Rozelle Rule govern when a player played out his option and signed with another team. Assuming, without deciding, that the 1970 agreement embodied a similar understanding, we proceed to a consideration of whether the agreements fall within the scope of the nonstatutory labor exemption. . . .

Applying these principles to the facts presented here, we think it clear that the alleged restraint on trade effected by the Rozelle Rule affects only the parties to the agreements sought to be exempted. Accordingly, we must inquire as to the other two principles: whether the Rozelle Rule is a mandatory subject of collective bargaining, and whether the agreements thereon were the product of bona fide arm's-length negotiation. . . .

In view of the foregoing, we hold that the agreements between the clubs and the players embodying the Rozelle Rule do not qualify for the labor exemption. The union's acceptance of the status quo by the continuance of the Rozelle Rule in the initial collective bargaining agreements under the circumstances of this case cannot serve to immunize the Rozelle Rule from the scrutiny of the Sherman Act.

We turn, then, to the question of whether the Rozelle Rule, as implemented, violates §1 of the Sherman Act. . . . The district court found the Rozelle Rule to be a per se violation of the Act. Alternatively, the court held the Rule to be violative of the Rule of Reason standard.

The clubs and the Commissioner first urge that the only product market arguably affected by the Rozelle Rule is the market for players' services, and that the restriction of competition for players' services is not a type of restraint proscribed by the Sherman Act.

We hold that restraints on competition within the market for players' services fall within the ambit of the Sherman Act. . . .

In view of the foregoing, we think it more appropriate to test the validity of the Rozelle Rule under the Rule of Reason. . . .

In defining the restraint on competition for players' services, the district court found that the Rozelle Rule significantly deters clubs from negotiating with and signing freeagents; that it acts as a substantial deterrent to players playing out their options and becoming free agents; that it significantly decreases players' bargaining power in contract negotiations; that players are thus denied the right to sell their services in a free and open market; that as a result, the salaries paid by each club are lower than if competitive bidding were allowed to prevail; and that absent the Rozelle Rule, there would be increased movement in interstate commerce of players from one club to another.

We find substantial evidence in the record to support these findings. . . .

We agree that the asserted need to recoup player development costs cannot justify the restraints of the Rozelle Rule. That expense is an ordinary cost of doing business and is not peculiar to professional football. Moreover, because of its unlimited duration, the Rozelle Rule is far more restrictive than necessary to fulfill that need.

We agree, in view of the evidence adduced at trial . . . with respect to existing players turnover by way of trades, retirements and new players entering the League, that the club owners' arguments respecting player continuity cannot justify the Rozelle Rule. We concur in the district court's conclusion that the possibility of resulting decline in the quality of play would not justify the Rozelle Rule. We do recognize, as did the district court, that the NFL has a strong and unique interest in maintaining competitive balance among its teams. The key issue is thus whether the Rozelle Rule is essential to the maintenance of competitive balance, and is no more restrictive than necessary. The district court answered both of these questions in the negative.

We need not decide whether a system of inter-team compensation for free agents moving to other teams is essential to the maintenance of competitive balance in the NFL. Even if it is, we agree . . . that the Rozelle Rule is significantly more restrictive than necessary to serve any legitimate purposes. . . .

In sum, we hold that the Rozelle Rule, as enforced, unreasonably restrains trade in violation of Section 1 of the Sherman Act.

Conclusion

In conclusion, although we find that non-labor parties may potentially avail themselves of the nonstatutory labor exemption where they are parties to collective bargaining agreements pertaining to mandatory subjects of bargaining, the exemption cannot be invoked where, as here, the agreement was not the product of bona fide arm's-length negotiations. Thus, the defendants' enforcement of the Rozelle Rule is not exempt from the coverage of the antitrust laws. Although we disagree with the district court's determination that the Rozelle Rule is a per se violation of the antitrust laws, we do find that the Rule, as implemented, contravenes the Rule of Reason and thus constitutes an unreasonable restraint of trade in violation of of the Sherman Act.

We note that our disposition of the antitrust issue does not mean that every restraint on competition for players' services would necessarily violate the antitrust laws. Also, since the Rozelle Rule, as implemented, concerns a mandatory subject of collective bargaining, any agreement as to interteam compensation for free agents moving to other teams, reached through good faith collective bargaining, might very well be immune from antitrust liability under the nonstatutory labor exemption.

It may be that some reasonable restrictions relating to player transfers are necessary for the successful operation of the NFL. The protection of mutual interests of both the players and the clubs may indeed require this. We encourage the parties to resolve this question through collective bargaining. The parties are far better situated to agreeably resolve what rules governing player transfers are best suited for their mutual interests than are the courts. However, no mutual resolution of this issue appears within the present record.

Therefore, the Rozelle Rule, as it is presently implemented, must be set aside as an unreasonable restraint of trade.

With the exception of the district court's finding that implementation of the Rozelle Rule constitutes a per se violation of Section 1 of the Sherman Act and except as . . . otherwise modified . . . , the judgment of the district court is Affirmed. The cause is remanded to the district court for further proceedings consistent with this opinion.

In *Wood v. National Basketball Assn.*, O. Leon Wood, although a talented college player and a member of the 1984 U.S. Olympic basketball team, had the misfortune to be drafted as the second first-round player chosen by Philadelphia (the first was Charles Barkley, then known as the "Round Mound of Rebound"). He thus ran afoul of the salary cap so that he could be offered only the minimum salary. He sued on the grounds that the salary cap and college draft violated §1 of the Sherman Act and were not exempted by reason of the nonstatutory labor exemption.

WOOD v. NATIONAL BASKETBALL ASSOCIATION

809 F.2d 954 (2d Cir. 1986)

WINTER, Circuit Judge

O. Leon Wood, an accomplished point-guard from California State University at Fullerton and a member of the gold medal-winning 1984 United States Olympic basketball team, appeals from Judge Carter's dismissal of his antitrust action challenging certain provisions of a collective bargaining agreement between the National Basketball Association ("NBA"), its member-teams, and the National Basketball Players Association ("NBPA"). Wood contends that the "salary cap," college draft, and prohibition of player corporations violate Section 1 of the Sherman Act, 15 U.S.C. §1 (1982) and are not exempt from the Sherman Act by reason of the non-statutory "labor exemption." We disagree and affirm.

The challenged provisions are in part the result of the settlement of an earlier antitrust action brought by players against the NBA. *Robertson v. National Basketball Ass'n.* 72 F.R.D. 64 (S.D.N.Y. 1976) In that case, a class consisting of all NBA players challenged both the merger of the NBA with the now-defunct American Basketball Association and certain NBA employment practices, including the college draft system by which teams obtain the exclusive right to negotiate with particular college players. Following extensive pre-trial proceedings, the parties settled the case on April 29, 1976. The Settlement Agreement provided for the payment of $4.3 million to the class and for substantial modification of the practices attacked by the plaintiffs.

The Settlement Agreement is effective through the 1986-87 season. It modified the college draft system by limiting to one year the period during which a team has exclusive rights to negotiate with and sign its draftees. If a draftee remains unsigned at the time of the next year's draft, he may re-enter the draft. Most important, the Settlement Agreement instituted a system of free agency allowing veteran players to sell their services to the highest bidder subject only to their current team's right of first refusal that allows it to match the best offer.

On October 10, 1980, the NBA and NBPA signed a collective bargaining agreement that incorporated the provisions of the Settlement Agreement pertinent to this action. The 1980 collective agreement expired on June 1, 1982, however, and the 1982-83 season began before a new agreement had been reached. Negotiations between the NBA and the NBPA continued and centered on the league's insistence upon controls on the growth in players' salaries. The NBA claimed that increases in players' salaries resulting from free agency were in part responsible for mounting losses and that a number of its teams might face bankruptcy absent some stabilization of expenses. The NBPA, after reviewing the teams' financial data, reached an agreement in principle with the NBA on March 31, 1983, some 48 hours before a strike deadline set by the players. This agreement was memorialized in writing on April 18, 1983, in a Memorandum of Understanding. . . .

The Memorandum continued the college draft and free agency/first refusal provisions of the earlier agreements and, like those agreements, included provisions for fringe benefits such as pensions and medical and life insurance. However, the Memorandum also established a minimum for individual salaries and a minimum and maximum for aggregate team salaries. The latter are styled the salary cap provisions, even though they establish a floor as well as a ceiling. Under the salary cap, a team that has reached its maximum allowable team salary may sign a first-round draft choice like Wood only to a one-year contract for $75,000. An integral part of the method by which the floor and ceiling on aggregate team salaries were to be determined was a guarantee that the players would receive 53 percent of the NBA's gross revenues, including new revenues, in salaries and benefits. This combination of fringe benefits, draft, free agency, a floor and a ceiling on aggregate team salaries, and guaranteed revenue sharing was unique in professional sports negotiations.

Because the Memorandum altered certain terms and conditions of the Settlement Agreement, the NBA and NBPA jointly requested district court approval of a modification of the Settlement Agreement. After a hearing at which class members were invited to address the fairness and adequacy of the modification, Judge Carter approved it on June 13, 1983.

Against this background, the Philadelphia 76ers drafted Wood in the first round of the 1984 college draft. At the time of the draft, the 76ers' team payroll exceeded the amount permitted under the salary cap. The 76ers therefore tendered to Wood a one-year $75,000 contract, the amount stipulated under the salary cap. This offer was a formality, however, necessary to preserve its exclusive rights to sign him. In fact, the team informed Wood's agent of its intention to adjust its roster so as to enable it to negotiate a long-term contract with Wood for substantially more money. Wood understandably did not sign the proffered contract.

On September 13, 1984, he turned from the basketball court to the district court and sought a preliminary injunction restraining enforcement of the agreement between the NBA and NBPA and compelling teams other than the 76ers to cease their refusal to deal with him except on the terms set out in the collective bargaining agreement and Memorandum.

Judge Carter denied Wood's motion. *602 F. Supp. 525, [528] (S.D.N.Y. 1984)* He found that both the salary cap and college draft provisions affect only the parties to the collective bargaining agreement—the NBA and the players—involve mandatory subjects of bargaining as defined by federal labor laws, and are the result of bona fide arms-length negotiations. Both are proper subjects of concern by the Players Association. As such these provisions come under the protective shield of our national labor policy and are exempt from the reach of the Sherman Act.

Meanwhile, Wood signed a contract with the 76ers that provided for $1.02 million in total compensation over a four-year period, including a $135,000 signing bonus. Wood has since been traded.

DISCUSSION

Plaintiff views the salary cap, college draft and prohibition of player corporations as an agreement among horizontal competitors, the NBA teams, to eliminate competition for the services of college basketball players. As such, he claims, they constitute *per se* violations of Section 1 of the Sherman Act.

We may assume for purposes of this decision that the individual NBA teams and not the league are the relevant employers and that Wood would obtain considerably more favorable employment terms were the draft and salary cap eliminated so as to allow him to offer his services to the highest bidder among NBA teams. We may further assume that were these arrangements agreed upon by the NBA teams in the absence of a collective bargaining relationship with a union representing the players, they would be illegal and plaintiff would be entitled to relief.

The draft and salary cap are not, however, the product solely of an agreement among horizontal competitors but are embodied in a collective agreement between an employer or employers and a labor organization reached through procedures mandated by federal labor legislation.

Although the combination of the college draft and salary cap may seem unique in collective bargaining (as are the team salary floor and 53 percent revenue sharing agreement), the uniqueness is strictly a matter of appearance. The nature of professional sports as a business and professional sports teams as employers calls for contractual arrangements suited to that unusual commercial context. However, these arrangements result from the same federally mandated processes as do collective agreements in the more familiar industrial context. Moreover, examination of the particular arrangements arrived at by the NBA and NBPA discloses that they have functionally identical, and identically anticompetitive, counterparts that are routinely included in industrial collective agreements. . . .

The gravamen of Wood's complaint, namely that the NBA-NBPA collective agreement is illegal because it prevents him from achieving his full free market value, is therefore at odds with, and destructive of, federal labor policy. It is true that the diversity of talent and specialization among professional athletes and the widespread exposure and discussions of their "work" in the media make the differences in value among them as "workers" more visible than the differences in efficiency and in value among industrial workers. High public visibility, however, is no reason to ignore federal legislation that explicitly prevents employees, whether in or out of a bargaining unit, from seeking a better deal where that deal where that deal is inconsistent with the terms of a collective agreement.

Indeed, examination of the criteria that Wood advances as the basis for striking down the draft and salary cap reveals that there is hardly a collective agreement in the nation that would survive his legal theory. For example, Wood emphasizes his superior abilities as a point-guard and his selection in the first round of the college draft as grounds for enabling him to bargain individually for a higher salary. However, collective agreements routinely set standard wages for employees with differing responsibilities, skills, and levels of efficiency. Wood's theory would allow any employee dissatisfied with his salary relative to those of other workers to insist upon individual bargaining, contrary to explicit federal labor policy. . . .

Wood also attacks the draft and salary cap because they assign him to work for a particular employer at a diminished wage. . . . Wood further attacks the draft and salary cap as disadvantaging new employees. . . . Finally, Wood argues that the draft and salary cap are illegal because they affect employees outside the bargaining unit.

Wood's assertion that he would be paid more in the absence of the draft and salary cap also implies that others would receive less if he were successful. It can hardly be denied that the NBA teams would be more resistant to benefits guaranteed to all, such as pensions, minimum salaries, and medical and insurance benefits. In fact, the salary cap challenged by Wood is one part of a complex formula including minimum team salaries and guaranteed revenue sharing. . . .

Freedom of contract is particularly important in the context of collective bargaining between professional athletes and their leagues. Such bargaining relationships raise numerous problems with little or no precedent in standard industrial relations. As a result, leagues and player unions may reach seemingly unfamiliar or strange agreements. If courts were to intrude and to outlaw such solutions, leagues and their player unions would have to arrange their affairs in a less efficient way. It would also increase the chances of strikes by reducing the number and quality of possible compromises.

The issues of free agency and entry draft are at the center of collective bargaining in much of the professional sports industry. It is to be expected that the parties will arrive at unique solutions to these problems in the different sports both because sports generally differ from the industrial model and because each sport has its own peculiar economic imperatives. The NBA/NBPA agreement is just such a unique bundle of compromises. The draft and the salary cap reflect the interests of the employers in stabilizing salary costs and spreading talent among the various teams. Minimum individual salaries, fringe benefits, minimum aggregate team salaries, and guaranteed revenue sharing reflect the interests of the union in enhancing standard benefits applicable to all players. The free agency/first refusal provisions in turn allow individual players to exercise a degree of individual bargaining power. Were a court to intervene and strike down the draft and salary cap, the entire agreement would unravel. This would force the NBA and NBPA to search for other avenues of compromise that would be less satisfactory to them than the agreement struck down. It would also measurably increase the chances of a strike. We decline to take that step.

We also agree with the district court that all of the above matters are mandatory subjects of bargaining under 29 U.S.C. §158(d). Each of them clearly is intimately related to "wages, hours, and other terms and conditions of employment." Indeed, it is precisely because of their direct relationship to wages and conditions of employment that such matters are so controversial and so much the focus of bargaining in professional sports. Wood's claim for damages, for example, is based on an allegation of lost wages. . . . It is true that the combination of the draft and salary cap places new players coming out of college ranks at a disadvantage. However, . . . that is hardly an unusual feature of collective agreements. In the industrial context salaries, promotions, and layoffs are routinely governed by seniority, with the benefits going to the older employees, the burdens to the newer. Wood has offered us no reason whatsoever to fashion a rule based *on antitrust grounds* prohibiting agreements between employers and players that use seniority as a criterion for certain employment decisions. Even if some such arrangements might be illegal because of discrimination against new employees (players), the proper action would be one for breach of the duty of fair representation. . . . He reads those decisions as holding generally that a person outside the bargaining unit, in his case an unsigned first-round draft choice, who is injured in an anticompetitive fashion by a collective agreement may challenge that agreement on antitrust grounds. However, these cases are so clearly distinguishable that they need not detain us. . . .

Affirmed.

QUESTIONS AND DISCUSSION

1. The rule of reason test should be applied to the Rozelle Rule and other player restraints because professional football is different from traditional business and industrial settings. In *Mackey*, the court agreed with the NFL's contention that the league had some of the characteristics of a joint venture since no individual team is interested in driving another team out of business. If the league fails, no one team can survive.

2. A salary cap limits the total amount that each team can annually pay to its players. It might certainly limit the salary that particular players would be able to negotiate from their team. *Wood* held that the cap was exempt from antitrust analysis and that Leon Wood fell under the collective bargaining agreement's coverage even though, as a rookie, he entered the bargaining unit only after the CBA was negotiated.

3. The salary cap greatly limits the amount of income a particular player can earn. The NBA had a soft cap with one exception being that a team can resign its own players regardless of cap limitations. Caps create a pseudoscience, "capology," where it seems that everyone tries to avoid it. In the case of journeyman center Chris Dudley (BA, economics, Yale), he was offered seven years for about $20.7 million from his old team and

about $10.5 million (the maximum allowed under their cap) for seven years from his new team, plus a one-year out provision, which allows the player the option to terminate after one year. If the player chooses that option, then his current team can sign him without the cap. This loophole has now been closed through collective bargaining; obviously, it existed and thrived only with the active participation of management. *Bridgeman v. NBA (In re Dudley)*, 838 F. Supp 172 (D.N.J. 1993). Should cap penalties be directed at management instead? *See also* Hertz, *The NBA and the NBPA Opt to Cap Off the 1988 C.B.A. with a Full Court Press*: In re Chris Dudley, 5 Marq. Sports L.J. 251 (1995); Patterson, *The NBA Salary Cap, Dead, or Alive*, 19 T. Marshall L. Rev. 535 (1994).

4. In *NBA v. Williams,* 45 F.3d 684 (2d Cir. 1995), the Second Circuit used *Powell v. NFL*, 930 F.2d 1293 (8th Cir. 1989), and the nonstatutory labor exemption to protect certain provisions. The court declared these provisions legal so that their viability would continue after the formal expiration of the CBA. What options are available to athletes who do not want their marketability limited by these player restriction procedures? What options are available to the union if they wanted to limit these restrictions on behalf of their members? *See also* Doyle, *A Look into the Future of Professional Sports Labor Disputes* (NBA v. Williams), 11 Santa Clara Computer & High Tech. L.J. 403 (1991); Gould, *Now Wait a Minute, Casey: Baseball and the Salary Cap in Light of* NBA v. Williams, 13 Ent. & Sports Law. 9 (1995).

5. In *Brown v. Pro Football, Inc.*, 518 U.S. 231 (1996), the Supreme Court held that the NFL's Developmental Squad with its $1,000 per week salary and its obvious restrictive tendencies, was immune from antitrust analysis under the nonstatutory labor exemption. And that the exemption continues after the expiration of the agreement and impasse. Justice Stevens's dissent in *Brown* reminded the sports community that exemptions should be construed narrowly. *Id.* at 257. The majority opinion allows a broad interpretation. Is the dissent a better approach in the world of sports where a career is brief and at best problematic? *See also* Leslie, Brown v. *Pro Football*, Inc., 82 Va. L. Rev. 69 (1996); Tyras, *Players v. Owners: Collective Bargaining and Antitrust After* Brown v. Pro Football, Inc., 1 U. Pa. J. Lab. & Emp. L. 297 (1998).

C. EXEMPTIONS

As mentioned above, organized sports appear to resonate with monopolistic policies, and as such, the antitrust law would appear to be violated at every turn. However, even though there are prima facie violations, they are deemed to be legal because of various exemptions. In fact, the exemptions have all but swallowed the rule.

The major exemptions to the antitrust laws in sports are the baseball exemption, the labor exemption, the NFL exemptions, and the nonstatutory labor exemption. The baseball exemption is an anomaly that developed through case law; it was refined and (slightly) limited by the Curt Flood Act of 1998 (the exception was repealed only as it relates to the employment of major league baseball players).

The statutory labor exemption comes from the Clayton Act (15 U.S.C. §§12 *et seq*) and the Norris LaGuardia Act (29 U.S.C. §§101-115), in which unions are allowed to enter into agreements that might eliminate competition from other unions and create monopolies of all union activities. <u>Management cannot claim this exemption.</u>

Professional football was able to persuade Congress to promulgate various exemptions. One such exemption allows the NFL and the TV networks to pool and sell a unitary television package (15 U.S.C. §1291). Another exemption allows for the blackout of nonlocal games telecast into home territories when the home team is playing; it also permits the blackout of home games in the home territory (15 U.S.C. §1292). Finally, the last NFL exemption specifically allowed merger of the combined AFL and NFL draft systems (15 U.S.C. §1291).

The nonstatutory labor exemption is the major exemption that has all but eliminated the Sherman Act as a viable regulator of management excesses. This exemption is a derivative of the statutory labor exemption that protects union activity from the purview of the antitrust laws. The nonstatutory labor exemption is based on the policy that favors collective bargaining and gives it preference over the antitrust laws. The exemption applies when the restraint on trade affects only the parties to the agreement, where the restraint concerns a mandatory subject of collective bargaining, and where the provision in question is a product of bona fide, arm's-length bargaining.

1. Baseball

Baseball's exemption continues to the present and in effect protects from antitrust scrutiny all things that are connected to the game of baseball. The celebrated case of *Flood v. Kuhn* allowed the reserve clause to survive on a strict stare decisis basis.

FLOOD V. KUHN

407 U.S. 258 (1972)

Mr. Justice BLACKMUN delivered the opinion of the Court.

For the third time in 50 years the Court is asked specifically to rule that professional baseball's reserve system is within the reach of the federal antitrust laws. . . .

I. The Game

It is a century and a quarter since the New York Nine defeated the Knickerbockers 23 to 1 on Hoboken's Elysian Fields June 19, 1846, with Alexander Jay Cartwright as the instigator and the umpire. The teams were amateur, but the contest marked a significant date in baseball's beginnings. That early game led ultimately to the development of professional baseball and its tightly organized structure.

The Cincinnati Red Stockings came into existence in 1869 upon an outpouring of local pride. With only one Cincinnatian on the payroll, this professional team traveled over 11,000 miles that summer, winning 56 games and tying one. Shortly thereafter, on St. Patrick's Day in 1871, the National Association of Professional Baseball Players was founded and the professional league was born.

The ensuing colorful days are well known. The ardent follower and the student of baseball know of General Abner Doubleday; the formation of the National League in 1876; Chicago's supremacy in the first year's competition under the leadership of Al Spalding and with Cap Anson at third base; the formation of the American Association and then of the Union Association in the 1880's; the introduction of Sunday baseball; interleague warfare with cut-rate admission prices and player raiding; the development of the reserve "clause"; the emergence in 1885 of the Brotherhood of Professional Ball Players, and in 1890 of the Players League; the appearance of the American League, or "junior circuit," in 1901, rising from the minor Western Association; the first World Series in 1903, disruption in 1904, and the Series' resumption in 1905; the short-lived Federal League on the majors' scene during World War I years; the troublesome and discouraging episode of the 1919 Series; the home run ball; the shifting of franchises; the expansion of the leagues; the installation in 1965 of the major league draft of potential new players; and the formation of the Major League Baseball Players Association in 1966.

Then there are the many names, celebrated for one reason or another, that have sparked the diamond and its environs and that have provided tinder for recaptured thrills, for reminiscence and comparisons, and for conversation and anticipation in-season and off-season: Ty Cobb, Babe Ruth, Tris Speaker, Walter Johnson, Henry Chadwick, Eddie Collins, Lou Gehrig, Grover Cleveland Alexander, Rogers Hornsby, Harry Hooper, Goose Goslin, Jackie Robinson, Honus Wagner, Joe McCarthy, John McGraw, Deacon Phillippe, Rube Marquard, Christy Mathewson, Tommy Leach, Big Ed Delahanty, Davy Jones, Germany Schaefer, King Kelly, Big Dan Brouthers, Wahoo Sam Crawford, Wee Willie Keeler, Big Ed Walsh, Jimmy Austin, Fred Snodgrass, Satchel Paige, Hugh Jennings, Fred Merkle, Iron Man McGinnity, Three-Finger Brown, Harry and Stan Coveleski, Connie Mack, Al Bridwell, Red Ruffing, Amos Rusie, Cy Young, Smokey Joe Wood, Chief Meyers, Chief Bender, Bill Klem, Hans Lobert, Johnny Evers, Joe Tinker, Roy Campanella, Miller Huggins, Rube Bressler, Dazzy Vance, Edd Roush, Bill Wambsganss, Clark Griffith, Branch Rickey, Frank Chance, Cap Anson, Nap Lajoie, Sad Sam Jones, Bob O'Farrell, Lefty O'Doul, Bobby Veach, Willie Kamm, Heinie Groh, Lloyd and Paul Waner, Stuffy McInnis, Charles Comiskey, Roger Bresnahan, Bill Dickey, Zack Wheat, George Sisler, Charlie Gehringer, Eppa Rixey, Harry Heilmann, Fred Clarke, Dizzy Dean, Hank Greenberg, Pie Traynor, Rube Waddell, Bill Terry, Carl Hubbell, Old Hoss Radbourne, Moe Berg, Rabbit Maranville, Jimmie Foxx, Lefty Grove. The list seems endless.

And one recalls the appropriate reference to the "World Serious," attributed to Ring Lardner, Sr.; Ernest L. Thayer's "Casey at the Bat,"[4] the ring

---

[4] Millions have known and enjoyed baseball. One writer knowledgeable in the field of sports almost assumed that everyone did until, one day, he discovered otherwise:

I knew a cove who'd never heard of Washington and Lee,

of "Tinker to Evers to Chance";[5] and all the other happenings, habits, and supersitions about and around baseball that made it the "national pastime" or, depending upon the point of view, "the great American tragedy."[6]

II. The Petitioner

The petitioner, Curtis Charles Flood, born in 1938, began his major league career in 1956 when he signed a contract with the Cincinnati Reds for a salary of $4,000 for the season. He had no attorney or agent to advise him on that occasion. He was traded to the St. Louis Cardinals before the 1958 season. Flood rose to fame as a center fielder with the Cardinals during the years 1958-1969. In those 12 seasons he compiled a batting average of .293. His best offensive season was 1967 when he achieved .335. He was .301 or better in six of the 12 St. Louis years. He participated in the 1964, 1967, and 1968 World Series. He played errorless ball in the field in 1966, and once enjoyed 223 consecutive errorless games. Flood has received seven Golden Glove Awards. He was co-captain of his team from 1965-1969. He ranks among the 10 major league outfielders possessing the highest lifetime fielding averages.

But at the age of 31, in October 1969, Flood was traded to the Philadelphia Phillies of the National League in a multi-player transaction. He was not consulted about the trade. He was informed by telephone and received formal notice only after the deal had been consummated. In December he complained to the Commissioner of Baseball and asked that he be made a free agent and be placed at liberty to strike his own bargain with any other major league team. His request was denied.

Flood then instituted this antitrust suit in January 1970 in federal court for the Southern District of New York. The defendants (although not all were named in each cause of action) were the Commissioner of Baseball, the presidents of the two major leagues, and the 24 major league clubs. In general,

---

Of Caesar and Napoleon from the ancient jamboree. But, bli'me, there are queerer things than anything like that,
For here's a cove who never heard of "Casey at the Bat"!
Ten million never heard of Keats, or Shelley, Burns or Poe.
But they know "the air was shattered by the force of Casey's blow";
They never heard of Shakespeare, nor of Dickens, like as not,
But they know the somber drama from old Mudville's haunted lot.
He never heard of Casey! Am I dreaming? Is it true?
Is fame but windblown ashes when the summer day is through?
Does greatness fade so quickly and is grandeur doomed to die
That bloomed in early morning, ere the dusk rides down the sky?

"He Never Heard of Casey", Grantland Rice, The Sportlight, New York Herald Tribune, June 1, 1926, p. 23.
    [5] These are the saddest of possible words,

"Tinker to Evers to Chance."
Trio of bear cubs, and fleeter than birds, "Tinker to Evers to Chance."
Ruthlessly pricking our gonfalon bubble,
Making a Giant hit into a double — Words that are weighty with nothing but trouble:
"Tinker to Evers to Chance."

Franklin Pierce Adams, Baseball's Sad Lexicon
    [6] George Bernard Shaw, The Sporting News, May 27, 1943, p. 15, col. 4.

the complaint charged violations of the federal antitrust laws and civil rights statutes, violation of state statutes and the common law, and the imposition of a form of peonage and involuntary servitude contrary to the Thirteenth Amendment and 42 U.S.C. 1994, 18 U.S.C. §1581, and 29 U.S.C. §§102 and 103. Petitioner sought declaratory and injunctive relief and treble damages.

Flood declined to play for Philadelphia in 1970, despite a $100,000 salary offer, and he sat out the year. After the season was concluded, Philadelphia sold its rights to Flood to the Washington Senators. Washington and the petitioner were able to come to terms for 1971 at a salary of $110,000. Flood started the season but, apparently because he was dissatisfied with his performance, he left the Washington club on April 27, early in the campaign. He has not played baseball since then. . . .

IV. The Legal Background

A

Federal Baseball Club v. National League, 259 U.S. 200 (1922), was a suit for treble damages instituted by a member of the Federal League (Baltimore) against the National and American Leagues and others. The plaintiff obtained a verdict in the trial court, but the Court of Appeals reversed. The main brief filed by the plaintiff with this Court discloses that it was strenuously argued, among other things, that the business in which the defendants were engaged was interstate commerce; that the interstate relationship among the several clubs, located as they were in different States, was predominant; that organized baseball represented an investment of colossal wealth; that it was an engagement in moneymaking; that gate receipts were divided by agreement between the home club and the visiting club; and that the business of baseball was to be distinguished from the mere playing of the game as a sport for physical exercise and diversion. See also 259 U.S., at 201-206. . . .

In the years that followed, baseball continued to be subject to intermittent antitrust attack. The courts, however, rejected these challenges on the authority of Federal Baseball. In some cases stress was laid, although unsuccessfully, on new factors such as the development of radio and television with their substantial additional revenues to baseball. For the most part, however, the Holmes opinion was generally and necessarily accepted as controlling authority. . . .

C

The Court granted certiorari, 345 U.S. 963 (1953), in the *Toolson, Kowalski*, and *Corbett* cases, cited in rm 12 and 13 [deleted from this excerpt], and, by a short percuriam (Warren, C.J., and Black, Frankfurter, Douglas, Jackson, Clark, and Minton, JJ.), affirmed the judgments of the respective courts of appeals in those three cases. Toolson v. New York Yankees, Inc., 346 U.S. 356 (1953). Federal Baseball was cited as holding "that the business of providing public baseball games for profit between clubs of professional baseball players was not within the scope of the federal antitrust laws," 346 U.S., at 357. . . .

[There are] four reasons for the Court's affirmance of *Toolson* and its companion cases (a) Congressional awareness for three decades of the Court's ruling in Federal Baseball, coupled with congressional inaction. (b) The fact that baseball was left alone to develop for that period upon the understanding that the reserve system was not subject to existing federal antitrust laws. (c) A reluctance to overrule Federal Baseball with consequent retroactive effect. (d) A professed desire that any needed remedy be provided by legislation rather than by court decree. The emphasis in Toolson was on the determination, attributed even to Federal Baseball, that Congress had no intention to include baseball within the reach of the federal antitrust laws Two Justices (Burton and Reed, JJ.) dissented, stressing the factual aspects, revenue sources, and the absence of an express exemption of organized baseball from the Sherman Act. 346 U.S., at 357. . . .

V

In view of all this, it seems appropriate now to say that:

1. Professional baseball is a business and it is engaged in interstate commerce.
2. With its reserve system enjoying exemption from the federal antitrust laws, baseball is, in a very distinct sense, an exception and an anomaly. Federal Baseball and Toolson have become an aberration confined to baseball.
3. Even though others might regard this as "unrealistic, inconsistent, or illogical," the aberration is an established one, and one that has been recognized not only in Federal Baseball and Toolson, but in Shubert, International Boxing, and Radovich, as well, a total of five consecutive cases in this Court. It is an aberration that has been with us now for half a century, one heretofore deemed fully entitled to the benefit of stare decisis, and one that has survived the Court's expanding concept of interstate commerce. It rests on a recognition and an acceptance of baseball's unique characteristics and needs.
4. Other professional sports operating interstate — football, boxing, basketball, and, presumably, hockey[19] and golf[20] — are not so exempt.
5. The advent of radio and television, with their consequent increased coverage and additional revenues, has not occasioned an overruling of Federal Baseball and Toolson.
6. The Court has emphasized that since 1922 baseball, with full and continuing congressional awareness, has been allowed to develop and to expand unhindered by federal legislative action. Remedial legislation has been introduced repeatedly in Congress but none has ever been enacted. The Court, accordingly, has concluded that Congress as yet has had no intention to subject baseball's reserve system to the reach of the antitrust statutes. This, obviously, has been deemed to be something other than mere congressional silence and passivity. . . .

Accordingly, we adhere once again to Federal Baseball and Toolson and to their application to professional baseball. We adhere also to International Boxing and Radovich and to their respective applications to professional

---

[19] Peto v. Madison Square Garden Corp., 1958 Trade Cases, 69, 106 (SDNY 1958).
[20] Deesen v. Professional Golfers' Assn., 358 F.2d 165 (CA9) cert. denied, 385 U.S. 846 (1966).

boxing and professional football. If there is any inconsistency or illogic in all this, it is an inconsistency and illogic of long standing that is to be remedied by the Congress and not by this Court. If we were to act otherwise, we would be withdrawing from the conclusion as to congressional intent made in Toolson and from the concerns as to retrospectivity therein expressed. Under these circumstances, there is merit in consistency even though some might claim that beneath that consistency is a layer of inconsistency. . . .

The conclusion we have reached makes it unnecessary for us to consider the respondents' additional argument that the reserve system is a mandatory subject of collective bargaining and that federal labor policy therefore exempts the reserve system from the operation of federal antitrust laws. . . .

And what the Court said in Federal Baseball in 1922 and what it said in Toolson in 1953, we say again here in 1972; the remedy, if any is indicated, is for congressional, and not judicial, action.

The judgment of the Court of Appeals is affirmed.

Judgment affirmed.

Mr. Justice WHITE joins in the judgment of the Court, and in all but Part I of the Court's opinion.

Mr. Justice POWELL took no part in the consideration or decision of this case.

Mr. Chief Justice BURGER, [concurs]. . . .

Mr. Justice DOUGLAS, with whom Mr. Justice BRENNAN concurs, dissenting.

This Court's decision in Federal Baseball Club v. National League, 259 U.S. 200, made in 1922, is a derelict in the stream of the law that we, its creator, should remove. Only a romantic view[1] of a rather dismal business account over the last 50 years would keep that derelict in midstream. . . .

Mr. Justice MARSHALL, with whom Mr. Justice BRENNAN joins, [dissents]. . . .

In *Piazza v. Major League Baseball,* plaintiffs alleged that professional Major League Baseball frustrated their efforts to purchase the San Francisco Giants baseball club and relocate it to Tampa Bay, Florida.

PIAZZA V. MAJOR LEAGUE BASEBALL

831 F. Supp. 420 (E.D. Pa. 1993)

PADOVA, District Judge.

Plaintiffs allege that the organizations of professional major league baseball and an affiliated individual frustrated their efforts to purchase the San Francisco Giants baseball club (the "Giants") and relocate it to Tampa Bay, Florida. Plaintiffs charge these defendants with infringing upon their rights under the United States Constitution and violating federal antitrust laws and several state laws in the process. . . .

---

[1] While I joined the Court's opinion in Toolson v. New York Yankees, Inc., 346 U.S. 356, I have lived to regret it; and I would now correct what I believe to be its fundamental error.

With regard to plaintiffs' federal antitrust claims, defendants also claim exemption from antitrust liability under *Federal Baseball Club of Baltimore, Inc. v. National League of Professional Baseball Clubs*, 259 U.S. 200 (1922), and its progeny. For the following reasons, I will grant defendants' motion as to plaintiffs' direct claims under the Constitution; but I will deny defendants' motion in all other respects. As to defendants' assertion of exemption from antitrust liability, I hold that the exemption created by *Federal Baseball* is inapplicable here because it is limited to baseball's "reserve system."

I. *Background*
A. *The Allegations*

Plaintiffs are Vincent M. Piazza and Vincent N. Tirendi, both Pennsylvania residents, and PT Baseball, Inc. ("PTB"), a Pennsylvania corporation wholly owned by Piazza and Tirendi. Pursuant to a written Memorandum of Understanding ("Memorandum") dated August 18, 1992, Piazza and Tirendi agreed with four other individuals, all Florida residents, to organize a limited partnership for the purpose of acquiring the Giants. . . .

The Investors anticipated that they would form individual corporations to serve as general partners of the partnership. Accordingly, on August 26, 1992, PTB entered into a Limited Partnership Agreement (the "Partnership Agreement") with corporations owned by the other Investors. This Partnership Agreement implemented the intent of the Memorandum and created a partnership entity known as Tampa Bay Baseball Club, Ltd. (the "Partnership"). PTB agreed to contribute $27 million to the Partnership, making it the single largest contributor of Partnership capital.

Earlier, on August 6, 1992, the Investors had executed a Letter of Intent with Robert Lurie, the owner of the Giants, to purchase the Giants for $115 million. Pursuant to this Letter of Intent, Lurie agreed not to negotiate with other potential buyers of the Giants and to use his best efforts to secure from defendant Major League Baseball approval of the sale of the Giants to the Partnership and transfer of the team to the Suncoast Dome, located in St. Petersburg, Florida.

As required by the rules of Major League Baseball, the Partnership submitted an application to that organization on September 4, 1992 to purchase the Giants and move the team to St. Petersburg. In connection with this application, Major League Baseball and its "Ownership Committee" undertook or purported to undertake a personal background check on the Investors. On September 10, 1992, defendant Ed Kuhlmann, Chairman of the Ownership Committee, stated at a press conference that, among other things, the personal background check on the Investors had raised a "serious question in terms of some of the people who were part of that group" and that "a couple of investors will not be in the group." . . . Immediately following Kuhlmann at the news conference, Jerry Reinsdorf, a member of the Ownership Committee added that the Ownership Committee's concern related to the "out-of-state" money and that the "Pennsylvania People" had "dropped out."

As the only principals of the Partnership who reside in Pennsylvania, Piazza and Tirendi aver that the clear implication of Kuhlmann's and

Reinsdorf's comments, combined with the fact that Piazza and Tirendi are of Italian descent, was that the personal background check had associated them with the Mafia and/or other criminal or organized criminal activity. Piazza and Tirendi further allege that they have never been involved in such activity; nor had they "dropped out" of the Partnership. . . .

On the same day that the Partnership submitted its application to purchase and relocate the franchise, Kuhlmann directed Lurie to consider other offers to purchase the Giants, in knowing violation of Lurie's exclusive agreement with the Partnership. On September 9, 1992, Bill White, President of the National League, invited George Shinn, a North Carolina resident, to make an alternative bid to purchase the Giants in order to keep the team in San Francisco. An alternative offer was ultimately made by other investors to keep the Giants in San Francisco. Even though this offer was $15 million less than the $115 million offer made by the Partnership, Major League Baseball formally rejected the proposal to relocate the Giants to the Tampa Bay area on November 10, 1992.

Plaintiffs allege that Baseball never intended to permit the Giants to relocate to Florida and failed to evaluate fairly and in good faith their application to do so. They claim that to avoid relocation of the Giants, Baseball set out to "destroy the financial capability of the Partnership by vilifying plaintiffs." And in addition to preventing plaintiffs' purchase and relocation of the Giants, plaintiffs allege that Baseball's allegedly defamatory statements cost them the loss of a significant contract in connection with one of their other businesses, which depends upon "impeccable personal reputations."

B. *The Claims*
1. *Federal claims*

Plaintiffs first claim that the above actions of Baseball violated the First and Fifth Amendments to the United States Constitution by (1) depriving them of their liberty and property interests and privileges without due process of law, (2) denying them equal protection of the laws, and (3) impairing their freedom of contract and association. In this connection plaintiffs claim that Baseball's actions should be attributed to the federal government, to which the constraints of the U.S. Constitution apply, because the federal government has granted Baseball a unique exemption from the federal antitrust laws.

Plaintiffs next assert a claim under 42 U.S.C.A. §1983 (West 1981), alleging that Baseball acted under color of state law in unlawfully depriving them of the rights, privileges, immunities, freedoms, and liberties secured by Article IV, Section 2 of the U.S. Constitution, as well as the First, Fifth and Fourteenth Amendments. Plaintiffs claim that Baseball's actions took place under color of state law because (a) Baseball is exempt from liability under state antitrust laws; (b) there is a close nexus and symbiotic relationship between Baseball and state and local governments; and (c) Baseball acted in concert with the City of San Francisco to prevent the Giants from being relocated.

Plaintiffs' final federal claim asserts violations of sections 1 and 2 of the Sherman Anti-Trust Act, 15 U.S.C.A. §§1 and 2 (West 1973 & Supp. 1993). Plaintiffs claim that Baseball has monopolized the market for Major League Baseball teams and that Baseball has placed direct and indirect restraints on the purchase, sale, transfer, relocation of, and competition for such teams. Plaintiffs allege that these actions have unlawfully restrained and impeded plaintiffs' opportunities to engage in the business of Major League Baseball. . . .

II. *DISCUSSION* . . .

D. *Antitrust*

Baseball next moves to dismiss plaintiffs' claims under sections 1 and 2 of the Sherman Anti-Trust Act ("Sherman Act"), 15 U.S.C.A. §§1 and 2 (West 1973 & Supp. 1993), and offers the following three reasons why these claims should be dismissed: (1) plaintiffs have failed to allege that Baseball's actions restrained competition in a relevant market; (2) plaintiffs have no standing to assert a Sherman Act claim; and (3) Baseball is exempt from liability under the Sherman Act. I will address each argument in turn.

1. *Relevant Market*

Absent a *per se* violation, which neither party argues has been alleged here, a cause of action under the Sherman Act requires, *inter alia,* an allegation of injury to competition in relevant product and geographic markets. *See Mid-South Grizzlies v. National Football League*, 720 F.2d 772, 785-88 (3d Cir. 1983), *cert. denied,* 467 U.S. 1215 (1984); *Fleer Corp. v. Topps Chewing Gum, Inc.,* 658 F.2d 139, 147 (3d Cir. 1981). Baseball argues that plaintiffs have not alleged an injury to competition in a relevant product market because plaintiffs were seeking to *join* Baseball, rather than *compete* with it. . . .

2. *Standing*

The principles of standing applicable to alleged violations of sections 1 and 2 of the Sherman Act are the same as those applicable to questions of standing under section 4 of the Clayton Act, 15 U.S.C.A. §15 (West Supp. 1993). . . .

3. *Exemption from Antitrust Liability*

I now turn to the heart of Baseball's motion to dismiss plaintiffs' Sherman Act claim — that in *Federal Baseball Club of Baltimore, Inc. v. National League of Professional Baseball Clubs, Inc.,* 259 U.S. 200 (1922); *Toolson v. New York Yankees,* 346 U.S. 356 (1953); and *Flood v. Kuhn,* 407 U.S. 258 (1972), the United States Supreme Court exempted Baseball from liability under the federal antitrust laws. Plaintiffs do not deny that these cases recognize some form of exemption from antitrust liability related to the game of baseball, but argue alternatively that the exemption either does not apply in this case, cannot be applied as a matter of law to the facts of this case, or should no longer be recognized at all.

a. *Evolution of the exemption.* Writing for a unanimous Supreme Court over seventy years ago, Justice Holmes affirmed a judgment of the Court of Appeals of the District of Columbia and held that the business of giving exhibitions of baseball games for profit does not constitute trade or commerce within the meaning of the Sherman Act, and thus the Act does not apply to that business. *See Federal Baseball,* 259 U.S. at 208-09, and the underlying decision of the Court of Appeals, *National League of Professional Baseball Clubs v. Federal*

Baseball Club of Baltimore, Inc., 269 F. 681 (C.C.D.C. 1920) *("D.C. Opinion")*. The plaintiff in that case, Federal Baseball of Baltimore, Inc. ("Federal Baseball"), owned a franchise in the Federal League of Professional Baseball Clubs until dissolution of that league in 1915 pursuant to an agreement with the National League and American League of Professional Baseball Clubs. *D.C. Opinion*, 269 F. at 682. With the demise of the Federal League, Federal Baseball was left without an organization within which to compete, and subsequently brought suit against the National and American Leagues, among others, for violation of the Sherman Act. *Id.* A jury found in favor of Federal Baseball, awarding it $240,000 in treble damages, costs, and attorneys fees.

The gravamen of Federal Baseball's case was the alleged anticompetitive impact of what is known as the "reserve clause" in the yearly contracts of players in the National and American Leagues. *Id.* at 687-88. The reserve clause bound a player to either enter a new contract with the same team in the succeeding year of the player's contract or be considered ineligible by the National and American Leagues to serve any baseball club. *Id.* at 687. Because of this restrictive provision, the Federal League and its constituent clubs were unable to obtain players who had contracts with the National and American Leagues, the effect of which, as found by the jury, was to damage Federal Baseball. *Id.* at 682, 687.

The Court of Appeals reversed the jury's verdict and remanded, making four significant findings. First, and quite simply, the court found that the business in which the defendants were engaged was the business of giving exhibitions of the game of baseball. *Id.* at 684.

Second, the court found that "[a] game of baseball is not susceptible of being transferred, . . . [and] [t]he transportation in interstate commerce of the players and the paraphernalia used . . . was but an incident to the main purpose of the [defendants], namely, the production of the game." *Id.* at 684-85. Thus, the court reasoned, a baseball exhibition could not be considered interstate commerce, and the business of giving such an exhibition could not be subject to the Sherman Act. *Id.*

The third finding of the Court of Appeals was that, despite the fact that the giving of an exhibition was not interstate commerce, there were interstate components of Federal Baseball's business, the direct interference with which was redressable under the Sherman Act. *Id.* at 686. These interstate features included such things as the movement of players and their paraphernalia from place to place across state lines. *Id.* The court found that if unlawful anticompetitive activity directly interfered with the business of moving the players or their equipment, as opposed to the exhibition of the game itself, the Sherman Act would apply. *Id.*

Finally, the Court of Appeals found that the reserve clause only indirectly, if at all, affected the interstate aspects of Federal Baseball's business (the business of moving players and their equipment), which was not sufficient to give rise to a Sherman act violation. *Id.* at 687-88.

These four findings can be condensed into two reasons why the Court of Appeals found that the reserve clause did not offend the Sherman Act. First, the anticompetitive impact of the reserve clause on the business of giving a baseball exhibition was not redressable as a matter of law under the Sherman

Act, such business found not to be interstate commerce. Second, the reserve clause had, at best, only an incidental impact on the portion of Federal Baseball's business that was considered interstate commerce.

The Supreme Court affirmed. The Court agreed that the defendants' exhibitions of baseball games "are purely state affairs," lacking the character of interstate commerce. *Federal Baseball,* 259 U.S. at 208. From this, the Court reasoned, "[i]f we are right the plaintiff's business is to be described the same way and the restrictions by contract that prevented the plaintiff from getting players to break their bargains [the reserve clause] and the other conduct charged against the defendants [buying up Federal League clubs] were not an interference with commerce among the States." *Id.* at 209.

The Supreme Court next addressed the exemption in *Toolson v. New York Yankees, Inc.,* 346 U.S. 356 (1953), a *per curiam* opinion affirming decisions of the Sixth and Ninth Circuits. . . .

The next and most recent time the Supreme Court directly considered the exemption was in *Flood v. Kuhn,* 407 U.S. 258 (1972). Like *Toolson,* the plaintiff in *Flood* was a professional baseball player dissatisfied with the reserve clause in his contract and the "reserve system" generally. . . .

b. *Discussion: Scope of the exemption.* In each of the three cases in which the Supreme Court directly addressed the exemption, the factual context involved the reserve clause. Plaintiffs argue that the exemption is confined to that circumstance, which is not presented here. Baseball, on the other hand, argues that the exemption applies to the "business of baseball" generally, not to one particular facet of the game.

Between 1922 and 1972, Baseball's expansive view may have been correct. . . .

In 1972, however, the Court in *Flood v. Kuhn* stripped from *Federal Baseball* and *Toolson* any precedential value those cases may have had beyond the particular facts there involved, *i.e.,* the reserve clause. The *Flood* Court employed a two-prong approach in doing so. First, the Court examined the analytical underpinnings of *Federal Baseball* — that the business of exhibiting baseball games is not interstate commerce. In the clearest possible terms, the Court rejected this reasoning, removing any doubt that "[p]rofessional baseball is a business . . . engaged in interstate commerce." *Flood,* 407 U.S. at 282.

Having entirely undercut the precedential value of the *reasoning of Federal Baseball,* the Court next set out to justify the continued precedential value of the *result* of that decision. . . .

[T]he *Flood* Court viewed the *disposition* in *Federal Baseball* and *Toolson* as being limited to the reserve system, for baseball developed between 1922 and 1953 with the understanding that its *reserve system,* not the game generally, was exempt from the antitrust laws. This reading of *Flood* is buttressed by (1) the reaffirmation in *Flood* of a prior statement of the Court that "'*Toolson* was a narrow application of the doctrine of *stare decisis,*'" *id.* at 276 (quoting *Shubert,* 348 U.S. at 228-30, and (2) the *Flood* Court's own characterization, in the *first sentence* of its opinion, of the *Federal Baseball, Toolson,* and *Flood* decisions: "For the third time in 50 years the Court is asked *specifically* to rule that professional baseball's *reserve system* is within the reach of the antitrust laws." *Id.* at 259, (emphasis added) (footnote omitted).

Viewing the dispositions in *Federal Baseball* and *Toolson* as limited to the reserve clause, the *Flood* Court then turned to the reasons why, even though analytically vitiated, the precise results in *Federal Baseball* and *Toolson* were to be accorded the continuing benefit of *stare decisis*. Like *Toolson,* the *Flood* Court laid its emphasis on continued positive congressional inaction and concerns over retroactivity. *Id.* at 283-84. In particular, the *Flood* Court "concluded that Congress as yet has had no intention to subject baseball's *reserve system* to the reach of the antitrust statutes." *Id.* at 283 (emphasis added). Finally, the Court acknowledged that "[w]ith its *reserve system* enjoying exemption from the federal antitrust laws, baseball is, in a very distinct sense, an exception and an anomaly. *Federal Baseball* and *Toolson* have become an aberration confined to baseball." *Id.* at 282 (emphasis added). Thus in 1972, the Supreme Court made clear that the *Federal Baseball* exemption is limited to the reserve clause. . . .

Applying these principles of *stare decisis* here, it becomes clear that, before *Flood,* lower courts were bound by both the *rule* of *Federal Baseball* and *Toolson* (that the business of baseball is not interstate commerce and thus not within the Sherman Act) and the *result* of those decisions (that baseball's reserve system is exempt from the antitrust laws). The Court's decision in *Flood,* however, effectively created the circumstance referred to by the Third Circuit as "result stare decisis," from the English system. In *Flood,* the Supreme Court exercised its discretion to invalidate the *rule* of *Federal Baseball* and *Toolson.* Thus no rule from those cases binds the lower courts as a matter of *stare decisis.* The only aspect of *Federal Baseball* and *Toolson* that remains to be followed is the result or disposition based upon the facts there involved, which the Court in *Flood* determined to be the exemption of the reserve system from the antitrust laws. . . .

For these reasons, I conclude that the antitrust exemption created by *Federal Baseball* is limited to baseball's reserve system, and because the parties agree that the reserve system is not at issue in this case, I reject Baseball's argument that it is exempt from antitrust liability in this case.

III. Conclusion

Baseball's motion to dismiss is granted in part and denied in part. Plaintiffs' direct claims under the U.S. Constitution are dismissed. In all other respects the motion is denied. Because I have not dismissed all of plaintiffs' claims over which this Court has original jurisdiction, I will continue to exercise supplemental jurisdiction over plaintiffs' state law claims. *See* 28 U.S.C.A. §1367 (West Supp. 1993).

An appropriate order follows.

ORDER

And Now, this 4th day of August, 1993, upon consideration of Defendants' Motion to Dismiss the Complaint (Docket Entry No. 3) and all papers filed in support thereof and in response thereto, and after oral argument, it is hereby ordered that said motion is granted in part and denied in part for the reasons stated in the accompanying Opinion, as follows:

1. Plaintiffs' direct claims under the U.S. Constitution (Count I) are dismissed.
2. In all other respects, defendants' motion is denied.

———————

Piazza is only a federal district court case and thus has limited jurisdiction. It held that the proposed sale and relocation of a baseball team was not protected by baseball's antitrust exemption. However, the Supreme Court of Minnesota in *Minnesota Twins Partnership* held that the proposed sale and relocation of a professional baseball team, by virtue of baseball's contraction scheme, was an integral part of the business of professional baseball and thus exempt from antitrust.

MINNESOTA TWINS PARTNERSHIP V. STATE

592 N.W.2d 847 (Minn. 1999)

Paul H. ANDERSON, Justice.

We are asked to determine if appellants must comply with civil investigative demands issued by the Minnesota Attorney General's Office. The Attorney General is requesting information on the proposed sale and relocation of the Minnesota Twins baseball franchise to North Carolina and a potential boycott of Minnesota by Major League Baseball in violation of state antitrust laws. The appellants allege that their conduct is exempt from Minnesota's antitrust laws because the United States Supreme Court has held that the business of professional baseball is exempt from compliance with federal antitrust laws. The district court rejected this argument and issued an order compelling compliance with the civil investigative demands. The Minnesota Court of Appeals denied review, holding that the issues presented were "premature." Appellants now ask us to reverse the court of appeals' denial of review and remand the matter to that court to consider the issues on the merits. We instead reverse the district court's order to compel compliance with the civil investigative demands and remand.

The facts are not in dispute. Early in October 1997, Carl R. Pohlad, on behalf of the Minnesota Twins Partnership, announced that he had signed a letter of intent to sell the Twins to North Carolina businessman Donald C. Beaver and the other investors of North Carolina Major League Baseball, L.L.C. (NCMLB). The sale was contingent on the Minnesota Legislature's refusal to authorize public funding for a new baseball stadium by November 30, 1997. Within days of the announcement of the proposed sale, a delegation from Minnesota, including then-Governor Arne H. Carlson and key legislators, traveled to Milwaukee to confer with then-Acting Commissioner of Major League Baseball Allan "Bud" Selig. Selig told the delegation that if a publicly-funded stadium was not authorized and built, the other Major

League Baseball (MLB) team owners would approve the Twins' move from Minnesota. The Minnesota Legislature subsequently rejected all stadium bills introduced in the special legislative session called by Governor Carlson.

On December 17, 1997, the Attorney General served the Twins with civil investigative demands (CIDs) as part of an investigation into possible violations of state antitrust laws. . . . The CIDs served on the Twins requested a broad array of documents concerning, among other things, the financial viability of the Hubert H. Humphrey Metrodome (the Twins' current stadium), the methods used by other professional baseball teams to obtain new stadia, the potential purchase of the Twins by Beaver and his group of North Carolina investors, and the 1961 relocation of the Washington Senators to Minnesota. . . .

The court of appeals denied review in an order opinion, holding that the question of professional baseballs exemption from antitrust laws under either federal caselaw or the Commerce Clause was "premature." The court's order stated specifically that the Twins retained the right to raise the exemption as an affirmative defense should prosecution occur. The Twins appealed, arguing that the court of appeals erred in not reaching the merits of the argument that professional baseball's exemption from federal antitrust laws precluded prosecution under state antitrust laws. . . .

In several cases following *Toolson,* the Supreme Court made it clear that professional baseball's exemption rested on "a narrow application of the rule of *stare decisis*" applicable only to baseball. . . .

[The Court discusses *Federal Baseball* and *Toolson.*]

The Supreme Court's most recent and most thorough look at professional baseball's exemption came in *Flood v. Kuhn,* 407 U.S. 258, (1972). Like *Toolson, Flood* involved a challenge to baseball's reserve system. . . .

The Supreme Court affirmed in an opinion written by Justice Harry A. Blackmun. *Flood,* 407 U.S. at 258. In *Flood,* the Court delineated the circumstances surrounding *Federal Baseball* in subsequent cases. *Id.* at 269-80. The pattern that emerges is clear: the exemption set forth in *Federal Baseball* is limited strictly to professional baseball, and despite frequent invitations to review the issue, Congress has allowed the anomalous exemption to remain. *Id.* at 281-82. The Court acknowledged that the legal footings for the exemption were no longer valid, stating that "[p]rofessional baseball is a business and it is engaged in interstate commerce," but held that baseball remained exempt from federal antitrust law under the stare decisis of *Federal Baseball* and *Toolson.*

While engagingly written, the *Flood* opinion is not clear about the extent of the conduct that is exempt from antitrust laws. The opinion begins by identifying the issue as whether "professional baseball's *reserve system* is within the reach of the federal antitrust laws." *Flood,* 407 U.S. at 259 (emphasis added). The facts before the Supreme Court clearly implicated only the reserve clause. *Id.* at 264-66. However, the holding is broader, stating that "we adhere once again to *Federal Baseball* and *Toolson* and to their application *to professional baseball.*" *Id.* at 284 (emphasis added). Thus, when interpreting the scope of *Flood,* we are seemingly offered the choice between either a narrow or a broad reading of professional baseball's antitrust exemption.

The "great weight of federal cases" hold that *Flood* exempts the entire business of baseball from federal and state antitrust claims. . . .

A different interpretation of *Flood* can be found in *Piazza v. Major League Baseball,* 831 F. Supp. 420 (E.D. Pa. 1993). *Piazza* was precipitated by a situation analogous to the one before this court—the threatened move of the San Francisco Giants baseball club to Florida. *Id.* at 422-23. A partnership of investors, including plaintiff Vincent Piazza, signed a letter of intent with Robert Lurie, the owner of the Giants, to purchase the team for $115 million. *Id.* at 422. The chair of MLB's Ownership Committee directed Lurie to negotiate with other potential purchasers in violation of the letter of intent and the Ownership Committee refused to grant the partnership the necessary permission to purchase and move the team. *Id.* at 422-23. The team was eventually sold to a group of San Francisco investors for $15 million less than Piazza's partnership had offered.

Piazza sued MLB on a number of grounds, including violations of the Sherman Antitrust Act. *Piazza,* 831 F. Supp. at 423-24. MLB moved to dismiss arguing that "plaintiffs' federal claims fail to state a cause of action" and that the court lacked subject matter jurisdiction. *Id.* at 421. The *Piazza* court interpreted the Supreme Court's statement in *Flood* that baseball was a business engaged in interstate commerce as limiting the scope of the exemption to the reserve clause at issue in *Flood* and *Toolson. Id.* at 435-38. Hence, the *Piazza* court reasoned, the broad exemption articulated by other courts is an inappropriate application of stare decisis that erroneously expands professional baseball's exemption beyond the facts of *Flood* and *Toolson. Id.* at 437-48. Even applying a broad exemption, the court concluded that the ownership of baseball franchises had not been analyzed in light of *Federal Baseball* and therefore a factual record was necessary before a determination could be made.

In the present case, the Ramsey County District Court found *Piazza* to be more persuasive than other federal cases that outlined a broader exemption. The court concluded that "the ruling in *Flood* confines [baseball's] antitrust exemption to the narrow area of the reserve clause." Because the state's allegations "go far beyond the question of the reserve system," the court issued an order compelling compliance with the CIDs. . . .

The *Piazza* opinion is a skillful attempt to make sense of the Supreme Court's refusal to overrule *Federal Baseball,* an opinion generally regarded as "not one of Mr. Justice Holmes' happiest days." But *Piazza* ignores what *is* clear about *Flood*—that the Supreme Court had no intention of overruling *Federal Baseball* or *Toolson* despite acknowledging that professional baseball involves interstate commerce. Although the facts of *Flood* deal only with baseball's reserve system, the court's conclusion in *Flood* is unequivocal. . . .

As intellectually attractive as the *Piazza* alternative is, we are compelled to accept the paradox the Supreme Court acknowledged in *Flood* when it declined to overrule *Federal Baseball.* . . .

We choose to follow the lead of those courts that conclude the business of professional baseball is exempt from federal antitrust laws. Further, we conclude that the sale and relocation of a baseball franchise, like the reserve clause discussed in *Flood,* is an integral part of the business of professional baseball and falls within the exemption. . . . Because as a matter of law the Attorney

General is precluded from prosecuting the Twins on these antitrust allegations, the district court erred when it issued an order compelling compliance with the CID's. The Twins are entitled to a protective order under Minn. R. Civ. P. 26.03.

We reverse the court of appeals and remand this matter to the district court for proceedings consistent with this opinion.

Minnesota Twins Partnership is consistent with the Curt Flood Act, in that even though the act partially repeals baseball's exemption, it still exempts franchise relocation and ownership transfer.

CURT FLOOD ACT OF 1998

15 U.S.C. §27

Section 1. Short Title.

This Act may be cited as the "Curt Flood Act of 1998."

Section 2. Purpose.

It is the purpose of this legislation to state that major league baseball players are covered under the antitrust laws (i.e., that major league baseball players will have the same rights under the antitrust laws as do other professional athletes, e.g., football and basketball players), along with a provision that makes it clear that the passage of this Act does not change the application of the antitrust laws in any other context or with respect to any other person or entity.

Section 3. Application of the Antitrust Laws to Professional Major League Baseball.

The Clayton Act (15 U.S.C. §§12 *et seq.*) is amended by adding at the end the following new section:

> Sec. 27 (a) Subject to subsections (b) through (d), the conduct, acts, practices, or agreements of persons in the business of organized professional major league baseball directly relating to or affecting employment of major league baseball players to play baseball at the major league level are subject to the antitrust laws to the same extent such conduct, acts, practices, or agreements would be subject to the antitrust laws if engaged in by the person in any other professional sports business affecting interstate commerce.
>
> (b) No court shall rely on the enactment of this section as a basis for changing the application of the antitrust laws to any conduct, acts, practices, or agreements other than those set forth in subsection (a). This section does not create, permit or imply a cause of action by which to challenge under the antitrust laws, or otherwise apply the antitrust laws to, any conduct, acts, practices, or agreements that do not directly relate to or affect employment of major league baseball players to play baseball players to play baseball at the major league level.

2. Nonstatutory Labor Exemption

The so-called nonstatutory labor exemption allows for union-management clauses to receive antitrust protection if they are the result of bona fide, arm's-length negotiation on mandatory subjects of collective bargaining. *Powell v. NFL* holds that this exemption continues even after the parties have reached impasse in their negotiation.

POWELL V. NATIONAL FOOTBALL LEAGUE

930 F.2d 1293 (8th Cir. 1989)

John R. GIBSON, Circuit Judge.

The National Football League appeals from a district court order which denied the League's motion for partial summary judgment, ruling that the nonstatutory labor exemption to the antitrust laws expires when, as here, the parties have reached "impasse" in negotiations following the conclusion of a collective bargaining agreement. This antitrust action was brought by Marvin Powell, eight other professional football players, and the players' collective bargaining representative, the National Football League Players Association (hereinafter the "Players").[1] Although this action also includes claims that both the League's college draft and its continued adherence to its uniform Player Contract constitute unlawful player restraints, the only League practice at issue in this interlocutory appeal is that provision of the Players' collective bargaining agreement establishing a "Right of First Refusal/Compensation" system. These employment terms restrict the ability of players to sign with other teams, a right commonly termed "free agency." On appeal, the League contends that the challenged practices are the product of bona fide, arm's-length collective bargaining and therefore are governed by federal labor law to the exclusion of challenge under the Sherman Act, 15 U.S.C. §§1-7 (1982). The Players, on the other hand, argue that the labor exemption to the antitrust laws expires when parties reach "impasse" in negotiations, and that the First Refusal/Compensation system therefore may be challenged as an unlawful restraint of trade. As we conclude that this action is at present governed by federal labor law, and not antitrust law, we reverse. . . .

I

This is not the first time that this court has considered whether a labor exemption shields the League from antitrust liability for the restraints it imposes on its players. In *Mackey v. National Football League*, 543 F.2d 606 (8th Cir. 1976), *cert. dismissed*, 434 U.S. 801 (1977), the League appealed from a district court ruling that the "Rozelle Rule," a restraint on competition for player services, violated section 1 of the Sherman Act. We first analyzed the statutory labor exemption to the application of the antitrust laws, observing that while the exemption applies to legitimate labor activities unilaterally undertaken by a union in furtherance of its own interest, it does not extend

---

[1] Powell is president of the National Football League Players Association. . . .

to concerted action or agreements between unions and nonlabor groups such as employers. *Id.* at 611. We further held, however, that employer groups such as the League may invoke the nonstatutory labor exemption to their benefit where there has been an agreement between management and labor with regard to the challenged restraint. *Id.* at 612.

The Players contend that the League in essence asks this court to overrule *Mackey*. The Players argue that although in the case before us the Players' collective bargaining agreement has expired, the *Mackey* court conditioned its application of the labor exemption upon the existence of an agreement between the union and management and specifically referred to the existence of an agreement in two of its three requirements for invoking the labor exemption. *See Mackey*, 543 F.2d at 614. We cannot accept this interpretation. Our discussion in *Mackey* was couched in terms of "agreements" because in that case we were presented with unlawful restraints which, although initiated years before football players had been represented by a union, had been incorporated by two bargaining agreements. Against those facts, we held that the mere incorporation of unlawful restraints into a collective bargaining agreement without bona fide bargaining was not sufficient to place them beyond the reach of the Sherman Act. *Id.* at 616. . . .

Now that the 1982 Agreement is terminated, however, we must decide whether the nonstatutory labor exemption has also expired or, alternatively, whether under the circumstances of this case the exemption continues to protect the League from potential antitrust liability.

II

The district court adopted "impasse" as the point at which the nonstatutory labor exemption expires, holding that "once the parties reach impasse concerning player restraint provisions, those provisions will lose their immunity and further imposition of those conditions may result in antitrust liability." The court reasoned that its impasse standard "respects the labor law obligation to bargain in good faith over mandatory bargaining subjects following expiration of a collective bargaining agreement," and that it "promotes the collective bargaining relationship and enhances prospects that the parties will reach compromise on the issue." *Powell I,* 678 F. Supp. at 789. The League attacks the district court's standard as providing a union, such as the Players, with undue motivation to generate impasse in order to pursue an antitrust suit for treble damages. . . .

Upon the facts currently presented by this case, we are not compelled to look into the future and pick a termination point for the labor exemption. The parties are now faced with several choices. They may bargain further, which we would strongly urge that they do. They may resort to economic force. And finally, if appropriate issues arise, they may present claims to the National Labor Relations Board. We are satisfied that as long as there is a possibility that proceedings may be commenced before the Board, or until final resolution of Board proceedings and appeals therefrom, the labor relationship continues and the labor exemption applies. Since the matter before us concerns an interlocutory appeal, we need not decide issues left unresolved by this opinion.

III

In sum, we hold that the antitrust laws are inapplicable under the circumstances of this case as the nonstatutory labor exemption extends beyond impasse. We reverse the order of the district court and remand the case with instructions to enter judgment in defendants' favor on Counts I, II, and VIII of plaintiffs' amended complaint.

HEANEY, Senior Circuit Judge, [dissents]. . . .

LAY, Chief Judge, with whom McMILLIAN, Circuit Judge, joins, [dissents]. . . .

John R. GIBSON, Circuit Judge, [concurs] in the denial of the rehearing en banc, joined by WOLLMAN, Circuit Judge. . . .

In *Brown v. Pro Football, Inc.*, professional football players assigned to developmental squads of substitute players brought an antitrust class action against the professional football league challenging the league's unilateral imposition, after bargaining to the point of impasse, of fixed salary for developmental squad players. The Supreme Court held that the league's conduct in unilaterally imposing a fixed salary for developmental squad players fell within the scope of the nonstatutory labor exemption from antitrust liability.

BROWN V. PRO FOOTBALL, INC.

518 U.S. 231 (1996)

Justice BREYER delivered the opinion of the Court.

The question in this case arises at the intersection of the Nation's labor and antitrust laws. A group of professional football players brought this antitrust suit against football club owners. The club owners had bargained with the players' union over a wage issue until they reached impasse. The owners then had agreed among themselves (but not with the union) to implement the terms of their own last best bargaining offer. The question before us is whether federal labor laws shield such an agreement from antitrust attack. We believe that they do. This Court has previously found in the labor laws an implicit antitrust exemption that applies where needed to make the collective-bargaining process work. Like the Court of Appeals, we conclude that this need makes the exemption applicable in this case.

I

We can state the relevant facts briefly. In 1987, a collective-bargaining agreement between the National Football League (NFL or League), a group of football clubs, and the NFL Players Association, a labor union, expired. The NFL and the Players Association began to negotiate a new contract. In March 1989, during the negotiations the NFL adopted Resolution G-2, a plan that would permit each club to establish a "developmental squad" of up to six rookie or "first-year" players who, as free agents, had failed to secure a position on a regular player roster. Squad members would play in practice games and sometimes in regular games as substitutes for injured players. Resolution G-2 provided that the club owners would pay all squad members the same weekly salary.

The next month, April, the NFL presented the developmental squad plan to the Players Association. The NFL proposed a squad player salary of $1,000 per week. The Players Association disagreed. It insisted that the club owners give developmental squad players benefits and protections similar to those provided regular players, and that they leave individual squad members free to negotiate their own salaries.

Two months later, in June, negotiations on the issue of developmental squad salaries reached an impasse. The NFL then unilaterally implemented the developmental squad program by distributing to the clubs a uniform contract that embodied the terms of Resolution G-2 and the $1,000 proposed weekly salary. The League advised club owners that paying developmental squad players more or less than $1,000 per week would result in disciplinary action, including the loss of draft choices.

In May 1990, 235 developmental squad players brought this antitrust suit against the League and its member clubs. The players claimed that their employers' agreement to pay them a $1,000 weekly salary violated the Sherman Act. See *15 U.S.C. §1* (forbidding agreements in restraint of trade). The Federal District Court denied the employers' claim of exemption from the antitrust laws; it permitted the case to reach the jury; and it subsequently entered judgment on a jury treble-damages award that exceeded $30 million. The NFL and its member clubs appealed.

The Court of Appeals (by a split 2-to-1 vote) reversed. The majority interpreted the labor laws as "waiv[ing] antitrust liability for restraints on competition imposed through the collective-bargaining process, so long as such restraints operate primarily in a labor market characterized by collective bargaining." *50 F.3d, 1041, 1056 (C.A.D.C. 1995)*. The court held, consequently, that the club owners were immune from antitrust liability. We granted certiorari to review that determination. Although we do not interpret the exemption as broadly as did the Appeals Court, we nonetheless find the exemption applicable, and we affirm that court's immunity conclusion.

II

The immunity before us rests upon what this Court has called the "nonstatutory" labor exemption from the antitrust laws. The Court has implied this exemption from federal labor statutes, which set forth a national labor policy favoring free and private collective bargaining, which require good-faith bargaining over wages, hours, and working conditions, and which delegate related rulemaking and interpretive authority to the National Labor Relations Board (Board). . . .

B

The Government argues that the exemption should terminate at the point of impasse. After impasse, it says, "employers no longer have a duty under the labor laws to maintain the status quo," and "are free as a matter of labor law to negotiate individual arrangements on an interim basis with the union."

Employers, however, are not completely free at impasse to act independently. The multiemployer bargaining unit ordinarily remains intact; individual employers cannot withdraw. The duty to bargain survives; employers must stand ready to resume collective bargaining. And individual employers can negotiate individual interim agreements with the union only insofar as those agreements are consistent with "the duty to abide by the results of group bargaining." Regardless, the absence of a legal "duty" to act jointly is not determinative. This Court has implied antitrust immunities that extend beyond statutorily *required* joint action to joint action that a statute "expressly or impliedly allows or assumes must also be immune."

More importantly, the simple "impasse" line would not solve the basic problem we have described above. Labor law permits employers, after impasse, to engage in considerable joint behavior, including joint lockouts and replacement hiring. Indeed, as a general matter, labor law often limits employers to four options at impasse: (1) maintain the status quo, (2) implement their last offer, (3) lock out their workers (and either shut down or hire temporary replacements), or (4) negotiate separate interim agreements with the union. What is to happen if the parties cannot reach an interim agreement? The other alternatives are limited. Uniform employer conduct is likely. Uniformity—at least when accompanied by discussion of the matter—invites antitrust attack. And such attack would ask antitrust courts to decide the lawfulness of activities intimately related to the bargaining process.

The problem is aggravated by the fact that "impasse" is often temporary, it may differ from bargaining only in degree, it may be manipulated by the parties for bargaining purposes, and it may occur several times during the course of a single labor dispute, since the bargaining process is not over when the first impasse is reached. How are employers to discuss future bargaining positions during a temporary impasse? Consider, too, the adverse consequences that flow from failing to guess how an *antitrust* court would later draw the impasse line. Employers who erroneously concluded that impasse had *not* been reached would risk antitrust liability were they collectively to maintain the status quo, while employers who erroneously concluded that impasse *had* occurred would risk unfair labor practice charges for prematurely suspending multiemployer negotiations. . . .

For these reasons, we hold that the implicit ("nonstatutory") antitrust exemption applies to the employer conduct at issue here. That conduct took place during and immediately after a collective-bargaining negotiation. It grew out of, and was directly related to, the lawful operation of the bargaining process. It involved a matter that the parties were required to negotiate collectively. And it concerned only the parties to the collective-bargaining relationship. . . .

The judgment of the Court of Appeals is affirmed.

It is so ordered. . . .

———————

Powell held that the nonstatutory labor exemption survived the expiration of the collective bargaining agreement and impasse. The NFL was thus effectively protected from antitrust liability. After *Powell*, the National Football League Players Association decertified as the union in order to allow the players to seek redress through individual antitrust lawsuits free from the constraints of the nonstatutory labor exemption. On April 10, 1990, Freeman McNeil and seven others sued alleging that "Plan B" free agency violated the antitrust laws under a rule of reason analysis. *McNeil v. NFL*, 790 F. Supp. 871 (D. Minn. 1992). Plan B was implemented on February 1, 1989, and allowed clubs to protect 37 players. These players were allowed to move to other clubs, conditioned on traditional compensation procedures. All other players were "unrestricted." In June 1989, the NFL established "Developmental Squads," comprised of six rookie players who practiced with the team but played in games only in the event of injury to other players; each player was paid $1,000 per week. On May 9, 1990, Antony Brown and 234 Developmental Squad players challenged this scheme as violative of antitrust law. See *Brown v. Pro Football, Inc.*, 518 U.S. 231 (1996). On September 21, 1992, Reggie White and four others filed a class action suit challenging the NFL's right of first refusal/compensation rules, Plan B, the college draft, NFL player's contract, and preseason pay rules. A global settlement was reached in *White v. NFL*, 822 F. Supp. 1389 (D. Minn. 1993), the terms of which were adopted as part of the 1993.

Then, in 1996, the U.S. Supreme Court in *Brown* held that the nonstatutory labor exemption compelled unions to rely on labor law, not antitrust law, to resolve bargaining disputes after the expiration of the agreement and after impasse. This allows the unions the option of decertification as the only route in which antitrust can be used as a weapon in disputes with management. *See* Goplerud, *Collective Bargaining in the National Football League: A Historical and Comparative Analysis*, 4 Vill. Sports & Ent. L.J. 13 (1997).

QUESTIONS AND DISCUSSION

1. In *Powell*, the court held that the nonstatutory labor exemption continues after the expiration of the CBAs and continues even after the parties have reached impasse. The exemption also continues even if the policies in question, the "free-agent" and draft procedures, are actively loathed and vilified by the union.
2. Justice Marshall dissented in *Flood v. Kuhn*, 407 U.S. 258, 293 (1972) by introducing the nonstatutory labor exemption to sports:

   > Lurking in the background is a hurdle of recent vintage that petitioner still must overcome.
   >
   > In 1966, the Major League Players Association was formed. It is the collective-bargaining representative for all major league baseball players. Respondents argue that the reserve system is now part and parcel of the collective-bargaining agreement and that because it is a mandatory subject of bargaining, the federal labor statutes are applicable, not the federal antitrust laws. The lower courts did not rule on this agreement, having decided the case solely on the basis of the antitrust exemption.

This Court has faced the interrelationship between the antitrust laws and the labor laws before. The decisions make several things clear. First, "benefits to organized labor cannot be utilized as a cat's paw to pull employers' chestnuts out of the antitrust fires." Second, the very nature of a collective-bargaining agreement mandates that the parties be able to "restrain" trade to a greater degree than management could do unilaterally.

Finally, it is clear that some cases can be resolved only by examining the purposes and the competing interests of labor and antitrust statutes and by striking a balance. . . . In this case, petitioner Flood urges that the reserve system works to the detriment of labor. . . .

There is a surface appeal to respondents' argument that petitioner's sole remedy lies in filing a claim with the National Labor Relations Board, but this argument is premised on the notion that management and labor have agreed to accept the reserve clause. This notion is contradicted, in part, by the record in this case Petitioner suggests that the reserve system was thrust upon the players by the owners and that the recently formed players' union has not had time to modify or eradicate it. If this is true, the question arises as to whether there would then be any exemption from the antitrust laws in this case. Petitioner also suggests that there are limits to the antitrust violations to which labor and management can agree. These limits should also be explored. . . .

3. The Curt Flood Act partially repealed baseball's antitrust exemption. The repealing of the exemption, however, specifically does not apply to minor leagues and minor league reserve clauses; the "Professional Baseball Agreement" (the CBA); franchise relocation; club ownership rules; ownership transfer; the relationship between commissioner and owners; baseball marketing; the Sports Broadcasting Act of 1961, 15 U.S.C. §§1291 *et seq.*; the relationship with umpires; and "persons not in the business of organized professional Major League Baseball." Also, "[n]othing [here]. . . . affect[s] the application . . . of the nonstatutory labor exemption. . . ."

See also Bautista, *Congress Says, "Yooou're Out!!!" to the Antitrust Exemption of Professional Baseball: A Discussion of the Current State of Player-Owner Collective Bargaining and the Impact of the Curt Flood Act of 1998*, 15 Ohio St. J. Disp. Resol. 445 (2000); Criswell, *Repeal of Baseball's Longstanding Antitrust Exemption: Did Congress Strike Out Again?* 19 N. Ill. U.L. Rev. 545 (1999); Dyer, *The Curt Flood Act of 1998: After 76 Years Congress Lifts Baseball's Exemption on Labor Relations But Leaves Franchise Relocation Up to the Courts*, 3 T.M. Cooley J. Prac. & Clinical L. 247 (2000); Hamilton, *Congress in Relief: The Economic Importance of Revoking Baseball's Antitrust Exemption*, 38 Santa Clara L. Rev. 1223 (1998); Maculuso, *Bang the Gavel Slowly: A Call for Judicial Activism Following the Curt Flood Act*, 9 B.U. Pub. Int. L.J. 463 (2000); Sullivan, A Derelict in the Stream of Law: Overruling Baseball's Antitrust Exemption, 48 Duke L.J. 1265 (1999); Symposium: The Curt Flood Act, 9 Marq. Sports L.J. 307 (1999). Jones, *A Congressional Swing and Miss: The Curt Flood Act, Player Control, and the National Pastime*, 33 Ga. L. Rev. 639 (1999).

4. *Federal Baseball Club of Baltimore v. National League of Professional Baseball Clubs*, 259 U.S. 200(1922), was based on a league rivalry settlement, with

one club from the new league, Baltimore, claiming that it did not receive satisfactory treatment in the settlement agreement. The result was described as "not one of Mr. Justice Holmes' happiest days." *Salerno v. American League of Professional Baseball Clubs*, 429 F.2d 1003, 1005 (2d Cir. 1970). Justice Holmes saw baseball games as purely state affairs with the travel incidental, the result being that baseball did not operate in interstate commerce and thus not subject to the Sherman Act. *Piazza*, as a district court case, of course, could not overrule *Flood*, which admitted that the exemption was "an inconsistency and illogic of long standing by Congress and not by the Court." *Flood*, 407 U.S. at 284. Congress did act in the Curt Flood Act of 1998 but revoked the exemption only for labor relations, and not for matters that involve franchise relocation, league expansion, or the minor leagues. Should Congress try another effort to more effectively revisit *Flood v. Kuhn*? *See* Champion, "*The Baseball Antitrust Exemption Revisited 21 Years After* Flood v. Kuhn," 19 T. Marshall L. Rev. 573 (1994); Jones, "A *Congressional Swing and Miss: The Curt Flood Act, Player Control, and the National Pastime*," 33 Ga. L. Rev. 639 (1999).

5. The Supreme Court in *Brown v. Pro. Football, Inc.*, effectively limited the reach and implications of the Curt Flood Act on the basis that now union members are essentially estopped from seeking antitrust relief due to the numbing effect of the nonstatutory exemption to the antitrust laws. What suggestions would you give to baseball's union management as regards future negotiation strategies?

D. LEAGUE VERSUS LEAGUE

In professional sports, when a new league attempts to compete with a more established league, one of the more typical responses is for the new league to sue the other league on antitrust grounds on the basis that there was an illegal monopolization of the relevant market. In *United States Football League v. National Football League*, the jury decided in favor of the USFL, finding that the NFL possessed monopoly power and was liable for damages to the USFL for willfully maintaining the power. However, the jury awarded only $1.00, which was trebled under the Clayton Act.

United States Football League v. National Football League

842 F. 2d 1335 (2d Cir. 1988)

Winter, Circuit Judge:

This appeal follows a highly publicized trial and jury verdict of $1.00. The plaintiff is a now-defunct professional football league that began play in this decade; the defendant is a football league founded nearly seventy years ago. The older of the two leagues, the National Football League, is a highly successful entertainment product. So many Americans watched NFL games between 1982 and 1986 that its twenty-eight teams shared $2.1 billion in rights fees from the three major television networks, and perhaps as much as $1 billion in gate receipts. The newer league, the United States Football League, began play in March 1983 with twelve teams and network and cable television contracts with the American Broadcasting Company ("ABC") and the Entertainment and Sports Programming Network ("ESPN"). After three seasons and losses in the neighborhood of $200 million, the USFL played its last game in July 1985. Meanwhile, in October, 1984, blaming its older competitor for its difficulties, the USFL instituted this litigation. Plans to play in the fall of 1986 were abandoned after the jury's verdict that is the principal subject of this appeal.

The USFL and certain of its member clubs brought this suit in the Southern District of New York against the NFL, its commissioner, Alvin R. "Pete" Rozelle, and twenty-seven of its twenty-eight member clubs. Seeking damages of $1.701 billion and appropriate injunctive relief, the USFL alleged that the NFL violated *Sections 1* and *2* of the Sherman Anti-Trust Act, *15 U.S.C. §§1* and *2 (1982)*, and the common law. Forty-eight days of trial before Judge Leisure produced a trial transcript of nearly 7100 pages and thousands of additional pages in exhibits.

After five days of deliberations, the jury found that the NFL had willfully acquired or maintained monopoly power in a market consisting of major-league professional football in the United States. The jury also found that the NFL's unlawful monopolization of professional football had injured the USFL. The jury awarded the USFL only $1.00 in damages, however, an amount that, even when trebled, was no consolation for the USFL. . . .

SUMMARY

We briefly summarize our principal rulings. The jury's finding of illegal monopolization of a market of major-league professional football was based upon evidence of NFL attempts to co-opt USFL owners, an NFL Supplemental Draft of USFL players, an NFL roster increase, and NFL conduct directed at particular USFL franchises. These activities, however, were hardly of sufficient impact to support a large damages verdict or to justify sweeping injunctive relief. For that reason, the USFL candidly admits that "at the heart of this case" are its claims that the NFL, by contracting with the three major networks and by acting coercively toward them, prevented the USFL from acquiring a network television contract indispensable to its survival. The jury expressly rejected the television claims.

The jury was clearly entitled by the evidence to find that the NFL's fall contracts with the three networks were not an anticompetitive barrier to the USFL's bidding against the NFL to acquire a network contract. Moreover, there was ample evidence that the USFL failed because it did not make the painstaking investment and patient efforts that bring credibility, stability and public recognition to a sports league. In particular, there was evidence that the USFL abandoned its original strategy of patiently building up fan loyalty and public recognition by playing in the spring. The original plan to contain costs by adherence to team salary guidelines was discarded from the start. Faced with rising costs and some new team owners impatient for immediate parity with the NFL, the idea of spring play itself was abandoned even though network and cable contracts were available. Plans for a fall season were therefore announced, thereby making 1985 spring play a "lame-duck" season. These actions were taken in the hope of forcing a merger with the NFL through the threat of competition and this litigation. The merger strategy, however, required that USFL franchises move out of large television markets and into likely NFL expansion cities. Because these moves further eroded fan loyalty and reduced the value of USFL games to television, the USFL thereby ended by its own hand any chance of a network contract.

Notwithstanding the jury's evident conclusions that the USFL's product was not appealing largely for reasons of the USFL's own doing and that the networks chose freely not to purchase it, the USFL asks us to grant sweeping injunctive relief that will reward its impatience and self-destructive conduct with a fall network contract. It thus seeks through court decree the success it failed to achieve among football fans. Absent a showing of some unlawful harm to competition, we cannot prevent a network from showing NFL games, in the hope that the network and fans will turn to the USFL. The Sherman Act does not outlaw an industry structure simply because it prevents competitors from achieving immediate parity. This is particularly so in the case of major-league professional football because Congress authorized a merger of the two leagues existing in 1966 and thus created the industry structure in question. . . .

CONCLUSION

For the foregoing reasons, we affirm the jury's verdict and the judgments entered thereon. We thus need not consider the NFL's conditional cross-appeal.

Affirmed.

QUESTIONS AND DISCUSSION

1. *USFL v. NFL*, 704 F. Supp. 474 (S.D.N.Y. 1989). Is the claim for attorney fees disingenuous?

    . . . The USFL makes the present application for attorney's fees.

    After trial, the jury found the NFL liable on the USFL's first claim of actual monopolization, concluding that the NFL had willfully acquired or maintained monopoly power in a relevant market consisting of major league professional football in the United States. The jury also found that the NFL's unlawful monopolization of a relevant market had caused injury to plaintiffs' business or property. Despite these findings, the jury chose to award only nominal damages of $1.00 as a result of the NFL's unlawful conduct. . . .

    The issues presented by this petition basically fall into three categories: 1) the adequacy of the documentation of the fees; 2) whether the USFL should receive attorney's fees at all; and 3) the proper amount of those fees. Additionally, the NFL contests the costs application of the USFL. . . .

    The NFL concedes, as it must, that a prevailing antitrust plaintiff is entitled to a mandatory award of attorney's fee under section 4 of the Clayton Act. The NFL makes the only real argument left to make, namely, that the USFL, despite the jury's finding on the monopolization claim, was not a "prevailing party." . . .

In sum, the jury's finding of injury and an antitrust violation precludes the NFL's arguments that the USFL was not a prevailing party under Section 4 of the Clayton Act. The award of counsel fees itself is therefore a non-issue. A reasonable fee award under the statute is mandatory. . . .

Consideration of the relevant factors in determination of a "reasonable" fee, however, at least partially supports the USFL's contention that the full amount requested is itself reasonable. It is not seriously disputed that the time and labor required, the novelty and difficulty of the issues, the skill required of counsel, comparison with customary fees, time limits imposed by circumstances, and experience, reputation and ability of counsel all point strongly to a maximum award. . . .

2. The most interesting cases occur when an upstart league attempts to compete with a more established league. This not only pertains to antitrust, but also to blacklisting, contract jumping, tortious interference with a business relationship, signing bonuses, and the like.

3. *USFL v. NFL* is infamous since although the jury found for the USFL it awarded only $1 (in antitrust, the damages are trebled, so the total award was $3). This case, of course, essentially ended the USFL. But the USFL's successful lawyers sued for attorneys fees and were awarded over $5.5 million ($5,515,290.81). Should the court have readjusted the original award to a figure that might synchronize more logically with the award of attorneys fees?

4. In *AFL v. NFL*, 323 F.2d 124 (4th Cir. 1963), the American Football League sued the older, more established National Football League on the basis that it monopolized all the best markets. The court held that the NFL did not have the power to monopolize the relevant market and that it did not attempt a conspiracy to monopolize the market. In short, the court in *AFL v. NFL* held that any NFL monopoly was a natural monopoly that does not violate antitrust laws unless the natural monopoly was misused to gain a competitive advantage. The NFL had previously acquired markets that the latecomer AFL thought desirable. The NFL was not required to surrender any, or all, of its advantageous sites to the second league simply to enable the latecomer to compete more effectively. But, one must acquire a natural monopoly by means which are neither exclusionary, unfair, nor predatory.

5. The Memphis Southmen was a team in the World Football League. This league opened in 1974 and closed midway through the 1975 season. The team then reorganized with players from two other WFL teams, renamed itself the Grizzlies, and applied for an NFL franchise. Their application was rejected, and they sued the NFL for antitrust violations. The court held that the NFL's refusal to add this new team to the league did not affect market competition because no other NFL teams were located near Memphis. *Mid-South Grizzlies v. NFL*, 720 F.2d 772 (3d Cir. 1983).

E. FRANCHISE RELOCATION AND ARENA FINANCING

From 1990 through 2000, 48 major league stadiums and arenas were constructed worth approximately $9 billion. Sports facility financing requires revenue streams to support multiple issues of debt whether the financing is public, private, or hybrid. There are many potential sources of income, which may include sale of naming rights, rental payments, and revenue from stadium operations such as concessions, novelties, parking, gate, luxury boxes suites, PSLs (permanent seat licenses), and advertising. Part of the financing cones from bond issues, which are commonly backed by public sources such as general obligation pledges, annual appropriations, and specific taxes. Creative financial packages are often arranged and include sales taxes, surcharge or ticket purchases, special lottery and gaming revenues, hotel taxes, tourist development taxes, rental car taxes, liquor and tobacco taxes, and airport departure taxes.

Los Angeles Memorial Coliseum Commission v. NFL involves antitrust litigation against a NFL rule that stipulated that three-quarters of all NFL teams must approve the relocation of a franchise into the home territory of another team. The rule was held to violate antitrust laws since the NFL was not a single entity and the rule was an unreasonable restraint of trade.

L.A. MEMORIAL COLISEUM COMMISSION V. NATIONAL FOOTBALL LEAGUE

726 F. 2d 1381 (9th Cir. 1983)

J. Blaine ANDERSON, Circuit Judge:

These appeals involve the hotly contested move by the Oakland Raiders, Ltd. professional football team from Oakland, California, to Los Angeles, California. We review only the liability portion of the bifurcated trial; the damage phase was concluded in May 1983 and is on a separate appeal. After a thorough review of the record and the law, we affirm.

I. FACTS

In 1978, the owner of the Los Angeles Rams, the late Carroll Rosenbloom, decided to locate his team in a new stadium, the "Big A," in Anaheim, California. That left the Los Angeles Coliseum without a major tenant. Officials of the Coliseum then began the search for a new National Football League occupant. They inquired of the League Commissioner, Pete Rozelle, whether an expansion franchise might be located there but were told that at the time it was not possible. They also negotiated with existing teams in the hope that one might leave its home and move to Los Angeles.

The L.A. Coliseum ran into a major obstacle in its attempts to convince a team to move. That obstacle was Rule 4.3 of Article IV of the NFL Constitution. In 1978, Rule 4.3 required unanimous approval of all the 28 teams of the League whenever a team (or in the parlance of the League, a "franchise") seeks to relocate in the home territory of another team. . . .

In this case, the L.A. Coliseum was still in the home territory of the rams.

The Coliseum viewed Rule 4.3 as an unlawful restraint of trade in violation of §1 of the Sherman Act, 15 U.S.C. §1, and brought this action in September of 1978. The district court concluded, however, that no present justiciable controversy existed because no NFL team had committed to moving to Los Angeles. 468 F. Supp. 154 (C.D. Cal. 1979).

The NFL nevertheless saw the Coliseum's suit as a sufficient threat to warrant amending Rule 4.3. In late 1978, the Executive Committee of the NFL, which is comprised of a voting members of each of the 28 teams, met and changed the rule to require only three-quarters approval by the members of the League for a move into another team's home territory.

Soon thereafter, A1 Davis, managing general partner of the Oakland Raiders franchise, stepped into view. His lease with the Oakland Coliseum had expired in 1978. He believed the facility needed substantial improvement and he was unable to persuade the Oakland officials to agree to his terms. He instead turned to the Los Angeles Coliseum.

Davis and the L.A. Coliseum officials began to discuss the possibility of relocating the Raiders to Los Angeles in 1979. In January, 1980, the L.A. Coliseum believed an agreement with Davis was imminent and reactivated its lawsuit against the NFL, seeking a preliminary injunction to enjoin the League from preventing the Raiders' move. The district court granted the injunction, 484 F. Supp. 1274 (1980), but this court reversed, finding that an adequate probability of ineparable injury had not been shown 634 F.2d 1197 (1980).

On March 1, 1980 Al Davis and the Coliseum signed a "memorandum of agreement" outlining the terms of the Raiders relocation in Los Angeles. At an NFL meeting on March 3, 1980, Davis announced his intentions. In response, the League brought a contract action in state court, obtaining an injunction preventing the move. In the meantime, the City of Oakland brought its much-publicized eminent domain action against the Raiders in its effort to keep the team in its original home. The NFL contract action was stayed pending the outcome of this litigation, but the eminent domain action is still being prosecuted in the California courts.

Over Davis objection that Rule 4.3 is illegal under the antitrust laws, the NFL teams voted on March 10, 1980, 22-0 against the move, with five teams abstaining. That vote did not meet the new Rule 4.3's requirement of three-quarters approval. . . .

II. SHERMAN ACT §1

The jury found that Rule 4.3 violates §1 of the Sherman Act, 15 U.S.C. §1. . . . The rule of reason requires the factfinder to decide whether under all the circumstances of the case the agreement imposes an unreasonable restraint on competition. . . .

A. Single Entity

The NFL contends the league structure is in essence a single entity, akin to a partnership or joint venture, precluding application of Sherman Act section 1 which prevents only contracts, combinations or conspiracies in restraint of trade. The Los Angeles Coliseum and Raiders reject this position and assert the League is composed of 28 separate legal entities which act independently. . . .

For the foregoing reasons, we affirm the district court's rejection of the NFL's single entity defense. Of course, the singular nature of the NFL will need to be accounted for in discussing the reasonableness of the restriction on team movement, but it is not enough to preclude §1 scrutiny. The NFL's related argument that Rule 4.3 is valid as a restraint ancillary to a joint venture agreement will be discussed in the rule of reason analysis that follows. Contrary to the NFL's apparent belief, the ancillary restraint doctrine is not independent of the rule of reason. . . .

1. Relevant Market

The NFL contends it is entitled to judgment because plaintiffs failed to prove an adverse impact on competition in a relevant market. The NFL's claim that it is entitled to judgment notwithstanding the verdict is governed by the same standards as a motion for directed verdict, discussed above. The court is not permitted to account for witness credibility, weigh the evidence or reach a different result it finds more reasonable as long as, viewing the evidence in a light most favorable to the nonmoving party, the jury's verdict is supported by substantial evidence. . . .

In the present case, the parties entered a stipulation regarding relevant market evidence because the time allowed for witnesses in the second trial was restricted by the trial court. The stipulation provided that no experts would be called to testify on the subject. Instead, the transcripts and exhibits used by the economic experts were deemed incorporated in the record and admitted in evidence at the retrial, allowing counsel to argue market issues as if the experts had testified before the jury. Our review shows, however, that neither the transcripts nor the exhibits were placed before the jury. We are surprised that in a trial of this magnitude these able attorneys would neglect such important evidence. Upon a careful review of the record, however, we find that testimony of others was sufficient to cover the subject where necessary, and to guide the jury's finding that Rule 4.3 is an unreasonable restraint of trade. . . .

We conclude with one additional observation. In the context of this case in particular, we believe that market evidence, while important, should not become an end in itself. Here the exceptional nature of the industry makes precise market definition especially difficult. To a large extent the market is determined by how one defines the entity: Is the NFL a single entity or partnership which creates a product that competes with other entertainment products for the consumer (e.g., television and fans) dollar? Or is it 28 individual entities which compete with one another both on and off the field for the support of the consumers of the more narrow football product? Of course, the NFL has attributes of both examples and a variety of evidence was presented on both views. In fact, because of the exceptional structure of the League, it was not necessary for the jury to accept absolutely either the NFL's or the plaintiff's market definitions. Instead, the critical question is whether the jury could have determined that Rule 4.3 reasonably served the NFL's interest in producing and promoting its product, i.e., competing in the entertainment market, or whether Rule 4.3 harmed competition among the 28 teams to such an extent that any benefits to the League as a whole were outweighed. As we find below, there was ample evidence for the jury to reach the latter conclusion. . . .

V. CONCLUSION

The NFL is an unique business organization to which it is difficult to apply antitrust rules which were developed in the context of arrangements between actual competitors. This does not mean that the trial court and jury were incapable of meeting the task, however. The lower court correctly applied and described the law. The reasonableness of a restraint is a "paradigm fact question," *Betaseed, Inc. v. U and I Inc.*, 681 F.2d 1203, 1228 (9th Cir. 1982), and our review of the record convinces us the jury had adequate evidence to answer that question.

We believe antitrust principles are sufficiently flexible to account for the NFL's structure. To the extent the NFL finds the law inadequate, it must look to Congress for relief.

The judgment finding the NFL liable to the Los Angeles Coliseum and the Raiders, and enjoining the NFL from preventing the Raiders from relocating in Los Angeles is Affirmed.

SPENCER WILLIAMS, District Judge, Sitting by Designation, [concurs] in part, [dissents] in part. . . .

In *Los Angeles Memorial Coliseum,* the court held that the NFL's rule on franchise relocation violated the antitrust laws. Essentially, the case allowed for the possibility of more team movement with an accompanying increase in the level of enticement, including building new stadiums and arenas, that non-NFL cities were now willing to engage in.

In *Seattle Totems Hockey Club, Inc. v. NHL,* the court held that the denial of a National Hockey League franchise to a minor league team did not rise to the level of an antitrust violation.

SEATTLE TOTEMS HOCKEY CLUB, INC. v. NATIONAL HOCKEY LEAGUE

783 F.2d 1347 (9th Cir. 1986)

CANBY, Circuit Judge:

This case arises out of the financial demise of plaintiff Seattle Totems, a hockey team of which plaintiffs Vincent H. D. Abbey and Eldred W. Barnes were principal officers, directors and shareholders. The Totems and Abbey and Barnes brought an antitrust action against the defendant National Hockey League (NHL) and some of its members. One member of that league is the Vancouver Canucks, owned by defendant Northwest Sports Enterprises, Inc. Northwest Sports counterclaimed, asserting certain breaches of contract by plaintiffs.

The district court dismissed plaintiffs' antitrust claims and directed a verdict granting part of defendants' counterclaim and denying the rest. We review both the dismissals and the directed verdict de novo, viewing the evidence in the light most favorable to the losing party. *Los Angeles Memorial Coliseum Com'n v. National Football League*, 726 F.2d 1381, 1387 (9th Cir.), *cert. denied*, 105 S. Ct. 397 (1984) (directed verdict). Because the antitrust and contract issues were tried separately, we review them separately here.

PART I. ANTITRUST

The Seattle Totems were a minor league hockey team that played in the Western Hockey League (WHL). They suffered financial difficulties, and in 1971, the WHL terminated their franchise. In 1972, Northwest Sports purchased 55.56% of the Totems' stock. Northwest Sports also agreed to assume the Totems' liabilities and to advance funds for their operations. Abbey and Barnes, who owned a 44.44% interest in the Totems, continued as shareholders and agreed to guarantee repayment of their pro rata share of Northwest Sports' advances to the Totems. The Totems regained their WHL franchise.

In 1971, the World Hockey Association (WHA), which is not a party to this action, was formed as a major professional hockey league. The WHA competed with the established major league, defendant NHL, for players, fans, and revenues.

With the emergence of a second major league, WHL owners concluded that WHL teams needed major league status to survive. In June 1972, the NHL and the WHL entered into an agreement called the "White Paper." The White Paper provided that, if the NHL expanded after the 1974-75 season, it would offer to WHL members at least one-half of any expansion franchises in four WHL cities. In June 1974, the NHL voted to award a conditional franchise to Abbey for Seattle to commence play in the 1976-77 season. The conditional franchise for Seattle expired because Abbey did not fulfill the conditions. The NHL did not award a conditional or final franchise for Seattle to anyone else. The Totems did not seek or receive a WHA franchise.

On appeal, the Totems challenge the district court's dismissal of their antitrust claims that the alleged NHL monopoly wrongfully denied Totems an NHL franchise, denied them the opportunity to join the WHA, and destroyed the WHL. We affirm.

I. The Seattle NHL Franchise

The district court dismissed the Totems' claim for damages for their failure to receive an NHL franchise. The district court found that "any denial of an NHL franchise to plaintiffs . . . was procompetitive, rather than anti competitive in its effect and hence not violative of the anti-trust laws."

The Totems argue that they were injured by an NHL monopoly that allegedly violated the antitrust laws. They contend that the NHL and its member teams have monopolized professional hockey in North America. The Totems cite a number of agreements and practices through which the NHL achieved the alleged monopoly. The Totems claim that the NHL monopoly was "exercised to exclude competition and to obtain total control over all major league professional hockey franchises, including the purchase prices paid therefor [sic]."

The offense of monopolization (15 U.S.C. §2) consists of the willful acquisition or maintenance of monopoly power in the relevant market and the existence of actual injury to competition in that market. "To establish anticompetitive market effect, the plaintiff must prove that the defendant's actions caused a decrease in competition in the relevant market." A plaintiff has the burden to plead and prove that the defendant's actions harmed competition, not that the actions harmed plaintiff in its capacity as a competitor.

The Totems were not competing with the NHL; they were seeking to join it. They were granted a conditional NHL franchise but failed to fulfill the conditions precedent to obtaining a final franchise. The WHA was competing as a major professional hockey league at that time. Without an NHL franchise Seattle constituted a potential WHA site, and the denial, if any, of an NHL franchise under these circumstances did not injure competition. *See Mid-South Grizzlies v. National Football League,* 720 F.2d 772 (3d Cir. 1983), *cert. denied,* 467 U.S. 1215, (1984). There is no contention or showing that the denial was to protect any other major league team in the Seattle market; there was none. *See id.* at 787; *Los Angeles Memorial Coliseum Com'n,* 726 F.2d 1381 (antitrust violation to restrict entry of one NFL team into another team's market).

The Totems argue that there is more here than the mere denial of a sports franchise. They argue that there was a grand scheme on the part of the NHL to destroy the WHA by promising franchises to WHL teams so that those teams would not join the WHA. "Once peace had been made between the NHL and WHA, however, the NHL moved to avoid its responsibilities" under its White Paper agreement with the WHL. One of those alleged "moves" was apparently to deny Seattle a franchise. This argument misses the point. The Totems' allegations of wrongful conduct by the NHL do not establish that competition in the relevant market was injured by those acts. Consequently, the Totems have failed to meet their burden of proof on this issue.

II. Claim of Unlawful NHL Conduct toward the WHA

The district court dismissed the Totems' claim that they were denied an opportunity to join the WHA "for lack of evidence in the record as to the value of a Seattle franchise in that league." "An antitrust plaintiff who is excluded from the relevant market by anticompetitive activity is entitled to recover his lost profits." Alternatively, a plaintiff who is excluded from the relevant market may seek to recover the value of his business. A defendant, whose illegal conduct excluded others from the relevant market, should not benefit because its actions make it more difficult for the plaintiff to establish the amount of its injury. There must, however, be sufficient evidence from which a jury could determine the amount of damages, and the plaintiff bears the burden of anticipating a hypothetical free market in establishing the amount of his injury. The trier of fact is allowed to act on probative and inferential proof in determining those damages, although the award may be an approximation.

The Totems allege that the NHL's anticompetitive activities caused the Totems to be unable to secure a WHA franchise. The district court found that the measure of the Totems' damages on this claim was the value of a WHA franchise in Seattle at the time it was foreclosed from joining the WHA, not the value of an NHL franchise at that time. The Totems, therefore, had the burden of establishing the value of a Seattle WHA team in a hypothetical economic free market. The Totems presented no evidence to establish that value. Consequently, there was not sufficient evidence from which a jury could have determined damages, and the trial judge properly dismissed this claim.

II. Destruction of WHL

The district court dismissed the Totems' claim that they were denied the opportunity to form a new major hockey league with other WHL teams. The court found a lack of evidence in the record to sustain that claim. Specifically, the court ruled that "[t]o recover on this claim plaintiffs must prove the intention and preparedness of the WHL clubs to form such a league." The court held that there was no evidence in the record to sustain an affirmative finding upon either element, and that "[t]here is in fact much evidence to the contrary." In addition, the Totems presented no evidence of the value of a Seattle franchise in such a league.

The WHL teams opted not to join the WHA or to form an independent major hockey league. Instead, they entered into the White Paper agreement with the NHL for purposes of obtaining NHL franchises. The record, therefore, supports the district judge's ruling.

The district judge ruled in a separate order, on the Totems' claim that the NHL's allegedly monopolistic activities caused the destruction of the WHL. The judge found that the assertion of this claim was untimely and that it would be prejudicial to defendants to allow it to be asserted. In addition, the district judge found that the claim was not supported by testimony.

We have reviewed the record and conclude that the district judge did not abuse his discretion by this separate ruling. In addition, the lack of evidence as to the value of a Seattle WHL franchise (whether minor or major league) independent of the NHL in a hypothetical economic free market deprived the jury of sufficient information from which to determine damages for such a claim.

PART II. Northwest Sports' Counterclaim

In 1972, Northwest Sports acquired a 55.56% interest in the Totems. Abbey and Barnes owned a 44.44% interest in the Totems. Abbey, Barnes and Northwest Sports entered into an agreement, dated April 7, 1972 (the 1972 Agreement). This contract provided that Northwest Sports would advance funds to enable the Totems to operate, that Abbey and Barnes would guarantee to Northwest Sports repayment of 44.44% of all moneys advanced by Northwest Sports to the Totems, and that if a National Hockey League (NHL) franchise were granted to the Totems for Seattle, Abbey and Barnes would purchase Northwest Sports' 55.56% interest in the Totems. Abbey and Barnes subsequently agreed to pay to Northwest Sports interest on the repayable 44.44% share of the advances.

On June 12, 1974, the NHL announced the award of a "conditional" franchise to Abbey, as representative of Seattle, to commence play in the 1976-77 season. The award of the franchise was subject to several conditions, including the requirements that a long-term arena lease be obtained and that certain franchise payments be made.

Prior to the NHL's announcement of the award of a conditional franchise to Seattle, Abbey, Barnes and Northwest Sports negotiated the 1974 Agreement. The 1974 Agreement set out the terms for the repurchase of Northwest Sports' shares in the Totems by Abbey and Barnes and provided that Abbey and Barnes would repay the advances made by Northwest Sports to the Totems. A condition precedent to the 1974 Agreement was that the NHL announce, before June 30, 1974, the award of a franchise to Seattle.

Northwest Sports counterclaimed against Abbey and Barnes for breach of the 1972 and the 1974 agreements. The district court rejected a defense theory raised by Abbey and Barnes that Northwest Sports had made it impossible for them to perform the agreements. The district court found that Abbey and Barnes had breached the 1972 Agreement. The court accordingly directed a partial verdict in favor of Northwest Sports. The district court ruled that Northwest Sports was not entitled to reimbursement for player development costs under the 1972 Agreement. With regard to the 1974 Agreement, the district court entered a directed verdict in favor of Abbey and Barnes finding that a condition precedent to that agreement had not been fulfilled. Abbey and Barnes appeal, and Northwest Sports cross-appeals. We affirm the rejection of the contractual interference defense appealed by Abbey and Barnes, and reverse and remand with regard to both issues raised by Northwest Sports on its cross-appeal.

I. "Impossible Performance" Defense

In granting a partial directed verdict for Northwest Sports on its claims under the 1972 Agreement, the district court rejected the contention of Abbey and Barnes that the jury should decide whether they were relieved of their repayment obligation because Northwest Sports had rendered their performance impossible by its failure to provide an accounting and by its refusal to provide to Abbey the original Seattle Totems' stock certificates.

One party to a contract who prevents another party from performing his promise cannot recover for the nonperformance of that promise. *Hydraulic Supply Mfg. Co. v. Mardesich,* 57 Wash. 2d 104, 352 P.2d 1023, 1024 (1960) (vessel left harbor before refrigerator plant had been reassembled, thereby preventing company from completing testing of its work; shipowners could not recover from company for damages allegedly resulting from improper repair). The purpose of this rule is to prevent a party from benefiting by its wrongful acts. *Wolk v. Bonthius,* 13 Wash. 2d 217, 124 P.2d 553, 554 (1942).

Abbey and Barnes rely on *United States ex rel Acme Granite & Tile Co. v. F. D. Rich Co.,* 437 F.2d 549, 553 (9th Cir. 1970), *cert. denied,* 404 U.S. 823, (1971). That case involved an action by a subcontractor (Acme) for damages against the prime contractor (F. D. Rich Co.) on an army housing project. Acme had refused to proceed with plastering on the project after the Army inspector revoked his approval of some of the houses because of defective framing by another subcontractor. Corrective measures were taken by the framing contractor, but their quality was in dispute. An impasse developed, and Rich declared Acme in default and employed another contractor to finish the work. 437 F.2d at 551. The court concluded that the district court's entry of a judgment notwithstanding the verdict was improper because "there was a question of fact whether Rich, by its failure to have B & G correct the defective framing job, prevented Acme from going ahead with its obligations under the contract." 437 F.2d at 553.

The situation here is not parallel to that in *Acme Granite*. The 1972 Agreement does not provide that Northwest Sports is required to give an accounting to Abbey and Barnes before the repayment obligation of Abbey and Barnes arises. That obligation arose with each advance made by Northwest Sports to the Totems. Abbey and Barnes do not contend that Northwest Sports failed to make the contracted-for advances to the Totems. While Abbey and Barnes may have hoped to receive an NHL franchise, the fact that they did not, whether or not that failure was due to any wrongful act of Northwest Sports, does not excuse them of their obligation under the 1972 Agreement to repay Northwest Sports 44.44% of moneys advanced or paid on behalf of the Totems. That obligation was not conditioned upon obtaining an NHL franchise.

Northwest Sports, therefore, did not interfere with the ability of Abbey and Barnes to perform, nor did Northwest Sports make performance physically impossible. *See Acme Granite*, 437 F.2d at 553; *Hydraulic Supply Mfg. Co.*, 352 P.2d at 1024. The district court did not err in rejecting the impossible performance defense and directing a verdict in favor of Northwest Sports on Abbey and Barnes' breach of their repayment obligation under the 1972 contract. We affirm.

II. "All Moneys Advanced"

The 1972 Agreement provides that Abbey and Barnes agreed to pay Northwest Sports 44.44% of "all moneys advanced by Northwest to Totems or paid by Northwest on behalf of Totems. . . ." The trial judge ruled, as a matter of law, that Northwest Sports was entitled to recover from Abbey and Barnes 44.44% of the advances made by Northwest to the Totems, "other than those advances which were made for player development." The judge reasoned that advances for player development were made primarily for the benefit of Northwest Sports' Vancouver hockey club not for the Totems. The judge based his conclusion in part on the fact that, for Canadian tax purposes, the Vancouver club and Northwest Sports treated player development costs as expenses incurred by the Vancouver club and Northwest Sports, not as costs of the Totems for which Northwest Sports was making advances.

Northwest Sports argues that the contractual term "all moneys advanced" is not ambiguous and that the trial court erred in admitting extrinsic evidence of Northwest Sports' tax treatment of the advances. Abbey and Barnes point to the compound nature of the provision which could be rewritten as "all moneys advanced by Northwest to Totems" and "all moneys paid by Northwest on behalf of Totems." Abbey and Barnes contend that the term "advanced" referred to sums expended by Northwest Sports to enable the Totems to pay several of its outstanding debts and liabilities that existed prior to or at the time Northwest Sports acquired its shares of the Totems stock, whether Northwest made the advances before or after the date of the 1972 Agreement. On the other hand, "all moneys paid on behalf of Totems" must, Abbey and Barnes argue, be read to exclude sums paid for player development costs because those sums were "paid to the Totems for the purpose of training players for the NHL, and thus Vancouver's benefit." . . .

The issue here is whether player development costs paid by Northwest Sports fall within the scope of the reimbursement provision. In order to determine whether those payments were made "on behalf of" the Totems, the court properly admitted extrinsic evidence to determine the purpose of those payments, but not to expand, vary or contradict the terms of the contract. *See Morgan v. Stokely-Van Camp, Inc.*, 34 Wash. App. 801, 663 P.2d 1384, 1388 (1983). Northwest Sports contends that the trial court incorrectly evaluated that evidence in determining that amounts paid by Northwest Sports for player development costs did not constitute recoverable advances. We agree.

The trial court characterized all sums paid by Northwest Sports after the commencement of the 1972-73 season as player development costs. Prior to that point, Northwest Sports had advanced $595,000. During and after the 1972-73 season Northwest Sports advanced over a million dollars to the Seattle Totems. The Totems then billed Northwest Sports for that amount as "cost of developing players" for the Vancouver Hockey Club, Ltd. These costs included salary, FICA, workman's compensation and bonuses.

Northwest Sports acknowledges that it intended to use the Totems as Vancouver's development club to train young hockey players before they entered major league competition, replacing its development club in Rochester, New York. Northwest Sports' tax treatment of the advances as player development costs is also probative on the issue of whether these payments were on behalf of the Totems. Nevertheless, the "paid on behalf of Totems" provision would be rendered meaningless if we construe it to exclude all advances by Northwest Sports to the Totems for operating expenses incurred by the Totems after Northwest Sports' acquisition of its majority interest.

The payments by Northwest Sports benefited the Totems directly, because they enabled the club to operate. Vancouver benefited also, because it was able to use the Seattle club to develop future major league players. We, therefore, conclude that the parties intended that Northwest Sports be reimbursed by Abbey and Barnes for all sums paid to the Totems to enable the club to continue in existence whether or not those sums also constituted payments for player development expenses of Northwest Sports. We reverse the partial directed verdict entered in favor of Abbey and Barnes and remand to the district court for entry of judgment in accordance with this opinion on Northwest Sports' breach of contract claim arising out of the 1972 Agreement.

III. Condition Precedent — 1974 Agreement

Northwest Sports contends that the district court erred in ruling, as a matter of law, that the condition precedent in the 1974 Agreement had not been met and by directing judgment for Abbey and Barnes on Northwest Sports' breach of contract claim arising out of the 1974 Agreement. . . .

On June 12, 1974, the NHL announced that it would grant a franchise to the Abbey group, subject to the fulfillment of several conditions. The district court found that the announcement of the grant of a conditional franchise to the Abbey group on behalf of Seattle did not satisfy the condition precedent because "the 1974 agreement was conditioned upon the announcement of the granting of an *actual* NHL franchise, which never occurred." (Emphasis added.)

The ambiguity in the 1974 contract arises from the parties' failure to specify whether they meant the announcement of a conditional franchise *or* the announcement of an actual or final franchise *or* the announcement of any kind of franchise, conditional or final. The record shows that Northwest Sports owned one NHL team and that the 1972 Agreement provided for the buyback of Totems' stock for Northwest Sports if the Totems were awarded an NHL franchise. The 1974 Agreement, which provided the terms of the buyback, conditioned its effectiveness on the announcement of "a" franchise before a specified date.

It is significant that the 1974 Agreement required only an announcement, not the actual award of a franchise. In addition, it was apparently not unusual for the NHL to condition franchise awards upon the receipt of franchise payments and assurance of a facility. The parties may not have even contemplated that, once the long-awaited Seattle NHL franchise was granted, Abbey and Barnes would be unable to obtain the necessary financial backing and that a conditional franchise would not mature to an actual franchise.

We conclude that the parties intended the 1974 Agreement to be effective upon the announcement that Seattle would get a franchise, even if that announcement was conditioned on the securing of a facility and the making of franchise payments. Had Abbey and Barnes complied with those conditions, and the 1974 agreement, they would have been full owners of the Totems at the time a franchise was entered into. The district court erred by interpreting the condition precedent in the 1974 Agreement to require the announcement by the NHL of the grant of an "actual" franchise to Seattle. We reverse the district court's dismissal of Northwest Sports' counterclaim for breach of the 1974 Agreement and remand.

Affirmed as to appeal; reversed and remanded as to cross appeal.

In short, plaintiff's attempt to obtain an expansion franchise in *Seattle Totems Hockey Club, Inc. v. NHL* was rejected.

In *St. Louis Convention & Visitors Commission v. NFL,* plaintiffs failed in their attempt to argue that the league's relocation rule was the reason behind a lack of franchises showing an interest in relocating to St. Louis.

St. Louis Convention & Visitors Commission v. National Football League

154 F.3d 851 (8th Cir. 1998)

MURPHY, Circuit Judge.

After St. Louis lost its professional football team to Phoenix in 1988, extensive efforts began to obtain another team and resulted in the successful relocation of the Los Angeles Rams in 1995. Many millions of dollars were spent in order to accomplish the relocation, and the St. Louis Convention and

Visitors Center (CVC) sued the National Football League and twenty four of its member teams (collectively the NFL) alleging that these expenditures were made necessary by actions of the NFL in violation of antitrust and tort law. The case was tried before a jury for over four weeks before it ended in a judgment in favor of the NFL. CVC appeals the dismissal of its claim for Sherman Act conspiracy and tortious interference with contract. The NFL cross appeals the refusal of the district court to rule that the league and the member teams do not amount to a single entity for antitrust purposes. We affirm the judgment.

I

A

The move of the St. Louis Cardinals football team to Phoenix in 1988 caused the Missouri state legislature, the city of St. Louis and the surrounding county to undertake to find a replacement by the beginning of the 1995 season. The legislature assigned the effort to procure a team to CVC, a body previously created by the Missouri legislature and empowered to promote the convention and tourism business in St. Louis. The initial goal was to obtain one of the two NFL expansion franchises to be established in 1993. In order to attract a team the city resolved to build a convention center in downtown St. Louis called America's Center which would include a new football stadium. The football stadium was called the Trans World Dome, and its $258 million cost was paid from state and local government funds. The stadium lease was assigned to CVC which became its manager and initially subleased the right to present football in the dome to private parties.

Problems associated with control over the lease and the potential ownership group caused St. Louis to be passed over in the NFL's expansion voting. The new franchises were awarded to Jacksonville, Florida and Charlotte, North Carolina. This forced the St. Louis football enthusiasts to adopt another strategy, and they turned their attention toward attracting an existing team. They founded a civic organization called FANS, Inc. (Football at the New Stadium), to assist their efforts. FANS, acting on behalf of CVC, then approached the Los Angeles Rams and began to negotiate a deal for the team to move to St. Louis. As a result a written agreement was eventually signed by CVC and the Rams.

The NFL League Constitution and Bylaws require a favorable vote by three fourths of the team owners to permit relocation, and the proposal for the Rams to move was initially voted down by the owners. It was later approved after the Rams agreed to pay the NFL a $29 million relocation fee. CVC eventually agreed with the Rams to pay $20 million of this fee, despite a clause in their contract allowing CVC to cancel if the fee were to exceed $7.5 million.

The Rams began playing in St. Louis in 1995, and in that year CVC was unable to make some of the payments owed to the team. CVC then brought this suit against the league and twenty four of its member teams. It also made an agreement with the Rams that they would receive half of any recovery obtained in the case in return for forgiveness of the money CVC owed them. The theory CVC presented at trial was that the league's relocation rules and the way they had been applied had created an atmosphere in which teams were unwilling to relocate. It contended that this anti-relocation atmosphere had discouraged interested teams from bidding on the St. Louis lease. The result was a one buyer market which forced the CVC to give more favorable lease terms than it would have in a competitive market.

B

The league was formed in 1966 by a union of the American Football League and the National Football League, and it functions as the governing body of a joint venture of thirty professional Football teams producing "NFL football." The teams are independently owned and managed by different business interests. The league is organized through the League Constitution and Bylaws, an agreement among team members that sets out rules for league management of matters such as game rules, game schedules, team ownership, and location of teams. Most decisions affecting the league are made by vote of team representatives at NFL meetings. When NFL members decided to create two new team franchises for 1993, representatives from various cities made presentations to team owners in order to win a franchise.

St. Louis political leaders and business people were among those who made presentations to the league, and they emphasized the benefits an NFL team could expect from the stadium lease and the city. But there were problems with the St. Louis application for a team. At the time of the expansion decisions the exclusive right to use the Trans World Dome for professional football games was held by St. Louis NFL, Inc., which was controlled by two St. Louis businessmen, Jerry Clinton who owned one third and Jim Orthwein who owned the remaining two thirds. The fact that rights to lease the stadium for football were held by individuals who were unrelated to CVC caused the owners to pass over St. Louis as the site of an expansion team.

CVC's next option was to arrange for an existing team to leave its home city and relocate to St. Louis. Community members formed the civic organization FANS, Inc. in January of 1994, headed by former Senator Thomas Eagleton, to accomplish the task which they were increasingly anxious to complete. Around this time Congressman Richard Gephardt alerted FANS that the Los Angeles Rams were considering relocating from their stadium in Anaheim, California. He had seen a newspaper report that the Rams were discussing a possible move to Baltimore, Maryland. Congressman Gephardt concluded that since Baltimore had been one of St. Louis' main competitors during the expansion process, the city should follow Baltimore's lead and approach the Rams. FANS then contacted John Shaw, the Rams president, and began negotiations on a relocation agreement and stadium lease. During this period, St. Louis was competing with Hartford and Anaheim in addition to Baltimore.

FANS made an initial presentation to the Rams, but talks ended because of problems with Clinton and Orthwein having control over the lease and because FANS had leaked information about the negotiations to the press, including the Rams' list of features it desired in a new stadium (the "wish list"). Discussions resumed only after CVC gained control over the lease, and the Rams told CVC that they would discontinue any business dealings if the CVC approached any other team about moving to St. Louis. CVC never contacted any other team to solicit a bid on the lease. CVC considered it the better course to focus on only one team, and it believed its presentation during the expansion process should have been sufficient to stimulate the interest of other teams.

The Rams and CVC eventually agreed on a lease. The Rams agreed to pay to CVC $25,000 rent per game, plus half of the game day expenses. In return the Rams would receive all of the ticket revenue from Rams games, 75% of the first $6 million in advertising revenue and 90% of the remainder, 100% of the profit from the concessions at Rams games and a portion of the concessions profit from other events. Rams president John Shaw estimated the lease would produce approximately $40 million per season in revenue for the Rams. CVC agreed to a number of other obligations, including promises to pay $28 million to fulfill bond obligations which the Rams owed on Anaheim Stadium, to build a $9.9 million training facility for the team, and to pay the team's moving costs. Once the Rams and CVC reached their agreement, the Rams presented their relocation application to the league owners for approval in March, 1995.

C

Relocation decisions by the NFL come under Article 4.3 of the league constitution which provides that "[n]o member club shall have the right to transfer its franchise or playing site to a different city, either within or outside its home territory, without prior approval by the affirmative vote of three-fourths of the existing member clubs of the league." While not expressed in the governing documents, the league claims the right to assess a relocation fee on any team seeking to move. At the time CVC was dealing with the Rams, the NFL had levied one previous relocation fee; the Cardinals had been assessed $7.5 million for their move to Phoenix.

After a successful antitrust challenge to an application of Article 4.3 to the relocation of the Oakland Raiders to Los Angeles, *see Los Angeles Memorial Coliseum Comm'n v. NFL*, 726 F.2d 1381 (9th Cir. 1984) (*Raiders I*), the NFL commissioner had issued procedures for obtaining league approval of any proposed relocation and nine non exclusive factors (the guidelines) that team owners should consider in deciding how to vote on a move. No guidelines have been promulgated on the imposition or computation of a relocation fee. Under the rules in effect at the time of the Rams move, a NFL team which wanted to move would negotiate a lease and relocation agreement with its new landlord and then apply to the league for permission to relocate. Only the moving team participated in the NFL application process; the new landlord had no direct involvement.

Owners voted down the initial application by the Rams because of disagreements between the league and the team on several of the relocation terms, including payment of a relocation fee, sharing of revenues from the sale of "personal seat licenses" (options to purchase tickets), and possible indemnification of the league for television payments it might owe as a consequence of the move. After the initial league vote, and in anticipation of the assessment of a relocation fee, CVC agreed with the Rams it would pay up to $7.5 million of any fee. Either party had the right to void the agreement should the fee exceed that amount.

The Rams and the NFL reentered negotiations, and the NFL commissioner said that the relocation could be approved if the Rams would pay a higher fee. The NFL had "the right to assess whatever fee they thought necessary" since the initial relocation proposal had not satisfied the league guidelines. The Rams then agreed to pay a $29 million relocation fee, to forgo any share in the next two relocation fees levied by the league, to share $17 million in personal seat license revenue with the NFL, and to indemnify the league for up to $12.5 million of any extra expenses arising from the league's television contract. The Rams relocation was approved on April 12, 1995.

The agreement between CVC and the Rams about CVC's obligating itself on any relocation fee was not revealed to the NFL owners during these negotiations, and it does not appear that the owners were informed about it until after the April 12 vote. Following the vote, the Rams and CVC once again entered negotiations, this time on how the charges assessed by the NFL on the Rams would be paid. The parties agreed in June of 1995 that CVC would pay $20 million of the relocation fee and that CVC would be directly liable to the NFL for its payment. CVC did not exercise the agreement's escape clause, and the Rams began playing in St. Louis in 1995. During that year CVC experienced difficulties meeting its financial obligations to the Rams and did not pay approximately $14 million of the amount due. CVC and Rams president Shaw then agreed that CVC would sue the NFL and that the Rams would receive a right to half of any recovery in place of the payments due.

II

A

CVC filed this case against the league and twenty four member teams on December 18, 1995, claiming that their actions had violated Sections 1 and 2 of the Sherman Antitrust Act, 15 U.S.C. §§1, 2, and that the imposition of the high relocation fee tortiously interfered with CVC's contract with the Rams. CVC's theory was that Article 4.3, the accompanying guidelines, and their application over time functioned as an agreement among the league and the individual teams to restrain relocations, creating an atmosphere which deterred teams from moving and therefore from bidding on the Trans World Dome lease. It contended that the Rams were the only team willing to take the risk of an attempted relocation so they were the only bidder on the lease. As a consequence the Rams were able to obtain very favorable terms from CVC which caused it to lose between $77 and $122 million. CVC requested damages under the Clayton Act which, if established, would be trebled to between $241 and $366 million, and attorney fees. *See* 15 U.S.C. §15. The tortious interference claim was based on the theory that the $29 million relocation fee assessed on the Rams was levied through economic duress, since its only choices were to agree to increase its share of the fee from $7.5 million to $20 million or abandon the deal with the Rams. It asserted that the fee made its contract with the Rams substantially more burdensome which constituted tortious interference under Missouri law, as did the use of economic duress. . . .

The NFL moved for judgment as a matter of law at the close of CVC's case, after four weeks of evidence, and the district court granted the motion as to two of CVC's three remaining claims. The court found that CVC had failed to present evidence that the relocation fee caused a breach in its lease agreement with the Rams, and breach is a necessary element of tortious interference under Missouri law. CVC instead modified its agreement with the Rams to accommodate the size of the fee. The court also found that there had been no evidence that the NFL had intended to interfere with the contract, another required element under state law. Judgment was granted in the NFL's favor on the Section 2 claim as well, since CVC had not shown that the NFL had a monopoly in the professional football market or that there was a secondary market in NFL stadia. CVC has not appealed the ruling on the Section 2 claim. The court permitted the Section 1 claim to proceed, despite expressing misgivings about CVC's case.

After the NFL had presented two days of evidence and was close to finishing its case, the court convened the charge conference to prepare for submission of the Section 1 claim to the jury. The parties again disagreed about whether CVC could make a submissible case by showing that the NFL's rules and actions must have been what had prevented other teams from bidding on the Trans World Dome lease, as opposed to showing that there had been a connection in fact between the allegedly anticompetitive behavior and the absence of competitive bidding. CVC was asked to explain its Section 1 theory at the conference. Counsel responded that "this application and enforcement of the relocation policies had a very substantial deterrent effect upon anybody but the Rams entering into negotiations with CVC." At this point the NFL moved again for judgment as a matter of law. It argued that without a showing that the NFL's rules and actions had in fact deterred bidding on the St Louis lease, CVC's claim was in essence a per se attack on Article 4.3 and the guidelines, and the court had already indicated that the rule of reason was the proper method of analysis.

After further briefing and oral argument, the court described the critical question as whether there was evidence tending to show that "the alleged restraint arises out of 'the agreement of the teams to adopt Article 4.3 to empower the commissioner to adopt and promulgate rules in enforcing 4.3 which has resulted in conduct which has precluded teams from coming to bid competitively in St. Louis.'" In other words, in order to go to the jury CVC had to show more than a theoretical connection between the allegedly anticompetitive actions and the events surrounding the Rams move to St. Louis.

Since the court concluded that CVC had presented no evidence to show that the NFL's rule and the guidelines actually had caused league teams other than the Rams to refrain from competitive bidding on the Trans World Dome lease, it granted the Rule 50 motion. CVC had not shown that it had either tried to learn if other teams might be interested in relocating, that there were teams actually interested in moving to St. Louis, or that the failure of the others to bid on the lease was due to the NFL's policies and acts. There was no showing that there had been interested teams who had failed to contact CVC or that at the time CVC was seeking a team there were team owners who had not bid because of past application of league rules or acts of the commissioner to stop relocations. Finally, the court held that CVC had failed to present evidence of antitrust injury. It said there had been no evidence that collusive activity of the league and member teams reduced competitive bidding and that the opinion testimony of CVC's expert on damages lacked foundation in the record and was not consistent with its theory of liability.

III

CVC's appeal from the judgment focuses on the dismissal of its claim under Section 1 of the Sherman Act and of its claim for tortious interference with contract. It seeks a new trial. CVC argues that its evidence was sufficient to establish a Section 1 violation, contending that it had shown a connection in fact between the NFL rules and actions and the lack of competitive bidding on the lease. It also argues that the tortious interference claim should not have been dismissed because it had established both economic duress and actions which made its agreement with the Rams more burdensome. The NFL responds that CVC did not produce sufficient evidence and no evidence that it sought bids from other teams or that other teams were even in a position to move. The league and teams also suggest that Article 4.3 and the related guidelines could not have affected the number of bidders on the lease because the rules did not become relevant until after the agreement between the Rams and CVC was completed and the Rams made their application to move, in other words well after any bidding period. Finally, the NFL argues that CVC was unable to show there were not independent reasons for the absence of other bids, especially since other owners did not know that the St. Louis lease problems which surfaced during the expansion period had been corrected or that certain acts alleged to have been taken by the commissioner to prevent team relocation had occurred.

The league and teams also cross appeal. They challenge the district court ruling that they were collaterally estopped from arguing that they are a single economic enterprise incapable of conspiracy under Section 1 of the Sherman Act. . . . They seek reversal of the collateral estoppel ruling and dismissal of CVC's Section 1 claim on the ground that they amount to a single economic enterprise. . . .

Section 1 of the Sherman Antitrust act makes it unlawful to form a conspiracy in restraint of trade. 15 U.S.C. §1. . . .

In order to prevail under Section 1, CVC must prove that: (1) there was an agreement among the league and member teams in restraint of trade; (2) it was injured as a direct and proximate result; and (3) its damages are capable of ascertainment and not speculative. . . .

CVC did not present evidence tending to show that there was even one other team besides the Rams that failed to bid on its lease because of the NFL rules and past applications of them. . . .

CVC presented no evidence to exclude the possibility that the owners who did not bid on the St. Louis lease were acting for independent business reasons rather than pursuant to the alleged agreement in restraint of trade. . . .

The district court rested its summary judgment ruling on the issue of causation. In order to satisfy the causation element of a Section 1 case, CVC had to show that the NFL's anticompetitive acts were an actual, material cause of the alleged harm to competition. . . .

The district court found it particularly significant that CVC had not presented evidence to show that it had sought bids from other teams. . . .

The district court also ruled that CVC failed to present evidence to make out a submissible case of antitrust injury. CVC says that its evidence tended to prove that the NFL's policies caused a reduction in competitive bidding which is an antitrust injury. The NFL replies that the theory of CVC's case was that the very existence of Article 4.3 and the guidelines limited team bidding. It did not show that they operated to make CVC's financial obligations greater than they should have been, there was no antitrust injury. The league and team also argue that the rules did not result in a reduction in output of the number of NFL games, teams, or stadia which would be necessary to show antitrust injury. . . .

In sum, CVC did not make out a claim under Section 1 of the Sherman Act, and appellees were entitled to judgment as a matter of law. . . .

CVC also claims that the NFL tortiously interfered with its contract with the Rams by charging the $29 million relocation fee after initially voting down the Rams' application to move. CVC argues that it was forced to pay the fee because of economic duress and that the required fee made its obligations to the Rams substantially more burdensome. The NFL responds that CVC failed to establish several of the essential elements of a tortious interference claim under Missouri law. The district court dismissed this claim because of lack of evidence of a breach induced by the NFL's conduct or of any intentional interference. . . .

CVC had ample opportunity to prove the causes of action that are the subject of its appeal, and it took some four weeks to put in its evidence at trial. The many legal issues were briefed and argued by the parties before the district court ruled on them. Since CVC failed to produce sufficient evidence to make out essential elements required under Section 1 of the Sherman Act and under Missouri law on tortious interference, the league and the member teams were entitled to judgment as a matter of law. CVC has not shown on its appeal that it should have a new trial, and the cross appeal is dismissed as moot. Accordingly, we affirm the judgment of the district court.

Plaintiffs in *St. Louis Convention & Visitors Commn. v. NFL* failed to show a causal connection between the alleged negative effect of the relocation rules and the lack of interest in relocating and accepting their stadium lease offer.

The gist behind the litigation in *VKK Corp. v. NFL* was that the NFL illegally conspired to prohibit plaintiff's team from relocating to a new city.

VKK CORP. v. NATIONAL FOOTBALL LEAGUE

244 F.3d 114 (2d Cir. 2001)

SACK, Circuit Judge:

On November 16, 1994, plaintiff Victor K. Kiam, II ("Kiam"), and two entities through which he controlled the New England Patriots, brought suit in the United States District Court for the Southern District of New York against the National Football League (the "NFL"), twenty-two of its member clubs (with the NFL, collectively the "NFL defendants"), and two entities involved in the ultimately successful campaign to locate an NFL football team in Jacksonville, Florida-Touchdown Jacksonville, Ltd., and Touchdown Jacksonville, Inc. The plaintiffs allege that the defendants violated the Sherman Antitrust Act by preventing Kiam from moving the Patriots out of New England. The defendants assert that the plaintiffs are barred from maintaining this action because they released all claims against the defendants, including the antitrust claims, in a formal written release. Following a jury trial limited to the plaintiffs' claim of economic duress, the jury returned a verdict for the defendants. The district court then granted the defendants' motion for summary judgment with respect to the plaintiffs' remaining claims.

STANDARD OF REVIEW

We review the district court's grant of summary judgment *de novo,* construing the evidence in the light most favorable to the non-moving party. . . .

We may affirm the award of summary judgment on any ground with adequate support in the record. Insofar as we decide this appeal in favor of the NFL defendants, we do so purely as a matter of law rather than on the basis of the jury verdict in the district court. We therefore set forth the facts in the light most favorable to the plaintiffs.

BACKGROUND

The New England Patriots is a member club of the National Football League. From 1988 through 1992, Kiam, through two corporations, VKK Corporation and VKK Patriots, Inc. (Kiam and the corporations collectively "VKK"), was the majority owner of the Patriots. During the period relevant to this appeal, the Patriots played their home games in Foxboro, Massachusetts. VKK alleges that when it assumed control of the Patriots, the team was experiencing substantial financial difficulties stemming in part from the inadequate facilities at Foxboro and the restrictive lease that kept the Patriots there.

As a condition precedent to the approval of his purchase of the Patriots, in September of 1988, Kiam signed a contract in which VKK agreed to comply with the NFL's constitution and bylaws and to obtain advance approval from the NFL of any transfer of ownership of the Patriots. VKK further agreed to "continue to operate the Patriots' franchise within its existing home territory, unless a transfer of the franchise . . . to a different city is approved by the member clubs of the League." In 1989, shortly after VKK assumed ownership of the Patriots, Paul Tagliabue, who had succeeded Rozelle as NFL

Commissioner, issued a statement declaring that the sale of any club would only "become effective if approved by the affirmative vote of . . . [at least] three-fourths . . . of the members of the League."

The VKK-owned Patriots' first two seasons were not profitable, and Kiam was required personally to guarantee loans and use personal funds to cover the resulting cash flow shortages. In an attempt to resolve the Patriots' financial situation, Kiam unsuccessfully negotiated with Boston city officials for a new stadium. In 1990, with no prospects for a new stadium in New England, Kiam decided that it was necessary to consider moving the Patriots to another region of the country. Kiam claims that before buying the team he had received assurances from then-Commissioner Pete Rozelle that if a new stadium could not be secured in New England, such a move would be allowed.

At the time Kiam began to seek the Patriots' relocation, several cities were attempting to obtain NFL franchises. Because few new franchises were being created, groups in many of these cities sought to lure existing teams. One such group was Touchdown Jacksonville, Inc. ("TJI"), created "[t]o secure the NFL franchise for the City of Jacksonville." In the Spring of 1991, representatives of VKK and TJI held a series of meetings about the possibility of relocating the Patriots to Jacksonville.

Representatives of TJI informed the NFL of their meetings with VKK and indicated that they were close to a deal that would bring the Patriots to Jacksonville. As to the plan, TJI told the NFL, according to testimony of the NFL Director of Planning, that "we are going to do what you tell us to do." The NFL told TJI, according to a TJI consultant involved in the negotiations, that the NFL "did not favor the move," and that if TJI wanted the support of the NFL, which TJI needed to procure a franchise, it should cease negotiations with the Patriots. As a result of the NFL comments, the consultant testified, TJI "ceased pursuing discussions with the Patriots."

Several months later, in the fall of 1991, a new Touchdown Jacksonville entity was created: Touchdown Jacksonville, Ltd. ("TJL"). The president of TJI, David Seldin, was also the president of the corporate general partner of TJL. Seldin testified that in October of 1991, TJI "transferred some of its assets to [TJL] to enable [TJL] to seek an NFL expansion franchise for the city of Jacksonville." In November 1993, the NFL awarded an expansion franchise to TJL, which then changed its name to Jacksonville Jaguars, Ltd.

In 1991, Kiam informed Commissioner Tagliabue that Kiam was financially compelled to move the Patriots out of New England. Tagliabue responded that he opposed such a move and that the Patriots would not be allowed to relocate. According to Kiam's lawyer at the time, Tagliabue opposed the move because "he was, in principle, just against the concept of moving," and because he was concerned about losing the television revenues the NFL received because of "the strength of the so-called New England territory."

Meanwhile, Kiam had gone further into debt in order to meet the Patriots' expenses. He told the NFL that if he did not receive a loan he would be compelled to relocate the team immediately. In response, the NFL increased the Patriots' debt limit by $10 million but required that VKK agree not to move the team before the end of the 1993 season. VKK asserts that even with this increased debt limit it was required to sell the team in order to raise enough cash for Kiam to meet his obligations.

Prospective purchasers of the Patriots knew that any sale of the team required approval by the NFL. VKK claims that the NFL thereby lowered the value of the franchise by limiting the pool of prospective purchasers to those interested in owning the team in New England. The NFL eventually approved the sale of the Patriots to one James Orthwein, but only after he signed an "iron clad commitment" not to move the team to his hometown of St. Louis.

In April 1992, just weeks before the sale was scheduled to close, the NFL informed Kiam and Orthwein that the League had a "release policy" under which the league would not approve a sale unless Kiam, on behalf of VKK, signed a release of all claims against the NFL, including potential antitrust claims. Orthwein appeared ready to rescind the deal unless Kiam signed such a release and proceeded to closing. Kiam signed the release demanded of him (the "Release") on May 8, 1992. Three days later, on May 11, 1992, the transaction closed.

Some two and one half years later, on November 16, 1994, VKK filed the complaint in this action, asserting federal antitrust claims against the NFL, twenty-two member clubs, and TJL. The complaint alleged that the defendants violated the Sherman Act by engaging in monopolistic and conspiratorial conduct that illegally lowered the value of the Patriots and had anticompetitive effects in several markets. VKK attempted to avoid the effect of the terms of the Release by asserting that Kiam had signed it under economic duress, that it was itself an instrument of the anticompetitive conduct complained of under the Sherman Act and therefore void or voidable under the "part and parcel" doctrine, which holds that a release is invalid if it is an integral part of a scheme to violate the antitrust laws, and that the Release was not binding because VKK received no consideration in return. VKK also claimed that Kiam did not know that the Release had been part of a conspiracy among the defendants until the fall of 1993, a year before this suit was begun, when he read a newspaper article outlining the defendants' behavior in blocking the relocation of the Patriots to Jacksonville.

The action was originally assigned to Judge John E. Sprizzo, who stayed all merits discovery, allowing discovery to proceed only on the issues concerning the validity of the Release, pending resolution of a motion for summary judgment made by the defendants. While the motion was pending, VKK moved to amend the complaint to add TJI as a defendant, arguing that it had not realized that the entity it had negotiated with in 1991 was TJI not TJL. On April 3, 1998, Judge Sprizzo denied the motion for summary judgment and allowed the plaintiffs to amend their complaint to add TJI.

The case was then bifurcated. A jury trial was to be held on the enforceability of the Release, although it was unclear which of the plaintiffs' theories could be argued before the jury in that trial. Before the trial started, the case was reassigned to Judge Milton Pollack. Judge Pollack limited the trial to the issue of economic duress. The jury returned a verdict for the defendants.

The defendants then moved again for summary judgment on the remaining claims. On June 22, 1999, the district court granted the motion, holding that the Release was supported by valid consideration, that it was not unenforceable as "part and parcel" of a Sherman Act violation, that the claims against TJI-a party added to the complaint after the statute of limitations had run-did not relate back to those against TJL under the requirements set forth in Fed.R.Civ.P. 15(c) and were therefore time-barred, that the Release applied to TJL, and that there were no questions of fact on the merits of the antitrust claims against the Jacksonville defendants. *See VKK Corp. v. National Football League*, 55 F. Supp. 2d 196 (S.D.N.Y. 1999) ("*VKK*").

This appeal followed.

DISCUSSION

I. The Validity of the Release

The defendants claim that VKK was barred from bringing suit against them by the Release. VKK challenges the validity of the Release on three bases: (1) that it was signed under economic duress; (2) that it was "part and parcel" of the defendants' antitrust violation; and (3) that VKK received no consideration in exchange for it. . . .

We are not altogether in disagreement with VKK's assertion that despite these general principles, the time after which VKK was required to act promptly in order effectively to disclaim the Release began to run not at the time of its execution, but when Kiam learned of the conspiracy about which he and the two VKK companies complain. Not until then could they lay his economic duress at the door of the defendants and seek to renounce the Release in order to pursue their antitrust claims against the defendants. . . .

While we do not reject VKK's theory, neither do we find it applicable to the facts of this case. . . .

B. "Part and Parcel" Doctrine

VKK mounts a second challenge to the validity of the Release under the "part and parcel" doctrine. . . .

We think that those asserted consequences of Kiam's signing of the Release are insufficient to render the Release an integral part of the alleged conspiracy. . . .

We conclude, therefore, that whatever the status of the part and parcel doctrine, the Release was not invalid under it because it was not an integral part of the NFL defendants' alleged conspiracy. . . .

C. Absence of Consideration

VKK asserts, finally, that the Release fails for want of consideration. . . .

II. Whether TJI Was a properly Added Party

While we thus agree that the action against the NFL defendants was properly dismissed, we conclude that the district court erred in granting summary judgment to TJI and TJL. . . .

B. Coverage of the Jacksonville Defendants by the Release

The claims against TJI and TJL cannot be dismissed based on the Release because the Release does not cover TJI or TJL. The district court concluded that the Release unambiguously included TJL and therefore granted TJL summary judgment. *VKK*, 55 F. Supp. 2d at 209-10. We disagree.

Under New York law, "the initial interpretation of a contract 'is a matter of law for the court to decide.'" . . .

The district court concluded that the "plain, unambiguous language of the Release confirms that . . . [TJL] is within its scope" because TJL is a member club of the NFL and a successor "to the NFL and/or to the 28 predecessor member clubs." *VKK*, 55 F. Supp. 2d at 209-10. The district court also found "that the Release was intended to cover all member clubs of the NFL, including member clubs at the time any 'future . . . claims' might be brought by the plaintiffs." *VKK*, 55 F. Supp. 2d at 209. We disagree. . . .

Our conclusion that the Release does not cover future member clubs such as TJL is supported by the principle of *expressio unius est exclusio alterius*. The NFL and its member clubs are sophisticated commercial actors who could have specifically referred to future member clubs had they intended to include them in the Release. The Release refers to "past, present, and future . . . Releasors" but makes no mention of future "Releasees," leading us to conclude that the parties to the Release did not intend to include future member clubs. . . .

Finally, TJI has never been a member or affiliate of the NFL or a successor or affiliate of a member club. Whether or not future members are included within the Release, TJI is not covered.

III. The Antitrust Claims

Section 1 of the Sherman Antitrust Act makes it unlawful to enter into a conspiracy in restraint of trade. 15 U.S.C. §1. While some restraints of trade are illegal per se, others, such as trade restrictions by sports leagues, are analyzed to determine whether the restriction's "harm to competition outweighs any procompetitive effects." *St. Louis Convention & Visitors Comm'n v. Nat'l Football League*, 154 F.3d 851, 861 (8th Cir. 1998); *Los Angeles Mem'l Coliseum Comm'n*, 726 F.2d at 1391. In order to prevail under section 1, a plaintiff must show that: "(1) there was an agreement among . . . [the defendants] in restraint of trade; (2) [the plaintiff was] injured as a direct and proximate result; and (3) its damages are capable of ascertainment and not speculative." *St. Louis Convention & Visitors Comm'n*, 154 F.3d at 861.

The district court, as an alternative ground for granting summary judgment to TJL and TJI, concluded that there was no evidence of a conspiracy among the NFL, TJI, and TJL defendants. *VKK*, 55 F. Supp. 2d at 210-11. We hold that that was an issue of fact that could not be resolved by means of summary judgment on the current record. . . .

CONCLUSION

We therefore affirm the judgment of the district court with respect to VKK's claims against the NFL defendants but vacate and remand the judgment with respect to VKK's claims against TJI and TJL for further proceedings not inconsistent with this opinion. While we understand that this leaves the NFL dog of this litigation quite dead but the TJI/TJL tail still wagging, the result is a necessary outgrowth of the fact that at this point, only the validity and operation of the Release have been fully litigated. The Release protects the NFL defendants but not TJI or TJL.

QUESTIONS AND DISCUSSION

1. *Los Angeles Memorial Coliseum* noted the shift of antitrust strategizing; here, the team owners themselves use antitrust to gain advantage from the league, usually in the form of attempts to relocate their franchise.

2. *In San Francisco Seals, Ltd. v. NHL*, 379 F. Supp. 966 (C.D. Cal. 1974), an individual hockey franchise wanted to move from San Francisco to Vancouver. The court held that the team was not competing economically with the league and the other teams. Accordingly, the league's relocation rules did not restrain trade within the relevant market. Also, the Seals did not have standing to sue the league and the other teams for an alleged §2 Sherman Act violation of monopolizing the business of major league hockey since an individual team was not within the target area with respect to the claimed conspiracy.

3. However, in *Los Angeles Memorial Coliseum Commission v. NFL*, the court held that the NFL was not a single entity since each team had a separate identity independent from the league. If it was a single entity, then it would be impossible to conspire with itself to restrain trade. But here, the league is simply a group of individual competitors whose joint votes on league matters could constitute an illegal group boycott. Grauer, *The Use and Misuse of the Term "Consumer Welfare": Once More to the Mat on the Issue of Single Entity Status for Sports Leagues under §1 of the Sherman Antitrust Act*, 64 Tulane L. Rev. 71 (1989); Jacobs, *Professional Sports Leagues, Antitrust, and the Single Entity Theory: A Defense of the Status Quo*, 67 Ind. L.J. 25 (1991); Mitten & Burton, *Professional Sports Franchise Relocations from Private Law and Public Law Perspective: Balancing Marketplace Competition, League Autonomy, and the Need for a Level Playing Field*, 56 Md. L. Rev. 57 (1997); *See* Note, *Who Said, "There's No Place Like Home?" Franchise Relocation in Professional Sports*, 10 Loyola Enter. L.J. 163 (1990).

4. But, in *Fraser v. Major League Soccer*, 97 F. Supp. 2d 130 (D. Mass. 2000), Major League Soccer was deemed to be a single entity. Thus its teams and existing owners are incapable of conspiring among themselves to restrain trade in violation of §1 of the Sherman Act.

5. In *Los Angeles Memorial Coliseum Commn. v. NFL*, 791 F.2d 1356 (9th Cir. 1986), a bifurcated proceeding on damages, both team and stadium had antitrust standing to recover treble damages. The Court affirmed the trebled damage verdict in favor of the Coliseum but vacated the Raiders' antitrust damage recovery. The award to the Coliseum was in the amount of $14,580,243; the Raiders' award of $34,633,146 was remanded for a determination in the amount of set-off due the NFL for the lost value of the Los Angeles area franchise opportunity. *See also Seattle Totems Hockey Club, Inc. v. NHL*, 783 F.2d 1347 (9th Cir. 1986) (plaintiff's expansion franchise was rejected).

6. Plaintiff's theory in *St. Louis Convention & Visitors Comm. v. NFL.*, 154 F.3d 851 (8th Cir. 1998), "was that the league's relocation rules and the way

they had been applied had created an atmosphere in which teams were unwilling to relocate. It contended that this anti-relocation atmosphere had discouraged interested teams from bidding on the St. Louis lease." *Id.* at 853. The commission failed to show a causal connection between league rules regulating relocation and the absence of more than one relocation candidate to their attractive stadium lease offer. Would the outcome be different if there were two suitors? *See generally* Shropshire, *The Sports Franchise Game: Cities in Pursuit of Stadiums, Arenas, Sports Franchises and Events* (1995); Fisher, Maxwell & Schouten, *The Economics of Sports Leagues and the Relocation of Teams: The Case of the St. Louis Rams,* 10 Marq. Sports L.J. 193 (2000); Leone, *No Team, No Peace: Franchise Free Agency in the NFL,* 97 Colum. L. Rev. 473 (1997); Tygart, *Antitrust's Impact on the NFL and Team Relocation,* 7 Sports Law. J. 29 (2000).

7. Plaintiff's chief complaint in *VKK Corp. v. NFL* was that the NFL had illegally conspired to prohibit him from relocating the New England Patriots. The jury returned a verdict for the NFL on the severed issue of whether the former owner's signing of a condition for obtaining the NFL's approval for the sale of his majority interest to another was made under economic duress. The release was held dispositive, and plaintiff's claims were dismissed. Can you think of other claims that might have proven more successful? *See* Ritucco, *Contracts and Antitrust — Economic Duress and Anti-Competitive Practices — Coercive Tactics Utilized by the NFL to Prevent Franchise Relocation — VKK* Corp. v NFL; 12 Seton Hall J. Sport L. 149 (2002). *See generally* Bordson, *Public Sports Stadium Funding: Communities Being Held Hostage by Professional Sports Team Owners,* 21 Hamline L. Rev. 505 (1998); Negrin, *If You Build It, They Might Stay: Unconscionability in Modern Sports Stadium Leases,* 30 Pub. Cont. L.J. 503 (2001); Panel I (Leccese, *et al.*), *Stadium Finance, Naming Rights & Team Relocation,* 12 Fordham Intell. Prop. Media & Ent. L.J. 291 (2002); Smith, *History, Rivalry, Envy, and Relocation: Will the Sale of the New York Jets Give Rise to a New Stadium?* 7 Sports Law. J. 309 (2000).

8. *See King County v. Taxpayers of King City.,* 949 P.2d 1260 (Wash. 1997), involving a challenge to state legislation and local implementing ordinances for financing and constructing of new football stadium. Note that local governments regularly acquire stadium sites through the use of eminent domain power. Could this be a political negative? *See generally* Acton & Campbell, *Public Funding of Sports Stadiums and Other Recreational Facilities: Can the Deal Be "Too Sweet"?* 29 Stetson L. Rev. 877 (1998); Senkiewicz, *Stadiums and Arena Financing Who Should Pay?* 8 Seton Hall J. Sport L. 575 (1998).

9. *See NBA v. SDC Basketball Club, Inc.,* 815 F.2d 262 (9th Cir. 1987) (application of federal antitrust laws to a sports league's effort to restrain the movement of a member franchise). Teams attempt to use the threat of relocation to gain a better stadium deal. Is that fair? Should city loyalty be mandated by law? *See generally* Chapin, *The Political Economy of Sports Facility Location: an End-of-the-Century Review and Assessment,* 10 Marq. Sports L.J. 361 (2000); Greenberg, Stadium *Financing and Franchise Relocation Act of 1999,* 10 Marq. Sports L.J. 383 (2000); Oram, *The Stadium*

Financing and Franchise Relocation Act of 1999, 2 Va. J. Sports & L. 184 (2000).

10. *Sullivan v. NFL*, 34 F.3d 1091 (1st Cir. 1994), involved (1) the NFL's policy that a three-quarter's vote of all NFL owners must be approved for all transfers of ownership interests in an NFL team, and the (2) NFL's uncodified policy against sale of ownership interest in the club through public offerings. The Sherman Act was violated by preventing the team's owner from selling 49% of Patriots to the public in an equitable offering. *See* Grauer, *The Use and Misuse of the Term "Consumer Welfare": Once More to the Mat on the Issue of the Sherman Act*, 64 Tul. L. Rev. 71 (1989); Krause, *The NFL's Ban on Corporate Ownership: Violating Antitrust to Preserve Traditional Ownership — Implications Arising from W.H. Sullivan's Antitrust Suit*, 2 Seton Hall J. Sports L. 255 (1992); Lopatka & Herndon, *Antitrust and Sports Franchise Ownership Restraints: A Sad Tale of Two Cases*, 42 Antitrust Bull 749 (1997).

11. In *Chicago Professional Sports Ltd. Partnership v. NBA*, 95 F.3d 593 (7th Cir. 1996), the Chicago Bulls and their parent TV superstation, WGN, sued NBA and its rule that limited the number of games that each superstation could carry to 20. The court held in a limited characterization that the NBA was a joint venture and applied a rule of reason analysis in determining that the 20-game limit violated the Sherman Act. What is the difference between the NBA here and the NFL in *Los Angeles Memorial Coliseum*? See Fogel, fisher et al., *The Economics of Sports Leagues — The Chicago Bulls Case*, 10 Marq Sports L.J. 1 (1999); *The "Superstation," the NBA, and Antitrust: An Analysis of* Chicago Professional Sports Ltd. Partnership v. NBA," 47 Rutgers L. Rev. 1195 (1995); Shacknai, *Sports Broadcasting and the Antitrust Laws: Stay Tuned for Baseball After the Bulls Romp in Court*, 1 Sports Law. J. 1 (1994)

F. AMATEUR SPORTS

The role of the antitrust laws to regulate monopolistic tendencies in organized sports is also important in amateur sports. In the *Board of Regents* decision, the Supreme Court declared that the NCAA's football television plan was unlawful under a rule of reason analysis. The NCAA's TV package was an unreasonable restraint of trade. The NCAA's plan restricted the total number of football games an NCAA member could televise, and also stopped member schools from selling TV rights except in accordance with the NCAA plans. The Court rejected the NCAA's following arguments: the TV plan was not arranged to preserve the competitive plan since it was not intended to equalize competition; the NCAA did not regulate the money that schools spent on their football programs and the NCAA gave control to schools that either did not have football or would not be affected by the restrictions. By rejecting these arguments, this decision immediately set the networks free to negotiate TV contracts with the major football schools.

NATIONAL COLLEGIATE ATHLETIC ASSOCIATION v. BOARD OF REGENTS

468 4.5. 85 (1984)

Justice STEVENS delivered the opinion of the Court.

The University of Oklahoma and the University of Georgia contend that the National Collegiate Athletic Association has unreasonably restrained trade in the televising of college football games. After an extended trial, the District Court found that the NCAA had violated §1 of the Sherman Act and granted injunctive relief. 546 F. Supp. 1276 (WD Okla. 1982). The Court of Appeals agreed that the statute had been violated but modified the remedy in some respects. 707 F.2d 1147 (CA10 1983). We granted certiorari, 464 U.S. 913 (1983), and now affirm.

I. The NCAA

Since its inception in 1905, the NCAA has played an important role in the regulation of amateur collegiate sports. It has adopted and promulgated playing rules, standards of amateurism, standards for academic eligibility, regulations concerning recruitment of athletes, and rules governing the size of athletic squads and coaching staffs. In some sports, such as baseball, swimming, basketball, wrestling, and track, it has sponsored and conducted national tournaments. It has not done so in the sport of football, however. With the exception of football, the NCAA has not undertaken any regulation of the televising of athletic events.

The NCAA has approximately 850 voting members. The regular members are classified into separate divisions to reflect differences in size and scope of their athletic programs. Division I includes 276 colleges with major athletic programs; in this group only 187 play intercollegiate football. Divisions II and III include approximately 500 colleges with less extensive athletic programs. Division I has been subdivided into Divisions I-A and I-AA for football.

Some years ago, five major conferences together with major football-playing independent institutions organized the College Football Association (CFA). The original purpose of the CFA was to promote the interests of major footballplaying schools within the NCAA structure. The Universities of Oklahoma and Georgia, respondents in this Court, are members of the CFA.

History of the NCAA Television Plan

In 1938, the University of Pennsylvania televised one of its home games. From 1940 through the 1950 season all of Pennsylvania's home games were televised. That was the beginning of the relationship between television and college football.

On January 11, 1951, a three-person "Television Committee," appointed during the preceding year, delivered a report to the NCAA's annual convention in Dallas. Based on preliminary surveys, the committee had concluded that "television does have an adverse effect on college football attendance and unless brought under some control threatens to seriously harm the nation's overall athletic and physical system." The report emphasized that "the television problem is truly a national one and requires collective action by the colleges." As a result, the NCAA decided to retain the National Opinion Research Center (NORC) to study the impact of television on live attendance, and to declare a moratorium on the televising of football games. A television committee was appointed to implement the decision and to develop an NCAA television plan for 1951.

The committee's 1951 plan provided that only one game a week could be telecast in each area, with a total blackout on 3 of the 10 Saturdays during the season. A team could appear on television only twice during a season. The plan also provided that the NORC would conduct a systematic study of the effects of the program on attendance. The plan received the virtually unanimous support of the NCAA membership; only the University of Pennsylvania challenged it. Pennsylvania announced that it would televise all its home games. The council of the NCAA thereafter declared Pennsylvania a member in bad standing and the four institutions scheduled to play at Pennsylvania in 1951 refused to do so. Pennsylvania then reconsidered its decision and abided by the NCAA plan.

During each of the succeeding five seasons, studies were made which tended to indicate that television had an adverse effect on attendance at college football games. During those years the NCAA continued to exercise complete control over the number of games that could be televised.

From 1952 through 1977 the NCAA television committee followed essentially the same procedure for developing its television plans. It would first circulate a questionnaire to the membership and then use the responses as a basis for formulating a plan for the ensuing season. The plan was then submitted to a vote by means of a mail referendum. Once approved, the plan formed the basis for NCAA's negotiations with the networks. Throughout this period the plans retained the essential purposes of the original plan. See 546 F. Supp., at 1283. Until 1977 the contracts were all for either 1- or 2-year terms. In 1977 the NCAA adopted "principles of negotiation" for the future and discontinued the practice of submitting each plan for membership approval. Then the NCAA also entered into its first 4-year contract granting exclusive rights to the American Broadcasting Cos. (ABC) for the 1978-1981 seasons. ABC had held the exclusive rights to network telecasts of NCAA football games since 1965. Id., at 1283-1284.

The Current Plan

The plan adopted in 1981 for the 1982-1985 seasons is at issue in this case. This plan, like each of its predecessors, recites that it is intended to reduce, insofar as possible, the adverse effects of live television upon football game attendance. It provides that "all forms of television of the football games of NCAA member institutions during the Plan control periods shall be in accordance with this Plan." App. 35. The plan recites that the television committee has awarded rights to negotiate and contract for the telecasting of college football games of members of the NCAA to two "carrying networks." Id., at 36. In addition to the principal award of rights to the carrying networks, the plan also describes rights for a "supplementary series" that had been awarded for the 1982 and 1983 seasons, as well as a procedure for permitting specific "exception telecasts." . . .

Thus, although the current plan is more elaborate than any of its predecessors, it retains the essential features of each of them. It limits the total amount of televised intercollegiate football and the number of games that any one team may televise. No member is permitted to make any sale of television rights except in accordance with the basic plan.

Background of this Controversy

Beginning in 1979 CFA members began to advocate that colleges with major football programs should have a greater voice in the formulation of football television policy than they had in the NCAA. CFA therefore investigated the possibility of negotiating a television agreement of its own, developed an independent plan, and obtained a contract offer from the National Broadcasting Co. (NBC). This contract, which it signed in August 1981, would have allowed a more liberal number of appearances for each institution, and would have increased the overall revenues realized by CFA members.

In response the NCAA publicly announced that it would take disciplinary action against any CFA member that complied with the CFA-NBC contract. The NCAA made it clear that sanctions would not be limited to the football programs of CFA members, but would apply to other sports as well. On September 8, 1981, respondents commenced this action in the United States District Court for the Western District of Oklahoma and obtained a preliminary injunction preventing the NCAA from initiating disciplinary proceedings or otherwise interfering with CFA's efforts to perform its agreement with NBC. Notwithstanding the entry of the injunction, most CFA members were unwilling to commit themselves to the new contractual arrangement with NBC in the face of the threatened sanctions and therefore the agreement was never consummated. . . .

II

There can be no doubt that the challenged practices of the NCAA constitute a "restraint of trade" in the sense that they limit members' freedom to negotiate and enter into their own television contracts. In that sense, however, every contract is a restraint of trade, and as we have repeatedly recognized, the Sherman Act was intended to prohibit only unreasonable restraints of trade. . . .

III

Because it restrains price and output, the NCAA's television plan has a significant potential for anticompetitive effects. The findings of the District Court indicate that this potential has been realized. The District Court found that if member institutions were free to sell television rights, many more games would be shown on television, and that the NCAA's output restriction has the effect of raising the price the networks pay for television rights. Moreover, the court found that by fixing a price for television rights to all games, the NCAA creates a price structure that is unresponsive to viewer demand and unrelated to the prices that would prevail in a competitive market. And, of course, since as a practical matter all member institutions need NCAA approval, members have no real choice but to adhere to the NCAA's television controls. . . .

Thus, the NCAA television plan on its face constitutes a restraint upon the operation of a free market, and the findings of the District Court establish that it has operated to raise prices and reduce output. Under the Rule of Reason, these hallmarks of anticompetitive behavior place upon petitioner a heavy burden of establishing an affirmative defense which competitively justifies this apparent deviation from the operations of a free market. . . . We turn now to the NCAA's proffered justifications.

IV

The District Court did not find that the NCAA's television plan produced any procompetitive efficiencies which enhanced the competitiveness of college football television rights; to the contrary it concluded that NCAA football could be marketed just as effectively without the television plan. There is therefore no predicate in the findings for petitioner's efficiency justification. Indeed, petitioner's argument is refuted by the District Court's finding concerning price and output. If the NCAA's television plan produced procompetitive efficiencies, the plan would increase output and reduce the price of televised games. The District Court's contrary findings accordingly undermine petitioner's position. . . . Here production has been limited, not enhanced. No individual school is free to televise its own games without restraint. The NCAA's efficiency justification is not supported by the record. . . .

V

Throughout the history of its regulation of intercollegiate football telecasts, the NCAA has indicated its concern with protecting live attendance. This concern, it should be noted, is not with protecting live attendance at games which are shown on television; that type of interest is not at issue in this case. Rather, the concern is that fan interest in a televised game may adversely affect ticket sales for games that will not appear on television. . . .

There is, however, a more fundamental reason for rejecting this defense. The NCAA's argument that its television plan is necessary to protect live attendance is not based on a desire to maintain the integrity of college football as a distinct and attractive product, but rather on a fear that the product will not prove sufficiently attractive to draw live attendance when faced with competition from televised games. At bottom the NCAA's position is that ticket sales for most college games are unable to compete in a free market. The television plan protects ticket sales by limiting output-just as any monopolist increases revenues by reducing output. By seeking to insulate live ticket sales from the full spectrum of competition because of its assumption that the product itself is insufficiently attractive to consumers, petitioner forwards a justification that is inconsistent with the basic policy of the Sherman Act. "[T]he Rule of Reason does not support a defense based on the assumption that competition itself is unreasonable."

VI

Petitioner argues that the interest in maintaining a competitive balance among amateur athletic teams is legitimate and important and that it justifies the regulations challenged in this case. We agree with the first part of the argument but not the second. . . .

The television plan is not even arguably tailored to serve such an interest. It does not regulate the amount of money that any college may spend on its football program, nor the way in which the colleges may use the revenues that are generated by their football programs, whether derived from the sale of television rights, the sale of tickets, or the sale of concessions or program advertising. The plan simply imposes a restriction on one source of revenue that is more important to some colleges than to others. There is no evidence that this restriction produces any greater measure of equality throughout the NCAA than would a restriction on alumni donations, tuition rates, or any other revenue-producing activity. At the same time, as the District Court found, the NCAA imposes a variety of other restrictions designed to preserve amateurism which are much better tailored to the goal of competitive balance than is the television plan, and which are "clearly sufficient" to preserve competitive balance to the extent it is within the NCAA's power to do so. And much more than speculation supported the District Court's findings on this score. No other NCAA sport employs a similar plan, and in particular the court found that in the most closely analogous sport, college basketball, competitive balance has been maintained without resort to a restrictive television plan.

Perhaps the most important reason for rejecting the argument that the interest in competitive balance is served by the television plan is the District Court's unambiguous and well-supported finding that many more games would be televised in a free market than under the NCAA plan. The hypothesis that legitimates the maintenance of competitive balance as a procompetitive justification under the Rule of Reason is that equal competition will maximize consumer demand for the product. The finding that consumption will materially increase if the controls are removed is a compelling demonstration that they do not in fact serve any such legitimate purpose.

VII

The NCAA plays a critical role in the maintenance of a revered tradition of amateurism in college sports. There can be no question but that it needs ample latitude to play that role, or that the preservation of the student-athlete in higher education adds richness and diversity to intercollegiate athletics and is entirely consistent with the goals of the Sherman Act. But consistent with the Sherman Act, the role of the NCAA must be to preserve a tradition that might otherwise die; rules that restrict output are hardly consistent with this role. Today we hold only that the record supports the District Court's conclusion that by curtailing output and blunting the ability of member institutions to respond to consumer preference, the NCAA has restricted rather than enhanced the place of intercollegiate athletics in the Nation's life. Accordingly, the judgment of the Court of Appeals is affirmed.

Justice WHITE, with whom Justice REHNQUIST joins, [dissents]. . . .

QUESTIONS AND DISCUSSION

1. *NCAA v Board of Regents* concerned the NCAA's packaging television broadcasts of college football games. The NCAA's plan was held to be violative of the Sherman Act under a rule of reason analysis. Interestingly, the dissent was written by the late Justice Byron "Whizzer" White, an outstanding All-American halfback at the University of Colorado. To him, and remember he played in the 1930s, it was all about education, and the TV packaging was just another facet of the educational process. The majority Stevens J, saw this package as an unreasonable restraint of trade since it restricted the total number games that an NCAA member could televise. By limiting the output and curtailing the big schools' ability to respond to network offers, the NCAA was found to restrict the trade of these colleges. Was this a correct decision? Or is it the tail wagging the dog? Should the TV package monies be distributed evenly among all Division 1A schools? *See* Carstensen & Olszowka, *Antitrust Law, Student-Athletes and the NCAA; Limiting the Scope Conduct of Private Economic Regulation*, 1995 Wis. L. Rev. 545.

2. In *Law v. NCAA*, 902 F. Supp 1394 (D. Kan. 1995), the NCAA's "restricted earnings coach rule" was deemed to be an antitrust violation. As in *Board of Regents*, the NCAA could not meet the burden of establishing that the rule actually promoted a legitimate, procompetitive objective. *See* Leduc, Law v. NCAA: *A Guide to How Courts Will Treat Future Antitrust Challenges to NCAA Regulations*, 26 J.C. & U.L. 139 (1999); Sacks, *The Restricted Earnings Coach Under Sherman Act Review*, 4 Sports Law. J. 13 (1997).

3. In *Smith v. NCAA*, 139 F.3d 180 (3d Cir. 1998), Renee Smith, a college volleyball player, sued the NCAA on the grounds that their "Postbaccalaureate Bylaw" (14.1.8.2) violated the Sherman Act and Title IX of the Education Amendments. She breezed through college and went to law school; she wanted to use her years of remaining eligibility while in law school, which was a different school than her undergraduate university. The court held that the NCAA's eligibility rules were not connected to their commercial and business activities (like TV packaging); therefore, the Sherman Act did not apply.

4. In *United States v. Walters*, 711 F. Supp. 1435 (N.D.Ill. 1989), the court held that the NCAA's eligibility rules that restricted compensation to students and the penalities that enforced those rules did not violate antitrust. *Board of Regents* implied a message that eligibility rules and TV packages were apples and oranges and that the eligibility rules are justifiable means of encouraging competition among amateur teams and therefore procompetitive because they enhance public interest in intercollegiate sports.

5. As a result of the NCAA's Death Penalty enacted against Southern Methodist University, SMU's alumni, football players, and cheerleaders sued the NCAA for antitrust violations that resulted from NCAA rule enforcement that restricted benefits in the form of continued football that

would have accrued to plaintiffs. The court held that the NCAA's eligibility rules did not violate the antitrust laws, and that alumni and cheerleaders lacked antitrust standing. The loss of an opportunity to lead cheers at a football game as a result of SMU suspension did not qualify as an injury to business or property, and thus cheerleaders lacked standing to obtain damages for alleged antitrust violations by NCAA. *See McCormack v. NCAA*, 845 F.2d 1338 (5th Cir. 1988). *See generally* Greene, *Regulating the NCAA: Making the Calls Under the Sherman Antitrust Act and Title IX*, 52 Me. L. Rev. 81 (2000); Mitten, *Applying Antitrust Law to NCAA Requirements of "Big Time" College Athletics: The Need to Shift from Nostalgic 19th & 20th Century Ideals of Amateurism to the Economic Realities of the 21st Century*, 10 Marq. Sports L. Rev. 1 (2000); Pekron, *The Professional Student-Athlete: Undermining Amateurism as an Antitrust Defense in NCAA Compensation Challenges*, 24 Hamline L. Rev. 24 (2000).

6. In *Behagen v. Amateur Basketball Assn.*, 884 F.2d 524 (10th Cir. 1988), a basketball player, Ron Behagen, sued both an international basketball association and the American Amateur Basketball Association for their refusal to reinstate him to amateur status. The court held that the actions of the amateur basketball association were exempt from the federal antitrust laws since the control of amateur sports by the association was in direct compliance with both the intent and the wording of the Amateur Sports Act (36 U.S.C. §§371-382b, §§391-396); thus the antitrust claim was barred by the express intent by Congress.

CHAPTER 6

TORTS

The most prevalent cause of action to recover for athletic injuries is in **Negligence**. Negligence is conduct that falls below the reasonable person standard—what a reasonable person would do under similar circumstances. In sports, there are a myriad of possible variations of what that standard is as it relates to the different types of athletic activity.

The cause of action against medical personnel who are negligent is known as **Medical Malpractice**. It is bad or unskilled practice by a physician or other medical professional. In the area of medicine in sports, the medical professional possesses certain duties which, if breached, could trigger malpractice liability. The threshold question is identifying whether the 'team physician' is an employee of the team or an independent contractor.

Facility Liability is the area of law in which owners or operators of sports arenas and stadiums are liable if the design or maintenance of the structure is negligent. The duty of the owner-operator is based on determining the status of the injured party (trespasser, licensee, or invitee) who has entered the premises.

Products Liability actions are those that involve defective sports equipment. The manufacturers of sports equipment, such as football helmets, must abide by the duty of reasonable care in their manufacture and design. The equipment must be reasonably safe when used for its intended purpose and in the intended manner.

An action against an individual's reputation is termed **Defamation**. Sportswriters thrive on making negative comments about athletes and coaches. These statements are defamatory if they are published, false, cause damage to a person's reputation, and are not privileged. **Invasion of Privacy**, which is related to defamation, is the right to protect one's privacy.

Participant and Spectator Injuries may also be actionable in negligence if the injury was a result of action or inaction that fell below a recognized standard of care.

Similarly, **School, Coach and Referee Liability** is a possibility if there is a breach of duty. Schools have a duty to warn, instruct, hire competent coaches, properly supervise, and maintain equipments and facilities. Coaches have a duty to prepare participants, maintain equipment and facilities, and properly supervise. Referees have a duty to enforce rules, protect participants, warn of danger, anticipate reasonably foreseeable dangers, and control and properly supervise the flow of the game.

Many **Tort Defenses** historically have been used by sports injury defendants to avoid liability. Since participation in sports is usually voluntary, a participant or spectator who assumes the risk created by another's conduct cannot recover when harm in fact occurs.

An alternative recovery method to torts is **Workers' Compensation** for employees who are injured on the job. It is like a tort defense since, when applicable, it is the sole method of recovery and is used by employers to avoid the tort system.

A. NEGLIGENCE

Negligence is any conduct that falls below the reasonable man standard. Negligence in sports is measured against the particular facts and circumstances of each and every case. The defendant's negligent act or omission must be the proximate cause of the athlete's injury. In short, there must be an established duty of care, a breach of that duty, a proximate cause between defendant's action and the injury, and damages that result from that breach.

Recovery for injuries in sports-related activities was covered by Justice Cardozo's maxim that "the timorous may stay at home."[1] It was assumed that one voluntarily embraced any danger that might occur. Slowly, the courts began to understand that "some . . . restraints of civilization must accompany every athlete onto the playing field."[2]

1. Duty of Care

The first element in a successful negligence action is to determine whether a duty existed between the injured participant or spectator and the defendant. Without a duty, there is no negligence. An actionable duty — a duty strong enough to support a claim for relief — is not an exact formula. Rather, it is the sum total of policy considerations that might entitle the injured party to some type of protection. A duty can be created by common law, statute, contract, or policy.

In *Kleinknecht v. Gettysburg College*, the court found that the college owed a duty to a deceased lacrosse player based on the relationship between the athlete and the school and the foreseeability of the injury.

KLEINKNECHT V. GETTYSBURG COLLEGE

989 F.2d 1360 (3d Cir. 1993)

HUTCHINSON, Circuit Judge.

Suzanne W. Kleinknecht and Richard P. Kleinknecht (collectively "the Kleinknechts") appeal an order of the United States District Court for

---

[1] *Murphy v. Steeplechase Amusement Co.*, 166 N.E. 173 (N.Y. 1929).
[2] *Nabozny v. Barnhill*, 334 N.E.2d 258 (Ill. Ct. App. 1975).

the Middle District of Pennsylvania granting summary judgment to appellee Gettysburg College ("the College"). . . .

I. Procedural History

Drew Kleinknecht died of cardiac arrest on September 16, 1988, while a student at the College and during a practice session of its intercollegiate lacrosse team. His parents filed this wrongful death and survival action against the College on August 15, 1990. . . .

II. Factual History

In September 1988, Drew Kleinknecht was a twenty-year-old sophomore student at the College, which had recruited him for its Division III intercollegiate lacrosse team. The College is a private, four year liberal arts school. In 1988, it had an enrollment of about two thousand students and supported twenty one intercollegiate sports teams involving approximately 525 male and female athletes.

Lacrosse is a contact sport. In terms of sports-related injuries at the College, it ranked at least fourth behind football, basketball, and wrestling, respectively.

Lacrosse players can typically suffer a variety of injuries, including unconsciousness, wooziness, concussions, being knocked to the ground, and having the wind knocked out of them. Before Drew died, however, no athlete at the College had experienced cardiac arrest while playing lacrosse or any other sport.

In September 1988, the College employed two full-time athletic trainers, Joseph Donolli and Gareth Biser. Both men were certified by the National Athletic Trainers Association, which requires, inter alia, current certification in both cardio-pulmonary resuscitation ("CPR") and standard first aid. In addition, twelve student trainers participated in the College's sports program. The trainers were stationed in the College's two training room facilities at Musselman Stadium and Plank Gymnasium.

Because lacrosse is a spring sport, daily practices were held during the spring semester in order to prepare for competition. Student trainers were assigned to cover both spring practices and games. Fall practice was held only for the players to learn "skills and drills," and to become acquainted with the other team members. No student trainers were assigned to the fall practices.

Drew participated in a fall lacrosse practice on the afternoon of September 16, 1988. Coaches Janczyk and Anderson attended and supervised this practice. It was held on the softball fields outside Musselman Stadium. No trainers or student trainers were present. Neither coach had certification in CPR. Neither coach had a radio on the practice field. The nearest telephone was inside the training room at Musselman Stadium, roughly 200-250 yards away. The shortest route to this telephone required scaling an eight-foot high cyclone fence surrounding the stadium. According to Coach Janczyk, he and Coach Anderson had never discussed how they would handle an emergency during fall lacrosse practice.

The September 16, 1988 practice began at about 3:15 p.m. with jogging and stretching, some drills, and finally a "six on six" drill in which the team split into two groups at opposite ends of the field. Drew was a defenseman and was participating in one of the drills when he suffered a cardiac arrest. According to a teammate observing from the sidelines, Drew simply stepped away from the play and dropped to the ground. Another teammate on the sidelines stated that no person or object struck Drew prior to his collapse.

After Drew fell, his teammates and Coach Janczyk ran to his side. Coach Janczyk and some of the players noticed that Drew was lying so that his head appeared to be in an awkward position. No one knew precisely what had happened at that time, and at least some of those present suspected a spinal injury. Team captain Daniel Polizzotti testified that he heard a continuous "funny" "gurgling" noise coming from Drew, and knew from what he observed that something "major" was wrong. Other teammates testified that Drew's skin began quickly to change colors. One team member testified that by the time the coaches had arrived, "Drew was really blue."

According to the College, Coach Janczyk acted in accordance with the school's emergency plan by first assessing Drew's condition, then dispatching players to get a trainer and call for an ambulance. Coach Janczyk himself then began to run toward Musselman Stadium to summon help. . . .

The parties do not dispute that Polizzotti, the team captain, ran toward the stadium, where he knew a training room was located and a student trainer could be found. In doing so, Polizzotti scaled a chain link fence that surrounded the stadium and ran across the field, encountering student trainer Traci Moore outside the door to the training room. He told her that a lacrosse player was down and needed help. She ran toward the football stadium's main gate, managed to squeeze through a gap between one side of the locked gate and the brick pillar forming its support, and continued on to the practice field by foot until flagging a ride from a passing car. In the meantime, Polizzotti continued into the training room where he told the student trainers there what had happened. One of them phoned Plank Gymnasium and told Head Trainer Donolli about the emergency.

Contemporaneously with Polizzotti's dash to the stadium, Dave Kerney, another team member, ran toward the stadium for assistance. Upon seeing that Polizzotti was going to beat him there, Kerney concluded that it was pointless for both of them to arrive at the same destination and changed his course toward the College Union Building. He told the student at the front desk of the emergency on the practice field. The student called his supervisor on duty in the building, and she immediately telephoned for an ambulance.

Student trainer Moore was first to reach Drew. She saw Drew's breathing was labored, and the color of his complexion changed as she watched. Because Drew was breathing, she did not attempt CPR or any other first aid technique, but only monitored his condition, observing no visible bruises or lacerations.

By this time, Coach Janezyk had entered the stadium training room and learned that Donolli had been notified and an ambulance called. Coach Janczyk returned to the practice field at the same time Donolli arrived in a golf cart. Donolli saw that Drew was not breathing, and turned him on his back to begin CPR with the help of a student band member who was certified as an emergency medical technician and had by chance arrived on the scene.

The two of them performed CPR until two ambulances arrived at approximately 4:15 p.m. Drew was defibrillated and drugs were administered to strengthen his heart. He was placed in an ambulance and taken to the hospital, but despite repeated resuscitation efforts, Drew could not be revived. He was pronounced dead at 4:58 p.m. . . .

Prior to his collapse on September 16, 1988, Drew had no medical history of heart problems. The Kleinknechts themselves describe him as "a healthy, physically active and vigorous young man" with no unusual medical history until his death. In January 1988, a College physician had examined Drew to determine his fitness to participate in sports and found him to be in excellent health. The Kleinknecht's family physician had also examined Drew in August 1987 and found him healthy and able to participate in physical activity.

Medical evidence indicated Drew died of cardiac arrest after a fatal attack of cardiac arrhythmia. Postmortem examination could not detect the cause of Drew's fatal cardiac arrhythmia. . . . [H]e was not in play when he suffered his cardiac arrest. . . .

III. Issues on Appeal

The Kleinknechts present three general issues on appeal. They first argue that the district court erred in determining that the College had no legal duty to implement preventive measures assuring prompt assistance and treatment in the event one of its student athletes suffered cardiac arrest while engaged in school-supervised intercollegiate athletic activity. Second, the Kleinknechts maintain that the district court erred in determining that the actions of school employees following Drew's collapse were reasonable and that the College therefore did not breach any duty of care. . . .

IV. Analysis
1. The Duty of Care Issue

Whether a defendant owes a duty of care to a plaintiff is a question of law. . . . In order to prevail on a cause of action in negligence under Pennsylvania law, a plaintiff must establish: (1) a duty or obligation recognized by the law, requiring the actor to conform to a certain standard of conduct; (2) a failure to conform to the standard required; (3) a causal connection between the conduct and the resulting injury; and (4) actual loss or damage resulting to the interests of another.

The Kleinknechts assert three different theories upon which they predicate the College's duty to establish preventive measures capable of providing treatment to student athletes in the event of a medical emergency such as Drew's cardiac arrest: (1) existence of a special relationship between the College and its student athletes; (2) foreseeability that a student athlete may suffer cardiac arrest while engaged in athletic activity; and (3) public policy. . . .

a. Special Relationship

The Kleinknechts argue that the College had a duty of care to Drew by virtue of his status as a member of an intercollegiate athletic team. The Kleinknechts argue that a college or university owes a duty to its intercollegiate athletes to provide preventive measures in the event of a medical emergency. . . .

The Supreme Court of Pennsylvania has not specifically addressed the issue whether schools owe its athletes a duty based on that special relationship. . . .

Here, . . . Drew was not acting in his capacity as a private student when he collapsed. Indeed, the Kleinknechts concede that if he had been, they would have no recourse against the College. There is a distinction between a student injured while participating as an intercollegiate athlete in a sport for which he was recruited and a student injured at a college while pursuing his private interests, scholastic or otherwise. This distinction serves to limit the class of students to whom a college owes the duty of care that arises here. Had Drew been participating in a fraternity football game, for example, the College might not have owed him the same duty or perhaps any duty at all. There is, however, no need for us to reach or decide the duty question either in that context or in the context of whether a college would owe a duty towards students participating in intramural sports. On the other hand, the fact that Drew's cardiac arrest occurred during an athletic event involving an intercollegiate team of which he was a member does impose a duty of due care on a college that actively sought his participation in that sport. We cannot help but think that the College recruited Drew for its own benefit, probably thinking that his skill at lacrosse would bring favorable attention and so aid the College in attracting other students. . . .

In conclusion, we predict that the Supreme Court of Pennsylvania would hold that the College owed Drew a duty of care in his capacity as an intercollegiate athlete engaged in school-sponsored intercollegiate athletic activity for which he had been recruited.

b. Foreseeability

This does not end our inquiry, however. The determination that the College owes a duty of care to its intercollegiate athletes could merely define the class of persons to whom the duty extends, without determining the nature of the duty or demands it makes on the College. Because it is foreseeable that student athletes may sustain severe and even life threatening injuries while engaged in athletic activity, the Kleinknechts argue that the college's duty of care required it to be ready to respond swiftly and adequately to a medical emergency. . . . The type of foreseeability that determines a duty of care, as opposed to proximate cause, is not dependent on the foreseeability of a specific event. . . . Only when even the general likelihood of some broadly definable class of events, of which the particular event that caused the plaintiff's injury is a subclass, is unforeseeable can a court hold as a matter of law that the defendant did not have a duty to the plaintiff to guard against that broad general class of risks within which the particular harm the plaintiff suffered befell. . . . Even this determination that the harm suffered was foreseeable fails to end our analysis. If a duty is to be imposed, the foreseeable risk of harm must be unreasonable. . . .

Having determined that it is foreseeable that a member of the College's interscholastic lacrosse team could suffer a serious injury during an athletic event, it becomes evident that the College's failure to protect against such a risk is not reasonable. . . . This Court recognizes only that under the facts of this case, the College owed a duty to Drew to have measures in place at the lacrosse team's practice on the afternoon of September 16, 1988 in order to provide prompt treatment in the event that he or any other member of the lacrosse team suffered a life-threatening injury. . . .

Our holding is narrow. It predicts only that a court applying Pennsylvania law would conclude that the College had a duty to provide prompt and adequate emergency medical services to Drew, one of its intercollegiate athletes, while he was engaged in a school-sponsored athletic activity for which he had been recruited. Whether the College breached that duty is a question of fact. If the factfinder concludes that such a breach occurred, we think that the question whether that breach was the proximate or legal cause of Drew's death would likewise be a question of fact. . . .

c. Public Policy

Finally, the Kleinknechts argue that the College owed a duty of care to Drew based on public policy considerations. . . .

2. The Reasonableness of the College's Actions

On the duty question, it remains only for us to address the district court's second holding that the conduct of the College's agents in providing Drew with medical assistance and treatment following his cardiac arrest was reasonable. The court based this determination in part, if not in whole, on its conclusion that the College had no duty to consider what emergency assistance measures would be necessary were one of its student athletes to suffer a cardiac arrest during athletic activity. . . .

V. Conclusion

The district court's holding that the College's duty of care to Drew as an intercollegiate athlete did not include, prior to his collapse, a duty to provide prompt emergency medical service while he was engaged in school sponsored athletic activity will be reversed. The district court's holding that the College acted reasonably and therefore did not breach any duty owed to Drew following his collapse will likewise be reversed. We will remand this matter to the district court for further proceedings consistent with this opinion. We will reverse the district court's conclusion that the College is entitled to immunity under the Good Samaritan law.

2. Standard of Care and Breach of Duty

Duty is the key to negligence. In discovering whether a breach of duty occurred, one must determine if defendant's conduct fell below an applicable standard of care; for example, a violation of a league safety rule in softball might constitute an actionable duty if that rule is recognized as a standard of care that was created for the protection of participants.

The level of the standard of care varies with the plaintiff's circumstances. The more foreseeable the injury is, the higher the standard. For example, the standard of care would be one of extreme caution for an already injured base-ball player who is about to be taken off the field in a stretcher. It is not necessary to have a specific standard of care as created by a safety rule or a phys-ical education standard to maintain a negligence action. Absent a specific applicable rule, the standard of care is a reasonable person acting under similar circumstances.

A duty is determined to have been breached when there is sufficient evi-dence for a jury to conclude so. (At that point, the next question becomes whether the jury could reasonably infer that defendant's breach was the injury's proximate cause.) The question of breach is for the trier of facts (that is, the jury) unless the evidence is so obvious that no reasonable minds could differ. This determination is made on a case-by-case basis.

3. Proximate Cause

Proximate cause is the next element in determining negligence. Proximate cause is the connection between the negligent act and the resultant injury. The breach of the duty must be the injury's proximate cause. This too is a fact question and is decided by a jury on a case-by-case basis. Proximate cause is that which, in natural and continuous sequence, unbroken by an efficient intervening cause, produces the injury, without which the injury would not have occurred. It is not necessary to eliminate all of the other potential causes. It is enough to prove a sufficient evidentiary basis from which causa-tion can reasonably be inferred. This causation must only be a substantial factor in bringing about the injury; however, it does not have to be the only factor.

4. Damages

The last element in the negligence equation is that the injured athlete must prove up damages. Negligence requires that the plaintiff must suffer some damages. Because sports are action oriented, participants are prone to physical injuries as a result of negligent physical contact. As a result, damages are usually easy to prove; the only requirement is that an actual loss of damages must result to the interest of another. Nominal damages alone, where no actual loss has occurred, are insufficient to sustain a cause of action.

QUESTIONS AND DISCUSSION

1. The legal field of torts encompasses intentional torts and negligence. Torts are a civil, noncriminal avenue of redress for injuries. Intentional torts, such as assault and battery, are less important in sports because of the voluntary nature of athletic participation. In *Ginsberg v. Hontas*, 545 So. 2d 1154 (La. Ct. App. 1989), defendant in a softball game owed the injured player a duty to act reasonably, which meant to play fairly according to the rules of the game and to refrain from any wanton or reckless conduct that is likely to result in harm or injury to another. The duty owed by the

defendant is to act reasonably under the circumstances. Is this a useful standard? The requirement that an athlete acts with reasonable and ordinary care under the circumstances is translated into golf so that a golfer is required only to exercise ordinary care for the safety of persons reasonably within the zone of danger. That means that there is no duty to give advance warning to persons who are on contiguous holes or fairways and not in the line of play, if danger to them is not reasonably anticipated. *See Ludwikoski v. Kurotsu*, 840 F. Supp. 826 (D. Kan. 1993).

2. Johnny Golfer is in a foursome at the local golf course. He has the longest drive and goes to his ball before the others hit their second shots. He hides behind a tree to protect himself but grows impatient and sticks his head out. He is immediately struck with a shank shot by another member of the foursome. Should Johnny Golfer recover for his injuries? *See Schmidt v. Youngs*, 544 N.W.2d 743 (Mich. Ct. App. 1996).

3. In *Kleinknecht*, a duty of care arose because of the special relationship between a college and a recruited athlete. How about intramural lacrosse instead? In that scenario, plantiff would not recover. Is that fair? Although special relationships have many times created a duty (for example, train conductor and passenger; teacher and student), *Kleinknecht* was the first time that this rule was applied to this particular type of relationship. *See* Champion, *The Evolution of a Standard of Care for Injured Athletes: A Review of* Kleinknecht *and Progeny,* 1 Va. J. Sports & Ent. L. 290 (1999); Hollingsworth, Kleinknecht v. Gettysburg College: *What Duty Does a University Owe Its Recruited Athlestes?* 19 T. Marshall L. Rev. 711 (1994); McGirt, Do Universities Have a Special Duty of Care to Protect Student-Athletes from Injury? 6 vill. Sports & Ent. L.J. 219 (1999).

4. Bronco Smith, a collegiate scholarship football player, is injured during practice and collapses unconscious on the sideline. The trainer examines plaintiff but allows an assistant, without instructions, to accompany plaintiff to the hospital. A month later Bronco is "kicked in the head" during a game and collapses unconscious. This time at the hospital he undergoes a complete examination, where it is discovered that he had suffered a chronic subdural hematoma of three to four weeks duration. As a result of his injuries, plaintiff suffers severe and permanent neurological damage. It is undisputed that a CT scan after the first injury would have helped reveal the original subdural hematoma. In Bronco's lawsuit against the college and the trainer, who will win and why? *See Pinson v. Tennessee*, 1995 Tenn. App. LEXIS 807.

5. In *Davidson v. University of N.C. at Chapel Hill*, 543 S.E. 2d 920 (N.C. Ct. App. 2001), the court found that a special relationship existed between an injured JV cheerleader and the university, in that the defendant voluntarily undertook to educate the cheerleaders on safety, which thus created a separate duty of care. Could *Davidson* have been decided without *Kleinknecht*? What are their similarities? What are their differences? *See also* Hefferan, 'Taking One for the Team: Davidson vs. University of North Carolina *and the Duty of Care Owed by Universities to Their Student-Athletes,'* 37 Wake Forest L. Rev. 589 (2002).

6. A park commission was liable for injuries suffered when a softball player's foot slipped into a hole concealed under a base that was not connected to its shaft. The umpire warned of a "loose base," but that was insufficient to apprise the injured player of the concealed hole under an unattached base. The commission owed a duty of ordinary and reasonable care under the circumstances to properly maintain and operate and the softball field. Since the warning was inadequate, the commission did not fulfill its duty of reasonable care. The defective base presented an unreasonable risk of injury and the warning failed to place her on notice of the defect. *See Politz v. Recreation & Park Commn.*, 619 So. 2d 1089 (La. Ct. App. 1993).

7. A duty can also arise by way of statute. In *Northcutt v. Sun Valley Co.*, 787 P.2d 1159 (Idaho 1990), a statute limited liability for Idaho ski area operators (*I.C.* §§6-1109 to 6-1109). In *Northcutt*, a skier was injured when another skier collided with him and the forced him into a signpost. The operator had no duty to eliminate, control, or lessen the inherent risks of the sport beyond those stated in the act. Although there was a statutory duty to post signs, there was no duty to accomplish this to any standard of care; therefore, the operator was not liable for the improper placement of guiding signs. Also, the operator had only a duty to provide a ski patrol that met the standards of the national ski patrol system. It was not the operator's duty to provide patrol members to chase down the individual who caused plaintiff's injuries. Thus, Sun Valley was not liable for their failure to determine the skier's identity.

8. A violation of a safety rule could constitute an actionable duty if that rule is recognized as a standard of care that is created for the protection of participants. *See Nabozny v. Barnhill*, 334 N.E. 2d 258 (Ill. Ct. App. 1975).

9. In some instances, a school is held to the same degree of care as the children's parents. The school is *in loco parentis*, and the applicable standard is that of reasonably prudent parents acting under similar and comparable circumstances. But there is no duty under the doctrine of *in loco parentis* for a college and its coach to prevent an adult student from becoming excessively intoxicated with resulting severe bodily injury to himself while on a college-sponsored expedition at an out-of-state resort. *See Albano v. Colby College*, 822 F. Supp. 840 (D. Me. 1993).

B. MEDICAL MALPRACTICE

Medical malpractice in sports centers on lawsuits against doctors and medical personnel that administer to athletes. Since top physical shape is a prerequisite to continued competition, it is quite understandable why there is so much emphasis on the doctor-athlete relationship and the reliability of various medical examinations. Malpractice is bad medical practice. In the medical sports area, medical personnel's duties toward their athlete-clients can include the duty to disclose, the duty to instruct, the duty to disclose whether the physician is employed by a third party, and the duty to disclose medical negligence. A violation of any of these duties could be the basis for a successful medical malpractice suit. The extent of the duty is evaluated by a standard of conduct that takes into account the skill and knowledge of the medical community as a whole.

1. Doctors and Sports

Doctors provide all the various examinations in sports that allow athletes to continue competition. There are preseason physicals, post-injury examinations, and the examination that gives clearance to the athlete to return to active competition after an injury has healed. A doctor-patient relationship exists when there is mutual acceptance. A consent to treat must be obtained from the athlete or the athlete's guardian if he or she is a minor.

Chuy v. Philadelphia Eagles explores the duties of the team physician in properly disseminating inaccurate information about a player's physical condition.

CHUY v. PHILADELPHIA EAGLES FOOTBALL CLUB

595 F.2d 1265 (3d Cir. 1979)

ROSENN, Circuit Judge.

This appeal presents several interesting questions growing out of the employment by the Philadelphia Eagles Football Club ("the Eagles") of a former professional player, Don Chuy ("Chuy"). The unexpected and unfortunate termination of Chuy's employment evoked charges by him that the Eagles had not played the game according to the rules when Chuy blew the whistle terminating his football career. . . .

I. Background

Chuy joined the Eagles in 1969, having been traded from the Los Angeles Rams, another professional football club with which he had played for a half dozen years. On June 16, 1969, he met with the Eagles general manager, Palmer "Pete" Retzlaff, in Philadelphia, Pennsylvania, to negotiate a contract with the Eagles for the 1969, 1970, and 1971 football seasons. The parties concluded their negotiations by executing three National Football League (NFL) standard form player contracts on June 16, 1969, covering the 1969, 1970, and 1971 football seasons respectively at a salary of $30,000 for each season, with a $15,000 advance for the 1969 season.

The contracts each contained a standard NFL injury-benefit provision entitling a player injured in the performance of his service to his salary "for the term of his contract." Chuy sustained a serious injury to his shoulder during his first season in a game between the Eagles and the New York Giants in November, 1969. Sidelined for the remainder of the season, Chuy had to be hospitalized for most of December, 1969. During the hospitalization, his diagnosis revealed a pulmonary embolism, a blood clot in his lung, which marked the end of his professional athletic career. Following the advice of his physician, Chuy decided to retire from professional football and notified the Eagles of his intention. At the same time, Chuy requested that the Eagles pay him for the remaining two years of what he asserted was a three-year contract.

The Eagles requested that Chuy submit to a physical examination which Dr. Dick D. Harrell conducted in March, 1970. After extensive tests, Dr. Harrell concluded that Chuy suffered from an abnormal cell condition, presumably stress polycythemia, which may have predisposed him to the formation of dangerous blood clots. He therefore recommended to the Eagles that Chuy should "not be allowed to participate further in contract sports." Shortly after receiving Dr. Harrell's recommendation, General Manager Retzlaff informed Hugh Brown, a sports columnist for the Philadelphia Bulletin, that Chuy had been advised to quit football because of his blood clot condition. Brown thereupon telephoned Dr. James Nixon, the Eagles' team physician, for further information on Chuy's medical status.

On April 9, 1970, Hugh Brown's by-lined column in the Philadelphia Bulletin carried an account of Chuy's premature retirement. . . .

The Associated Press wire service picked up the story and articles appeared the next day in newspapers throughout the country, including the Los Angeles Times. The articles reported that Chuy had been "advised to give up football and professional wrestling because of a blood condition" and that, according to Dr. James Nixon, the Eagles' physician, "Chuy is suffering from polycythemia vera. Nixon said it is considered a threat to form blood clots."

After reading the Los Angeles Times article, Chuy testified that he panicked and immediately called his personal physician, Dr. John W. Perry. Dr. Perry informed Chuy that polycythemia vera was a fatal disease but that, from his records, Chuy did not have that disease. Dr. Perry added that he would run a series of tests to confirm his diagnosis. Chuy testified that he became apprehensive, despite Dr. Perry's assurances, broke down emotionally, and, frightened by the prospect of imminent death, refused to submit to any tests. Chuy stated that for the next several months, he could not cope with daily routines and he avoided people. He returned to Dr. Perry, who gave him numerous tests which disproved the presence of polycythemia vera. Nonetheless, Chuy testified that he continued to be apprehensive about death and that marital difficulties also developed. . . .

The judgment of the district court will be affirmed. The parties to bear their own costs.

Gardner v. Holifield shows the relationship between a scholarship athlete and the university physician who allegedly failed to properly identify the extent of the athlete's illness, which caused his death, or to implement an appropriate course of treatment.

GARDNER V. HOLIFIELD

639 So. 2d 652 (Fla. Dist. Ct. App. 1994)

KAHN, Judge.

This is a medical malpractice action brought by Gladys Gardner, Roosevelt Gardner's surviving mother and the personal representative of his estate, against Edward W. Holifield, a Tallahassee physician. Mrs. Gardner alleges that one or more acts of negligence committed by Dr. Holifield in his capacity as a private physician contributed to Roosevelt Gardner's death from Marfan's Syndrome at the age of eighteen. Acting upon Dr. Holifield's motion, the trial court entered summary judgment in favor of Dr. Holifield and against Gardner. Because we agree with Mrs. Gardner that the trial judge erroneously resolved disputed issues of fact against her as the nonmoving party, we reverse and do not reach Gardner's remaining issue.

Roosevelt Gardner entered Florida A & M University (FAMU) in the fall of 1988 on a basketball scholarship. On September 6th of that year, Roosevelt went to the FAMU clinic for a basketball physical. Dr. Holifield, employed at that time as the medical director of FAMU Student Health Center, performed the physical examination. Dr. Holifield diagnosed Roosevelt as possibly suffering from Marfan's Syndrome, a potentially lethal connective tissue disorder often characterized by cardiovascular irregularities. In order to confirm the diagnosis, Dr. Holifield referred Roosevelt to radiologists for chest x-rays and to an ophthalmologist to check for an eye condition that frequently accompanies Marfan's. Dr. Holifield ordered two echocardiograms, the first performed on September 6, 1988, and the second performed on September 22, 1988. The echocardiograms were done at Tallahassee Memorial Regional Medical Center (TMRMC). Dr. Holifield read the echocardiogram tapes, issued interpretive reports on TMRMC letterhead, and received compensation personally through a services contract with TMRMC. Six months after being initially seen by Dr. Holifield, 18-year-old Roosevelt Gardner collapsed at a service station and died.

In her suit, Mrs. Gardner alleges that Dr. Holifield failed to properly identify the extent of Roosevelt's illness or to implement an appropriate course of treatment. . . .

Mrs. Gardner initially brought this wrongful death action against Dr. Holifield, individually, in his capacity as a private physician treating Roosevelt, and against FAMU, where Dr. Holifield served as Director of Student Health Services. . . . Mrs. Gardner then settled her case against FAMU and proceeded solely against Dr. Holifield individually.

On appeal, Mrs. Gardner claims that the record is in factual conflict as to whether Dr. Holifield acted at least partly as a private cardiologist when he treated Roosevelt Gardner for Marfan's Syndrome. She specifically notes several matters of record which she believes were overlooked by the trial court. These matters can be briefly summarized. The FAMU clinic, by the terms of its own Operational Manual, provides only routine services and does not treat serious illnesses. Accordingly, Mrs. Gardner infers that Dr. Holifield was acting beyond the scope of the clinic's function in his duties as director when he followed up with Roosevelt after the initial diagnosis of Marfan's Syndrome, a condition not characterized as minor. The clinic's Operational Manual states, "If specialized care is indicated, the student will be referred to a local physician. The student is responsible for his own bill." Dr. Holifield referred Roosevelt to an ophthalmologist and radiologist, but made no referral to a cardiologist. Nothing that Dr. Holifield holds himself out as a cardiologist, Mrs. Gardner suggests that Dr. Holifield was to function as the heart specialist.

Dr. Holifield ordered and interpreted two diagnostic echocardiograms. He prepared his reports on TMRMC letterhead and received direct compensation for reading the echocardiograms. Mrs. Gardner now argues that misinterpretation of these echocardiograms was part and parcel of the medical negligence she attributes to Dr. Holifield. . . .

State employees, including medical doctors, enjoy immunity from liability for negligence committed within the scope and course of their state employment. . . .

The question of scope of state employment presents a jury issue when it arises upon disputed facts. . . .

In the present case, it is clear that although Dr. Holifield did make referrals to other medical specialists, he never referred Roosevelt to another cardiologist after the initial examination revealed a potential heart condition. Dr. Holifield's decision to order and read the echocardiograms at TMRMC, considered in light of the matters raised by Mrs. Gardner's experts, leads, in our view, to competing inferences that may not properly be resolved in favor of the party moving for summary judgment. . . . A permissible inference from the lack of a referral is the one Mrs. Gardner has drawn, i.e., Dr. Holifield assumed responsibility for Roosevelt's condition as a private cardiologist. . . .

In light of the foregoing, it is obviously not necessary for us to reach the issue of whether the trial court improperly granted summary judgment while discovery requests and motions to compel were pending. On remand, however, the parties should attempt to resolve any matters concerning discovery with the trial court providing controlling guidance regarding any disputes.

Reversed and remanded.

2. Duty to Disclose and Informed Consent

A patient must make meaningful decisions about his course of treatment. The player's consent must be informed: The doctor has a related duty to disclose all possible side effects so that the patient will have sufficient information to make an informed decision. The duty to disclose includes the duty to inform the athlete that he must seek additional medical advice. The athlete's consent should be in writing and should be clear and understandable in terms and in scope.

In *Krueger v. San Francisco 49ers,* the injured professional football player successfully brought an action for fraudulent concealment against his employer for the actions of a team physician who "patched him up" year after year and allowed him to continue to play without revealing the true extent of his injuries, which were sufficient to permanently disable him.

KRUEGER V. SAN FRANCISCO FORTY NINERS

189 Cal. App. 3d 823 (1987)

NEWSOM, J.

On August 19, 1980, appellant filed a complaint for damages and declaratory relief against respondent San Francisco Forty Niners. . . . [T]he case proceeded to court trial on the sole cause of action for fraudulent concealment of medical information. The trial court found in favor of respondent and this appeal followed.

Appellant began playing professional football with the San Francisco Forty Niners (hereafter respondent or the 49'ers) in 1958. He was a defensive line-man for the 49'ers until retiring in 1973, missing only parts of two seasons due to injuries. During his career, however, appellant played despite suffering numerous injuries. He broke his arm and the ring finger on each hand, cracked or broke his nose "innumerable times," suffered multiple dislocations of the fingers and thumbs on both hands, incurred a "blow-out" fracture of the right ocular orbit, developed an eye infection or "pterygium" caused by a foreign substance becoming lodged in the eye, sprained his right knee, and developed hypertension, among other maladies.

The injuries and damages to appellant's left knee are the focus of the present suit. While in college in 1955, appellant had surgery on his left knee to repair a torn meniscus. Then, in October of 1963, he ruptured the medial collateral ligament in his left knee. Dr. Lloyd Taylor, a physician who treated 49'ers players, performed an operation on the knee which, appellant was told, effectuated a "good repair." Thereafter, appellant engaged in reha-bilitative therapy with the team trainer and was given a knee brace which he later wore while playing until he removed it in 1967.

Dr. Taylor noted in his report of the operation that the anterior cruciate ligament — the function of which is to prevent the tibia from shifting forward on the femur — appeared to be "absent" from appellant's left knee. Such an injury can produce instability in the knee, particularly if combined with other injuries. According to appellant, he was not told that his left knee evidently lacked the anterior cruciate ligament.

In the spring of 1964, appellant began experiencing pain and considerable swelling in his left knee. He again received treatment from physicians retained by the 49'ers, specifically Dr. Taylor and Dr. Lloyd Milburn, which consisted of aspiration of bloody fluid from the knee by means of a syringe and con-temporaneous injection of novocain and cortisone, a steroid compound.

Appellant testified that he received approximately 50 such "Kepplemann" treatments during 1964, and an average of 14 to 20 per year from 1964 to 1973. Dr. Milburn could not recall administering Kepplemann treatments with such frequency, and testified that his records indicated only seven such treatments. Appellant also testified that he was never advised by the 49'ers medical staff of the dangers associated with steroid injections in the knee, such as possible rupturing of tendons, weakening of joints and cartilage, and destruction of capillaries and blood vessels. He also offered expert medical testimony that the adverse effects of steroids were known at that time. The same medical expert also testified that the number of steroid injections appel-lant claimed to have undergone would have been inappropriate and quite "unusual."

Appellant's left knee continued to plague him during his football career, and in 1971 he underwent another operation performed by Dr. Taylor to remove "loose bodies" in the knee resulting from chronic chondromalacia, patella-thinning and loss of cartilage on the undersurface of the kneecap, a condition fully consistent with known adverse reaction to prolonged steroid use. X-rays taken between 1964 and 1971 revealed "degenerative post-traumatic changes" in appellant's left knee joint. Appellant testified—without contradiction—that he was not told of either of these afflictions by the 49'ers medical staff.

Krueger also testified that he suffered a "hit" on the outside of the knee during a game in 1970. He felt a piece of the knee break off. Notwithstanding the obvious severity of the injury, appellant was given Empirin codeine and directed to return to the game. For the remainder of the season he could feel a "considerable piece of substance" dislodged on the outside of his left knee joint; nevertheless, he played the remaining five games of the season. At no time did the team doctors ever advise him that he risked permanent injury by continuing to play without surgery. Krueger testified unequivocally that, had he been advised not to play, he would have followed that advice. . . .

Appellant retired from football following the 1973 season. In April of 1974, he entered St. Mary's Hospital for a rhinoplasty and complete physical examination which, however, did not include either X-raying or testing of his knees. Neither Dr. Milburn, who had arranged the physical, nor any other orthopedist examined him at that time.

Not until 1978 was appellant treated again for his injured knee. At that time, he received a Kepplemann treatment from Dr. Milburn, and X-rays were taken of both legs. According to appellant it was not until this visit to Dr. Milburn in 1978 that he was shown X-rays of his knees and advised for the first time that he suffered from chronic and permanent disability in the knee.

Defendant was referred to Dr. Taylor, who subsequently performed on him a tibial osteotomy, which is a shaving of planes from the leg bone followed by regrafting of the tendons and ligaments to the bone. The operation did nothing to alleviate appellant's severe discomfort, and in fact, he thereafter developed calcification in the knee and suffered greater pain than had been the case before the surgery. He presently suffers from traumatic arthritis and a crippling degenerative process in the left knee. He cannot stand up for prolonged periods, and cannot run. He is also unable to walk on stairs without severe pain. His condition is degenerative and irreversible.

On this appeal Krueger argues error in the trial court's finding that he failed to prove all of the elements of fraudulent concealment. Pivotally, the court found that appellant would have continued to play football even if he had been advised of the nature and extent of his injuries—a finding which negated the element of proximate cause. . . .

Respondent submits that the record fails to substantiate appellant's claim that medical information was concealed from him. We disagree. Appellant testified unequivocally that the team's physicians never disclosed to him the adverse effects of steroid injections, or the true nature and extent of the damage to his left knee, particularly the dangers associated with the prolonged violent traumatic impact inherent in professional football. Nor, he testified, was he informed that X-rays taken of his legs revealed the severely degenerated condition of his left knee. . . .

In our opinion, the duty of full disclosure within the context of a doctor-patient relationship defines the test for concealment or suppression of facts . . . The failure to make such disclosure constitutes not only negligence, but where the requisite intent is shown-fraud or concealment as well. A physician cannot avoid responsibility for failure to make full disclosure by simply claiming that information was not withheld. . . .

[Here] . . . the requisite disclosure was never made.

The element of intent also must be established in all fraudulent concealment cases. . . .

Nevertheless, we think the record unequivocally demonstrates that, in its desire to keep appellant on the playing field respondent consciously failed to make full, meaningful disclosure to him respecting the magnitude of the risk he took in continuing to play a violent contact sport with a profoundly damaged left knee. . . .

Accordingly, we conclude there is no substantial evidence to support the judgment entered by the trial court; and conversely, that appellant established all the elements of a fraudulent concealment case based upon non-disclosure of material medical information. . . .

QUESTIONS AND DISCUSSION

1. Malpractice is a bad or unskilled practice by a physician or other medical professional. In the medical sports arena, the duty can include the duty to instruct, the duty to disclose whether the physician is employed by a third party (e.g., a sports team), and a duty to disclose medical negligence. The key is whether the doctor in question was a team doctor. *See generally* Mitten, *Team Physicians and Competitive Athletes: Allocating Legal Responsibilities for Athletic Injuries,* 55 U. Pitt. L. Rev. 129 (1993); Salares, *Preventing Medical Malpractice of Team Physicians in Professional Sports: A Call for the Players Unions to Hire the Team Physicians in Professional Sports,* 4 Sports Law. J. 235 (1997).

2. The team doctors in *Krueger* fraudently concealed medical information from Charlie Krueger. Without this information, he was unable to make an informed decision about whether to continue playing professional football. Should the football player take some responsibility for continuing to play even after repeated injuries; or, is Krueger merely an example of an extreme case that is actionable only as a result of the numerous and repeated times that Charlie was "duped" about his condition?

3. The element of a cause of action in fraudulent concealment of medical information are a misrepresentation or suppression of a material fact, knowledge of any falsity, intent to induce reliance, actual and justifiable reliance, and resulting damages. Additionally, the athlete must prove that he would not have played or undergone the medical treatment that caused the harm if he has been properly informed of the material risks of doing so. *See* W. Page Keeton, et al., *Prosser & Keeton on the Law of Torts* §105 at 725 (5th ed. 1984). The doctor has the duty of full disclosure. "A physician cannot avoid responsibility for failure to make full disclosure by simply claiming that information was not withheld." The team doctor administered questionable steroids, and Kreuger was directed to use

amphetamines during games. Krueger sued for fraudulent concealment; are there any other legal alternatives available to Krueger? *See* Caldarone, Professional Team Doctors: Money, Prestige, and Ethical Dilemmas, 9 Sports Law. J. 131 (2002); Hanson, 'The Informed Consent and the Scope of a Physician's Duty of Disclosure,' 77 N.D.L. Rev. 71 (2001); Hecht, 'Legal and Ethical Aspects of Sports-Related Concussions: The Merrill Hoge Story,' 12 Seton Hall J. Sport L. 1 (2002); Keim, 'Physicians for Professionals Sports Teams: Health Care Under the Pressure of Economic and Commercial Interests,' 9 Seton Hall J. Sport L. 196 (1999); Polsky, 'Winning Medicine: Professional Sports Team Doctors' Conflicts of Interest,' 145 Contemp. Health L. & Poly. 503 (1998); Woodlief, 'The Trouble with Charlie: Fraudulent Concealment of Medical Information in Professional Football,' 9 Ent. & Sports Law. 3 (1991). *See also Sherwin v. Indianapolis Colts, Inc.,* 752 F. Supp. 1172 (N.D.N.Y. 1990) (former professional football player's claims that team and team doctor failed to provide medical care was subject to the collective bargaining agreement's mandatory grievance arbitration procedures).

4. The tragic March 1990 death of collegiate basketball star Hank Gathers, who collapsed at center court, is a classic example of the interaction between athlete and doctor, the possible conflicts of interest between team and doctor, and the perceived need for collegiate basketball players to showcase their talent as much as possible, regardless of medical opinion or physical condition, in the hope of securing a lucrative professional contract. Although he had a previous problem with arrhythmia, his doctor allowed him to play under certain conditions.

This was a case of heart failure: He had collapsed earlier in the season, was put on medication, and, after several weeks away from basketball, was then allowed to compete. There were real questions about the dosage of the medication, the advice given to him by the doctors, and the wisdom of allowing his return to basketball. His heirs sued on various legal grounds, and the case was settled in 1992. This case calls into question the loyalty of the doctor: Is his first obligation to the player or the employer? Davis, *"Fixing" the Standard of Care: Motivated Athletes and Medical Malpractice,'* 12 Am. J. Trial Advoc. 715 (1988); *See also* Issacs, *'Conflicts of Interest for Team Physicians in Light of Gathers,'* 2 Alb. L.J. Sci. & Tech. 147 (1992); Jones, *'Collegiate Athletes: Illness or Injury and the Decisior to Return to Play,'* 40 Buff. L. Rev. 113 (1992); Mitten, *'Amateur Athletes with Handicaps or Physical Abnormalities: Who Makes the Participation Decision?'* 71 Neb. L. Rev. 987 (1992); Niles & West, *'In Whose Interest? The Return of the Injured Athlete to Competition,'* 25 Brief 8 (1996); Note, *'A High Price to Compete: The Feasibility of Waivers for Injuries to Athletes with High Medical Risks,'* 79 Ky. L.J. 867 (1990-91). *See generally* Connaughton & Spengler, *'Automated External Defibrillators in Sport and Recreational Settings: An Analysis of Immunity Provisions in State Legislations,'* 11 J. Legal Aspects Sport 51 (2001); Frenkel, *'Sports Medicine and the Law,'* 21 Med. & L. 201 (2002); Hekmat, *'Malpractice During Practice: Should NCAA Coaches Be Liable for Negligence?'* 22 Loy. L.A. Ent. L. Rev. 613 (2002); Mitten, Annot., *'Medical Malpractice Liability of Sports Medicine Care Providers for Injury to, or Death of, Athlete,'* 33 A.L.R. 5th

619 (1995); Westbury, *'General Provisions: Provide Immunity to Physicians Rendering Uncompensated Services to Non-professional Athletes,'* 10 Ga. St. U. L. Rev. 230 (1993). *See also Gardner v. Holifield,* 639 So. 2d 652 (Fla. Ct. App. 1994) (shows relationship between a scholarship athlete and the university physician who allegedly failed to properly identify the extent of the athlete's illness, which caused his death, or to implement an appropriate course of treatment).

C. FACILITY LIABILITY

Many lawsuits in sports negligence are against stadium owners and operators. The question is, what duty does the owner-operator owe to spectators? The court in *Atkins v. Glen Falls City School Dist.* discusses the relatively typical question of how much screening must the owner-operator of a baseball facility provide for the protection of spectators.

AKINS V. GLEN FALLS CITY SCHOOL DISTRICT

424 N.E.2d 531 (N.Y. 1981)

JASEN, J.:

On this appeal, we are called upon to define the scope of the duty owed by a proprietor of a baseball field to the spectators attending its games. The specific question presented is whether such an owner, having provided protective screening for the area behind home plate, is liable in negligence for the injuries sustained by a spectator as a result of being struck by a foul ball while standing in an unscreened section of the field.

In the early afternoon of April 14, 1976, plaintiff attended a high school baseball game that was being played on a field owned and maintained by defendant Glens Falls City School District. The field was equipped with a backstop 24 feet high and 50 feet wide. This backstop was located 60 feet behind home plate and was positioned in front of bleachers that could seat approximately 120 adults. There was additional standing room behind the backstop as well. Two chain link fences, three feet in height, ran from each end of the backstop along the base lines to a distance approximately 60 feet behind first and third base.

Plaintiff arrived while the game was in progress and elected to view the contest from a position behind the three-foot fence along the third base line, approximately 10 to 15 feet from the end of the backstop and 60 feet from home plate. As there were no seating facilities for spectators along the base lines, plaintiff had to stand in order to watch the game. At the time, other spectators were also standing along the base lines behind the three-foot fence. There was, however, no proof that the screened bleachers behind home plate were filled or that plaintiff was prevented from watching the game from behind the backstop. Approximately 10 minutes after arriving at the baseball field, plaintiff was struck in the eye by a sharply hit foul ball, causing her serious and permanent injury.

... [D]efendant ... [a]lleg[es] that the school district was negligent in failing to provide safe and proper screening devices along the base lines of its field, plaintiff sought judgment against the school district in the sum of $250,000. ...

Cases involving the liability of an owner of a baseball field for the injuries sustained by those attending its games are not altogether foreign to the courts of this State. Indeed, the doctrine of assumption of risk has had extensive application in a number of cases involving spectators struck by misguided baseballs. ...

As was aptly summarized by Chief Judge Cardozo, the spectator at a sporting event, no less than the participant, "accepts the dangers that inhere in it so far as they are obvious and necessary, just as a fencer accepts the risk of a thrust by his antagonist or a spectator at a ball game the chance of contact with the ball. The timorous may stay at home." (*Murphy v. Steeplechase Amusement Co.*, 250 NY 479, 482-483.) However, ... these cases arose prior to the adoption of the comparative negligence rule ... [a]s a result there is no case law in this State which defines the duty of care owed by a proprietor of a baseball field to its spectators. We now define that duty.

At the outset, it should be stated that an owner of a baseball field is not an insurer of the safety of its spectators. Rather, like any other owner or occupier of land, it is only under a duty to exercise "reasonable care under the circumstances" to prevent injury to those who come to watch the games played on its field. ... The perils of the game of baseball, however, are not so imminent that due care on the part of the owner requires that the entire playing field be screened. Indeed, many spectators prefer to sit where their view of the game is unobstructed by fences or protective netting and the proprietor of a ball park has a legitimate interest in catering to these desires. Thus, the critical question becomes what amount of screening must be provided by an owner of a baseball field before it will be found to have discharged its duty of care to its spectators ... have adopted a two-prong standard in defining the scope of an owner's duty to provide protective screening for its patrons. Under the majority rule, the owner must screen the most dangerous section of the field — the area behind home plate — and the screening that is provided must be sufficient for those spectators who may be reasonably anticipated to desire protected seats on an ordinary occasion. We believe this to be the better rule and adopt this definition of the duty owed by an owner of a baseball field to provide protective screening for its spectators.

We hold that, in the exercise of reasonable care, the proprietor of a ball park need only provide screening for the area of the field behind home plate where the danger of being struck by a ball is the greatest. Moreover, such screening must be of sufficient extent to provide adequate protection for as many spectators as may reasonably be expected to desire such seating in the course of an ordinary game. In so holding, we merely recognize the practical realities of this sporting event ... many spectators attending such exhibitions desire to watch the contest taking place on the playing field without having their view obstructed or obscured by a fence or a protective net. In ministering to these desires, while at the same time providing adequate protection in the most dangerous area of the field for those spectators who wish to avail themselves of it, a proprietor fulfills its duty of reasonable care under such circumstances.

This is not to say that, by adequately screening the area of the field where the incidence of foul balls is the greatest, the risks inherent in viewing the game are completely eliminated. Rather, even after the exercise of reasonable care, some risk of being struck by a ball will continue to exist. Moreover, we do not attempt to prescribe precisely what, as a matter of law, are the required dimensions of a baseball field backstop. Nor do we suggest that where the adequacy of the screening in tetras of protecting the area behind home plate properly is put in issue, the case should not be submitted to the jury. We merely hold that where a proprietor of a ball park furnishes screening for the area of the field behind home plate where the danger of being struck by a ball is the greatest and that screening is of sufficient extent to provide adequate protection for as many spectators as may reasonably be expected to desire such seating in the course of an ordinary game, the proprietor fulfills the duty of care imposed by law and, therefore, cannot be liable in negligence. . . .

In this case, it is and equipped its field with a backstop which was 24 feet high and 50 feet wide. Plaintiff presented no evidence that this backstop was inadequate in terms of providing protection . . . for those who might reasonably be expected to desire such protection. Under circumstances, having provided adequate protection for those spectators seated, or standing, in the area behind home plate, liability may not be imposed on the school district for failing to provide additional screening along the base lines of its field where the risk of being struck by a stray ball was considerably less. . . . Accordingly, the order of the Appellate Division should be reversed, with costs, and the complaint dismissed.

Chief Judge COOKE (dissenting). The majority today engages in an unfortunate exercise in Judicial rule making in an area that should be left to the jury. This attempt to precisely prescribe what steps the proprietor of a baseball field must take to fulfill its duty of reasonable care is unwarranted and unwise. Furthermore, the provision of CPLR 1411, providing that contributory negligence or assumption of the risk "shall not bar recovery," should not be disregarded. I therefore dissent and vote to affirm.

As the majority recognizes, the proprietor of a baseball field owes the same duty to spectators that any landowner owes to a person who comes onto the owner's property—"reasonable care under the circumstances." (*Basso v. Miller,* 40 NY2d 233, 241; see, also, *Scurti v. City of New York,* 40 NY2d 433). This duty requires that the landowner "must act as a reasonable man in maintaining his property in a reasonably safe condition in view of all the circumstances, including the likelihood of injury to others, the seriousness of the injury, and the burden of avoiding the risk" (*Basso v. Miller,* 40 NY2d 233, 241, supra, quoting *Smith v. Arbaugh's Rest.,* 469 F2d 97, 100).

The majority errs, however, in deciding as a matter of law exactly what steps by a baseball field proprietor will constitute reasonable care under the circumstances, Such a determination, by its very dependence upon the "circumstances," hinges upon the facts of the individual situation and should be left for the jury. Indeed, those exceptions to this rule that have been made by courts occur only in those narrow classes of cases where an identical set of facts is likely to recur with regularity. . . .

1. Status of Injured Party

The threshold question in a facility liability suit is the status of the injured party who has entered the premises. Is he or she an invitee, licensee, or trespasser? With each categorization there is a different standard of care on the part of the facility owner or operator. Usually, participants and spectators are business invitees. The duty owed to an invitee is one of ordinary care, which includes protection from negligence and reasonably discoverable third-party hazards. This includes an obligation to inspect premises and make them safe for a visit.

2. Unreasonably Hazardous Conditions

Owners are liable if they have prior knowledge of unreasonably hazardous conditions. In *Wilkinson v. Hartford Accident & Indemnity Co.*, prior knowledge of a reasonably discoverable but unreasonably dangerous condition was shown by a previous event when a visiting coach walked into the same glass panel.

WILKINSON V. HARTFORD ACCIDENT & INDEMNITY CO.

411 So. 2d 22 (La. 1982)

MARCUS, Justice.

David L. Wilkinson, individually and as administrator of the estate of his minor son, David Len Wilkinson, instituted this action against Joseph L. Rivers, Rapides Parish School Board, and Hartford Accident and Indemnity Company to recover damages for personal injuries sustained by David Len in an accident that occurred in the gymnasium lobby of the Glenmora High School. Hartford was the general liability insurer of the school board. After trial on the merits, the trial judge rendered judgment in favor of defendants and against plaintiff dismissing plaintiff's suit at his cost. In written reasons for judgment, the trial judge, while finding no negligence on the part of Rivers, concluded that the school board was negligent but denied recovery to plaintiff because of the contributory negligence of David Len. The court of appeal affirmed. On application of plaintiff we granted certiorari to review the correctness of that decision.

The facts are generally not in dispute. On November 8, 1978, David Len Wilkinson, age 12, attended his seventh grade physical education class conducted by Joe Rivers athletic coach, in the high school gymnasium. The gymnasium was originally constructed in 1965 with ordinary glass installed in all windows. When entering the gymnasium through the front doors, the first area encountered is a lobby or foyer extending from left (south) to right (north) about seventy feet with glass panels extending from the floor to the ceiling at each end of the lobby. A concession stand is located immediately in front of the entrance doors, about seven feet back, and rest room facilities are located on either side of the front doors. A water fountain is outside each rest room. To reach the spectator area from the front door of the gymnasium, it is necessary to walk into the lobby, turn left or right and walk about thirty feet in either direction to a door which leads from the lobby to the bleachers. Each door is about five feet from the glass panels at the end of the lobby. There is a wall immediately behind the concession stand with openings or doorless "portages" on either side which provide direct access between the lobby and the basketball court. The panel at the north end of the lobby was safety glass (the original plate glass panel having been replaced several years earlier following an incident in which a visiting coach walked through the glass) and the south panel was the original plate glass.

On the day of the accident, the physical education class was being conducted on the east half of the basketball court (side nearer to the lobby). Another class was being conducted on the other half. Coach Rivers had divided the boys into about six teams of five boys each. Relay races were being conducted between two teams at a time. At the conclusion of each race, the participants were instructed to sit along the inside east wall of the gymnasium and await their next turn. Coach Rivers was supervising the races at the time. While the boys had been instructed not to linger or engage in horseplay in the lobby, they were permitted to go into the lobby to get water from the fountains. Following one of the races, David Len and the other members of his team went into the lobby to get a drink of water from the north fountain. It was decided at that time to conduct a race of their own between David Len and another boy in order to determine the order they should be positioned in the next race. The race was to be from the north water fountain to the south glass panel and back again. The other boy reached the panel first and turned but when David Len reached the glass panel, running at his full speed, he pushed off the panel with both hands causing the glass to break. He fell through the glass on to the outside. He sustained multiple cuts on his arms and right leg and was bleeding profusely. Coach Rivers came immediately to the scene and administered first aid. David Len was then taken to the hospital for further treatment. After the accident, the school board replaced the south panel with safety glass.

The issues presented are the alleged negligence of Coach Rivers in failing to properly supervise the physical education class and/or that of the school board in maintaining a plate glass panel in the foyer of the gymnasium and if either or both was negligent, whether plaintiff's action is barred by the contributory negligence of David Len. . . .

The trial court found that the negligence of the school board was a cause of the accident. A school board is liable if it has actual knowledge or constructive knowledge of a condition unreasonably hazardous to the children under its supervision. . . . Accordingly, we conclude that the school board was negligent, [and had actual or constructive knowledge of the dangerous condition]. . . .

[The court also held that David Len was not quilty of contributory negligence.]

. . . [T]he negligence of the Rapides Parish School Board was the sole cause of the accident and the school board is responsible to plaintiff for damages sustained by David Len as a result of the accident. . . .

For the reasons assigned, the judgment of the court of appeal is reversed and the case is remanded to the court of appeal to consider the issue of the amount of damages not reached in its original opinion. . . .

3. Minors

The standard of care for the owner-operator also changes with the type of person who enters the premises, for example, if the invitee is a minor, a disabled person, or a senior citizen. With minor invitees, the question is whether he or she is capable of appreciating the risk involved in either watching or participating in a sport.

City of Atlanta v. Merritt discusses another relatively common situation in which the court must decide whether a minor baseball spectator assumes the risk of being struck by a foul ball. In suits of this type, most courts find for the defendant on the grounds that the injured minor either knew or should have known of the potential for danger. However, in *Merritt,* the court held that a factual question existed as to whether the injured eight-year-old appreciated the risk of watching the game in the unscreened, high-risk picnic area adjacent to the right field line.

CITY OF ATLANTA V. MERRITT

323 S.E.2d 680 (Ga. Ct. App. 1984)

BENHAM, Judge.

Appellee sued appellant for damages incurred when appellee, an 8-year-old at the time of the incident here involved, was struck in the face by a foul ball during a baseball game appellee attended at Atlanta-Fulton County Stadium, a sports facility operated by appellant. Appellee's theory of recovery is that the design and maintenance of the facility is negligently defective because the area from which appellee was watching the game when he was injured, the picnic area adjacent to the right field foul line, is not adequately screened from the playing field. This appeal from the trial court's denial of appellant's motion for summary judgment was filed in this court pursuant to our grant of appellant's petition for permission to file an interlocutory appeal.

1. Appellant relies on *Hunt v. Thomasville Baseball Co.,* 80 Ga.App. 572, 56 S.E.2d 828 (1949), for the proposition that spectators at baseball games are presumed to be aware of the dangers attendant thereto, and on *Abee v. Stone Mtn., etc., Assn.,* 169 Ga.App. 167, 312 S.E.2d 142 (1983), for the proposition that a child of tender years may be held to have assumed the risk of injury as a matter of law. Based on those cases, appellant asserts that it is entitled to judgment as a matter of law.

" 'Infants under fourteen years of age . . . assume the risk of those patent, obvious, and known dangers which they are able to appreciate and avoid.' [Cit.] Although whether assumption of risk on the part of a child bars recovery is peculiarly a question for the jury' [cit.], if the facts are so plain and palpable that they demand a finding by the court as a matter of law', the trial court may make that determination on summary adjudication without the intervention of a jury. [Cit.]"*Abee,* supra, at 69, 312 S.E.2d 142. In *Abee,* the record included a deposition of the plaintiff on which this court relied heavily in establishing that the plaintiff was aware of the risk of injury and voluntarily assumed that risk. The record of the present case is not so complete and there is nothing in it which demands the conclusion that appellee understood the risk of occupying the place he occupied and assumed that risk. In light of appellee's age and the lack of evidence in the record concerning his ability to appreciate the risk and his actual understanding of the risk, we hold that *Hunt,* supra, which did not involve a child, does not apply so as to demand a ruling that appellee, as a matter of law, assumed the risk of the injury he sustained.

2. Appellant has offered this court citations from several foreign jurisdictions to support its argument that it has fully discharged its duty to protect spectators from foul balls by providing protected seating behind home plate. Representative of those cases is *Akins v. Glens Falls City School Dist.,* 53 N.Y.2d 325, 441 N.Y.S.2d 644, 424 N.E.2d 531 (1981), where it was held that "in the exercise of reasonable care, the proprietor of a ball park need only provide screening for the area of the field behind home plate where the danger of being struck by a ball is the greatest. Moreover, such screening must be of sufficient extent to provide adequate protection for as many spectators as may reasonably be expected to desire such seating in the course of an ordinary game." 424 N.E.2d at 533.

Once again, we find that the record of this case does not establish appellant's entitlement to judgment as a matter of law. The New York court in *Akins,* supra, noted that it did not "suggest that where the adequacy of the screening in terms of protecting the area behind home plate properly is put in issue, the case should not be submitted to the jury." *Id.,* 424 N.E.2d 534. Appellee has done in this case what the Akins court anticipated: he has alleged that the design of the stadium is deficient in that the particular area which he occupied is a high-risk area which is unprotected and that the allegedly negligent design caused his injury. Appellant has not pierced those allegations by producing facts to refute them. Nor has appellant shown by evidence that there is sufficient screen-protected seating available for as many spectators as may reasonably be expected to desire such seating in the course of an ordinary game. Considering appellant's burden as movant for summary judgment to affirmatively negative appellee's claim by evidence (*Rogin v. Dimensions South Realty,* 153 Ga.App. 75, 264 S.E.2d 555 (1980)), and the fact that there is no such evidence in the record of this case, we are compelled to hold that appellant has not demonstrated entitlement to judgment as a matter of law on the basis of its theory that no duty to appellee was breached.

3. Appellant contends that appellee cannot recover because the sole proximate cause of appellee's injuries was the negligence of his parents in taking him into a place of danger. *Stroud v. Willingham,* 126 Ga.App. 156, 190 S.E.2d 143 (1972). However, since we have ruled in the preceding division of this opinion that questions of fact remain with regard to whether the design of appellant's facility is defective and whether that allegedly negligent design

caused appellee's injury, logic compels the conclusion that we cannot say, based on the record of this case as it now exists, that the proximate cause of appellee's injuries was negligence on the part of his parents.

Since appellant has not demonstrated its entitlement to judgment as a matter of law by producing evidence affirmatively showing that appellee cannot recover, the trial court was correct in denying appellant's motion for summary judgment.

Judgment affirmed.

QUESTIONS AND DISCUSSION

1. Chief Justice Cooke in *Akins* dissented, noting that "[t]he majority has in effect undertaken the task of prescribing the size, shape and location of backstops and other protective devices that will satisfy a baseball field owner's duty of reasonable care under the circumstances." Is that wise? Does a court possess the requisite expertise to delineate safety and security measures in sports?

2. The standard of care changes if the invitee is a minor. The question is whether a minor is capable of appreciating participating in a sport.

3. In *Merritt*, the factual question was whether the injured eight-year-old was able to appreciate the risk of occupying the place that he occupied and whether the design of the screening was negligent in that it ignored the high-risk area of the unprotected picnic grounds area adjacent to the right field foul line.

4. A business proprietor who holds his business out to the public for entry is subject to liability for bodily harm caused by accident, negligence, or intentionally harmful acts of third persons. That is, if the proprietor, by the exercise of reasonable care, could have discovered that such acts were being done or were about to be done, then he should have protected the public by controlling these third persons or by offering a warning. But proprietors are not bound to anticipate unforeseeable independent acts of third persons; only when one can reasonably anticipate is there a duty to take some sort of precautionary measures.

5. The owner-occupier owes a duty to discover, correct, and protect invitees from unreasonable risk of harm. In a case where an invitee slipped on a boat dock at a state park, allegedly due to the result of an unreasonably dangerous accumulation of algae and slime on the wood dock, the question was, did water on the dock create an unreasonable risk of harm? *See Douglas v. State ex rel Dept. of Culture Recreation & Tourism,* 636 So.2d 1098 (La. Ct. App. 1994).

6. The possessor is liable to a business invitee for a condition of the land if defendant (1) either created, knew, or by exercise of reasonable care would have discovered the condition; (2) should have realized that it involved an unreasonable risk of harm; (3) should have expected that an invitee either (a) would not discover or realize the danger, or (b) would fail to protect himself; (4) failed to use reasonable care to protect invitee against the danger, and (5) the condition was the proximate cause of plaintiff's injury.

7. A steep and hilly golf-cart path has a concealed 180 degree hairpin turn. First-time users speed down the hill, the brakes on the cart lock, and the cart crashes and tips over at the turn. Under the circumstances, is this an unreasonably hazardous condition? *See American Golf Corp. v. Manley*, 473 S.E.2d 161 (Ga. Ct. App. 1996). *See also* Devoto, *'Injury on the Golf Course: Regardless of Your Handicap Escaping Liability Is Par for the Course,'* 44 Def. L.J. 333 (1995); Grieme, 'Developer Liability for "Sub-Par" Golf,' 11 Prob. & Prop. 8 (1997).

8. A horse show participant was injured when she struck a utility guywire appurtenant to the horse arena. Plaintiff escaped summary judgment on the grounds that the

> . . . Riding Club may have been negligent in failing to remove or relocate the guywire in question or in failing to warn the horse show participants by flags or otherwise, of its location. Furthermore, they may have also been negligent in failing to provide proper lighting in or near the arena.

Uhler v. Evangeline Riding Club, 525 So. 2d 550, 553 (La. Ct. App. 1988). Of these several issues of material fact, is there any one issue alone that if decided to plaintiff's favor would assure her recovery?

D. PRODUCTS LIABILITY

Products liability law in sports was once associated almost solely with football helmets. This is no longer the case. It is now the method of recovery for an athletic participant who is injured as a result of defective equipment. The three most prevalent theories of recovery are negligence (liability), strict liability, and warranty (liability).

1. Sports Equipment

Items and equipment in sports that have been alleged to be defective have included football helmets, golf carts, lawn darts, softball bases, ski bindings, jet-skis, outboard propeller guards, roller skates, three-wheel ATV's, racing bikes, exercise machines, Astroturf, trampolines, aluminum bats, diving boards, and basketball courts. Equipment manufacturers must meet state-regulated standards of safety and care in the product's design, manufacture, and use. Additionally the supplier and seller may also be liable for negligence if they fail to exercise reasonable care: the manufacturer must assure that the product is reasonably safe when used for the intended purpose and in the intended manner, and the manufacturer must meet the standard of reasonable care in the manufacture and design of sports equipment.

2. Strict Liability

Strict liability is liability without fault. Strict liability is imposed for reasons of public policy. Sports equipment suppliers are liable if they sell unreasonably dangerous sports equipment that is harmful as a result of a defective condition. The manufacturer is liable to the ultimate consumer if the seller is in the business of selling the product and the product has not been substantially changed or altered.

A product is defective if it is not reasonably fit for the purposes for which it was sold. In sports, of course, each piece of safety (protective) equipment is specifically designed and manufactured for a particular safety or functional objective. By using proper instructions and warnings, a seller may avoid liability, if when followed properly, injury would be avoided. The seller can assume that the athlete will read, understand, and follow these instructions.

In *Everett v. Bucky Warren, Inc.*, a hockey coach's decision to supply helmets with a design defect, when other, safer helmets were available, was sufficient to create a product liability claim.

EVERETT V. BUCKY WARREN, INC.

380 N.E.2d 653 (Mass. 1978)

In this case the plaintiff seeks damages from the suppliers of a protective helmet he was wearing when, while playing in a hockey game, he was struck in the head by a puck and was seriously injured. The question before us is whether, on the various counts brought under both negligence and strict liability theories, the evidence was sufficient to support the verdicts for the plaintiff.

. . . [T]his case revolves around the design of the protective helmet worn by the plaintiff when he was injured. It is described as a three-piece helmet because its protective components are three sections of high-impact plastic lined on the inside with shock foam. One piece covers the back of the head, extending from the nape up about six inches, and running horizontally between positions slightly behind each ear; the second piece, approximately two inches wide, rings the front of the head from the same positions, thus covering the forehead; and the third piece joins the tops of these two sections and covers the top of the head. This top piece is loosely connected to the other two sections by six strips of leather, each $1\frac{1}{2}$ to $1\frac{3}{4}$ inches in width and $1\frac{1}{2}$ to 2 inches in length. The side pieces are linked by a $\frac{3}{4}$ inch wide elastic strap, whose length is adjustable. The result of this three-piece design and loose method of linking the sections is that there are gaps within the helmet where no plastic piece covers. The gap between the top piece and the two side pieces ranges from $\frac{1}{2}$ to $\frac{3}{4}$ of an inch. The gaps between the two side pieces vary with the size of the wearer's head and the tension with which the elastic straps are adjusted, and range from zero to $\frac{3}{4}$ of an inch. This three-piece design, characterized by the internal gaps, was somewhat unique, and there were available at the time of the plaintiff's injury and for some time prior thereto helmets that were designed as one-piece units and were therefore without such gaps.

When the injury occurred the plaintiff, who was approximately nineteen years old, was a post-graduate student and a member of the hockey team at the defendant New Preparatory School (New Prep) in Cambridge, Massachusetts. On January 10, 1970, the New Prep team went to Providence, Rhode Island, to play the Brown University freshman team. During the game the plaintiff, a defenseman, attempted to block the shot of a Brown player by throwing himself into a horizontal position on the ice, about ten to fifteen feet in front of the shooting player and perpendicular to the intended line of flight of the puck. The puck struck the plaintiff above and slightly back from his right ear, and penetrated into the gap of the helmet formed where the three helmet sections came together. As a result of this penetration the puck hit his head and caused a fracture of the skull. This serious injury subsequently required that a plate be inserted in the plaintiff's skull, and caused the plaintiff to have headaches that will continue indefinitely.

The helmet was being worn by the plaintiff on the night of his injury as a result of its being supplied to him through the following process. The helmet was manufactured by J. E. Pender (Pender), a proprietorship engaged in the manufacture of sporting goods and represented in this action by the defendant George Whittie, executor of the will of James E. Pender. In 1967 through 1969 Pender sold at least fourteen helmets of the type worn by the plaintiff to the defendant Bucky Warren, Inc. (Bucky Warren), a retailer in sporting goods, which in turn sold them to New Prep. The helmets had been specially ordered by Owen Hughes, the coach of the New Prep team, who was the person authorized by the school to make such purchases. They were painted in the colors of the school to match the team uniforms. Each player on the plaintiff's team was supplied with one of these helmets for practice and games use, although Hughes's testimony indicated that, had a player so wished, he could have worn a different helmet of his own choosing. Rather than purchasing his own helmet, the plaintiff chose to wear the one supplied to him by the school authorities.

The plaintiff brought this action claiming that, because of the gaps, the Pender helmet was defectively designed, and that therefore all three defendants, Pender, Bucky Warren, and New Prep, were liable to him in negligence for supplying him the helmet, and that the defendants Pender and Bucky Warren were also liable to him in tort on a strict liability theory. . . . The jury found that all three defendants were negligent, that the helmet was not in a reasonably safe condition when sold by Pender and Bucky Warren, that the plaintiff's injury was caused by the condition of the helmet and the negligence of the defendants, and that the plaintiff himself neither assumed the risk of the injury nor was contributorily negligent. The plaintiff was awarded $85,000 in damages. After proper motions the judge, notwithstanding the jury verdicts, entered judgments in favor of all defendants on the negligence counts, holding that, as matter of law, the plaintiff assumed the risk of his injury. He entered judgment for the plaintiff for $85,000 on the strict liability counts, however, on the ground that assumption of the risk was not a defense to this cause of action. Appeals and cross-appeals were claimed, and we granted an application for direct appellate review . . . .

A third-party action was filed by the defendant Pender against the defendant New Prep. The issues raised here are whether there was sufficient evidence for the jury to find that: (a) the defendants Pender and New Prep were negligent, (b) the plaintiff was not negligent and did not assume the risk of his injury, and (c) the helmet was defective and unreasonably dangerous as sold by Pender and Bucky Warren. . . .

1. Negligence. "A manufacturer is under a duty to use reasonable care to design a product that is reasonably safe for its intended use." . . . We hold that this evidence was sufficient to support the answer of the jury that Pender was negligent in the design of the helmet.

We reach a similar conclusion with regard to the defendant New Prep. . . . [T]he issue with regard to New Prep is whether "it was bad practice for a hockey coach to supply the plaintiff with the helmet in question and whether the supplying of said helmet to the plaintiff was causally related to his injuries." . . . There was sufficient evidence to permit the jury to decide whether, in these circumstances, the supplying of the helmet to the plaintiff was negligent conduct.

Having determined that the jury were warranted in finding negligence on the parts of the defendants, we turn now to a consideration of the defenses of assumption of the risk and contributory negligence. . . .

2. Strict liability in tort. The plaintiff claims that the three-piece design of the Pender helmet, with the gaps in it, was defective and unreasonably dangerous as defined in the Restatement, and therefore that the manufacturer and retailer are liable to him. We hold that there was sufficient evidence to reach the jury on this theory. For a product to be in a defective condition it does not have to be the result of errors made during the manufacturing process; it is defective as well "when it is properly made according to an unreasonably dangerous design" and does not meet a consumer's reasonable expectation as to its safety. The focus is on the design itself, not on the manufacturer's conduct. Factors that should be weighed in determining whether a particular product is reasonably safe include "the gravity of the danger posed by the challenged design, the likelihood that such danger would occur, the mechanical feasibility of a safer alternative design, the cost of an improved design, and the adverse consequences to the product and to the consumer that would result from an alternative design. In this case the gravity of the danger posed by the three-piece design was demonstrated by the injuries to the plaintiff. There was substantial evidence that tended to show that helmets of the one-piece design were safer than the Pender model, that these one-piece helmets were in manufacture prior to the plaintiff's injury, and that, while more expensive than the Pender helmets, they were not economically unfeasible. This evidence provided a sufficient basis for the jury's findings that the helmet was "unreasonably dangerous." . . .

4. The judgments on the strict liability counts are affirmed. The judgments on the negligence counts are reversed with instructions that judgments be entered on the verdicts.

So ordered.

3. Warranty Liability

Another theory of recovery under product's liability is breach based on contract. A warranty is a promise about the product's quality and condition. If the product does not meet the promise's expectations, then the warranty is breached and the seller is liable for the resulting damage. There are two types of warranties: express and implied. The express warranty is specifically "expressed" by the manufacturer or seller's statements or conduct. The implied warranty, more commonly known as the implied warranty of merchantability (or fitness for ordinary use), is breached when a specific piece of sports equipment does not meet its label's "implied" representations (and therefore is not fit for the ordinary use for which it was sold).

QUESTIONS AND DISCUSSION

1. When the sports product in question is dangerous, for example, a golf cart, the manufacturer has a duty to warn of potential hazards even if it was properly used. *See, e.g.*, Eichstadt, *'Release Me Not: Products Liability and Ski Bindings Injuries — A Source for Model Sports Principles,'* 19 T. Marshall L. Rev. 551 (1994).
2. But warnings are not required when the danger is obvious or when the user already knows of the product's dangerous propensities (for example, that the sharp blades of ice skates can cut you). *See, e.g.*, Duff, *'Game Plan for Successful Products Liability Action Against Manufacturers of Artificial Turf,'* 5 Seton Hall J. Sports L. 223 (1995).
3. Warnings must perform the function of adequately explaining how to reduce the potential for risk. A warning is inadequate if (1) it does not particularize the risk that the product presents; (2) if it is inconsistent with how the product will be used; (3) if it does not provide the reason for the warning; or (4) if the warning was not designed in a manner that is intended to reach the foreseeable user.
4. *Everett v. Bucky Warren, Inc.,* explained the particular factors that will determine if a product's design (here, a three-piece hockey helmet) is reasonably safe; they are (1) the gravity of the danger posed by the design defect; (2) the likelihood that danger will occur; (3) the mechanical feasibility of a safer design; (4) the cost of an improved design; and (5) the adverse consequences that might result from an alternative design. *See, e.g.*, Merritt, *'The Football Helmet v. Products Liability,'* 39 Fedn. Ins. & Corp. Coun. Q. 393 (1989); Sullivan, *'Football Helmet Products Liability: A Survey of Cases and Call for Reform,'* 3 Sports Law. J. 233 (1996). *See generally* Kochman, *'The "Fun Defense": Assuming the Risk of Recreational Equipment,'* 35 For Def. 28 (1993).
5. Products liability differs from state to state. However, one general requirement, at least to some extent, is that there must be "privity" if one is to effectively sue under warranty liability. Privity is that direct line that extends from manufacturer to the consumer. It is a relationship between parties that is sufficiently close and direct so as to support a legal claim on behalf of the plaintiff against the other person with whom this relationship exists. Would privity extend from the manufacturer to a high school star student-athlete who is injured when a defective aluminum bat that was purchased, owned, controlled, and maintained by the high school splits in his hand while batting and severely injures him, effectively

terminating his Rice University scholarship and his promising hopes for a successful professional career? What are his damages?

6. Along with privity or the lack thereof, there are other defenses that the manufacturer or seller can assert to defeat a claim based on the product liability of an allegedly defective piece of sports equipment. Professor Dobbs identifies the following categories of defenses: contributory (comparative) negligence and assumed risk; unforeseeable misuse, alteration, and modification; disclaimers and limitations on liability; statutory defenses; compliance with or preemption by statute; and statutes of limitations. See generally Dobbs, *The Law of Torts* §§369-374 at 1020-1039. Professor Dobbs continues that

> [d]ifferences among the courts make a statement of the rules of comparative fault and assumed risk unreasonably complicated. But the mainstream thought in products liability actions presently holds that (1) conduct amounting to contributory fault reduces the plaintiff's damages under the comparative fault rules, and (2) assumed risk is now ordinarily regarded as a species of fault also treated under the comparative fault rules, except that (3) some assumed risk may turn out upon analysis to be an obscure way of saying that the product was not defective or that a superseding course insulated the manufacturer from liability.

Id., §369 at 1020. Another type of defense is called incurred risk. In a ski binding strict liability and negligence action, the manufacturer used this defense along with a signed sales slip release that acknowledged the fact that bindings will not release under all circumstances. "Incurred risk involves a mental state of venturousness on the part of the actor against whom it is asserted, and requires a subjective analysis of the actors actual knowledge and voluntary acceptance." *Moore v. Sitzmark Corp.*, 555 N.E.2d 1305, 1308 (Ind. Ct. App. 1990). The proper definition of the risk that the skier may or may not have incurred must be determined. The sales slip release only released injuries that were incurred as a result of the inherent nature of the bindings and not damages that might have resulted from their alleged negligent design. Are there any risks in a suit that alleges defective bindings that would not be "incurred"?

7. In an elementary school gym class, an 11-year-old was struck in the eye with a hockey stick. The injured student claimed that he based his behavior on defendant misrepresentations that "Cosom Hockey" could be played safely without eye protection. Plaintiff argued that these representations rendered defendants liable on theories of negligence, including a failure to warn, negligent misrepresentation, and breach of warranty. Plaintiff sued the game's manufacturer, even though the identity of the stick's manufacturer was never determined. Plaintiff's theory of the case was that the game, not the stick, was the defective product. The court held that plaintiff's causes of action cannot be based on a dissemination of product literature or the rules of the game, in the absence of evidence that the injuries were caused by any equipment made or supplied by defendant. Is this in actuality a privity defense? *See Garcia v. Kusan, Inc.*, 655 N.E.2d 1290 (Mass. Ct. App. 1995).

E. DEFAMATION

Sports in America cause great discussion, varied opinion, and even heated debate. Because of this, there is always a possibility that athletes will be defamed by journalists, sportswriters, media personalities, or others. The question is whether specific statements are defamatory, and if so, are they actionable. Defamation is a "taking from one's reputation." Statements are defamatory if they are published, false, and cause damage to an athlete's reputation. There are two forms of defamatory publication: libel and slander. Libel originally referred to written or printed work while slander was oral. This distinction has become blurred in recent years. The slandered athlete must prove actual damages; but there are four exceptions that impute slander per se and are actionable per se. These imputations refer to accusations regarding crimes; loathsome diseases; adverse affect on trade, business, or profession; or unchastity to a woman.

1. Public Figures

It is pivotal in defamation to determine if the plaintiff is a public figure. Public figures and public officials must meet the burden of proof of actual malice before they can maintain a successful suit in defamation. The media is entitled to act on the assumption that public people have voluntarily exposed themselves to an increased risk of defamatory falsehood. Athletes are usually deemed to be limited public figures.

The plaintiff in *Nussbaumer v. Time, Inc.*, the assistant general manager of the Cleveland Browns, was determined to be a public figure where an article, five years after the event, characterized him as "spying" on a team meeting. In this position, he was responsible for conducting player trades and the college draft, and negotiating with players.

The coach, Forrest Gregg, was conducting a team meeting when he discovered Nussbaumer surreptitiously listening. He then pulled Nussbaumer into the meeting and yelled at him in front of the players. Nussbaumer was relieved of his duties that same day. Five years later, in a *Sports Illustrated* article on Coach Gregg, it categorized this incident as Nussbaumer spying for the front office at the time he was caught.

NUSSBAUMER V. TIME, INC.

---

13 Media L. Rep. 1753 (Ohio Ct. App. 1986)

NAHRA, Judge.

Robert Nussbaumer, plaintiff-appellant, appeals the Court of Common Pleas' decision granting summary judgment to Time Magazine and Paul Zimmerman. The court based its decision of this libel case on two determinations. First the article was held to be substantially true. Second, the appellant was held to be a public figure; as such he was required to demonstrate "actual malice" on the part of the defendants. The following facts give rise to this appeal.

Robert Nussbaumer played professional football from 1946 to 1951. Following his retirement as a player, he became a scout for the St. Louis Cardinals Football Club. He worked in this capacity for Detroit and Cleveland. In Cleveland, he became a Vice President of the Club and the Player Personnel Director (Director). As Director, he was responsible for conducting player trades and the college draft, and negotiating with players.

He held this position during the 1977 football season. The team had started strong in 1977 but by December it had disintegrated. As the team fortunes faded, media coverage of the coach and the management intensified. Coach Forrest Gregg was rumored to be on the verge of being fired. Gregg's relationship with the team owner, Art Modell, was at the core of this controversy.

During the middle of this furor, the incident which forms the basis of this libel case took place; Gregg was conducting a team meeting when he discovered Nussbaumer surreptitiously listening. He pulled Nussbaumer into the meeting and yelled at him in front of the whole team. Nussbaumer was relieved of his duties the same day. A press release announced that he resigned.

Gregg, who was fired by the Browns two weeks later, subsequently became the coach of the Cincinnati Bengals. The Bengals were in the 1982 Super Bowl. Prior to the game, Sports Illustrated ran an article entitled "What's New? These Two" which recapped the careers of the head coaches of the opposing teams. In the portion of the article that focused on Gregg's career, the author, Paul Zimmerman, referred to the incident which lead to Nussbaumer's discharge. The article said Nussbaumer was spying for the front office (management) at the time he was caught.

Nussbaumer sued Time, Inc., Sports Illustrated's parent corporation, and Zimmerman for libel. The trial court granted summary judgment. It concluded that the version printed in the article was substantially true when compared to Nussbaumer's version.

The court also determined that Nussbaumer was a public figure. A public figure must demonstrate actual malice before he can maintain a successful libel suit.

The appellant filed a timely appeal.

I

The appellant's first assignment of error is:

I. THE TRIAL COURT ERRED IN GRANTING THE APPELLEES' MOTION FOR SUMMARY JUDGMENT–REASONABLE MINDS COULD ONLY CONCLUDE THAT THE STATEMENTS IN THE ARTICLE WERE ABSOLUTELY UNTRUE AND DEFAMATORY.

The trial court determined that the Sports Illustrated article entitled "What's New? These Two", published January 25, 1982, (the article) did not materially vary from the facts as related by Nussbaumer. Slight and unimportant inaccuracies will not prevent a finding of truth if the "gist" or "sting" of the charges is justified by a showing of its essential elements. A comparison of Nussbaumer's version with the article demonstrates that the gist is the same.

Nussbaumer contends that he was standing in a seldomly used side hallway outside the door to the room where the team meeting was taking place. He was eavesdropping on a team meeting being conducted by the coach, Forrest Gregg. Nussbaumer admits to deliberately standing outside the door and surreptitiously listening to the meeting for three minutes. Gregg suddenly opened the door and pulled him into the room. Gregg said "If you want to listen to what's going on in a team meeting, why the hell don't you come in and listen to it." The meeting was immediately adjourned. Later that afternoon Peter Hadhazy, the team's general manager, fired him because of the incident.

The article gave the following version of this incident:

Next year was up and down, and Gregg began learning about the underside of the NFL/Every word from his team meetings, everything spoken to his players was finding its way to the front office. There was obviously a spy, but who? Gregg knew it wasn't one of his coaches. Whenever a team meeting was going on, the noise from a heater in the next room would suddenly stop. Someone was turning it off, to listen more carefully. Finally there was a Monday meeting after a game with the Rams, a 9-0 loss. There was a noise from the closet. The door was pulled open and there was the spy, Bob Nussbaumer, the player personnel director. It was an embarrassing situation, but the message soon came down to Gregg. If you talk about what went on here, you'll never get another job in the NFL.

To this day Modell denies having any hand in the matter. "When I found out about the incident, I fired Nussbaumer on the spot," Modell says. "Whatever he was doing it for, he wasn't reporting to me. As far as Gregg's being blackballed, that's a total lie. We don't work that way. We've always run a clean operation."

The appellant contends that the story varies from his version in several respects:

1. Appellant did not "spy" on Gregg's team meeting. He was attracted to the loud shouting and stood outside the door to find out what what (sic) going on.
2. The incident did not occur after the Browns loss to the Rams, but after a loss to the Chargers.
3. He was not secretly hiding in a closet. He was standing outside a door.
4. There was no heater to be turned off to hear the team meeting in the next room.
5. He was not fired on the spot by Modell but kept on the payroll for more than a year.

The argument that he was eavesdropping rather than spying is premised on the appellant's definition of spying. The appellant contends that a spy is somebody working for the other side. . . .

A court must choose the most innocent definition possible when determining if a party has been libeled. The trial court correctly determined that the use of the term spy, given the conceded facts, was not defamatory.

The second inaccuracy is that the incident occurred after a loss to the San Diego Chargers instead of the loss to the Los Angeles Rams. Aside from a factual error, the appellant does not show why this inaccuracy matters.

The third factor the appellant relies on to distinguish his facts from those in the article is that he was standing in a side hall instead of a bathroom. The appellant admitted that he was in a secluded side hallway purposefully listening to the team meeting. He knew that he could not be observed by anyone in the meeting. In this context, the difference between standing in a hallway and standing in a bathroom is immaterial.

The fourth alleged difference is that he did not turn a heater off. Again, given the context of this incident this is a difference without distinction.

Finally, he argues that Modell kept him on the payroll for a year instead of firing him immediately, as the article reported. The appellant stated in his deposition that he was discharged by the General Manager the afternoon the incident took place. His duties ceased and notice of his resignation was given to the media. The fact that Model chose to give him his salary until he found a new job does not affect the accuracy of the report that he was fired immediately.

The appellant also contends that the article states that he was engaged in a season long spying campaign. He only conceded that one incident took place. However, he has not controverted Forrest Gregg's testimony that Gregg's secretary had told him (Gregg) that Nussbaumer would frequently eavesdrop on conversations in Gregg's office by going into an adjoining bathroom and turning off the light (a noisy fan would come on with the light). Gregg testified that he and the secretary had a series of hand signals that would signal when Nussbaumer was listening.

The conceded facts are substantially true when compared to the article. The trial court correctly granted summary judgment on this basis.

II

The appellant's second assignment of error is:

II. THE TRIAL COURT ERRED IN HOLDING THE APPELLANT TO BE A PUBLIC FIGURE.

The trial court correctly concluded that Nussbaumer was a "public figure"; summary judgment was properly granted because the supporting evidence demonstrates the appellant cannot meet his burden of showing Time acted with actual malice.

The Supreme Court has held that certain individuals must meet a heightened burden (actual malice) before they can maintain a successful libel suit. The court has held that the First Amendment of the Federal Constitution requires two categories of individuals to meet this threshold: public officials and public figures. *Gertz v. Robert Welch, Inc.* (1974), 418 U.S. 323. Nussbaumer, through his role with the Browns, is a public figure.

The *Gertz* court gave the following definition of a public figure: "The *New York Times* standard defines the level of constitutional protection appropriate to the context of defamation of a public person. Those, who by reason of the notoriety of their achievements or the vigor and success with which they seek the public's attention, are properly classed as public figures. . . ." . . .

In the instant case, Nussbaumer held a high profile job with an organization that curries and thrives on media attention. The Cleveland Browns Football Club is a business whose product is sold by having people buy tickets or watch their games on television. Media attention is a critical tool used to attract and keep the public's interest. During the football season, the local paper daily carries at least one story on the team. In fact, part of Nussbaumer's job was to facilitate this coverage by informing the media about things that affect the club's performance, i.e., injuries, contract status of players, strategies, etc.

The managing of a professional club attracts acute coverage. Decisions controlling what player will be on the field, coaching, and general management philosphy are publicized. News conferences are frequently held to announce changes that affect this area.

When Nussbaumer accepted a front office job with the Browns, he stepped into the public eye. He was in charge of player selection. He helped arrange player trades with other clubs, select possible choices in the college player draft, and helped negotiate contracts with players on the team roster. All of these chores directly affect who will be playing for the team; hence, they attract a continuing media coverage.

The relationship between the individuals charged with managing the team is also predictably in the limelight. Disagreements over players, coaching philosophy, or just personality clashes are predictably given great attention by the media. Each season the media covers dozens of stories stemming from office gossip or office politics. Stories of the firing of a coach because of a disagreement with the management are common.

An individual involved in the management of professional sports teams has voluntarily stepped into the public eye. The organization he works for attracts and courts such attention that he is a public figure at least for the limited purpose of stories related to his job.

The article dealt solely with the management of the Browns. It stated that Nussbaumer was spying on the head coach for the front office. Nussbaumer should be required to demonstrate actual malice on the part of the defendants.

This conclusion is consistent with the restricted definition of public figure given by the Ohio Supreme Court in *Milkovich v. The News-Herald, et al.* (1984), 15 Ohio St. 3d 292. Milkovich, a high school wrestling coach, was held not to be a public figure. A high school wrestling coach is primarily an educator and a teacher. In contrast, professional sports is a business that requires and facilitates media coverage. A front office employee of a sports franchise in a policy making position has elected to enter the public eye and has assumed the risk of greater public exposure.

Summary judgment was correctly granted because no evidence was presented which would demonstrate actual malice. Nussbaumer was required to demonstrate that the statement was made "with 'actual malice' — that is, with knowledge that it was false or with reckless disregard of whether it was false or not." *New York Times v. Sullivan* (1964), 376 U.S. 254. . . .

Judgment affirmed. . . .

2. Defenses

There are various defenses available to defendants in actions based on defamation: for example, truth, fair comment, or privilege. The most prevalent defense in actions based on the defamation of athletes by sportswriters is the doctrine of fair comment. Everyone has a right to comment on matters of public interest if it is done fairly and with an honest purpose. Athletes, as public individuals, must expect critical reviews. However, they cannot effectively complain unless they are in fact falsely accused of wrongdoing.

In *Stepien v. Franklin,* the former owner of the NBA's Cleveland Cavaliers was lambasted by a radio sports talk show host; but these diatribes were viewed as opinions and protected by the First Amendment (for example, "stupid," "dumb," "buffoon," "nincompoop," "scum," "a cancer," "an obscenity," "gutless liar," "unmitigated liar," "pathological liar," "egomaniac," "nuts," "crazy," "irrational," "suicidal," "lunatic"). Opinions are not capable of defamatory content. However, assertions of fact are unprotected and thus capable of a defamatory meaning. Therefore, sports commentary that carries with it a "mixed opinion" is capable of implying an underlying defamatory fact and therefore is actionable. *Milkovich v. Lorain Journal Co.,* 497 U.S. 1 (1990).

STEPIEN V. FRANKLIN

528 N.E.2d 1324 (Ohio Ct. App. 1988)

This cause of action arises as a result of an action for slander and intentional infliction of emotional distress by the appellant, Theodore J. Stepien, against the appellee, Peter J. Franklin. . . .

Theodore J. Stepien ("Stepien") is the former President of the Cleveland Professional Basketball Company, more commonly known as the Cleveland Cavaliers. The Cleveland Cavaliers is a professional damages basketball franchise operated under the auspices of the National Basketball Association ("NBA"). In addition to his position with the Cavaliers, appellant was with actalso the President and sole shareholder of Nationwide Advertising Service, Inc., the largest personnel recruitment advertising company in the world with offices throughout the United States and Canada. Nationwide was also the principal shareholder of the Cavaliers. Appellant's tenure as president of the Cavaliers began in June 1980 and he remained in that position until the team . . . was sold . . . in May 1983.

Peter J. Franklin ("Franklin") is the host of a radio sports talk show known as "Sportsline." During the period in question, Sportsline was regularly broadcast Monday through Friday, 7:00 p.m. to midnight, unless it was pre-empted by a live sports event.

Franklin principally employed an audience call-in format—listeners are encouraged to call in and give their opinions and/or solicit Franklin's opinion about sports. Sportsline is entertainment, designed to encourage and capitalize on the considerable public interest in professional sports. The style of radio and television personalities who host talk shows such as Sportsline varies widely, from the erudite analysis of William F. Buckley to the insults of Joan Rivers. Franklin's style, which is immediately apparent from listening to his show, is an extreme version of the "insult" genre of entertainment. Franklin is often loud, opinionated, rude, abrasive, obnoxious and insulting. In a manner reminiscent of the popular comedian Don Rickles, Franklin frequently hangs up on his callers and/or calls them insulting names.

The period when Stepien was the President of the Cavaliers, June 1980 to May 1983, is also the time period in which the alleged slander and emotional distress took place.

The appellant, after becoming President of the Cavaliers, immediately began an aggressive style of management that involved making numerous player transactions and staff appointments. The appellant went through more than fifty players and six coaches in two and one-half years, including the hiring and firing of one coach twice. This aggressive style of management and the lack of the Cavaliers' success thereafter resulted in appellant's receiving a great deal of unfavorable criticism in the press, nationally and locally.

The factual background specifically relevant to the alleged defamatory statements can be broken down into three general topics:

1. National Basketball Association's moratoriums on trading;
2. The finances of the Cavaliers; and
3. The proposed sale of the team and move to Toronto.

Many of Franklin's alleged defamatory statements complained of herein consisted of those that challenged the appellant's ability to manage an NBA team. These remarks by Franklin involved Cavaliers' player transactions and the league's subsequent reaction to them. In November 1980, the Cavaliers engaged in the abovestated trades that resulted in the team's trading away several first round draft choices. These trades were criticized by most observers and fans as being detrimental to the Cavaliers. In response, the NBA Commissioner imposed a restriction referred to as a "moratorium on trades" involving the Cavaliers. The restriction permitted the team to make trades, but only upon consulting with the league office and obtaining final approval. After a short while, the moratorium was lifted, but in February 1983, a second moratorium occurred. This restriction required the Cavaliers to give the NBA twenty-four hours to consider any trade and was apparently motivated by the NBA's concern that the Cavaliers' troubles might lead them to make unwise player transactions in order to raise operating capital. The Cavaliers' financial problems were acute. The appellant considered many options to alleviate this problem. Between January and April 1983, the appellant explored several possibilities including selling the team to out-of-town buyers, selling the team to a local buyer, or retaining ownership and moving the team to Toronto. During this period, the media harshly criticized the appellant for not completing the sale and for proposing that the team move away from Cleveland.

There is no question that during the appellant's three-year period of ownership of the Cavaliers, Franklin was a harsh and critical commentator. His descriptions of appellant, extracted from tapes of the show provided to this court, include "stupid," "dumb," "buffoon," "nincompoop," "scum," "a cancer," "an obscenity," "gutless liar," "unmitigated liar," "pathological liar," "egomaniac," "nuts," "crazy," "irrational," "suicidal," "lunatic," etc. . . .

In this case, appellant asserts that summary judgment was inappropriate due to the fact the lower court incorrectly applied the "totality of circumstances" analysis set forth in Scott v. News-Herald. . . . The Scott analysis uses four factors to determine whether a published statement is a constitutionally protected opinion or an actionable defamatory remark. The factors to be considered are:

1. The specific language used;
2. Whether the truth or falsity of the statement is verifiable;
3. The specific context of the statement; and
4. The broader social context in which the statement appeared. . . .

This court finds, as the trial court found, that Franklin's comments were constitutionally protected opinion. As in Scott, the arena of sports is "a traditional haven for cajoling, invective, and hyperbole," and therefore the reasonable reader was on notice that this was a statement of opinion. *Scott*, 496 N.E.2d at 708-709. The appellant would have us believe that the statistical demographics of Franklin's audience is tantamount to deciding whether his remarks were defamatory. Again, if we are to have a free exchange of ideas, thoughts and discussion, we cannot place on a commentator the burden to protect against listeners who are not reasonable. . . .

In the cause before this court, the plaintiff is a public figure. Public figures, having thrust themselves into the public eye, cannot prevent others from criticizing or insulting them for their acts or deeds. This is especially true when the public figure is a professional basketball team "owner" and the antagonism and criticism is from a member of the media.

Public figures who thrust themselves into the public eye must bear the discomfort of criticisms levied upon their public actions or statements . . . Stepien admitted he made many bold moves in his ownership of the Cleveland Cavaliers. Many of these moves caused heated disputes among fans, media, and the NBA. In this context, Stepien must expect critical commentary. Stepien also considered moving the team to Toronto. This speculative move was also highly controversial. Writers and fans cannot be expected to remain mute when "their" team might leave the Cleveland area. Having engaged in such conduct, the expected response was quite normal, although harsh.

Appellee, Peter J. Franklin, commented about a public figure concerning controversial situations. The court cannot award an emotional distress claim based on Franklin's ill will to Stepien. Therefore, assignment of error number two is not well-taken and the trial court's decision is affirmed. . . .

In *Falls v. The Sporting News Publishing Co.*, a sportswriter was deemed to be a public figure with regard to his sports writing activities.

FALLS V. THE SPORTING NEWS PUBLISHING CO.

899 F. 2d 1221 (6th Cir. 1990)

PER CURIAM.

Plaintiff Joseph F. Falls, a sportswriter, appeals from an order granting summary judgment to the defendants in this diversity action brought under Michigan law for wrongful discharge and defamation. The district court found that the plaintiff was an independent contractor and thus lacked the rights that he would have had as an employee. The court found further that the plaintiff is a public figure and could not show that the defendants made false statements about him knowingly or recklessly. The plaintiff argues that genuine issues of fact exist as to all of these matters. We disagree, and we shall affirm the judgment of the district court.

I

At the time he commenced this suit Mr. Falls was 57 years old. He had been a sportswriter for over 35 years, and he had risen to the position of sports editor of *The Detroit News.*

In 1963, as a sideline, Mr. Falls began writing a weekly column for another paper, *The Sporting News,* which is published by defendant Sporting News Publishing Co. That relationship existed until June of 1985, when defendant Tom Barnidge, *The Sporting News'* then-new 37-year-old editor, terminated it. Mr. Barnidge allegedly told Mr. Falls that he "no longer fit our image." Sporting News discharged two other older columnists at the same time and hired three younger ones.

On June 19, 1985, in response to a reader's letter expressing displeasure with the dropping of Mr. Falls' column, Editor Barnidge wrote that "I know that Joe brightened a lot of hearts with his column through the years but we felt it was time to make a change, with more energetic columnists who attend more events and are closer to today's sports scene."

In a September 17, 1985, sports page "cover story" in *USA Today* discussing the changes at *The Sporting News,* defendant Richard Waters, president and chief executive officer of Sporting News, was quoted as saying that "[t]hose who seem to have reached maturity and are on the downswing are giving way to some of the up-and-coming young writers who we think deserve a chance." These two statements form the basis for the defamation claim.

Mr. Falls filed a timely federal court action charging age discrimination in violation of Michigan's Elliot-Larsen Civil Rights Act, Mich.Comp. Laws §§37.2101, *et seq.;* intentional, reckless, and negligent defamation; and knowing or reckless injurious falsehood. Without answering the complaint, the defendants moved for summary judgment. The district court granted the motion, finding (a) that Mr. Falls was an independent contractor not protected under Elliot-Larsen, and (b) that the statements were privileged opinions.

This court vacated the judgment and remanded the case. *Falls v. Sporting News Publishing Co.,* 834 F.2d 611 (6th Cir. 1987). We expressed concern about the granting of summary judgment on the age discrimination count while discovery was still pending, and we observed that it was not clear what test the district court had used in finding that the plaintiff was an independent contractor. *Id.* at 614. We rejected the district court's finding that the statements of Messers. Barnidge and Waters were protected opinions. *Id.* at 614-16. We remanded the injurious falsehood claim so that the plaintiff would have an opportunity to amend his pleadings and attempt to prove the elements of the tort. *Id.* at 617.

After the completion of discovery, defendants again moved for summary judgment. Again the motion was granted. *Falls v. Sporting News Publishing Co.,* 714 F. Supp. 843 (E.D. Mich. 1989). The district court undertook an exhaustive analysis of the factors bearing on whether an individual is an independent contractor, and found that this was what the plaintiff was. *Id.* at 844-46. The court went on to hold that the plaintiff was a public figure, and that on the uncontested facts no inference could be drawn that the statements were made with knowing or reckless disregard for the truth. *Id.* at 846-48. The court noted that plaintiff did not amend his complaint to allege the elements of injurious falsehood, and it granted summary judgment to the defendants in all respects. *Id.* at 848.

II

Whether one is an employee or independent contractor under Michigan law depends, as the district court correctly noted, on "economic reality." . . .

"Control of the worker's duties, payment of wages, authority to hire and fire, and responsibility for the maintenance of discipline, are all factors to be considered, but no one factor is controlling. . . . Whether TSN was plaintiff's employer, then, will depend upon the economic realities of their relationship, and among the relevant factors that will demonstrate an employment relationship are those listed above, as well as whether the duties performed by plaintiff were an integral part of TSN's business and contributed to the accomplishment of a common goal. . . . Establishment of an independent contractor relationship would require a convincing accumulation of factors indicating that plaintiff's services were rendered in the course of his pursuit of his separate business enterprise of selling those services." 834 F.2d at 614 (citations omitted).

The district court found, and we agree, that the plaintiff's work was integral to the success of *The Sporting News*. See 714 F.Supp. at 845. The issue is not, as defendants urge, whether the plaintiff is personally integral to the organization's success. Very few employees are so key that their employers could not function without them. The issue is whether the type of work done by the individual is integral to the success of the organization. Here Mr. Falls worked as a writer. Without written stories, there could be no *Sporting News*.

The district court also found that Sporting News exercised control over the plaintiff's work. This finding is more problematical, in our view. The defendants certainly had the right to edit the plaintiff's columns, and they sometimes asked him to write on a general topic such as the Super Bowl or the World Series. But Mr. Falls usually could write on any topic he wished, and even when given a general topic he could pick any aspect of that topic. Mr. Falls was not the type of writer-employee who is assigned a team or a sport and told how to cover it.

Regardless of how the question of control is resolved, however, we agree with the district court that the financial arrangements under which Mr. Falls wrote for *The Sporting News* militate strongly in favor of the conclusion that he was an independent contractor. Mr. Falls received $90 per column, which came to over $4,000 per year. If he did not produce a column, he did not get paid for it. His salary at *The Detroit News* was $89,000 per annum. *The Detroit News* paid all of Mr. Falls' fringe benefits; Sporting News paid none.

Sporting News paid none of Mr. Falls' expenses, and he deducted his expenses on his income tax returns. His receipts from Sporting News were reported not on a W-2 employee form, but on a Form 1099 (miscellaneous receipts), with no withholding and no social security deductions. His own returns listed his Sporting News receipts on Schedule C, which is used for income from sole-proprietorship businesses or professions. Mr. Falls' own tax returns indicate that *The Detroit News* was his only employer.

It is true that Sporting News paid Mr. Falls for every column he turned in, whether the column was run or not. But the more significant fact is that he was paid only when he produced a column. Once the column became the property of Sporting News, the publication could do with it what it pleased. *The Detroit News,* by contrast, paid Mr. Falls the same amount every week, even though his output (which ranged between 5 and 21 columns per week) was far from constant. It is clear from the undisputed facts that Mr. Falls was merely doing piecework for Sporting News. No rational jury could find otherwise, and summary judgment was therefore appropriate.

III

We turn now to Mr. Falls' defamation claim. If the plaintiff is a public figure, he must establish by clear and convincing proof that the defamatory statements were made with knowing or reckless disregard for their truth. *New York Times Co. v. Sullivan,* 376 U.S. 254 (1964). Under Michigan law, if the plaintiff is a private person, the statements must have been made negligently at least. *Ledl v. Quik Pik Food Stores, Inc.,* 133 Mich. App. 583, 349 N.W.2d 529 (1984) (per curiam).

The United States Supreme Court has defined two classes of public figures:

> For the most part those who attain this status have assumed roles of especial prominence in the affairs of society. Some occupy positions of such persuasive power and influence that they are deemed public figures for all purposes. More commonly, those classed as public figures have thrust themselves to the forefront of particular public controversies in order to influence the resolution of the issues involved. In either event, they invite attention and comment. *Gertz v. Robert Welch, Inc.,* 418 U.S. 323, 345 (1974).

Whether one is a public figure is a question of law to be determined by the courts. The district court found that Mr. Falls "is a public figure with regard to his sports writing activities." 714 F. Supp. at 847.

The plaintiff argues that he is not a public figure because he did not thrust himself into a controversy over his firing. This is not the test. The real question is whether Mr. Falls' career as a sportswriter made him a public figure for purposes of commentary on him as a sportswriter. Mr. Falls did choose to thrust his writing into the public eye, and he did "enjoy significantly greater access to the channels of effective communication and hence had a more realistic opportunity to counteract false statements than private individuals normally enjoy." *Gertz,* 418 U.S. at 344. According to the *USA Today* story, *The Sporting News* had a circulation of 700,000 in 1985. Given his weekly appearances before an audience of that size, Mr. Falls cannot persuasively claim to be a private figure.

That being so, we must determine whether a reasonable jury could find, by clear and convincing evidence, that the defendants made the statements with "actual malice" — *i.e.*, while realizing the statements were false or while subjectively entertaining serious doubt as to their truth.

Pointing to Mr. Waters' deposition testimony that he read the plaintiff's column only four or five times a year for four years, Mr. Falls argues that "Waters had an insufficient base upon which to construct any objective analysis of whether Plaintiff was 'past his peak' as a writer." The issue, however, is not whether Mr. Waters had a sufficient objective basis for making the remark, but whether he really entertained serious doubt about its truth. Mr. Waters testified that he found Mr. Falls' columns increasingly boring; there is no evidence to the contrary.

As to Mr. Barnidge's statement regarding "more energetic columnists who attend more events and are closer to today's sports scene," the plaintiff points to several parts of Mr. Barnidge's deposition testimony to support his claim of actual malice. Mr. Barnidge said he knew that Mr. Falls traveled extensively in connection with his job as sports editor of *The Detroit News;* that he could not recall any specific sporting events that Mr. Falls should have covered but did not; that his problem with Mr. Falls' writing was one of "intellectual industry" rather than "physical industry;" that he could not think of any specific sports figures with whom Mr. Falls should have been in touch, but was not; and that he did not feel that Mr. Falls was "too old to get up in the morning and do his job." With regard to the decision to drop Mr. Falls' column, Mr. Barnidge said that "[t]he number of events that he covered or the location of them had absolutely no bearing on my decision." As to the replacement columnists, Mr. Barnidge said he did not know if they had contacts within the sports world that Mr. Falls did not have and he had no numerical evidence that they attended more events that Mr. Falls. On the other hand, as noted by the district court, the following exchange did occur:

> Q: You further say, "Verdi, Gergen and Downey [the replacement columnists] attend more events."
> What events did they attend that were more than what Joe Falls had attended?
> A: I guess again this is my impression. It's my opinion, and I cannot give you numerical numbers as to how many events they attend or why there are more. Joe Gergen goes to the Final Four every year. I've never seen Joe Falls at the Final Four. Is that a specific?
> Q: That gives me a specific. Anything other than the Final Four that you know of that those three attended that in your opinion made you feel they attended more events?
> A: Again it was the material that they produced as a result of attending events and interviewing athletes, being on the scene that impressed me.

As with Mr. Waters, the most that can be said is that the remarks were ill-considered, lacked a reasonable basis in fact, and were negligently made. Unprofessional terminology and an intemperate tone do not satisfy the actual malice standard. The plaintiff himself testified that he knew of no facts that would demonstrate that the defendants made false statements about him with actual malice:

> Q: Are there any facts or reasons that you know of that would lead you to conclude or that you know of as to why those men would have lied about you or your column writing ability?
>
> A: Again, we are talking about opinion and what is subjective and I can argue with them. I am not calling them liars. I'm just saying that they said what they said and it defamed me. I felt very embarrassed by it.

Mr. Falls also testified that he knew of no facts that suggested to him that the defendants were expressing anything other than honestly held beliefs about his writing.

There is no evidence that Mr. Barnidge entertained serious doubts about the truth of what he said. No reasonable jury could find clear and convincing evidence of actual malice by either Mr. Barnidge or Mr. Waters, and therefore summary judgment was appropriate.

The judgment of the district court is affirmed.

QUESTIONS AND DISCUSSION

1. "If I were smart enough to know what I'd do two weeks from now I'd be smart enough to be a sports writer." John Madden, quoted in Parietti, *The Greatest Sports Excuses, Alibis, and Explanations* 245 (1990), quoted with approval in *Washington v. Smith*, 893 F. Supp. 60 (D.D.C. 1995). *Washington v. Smith* involves a sportswriter's preseason attempt to predict the likely contenders for the 1992-1993 women's college basketball championship. The sportswriter disparaged the coach of the University of Kansas Lady Jayhawks by opining that "playing to their ability is usually sabotaged by suspect coaching. This season should prove no different." *Id.* The question is whether this is a *Milkovich*-type "mixed opinion." The court held that the reader of a sports preview magazine understands that a considerable portion of the magazine's content is subjective opinion. Plaintiff will recover only if she could show that no reasonable person could find that the characterizations were supportable interpretations of the underlying facts. This the plaintiff in *Washington v. Smith* could not do. What additional comments could the sportswriter append to his original preview that would make a stronger case for plaintiff's attempt to find a "mixed opinion" capable of implying underlying defamatory facts?

2. A TV sports commentator called a soccer player a quitter and then, at the end of the broadcast, took a photograph of the athlete, drew a mustache and beard, spat on it, laid it on the floor, and jumped on it. Is that defamatory? The Colorado Court of Appeals said it was not. Mere opinions are not actionable; and since the athlete decided not to play during the playoffs, the comments were not capable of defamatory meaning. *Brooks v. Paige*, 773 P.2d 1098 (Colo. Ct. App. 1988).

3. As regards an athlete's public figure status, they are usually deemed to be a limited public figure. There are many personal factors in an athlete's life, which although they may affect his career, are not the proper subject of unlimited publication.

4. In *Woy v. Turner*, 573 F. Supp. 35 (N.D. Ga. 1983), Bucky Woy, the agent, became a limited public figure when he thrust himself into the forefront of a public controversy during a contract dispute by using the media, through press conferences, to help make his point.

5. The U.S. Supreme Court has defined two classes of public figures: "For the most part those who attain this status have assumed roles of especial prominence in the affairs of society. Some occupy positions of such persuasive power and influence that they are deemed public figures for all purposes. More commonly, those classed as public figures have thrust themselves to the forefront of particular public controversies in order to influence the resolution of the issues involved. In either event, they invite attention and comment." *Gertz v. Robert Welch, Inc.*, 418 U.S. 323, 345 (1974).

6. In *Falls v. The Sporting News Publishing Co.*, the court held that Falls was a public figure with regard to his sports writing activities. As such, he could not prove actual malice under the *New York Times* standard. This standard (*New York Times v. Sullivan*, 276 U.S. 254 (1976)) requires that false comments about public figures must be knowingly and in reckless disregard of the truth to be actionable. At worst, his former employer's remarks were ill-considered. Unprofessional terminology and an intemperate tone do not satisfy the actual malice standard. *Lins v. Evening News Assn.*, 436, 342 N.W. 2d 573, 582 (Mich. Ct. App. 1983).

7. In determining whether an alleged defamatory statement was an opinion or statement of fact, the standard to be applied is the totality of the circumstances. This includes specific language, whether the statement is verifiable, the general context of the statement, and the broader context in which the statement appears. *Scott v. News-Herald*, 496 N.E.2d 699 (Ohio 1986).

8. Once you attain public figure status, you can slip back into the status of a private person through the auspices of the rule of repose. In *Dempsey v. Times, Inc.*, 252 N.Y.S.2d 186 (Sup. Ct. 1964), *aff'd*, 254 N.Y.S.2d 80 (App. Dir. 1964), the heavyweight boxing champion, Jack Demsey, was defamed 45 years after the alleged event in a *Sports Illustrated* article in which his manager claimed that he had loaded Dempsey's gloves with plaster-of paris. The court held that reaching back that far was not within the *New York Times* standard, therefore, the recitation of the glove incident was not cloaked by the veil of privilege.

F. INVASION OF PRIVACY

Related to defamation is the right to protect one's privacy. This protects the athlete from distress created by the public exposure to accurate but private facts. Privacy is "the right to be left alone; to live one's life as one chooses free from assault, intrusion or invasion except as they can be justified by the clear needs of community living under a government of law." *Rosenbloom v. Metromedia, Inc.*, 403 U.S. 29 (1971). But, to the extent the athlete is a public figure, the *New York Times* actual malice standard, *New York Times Co. v. Sullivan*, 376 U.S. 254 (1964), will apply since to recover the athlete must prove that the defendant published the report with knowledge of its falseness (or reckless disregard of the truth). *See Time, Inc. v. Hill*, 385 U.S. 374, 388, (1967). Invasion of privacy suits in sports deal with the athletes' private lives as opposed to their lives as athletes, or it applies in situations where the publisher is not entitled to the constitutional privilege on the basis of maliciousness.

Analogous to the right of privacy is an athlete's right to his commercial representation. In *Ali v. Playgirl, Inc.*, an unauthorized representation of Muhammad Ali was used for commercial purposes. The court held that the right of publicity recognizes the commercial value of a non-newsworthy pictorial representation of a prominent athlete and protects the proprietary interest in the profitability of his public persona.

Ali v. Playgirl, Inc.

447 F. Supp. 723 (S.D.N.Y. 1978)

Plaintiff Muhammad Ali, a citizen of Illinois and until recently the heavyweight boxing champion of the world, has brought this diversity action for injunctive relief and damages against defendants Playgirl, Inc., a California corporation, Independent News Company ("Independent"), a New York corporation, and Tony Yamada, a California citizen, for their alleged unauthorized printing, publication and distribution of an objectionable portrait of Ali in the February, 1978 issue of Playgirl Magazine ("Playgirl"), a monthly magazine published by Playgirl, Inc., and distributed in New York State by Independent. The portrait complained of depicts a nude black man seated in the corner of a boxing ring and is claimed to be unmistakably recognizable as plaintiff Ali. Alleging that the publication of this picture constitutes, inter alia, a violation of his rights under Section 51 of the New York Civil Rights Law (McKinney March 3, 1976) and of his related common law "right of publicity", Ali now moves for a preliminary injunction directing defendants Playgirl, Inc. and Independents to cease distribution and dissemination of the February, 1978 issue of Playgirl Magazine, to withdraw that issue from circulation and recover possession of all copies presently offered for sale, and to surrender to plaintiff any printing plates or devices used to reproduce the portrait complained of. For the reasons which follow and to the extent indicated below, plaintiff's motion for a preliminary injunction is granted.

The Facts . . .

At the preliminary injunction hearing on February 2, counsel stated that the February issue of Playgirl containing the allegedly unlawful portrait of Ali was then scheduled to go "off sale," that is, to be removed from newsstand circulation on February 4.

Discussion

This court concludes that plaintiff has satisfied the standard established in this Circuit for determining whether a preliminary injunction should issue . . .

Defendants do not, and indeed cannot, seriously dispute the assertion that the offensive drawing is in fact Ali's "portrait or picture . . ." Even a cursory inspection of the picture which is the subject of this action strongly suggests that the facial characteristics of the black male portrayed are those of Muhammad Ali. The cheekbones, broad nose and wideset brown eyes, together with the distinctive smile and close cropped black hair are recognizable as the features of the plaintiff, one of the most widely known athletes of our time. In addition, the figure depicted is seated on a stool in the corner of a boxing ring with both hands taped and outstretched resting on the ropes on either side. Although the picture is captioned "Mystery Man," the identification of the individual as Ali is further implied by an accompanying verse which refers to the figure as "the Greatest." This court may take judicial notice that plaintiff Ali has regularly claimed that appellation for himself and that his efforts to identify himself in the public mind as "the Greatest" have been so successful that he is regularly identified as such in the news media.

Finally, defendants concede that Ali did not consent to the inclusion of his likeness in the February, 1978 Playgirl Magazine. Defendants contend, however, that even if their use of Ali's likeness is determined to be unauthorized and for trade purposes . . . the statutory right of privacy does not extend to protect "someone such as an athlete who chooses to bring himself to public notice, who chooses, indeed, as clearly as the plaintiff here does to rather stridently seek out publicity."

Accordingly, this right of publicity is usually asserted only if the plaintiff has "achieved in some degree a celebrated status." In the instant case, it is undisputed that plaintiff Ali has achieved such a "celebrated status" and it is clear to this court that he has established a valuable interest in his name and his likeness. There can be little question that defendants unauthorized publication of the portrait of Ali amounted to a wrongful appropriation of the market value of plaintiff's likeness . . .

As has been noted, in the course of his public career plaintiff has established a commercially valuable proprietary interest in his likeness and reputation, analogous to the good will accumulated in the name of a successful business entity. To the extent that defendants are unlawfully appropriating this valuable commodity for themselves, proof of damages or unjust enrichment may be extremely difficult." In virtually identical circumstances it has been observed that "a celebrity's property interest in his name and likeness is unique, and therefore there is no serious question as to the propriety of injunctive relief." . . . Furthermore, defendants appear not only to be usurping plaintiff's valuable right of publicity for themselves but may well be inflicting damage upon this marketable reputation. As described previously, the "likeness" of Ali which has been published is a full frontal nude drawing, not merely a sketch or photograph of him as he appears in public. Damages from such evident abuse of plaintiff's property right in his public reputation are plainly difficult to measure by monetary standards.

This court also notes that, although it appears that routinely scheduled newsstand circulation of the contested issue of Playgirl Magazine has ceased, it is established that voluntary cessation of illegal conduct does not deprive the court of the power to grant injunctive relief. . . .

Defendant Playgirl, Inc., is hereby enjoined from further distribution and dissemination of any copies of the February, 1978 issue of Playgirl Magazine containing the portrait complained of, and shall neither transfer nor remove from the jurisdiction any such copies presently in its custody, as well as the printing plates or devices used to reproduce the portrait, until further order of the court. Defendant Independent News is hereby directed to retain in its possession . . . those copies of the February 1978 issues of Playgirl Magazine it has recovered and impounded.

So ordered.

QUESTIONS AND DISCUSSION

1. In *Spahn v. Julian Messner, Inc.*, 274 N.Y.S.2d 877 (N.Y. 1966), a fictitious biography of a Hall of Fame baseball player was held to be unauthorized exploitation of his personality for purposes of trade. Although Warren Spahn gave away his public privacy, he maintained the right to secure privacy in his personal nonpublic life.
2. In *Zacchini v. Scripps-Howard Broadcasting Co.*, 433 U.S. 562, (1977), the Supreme Court gave the "human cannonball" the power to protect his publicity rights in that it did not immunize the television station from liability for televising Zacchini's entire act.
3. In *Ali v. Playgirl,* there was a cartoon-like drawing of a nude black man seated with boxing gloves in the corner of a boxing ring and indicated as "mystery man" but labeled in an accompanying verse as "The Greatest." This distinct and clear reference to Muhammad Ali was found to violate his celebrity publicity rights. Without the addendum of "The Greatest," which was undoubtedly the nom de guerre that Ali chose for himself, would the court still have found that this likeness violated Ali's publicity rights?
4. Deon Thomas, an All-American high school basketball player, told an assistant basketball coach at one school about the alleged inducements he was offered from another school. The coach recorded these conversations and promptly relayed them to the NCAA. Thomas sued on three variations of privacy tort: intrusion upon the seclusion of another, publicity given to private life (unwarranted publicity), and publicity that places a person in a false light. The court found no privacy violations. *See Thomas v. Pearl*, 998 F.2d 447 (7th Cir. 1993). *See also* Hochbert, '*Athletes and the Right to Privacy,*' 7 Sports Law. 2 (1989-1990); Margolies, '*Sports Figures Right of Publicity,*' 1 Sports Law. J. 359 (1994); Stapleton & McMurphy, '*The Professional Athlete's Right of Publicity,*' 10 Marq Sports L.J. 23 (1999).
5. An artist's representation of photographs of Joe Montana in the Super Bowl as rendered in the *San Jose Mercury Nerve* were quickly reproduced as posters and made available for sale to the general public. Montana sued for

commercial misappropriation of his name, photograph, and likeness. The court found against Montana on the grounds that no cause of action exists for the publication of matters in the public interest, which rests on the right of the public to know and the freedom of the press to print it. The "full page newspaper accounts of Super Bowls XXIII and XXV and of the 49'ers four championships in a single decade constituted publication of matters in the public interest entitled to First Amendment protection." The reproductions are similarly protected because Montana's name and likeness appeared on the posters for the same reason that they appeared on the original newspaper front pages: because he was a preeminent player in a contemporaneous newsworthy event. *Montana v. San Jose Mercury News, Inc.*, 40 Cal Rptr. 2d 639, 640-641 (Cal. Ct. App. 1995).

G. PARTICIPANT AND SPECTATOR INJURIES

Participants and spectators are on the front line for possible injuries and potential legal redress. Historically, many very potent defenses made successful lawsuits difficult. In many states, for example, there is a presumption that in the usual course of sporting activities, participants and spectators will assume the normal and ordinary risks of playing or watching the game. Accordingly, most successful lawsuits are based on those risks that are neither ordinary nor expected.

1. Participants Generally

Participants assume the risk of unintentional injuries, but do not assume the risk of injuries that are intentionally inflicted or result from a disregard for safety. However, an injured participant cannot recover from another participant if the latter did not breach a recognized duty of care. For example, in *Griggas v. Clauson*, liability was found when a basketball player struck an unprovoked blow to an opponent whose back was turned.

GRIGGAS V. CLAUSON

128 N.E.2d 363 (Ill. Ct. App. 1955)

EOVALDI, Justice.

This is an appeal by defendant from a judgment for $2000 entered on the verdict of a jury for injuries sustained by plaintiff for an alleged assault and battery during a basketball game.

In his complaint, plaintiff charged that while he and defendant were participating on opposing teams and while plaintiff had his back to defendant, defendant maliciously, wantonly and wilfully and without provocation assaulted plaintiff and with his fist repeatedly struck plaintiff violently in the head and knocked plaintiff unconscious to the floor; plaintiff suffered . . . lacerations abrasions, contusions, concussions, and other injuries, both temporary and permanent, and has been unable to go about his affairs and duties . . . lost a four-year scholarship.

On the evening in question, plaintiff, 19 years old, was a member of and playing center for an amateur basketball team known as the Rockford Athletic Club Basketball Team. . . . If the testimony on behalf of appellee is true, he was subjected to a wanton and unprovoked assault and was struck at a time when he had his back to defendant. The statements of defendant at the time plaintiff was lying on the floor and during part of the time that plaintiff was unconscious, show the true state of his mind, contrary to his testimony that plaintiff was injured as they were jumping for the ball. Considering the injuries sustained by the plaintiff, the time he was in the hospital, the doctor and hospital bills of $362.10, and the fact that the jury was entitled to grant exemplary damages, we cannot say that the verdict is excessive. . . . We have examined the record and do not find that the verdict is manifestly against the weight of the testimony. Under these circumstances we have no right to set aside the jury's finding. The judgment of the circuit court accordingly is affirmed. Judgment affirmed.

2. Violation of Safety Rules and Unsportsmanlike Conduct

A participant can avoid the defenses of assumption of risk and contributory negligence by basing her cause of action on defendant's violation of a safety rule. *See Nabozny v. Barnhill*, 334 N.E.2d 258 (Ill. Ct. App. 1975). Similarly, recovery may be allowed when a plaintiff was injured through defendant's unsportsmanlike conduct. *See Bourque v. Duplechin*, 331 So. 2d 40 (La. Ct. App. 1976).

In *Nabozny v. Barnhill*, defendant violated the safety rule that prohibits contact with the goal keeper in soccer, when the goal keeper is holding the ball in the penalty area.

NABOZNY V. BARNHILL

334 N.E.2d 258 (Ill. Ct. App. 1975)

ADESKO, Justice

Plaintiff, Julian Claudio Nabozny, a minor, by Edward J. Nabozny, his father, commenced this action to recover damages for personal injuries allegedly caused by the negligence of defendant, David Barnhill. . . .

A soccer match began between two amateur teams at Duke Child's Field in Winnetka, Illinois. Plaintiff was playing the position of goalkeeper for the Hansa team. Defendant was playing the position of forward for the Winnetka team. Members of both teams were of high-school age. Approximately twenty minutes after play had begun, a Winnetka player kicked the ball over the midfield line. Two players, Jim Gallos (for Hansa) and the defendant (for Winnetka) chased the free ball. Gallos reached the ball first. Since he was closely pursued by the defendant, Gallos passed the ball to the plaintiff, the Hansa goalkeeper. Gallos then turned away and prepared to receive a pass from the plaintiff. The plaintiff, in the meantime, went down on his left knee, received the pass, and pulled the ball to his chest. The defendant did not turn away when Gallos did, but continued to run in the direction of the plaintiff and kicked the left side of plaintiff's head causing plaintiff severe injuries.

All of the occurrence witnesses agreed that the defendant had time to avoid contact with plaintiff and that the plaintiff remained at all times within the "penalty area," a rectangular area between the eighteenth yard line and the goal. . . .

[T]he game in question was being played under 'F.I.F.A.' rules. . . . those rules prohibited all players from making contact with the goalkeeper when he is in possession of the ball in the penalty area. . . . Under "F.I.F.A." rules, any contact with a goalkeeper in possession in the penalty area is an infraction of the rules, even if such contact is unintentional. . . . The . . . contact in question . . . should not have occurred. Additionally, goalkeeper head injuries are extremely rare in soccer. As a result of being struck, plaintiff suffered permanent damage to his skull and brain.

The initial question presented by this appeal is whether, under the facts in evidence, such a relationship existed between the parties that the court will impose a legal duty upon one for the benefit of the other. . . .

This court believes that the law should not place unreasonable burdens on the free and vigorous participation in sports by our youth. However, we also believe that organized, athletic competition does not exist in a vacuum. Rather, some of the restraints of civilization must accompany every athlete onto the playing field. One of the educational benefits of organized athletic competition to our youth is the development of discipline and self control.

Individual sports are advanced and competition enhanced by a comprehensive set of rules. Some rules secure the better playing of the game as a test of skill. Other rules are primarily designed to protect participants from serious injury.

For these reasons, this court believes that when athletes are engaged in an athletic competition; all teams involved are trained and coached by knowledgeable personnel; a recognized set of rules governs the conduct of the competition; and a safety rule is contained therein which is primarily designed to protect players from serious injury, a player is then charged with a legal duty to every other player on the field to refrain from conduct proscribed by a safety rule. A reckless disregard for the safety rule. A reckless disregard for the safety of other players cannot be excused. To engage in such conduct is to create an intolerable and unreasonable risk of serious injury to other participants. . . . Under the facts presented in the case at bar, we find such a duty clearly arose. Plaintiff was entitled to legal protection at the hands of the defendant. The defendant contends he is immune from tort action for any injury to another player that happens during the course of a game, to which theory we do not subscribe.

It is our opinion that a player is liable for injury in a tort action if his conduct is such that it is either deliberate, wilful or with a reckless disregard for the safety of the other player so as to cause injury to that player, the same being a question of fact to be decided by a jury.

Defendant also asserts that plaintiff was contributorily negligent as a matter of law, and, therefore, the trial court's direction of a verdict in defendant's favor was correct. We do not agree. . . .

Using the standard set out in Pedrick v. Peoria & Eastern R. R. Co., 37 Ill.2d 494, 229 N.E.2d 504, for determining both freedom from negligence and contributory negligence as matters of law, we conclude that the trial court erred in directing a verdict in favor of defendant. It is a fact question for the jury.

This cause, therefore, is reversed and remanded to the Circuit Court of Cook County for a new trial consistent with the views expressed in this opinion.

Reversed and remanded.

In *Bourque v. Duplechin*, 31 So. 2d 40 (La. Ct. App. 1976), plaintiff, Jerome Bourque, Jr., filed suit to recover damages for personal injuries received in a softball game against Adrien Duplechin, a member of the opposing team who inflicted the injuries. The court held that a participant does not assume the risk of injury from fellow players acting in an unexpected or unsportsmanlike way with a reckless lack of concern for others participating.

BOURQUE V. DUPLECHIN

331 So. 2d 40 (La. Ct. App. 1976)

WATSON, Judge.

Plaintiff, Jerome Bourque, Jr., filed this suit to recover damages for personal injuries received in a softball game. Made defendants were Adrien Duplechin, a member of the opposing team who inflicted the injuries, and Duplechin's liability insurer, Allstate Insurance Company. The trial court rendered judgment in favor of plaintiff against both defendants and defendants have appealed. We affirm.

Both Duplechin and Allstate contend that the trial court erred: in not finding that Bourque assumed the risk of injury by participating in the softball game; and in failing to find that Bourque was guilty of contributory negligence. Defendant Duplechin also contends that the trial court erred in finding him negligent and in finding that the injury to plaintiff Bourque occurred four to five feet away from the second base position in the general direction of the pitcher's mound. Allstate further contends that the trial court erred in finding coverage under its policy which excludes injury intended or expected by the insured.

On June 9, 1974, Bourque was playing second base on a softball team fielded by Boo Boo's Lounge. Duplechin, a member of the opposing team sponsored by Murray's Steak House and Lounge, had hit the ball and advanced to first base. A teammate of Duplechin's, Steve Pressler, hit a ground ball and Duplechin started to second. The shortstop caught the ground ball and threw it to Bourque who tagged second base and then stepped away from second base to throw the ball to first and execute a double play. After Bourque had thrown the ball to first base, Duplechin ran at full speed into Bourque. As Duplectin ran into Bourque, he brought his left arm up under Bourque's chin. The evidence supports the trial court's factual conclusion that the collision occurred four or five feet away from the second base position in the direction of the pitcher's mound. Duplechin was thrown out of the game by the umpire because of the incident.

Pertinent to the trial court's decision was the following testimony:

Plaintiff Bourque, age 22 at the time of trial, testified that he is 5 7 tall. He was well out of the way when he was hit, standing four or five feet from second base and outside the base line. He knew there was a possibility of a runner sliding into him but had never imagined what actually happened, which he regarded as unbelievable under the circumstances.

Gregory John Laborde, a student at Tulane Law School, testified that he witnessed the incident from the dugout along the first base line and saw Duplechin turn and run directly toward Bourque who was standing four or five feet from second base toward home plate. Duplechin did not attempt to slide or decrease his speed and his left arm came up under Bourque's chin as they collided. Duplechin had to veer from the base path in order to strike Bourque.

Donald Frank Lockwood, baseball coach at USL, testified as an expert witness that: softball is a noncontact sport; in a forced play to second such as this the accepted way to break up a double play is by sliding.

Steve Pressler, who hit the ground ball that precipitated the incident, testified that the sides were retired as a result, because the collision was a flagrant violation of the rules of the game.

Duplechin admitted that he ran into Bourque while standing up in an attempt to block Bourque's view of first base and keep him from executing a double play. Duplechin also admitted that he was running at full speed when he collided with Bourque, a much smaller man. Duplechin attributed the accident to Bourque's failure to get out of the way.

Oral surgeon John R. Wallace saw Bourque following the accident and said the nature of the injury and the x-rays indicated that it was caused by a blow from underneath the jaw. Dr. Wallce characterized the injury as one that may have been common in football before the use of mouthpieces and faceguards.

While other testimony was presented, both cumulative and contradictory, the evidence summarized above provides a reasonable evidentiary basis for the trial court's conclusions.

There is no question that defendant Duplechin's conduct was the cause in fact of the harm to plaintiff Bourque. Duplechin was under a duty to play softball in the ordinary fashion without unsportsmanlike conduct or wanton injury to his fellow players. This duty was breached by Dupledhin, whose behavior was, according to the evidence, substandard and negligent. Bourque assumed the risk of being hit by a bat or a ball.

Bourque may also have assumed the risk of an injury resulting from standing in the base path and being spiked by someone sliding into second base, a common incident of softball and baseball. However, Bourque did not assume the risk of Duplechin going out of his way to run into him at full speed when Bourque was five feet away from the base. A participant in a game or sport assumes all of the risks incidental to that particular activity which are obvious and foreseeable. A participant does not assume the risk of injury from fellow players acting in an unexpected or unsportsmanlike way with a reckless lack of concern for others participating. Assumption of risk is an affirmative defense which must be proven by a preponderance of the evidence, and the record here supports the trial court's conclusion that Bourque did not assume the risk of Duplechin's negligent act.

There is no evidence in the record to indicate contributory negligence on the part of Bourque.

Allstate contends on appeal that there is no coverage under its policy, because its insured, Duplechin, committed an intentional tort and should have expected injury to result. However, while Duplechin's action was negligent and perhaps even constitutes wanton negligence, the evidence is that he did not intend the harm that result. . . .

Duplechin was not motivated by a desire to injure Bourque. Duplechin tried to break up a double play with a reckless disregard of the consequences to Bourque. Duplechin's action was negligent but does not present a situation where the injury was expected or intended. There is coverage under Allstate's policy.

The trial court awarded plaintiff Bourque $12,000 for his pain and suffering and $1,496.00 for his special damages. There is no dispute about the amount awarded. Bourque's jaw was fractured; his chin required plastic surgery; seven teeth were broken and had to be crowned; and one tooth was replaced by a bridge.

There is no manifest error in the trial court's conclusions which we summarize as follows: plaintiff Bourque's injuries resulted from the negligence of defendant Duplechin; Bourque was not guilty of contributory negligence and did not assume the risk of this particular accident; and defendant Allstate did not prove that coverage was excluded under the terms of its policy.

For the foregoing reasons, the judgment of the trial court is affirmed at the cost of defendants-appellants, Adrien Duplechin and Allstate Insurance Company.

Affirmed. . . .

3. Professional Sports

The key to recovery in both *Nabozny v. Barnhill* and *Bourque v. Duplechin* is that the cause of the injury must be a result of wanton misconduct. Mere negligence is insufficient to establish a predicate for a successful cause of action. The case of *Hackbart v. Cincinnati Bengals*, 435 F. Supp. 352 (D. Colo. 1977) *(Hackbart I)*, rev'd, 601 F.2d 516 (10th Cir. 1979) *(Hackbart II)*, allows for recovery for injuries sustained in the course of a professional football game if they result from wanton misconduct and are not directly related to the flow of the game.

HACKBART v. CINCINNATI BENGALS

601 F.2d 516 (10th Cir. 1979)

WILLIAM E. DOYLE, Circuit Judge.

The question in this case is whether in a regular season professional football game an injury which is inflicted by one professional football player on an opposing player can give rise to liability in tort where the injury was inflicted by the intentional striking of a blow during the game.

The injury occurred in the course of a game between the Denver Broncos and the Cincinnati Bengals, which game was being played in Denver in 1973. The Broncos' defensive back, Dale Hackbart, was the recipient of the injury and the Bengals' offensive back, Charles "Booby" Clark, inflicted the blow which produced it. . . .

Clark was an offensive back and just before the injury he had run a pass pattern to the right side of the Denver Broncos' end zone. The injury flowed indirectly from this play. The pass was intercepted by Billy Thompson, a Denver free safety, who returned it to midfield. The subject injury occurred as an aftermath of the pass play.

As a consequence of the interception, the roles of Hackbart and Clark suddenly changed. Hackbart, who had been defending, instantaneously became an offensive player. Clark, on the other hand, became a defensive player. Acting as an offensive player, Hackbart attempted to block Clark by throwing his body in front of him. He thereafter remained on the ground. He turned, and with one knee on the ground, watched the play following the interception.

The trial court's finding was that Charles Clark, "acting out of anger and frustration, but without a specific intent to injure . . . stepped forward and struck a blow with his right forearm to the back of the kneeling plaintiff's head and neck with sufficient force to cause both players to fall forward to the ground." Both players without complaining to the officials or to one another, returned to their respective sidelines since the ball had changed hands and the offensive and defensive teams of each had been substituted. Clark testified at trial that his frustration was brought about by the fact that his team was losing the game.

Due to the failure of the officials to view the incident, a foul was not called. However, the game film showed very clearly what had occurred. Plaintiff did not at the time report the happening to his coaches or to anyone else during the game. However, because of the pain which he experienced he was unable to play golf the next day. He did not seek medical attention, but the continued pain caused him to report this fact and the incident to the Bronco trainer who gave him treatment. Apparently he played on the specialty teams for two successive Sundays, but after that the Broncos released him on waivers. (He was in his thirteenth year as a player.) He sought medical help and it was then that it was discovered by the physician that he had a serious neck fracture injury. . . .

I. THE ISSUES AND CONTENTIONS

1. Whether the trial court erred in ruling that as a matter of policy the principles of law governing the infliction of injuries should be entirely refused where the injury took place in the course of the game. . . .

5. The final issue is whether the evidence justifies consideration by the court of the issue of reckless conduct as it is defined in A.L.I. Restatement of the Law of Torts Second, s 500, because (admittedly) the assault and battery theory is not available because that tort is governed by a one-year statute of limitations.

II. WHETHER THE EVIDENCE SUPPORTED THE JUDGMENT

The evidence at the trial uniformly supported the proposition that the intentional striking of a player in the head from the rear is not an accepted part of either the playing rules or the general customs of the game of professional football. . . .

Thus the district court's assumption was that Clark had inflicted an intentional blow which would ordinarily generate civil liability and which might bring about a criminal sanction as well, but that since it had occurred in the course of a football game, it should not be subject to the restraints of the law; that if it were it would place unreasonable impediments and restraints on the activity. The judge also pointed out that courts are illsuited to decide the different social questions and to administer conflicts on what is much like a battlefield where the restraints of civilization have been left on the sidelines.

We are forced to conclude that the result reached is not supported by evidence.

III. WHETHER INTENTIONAL INJURY IS ALLOWED BY EITHER WRITTEN RULE OR CUSTOM

Plaintiff, of course, maintains that tort law applicable to the injury in this case applies on the football field as well as in other places. . . .

The general customs of football do not approve the intentional punching or striking of others. . . .

IV. WAS IT LEGALLY JUSTIFIABLE FOR THE TRIAL COURT TO HOLD, AS A MATTER OF POLICY, THAT JURISDICTION SHOULD NOT BE ASSUMED OVER THE CASE IN VIEW OF THE FACT THAT IT AROSE OUT OF A PROFESSIONAL FOOTBALL GAME? . . .

V. IS THE STANDARD OF RECKLESS DISREGARD OF THE RIGHTS OF OTHERS APPLICABLE TO THE PRESENT SITUATION?

The Restatement of Torts Second, s 500, distinguishes between reckless and negligent misconduct. Reckless misconduct differs from negligence, in that negligence consists of mere inadvertence, lack of skillfulness or failure to take precautions; reckless misconduct, on the other hand, involves a choice or adoption of a course of action either with knowledge of the danger or with knowledge of facts which would disclose this danger to a reasonable man. . . .

Therefore, recklessness exists where a person knows that the act is harmful but fails to realize that it will produce the extreme harm which it did produce. It is in this respect that recklessness and intentional conduct differ in degree.

In the case at bar the defendant Clark admittedly acted impulsively and in the heat of anger, and even though it could be said from the admitted facts that he intended the act it could also be said that he did not intend to inflict serious injury which resulted from the blow which he struck. . . .

In sum, having concluded that the trial court did not limit the case to a trial of the evidence bearing on defendant's liability but rather determined that as a matter of social policy the game was so violent and unlawful that valid lines could not be drawn, we take the view that this was not a proper issue for determination and that plaintiff was entitled to have the case tried on an assessment of his rights and whether they had been violated.

The trial court has heard the evidence and has made findings. The findings of fact based on the evidence presented are not an issue on this appeal. Thus, it would not seem that the court would have to repeat the areas of evidence that have already been fully considered. The need is for a reconsideration of that evidence in the light of that which is taken up by this court in its opinion. We are not to be understood as limiting the trial court's consideration of supplemental evidence if it deems it necessary.

The cause is reversed and remanded for a new trial in accordance with the foregoing views.

4. Spectators Generally

Spectators run the risk of injury while observing a sports event. Spectator injuries can occur from foul balls, errant pucks, thrown bats, clumsy fullbacks, misthrown javelins, and so on. But regardless of the severity of the injury, spectators do not recover for injuries that result from ordinary and foreseeable risks that are inherent to that particular sport because, legally, they have assumed those risks. However, they do not assume the risks of intentional harm from a participant.

Also, spectators do not assume the risk of a stadium operator's failure to meet his duty of care. The owners are business inviters and are liable for conditions that cause harm: if they knew or should have known that the condition posed an unreasonable risk, that the spectators could not have discovered and protected against this risk, and if the owner failed to exercise reasonable care for their protection. The duty is to maintain the premises in a reasonably safe condition and to supervise the conduct of those on the premises so as to prevent injury. Spectators can assume that operators exercised reasonable care to make the stadium safe for the purposes of inviting spectators to attend and observe sporting events.

However, the owner-operator is not an insurer of the spectator's safety. The injured spectator must prove that the acts were a breach of duty and that the breach was the proximate cause of the injury.

5. Baseball Spectators

Owners of baseball stadiums have a duty to provide screened seats for those spectators who wish them. But the stadium owner or operator does not have a duty to inform the spectators of the availability of the protected seats since their existence is obvious. *Dent v. Texas Rangers*, 764 S.W.2d 345 (Tex. Ct. App. 1989).

In *Schentzel v. Philadelphia National League Club*, 96 A.2d 181 (Pa. Super. Ct. 1953), plaintiffs traveled to Philadelphia to watch a "doubleheader" baseball game between the Cubs and the Phillies on June 5, 1949, at Shibe Park. Mrs. Schentzel, although aware of the game of baseball, was attending her first game. She was struck by a foul ball. The court concluded that such injuries are a matter of such common everyday practical knowledge as to be subject to judicial notice.

SCHENTZEL V. PHILADELPHIA NATIONAL LEAGUE CLUB

96 A.2d 181 (Pa. Super. Ct. 1953)

Ross, Judge.

In this action of trespass for personal injuries, damages were sought by the wife plaintiff (hereinafter referred to as plaintiff) for pain and suffering and by the husband plaintiff for expenses incurred by reason of his wife's injuries and for loss of consortium. The jury returned a verdict for the plaintiff and found against her husband. Defendant's motion for judgment n.o.v. was refused, and it has appealed to this Court.

On the afternoon of June 5, 1949, plaintiffs, residents of Allentown, traveled to Philadelphia to see a "doubleheader" baseball game between the Philadelphia Phillies and the Chicago Cubs. They arrived at Shibe Park, the scene of the games, and found a "tremendous crowd" at the various ticket windows. Plaintiff husband became part of a long ticket line. He testified that he was assured by the ticket seller that the seats being assigned to him were "pretty good" and that they were "back of the screen," as he desired them to be. During this alleged discussion the plaintiff stood nearby but it is not disclosed whether she heard or paid any attention to it. The seats, it developed, were located in the upper stand, on the first base side of the diamond, but not behind the protective screen, being removed therefrom by about 15 or 20 feet. The husband testified that when they reached their seats the first game was in the sixth or seventh inning of play, that on discovering the seats were not in the protected area he got up but saw it was impossible to return to the ticket window to exchange the tickets because of the crowd coming down the aisle, so resumed his seat. A minute or two later, or about ten minutes after he and plaintiff had originally been seated, plaintiff was struck by a foul ball.

Plaintiff testified that she had never seen a baseball game prior to the one at which she was injured, that she knew nothing about it, that she had seen televised games but had seen no balls go into the stands on television.

That the husband was thoroughly familiar with this particular hazard is established by his testimony on cross-examination. He stated, "There is a million foul balls, may be three or four or five in an inning, goes into the stand." . . .

Plaintiff contends that the legal duty owing her by defendant (which she claims was breached) consisted of 'exceptional precautions' toward its women patrons, many of whom are ignorant of the hazards involved in the game, and who are induced to attend by special invitation, as on afternoons when they are admitted free; that these exceptional precautions include extension of the screen coverage behind the batter's and catcher's positions to a wider area, still leaving "a few sections" for patrons who prefer to watch the game from unprotected areas. In substance the argument is tantamount to a request for a holding that a baseball club must at its peril always have available a seat behind the screen whenever a patron requests one. The plaintiff has furnished no proof that the screening of a wider area would have resulted in her being seated within it, thus, by inference, precluding her injury. She and her husband found on their arrival that "the place was packed" with a "tremendous crowd" during the sixth or seventh inning of the first game. It was the crowded condition, according to her husband, which prevented his return to the box office to exchange the tickets. Assuming an enlarged area of screenage, it does not necessarily follow that the crowd which arrived earlier would not have occupied the entire bloc of protected seats but would instead have left two seats vacant for their occupancy. . . .

In this case, plaintiff produced no evidence tending to show that defendant's screening of certain sections of its grandstand deviated from that customarily employed at other baseball parks. . . .

No claim is made that the screen was defective in structure. The only question of defectiveness relates to the extent of coverage. It is of record that the screen protected almost all the seats in five sections of defendant's upper stand and practically all of five sections in its lower stand. There is no evidence to indicate the number of sets behind the protective screen. Provided with such meagre background of evidence, the jury were nevertheless permitted to set a theoretical standard of due care upon which to predicate their finding of negligence. We think their verdict under these circumstances cannot represent more than mere conjecture. . . .

Plaintiff was a woman 47 years of age. There is nothing whatever in the record to support an inference that she was of inferior intelligence, that she had subnormal perception, or that she had led a cloistered life. Consequently, she must be presumed to have been cognizant of the neighborhood knowledge with which individuals living in organized society are normally equipped. We think the frequency with which foul balls go astray, alight in the grandstand or field, and are sometimes caught and retained by onlookers at baseball games is a matter of such common everyday practical knowledge as to be a subject of judicial notice. It strains our collective imagination to visualize the situation of the wife of a man obviously interested in the game, whose children view the games on the home television set, and who lives in a metropolitan community, so far removed from that knowledge as not to be chargeable with it. . . .

Plaintiff stresses the fact that her husband requested tickets of defendant's ticket seller calling for seats behind the protective screen and was prevented from exchanging them by the crowded condition of the aisles. That fact might be pertinent had she chosen to bring her action on the theory of assumpsit for breach of contract, but we do not see its relevancy to negligence. We do not thus place form over substance because in view of our decision it adds nothing to her case.

Judgment reversed and here entered for defendant.

In *Lawson v. Salt Lake Trappers, Inc.,* a minor spectator who was struck by a foul ball also assumed the risk of injury.

LAWSON V. SALT LAKE TRAPPERS, INC.

901 P.2d 1013 (Utah 1995)

DURHAM, Justice:

This is an appeal from a summary judgment in favor of defendants in a negligence action. The parents of a child who was struck by a foul ball at a baseball game brought a negligence action against the baseball organization, the Salt Lake Trappers, and Salt Lake City Corporation. Judge Timothy R. Hanson of the Third District Court granted summary judgment in favor of defendants, and plaintiffs appeal. We affirm.

On July 4, 1991, Brook Lawson and her parents attended a Salt Lake Trappers baseball game at Derks Field in Salt Lake City. Brook was six years old and went with her parents to see a fireworks display immediately following the baseball game. The Trappers were hosting the fireworks show to promote baseball game attendance and to celebrate Independence Day.

The Lawsons purchased their tickets when they arrived at the stadium. Because they were part of a group of ten, they purchased general admission tickets that would enable their group to sit together. The Lawsons' seats were located above first base, approximately 143 feet from home plate. The seats were about halfway from the top of the stands. No protective screening blocked foul balls where the Lawsons chose to sit. The only area at Derks Field with protective screening was directly behind home plate and along portions of the first and third baselines. The Lawsons did not request seats in a screened area.

During the game, a foul ball exited the playing field and struck Brook Lawson, causing head injuries. The Lawsons sued the Trappers and Salt Lake City, alleging negligence for failure to provide adequate protection to spectators from known dangers at the playing field. In addition, Brook's parents, James and Cheryl Lawson, claimed damages for negligent infliction of emotional distress. . . .

The Lawsons ask this court to reverse the trial court's order, arguing that (1) whether defendants breached a duty of care to Brook is a question of fact that should be tried to a jury; (2) the trial court misapplied the doctrine of assumption of risk; and (3) because James and Cheryl Lawson were within the "zone of danger" of the foul ball, their claim of negligent infliction of emotional distress should be tried to a jury. . . .

I. DUTY OF CARE

The first issue in this case is whether the Trappers or Salt Lake City owed a duty of care to the Lawsons. In *Hamilton v. Salt Lake City Corp.,* 120 Utah 647, 237 P.2d 841, 843 (Utah 1951), this court held that a baseball facility "must use reasonable care in providing a reasonably safe place for its patrons." Since that case was decided, the standard for "reasonable care" for a baseball park has been extensively explored in case law from other jurisdictions.

The majority rule is that an owner of a baseball stadium has a duty to screen the most dangerous part of the stadium and to provide screened seats to as many spectators as may reasonably be expected to request them on an ordinary occasion. Walter T. Champion Jr., *"At the Ol' Ball Game" and Beyond: Spectators and the Potential for Liability,* 14 Am.J. of Trial Advoc. 495, 500 (1990) [hereinafter Champion]. . . .

We are persuaded that the policy and rationale of the majority rule are sound. The majority rule insures that those spectators desiring protection from foul balls will be accommodated and that seats in the most dangerous area of the stadium will be safe. At the same time, the majority rule recognizes baseball tradition and spectator preference by not requiring owners to screen the entire stadium. Champion, at 500. Thus, we hold that the Trappers had a duty to screen the area behind home plate and to provide screened seats to as many spectators as would normally request such seats on an ordinary occasion.

We next examine defendants' compliance with this duty. The undisputed facts demonstrate that defendants provided protective screening behind home plate and partway along the first and third baselines.

In *Akins* [*v. Glen Falls City Sch. Dist.,* 441 N.Y.S.2d 644 (1981)], the plaintiff was struck by a foul ball while standing near the third baseline, ten to fifteen feet from the end of the backstop and sixty feet from home plate. 441 N.Y.S.2d at 645. . . .

Like the plaintiff in *Akins,* the Lawsons have not proffered any evidence that the screening at Derks Field was inadequate in terms of protecting spectators behind home plate. In fact, the record is silent as to the dimensions of the screen. Similarly, while the Lawsons allege that the screening failed to comply with "industry standards," they have not shown what the industry standards for protective screening are or how they differ from the screening provided by defendants. In the absence of such a showing, we agree with the trial court's conclusion that defendants complied as a matter of law with their initial duty of screening the area behind home plate.

Defendants' second duty was to provide protected seats to as many patrons as would normally request such seats on an ordinary occasion. The Lawsons have failed to demonstrate any breach of this duty. In fact, they do not address this issue. They did not request screened seating when they purchased their tickets, nor did they request to change seats after arriving in the unscreened grandstand area. Rather, the Lawsons chose to sit in an area that would accommodate their group. Because the Lawsons do not raise an issue of material fact concerning defendants' duty to provide a reasonable number of screened seats, the trial court correctly granted summary judgment.

II. ASSUMPTION OF RISK

As this court has previously noted, being struck by a foul ball is " 'one of the natural risks assumed by spectators attending professional games.' " . . .

III. NEGLIGENT INFLICTION OF EMOTIONAL DISTRESS

The final issue in this case is whether James and Cheryl Lawson have a claim for negligent infliction of emotional distress. This action requires that the plaintiff feared physical injury or peril.

The undisputed facts demonstrate that James and Cheryl Lawson did not actually witness the event in which their daughter was hit. Because they did not even see the foul ball, they cannot claim that the accident caused emotional distress from fear of injury; the speed of the accident actually prevented any apprehension or anticipation of harm. Furthermore, even if James and Cheryl Lawson had anticipated the harm, they do not proffer any evidence indicating that they experienced severe mental illness as a result of the incident. Thus, as a matter of law, the Lawsons do not have a claim for negligent infliction of emotional distress. Accordingly, the trial court properly granted defendants' motion for summary judgment on this point.

Having rejected all of the Lawsons' arguments, we affirm the trial court's order.

In *Benejam v. Detroit Tigers, Inc.*, an injured minor was hit by a baseball bat fragment.

BENEJAM V. DETROIT TIGERS, INC.

635 N.W.2d 219 (Mich. Ct. App. 2001)

BANDSTRA, C.J.

In this case, we are asked to determine whether we should adopt, as a matter of Michigan law, the "limited duty" rule that other jurisdictions have applied with respect to spectator injuries at baseball games. Under that rule, a baseball stadium owner is not liable for injuries to spectators that result from projectiles leaving the field during play if safety screening has been provided behind home plate and there are a sufficient number of protected seats to meet ordinary demand. We conclude that the limited duty doctrine should be adopted as a matter of Michigan law and that there was no evidence presented at trial that defendants failed to meet that duty. Further, we conclude that there is no duty to warn spectators at a baseball game of the well-known possibility that a bat or ball might leave the field. We therefore conclude that there is no evidence to support the verdict rendered on behalf of plaintiffs against defendant and we reverse and remand.

Facts

Plaintiff Alyssia M. Benejam, a young girl, attended a Tigers game with a friend and members of the friend's family and was seated quite close to the playing field along the third base line. the stadium was equipped with a net behind home plate, and the net extended part of the way down the first and third base lines. Although Alyssia was behind the net, she was injured when a player's bat broke and a fragment of it curved around the net. There was no evidence, and plaintiffs do not contend, that the fragment of the bat went through the net, that there was a hole in the net, or that the net was otherwise defective.

Plaintiffs sued the Tigers, claiming primarily that the net was insufficiently long and that warnings about the possibility of projectiles leaving the field were inadequate. The Tigers responded with motions before, during, and after trial arguing that, as a matter of law, plaintiffs could not or did not present any viable legal claim. Those motions were all denied by the trial court. Alyssia suffered crushed fingers as a result of the accident and the jury awarded plaintiffs noneconomic damages (past and future) totaling $917,000, lost earning capacity of $56,700 and $35,000 for past and future medical expenses. Damages are not at issue on appeal.

Standard of Review . . .
Standard of Care/Protective Screening

Defendant argues that although there is no Michigan law directly on point, other jurisdictions have balanced the safety benefits of providing a protective screen against the fact that such screening detracts from the allure of attending a live baseball game by placing an obstacle or insulation between fans and the playing field. The rule that emerges in these cases is that a stadium proprietor cannot be liable for spectator injuries if it has satisfied a "limited duty"—to erect a screen that will protect the most dangerous area of the spectator stands, behind home plate, and to provide a number of seats in this area sufficient to meet the ordinary demand for protected seats. In this case, there is no dispute that the Tigers constructed a protective screen behind home plate, and there was no evidence that the screen was insufficient to meet the ordinary demand for protected seating. Defendant argues the circuit court erred in failing to recognize the limited duty doctrine and in denying motions based on that doctrine for summary disposition, a directed verdict, and judgment notwithstanding the verdict.

Plaintiffs argue against application of the limited duty doctrine and contend that, under usual principles of premises liability, the circuit court correctly concluded that a jury question was presented. Defendant (an invitor) had a duty to exercise ordinary care and prudence and maintain premises reasonably safe for invitees like Alyssia. Plaintiffs argue that the jury verdict was supported by sufficient evidence that the defendant failed to fulfill this duty because it did not provide a screen extending long enough along the third (and first) base lines.

There is no Michigan case law directly on point. Our review of precedents from other jurisdictions finds overwhelming, if not universal, support for the limited duty rule that defendant advocates.

The logic of these precedents is that there is an inherent risk of objects leaving the playing field that people know about when they attend baseball games. Also, there is inherent value in having most seats unprotected by a screen because baseball patrons generally want to be involved with the game in an intimate way and are even hoping that they will come in contact with some projectile from the field (in the form of a souvenir baseball). In other words, spectators know about the risk of being in the stands and, in fact, welcome that risk to a certain extent. On the other hand, the area behind home plate is especially dangerous and spectators who want protected seats should be able to find them in this area. Balancing all of these concerns, courts generally have adopted the limited duty doctrine that prevents liability if there are a sufficient number of protected seats behind home plate to meet the ordinary demand for that kind of seating. If that seating is provided, the baseball stadium owner has fulfilled its duty and there can be no liability for spectators who are injured by a projectile from the field.

An oft-cited precedent, *Akins v. Glens Falls City School Dist.*, 53 N.Y.2d 325, 441 N.Y.S.2d 644, 424 N.E.2d 531 (1981), provides a good illustration of the reasoning employed. There, a spectator at a baseball game was permanently and seriously injured when a sharply hit foul ball struck her in the eye. *Id*. at 327, 441 N.Y.S.2d 644, 424 N.E.2d 531. . . .

We find *Akins* and similar precedents to be well-reasoned and persuasive. It seems axiomatic that baseball fans attend games knowing that, as a natural result of play, objects may leave the field with the potential of causing injury in the stands. It is equally clear that most spectators, nonetheless, prefer to be as "close to the play" as possible, without an insulating and obstructive screen between them and the action. In contrast, a smaller number of spectators prefer the protection offered by screening. The most dangerous part of the spectator stands is the area in the lower deck behind home plate and along each of the baselines. Certainly home plate is the center of the most activity on the field. Most notably, it is there that pitched balls, traveling at great speeds in a line that would extend into the stands, are often deflected or squarely hit into those stands. Quite logically, the limited duty rule protects a stadium owner that provides screening for this most dangerous area and, in so doing, accommodates baseball patrons who seek protected seating. Because the limited duty rule is based on the desires of spectators, it further makes sense to define the extent of screening that should be provided behind home plate on the basis of consumer demand.

Plaintiffs do nothing to argue substantively against the limited duty rule, but merely argue that baseball stadium cases should be governed by usual invitor-invitee principles, not any special "baseball rule." . . .

This case, tried under usual invitor-invitee principles of liability provides a good example. Plaintiff's expert testified that, on the basis of his review of accidents occurring over time in the spectator stands between first base and third base, reasonable safety precautions would include screening in that entire area. In another case, where an injury occurred farther down the base-line, testimony and argument would likely be adduced to support a further extension as "reasonably necessary" to protect fans. The logical result of having these cases governed by usual invitor-invitee principles of liability would be that warned against in *Akins, supra* at 331, 441 N.Y.S.2d 644, 424 N.E.2d 531: "[E]very spectator injured by a foul ball, no matter where he is seated or standing in the ball park, would have an absolute right to go to the jury on every claim of negligence." . . .

Applying the limited duty rule here, we conclude that plaintiffs have failed to provide any proof sufficient to find that liability could be imposed. Clearly, there was a screen behind home plate and there was no proof whatsoever that persons wanting seats protected by the screen could not be accommodated. To the contrary, uncontested testimony by Tigers ticket personnel established that protected seating is generally open and available to fans who want it. Accordingly, we conclude that the screening provided by defendant was sufficient under the limited duty doctrine applicable in this case.

Duty to Warn

Plaintiffs also argue that defendant failed to provide an adequate warning regarding the possibility that some object might come flying off the field and cause injury in the stands. However, we conclude that defendant did not have any duty to warn regarding this wellknown risk . . .

In any event, we conclude that . . . baseball stadiums have a duty to warn spectators of the risk that objects from the field might cause injury.

As discussed above, one of the premises of the universally adopted limited duty rule for protective screening is the fact that baseball spectators generally know that attending a game involves risks from off-field projectiles. Accordingly, precedents from other jurisdictions conclude that there is no duty to warn regarding this risk. . . .

We find these precedents to be compelling and persuasive. Further, having concluded that the limited duty rule should be adopted in Michigan partly on the premise that spectators know about the dangers of objects leaving the field, it would be inconsistent to impose a duty to warn of those dangers. . . .

Having concluded that under the facts of this case, defendant did not breach any duty to provide screening and was under no duty to provide a warning to plaintiffs regarding the risk of injury from objects leaving the field, we reverse the jury verdict and remand this matter for entry of an order finding no cause of action against defendant. We need not consider other arguments advanced by defendant in support of that result.

We reverse and remand. We do not retain jurisdiction.

QUESTIONS AND DISCUSSION

1. Liability was found when a catcher deliberately and without warning struck a batter. *Averill v. Luttrell*, 311 S.W.2d 812 (Tenn. Ct. App. 1957). *See also* Lazavoff, *Torts and Sports: Participant Liability to Co-Participants for Injuries Sustained During Competition*, 7 U. Miami Ent. & Sports L. Rev. 191 (1990); and Yasser, *In the Heat of Competition: Tort Liability of One Participant; Why Can't Participants Be Required to be Reasonable?* 5 Seton Hall J. Sport L. 253 (1995).

2. But, unlike *Bourque*, recovery was denied when a second baseman was injured as an unintended consequence of an opposing player's slide into the base. *Tavernier v. Maes*, 242 Cal. App. 2d 532 (1996). Do you see the difference between the two cases? Does it make sense?

3. Liability was denied when the bat slipped out of the hands of a batter and struck another player. *Gaspard v. Grain Dealers Mut. Ins. Co.*, 131 So. 2d 831 (La. Ct. App. 1961).

4. Recovery was also denied when a basketball player was accidentally struck by an opposing player. *Thomas v. Barlow*, 138 A. 208 (N.J. Sup. Ct. 1927).

Compare this case with *Griggas*. Do you see the reason why they were decided differently?

5. Recovery was denied for a minor who was injured while playing goalie in a floor hockey game. Participation in contact sports precluded recovery in negligence since the players were organized and coached. Also, shooting plastic pucks in an attempt to score was neither willful nor wanton conduct.

6. *Novak v. Lamar Ins. Co.*, 488 So. 2d 739 (La. Ct. App. 1986), is similar to *Tavernier* but unlike *Bourque*; under similar circumstances, the court denied recover for injuries to plaintiff/first baseman from a collision with defendant who was running to first base. The defendant was neither reckless nor unsportsmanlike; therefore, the risk of collision was reasonable and one that the softball player assumed.

7. Similarly, in *Niemczyk v. Burleson*, 538 S.W.2d 737 (Mo. Ct. App. 1976), defendant shortstop in a softball game ran across the infield and collided with plaintiff base runner as she was running from first to second base. A sports participant accepts reasonable dangers that are inherent to the sport, but only to the point that they are obvious and a usual incident to that sport. Here, the plaintiff sufficiently stated a claim on which relief could be granted on the grounds of negligence.

8. A rule violation establishes a duty only if the conduct was more than ordinary negligence, that is, either deliberate or willful conduct or conduct with a reckless disregard for the safety or others. *Oswald v. Township H.S. Dist.* 406 N.E.2d 157 (Ill. Ct. App. 1980).

9. *Schentzel* merges with *Jones v. Three Rivers Management Corp.*, 394 A.2d 546 (Pa. 1978), to establish the bottom line in baseball spectator injuries. In *Jones*, the injured spectator was struck while standing in the interior walkway of a stadium concourse. The court held that the *Schentzel* no-duty rule applies only to common, frequent, and expected risks, and in no way affects the duty of a sports facility to protect patrons from foreseeably dangerous conditions not inherent in the amusement activity. *See* Champion, *At the Ol' Ball Game and Beyond: Spectators and the Potential for Liability*, 14 Amer. J. Trial Advoc. 495 (1991).

10. In *Lawson v. Salt Lake Trappers, Inc.*, 901 P.2d 1013 (Utah 1995), an injured minor struck by a foul ball assumed the risk of injury. Also, the stadium owners did not breach their duty to provide adequate screened seating. The injured plaintiff was "six years old and went with her parents to see a fireworks display immediately following the baseball game." Does the additional lure of fireworks increase the potential liability of the stadium owner?

11. Similarly in *Benejam v. Detroit Tigers, Inc.*, 635 N.W.2d 219 (Mich. Ct. App. 2001), an injured minor was hit by a fragment of a baseball bat during a game. Again, the stadium owner did not breach the duty to provide adequate screening. Also, the proprietor had no duty to provide a warning regarding the risk of injury from objects leaving the baseball field. The risk was obvious and baseball spectators generally knew that attending a game involved risks from off-field projectiles. Here, although plaintiff "was behind the net, she was injured when a player's bat broke

and a fragment of it curved around the net." Should the fact that the injury was caused by a bat fragment, which is not an everyday occurrence, as opposed to a foul ball, which is, change the relationship sufficiently so that the stadium should be liable for the girl's injuries in this situation?

12. Assumption of risk to spectators has been extended to include errant softballs. *Arnold v. City of Cedar Rapids*, 443 N.W.2d 332 (Iowa 1989). Also, the definition of a spectator includes a father who was injured in a pregame softball warm-up while he stood around the in field as a bystander. *Clark v. Goshen Sunday Morning Softball League*, 493 N.Y.S.2d (1985). In *Friedman v. Houston Sports Auth.*, 731 S.W.2d 572 (Text. Ct. App. 1987), the court held that the stadium did not have a duty to warn an 11-year-old baseball spectator of the danger of being hit by a foul ball while in the area behind the first base dugout. Will the presence of a mascot change the equation as to whether a minor will be held to have assumed the risk of being struck by a foul ball?

13. In golf, the key is whether the defendant has reason to expect harm to the plaintiff from an obvious risk in circumstances where the plaintiff's attention might be distracted from the risk, causing him to forget to protect himself against that harm. *Baker v. Mid-Maine Med. Center*, 499 A.2d 464 (Me. 1985).

14. In *Brosko v. Hetherington*, 16 Pa. D&C 761 (C.P., 1931), an 11-year-old caddy in the first day of service was negligently struck by a golf ball without warning; the court held that the defendant has a duty to observe and warn if anyone was in an area where the ball could possibly travel if sliced.

H. SCHOOL, COACH, AND REFEREE LIABILITY

Schools, coaches, and referees are integral parts of both interscholastic sports and mandatory physical education. As such, they each possess a standard of care that when breached triggers an actionable negligence claim.

1. School Liability

Many of the cases against schools for sports injuries involve participants in interscholastic sports or students in mandatory physical education courses. These lawsuits against various school officials are usually based on one or more of the following alleged acts of negligence: failure to warn, failure to instruct, failure to supervise, failure to hire and train competent coaches and staff, and failure to provide safe facilities.

Once again, a duty must exist before an injured athlete can recover from a school district. With that duty, there must be some casual connection (or proximate cause) between the alleged negligence and injury. The duties owed an athlete can take the forms of adequate instruction, proper equipment, reasonable matching of opponents, nonnegligent supervision, and proper post-injury procedures. The school also has a duty to take protective precautions for spectators, which include protection from participant-inflicted injuries, reasonably expected rowdyism, and injuries resulting from overcrowded or defective bleachers.

A duty of a different sort was alleged to have been breached in *Ross v. Creighton*, where a former scholarship basketball player sues his college on the theory of "educational malpractice."

Ross v. Creighton University

957 F.2d 410 (7th Cir. 1992)

Mr. Ross' complaint advances three separate theories of how Creighton was negligent towards him. First, he contends that Creighton committed "educational malpractice" by not providing him with a meaningful education and preparing him for employment after college. Second, Mr. Ross claims that Creighton negligently inflicted emotional distress upon him by enrolling him in a stressful university environment for which he was not prepared, and then by failing to provide remedial programs that would have helped him survive there. Third, Mr. Ross urges the court to adopt a new cause of action for the tort of "negligent admission," which would allow recovery when an institution admits, and then does not adequately assist, a woefully unprepared student. The complaint also sets forth a contract claim, alleging that Creighton contracted to provide Mr. Ross "an opportunity . . . to obtain a meaningful college education and degree, and to do what was reasonably necessary . . . to enable [Mr. Ross] to obtain a meaningful college education and degree." It goes on to assert that Creighton breached this contract by failing to provide Mr. Ross adequate tutoring; by not requiring Mr. Ross to attend tutoring sessions; by not allowing him to "red-shirt," that is, to forego a year of basketball, in order to work on academics; and by failing to afford Mr. Ross a reasonable opportunity to take advantage of tutoring services. Mr. Ross also alleges that Creighton breached a promise it had made to him to pay for a college education. . . .

II. ANALYSIS

A. Guiding Principles . . .

B. The Negligence Claims

Mr. Ross advances three separate theories of how Creighton was negligent towards him: educational malpractice for not educating him, a new tort of "negligent admission" to an educational institution, and negligent infliction of emotional distress.

1. Educational Malpractice

Illinois courts have never ruled on whether a tort cause of action exists against an institution for educational malpractice. However, the overwhelming majority of states that have considered this type of claim have rejected it. . . .

Courts have identified several policy concerns that counsel against allowing claims for educational malpractice. First, there is the lack of a satisfactory standard of care by which to evaluate an educator. Theories of education are not uniform, and "different but acceptable scientific methods of academic training [make] it unfeasible to formulate a standard by which to judge the conduct of those delivering the services." Second, inherent uncertainties exist in this type of case about the cause and nature of damages. Factors such as the student's attitude, motivation, temperament, past experience and home environment may all play an essential and immeasurable role in learning. Consequently, it may be a "practical impossibility [to] prov [e] that the alleged malpractice of the teacher proximately caused the earning deficiency of the plaintiff student." . . .

2. "Negligent Admission"

In his complaint, Mr. Ross alleges that Creighton owed him a duty "to recruit and enroll only those students reasonably qualified and able to academically perform at Creighton." He then contends that Creighton breached this duty by admitting him, not informing him of how unprepared he was for studies there, and then not providing tutoring services or otherwise enabling him to receive a meaningful education. As a result, Mr. Ross underwent undue stress, which brought about, among other things, the incident at the motel.

We believe that Illinois would reject this claim for "negligent admission" for many of the same policy reasons that counsel against recognizing a claim for educational malpractice. First, this cause of action would present difficult, if not insuperable, problems to a court attempting to define a workable duty of care. Mr. Ross suggests that the University has a duty to admit only students who are "reasonably qualified" and able to perform academically. However, determining who is a "reasonably qualified student" necessarily requires subjective assessments of such things as the nature and quality of the defendant institution and the intelligence and educability of the plaintiff. Such decisions are not open to ready determination in the judicial process. Second, such a cause of action might unduly interfere with a university's admissions decisions, to the detriment of students and society as a whole. . . . [I]f universities and colleges faced tort liability for admitting an unprepared student schools would be encouraged to admit only those students who were certain to succeed in the institution. The opportunities of marginal students to receive an education therefore would likely be lessened. Also, the academic practice of promoting diversity by admitting students from disadvantaged backgrounds might also be jeopardized . . .

We read Mr. Ross' complaint to allege more than a failure of the University to provide him with an education of a certain quality. Rather, he alleges that the University knew that he was not qualified academically to participate in its curriculum. Nevertheless, it made a specific promise that he would be able to participate in a meaningful way in that program because it would provide certain specific services to him. Finally, he alleges that the University breached its promise by reneging on its commitment to provide those services and, consequently, effectively cutting him off from *any* participation in and benefit from the University's academic program. To adjudicate such a claim, the court would not be required to determine whether Creighton had breached its contract with Mr. Ross by providing *deficient* academic services.

Rather, its inquiry would be limited to whether the University had provided any real access to its academic curriculum at all.

Accordingly, we must disagree respectfully with our colleague in the district court as to whether the contract counts of the complaint can be dismissed at the pleadings stage. In our view, the allegations of the complaint are sufficient to warrant further proceedings. We emphasize, however, the narrow ground of our disagreement. We agree—indeed we emphasize—that courts should not "take on the job of supervising the relationship between them." We also recognize a formal university-student contract is rarely employed and, consequently, "the general nature and terms of the agreement are usually implied, with specific terms to be found in the university bulletin and other publications; custom and usages can also become specific terms by implication." Nevertheless, we believe that the district court can adjudicate Mr. Ross'; specific and narrow claim that he was barred from *any* participation in and benefit from the University's academic program without second-guessing the professional judgment of the University faculty on academic matters.

Conclusion

Accordingly, the judgment of the district court is affirmed in part and reversed and remanded in part for proceedings consistent with this opinion.

Affirmed in part, Reversed in part and Remanded.

2. Vicarious Liability

The great majority of lawsuits against school districts for injuries to athletes are based on the alleged negligent acts of their employees. In response, schools will claim that they are not responsible for their employees' actions or that the events are not school-sponsored. But an employer is vicariously liable for the wrongful acts of his servants. A principal is liable for the acts of his agents when the acts are performed within the scope of their employment. The theory of vicarious liability is used to bring liability of coach, referee, trainer, or grounds keeper under the school board's insurance coverage.

Agents of the school district might include coaches, aides, trainers, equipment managers, teachers, custodians, administrators, janitors, school principals, groundskeepers, and referees. The school board is vicariously liable for the actions of their agents (unless specific statutory immunity exists) if the alleged negligence occurred during the course of employment. Vicarious liability also may be applicable for nonemployees who are performing the functions of employees. The school board may be liable for the actions of these quasi-employees (for example, volunteers) under the doctrine of vicarious liability. The determination of their status is based on the amount and quality of the indices that connect the volunteer's actions to the board.

3. Coach Liability

A coach's duty is to use reasonable care to avoid the creation of foreseeable risks to the athlete under his or her supervision. The standard of reasonableness changes from sport to sport, but the degree of care increases if the activity is a contact sport.

A coach is also liable for the breach of certain duties, including duty to instruct on safety and ways to minimize injuries and duty to provide safe and effective equipment. Also, coaches cannot force previously injured athletes to participate and they must take reasonable steps to provide medical assistance.

A coach is not negligent if she has fulfilled her duty to exercise reasonable care for athletes under her supervision. This is satisfied by providing proper instructions or explaining how to play and also by showing due concern that the athlete is in proper condition. A coach satisfies this duty if all reasonable steps are taken to minimize the possibility of injury. The coach is liable only if she fails to exercise reasonable care for the protection of the players and the specific injury involved was a result of that failure.

In *Brahatcek*, the alleged failure to exercise reasonable care for the protection of the participant was in the nature of a failure to properly supervise ninth grade golf instruction.

BRAHATCEK V. MILLARD SCHOOL DISTRICT

273 N.W.2d 680 (Neb. 1979)

SPENCER, Chief Judge, Pro Tem.

This is a wrongful death action brought by Darlene Brahatcek as administration of the estate of her son, David Wayne Brahatcek, hereinafter called David, against Millard School District No. 17. David died as a result of being accidentally struck in the left occipital region of his skull by a golf club during a physical education class. Trial was had to the court. The District Judge entered judgment in favor of the plaintiff in the amount of $3,570.06 special damages, $50,000 general damages, and costs. Defendant appeals.

Defendant essentially alleges four assignments of error: (1) The insufficiency of the evidence; (2) the failure to find decedent contributorily negligent; (3) the failure to hold the negligence of the classmate who struck decedent was an intervening cause of death; and (4) the award of general damages was excessive. We affirm.

David, who was a ninth grade student 14 years of age, was injured on April 3, 1974, during a physical education class conducted in the gymnasium of Millard Central Junior High School. He was struck by a golf club swung by a fellow student, Mark Kreie. He was rendered unconscious and died 2 days later without regaining consciousness.

Mandatory golf instruction during physical education classes at the school began on Monday, April 1, 1974. Because decedent was absent from school on that day, his first exposure to the program was when his class next met on Wednesday, the day of the accident. Classes on both dates were conducted in the school gymnasium because of inclement weather. Instruction was coeducational. Decedent's class of 34 boys combined with a girls' physical education class having an enrollment of 23. Two teachers, one male and one female, were responsible for providing supervision and instruction. The faculty members present on Monday were Max Kurtz and Vickie Beveridge, at that time Vickie Lindgren.

On Monday, after attendance was taken, the students were gathered around in a semicircle and received instruction on the golf grip, stance, swing, etiquette, and safety. Mr. Kurtz then explained to them the procedure that would be followed in the gym.

With the bleachers folded up, the gym was nearly as wide as it was long. Approximately 12 mats were placed across the width of the gym, in two rows of six each. One row of mats was located in the south half of the gym about even with the free throw line on the basketball court. The other row was placed along the free throw line in the north half of the gym. The mats measured about 2 feet square and were spaced 10 to 12 feet apart. Each row contained approximately six mats. A golf club and three or four plastic "wiffle" balls were placed by each mat.

The students were divided into groups of four or five students and each group was assigned to the use of one of the mats. The boys used the mats on the south side of the gym and hit in a southerly direction. The girls used the mats on the north, and hit the golf balls in a northerly direction. At the start of the class all of the students were to sit along the center line of the basketball court between the two rows of mats. On the signal of one of the instructors one student from each group would go up to the assigned mat, tee up a ball, and wait for the signal to begin. After the student had hit all of the balls on the mat he was to lay the club down and return to the center of the gym. When all of the students were back at the center line, the next student in each group was directed to retrieve the balls and the procedure was repeated.

Mr. Kurtz was not present for class on Wednesday, the day of the accident, because his wife had just given birth to a baby. His place was taken by a student teacher, Tim Haley, who had been at the school for approximately 5 weeks and had assisted with four to six golf classes on Monday and Tuesday. At the beginning of the class on Wednesday, Mrs. Beveridge repeated the instructions which had been given by Mr. Kurtz on Monday. The groups were again divided. One student went up to each mat and Mrs. Beveridge testified she gave the signal for the first balls to be hit.

Plaintiff's decedent, who prior to the date of his death had never had a golf club in his hands, was either the second or third student to go up to the easternmost mat on the boys' side of the gym. He had difficulty and asked his group if anyone could help him. Mark Kreie, who had been the last to use the club, came forward and showed decedent how to grip the club and told him that he (Kreie) would take two practice swings then hit the ball. Decedent moved to the east and stood against the folded up bleachers about 10 feet to the rear of Kreie. Kreie looked over his shoulder to observe decedent before taking two practice swings. He then stepped up to the ball and took a full swing at it. Unaware that decedent had moved closer, he hit decedent with the club on the follow-through. During all of this time, Mr. Haley was helping another boy a few mats away. Mark did not know whether Mr. Haley saw decedent and him standing together at the mat. Mrs. Beveridge was positioned along the west end of the girls' line. . . .

Ike F. Pane, principal of Millard Central Junior High School, testified golf was a mandatory course of instruction. Golf instruction was provided to ninth grade students in April of 1974, with the first class on Monday, April 1, 1974.

Pane identified exhibit 9 as his schools written rules of instruction which stated the objectives to be achieved in teaching golf to the ninth grade class, and specifically setting forth in what manner or procedure the instruction be accomplished with safety. . . .

It is evident the instruction procedure used Monday was not followed on Wednesday. If it had been, the instructor would have observed the dilemma of the deceased and given him the instruction he had missed. Also, the students would not have been assisting one another. . . .

Recovery in this case is sought on the ground of lack of supervision. Where lack of supervision by an instructor is relied on to impose liability, such lack must appear as the proximate cause of the injury, with the result that the liability would not lie if the injury would have occurred notwithstanding the presence of the instructor.

In the instant case, we are dealing with a ninth grader who had never before swung a golf club. The instruction was conducted indoors, in close quarters. There was some testimony, which the trial court could have accepted, that the physical arrangement, which was contrary to defendant's suggestion, . . . would have prevented the opportunity for injury if followed. There is a question as to whether there was adequate safety instruction regarding the use of a golf club prior to the commencement of the class at which the fatal injury occurred. There is evidence, which the court could have accepted, that on the day the accident occurred the teaching procedure outlined by the regular instructor was not followed by the student teacher. The record would also indicate the student teacher may not have been properly informed as to the procedure to be followed. There is no question the trial judge could have found that, at the very best, there was ineffective observation and attention on the part of the student teacher when ordinary care or supervision would have prevented the occurrence which resulted in the death of David.

In this instance, working with ninth graders, who were not familiar with the rules of golf, and in the case of the deceased, who had never before been exposed to the game, includes a duty to anticipate danger that is reasonably foreseeable.

We have no difficulty in finding that the lack of supervision was a proximate cause of the death of David. "Proximate cause" as used in the law of negligence is that cause which in the natural and continuous sequence, unbroken by an efficient intervening cause, produces the injury and without which the injury would not have occurred.

Defendant contends that even if it were guilty of negligence its negligence was superseded by that of Mark Kreie, decedent's classmate, and Kreie's negligence was an efficient intervening cause which produced the injury.

Defendant further argues that the deceased is guilty of contributory negligence. One who is capable of understanding and discretion and who fails to exercise ordinary care and prudence to avoid obvious danger is negligent or contributorily negligent.

Whether or not a minor 14 years of age is of sufficient knowledge, discretion, and appreciation of danger that he may be subject to the defense of contributory negligence is generally a question of fact for the jury. The trial court in this instance must have found the deceased was not contributorily negligent. The golf instruction was a required subject. David, a ninth grader, had no understanding of the game and the record is not clear that he was properly warned of the apparent danger in the sport. If the testimony of Mark Kreie is accepted, Mark was complying with the directions of Mrs. Beveridge and giving help to another student. The mere fact there is a recognized amount of danger in the activity by reason of a swinging club is not contributory negligence unless the knowledge of the danger is made known to the child. The doing of an act with appreciation of the amount of danger is necessary in order to say as a matter of law a person is negligent. It cannot be said that deceased had sufficient knowledge of the danger involved, considering the fact he was not familiar with the game of golf and had never before had a golf club in his hands. He had not attended the first class where instruction and practice were provided. He had not received any instruction on any aspect of the game by any teacher prior to his attempted use of the club. The only instruction he received was that provided by the fellow student who struck the fatal blow.

The judgment of the trial court is affirmed.

In *Brahatcek*, the instructor's failure to properly supervise was held to be the cause of plaintiff's death. However, in *Vendrell v. School Dist. No.26, Malheur County*, 376 P.2d 406 (Or. 1962), the alleged negligent instruction of the football player was insufficient to show that the coach failed to exercise reasonable care for his players and that the injury was a result of that failure.

VENDRELL V. SCHOOL DISTRICT NO. 26, MALHEUR COUNTY

376 P.2d 406 (Or. 1962)

ROSSMAN, Justice.

This is an appeal by the defendant, School District No. 26C of Malheur County, from a judgment in the amount of $25,000 which the circuit court entered against it in favor of the plaintiff based upon a jury's verdict. The defendant school district lies in Malheur County and includes the city of Nyssa and more particularly Nyssa High School which it operates. August 24, 1953, a week before classes assembled in the high school, the plaintiff registered for football practice and play. He shortly enrolled in the school as a freshman. October 9, about six weeks after he had turned out for football and while playing as a member of the Nyssa High School team against the Vale High School team, he sustained the injury mentioned in Vendrell v. School District No. 26C, Malheur County et al, 226 Or. 263, 360 P.2d 282. He was the plaintiff in that action. The action now before us and the one just cited are based upon substantially the same complaint. Following the announcement of the decision just mentioned the complaint was amended by adding an additional charge of negligence and omitting all defendants except the school district. Since the acts of negligence, if any were established by the evidence, were those of the football coaches, the defendant's liability, if any, must be based upon the doctrine of respondeat superior. . . .

With three members dissenting, our former opinion ruled that since the defendant had obtained a policy of liability insurance as authorized by ORS 332.180, an action based upon charges of negligence could be maintained against it with recovery limited to the amount of the policy ($25,000). It also sustained the sufficiency of the complaint as the statement of a charge of negligence.

The present complaint, in charging the defendant with negligence, avers that at the time of the plaintiff's injury (1) he was "an inexperienced football player"; (2) he weighed 140 pounds; (3) he was "not physically corrdinated"; (4) his injury befell him when he was "tackled hard by two Vale boys"; (5) he had not received "proper or sufficient instructions"; and (6) he had not been furnished with "the necessary and proper protective equipment" for his person. The latter is the new charge which the third amended complaint added to the averments of negligence. The complaint also alleges that the plaintiff's injuries "were directly and proximately caused by the negligence of the defendant." The answer denied all allegations of negligence and of proximate cause. It alleged that (1) if any of plaintiff's protective equipment was improper or insufficient the fact was known to him, (2) he did not advise the defendant thereof, and (3) his neglect in that respect constitued contributory negligence upon his part. It further alleged that (a) the plaintiff knew that football was a body contact sport, (b) he willingly entered into it, and (c) he assumed its risks. The reply denied all new matter alleged in the answer. It averred that (1) the plaintiff "was never informed by the defendant as to the uses of protective equipment"; (2) the plaintiff was not informed of the dangers of playing football with ill fitting, improper equipment; (3) the defendant did not possess a sufficient quantity of equipment ot enable the players to obtain properly fitting gear, and (4) the defendant "had never explained the risk and hazards incidental to a football game, nor had defendant or its agents ever explained the full nature of the game of football to this plaintiff, or the hazards involved therein." . . .

We must therefore determine whether the evidence presented in this case showed that the defendant's coach failed "to exercise reasonable care for the protection of his players," and if so, whether the injury which the plaintiff sustained resulted therefrom.

Before entering Nyssa High School the plaintiff had completed the course of study offered by Nyssa Junior High School. The latter maintains a football team, two coaches and scheduled games. While a student in that school the plaintiff had constantly been a member of its football team. He played the position of left half-back, the same position that he was playing at the time of his injury.

Nyssa High School has about 300 students, two football coaches and a manager for the team. It played scheduled games with other high schools. The plaintiff was 15 years of age when he entered the high school — one year older than most pupils.

The plaintiff sustained his injury during the close of the fourth quarter of a game in which Nyssa's opponent was the Vale High School team. He was injured when he was tackled by two Vale players while he was carrying the ball.

As a witness the plaintiff described as follows what happened: "And I saw the Vale players in front of me and I knew I couldn't go any further so I put my head down and just ran into 'em and that is when I heard my neck snap." At that moment he suffered the injury for which he seeks redress in damages. It consists of a fracture of the fifth cervical vertebra of the neck.

We shall now consider the plaintiff's specifications of negligence, one by one.

The first specification of negligence states that when the plaintiff was injured he was "an inexperienced football player." . . .

Before the plaintiff had turned out on August 24, 1953, for football practice he had played for two years as a member of the football team of Nyssa Junior High School. Evidently, the training given to the football squad in the junior high school is substantial, for we note that the plaintiff mentioned that the squad was taught how to tackle, block, stiff-arm, carry the ball and keep the ball from the opponent. . . .

Before any student was accepted as a member of the Nyssa High School football squad it was necessary for him to be pronounced physically fit by a physician and for his parents to give their written consent. . . .

Football practice was conducted every afternoon, Monday through Thursday, for about two hours. No practice was maintained on Fridays because that was the day upon which the team played its games. . . .

The training of the squad consisted of a program of calisthenics, classes on physical conditioning and training rules. The calisthenics were intended to strengthen the body. One of them was called bull-neck exercise. It was engaged in for several minutes each day and was designed to strengthen the neck. . . .

The plaintiff practiced, so he testified, "most of the time" with what he termed the "varsity" team. He attended every practice session. . . .

Without further analysis of the evidence, we express our belief that it cannot warrant a finding that the plaintiff was "an inexperienced football player" at the time of his injury.

The second specification of negligence mentions the fact that the plaintiff weighed 140 pounds. Smith, Vale's half-back who tackled the plaintiff . . . weighed 130 to 135 pounds. . . .

We do not believe that the plaintiff's weight could furnish the basis for a finding of negligence upon the defendant's part. . . .

If the plaintiff, as he faced the tacklers, noticed anything unusual in the situation, he did not mention the fact as a witness, nor did he testify that the tacklers employed uncommon force. The fact that the plaintiff was "tackled hard by two Vale boys" establishes no negligence upon the defendant's part.

The sixth specification of negligence which we will consider before we proceed with the fifth, contends that the plaintiff had not been furnished with 'the necessary and proper protective equipment' for his person. . . .

The fifth specification of negligence presents the contention that the plaintiff did not receive "proper or sufficient instruction." We infer that the quoted words were intended to mean that the defendant's coaches (1) did not instruct the plaintiff adequately in the manner of playing the game of football, (2) should have told him that in playing football he might sustain injury, and (3) should have told him that if he lowered his head and used it as a battering ram injury to his spine might ensue.

The playing of football is a body-contact sport. The game demands that the players come into physical contact with each other constantly, frequently with great force. The linemen charge the opposing line vigorously, shoulder to shoulder. The tackler faces the risk of leaping at the swiftly moving legs of the ball-carrier and the latter must be prepared to strike the ground violently. Body contacts, bruises, and clashes are inherent in the game. There is no other way to play it. Nor prospective player need be told that a participant in the game of football may sustain injury. That fact is self evident. It draws to the game the manly; they accept its risks, blows, clashes and injuries without whimper.

No one expects a football coach to extract from the game the body clashes that cause bruises, jolts and hard falls. To remove them would end the sport. The coach's function is to minimize the possibility that the body contacts may result in something more than slight injury. The extensive calisthenics, running and other forms of muscular exercise to which the defendant's coaches subjected the defendant's squad were intended to place the players in sound physical condition so that they could withstand the shocks, blows and other rough treatment with which they would meet in actual play. As a further safeguard for the players' protection the defendant provided all of the players with protective equipment. Each player was taught and shown how to handle himself while in play so that a blow would fall upon his protective equipment and not directly upon his body. We have also noticed the fact that every player was instructed in the manner of (1) running while carrying the ball, (2) tackling an opposing player, and (3) handling himself properly when about to be tackled. . . .

The purpose of the extensive instructions and arduous practice was to enable the player not only to make for his team the maximum yardage but also to reduce to the minimum the possibility that an injury would befall him.

All of the football coaches who testified upon the subject swore, as we have seen, that the instructions and practice which were given to the defendant's football squad were adequate and were similar to that which they gave to their own players. No criticism was offered of the instructions and practice. Had the plaintiff followed the instructions that were given to him about holding his head up, his injury would not have occurred, assuming, of course, that the failure to hold up his head was the cause of his injury.

But the plaintiff says that the defendant's coaches had not told him that if he used his head as a battering ram an injury might befall him. One of the first lessons that an infant learns when he begins to toddle about on his feet is not to permit his head to collide with anything. Not only do his parents, playmates and teachers unite in teaching him that lesson, but every door, chair and other protruding object that is in the child's presence becomes a harsh but effective teacher that injury occurs if he bumps his head upon something. Less than two weeks before his lamentable injury befell him, the plaintiff was taught the lesson again that he had learned in his infancy. This time it was taught to him when he ran head-on into a player in the Parma game and split his head gear. When he discarded his ruined helmet and borrowed one from a team mate he saw from the split helmet in his own hands what could have happened to his head. No coach could have spoken to him more effectively.

The defendant was not the plaintiff's employer or his master. Its coaches were his teachers. He had the right — in fact, the duty — to ask the coaches questions concerning any matter which was not clear. . . . In turn, the coaches had the right to assume that he possessed the intelligence and stock of information of a normal young man. . . . Thus, they had the right to assume that he knew of the possibility of injury that comes to an individual who uses his head as a battering ram.

There is no express testimony in the record that the plaintiff struck any-one with his head. He swore that he lowered his head when he saw that he was about to be tackled, but neither he nor anyone else testified that he struck anyone with his head. The manner in which the play was made in which the plaintiff received his injury is left in doubt. . . .

We believe that the plaintiff assumed the risk attendant upon being tackled. The risk of injury that was inherent in being tackled was obvious. The plaintiff was throughly familiar with it. He had been tackled scores of times. The tackle in question was made fairly and according to the rules.

We believe that the defendant's coaches gave to the football squad adequate, standard instruction and practice. The record does not indicate that the defendant's coaches negligently omitted any detail; certainly it does not establish that the defendant's coaches omitted to perform any duty alleged by the complaint. As we have said, we believe that the plaintiff assumed all of the obvious risks of which tackling was one.

The defendant's motion for a directed verdict should have been sustained. The assignment of error reveals merit. The judgment of the circuit court is reversed, and the cause remanded with directions to enter judgment for the defendant.

4. Referee Liability

It is a referee's duty to properly supervise the athletic contest. Included in this duty is an obligation to enforce safety rules. If this duty is ignored or not properly performed, then both the referee and the school might be liable for negligence. In *Carabba v. Anacortes School Dist.*, a wrestling referee was held to be negligent for not properly supervising a match.

CARABBA V. ANACORTES SCHOOL DISTRICT

435 P.2d 936 (Wash. 1967)

DONWORTH, J.

This action was brought on behalf of Stephen Carabba, a minor, by his guardian ad litem to recover $500,000 for injuries sustained by Carabba while he was a participant in a high school wrestling match.

The amended complaint alleged that respondent school districts, acting through their agent, the referee, were negligent in the following particulars:

1. Failing to adequately supervise the contestants;
2. Allowing his [the referee's] attention to be diverted from the actions of the contestants;
3. Allowing an illegal and dangerous hold to be applied;
4. Failing to immediately cause the said hold to be broken;
5. Allowing the said hold to be prolonged for a substantial period of time;
6. Violating the provisions of the 1963 official Wrestling Guide of the National Collegiate Athletic Association.

Respondents denied that the referee was acting as their agent, denied the allegations of negligence, and affirmatively. . . . The trial court ruled out the affirmative defenses, and instructed the jury that the referee was the agent of respondents as a matter of law.

The case was submitted to the jury solely on the issues of the referee's negligence and damages.

During the course of their deliberations, the jury requested an additional instruction regarding the standard of care applicable to the referee, i.e. the standard of the reasonably prudent man or that of an ordinarily prudent referee. [T]he . . . court . . . told the jury that the standard . . . was that of the ordinarily prudent referee.

The jury thereafter returned a verdict for respondents. . . . The jury could have found, from the evidence presented, that on January 31, 1963, a wrestling meet was held at Anacortes High School between the wrestling teams of Anacortes High School and Oak Harbor High School. The meet was sponsored jointly by the student body associations of those two schools. The referee for this meet was Mr. Robert L. Erhart, a state trooper, and a member of the Northwest Wrestling Officials Association.

In essence, respondents contend that the school districts played no part in this wrestling competition; that the matches were sponsored by the associated student bodies, which are entities separate from the school districts; that the referee was qualified and selected by the referees' association, an entity separate and apart from either the school district or the student body associations; and that the referee, in the performance of his function, occupied the status of an independent contractor. This being the case, they contend, no liability may arise on the part of respondent school districts, however negligent the referee might have been.

. . . [A]ppellant contends that the school district respondents owed a nondelegable duty to protect the students participating in the interscholastic wrestling matches which took place on the school premises.

The duty owed by a school district to its pupils has been recently stated by this court to be:

[T]o anticipate reasonably foreseeable dangers and to take precautions protecting the children in its custody from such dangers. . . .

It is likewise clear that potential liability on the part of the school districts is not limited to those situations involving curricular activities. . . . However,

. . . one is never held to "assume the risk" of another's negligence or incompetence. . . .

Respondent Oak Harbor High School contends that the trial court should have submitted the issue of appellant's contributory negligence to the jury. But . . . the . . . trial court did not err in refusing to submit this issue to the jury.

We further find that respondent's proposed instruction bearing on the statutory exemption in the case of failure of athletic equipment was properly excluded by the trial court because it was not applicable to the facts of this case. . . . The trial court's judgment, dismissing appellant's action with prejudice and awarding respondents judgment for costs and disbursements, is reversed, and the cause is remanded for retrial to be conducted in accordance with the views expressed in this opinion.

QUESTIONS AND DISCUSSION

1. Coaches and teachers have a duty to supervise their student-athletes. However, supervisors do not have the duty to supervise every student every second in every possible area. *See Fagan v. Summers*, 948 P.2d 1227 (Wyo. 1972) (school district was not liable for student injured by stone-throwing incident in playground).
2. The schools also have a duty to maintain equipment and facilities. *See Tiemann v. Independent Sch. Dist. #740*, 331 N.W.2d 250 (Minn. 1983) (student injured during physical education instruction on a pommel horse with exposed holes).
3. Coaches too can be held personally liable. *See Mogabgab v. Orleans Parish Sch. Bd.*, 239 So. 2d 456 (La. Ct. App. 1970) (liability was found when a coach failed to summon medical aid in a timely fashion when a player showed symptoms of heat stroke).
4. In *Thomas v. Chicago Bd. of Educ.*, 395 N.E.2d 538 (Ill. 1979), sovereign immunity protected a coach since his failure to inspect defective football equipment was neither willful nor wanton.
5. In *Nydegger v. Don Bosco Preparatory High Sch.*, 495 A.2d 485 (N.J. Super. 1985), an injured high school soccer player sued the opposing coach for teaching his team to compete in an aggressive, "win-at-all-costs" manner. The court held that absent specific instruction to commit a wrongful act or instructing his players in techniques designed to increase risk of harm, the coach could not be responsible to the injured player.
6. Many states' legislators are alarmed by seemingly gratuitous lawsuits against volunteer referees, so they designed laws to eliminate suits against referees unless they are grossly negligent (for example, referee, in *Carabba* would be grossly negligent since he looked away in a sport where the potential for catastrophic injury is possible at any time unless the supervision is complete, intensive, and extensive). A New Jersey law provides for partial immunity for volunteer referees from civil suits for injuries that result from acts or omissions that occur during the ordinary course of their supervisory activities. N.J. Stat. Ann. §2A:62A-6.

I. TORT DEFENSES

1. Assumption of Risk

A stadium operator or team owner or a school district has many defenses at its command to summon against claims for injuries. The three most powerful are assumption of risk, contributory negligence, and comparative negligence. The doctrine of assumption of risk is to be used when a sports-related accident occurs. It can be defined as a voluntary assumption, expressed or implied, of a known and appreciated risk. For sports accidents, the injured athlete assumes only the ordinary risks of the game.

In *Ashcroft*, a jockey was injured when his horse veered across the race course toward an exit gap. Riding on a track with a negligently placed exit gap is not an inherent risk in the sport of horse racing.

ASHCROFT V. CALDER RACE COURSE, INC.

492 So. 2d 1309 (Fla. 1986)

Petitioner Ashcroft, a jockey racing at Calder Race Course, was injured when his horse veered across the race course and toward an exit gap. He lost control, fell to the ground, and was run over by another horse, rendering him a quadriplegic. He sued respondent Calder Race Course, Inc. for damages, alleging that Calder's negligent placement of the exit gap caused the accident and his resultant injury. The trial court, over Ashcroft's objection, instructed the jury on assumption of risk. The jury rendered a verdict finding Calder negligent and Ashcroft not negligent, but finding that Ashcroft had assumed the risk of the danger of which he complained. Damages of $10,000,000 were assessed. The trial court denied Calder's motion for judgment on the verdict in its favor and found Calder liable, but upon motion deemed the verdict excessive and granted Calder's motion for remittitur or, in the alternative, a new trial. The award reduced to $5,000,000 was declined by Ashcroft, and the cause was therefore subject to a new trial. On appeal, the district court found abundant evidence supporting the jury's finding that Ashcroft assumed the risk and reversed the trial court's order in failing to enter judgment for Calder.

This Court rejected the doctrine of contributory negligence as a complete bar to a plaintiff's recovery from a defendant whose negligence contributed to his injury. We rejected the doctrine of implied assumption of risk as a complete bar to a plaintiff's otherwise meritorious claim for recovery ... [H]owever, [not rejected is] the doctrine of express assumption of risk, including "express contracts not to sue for injury or loss which may thereafter be occasioned by the covenantee's negligence as well as situations in which actual consent exists such as where one voluntarily participates in a contact sport."

We had occasion to affirm the viability of the doctrine of express assumption of risk in the contact sport setting in *Kuehner*. We pointed out, however, that a participant in a contact sport does *not* automatically assume all risks except those resulting from deliberate attempts to injure. *Express* assumption of risk, as it applies in the context of contact sports, rests upon the plaintiff's voluntary consent to take certain chances. This principle may be better expressed in terms of waiver. When a participant volunteers to take certain chances he waives his right to be free from those bodily contacts inherent in the chances taken. Our judicial system must protect those who rely on such a waiver and engage in otherwise prohibited bodily contacts.

436 So. 2d at 80 (emphasis in original; citation omitted). Assuming that express assumption of risk applies to horse racing, it is clear from the above quotation that express assumption of risk waives only risks inherent in the sport itself. Riding on a track with a negligently placed exit gap is not an inherent risk in the sport of horse racing. We therefore find as a matter of law that there was no express assumption of risk with respect to the negligent placement of the exit gap and it was error for the judge to instruct the jury on assumption of risk.

The owner or occupier of land has a duty to exercise reasonable care for the protection of invitees.

A landowner who assumes the task of providing the physical facility upon which a sport is to be played has a duty to exercise reasonable care to prevent foreseeable injury to the participants that includes foreseeing that they may risk a known danger in order to participate. If injury occurs due to negligent maintenance of the facility, the landowner may be held liable.

The decision below is quashed. The cause is remanded with instructions to reinstate the jury verdicts and enter judgment.

It is so ordered.

In *Ashcroft*, the court held that a negligently placed gap was not the type of ordinary risk of the sport of horse racing that a jockey would be deemed to have assumed. However, in California, under both *Ford v. Gouin* and *Knight v. Jewett*, the doctrine of reasonable implied assumption is held to be a complete bar to recovery in sports injury cases.

FORD V. GOUIN

834 P.2d 724 (Cal. 1992)

As in the companion case of *Knight v. Jewett*, [834 P.2d 696 (hereinafter *Knight*)], the issue in this case is whether plaintiff's cause of action, arising out of an injury allegedly caused by the negligence of a coparticipant in an active sport, is barred under the assumption of risk doctrine. As explained in *Knight*, in light of the adoption of comparative fault principles in *Liv. Yellow Cab Co.*, the assumption of risk doctrine operates as a complete bar to a plaintiff's action only in instances in which, in view of the nature of the activity at issue and the parties' relationship to that activity, the defendant's conduct did not breach a legal duty of care owed to the plaintiff. As Knight also explains, in general the legal duty applicable to a coparticipant in an active sport simply is a duty to avoid either intentionally injuring another participant or engaging in conduct so reckless as to bring it totally outside the range of the ordinary activity involved in the sport. A coparticipant in an active sport ordinarily bears no liability for an injury resulting from conduct in the course of the sport that is merely careless or negligent.

On June 12, 1983, plaintiff Larry C. Ford was seriously injured while waterskiing in the "Warren Cut" channel of the Sacramento River Delta. At the time of the accident, plaintiff was skiing barefoot and backward. He was injured when the back of his head struck a tree limb that extended over the channel from one of the riverbanks.

After the accident, plaintiff filed this action against defendant Jack Gouin, a friend of plaintiff, who, at the time of the accident, was driving the boat that towed plaintiff. In his complaint, plaintiff alleged that the accident was proximately caused by defendant's negligence in driving the boat too close to the riverbank.

Plaintiff argues, however, that although a rule limiting a coparticipant's duty of care to the avoidance of intentionally injurious or reckless conduct appropriately may be applied to a "competitive" sport such as the touch football game involved in *Knight*, such a limited duty should not apply in the context of a "cooperative" sport such as waterskiing. Although most of the prior authorities cited in *Knight* did involve sports that are played in competing teams, the rationale of those decisions is, in our view, equally applicable to an active sport such as waterskiing even when it is engaged in on a noncompetitive basis.

As noted in Knight, the decisions that have recognized the existence of only a limited duty of care in a sports situation generally have reasoned that vigorous participation in the sport likely would be chilled, and, as a result, the nature of the sport likely would be altered, in the event legal liability were to be imposed on a sports participant for ordinary careless conduct. (*Knight*, at 318.) This reasoning applies to waterskiing. Even when a water-skier is not involved in a "competitive" event, the skier has undertaken vigorous, athletic activity, and the ski boat driver operates the boat in a manner that is consistent with, and enhances, the excitement and challenge of the active conduct of the sport. Imposition of legal liability on a ski boat driver for ordinary negligence in making too sharp a turn, for example, or in pulling the skier too rapidly or too slowly, likely would have the same kind of undesirable chilling effect on the driver's conduct that the courts in other cases feared would inhibit ordinary conduct in various sports. As a result holding ski boat drivers liable for their ordinary negligence might well have a generally deleterious effect on the nature of the sport of waterskiing as a whole. Additionally, imposing such liability might well deter friends from voluntarily assisting one another in such potentially risky sports. Accordingly, the general rule limiting the duty of care of a coparticipant in active sports to the avoidance of intentional and reckless misconduct, applies to participants engaged in noncompetitive but active sports activity, such as a ski boat driver towing a water-skier. Under the principles set forth in *Knight*, summary judgment in favor of defendant was properly entered.

2. Contributory Negligence

Contributory negligence occurs when an athlete or spectator with knowledge of a dangerous condition goes into that danger. Even though there might be negligence on the part of another, if plaintiff's own negligence is the proximate cause of the injury, then he will be barred from recovery. Contributory negligence is conduct that falls below standards that a plaintiff should meet for his own protection and that contributes to his injuries.

3. Comparative Negligence

The doctrines of assumption of risk and contributory negligence are complete bars to recovery; so in an attempt to ameliorate their harshness, many states have created comparative negligence statutes. This doctrine compares the fault of the defendant to the fault of the plaintiff. The statutes vary from state to state. The primary concern is that plaintiff be allowed to recover at least a portion of the damages if plaintiff's negligence is proportionally less than defendant's negligence.

4. Warnings and Releases

An old axiom that still retains validity is that courts favor warnings but dislike waivers (or releases). A warning in sports explains the inherent dangers that are involved in a certain activity; this is as opposed to a release that contractually releases a defendant from all participants injuries. Participants must be warned of a sport's inherent risks: the more dangerous the activity (example, scuba diving), the more important the warning becomes.

A waiver, or release, is an exculpatory agreement that attempts to relieve one party of all or part of their responsibility to another. Although they are allowed in certain circumstances, they are not favored by the law and are strictly construed against the benefiting party. If it is ambiguous in scope or purports to be releasing liability for intentional, willful, or wanton acts, then it is unenforceable. There are many ways in which a waiver may be voided: for it to be valid, it must be nonambiguous, specific as regards liability, not against public policy, not imply a waiver of gross negligence, and must not allow results that would indicate a large disparity in bargaining power. However, generally it is enforceable as long as it is sufficiently clear to show the party's intent that defendant is to be held harmless for any injury that is caused by defendant's own negligence.

In *Williams v. Cox Enterprises,* the court upheld a waiver in a 10,000 meter road race in which a participant suffered injuries as a result of heat prostration and exhaustion.

WILLIAMS V. COX ENTERPRISES

283 S.E.2d 367 (Ga. Ct. App. 1981)

The temperature on the morning of the race exceeded 85 degrees and the humidity 90 percent. As indicated previously, the course distance was 10,000 meters, or 6.2 miles. Participants in the race were required to pay a fee and sign an application form containing the following language: "In consideration of acceptance of this entry, I waive any and all claims for myself and my heirs against officials or sponsors of the 1977 Peachtree Road Race, for injury or illness which may directly or indirectly result from my participation. I further state that I am in proper physical condition to participate in this event. . . ." The application described the course as follows: "This is one of the most difficult 10,000-meter courses in America. . . . Heat and humidity, in addition to hills, make this a grueling 10,000-meter race."

The appellant testified that he is a *summa cum laude* graduate of Duke University, where he was a member of Phi Beta Kappa, and that he currently studied law at the University of Chicago. He admitted that he had read the quoted portions of the application and that he understood their meaning. He further testified that, as a former Atlanta resident, he knew from experience that the temperature and humidity on July 4 would be high and that extreme exertion under such conditions could cause the very conditions to which he succumbed. Held:

The appellant argues that the waiver was invalid because the event was so large and well-publicized that the sponsors were charged with a public duty to provide for the safety of the entrants. The general rule in Georgia is that a contractual waiver of liability for simple negligence is valid, the exception being where the waiver violates public policy.

2. The appellant also contends that the waiver was void due to a disparity in bargaining positions, arguing that because running and jogging had become such popular pastimes and because the Peachtree Road Race was "the only road race of its kind in the Atlanta area," he and the other partici- pants were under enormous pressure to enter it on whatever terms were offered to them. This proposition is, of course, ludicrous. It is clear from the appellant's deposition testimony that his decision to sign the waiver was the product of his own free will, unencumbered by anything remotely resembling duress or undue influence.

3. A recovery is also precluded under the assumption of risk doctrine. As indicated previously, the application described the course in very specific terms and warned that heat and humidity would make it a "grueling" one. The appellant admitted both that he read the warning and that he was already aware of the danger. Under these circumstances, any injury resulting to him from overheating and dehydration cannot reasonably be construed to have resulted from a breach of duty on the party of the appellee.

Judgment affirmed.

5. Immunities

Sometimes a tortfeasor may avoid liability on the basis that the particular activity or defendant is protected from liability based on doctrines of immu- nity, either sovereign or charitable. These immunities vary greatly from state to state and have numerous exceptions. Sovereign immunity avers that the state (and its instrumentalities) shall not be subject to suit without its consent. For example, in *Churilla v. School Dist.* 306 N.W.2d 381 (Mich. Ct. App. 1981), under Michigan law, the court found that the school board was immune from suits based on football injuries. Comparable to sovereign immunity is charitable immunity which, if applicable, provides protection from suits against charitable institutions.

Recreational Use Statutes

A variation on sovereign immunity are the recreational use statues, which substitute private landowners for governmental entities. Both types of immunities protect from suit those entities that perform a "state-like" function. Under these statutes, which also vary greatly from state to state, landowners who allow free recreational use of their property do not have a duty to keep their premises in a safe condition or a duty to warn of dangerous conditions. But if a fee is paid for use, the recreational use statute is inapplicable.

CHURILLA V. SCHOOL DISTRICT

306 N.W. 2d 381 (Mich. Ct. App. 1981)

BASHARA, Judge

This appeal involves the sole issue of whether the day-to-day operation of a public school, including the administration and supervision of a football program, is a governmental function and, therefore, entitled to immunity. We hold that a public school in the operation of its athletic program is entitled to immunity, and so affirm the order of the trial judge granting the school district's motion for summary judgment.

John Lawrence Churilla was a student at Oakwood Junior High School within the defendant school district. He was participating in a practice session of the school's football program when he allegedly made contact with an oncoming team member, sustaining injury.

Our Supreme Court appears to have determined that the operation of a public school is a governmental function. In *Bush v. Oscoda Area Schools*, 405 Mich. 716, 275 N.W.2d 268 (1979) Justice Levin reiterated the position of Justices Kavanagh, Fitzgerald, and himself that the day-to-day operation of a school is not a governmental function. See *Galli v. Kirkeby*, 398 Mich. 527, 531, 248 N.W.2d 149 (1976). He conceded that his position did not command the concurrence of a majority of the Court. *Bush*, 405 Mich. 727-728, 275 N.W.2d 268. In *Bush,* the remaining four justices agreed with Justice Levin's assessment that the "Kavanagh Levin Fitzgerald view" did not claim a majority of the Court.

The case of *Deaner v. Utica Community School Dist.*, 99 Mich. App. 103, 297 N.W.2d 625 (1980), presents facts similar to the case at bar. The minor in that matter was enrolled in a combative sports course and suffered severe injuries while engaged in a wrestling match in class.

The *Deaner* Court analyzed Justice Moody's position on governmental immunity in *Parker v. Highland Park,* 404 Mich. 183. 273 N.W.2d 413 (1978), and *Perry v. Kalamazoo State Hospital,* 404 Mich. 205. 273 N.W.2d 421 (1978) and applied it as follows:

> Operation of a public school presents factors similar to those relied on by Justice Moody to distinguish mental hospitals from general hospitals. The

government plays a pervasive role in the area of education, appropriating substantial state funds to that field and declaring education as a public policy. See Const. 1963, art. 8, §1. The number of private schools is inadequate to meet the educational needs of the public. Finally, while private schools exits to educate some students, the provision of a free and universal education is a uniquely governmental function. Therefore, we would find that the trial court was correct in granting summary judgment to the school district based on governmental immunity.

99 Mich. App. 108 See also, *Smith v. Mimnaugh,* 105 Mich. App. 209, 306 N.W.2d 454 (1981).

In *Lovitt v. Concord School Dist.,* 58 Mich. App. 593, 228 N.W.2d 479 (1975), plaintiff's decedent died of heat prostration during a particularly severe football practice session. Concluding that a school district is immune from tort liability under such circumstances, the Court cited *McDonell v. Brozo,* 285 Mich. 38, and *Cody v. Southfield-Lathrup School Dist.,* 25 Mich. App. 33, 181 N.W.2d 81 (1970), for the proposition that physical education activities have been held to constitute a governmental and not a proprietary function.

The Lovitt Court quoted with approval from Justice Dethmer's opinion in *Watson v. Bay City School Dist.,* 324 Mich. 1, 11, 36 N.W.2d 195 (1949)

> Here the football game was part of the school's physical education program. The function is inherently educational, a governmental function without doubt.

Finally, in *Richards v. Birmingham School Dist.,* 348 Mich. 490, 509-510, 83 N.W.2d 643 (1957), the Court stated:

> The football game played on November 25, 1948, must be considered as a part of the athletic activities of the school rather than as an independent contest. . . . Rather, the entire department is operated as a part of the school facilities and in furtherance of the objectives to be attained in educational lines. It may not be said that defendant district, in allowing athletic competition with other schools, is thereby engaging in a function proprietary in nature. On the contrary, it is performing a governmental function vested in it by law.

Affirmed.

BRONSON, Judge (dissenting).

I respectfully dissent . . . The question we are presented . . . is whether an extracurricular football program is of the essence of government. . . . I believe that an extracurricular football program is simply not of a uniquely governmental character or precipitated by governmental mandate. There is nothing uniquely governmental in the function of staging competitive athletic events. I also reject the idea that holding school districts liable for the negligent operations of a football program constitutes "an acceptable interference with government's ability to govern."

Nor do I believe a football program like the one in question here can only be accomplished through the government. It is true that the majority of football programs for high school aged participants are run through schools. . . . However, this factor is not dispositive and does not even clearly cut against the no-immunity view in this case. First, a number of extracurricular football programs are associated with private schools. Other football programs exist through private organizations and churches. Thus, there is an analogy to a similar function in the private sector. Second, if this factor were dispositive, I believe the result could be an anomalous situation in which school football programs would be entitled to immunity, but school baseball programs because of the greater number of private leagues would not be exempt. . . . I would reverse.

QUESTIONS AND DISCUSSION

1. Spectators do not assume the risk of unreasonable conduct by participants, for example, a ball player who intentionally throws his bat into the stands. But they do assume the risk of an errant bat if it slips out of the batter's hands. Is there a difference? Should there be a difference legally when the results are essentially the same?

   An interesting question is whether a spectator assumes the risk when his attention is diverted by matters that are not directly related to the sport, example, pesky mascots, fireworks, aggressive beer sellers, and the like. The answer appears to be if you're in the zone of danger (grandstands) and you're hit by a run-of-the mill foul ball, you probably assumed that risk since you were under implied notice that it might occur. *See Schentzel v. Philadelphia National League,* 96 A. 2d 181 (Pa. Super. Ct. 1953). On the other hand, if you're not in that grandstand zone, but in another less dangerous area, such as the inner corridor, you probably are not on guard to possible dangers and thus you would not have assumed the risk of the danger of being struck by a foul ball. See *Jones v. Three Rivers Management Corp.,* 380 A.2d 387 Pa. Super. Ct. 1977, rev'd 394 A.2d 546 (Pa. 1978).

2. A plaintiff must have knowledge to assume a risk; there must be a knowing assumption, which means that plaintiff has actual knowledge of the risk involved, or that it is imputed, because of certain observations from which he should have reasonably known that risk was involved. An example: Football coaches can assume that a player knows he may get hurt if he uses his head as a battering ram. The player has a duty to ask questions on matters of which he is uncertain; alternatively, coaches can assume that their players possess the intelligence, logic, and stock of information that a normal young, sports-oriented man would possess. It follows that a coach can assume that a player knows of the possibility of injury when he uses his head as a battering ram.

3. The doctrine of assumption of risk is being reviewed in many states. The view is that it is no longer necessary after the adoption of comparative negligence statutes. *See* Champion & Swygert, *Nonprofessional Sport-Related Injuries and Assumption of Risk in Pennsylvania: Is There Life After Rutter?* 54 Pa. B. Ass'n Q. 43 (Jan. 1983). "The term 'assumption of risk' is so apt to create mist that it is better to be banished from the scene." *McGrath v. American Cyanamid Co.,* 196 A.2d 238, 240 (N.J. 1968).

4. But in *Benitez v. New York City Bd. of Educ.,* 543 N.Y.S.2d 29 (N.Y. 1989), a high school football player was found to have assumed the risks of injury

even though he was tired and facing a losing battle in a mismatch. The court held that he was under no inherent compulsion to play.

5. State legislatures have promulgated various statutes to protect the recreational industries of roller skating, horseback riding, snowmobiling, and skiing. All these statutes attempt to memorialize as a matter of law that the injured parties in these activities have assumed, by their participation, the risk from dangers that are inherent to that recreational activity. *See, e.g.,* Georgia's Equine Activities Act (OCGA Sections 1-12-1 et seq.); N.J. Roller Skating Rink Safety & Fair Liability Act (N.J.J.A. 5:14-1-7:L. 1991, c. 28); Michigan's Roller Skating Safety Act (MCL 445 1721 *et seq.,* MSA 18.485(1) et seq.): Illinois Snowmobile Registration and Safety Act (625 ILCS 40/5-1(I) (West 1992)); Maine's Skiers and Tramway Passengers' Responsibilities Act, 26 M.R.S.A. Section 488 (1988); Massachusetts' Ski Safety Act (G.L.c. 143, Sections 71H-71S); Michigan's Ski Area Safety Act, MCL Section 408.321 *et seq.* (M.S.A. §18.483(1) *et seq.*), etc.

6. As regards California's attempt to understand assumption of risk, *see* Bradley, *Reasonable Implied Assumption of Risk as a Complete Defense in Sports Injury Cases (Knight v. Jewett,___),* 28 San Diego L. Rev. 477 (1991); Bianco, *The Dawn of a New Standard, Assumption of Risk Doctrine in a Post-Knight California,* 15 Whittier L. Rev. 1155 (1994). If defendant has control, there appears to be an exception carved out of *Knight and Ford,* which can be called the Gallardi/Tan coach/trainer exception. See *Knight v. Jewett,* 225 Cal. App. 886, (1990); *Gallardi v. Seahorse Riding Club,* 16 Cal. App. 4th 81 (1993). *See generally* Warrat, *Torts and Sporting Events: Spectator and Participant Injuries—Using Defendant's Duty to Limit Limit Liability as an Alternative to the Defense of Primary Implied Assumption of the Risk,* 31 U. Mem. L. Rev. 237 (2001).

7. Contributory negligence can be imposed only if plaintiff understood that the possibility of danger existed. For example, a 10-year-old student who was injured during a field hockey game was not contributorily negligent because he was incapable of appreciating the danger of active participation in connection with his physical condition of borderline hemophilia. *Lewis v. Dependent Sch. Dist. No. 10,* 808 P.2d 710 (Okla. App. 1990).

8. Plaintiff was injured when she collided with a group of people gathered near the bottom of a ski lift exit; the doctrine of comparative negligence applies if the injury was caused by a combination of skiing's inherent risk and operator negligence. *Jessup v. Mt. Bachelor, Inc.,* 792 P.2d 1232 (Or. Ct. App. 1990).

9. Courts dislike waivers; they're more inclined to approve waivers in cases such as *Williams v. Cox Enterprises* where the intrepid participant must by necessity possess the requisite amount of training, experience, and skill. But, absent the specificity of *Williams,* the court is more likely to disallow overly broad waivers. For example, in *Wagenblast v. Odessa School District,* 758 P.2d 968 (Wash. 1988), a waiver that public high school students were obliged to sign as a prerequisite for athletic participation, which released the district from all future acts of negligence, was invalid as against public policy.

10. An important way to interpret immunity questions is by applying the doctrine of discretionary immunity. This doctrine allows state officials and their employees to receive partial immunity but usually only for discretionary duties. State officials will ordinarily be liable then only while performing ministerial duties. Discretionary duties call for judgment; ministerial duties leave nothing to discretion. If a physical education teacher never engages in decision making that is relevant to developing and administering a curriculum, then his negligence does not involve decision making on the planning level; therefore, his activities would be classified as ministerial.

11. An injury during an informed basketball game at a Jewish Community Center: "A broken nose suffered in a basketball game has ballooned into a request that Maryland's century-old charitable immunity doctrine be judicially abrogated," However, the community center is an uninsured charitable organization devoted to religious, educational, and community welfare services; its assets are entirely committed to furthering its charitable purposes. Therefore, it is entitled to the application of Maryland's charitable immunity doctrine. *Abramson v. Reiss,* 638 A.2d 743 (Md. 1994).

12. Recreational use statutes usually protect landowners only from their own negligence. A seven-year, old was impaled on a large hook at the end of a broken swing, which became embedded in his groin; his older sister assisted him off the chain. Although the incident occurred at the municipality playground that charged no fee, their behavior was not protected by Massachusetts' recreational use statute (Mass. Gen. ch. 2, §17C) since defendant's conduct was willful, wanton, and reckless. Forbush v. City of Lynn, 625 N.E.2d 1370 (Mass. App. 1994).

J. WORKERS' COMPENSATION

Each state has a workers' compensation statute. It certainly is not a tort defense per se since it compensates injured citizens. However, it is often used as a defense by the tortfeasor to circumvent personal injury suits since, if an applicable statute exists, it is usually the sole remedy for recovery. Workers' compensation is a parallel system to torts that is created by state statutes and provides for employees to receive monetary compensation for employment-related injuries. These statutes usually allow recovery for professional athletes, college athletes on scholarship, and employees who are injured in job-related activities (for example, company softball teams). As regards injuries for professional athletes, there are a few states that specifically preclude professional athletes from coverage.

Generally, for coverage to be triggered, the injured person must be an employee who was injured by an accident while engaged in a job-related function. It is undoubted, by definition, that an injured professional athlete is an employee of the team. With college sports, the key question is whether the injured athlete is an employee for purposes of workers' compensation coverage. The general answer is that if the continued receipt of a job, free meals, or money is contingent upon continued sports participation, then a contract to play that sport is created and recovery is allowed. Employer-based sports injuries will receive coverage if the employer has brought the sporting activity within the course of employment. The more indices that indicate that the activity is within the course of employment, the better the chance that coverage applies. Examples of indices are championship trophy displayed, equipment paid for by employer, company logo embossed on uniforms, or copies of schedules passed out at work. Nonparticipants that might also be protected by Workers' compensation coverage include coaches, physical education teachers, team managers, stadium attendants, trainers, umpires, and referees.

At the same time, trainers and referees are often viewed as independent contractors and not employees for purposes of coverage. The question is, who has the right to control the details of their performance?

In *Waldrep*, an injured college football player was denied Workers' compensation coverage.

WALDREP V. TEXAS EMPLOYERS INSURANCE ASSOCIATION

21 S.W.2d 692 (Tx. Ct. App. 2000).

LEE YEAKEL, Justice.

Appellant Alvis Kent Waldrep, Jr. was awarded Workers' compensation benefits by the Texas Workers' Compensation Commission (the "Commission") for an injury he sustained while playing football for Texas Christian University ("TCU"). Appellee Texas Employers Insurance Association, in receivership, Texas Property and Casualty Insurance Guaranty Association appealed the award to the district court. Following a trial *de novo*, a jury found that Waldrep had failed to prove that he was an employee of TCU at the time of his injury. The district court rendered judgment that Waldrep take nothing against TEIA. Waldrep appeals the judgment, claiming that (1) he was an employee as a matter of law and (2) the district court erred in admitting and excluding certain evidence at trial. We will affirm the district court's judgment.

Background

Waldrep graduated from high school in Alvin, Texas in 1972. During his junior and senior years, TCU was among many schools interested in recruiting Waldrep, a young man known for his athletic ability as well as his good academic record. Tommy Runnels, a TCU assistant football coach, visited Waldrep frequently at his home and school, attempting to interest Waldrep in TCU's football and academic programs. During one home visit, Waldrep's mother asked Runnels what would happen if Waldrep were injured during his football career at TCU. Runnels assured Waldrep and his family that TCU would "take care of them" and emphasized that Waldrep would keep his scholarship even if he were injured and could not play football.

Waldrep was very impressed with the facilities at TCU and believed that his abilities would fit in well with TCU's football program. He was also aware that recruitment and his future involvement in athletics at TCU were governed by the rules of the Southwest Athletic Conference ("Southwest Conference") and the National Collegiate Athletic Association ("NCAA"). To affirm his intent to attend school at TCU and participate in TCU's football program, Waldrep signed two documents. First, Waldrep signed a pre-enrollment form ("Letter of Intent"), which demonstrated his formal desire to play football for TCU and penalized him if he decided to enter a different school within the Southwest Conference. Waldrep later signed a financial aid agreement ("Financial Aid Agreement"), ensuring that Waldrep's room, board, and tuition would be paid while attending TCU and that Waldrep would receive ten dollars per month for incidentals. This cash payment was generally referred to as "laundry money." Both documents were contingent on Waldrep's meeting TCU's admission and scholastic requirements for athletic awards.

In August 1972, Waldrep enrolled at TCU. In October 1974, while playing football for TCU against the University of Alabama, Waldrep was critically injured. He sustained a severe injury to his spinal cord and was paralyzed below the neck. Today, Waldrep has no sensation below his upper chest. In 1991, Waldrep filed a Workers' compensation claim for his injury. The Commission entered an award in his favor. TEIA appealed this decision to the district court. In a trial *de novo*, a jury found that Waldrep was not an employee of TCU at the time of his injury. The district court rendered judgment in favor of TEIA. On appeal, Waldrep presents five issues. The first addresses whether, as a matter of law, Waldrep was an employee of TCU. The final four challenge various evidentiary rulings made by the district court.

Discussion: status as an employee for workers' compensation purposes

By his first issue, Waldrep asserts that at the time of his injury he was an employee of TCU *as a matter of law*. . . . After hearing all of the evidence, the jury declined to find that Waldrep was an employee of TCU at the time of his injury. . . .

Therefore, the question presented to this Court is whether there is some evidence (more than a mere scintilla) supporting the jury's failure to find that Waldrep was an employee of TCU at the time of his injury. Stated another way, could any reasonable and fair-minded person conclude that Waldrep was not employed by TCU when injured? We answer this question affirmatively.

We are confronted with a situation novel to Texas jurisprudence: whether, for workers' compensation law purposes, a recipient of a scholarship or financial aid from a university becomes that university's employee by agreeing in return to participate in a university-sponsored program. . . .

Existence of Contract of Hire

For the purpose of workers' compensation law, the employer-employee relationship may be created *only* by a contract. Waldrep strongly urges that the Letter of Intent and Financial Aid Agreement are express contracts of hire that set forth the terms of Waldrep's "employment." However, we do not find these documents to be so clear. At best, they only partially set forth the relationship between Waldrep and TCU. By their terms, they generally bound Waldrep to TCU to the exclusion of other Southwest Conference schools, if he intended to participate in athletics, and extended him financial aid so long as he complied with the admission and scholastic requirements of TCU and the rules and regulations of both TCU and the Southwest Conference. These requirements, rules, and regulations are not specifically described in either of the agreements. Nor does the record in this case set them forth in any detail. The Letter of Intent and Financial Aid Agreement are also silent with regard to whether any rules or regulations of the NCAA would apply to Waldrep or affect his relationship with TCU. Yet it is undisputed that before Waldrep signed the Letter of Intent and Financial Aid Agreement, both he and TCU understood that his recruitment and future football career at TCU would be governed by and subject to the rules of the NCAA.

TEIA, on the other hand, posits that Waldrep clearly and simply did not have a contract of hire. . . .

On the facts of this record, any contract of hire must have been a contract whereby TCU hired Waldrep to attend the university, remain in good standing academically, and play football. However, if Waldrep played football for pay, he would have been a professional, not an amateur. The evidence reflects that the actions of both Waldrep and TCU were consistent with a joint intention that Waldrep be considered an amateur and not a professional. It is undisputed that before Waldrep signed the Letter of Intent and Financial Aid Agreement, both he and TCU understood that his recruitment and future football career at TCU would be governed by and subject to the rules of the NCAA. The record indicates that the NCAA's policies and rules in effect at that time exhibited a concerted effort to ensure that each school governed by these rules made certain that student-athletes were not employees. Indeed, the rules declared that the fundamental policy of the NCAA was "to maintain inter-collegiate athletics as an integral part of the educational program and the athlete as an integral part of the student body, and by so doing, retain a clear line of demarcation between college athletics and professional sports." *NCAA Manual* at 5. Following its policy, the evidence reflects that the NCAA rules made the principle of amateurism foremost and established several requirements to ensure that the student-athlete would not be considered a professional. . . .

Additionally, the record reflects that Waldrep and TCU did not treat the financial aid Waldrep received as "pay" or "income." . . .

The evidence further reflects that Waldrep and TCU intended that Waldrep participate at TCU as a *student*, not as an *employee*. . . .

Although the record in this case contains facts from which the jury could have found that Waldrep and TCU were parties to a contract of hire there is also probative evidence to the contrary. Viewing the evidence in the light most favorable to the jury's verdict, we hold that the record before us reflects more than a mere scintilla of evidence that Waldrep was not in the service of TCU under a contract of hire.

Right to Direct the Means or Details of Waldrep's Work

If, however, we assume the jury found that a contract existed between Waldrep and TCU, we must determine Whether there is some evidence concerning TCU's right to direct the means or details of Waldrep's "work." The definition of "employee" submitted to the jury correctly states the recognized test to determine whether an employer-employee relationship exists: the *right* of the employer to direct or control the means or details of the employee's work. . . .

The record reflects that TCU *exercised* direction and control over all of the athletes in its football program, including non-scholarship players, while they were participating in the *football program*. . . . The evidence is clear that TCU did not have the right to direct or control all of Waldrep's activities during his tenure at the school. . . .

The fact that the athletic department at TCU established practice and meeting times to be observed by those playing football does not establish that TCU had the *right* to direct and control all aspects of the players' activities while enrolled in the university. . . .

Conclusion

In conclusion, we note that we are aware college athletics has changed dramatically over the years since Waldrep's injury. Our decision today is based on facts and circumstances as they existed almost twenty six years ago. We express no opinion as to whether our decision would be the same in an analogous situation arising today; therefore, our opinion should not be read too broadly. Having disposed of all of the issues before us, we affirm the district court's judgment.

QUESTIONS AND DISCUSSION

1. In *King v. Edmonton Trappers Baseball Club*, 19 F 3d 27 (9th Cir. 1994), it was held that Florida's workers' compensation statute specifically excluded professional athletes from coverage.

2. However, in *Albrecht v. Industrial Comm.*, 648 N.E.2d 923 (Ill. Ct. App. 1995), under Illinois law, a professional football player whose career was ended by a back injury was able to successfully argue for the wage-loss differential between his former occupation and his current employment in the travel business.

3. As in *Albrecht, Tampa Bay Area NFL Football, Inc. v. Jarvis*, 668 So. 2d 217 (Fla. Ct. App. 1996), under Florida law, was also able to increase the player's benefits. In *Albrecht*, it was by way of a wage-loss differential; in *Jarvis*, the team was allowed to credit post-injury salary payments against only those Workers' compensation benefits that accrued during the term of his employment contract.

4. However, unlike *Jarvis*, the Louisiana Supreme Court in *Green v. New Orleans Saints*, 781 So. 2d 1199 (La. 2000), held that the team was entitled to a dollar-for-dollar offset for the total amount of worker's compensation payments.

5. For Workers' compensation coverage to apply to professional athletes, the first determination is whether the injured person is an employee. If he is not an employee, he is not covered. An injured horse jockey was employed and paid by the job as an independent contractor; he did not come under the control of the owner or trainer and therefore, was not an employee. *Munday v. Churchill Downs, Inc.*, 600 S.W.2d 487 (Ky. Ct. App. 1980).

6. For Workers' compensation coverage in some states, the injury must have resulted from an accident. The injury in *Palmer v. Kansas City Chiefs Football Club*, 621 S.W.2d 350 (Mo. Ct. App. 1981), occurred while an offensive guard was blocking. This was not an accident under the relevant statute, which defines it as trauma from unexpected or unforeseen events in the usual course of employee's occupation. The deliberate collision between human beings during a professional football game was not an accident; and the injury, in the usual course of his occupation, was not caused by an unexpected event.

7. *Waldrep v. Texas Employers Ins. Assn.*, 21 S.W.2d 692 (Tex. Ct. App. 2000), disallowed coverage on the basis that an injured scholarship athlete was not an employee at the time of the incident. *Quinones v. P. C. Richard & Son*, 707 A.2d 1372 (N.J. Super. Ct. 1998), on the other hand, dealt with a purely recreational arm wrestling match between claimant and his supervisor during working hours. However, coverage was also denied in *Quinones*.

7

CRIMINAL LIABILITY

The question of criminal liability for injuries that occur in sports is both interesting and subtle. The types of injury inflicted in a contact sport such as, football or hockey would most certainly be punishable criminally if not done on the playing field. But, of course, usually injury in these sports do not trigger criminal liability. Some degree of violence is inherent in sports. This is especially true in contact sports such as football, hockey, wrestling, and boxing. By definition, there is some degree of violent contact that is unavoidable in any contact sport. But there appears to be a quantum of unnecessary violence in today's professional sports, which has also spilled over to amateur sports. It is this unnecessary violence that might be controlled and punished through criminal penalties.

Violence in Sports appears to be on the rise, whether it is disgruntled parents or battling basketball players. Professional contracts, collective bargaining agreements, and amateur athletic association rules attempt to deter unnecessary violence. Also on the rise is **Spectator Violence**. As an indicia of the times, because of the popularity of ice hockey in Canada and the necessity of keeping in check its inherent violence, the **Canadian Approach** is a model in which Canadian prosecutors have more frequently used criminal laws against athletes who exhibit unnecessary violent contact.

A. VIOLENCE IN SPORTS

It appears that violence—or better yet, unnecessary violence—is increasing in sports. Although arguably this might appeal to some element within the fan base, it is not generally viewed by the leagues as a positive attribute of sportsmanship. The leagues try to decrease unnecessary violence through disciplinary rules. The standard player's contract and the collective bargaining agreement establish rules and procedures that penalize and control violent behavior that is not an inherent aspect of the sport.

Civil actions are another way to deter violence. These tort cases usually involve principles of negligence, vicarious liability, or assault and battery. On the whole, these civil actions have not been effective as a mechanism to decrease unnecessary violence in professional sports.

Violence can also be deterred by punishing the offenders criminally. The key question is whether the facts require the imposition of criminal sanctions or, more broadly, whether the particular penal laws are intended to be applied to conduct in sporting events. After that, one must determine if the elements of that particular crime (for example, battery), were present at the time of the incident. Sometimes the accused will claim a defense, usually, that the injured person consented to the injury by their voluntary participation. They may also counter with self-defense if the conduct was provoked.

Criminal actions are scarce in that the harm and violence is confined to the participants who know and assume the game's inherent risks, and the innocent public (unless you're an unlucky spectator) is not subjected to that risk of physical harm. Violent conduct usually is criminally actionable only if it falls outside the rules of that particular sport.

1. Assault and Battery

Assault and battery is the criminal offense that is most usually applicable when sports violence flairs. Battery is the unlawful application of force to the body of another person that results in injury. The question of unlawfulness is key to whether battery is relevant in the sports arena. Most penal codes have excepted sports violence by treating it as lawful. What might be unlawful on a city street might be perfectly lawful on a football field.

The elements of battery are a guilty state of mind, an act, a physical touching of the victim, and causation. The state of mind for battery does not require actual intent. Criminal negligence or a conscious disregard for known and serious risks is sufficient. Both of these states of mind allow for aggravated battery and can be punished as a felony when a deadly weapon is used or the causing of the serious injuries are a part of the criminal act. Potential deadly weapons abound in sports: for example, hockey sticks, baseball bats, bowling balls, javelins, arrows, (even) tennis rackets.

Assault was found in *State v. Floyd* as a result of a brawl in a YMCA basketball game.

STATE V. FLOYD

466 N.W.2d 919 (Iowa Ct. App. 1990)

Defendant was found guilty of two counts of assault without intent to inflict serious injury but causing bodily injury, a serious misdemeanor. . . . [On] August 15, 1988[,] [d]efendant had been participating in a four-on-four [YMCA] basketball game. . . . [T]he game was rough, though not . . . dirty . . . tempers were . . . hot. . . . Play was very physical, and the fouls were hard; there was considerable "hacking" and . . . shoving. . . . Each team was aggressive and sought to intimidate its opponent with deed and word.

. . . [P]assions were aroused when a member of defendant's team struck . . . a member of the opposing team, in the face. . . . Brown was ejected from the game but remained in the gymnasium. . . . The game score remained fairly even until the second half of play, when defendant's team pulled ahead by eight to ten points.

With three to five minutes left to play . . . defendant's cousin . . . was . . . fouled . . . in an attempt to steal the ball. The foul was a "reach-in" type that caught [him] . . . either in the face or on the arm. The referee stopped play to report Rogers' foul to the scorer.

With play still stopped . . . [they] exchanged words. [One of the victims allegedly] used a racial slur in response. [The cousin] . . . shoved [him], and the referee called a technical foul. . . . [He] . . . stepped back and raised his unclenched hands, [the cousin] hit [him] in the face with a fist, knocking [him] to the floor. Michael Kenealy, [his] teammate, had attempted to intervene, but failed and pushed [the cousin] away. . . . Two or three members of defendant's team then attacked Kenealy, hitting him from behind in the head and ribs. . . .

As these incidents unfolded . . . defendant left his team's bench area after play had been stopped and punches had been thrown. Defendant then assaulted [John] McHale and Gregg Barrier on the sidelines and Duane Barrier on the basketball court.

McHale, who was simply standing on the sidelines when disturbances began to occur on the court, suffered the worst from blows by defendant. Defendant hit McHale and knocked him to the floor. McHale suffered a concussion, severe hemorrhaging, and loss of brain tissue. He spent the next two days in intensive care. He has permanently lost the sense of smell, has some amnesia, and is at risk of epileptic seizures.

Leaving McHale unconscious on the floor and bleeding profusely, defendant attacked Gregg Barrier and Duane Barrier. Like McHale, Gregg Barrier was on the sidelines, but was returning from a water fountain. Gregg Barrier was able to cover up against defendant's punches to the back of his head and shoulders, and defendant did not seriously injure him.

Duane Barrier had been in the game when play had been halted. As Duane Barrier watched the incidents on the court, defendant approached and punched him in the side of the head. When Duane Barrier turned to see what had hit him, defendant hit him squarely on the nose. Duane Barrier suffered a severely deviated septum and required reconstructive surgery. . . .

The disturbance lasted a few minutes and even spread to the YMCA staff offices, where members of defendant's team beat . . . [the initial victim] as he attempted to call an ambulance for McHale.

The State filed two charges of willful injury . . . against defendant. He was convicted by a jury on two counts of the lesser included offense of assault causing bodily injury. . . . The trial court sentenced defendant to serve the maximum sentence of one year, for each conviction, and to serve these terms consecutively. . . . Defendant appeals, arguing he falls within the assault exception for voluntary participants in sporting events. . . . He further appeals, arguing that the trial court abused its discretion in sentencing him to consecutive maximum terms.

This is a case of first impression in this State, and one of a handful of reported criminal prosecutions for sports-related violence in North America. In *People v. Freer*, 381 N.Y.S.2d 976, 977-79 (Dist. Ct. 1976), an amateur football player was convicted of third degree assault. After a tackle and pileup, the defendant got up on one knee and punched the supine complainant in the eye.

We do not attempt an empirical definition of when persons are "voluntary participants in a sport." It is unnecessary for us to engage in such an exercise in this case. We have no doubt that defendant and his victims had been participants. Given that play had officially ceased, that an altercation had broken out, and that defendant and some of his victims had been on the sidelines and not engaged in play activities, it is clear that defendant and his victims were not, at that time, "voluntary participants in a sport." There simply is no nexus between defendant's acts and playing the game of basketball.

As discussed in Note, *Sports Violence as Criminal Assault: Development of the Doctrine by Canadian Courts*, 1986 Duke L.J. 1030, the Canadian courts have generally recognized that incidents that occur after cessation of play . . . are not part of the game. *Id.* at 1048-50 (citing *Re Duchesneau*, [1979] 7 C.R.3d 70, 83 (Que. Youth Trib.1978)). The Canadian courts have also recognized that such a bright-line rule, which is attractive because of its ease of application, cannot be blindly used without some evaluation of the circumstances. *Id.* (citing *Regina v. Leyte*, 13 C.C.C.2d 458, 459 (Ont. Prov. Ct. 1973)).

We reject defendant's suggestion that he is protected from prosecution for acts committed by him while he is on a playing surface until the final buzzer, gun, whistle, goal, or out. In carving out this exception, the legislature clearly contemplated a person who commits acts during the course of play, and the exception seeks to protect those whose acts otherwise subject to prosecution are committed in furtherance of the object of the sport. In addition, we recognize that there are difficult questions of to how much violence a "voluntary participant" consents, but because of our ruling, we need not address this issue.

We further reject defendant's contentions that our construction of the exception to the assault statute will either ruin competitive sporting or flood the courts with these cases. On the contrary, our decision does not mandate that all, or for that matter any, cases like this be prosecuted, and it certainly does not attempt to place in jeopardy all who commit acts otherwise subject to prosecution when play is supposed to have ceased. We are confident that in closer cases the inquiry necessarily will shift, and the reasonable foreseeability of the incident and the so-called "consent" defense will separate the cases with merit from those without. . . .

While there may be a continuum, or sliding scale, grounded in the circumstances under which voluntary participants engage in sport (e.g., professional or amateur) which governs the type of incidents in which an individual volunteers (i.e., consents) to participate, it seems clear that such distinctions have no application here because of the stoppage of play. . . .

We noted above our belief that an average reasonable basketball player is unprotected and unprepared for fist fights, and we think this is particularly so under the circumstances described above. The legislature obviously did not intend to protect a basketball player who, regardless of his status as "participant," launches random attacks from the sidelines on other players. At least for the game of basketball, such acts "create an unreasonable risk of serious injury or breach of peace." The facts — the permanent injuries sustained by two of defendant's victims — and the manner in which these injuries were inflicted support our assessment. . . .

We conclude that the sentencing court may have considered improper factors and, therefore, committed an abuse of discretion. . . . We must, therefore, set aside the sentence and remand for resentencing. . . .

Affirmed and remanded.

As in *Floyd*, the court in *State v. Shelley*, discussed possible criminal charges that could stem from a recreational basketball game. In both cases, the damage was inflicted by way of an intentional striking. Although consent can be a defense to an assault, it is unavailable if the conduct in question was not a reasonably foreseeable hazard.

State v. Shelley

929 P.2d 489 (Wash. Ct. App. 1997)

Grosse, Judge.

During a rough basketball game, Jason Shelley struck another player and broke his jaw in three places. He was convicted of assault in the second degree after the State successfully argued to the jury that Shelley intentionally punched the other player. On appeal, Shelley claims that he was entitled to argue that the victim consented to the possibility of injury when he decided to play pickup basketball. While we agree that consent may be a defense to assault in athletic competitions, Shelley has failed to establish a factual basis for that defense. Further, while we hold that the consent defense is not limited to conduct within the rules of the games, rather it is to the conduct and harm that are the reasonably foreseeable hazards of joint participation in an athletic contest, we conclude that Shelley's conduct was not a reasonably foreseeable hazard.

On March 31, 1993, Jason Shelley and Mario Gonzalez played "pickup" basketball on opposing teams at the University of Washington Intramural Activities Building (the IMA). Pickup games are not refereed by an official; rather, the players take responsibility for calling their own fouls. During the course of three games, Gonzalez fouled Shelley several times. Gonzalez had a reputation for playing overly aggressive defense at the IMA. Toward the end of the evening, after trying to hit the ball away from Shelley, he scratched Shelley's face, and drew blood. After getting scratched, Shelley briefly left the game and then returned.

Shelley and Gonzalez have differing versions of what occurred after Shelley returned to the game. According to Gonzalez, while he was waiting for play in the game to return to Gonzalez's side of the court, Shelley suddenly hit him. Gonzalez did not see Shelley punch him. According to Shelley's version of events, when Shelley rejoined the game, he was running down the court and he saw Gonzalez make "a move towards me as if he was maybe going to prevent me from getting the ball." The move was with his hand up "across my vision." Angry, he "just reacted" and swung. He said he hit him because he was afraid of being hurt, like the previous scratch. He testified that Gonzalez continually beat him up during the game by fouling him hard.

A week after the incident, a school police detective interviewed Shelley and prepared a statement for Shelley to sign based on the interview. Shelley reported to the police that Gonzalez had been "continually slapping and scratching him" during the game. Shelley "had been getting mad" at Gonzalez and the scratch on Shelley's face was the "final straw." As the two were running down the court side by side, "I swung my right hand around and hit him with my fist on the right side of his face." Shelley asserted that he also told the detective that Gonzalez waved a hand at him just before throwing the punch and that he told the detective that he was afraid of being injured.

Gonzalez required emergency surgery to repair his jaw. Broken in three places, it was wired shut for six weeks. His treating physician believed that a "significant" blow caused the damage. . . .

First, we hold that consent is a defense to an assault occurring during an athletic contest. This is consistent with the law of assault as it has developed in Washington. A person is guilty of second degree assault if he or she "[i]ntentionally assaults another and thereby recklessly inflicts substantial bodily harm." One common law definition of assault recognized in Washington is "'an unlawful touching with criminal intent.'" At the common law, a touching is unlawful when the person touched did not give consent to it, and was either harmful or offensive. . . .

If consent cannot be a defense to assault, then most athletic contests would need to be banned because many involve "invasions of one's physical integrity." Because society has chosen to foster sports competitions, players necessarily must be able to consent to physical contact and other players must be able to rely on that consent when playing the game. This is the view adopted by the drafters of the Model Penal Code. . . .

The more difficult question is the proper standard by which to judge whether a person consented to the particular conduct at issue.

The State argues that "when the conduct in question is not within the rules of a given sport, a victim cannot be deemed to have consented to this act." The trial court apparently agreed with this approach. Although we recognize that there is authority supporting this approach, we reject a reliance on the rules of the games as too limiting. . . .

The State argues the law does not allow "the victim to 'consent' to a broken jaw simply by participating in an unrefereed, informal basketball game." This argument presupposes that the harm suffered dictates whether the defense is available or not. This is not the correct inquiry.

The correct inquiry is whether the conduct of defendant constituted foreseeable behavior in the play of the game. Additionally, the injury must have occurred as a by-product of the game itself. In construing a similar statutory defense, the Iowa court required a "nexus between defendant's acts and playing the game of basketball." In *State v. Floyd,* a fight broke out during a basketball game and the defendant, who was on the sidelines, punched and severely injured several opposing team members. Because neither defendant nor his victims were voluntarily participating in the game, the defense did not apply because the statute "contemplated a person who commits acts during the course of play, and the exception seeks to protect those whose acts otherwise subject to prosecution are committed in furtherance of the object of the sport." As the court noted in *Floyd*, there is a "continuum, or sliding scale, grounded in the circumstances under which voluntary participants engage in sport . . . which governs the type of incidents in which an individual volunteers (*i.e.*, consents) to participate [.]" . . .

As a corollary to the consent defense, the State may argue that the defendant's conduct exceeded behavior foreseeable in the game. Although in "all sports players consent to many risks, hazards and blows," there is "a limit to the magnitude and dangerousness of a blow to which another is deemed to consent." This limit, like the foreseeability of the risks, is determined by presenting evidence to the jury about the nature of the game, the participants' expectations, the location where the game has been played, as well as the rules of the game.

Here, taking Shelley's version of the events as true, the magnitude and dangerousness of Shelley's actions were beyond the limit. There is no question that Shelley lashed out at Gonzalez with sufficient force to land a substantial blow to the jaw, and there is no question but that Shelley intended to hit Gonzalez. There is nothing in the game of basketball, or even rugby or hockey, that would permit consent as a defense to such conduct. Shelley admitted to an assault and was not precluded from arguing that the assault justified self-defense; but justification and consent are not the same inquiry.

Related to his consent argument, Shelley claims that the assault statute is vague when applied to sports altercations because it fails to provide either adequate notice of proscribed conduct, or standards to prevent arbitrary enforcement as to athletes who believe they can be rough because they are accustomed to unprosecuted rough play. . . . Shelley cannot claim the statute is facially vague; he may only argue that it is vague as applied to him.

Our holding that a defendant is entitled to argue that another player may legally consent to conduct that causes or threatens bodily harm if the conduct and the harm are reasonably foreseeable hazards of joint participation in a lawful, athletic contest or competitive sport cures any problem with vagueness. With this defense, an ordinary person should understand that intentionally punching a person in an athletic competition may result in criminal prosecution. . . .

We affirm. . . .

2. Inherently Violent Sports

In the inherently violent sports, the question is in what type of violent conduct can one use consent as a defense. Consent can be used as a defense to criminal charges that arise from injury if it is a reasonably foreseeable hazard of that sport and not a result of intentional conduct that is not reasonably related to that particular sport. But, an athlete cannot consent to intentional or reckless acts that are not reasonably related to the conduct of that particular sport.

Consent is effective as a defense to conduct that does not threaten or cause serious injury or to reasonably foreseeable conduct that results in reasonably foreseeable harm. It is difficult to distinguish between reasonably foreseeable conduct and injurious nonforeseeable harmful conduct. As a result, athletes are discouraged from seeking criminal charges against fellow participants. There are just no neat and predictable lines as to when a particular act will go beyond the established boundaries of the rules of the game and thus be eligible for criminal intervention.

QUESTIONS AND DISCUSSION

1. In *State v. Floyd*, the court based its decision at least in part on the fact that play had been stopped. Is that a realistic distinction? The players were still on the court and the game was not over yet.

2. *State v. Shelley* allowed the use of the consent defense in athletic injuries, but did not allow it under their particular facts since Shelley's conduct in punching a basketball player was not a reasonably foreseeable hazard of a basketball game.

3. Actions such as *State v. Floyd* and *State v. Shelley* are the exception rather than the rule. *See generally*, Carlsen & Walker, *The Sports Court: A Private System to Deter Violence in Professional Sports*, 55 S. Cal. L. Rev. 399 (1982); Hanson & Dennis, *Revisiting Excessive Violence in the Professional Sports Arena: Changes in the Past Twenty Years?* 25 Ind. L. Rev. 147 (1991); Karon, *Winning Isn't Everything, It's the Only Thing; Violence in Professional Sports: The Need for Federal Regulation and Criminal Sanctions*, 25 Ind. L. Rev. 147 (1991); Yasser, *In the Heat of Competition: Tort Liability of One Participant to Another; Why Can't Participants Be Required to be Reasonable?* 5 Seton Hall J. Sport L. 253 (1995); Cohen, Comment, *The Relationship Between Criminal Liability and Sports: A Jurisprudential Investigation*, 7 U. Miami Ent. & Sports L. Rev. 311 (1990); Mayes, Comment, *Tonya Harding's Case: Contractual Due Process, the Amateur Athlete, and the American Ideal of Fair Play*, 3 UCLA Ent. L. Rev. 109 (1995).

4. Probably the most famous incident in professional sports violence occurred during a National Basketball Association game in 1977 when Kermit Washington of the L.A. Lakers punched Rudy Tomjanovich of the Houston Rockets; Rudy was acting as a peace maker when Kermit saw a red jersey coming at him and landed with a right that caused a concussion, broken nose, broken jaw, skull fractures, facial lacerations, loss of blood, and leakage of brain cavity spinal fluid. Tomjanovich won a substantial jury award (nearly $3 million) in a suit for civil damages against the Lakers, as Washington's employer. His theory was that the Lakers were vicariously liable for his actions since they knew about and even encouraged his dangerous tendencies and reputation as evidenced by a front page *Sports Illustrated* cover that proclaimed him as one of the league's enforcers. Although not pursued, one can make good cases against Kermit Washington individually for both criminal charges and civil damages. Do you think these cases would have been successful?

B. SPECTATOR VIOLENCE

Spectator violence, both on and off the field, is not a new occurrence with events in baseball, basketball, hockey, football, and soccer. It is a world-wide phenomenon that appears to be mostly fueled by alcohol.

1. 'Hooliganism'

'Hooliganism' at European and Mexico's soccer matches is the most serious example of spectator violence. The majority of these incidents involve international fans. Often, sanctions against spectator violence include joint ventures by many countries. One example is the *European Convention on Spectator Violence and Misbehavior at Sports Events and in Particular Football Matches.*[1]

The English courts have taken a very uncompromising attitude towards 'hooliganism.' For example, Section 5 of the Public Disorder Act of 1936 has been widely used in the U.K. to combat soccer violence. This law allows for the provision that the mere presence of football (soccer) 'hooligans' might constitute an offense. Furthermore, England has enacted both the Sport Events (control of alcohol, etc.) Act of 1985 ('Sports Events Act') and the Public Order Act of 1986 (esp. §§30-37) that could both be used to exclude known 'hooligans' from attending matches and to arrest anyone for alcohol possession or consumption either en route via public conveyance or at the event.[2]

In the United States, rabid, inebriated baseball fans come closest to soccer hooligans. A professional baseball game between the Chicago Cubs and the Los Angeles Dodgers produced a fracas that involved about 25 players and fans.

WALTER CHAMPION,
THE GREAT DODGERS-WRIGLEY FIELD MELEE:
A BAR EXAM QUESTION IN THE MAKING?

2 Tex. Rev. Sports & Enter. L. 43 (2001)

I. Wrigley Field Erupts

In a world where the intrepid citizen-voyeur places a premium on living vicariously, whether it be through chat rooms or eavesdropping on *Survivor* episodes or even by dummying down to watch professional wrestling, it was a refreshing relief one hot and muggy Chicago afternoon when the great "Wrigley Field Melee" ensued right before our cable-enlarged corneas. This was the worst case scenario of what could happen when you toss into the pot a mix of variously incendiary ingredients including hostile fans, the humidity, and a paranoid and exposed outpost of bullpen soldiers. The brew had been stewing for quite awhile, and it was only right that it would boil over at

---

[1] *Reprinted in* 24 Intl. L. Mat. 1566-1572 (1985).
[2] *See generally* Bertini, Comment, '*A Survey of Domestic and International Sanctions Against Spectator Violence at Sports Events,*' 11 Hous. J. Intl. L. 415 (1989).

Wrigley Field, where the fans come not so much to cheer their heroes as to smite their enemies.

This cause celebre erupted on May 16, 2000 at Wrigley Field in Chicago during the bottom of the ninth inning of a game between the Chicago Cubs and the Los Angeles Dodgers, in which the Dodgers won 6 to 5 over the Cubs.

> . . . A fan seated behind the *uncovered* [author's emphasis**] visitors' bull-pen at Wrigley Field allegedly *struck* [**] back-up catcher Chad Kreuter and *took his cap* [**]. Kreuter *went into the stands* [**] and *his teammates and coaches followed* [**], *triggering fights* [**] that delayed play for nine minutes. Three fans were arrested and *charged with disorderly conduct* [**].[7]

Another result of the melee was that "[o]ne fan, Ronald Camacho of Chicago has filed a lawsuit *against both teams* [**] and several players, Kreuter among them, claiming Kreuter *choked* [**] him while other Dodgers *pummeled* [**] him. . . .

The Baseball Barons reacted quickly and aggressively and assessed "the largest mass suspension and harshest penalties stemming from one altercation in baseball history. Twenty Dodgers including three coaches and a non-roster bullpen catcher were suspended for a total of 89 games and fined $77,000.00. . . ." In their appeal the Dodgers and the union presented "Kreuter as a *victim* [**] and the others as *peacekeepers*, [**] who followed Kreuter into the stands to protect him and restore order. Videotapes, still photographs, and court records pertaining to some of the fans' *criminal backgrounds* [**] will make up the crux of that argument." However, on appeal, twelve Dodgers had their suspensions overturned. . . .

III. A Professor's Response

To begin with, as soon as Camacho entered the bullpen area, he was guilty of trespass to land. He who intentionally enters upon the land in possession of another is a trespasser and liable for the tort of trespass, unless the entry was privileged, which it certainly was not here.

Camacho then apparently struck Kreuter, yanked Kreuter's hat from his head, took possession of the hat and then absconded with it to the more friendly confines of the grandstand. Battery is the intentional, unauthorized harmful or offensive contact of another. It was a battery when Camacho struck Kreuter, even though the contact may not have been harmful, it was certainly offensive. Even if Camacho did not per se strike Kreuter before he yanked the hat, the mere taking of the hat would be sufficient to establish battery. The hat was so intimately associated with Kreuter's person, that it in effect became an extension of his person; therefore, an offensive contact with the hat would be sufficient to establish a battery. . . .

By removing the hat from Kreuter's head and then absconding with it, Camacho was guilty of the tort of conversion. . . . By taking the hat and leaving with it, Camacho interfered with Kreuter's chattel; this counts as a

---

[7] The icon [**], is used to emphasize those facts which the author deems to be legally significant . . .

conversion since the interference was substantial enough to warrant a forced sale to Camacho.

So, some fan jumps over the guardrail, trespasses on the hallowed bullpen, assaults you, takes *your* cap, and then retreats. What can you do? There is a limited privilege to re-take the chattel. . . . Camacho certainly did not resist; he fled. Arguably, under the doctrine of Recovery of Property, Kreuter and his allies had the right to re-take the hat, but the effort to recover the chattel must be prompt and continuous. Any undue lapse of time once the pursuit was commenced will mean that the owner is no longer privileged to fight himself back into possession, but must resort to the law. Kreuter and his mates charged into the stands immediately after the initial insult. Therefore, he was privileged, in essence, to fight his way back into possession of the hat. However, choking Camacho to re-obtain the hat was excessive, and thus he lost his limited privilege to re-take possession. Since there was no privilege, Kreuter's attack on Camacho was a simple assault and battery.

There are other privileges or defenses that the Dodgers could argue, most notably, self-defense and defense of others; but they are weak, since Camacho retreated and was no longer a continued physical threat to Kreuter. Obviously, chasing him en masse, pummeling, and choking was excessive and would effectively eliminate any privilege that might have been available.

Other than assault and battery against Kreuter and his teammates, Camacho's best alternative is to claim that his injuries occurred because of the Dodgers' negligent supervision of their players and the Cubs' negligent and inadequate security against participants charging the grandstands and attacking fans. Negligence though is usually based on foreseeability or a relationship between the various parties. Another problem that Camacho has is (probably) a lack of damages.

The owner or operator of the stadium also has a duty to the spectator. The key is the status of the injured party; here, Camacho was a business invitee. . . .

QUESTIONS AND DISCUSSION

1. The impetus of England's war on football hooliganism resulted from the Heysel disaster on May 29, 1985, where 38 people were killed in a soccer riot at Heysel Stadium in Brussels, Belgium. Liverpool fans crushed a fence that separated Italian fans; the wall collapsed, which caused a mass exit trampling hundreds of fans: 31 Italians, 4 Belgians, 2 Frenchmen and 1 Brit died; 437 people were injured. The legal reaction was swift; was it too lenient or too harsh? Can you think of any other approaches? *See* Gammon, *Day of Horror and Shame*, Sports Illustrated June 10, 1985, at 20-35; *English Soccer Clubs Are Banned from European Play Indefinitely*, N.Y. Times June 3, 1985, at 1C. *See generally* Salter, *The Judges Against The Football Fan: A Sporting Contest*, 36 N. Ir. Legal Q. 351 (1985); Bertini, Comment, *A Survey of Domestic and International Sanctions Against Spectator Violence at Sports Events*, 11 Hous. J. Intl. L. 415 (1989); Wallace, Comment, *The Men in Black and Blue: A Comment on Violence Against Sports Officials and State Legislative Reaction*, 6 Seton Hall J. Sport L. 341 (1996).

2. "The Wrigley Field Melee" article explains the types of legal problems that can develop from the interaction between fan and athlete. The violence could have created a myriad of both civil complaints and criminal charges. Which ones are they? Much was said in the Dodgers' defense that fan perpetrators had criminal backgrounds. Should these "elements" like the British "football hooligans" be banned from attendance? What constitutional concerns may arise if the United States banned "bleacher bums"?

3. Should the U.S. Congress react as swiftly and powerfully to the Wrigley Field debacle as the European international community reacted to Heysel? Other than the carnage, is there an essential difference? In the long run, is education a better approach than criminal sanctions?

4. Alcohol appears to be a catalyst in both events. Should it be universally banned at all sporting events? Should liquor company sponsorship of the players, teams, leagues, games, and tournaments be disallowed?

5. In Wrigley Field, should the Chicago district attorney vigorously prosecute the perpetrator, Ronald Camacho, who absconded with Kreuter's cap? What crimes would you allege? Should "special" criminal sanctions be established for spectator violence at sporting events? Should these sanctions be enhanced if the violators have consumed alcohol?

C. THE CANADIAN APPROACH

The courts in the United States have been reluctant to differentiate between the physical contact that is a part of a violent sport and the physical contact that is deemed to be criminal in nature. In Canada, because of ice hockey, the prosecutors have more often used the criminal laws against hockey players who have initiated violent contact toward hockey players on the opposing team. The major sticking point is the status of the consent defense. In the Canadian debate, three issues have evolved as regards consent: consent that is implied by participation, consent that is implied by specific acts, and a public policy limitation on ones' ability to consent.

An English case, *Regina v. Bradshaw*, like the Canadian cases is hesitant to find a sporting participant guilty of a criminal charge. In *Regina*, the deceased was struck by another soccer player who jumped in the air and struck the deceased with his knee in the stomach. The deceased died the next day as a result of ruptured intestines.

REGINA V. BRADSHAW

14 Cox Crim. Cas. 83 (1878)

William Bradshaw was indicted for the manslaughter of Herbert Dockerty at Ashby-de-la-Zouch, on the 28th day of February.

. . . [T]he injury which caused his death . . . [was] a football match . . . between the football clubs of Ashby-de-la-Zouche and Coalville, in which the deceased was a player on the Ashby side, and the prisoner was . . . on the Coalville side. The game was played according to . . . "Association Rules." After the game had proceeded about a quarter of an hour, the deceased was "dribbling" the ball along the side of the ground in the direction of the Coalville goal, when he was met by the prisoner, who was running towards him to get the ball from him or prevent its further progress; both players were running at considerable speed; on approaching each other, the deceased kicked the ball beyond the prisoner, and the prisoner, by way of "charging" the deceased, jumped in the air and struck him with his knee in the stomach. The two met, not directly but at an angle, and both fell. The prisoners got up unhurt, but the deceased rose with difficulty and was led from the ground. He died the next day, after considerable suffering, the cause of death . . . [was] a rupture of the intestines.

Witnesses . . . differed as to some particulars, those most unfavorable to the prisoner alleging that the ball had been kicked by the deceased and had passed the prisoner before he charged; that the prisoner had therefore no right to charge at the time he did, that the charge was contrary to the rules and practice of the game and made in an unfair manner, with the knees protruding; while those who were more favorable . . . stated that the kick by the deceased and the charge by the prisoner were simultaneous, and that the prisoner had therefore, according to the rules and practice of the game, a right to make the charge, though these witnesses admitted that to charge by jumping with the knee protruding was unfair. One of the umpires of the game stated that in his opinion nothing unfair had been done . . .

BRAMWELL, L.J., . . . "The question for you to decide is whether the death of the deceased was caused by the unlawful act of the prisoner. There is no doubt that the prisoner's act caused the death and the question is whether that act was unlawful. No rules or practice of any game whatever can make that lawful which is unlawful by the law of the land; and the law of the land says you shall not do that which is likely to cause the death of another. For instance, no persons can by agreement go out to fight with deadly weapons, doing by agreement what the law says shall not be done, and thus shelter themselves from the consequences of their acts. Therefore, in one way you need not concern yourselves with the rules of football. But, on the other hand, if a man is playing according to the rules and practice of the game and not going beyond it, it may be reasonable to infer that he is not actuated by any malicious motive or intention, and that he is not acting in a manner which he knows will be likely to be productive of death or injury. But, independent of the rules, if the prisoner intended to cause serious hurt to the deceased, or if he knew that, in charging as he did, he might produce serious injury and was indifferent and reckless as to whether he would produce serious injury or not, then the act would be unlawful. In either case he would be guilty of a criminal act and you must find him guilty; if you are of a contrary opinion you will acquit him." His Lordship . . . stat[ed] that no doubt the game was, . . . a rough one; but he was unwilling to decry the manly sports of this country, all of which were no doubt attended with more or less danger.

Verdict, not guilty.

The Canadian cases of *Regina v. Maki* and *Regina v. Green* both emanated from the same incident that occurred during the playing of a National Hockey League exhibition game. The charge of assault causing bodily harm was dismissed. The accused were acquitted. Both players consented to the type of injuries that were inflicted.

REGINA V. MAKI

14 D.L.R.3d 164 (Ont. Prov. Ct. 1970)

CARTER Prov. J.:

1. Mr. Maki is charged under §231(2) of the Criminal Code; "Assault causing Bodily Harm." The case is basically a simple one factually but complicated to some extent in that the alleged assault occurred during the playing of a National Hockey League exhibition game, and that there has not been such a prosecution in the past. The game was between the St. Louis Blues and the Boston Bruins played at the Ottawa Civic Centre in the City of Ottawa on 21st September 1969.

2. I have considered the facts carefully and although, as would be expected in such a fast-moving situation, there are some inconsistencies in the evidence, the occurrence appears to have taken place in the following manner.

3. I might say in reviewing the facts I gave a great deal of weight to the evidence of the referee Mr. Bodenistel and, of course, to the evidence of Mr. Maki himself. I found both to be credible witnesses as in fact were all the witnesses in the case.

4. At about the 11-minute mark of the first period, St. Louis had shot the puck into the Boston zone and behind and to the left of the Boston net, Mr. Maki and Mr. Green followed the puck into the area and collided at this point. Mr. Green pushed or punched Mr. Maki in the face with his glove and it would appear caused some injury to his mouth. At this point the referee signalled a delayed penalty for an infraction by raising his arm and play continued. The two players it would appear broke apart at this juncture, with Mr. Maki skating to the area in front of the Boston net, and the puck was moved into the centre ice area. There is some evidence of spearing by Maki against Green but this fact is in some considerable doubt. There is evidence that Mr. Maki was somewhat dazed as a result of the incident behind the net. . . .

5. At this point the two players came together again at some point in front of the Boston net, sticks swinging, and as a result Mr. Green's unfortunate injury occurred at this time. There is no doubt that Mr. Green swung at Mr. Maki first and struck him on the neck or shoulders. Mr. Maki states that Mr. Green then made another move or motion towards him with his stick and that Mr. Green's stick was above his shoulders and held by both hands. Mr. Maki then swung at Mr. Green and his stick hit Mr. Green's stick and glanced from there to the side of Mr. Green's head, causing the injuries in question. It seems clear from the photographs filed that this was the case, and that if Mr. Green's stick had not been raised as it was the blow would probably have landed on Green's shoulder. Most witnesses testified that the blow struck by Mr. Maki was a chopping blow from about a vertical position and was not, as one witness testified, a baseball-type swing. . . .

6. I will deal first with the law upon which I have based my decision — that is, self defence, as put forward by defence counsel.

7. This whole affair took place in a matter of two to five seconds, in a game noted for its speed and bodily contact. We have evidence to indicate that Mr. Green is a very aggressive, hard-hitting player and Maki, of course, is fully aware of this. . . .

9. The law in this regard . . . is that on a charge of this sort there must be an acquittal if the court is left in any doubt as to whether the accused was acting in self defence, that is, where self defence is raised as a defence. The court must also consider the reasonableness of the force used under the circumstances and the state of mind of the accused at the time in question. . . .

In cases where life and limb are exposed to no serious danger in the common course of things, I think that consent is a defence to a charge of assault, even when considerable force is used, as, for instance, in cases of wrestling, single-stick, sparring with gloves, football, and the like; but in all cases the question whether consent does or does not . . . take from the application of force to another its illegal character, is a question of degree depending upon circumstances.

14. Thus all players when they step onto a playing field or ice surface assume certain risks and hazards of the sport and in most cases the defence of consent as set out in s. 230 of the Criminal Code would be applicable. But as stated above, there is a question of degree involved and no athlete should be presumed to accept malicious, unprovoked or overly violent attack.

But a little reflection will establish that some limit must be placed on a player's immunity from liability. Each case must be decided on its own facts so it is difficult, if not impossible, to decide how the line is to be drawn in every circumstance. But injuries inflicted in circumstances which show a definite resolve to cause serious injury to another, even when there is provocation and in the heat of the game, should not fall within the scope of the implied consent.

15. The adoption of such principles in the future would, I feel certain, be a benefit to the players, of course, to the general public peace and in particular to young aspiring athletes who look to the professionals for guidance and example.

16. I would like at this point to thank counsel for the excellent manner in which the case was presented. Their arguments were extremely helpful to me and may form guide-lines in the future.

REGINA V. GREEN

16 D.L.R.3d 137 (Ont. Prov. Ct. 1970)

FITZPATRICK, Prov. Ct. J.: — Edward Joseph Green was charged that on or about September 21, 1969, at the City of Ottawa in the Regional Municipality of Ottawa-Carleton he unlawfully did assault one Wayne Maki. . . .

The incident out of which this charge arose occurred on the evening of September 21, 1969, when an exhibition game involving two National Hockey League teams, the Boston Bruins and the St. Louis Blues, was being played at the Ottawa Civic Centre. Mr. Green was a member of the Boston Bruins and had for some time played for that team and was a defenseman. Mr. Maki was at that time a member of the St. Louis Blues. . . .

I think it is necessary to say at this point that there is probably no more serious attack that can be made by one hockey player on another, in view of the hockey players themselves — and this is quite clear from the evidence — than the action of spearing . . . It is an extremely dangerous type of attack, directed as it very often is at the abdomen, which is relatively unprotected, and at the lower abdomen, and normally speaking it results in instant retribution, if the player who has been speared has not been hurt in the process and is unable to defend himself. . . .

There is not doubt that the players who enter the hockey arena consent to a great number of assaults on their person, because the game of hockey as it is played in the National Hockey League . . . could not possibly be played at the speed at which it is played and with the force and vigor with which it is played, and with the competition that enters into it, unless there were a great number of what would in normal circumstances be called assaults, but which are not heard of. No hockey player enters on to the ice of the National Hockey League without consenting to and without knowledge of the possibility that he is going to be hit in one of many ways once he is on that ice. . . .

. . . It is notable that the two most serious, grievous assaults that were committed that night — blows that caused most of the trouble, the blows that almost cost Mr. Green his life — were (a) the spearing of Mr. Green by Mr. Maki (which I have found to be a fact) and (b) the hitting of Mr. Green over the head by Mr. Maki.

. . . If that second blow had not been struck, if Mr. Maki had not struck Mr. Green, it is difficult for me to imagine that any charge would have been laid against Mr. Green. In other words, after the blow that was struck by Mr. Green on Mr. Maki . . . if nothing else had happened, it would appear to me the necessary penalties would have been called (as they were in the process of being called) and that incident might have merited a line or two in the sporting pages the next day, and perhaps a comment or two in the sports telecasts and the radio sports broadcasts that evening. But that would have been the end of it and no more would have happened.

. . . Mr. Green gave his evidence in what I considered to be a very forthright way. It was the evidence of a man who is very experienced in his sport, a man who undoubtedly plays boisterously, as he is paid to; he is well known and his reputation is well known, and other players respect that reputation, as they have to in the circumstances. He gave substantially the account I have given of the facts, with this addition, that he said this fracas originally started when Mr. Maki grabbed him by the back of the sweater. No other witness gave that evidence, but I must make this comment, that Mr. Green was in fact in the best position to know this, because this would have been done at very close quarters, and I have no doubt that it was in fact what did start the fracas. . . .

Mr. Green also said that when he had been speared, as he said, in the testicles by Mr. Maki, he then struck him a sort of half chop on the shoulder as a warning not to do it again, to desist, and this action happened almost simultaneously with or directly after the spearing by Mr. Maki. As I have previously said, this incident took place in a furious activity of a hockey game: it took place in a very few seconds; and I have no doubt from the evidence (which I have sifted and weighed) that the blow struck by Mr. Green was struck almost immediately after the blow—the much more serious blow in my opinion, the spearing—which had been struck at him by Mr. Maki. I do not think that Mr. Green was doing anything more in the circumstances than protecting himself. Mr. Maki himself said in his evidence that he did not remember spearing Mr. Green, but that if he had speared Mr. Green he would expect that Mr. Green would immediately retaliate.

We must remember that we are dealing with a hockey game. We are dealing with two competent hockey players at the peak of their form. We are not now dealing with the ordinary facts of life, the ordinary going and coming. We must remember that when we discuss the action of these men we are examining it within that forum and we are discussing it within the context in which the game is played, at high speed and obviously with people keenly on edge. In these circumstances I find as a fact that Mr. Green's action that night was instinctive and that all he was doing in effect was warning Mr. Maki not to do what he had done again. . . .

I want to make one thing quite clear. I am only deciding this particular case on this particular set of facts. It is quite probable that in other circumstances and given other sets of facts a charge of common assault might very well stand. However, I must make this comment, that given the permissiveness of the game and the risks that the players willingly undertake, I find it difficult to envision a circumstance where an offence of common assault as opposed to assault causing actual bodily harm could readily stand on facts produced from incidents occurring in the course of a hockey game played at that level. I am not talking about unprovoked savage attacks in which serious injury results. I am talking about these particular facts and these particular circumstances. . . .

Having examined all the evidence very carefully, and having examined in particular the series of events that happened on the boards that night behind the Boston net, even though the original blow, if you will, was a hitting of Mr. Maki in the face by Mr. Green with the glove—a common action which happens hundreds of times—in my opinion the real cause of this altercation was the spearing of Mr. Green by Mr. Maki; Mr. Green's action was instinctive, and I find it was more protective in his own interests than anything else of his own safety. Having regard to those circumstances, I find Mr. Green not guilty.

Accused acquitted.

QUESTIONS AND DISCUSSION

1. *Regina v. Bradshaw* fits well in the Canadian section since it can be viewed as a philosophic kin to the *Maki-Green* approaches to sports injuries. The *Bradshaw* type of legal analysis bore fruit many years later in North America. Lord Judge Bramwell, who opined that "he was unwilling to

decry the manly sports of this country," is precient as regards Justice Cardozo's 1929 maxim that the "timorous may stay at home."

> One who takes part in such a sport accepts the dangers that inhere in it so far as they are obvious and necessary, just as a fencer accepts the risk of a thrust by his antagonist or a spectator at a ballgame the chance of contact with the ball. The antics of the clown are not the poses of the cloistered cleric. The rough and boisterous joke, the horseplay of the crowd, evokes its own guffaws, but they are not the pleasures of tranquility. The plaintiff [injured when he was thrown from an amusement device called the "Flopper"] was not seeking a retreat for meditation. Visitors were tumbling about the belt to the merriment of onlookers when he made his choice to join them. He took the chances of a like fate, with whatever damage to his body might ensue from such a fall. The timorous may stay at home.

Murphy v. Steeplechase Amusement Co., Inc., 166 N.E. 173, 174-175 (N.Y. 1929). Posit the above with the Supreme Court of Oregon in 1962:

> The playing of football is a body-contact sport. The game demands that the players come into physical contact with each other constantly, frequently with great force. The linemen charge the opposing line vigorously, shoulder to shoulder. The tackler faces that risk of leaping at the swiftly moving legs of the ball-carrier and the latter must be prepared to strike the ground violently. Body contacts, bruises, and clashes are inherent in the game. There is no other way to play it. No prospective player need be told that a participant in the game of football may sustain injury. That fact is self evident. It draws to the game the manly: they accept its risks, blows, clashes and injuries without whimper.

Vendrell v. School Dist. No. 26C, Malheur County, 233 Or. 1, 15, 376 P.2d 406, 412-413 (Or. 1962). *Bradshaw* is criminal, but both *Murphy* and *Vendrell* were civil. Should their logic be applied to criminal prosecutions?

2. As regards the 'Canadian approach' per se, see Svoranos, Comment, *Fighting? It's All in a Day's Work on the Ice: Determining the Appropriate Standard of a Hockey Player's Liability to Another Player,* 7 Seton Hall J. Sport L. 487 (1997). The *Maki-Green* cases emanated from a highly publicized occurrence in a 1969 exhibition game in Ottawa between the Boston Bruins and the St. Louis Blues where Ted Green, star defenseman and "enforcer" for the Bruins, swung and hit Wayne Maki of the Blues on the head, Maki then turned and speared Green in the abdomen, who swung his stick at Maki's shoulder, who then ended the altercation by fracturing Green's skull. Ontario authorities were so upset that they filed against *both* players. Both players were acquitted in that there was at least reasonable doubt as to whether they had used more than proportionate force in self-defense. Should criminal prosecution be used as an "example" so as to deter future occurrences?

3. On the whole, criminal prosecutions of athletes have been rarely undertaken. Other than the 1969 Maki-Green altercation, Boston Bruin player Dave Forbes was prosecuted for attacking Minnesota player Henry Boucha in *State v. Forbes* (No. 63280 Minn. Dist. Ct., 4th Jud. Dist.,

judgment of mistrial entered August 12, 1975); the case ended with a hung jury; the prosecutor decided to not retry the case. Like *Maki* and *Green,* in *Regina v. Maloney*, 28 C.C.C.2d 323 (Ont. 1976), a Canadian jury acquitted Dan Maloney, a Detroit Red Wing, for an attack on Brian Glennie of the Toronto Maple Leafs. Why so few cases? Why so many acquittals?

CHAPTER 8

ATHLETIC ELIGIBILITY

The threshold question in sports participation, at least in amateur sports (and, if one thinks about it, professional sports also) is the question of eligibility: that is, is the athlete eligible to participate in that particular sport? In amateur sports (such as high school, collegiate, Olympic, and Little League), eligibility is defined as the decision by that particular sport's governing body as to whether a particular athlete or particular team is eligible to participate in a specific sport or specific event. The job of establishing eligibility under a particular rule or bylaw is the domain of the applicable governing association. The concern is usually whether a particular denial of eligibility is a violation of the athlete's constitutional or civil rights. The right of an athlete to participate in sports may be protected by the constitutional guarantees of due process and equal protection.

Amateur Sports are those sports in which the athletes do not operate under a direct pay for play scheme. **Scholarships** are ways for colleges and universities to attract athletes to their schools to play sports. By accepting the scholarships, the athlete enters into a relationship that typically requires that she maintain certain grade levels and perform as an athlete. **Eligibility** rules are those athletic association regulations that the athlete must follow to participate in that sport. In determining an athlete's eligibility, one must first ascertain if the association is a **State Actor.** The question is whether the association's actions are state action or fall under the color of state action. One method of restricting high school eligibility is based on state statutes commonly called **No Pass, No Play,** which link participation in extracurricular activities to achieving passing scores in the previous grading period.

Historically, eligibility to participate was hinged on paternalistic rules that limited participation based on the athlete's perceived disabilities. **The Challenged Athlete** now receives protection from the Americans with Disabilities Act, which requires reasonable accommodations for otherwise qualified disabled individuals.

A. AMATEUR SPORTS

As mentioned earlier, the distinction between amateur and professional sports is becoming more and more gray now that many college athletic programs are grooming grounds for professional sports.

Amateur sports divide into two basic forms: restricted and unrestricted competition. The former, which includes high school and collegiate competition, is restricted to essentially the same groups at different levels. The National Collegiate Athletic Association (NCCA) is one example. Competition is controlled and organized by athletic conferences, associations, or leagues. These organizations establish rules of competition within these groups; an important part of their duties is to promulgate, establish, and enforce the eligibility of the participants under their jurisdiction. Also, these organizations must determine if inappropriate conduct by players or teams violates the pertinent rules and regulations. If it does, the groups impose sanctions, if applicable, to either the individual athlete or to the particular school.

Unrestricted competition is open to all athletes. Olympic competition is one example. In the United States, Olympic competition is controlled by the United States Olympic Committee (USOC). Competition of this sort allows competition among all types of athletes and groups and does not restrict by age, college, or other criterion.

The status of the athlete — that is, whether the athlete is an amateur or a professional — is the determining factor in ascertaining whether the sport in question is an amateur sport. An amateur, by definition, cannot also be a professional. But again, the applicable categorizations are ambivalent, especially in the context of collegiate sports where a well-known amateur athlete can also be a quasi-professional since he is under scholarship and perhaps creating revenue in other ways. An athlete is deemed to be an amateur if it is so defined by the governing body of that particular sport and for that particular athlete. But the definition of an amateur athlete may change from one organization to another organization. An athlete might be an amateur under the USOCs rule, for example, but not an amateur under the NCAA rules.

Courts usually are reluctant to overrule an athletic organization's rules, regulations, and restrictions as regards its decision on eligibility, participation, and discipline of its members. As a general rule, courts do not interfere with the internal affairs of voluntary associations unless there is mistake, fraud, collusion, or arbitrariness. Absent the above, courts accept an athletic governing body's decisions and rules as conclusive. Voluntary associations may adopt reasonable bylaws, rules, and regulations that are valid and binding unless the rules violate law or public policy. Courts are not responsible for inquiring into the expediency, practicability, or wisdom of those rules and regulations. Courts do not substitute their interpretations of an organization's rules and regulations for those interpretations that are placed on these rules by the group itself so long as these interpretations are fair and reasonable.

In *Robinson v. Kansas State High School Activities Association, Inc.*, the court held that a state high school athletic association was a voluntary association and the fact that the state legislature allowed the athletic commission to make rules for interscholastic athletic competition did not constitute an unconstitutional delegation of legislative authority by default.

ROBINSON V. KANSAS STATE HIGH SCHOOL ACTIVITIES ASSOCIATION, INC.

917 P.2d 836 (Kan. 1996)

SIX, Justice:

This case addresses the rule-making authority of the Kansas State High School Activities Association, Inc. (KSHSAA). The district court after a bench trial enjoined enforcement of all KSHSAA rules, holding the rules are void ab initio because they are the product of an unconstitutional delegation of legislative power. According to the district court, the rules violate Article 2, § 1 of the Kansas Constitution. Additional issues concern whether: (1) the plaintiffs have standing to bring this action and (2) the unconstitutional delegation issue was properly before the district court for decision.

Two fathers, each with two minor sons who play basketball, sued KSHSAA, seeking relief from four rules concerning eligibility for high school and junior high school interscholastic basketball competition. The fathers sought a declaratory judgment, quo warranto, an order of mandamus, and a permanent injunction. The district court stayed the injunction, pending appeal. Our jurisdiction is under K.S.A. 60-2101(b) (a final judgment of the district court in which a Kansas statute was held to be unconstitutional).

We reverse and hold: (1) The fathers have standing; (2) the unconstitutional delegation issue is before us for review; and (3) KSHSAA's rules are not void and unenforceable as an unconstitutional delegation or sub-delegation of legislative power.

The fathers also alleged in district court that KSHSAA acted beyond its jurisdiction in adopting the questioned rules and that the rules were arbitrary and capricious. The merits of these theories were not addressed by the district court; thus, we do not reach them on appeal.

Facts

Brook Robinson is the father of Brook, Jr., a freshman at Wichita Southeast High School, and Brandon, now a 7th-grader. Both boys play basketball. Charles Gunter is the father of Chuck, a senior on the varsity basketball squad at Wichita Southeast, and Mario, a freshman at the same school.

The fathers challenge the following four KSHSAA rules: Article 5, Section 1 of Rule 33 ("three players to a squad rule"); Article 4, Section 1 of Rule 33 ("anti-competitive team camp rule"); Article 1, Section 1 of Rule 22 ("outside team rule"); and Section 1 of Rule 26 ("anti-clinic and private instruction rule"). The "three player rule" may have been repealed, thus possibly mooting the question of its validity.

The "anti-competitive team camp rule" prohibits basketball players from attending competitive team camps in summer or school-organized practices during spring or summer. The rule generally prohibits coaches from basketball-related contacts with their players during those times (except for a one-week team camp). Students may individually attend summer basketball camps that are not school-organized. Soccer and baseball do not have similar restrictions. The fathers desire that their sons have the freedom to attend competitive team camps in the summer, play in summer leagues with school teammates, receive summer instruction from their coaches, and have the freedom to decide what summer activities they will engage in without being penalized by KSHSAA.

The "outside team rule" prohibits a student from playing on both a school team and a non-school team during the basketball season. Mario and Brook, Jr., could not play YMCA basketball during the basketball seasons of their schools. Brandon will not be able to play YMCA and Salvation Army basketball without losing his eligibility, if he plays on a middle school team.

The "anti-clinic and private instruction rule" prohibits two or more players from receiving private instruction from non-school personnel during the basketball season. Former National Basketball Association stars have offered free clinics in the Wichita area, but this rule has prohibited Robinson's sons from attending.

KSHSAA has existed since 1910, beginning as a voluntary athletic association of some 50 high schools. It has handled rules violation cases involving interscholastic athletics since the 1920's. In 1937, it became the Activities Association and included speech and music in addition to athletics. It was first incorporated in 1956 as a nonprofit educational corporation, reorganized in 1958, under L. 1955, ch. 341, as amended by L. 1957, ch. 375, and reorganized again in 1969, in order to remain in compliance with statutory requirements. KSHSAA is currently organized under K.S.A. 1995 Supp. 72-130. At present, approximately 365 high schools (over 90% of Kansas high schools) and 400 junior high or middle schools are members of KSHSAA.

Discussion
Standing

KSHSAA argues that the fathers do not have standing to challenge the legality of the KSHSAA rules because they are not members of the KSHSAA. . . .

KSHSAA has waived any objections to the fathers as the real parties in interest

The District Court's Decision

In reaching the determination that an unconstitutional delegation of legislative power had taken place, the district court first concluded that KSHSAA is not a voluntary association. In arriving at that conclusion, the district court relied on the contract doctrine of coercion or duress. . . . The district court also compared KSHSAA's situation to *Bunger v. Iowa High School Athletic Association*, 197 N.W.2d 555 (Iowa 1972), noting that over 90% of the schools in Kansas belonged to the association. Although *Bunger* was not relied on, the district court concluded that "withdraw[al] from the Association as a means of exercising some form of voluntariness would be a meaningless act."

The voluntariness issue goes to the heart of the question of whether KSHSAA's rules are considered a matter of contract between its members or a delegated legislative function. The district court reasoned that the rules of KSHSAA should not be considered the rules of the member schools because membership in KSHSAA was not voluntary. Member schools had no choice on following the rules, even if they had voted against them.

The relationship of a voluntary association with its members is governed by contract law. . . .

KSHSAA has been characterized as a voluntary organization. . . . Therefore, according to KSHSAA, its rules are a matter of contract and not the result of any delegation of power from the legislature. We agree.

Section 1, Article 1, of the bylaws of KSHSAA provides that any accredited public or private high school may join the association by its principal subscribing to the rules of the association and the payment of annual dues. Member schools can seek to have a rule rescinded or changed through the board of directors. . . .

Nothing compels a high school to join KSHSAA or refrain from withdrawing its membership, if the school is willing to accept the consequences, however unpalatable. Schools are not required to have an interscholastic athletic program. We question the comparison of the KSHSAA-school relationship to the "coercive contract" situations in *Milling Co.*, 115 Kan. 712, 225 P. 86; *Delano*, 663 F.2d 990; and *Williamson*, 77 Kan. 502, 94 P. 807. . . .

Right for the Wrong Reason

The district court in deciding the case did not reach the fathers' allegations concerning the validity of the rules themselves. The fathers invite us to address their claim that KSHSAA lacks jurisdiction to adopt the rules as an alternative reason for affirming the district court. . . . The "right for the wrong reason" rule is applicable when we affirm the district court. Here we reverse. We decline the invitation.

Conclusion

The fathers have met the minimal requirements for standing. The unconstitutional delegation issue was sufficiently raised at a trial to place it before us on appeal. KSHSAA is a nonprofit corporation consisting of voluntary members. KSHSAA's rules are adopted by its members, through its board of directors, and each member school agrees to obey those rules. We find no unconstitutional delegation or sub-delegation under K.S.A. 72-130 *et seq.* of legislative power violating Article 2, § 1 of the Kansas Constitution.

The fathers' remaining theories in the case are: (1) KSHSAA lacks jurisdiction to adopt the questioned rules because the rules attempt to regulate non-school activities, and (2) the subject rules are arbitrary, capricious, and unreasonable. The district court will need to consider the merits of these two theories on remand.

Reversed and remanded.

In short, the Kansas Supreme Court held that the eligibility rules of the high school athletic association were not unconstitutional. In *Kirby*, the Supreme Court of Michigan determined that the high school association had full authority to regulate amateur athletics, in this case interscholastic sports, and that the athletes under its coverage were bound by the association's rulings.

KIRBY V. MICHIGAN HIGH SCHOOL ATHLETIC ASSOCIATION

585 N.W.2d 290 (Mich. 1998)

PER CURIAM.

The circuit court intervened in the 1995 Michigan High School Athletic Association team wrestling tournament, ordering that wrestlers from Lake Fenton Community High School be allowed to participate. Later, the circuit court entered a second order, holding the MHSAA in contempt. The Court of Appeals affirmed both orders. We reverse the judgment of the Court of Appeals and the orders of the circuit court.

I

In February 1995, the Michigan High School Athletic Association conducted its annual team wrestling tournament. As in some other sports, the format called for a number of teams to wrestle in a district tournament, with the district winners advancing to a regional tournament. Regional winners continued to the state quarterfinals.

On Wednesday, February 15, 1995, the New Lothrop High School wrestling team competed against the team from Lake Fenton Community High School in a district semifinal match. New Lothrop won by a single point, allowing it to advance to a district final match that same evening against Bentley High School.

On the bus ride home, the Lake Fenton coach looked again at the weigh-in sheet, and discovered that one of the victorious New Lothrop wrestlers had violated the rules by wrestling in the wrong weight category. The coach immediately telephoned the director of the district meet, but the director did not share the opinion that the wrestler was ineligible.

New Lothrop defeated Bentley in the district final, and thus prepared to advance to the regional tournament a week later, on Wednesday, February 22, 1995.

The Lake Fenton coach was correct — the New Lothrop wrestler had been ineligible. Pursuant to a rule in the MHSAA handbook, the penalty was that New Lothrop forfeited its district semifinal match against Lake Fenton. New Lothrop offered a written acknowledgment and apology on the day after the meet, February 16, 1995.

That same day (February 16), Bill Bupp, the assistant director of the MHSAA, ruled that no team from the district would advance to the regional tournament, scheduled for Goodrich High School on Wednesday, February 22. Mr. Bupp relied on an MHSAA policy that a team that has been defeated in single-elimination tournament play cannot advance, even if the apparently victorious team later forfeits. In his written statement to the affected schools, Mr. Bupp characterized the rule as a "long-standing MHSAA policy which has been applied without exception. . . ."

On Friday, February 17, 1995, Lake Fenton submitted a written request that New Lothrop's violation be treated as a forfeiture of only the single match won by the ineligible wrestler. Such an approach would make Lake Fenton the winner of the district semifinal match. In their letter, Lake Fenton's wrestling coach and athletic director said that they had discussed a plan to set up a match between Lake Fenton and Bentley in advance of the regional meet scheduled for Wednesday, February 22, 1995.

MHSAA Executive Director John E. Roberts responded in writing later on February 17. . . .

Plaintiff James E. Kirby, the father of one of the Lake Fenton Wrestlers, filed a February 17, 1995 complaint against the MHSAA in circuit court. Mr. Kirby sought an injunctive order compelling the MHSAA to conduct a match between Lake Fenton and Bentley, with the winner advancing to the regional tournament.

On February 17, the circuit court ordered the MHSAA to show cause why a preliminary injunction should not be entered. The matter was set for hearing at 3:30 p.m. on Wednesday, February 22, 1995.

On February 22, the plaintiffs filed an amended complaint that added Lake Fenton Community School District as a party plaintiff.

The hearing began at 4:39 p.m. on February 22. At Goodrich High School, the regional tournament was slated to begin at 5:30 p.m. There would be only one semifinal match, between Brown City High School and Marlette High School. In the other bracket, Goodrich High School drew a bye, since there was no opponent from the district where the forfeiture had occurred. The finals were set for 7:00 p.m. . . .

After hearing testimony and argument, the circuit court ruled that there was no formal MHSAA rule prohibiting Lake Fenton from advancing in this situation. Though the situation had been discussed in MHSAA memos and bulletins, the court concluded that the Lake Fenton students would draw adverse lessons if the MHSAA and the other parties followed a course not set forth in the MHSAA's formal rules.

The circuit court's conclusion was that the athletes from Lake Fenton "can go wrestle." The proceedings concluded at 6:50 p.m., as the circuit court entered this handwritten order: . . .

IT IS ORDERED
1. Lake Fenton Community School may wrestle in the Regional Tournament at Goodrich High School. . . .

In the meantime, the semifinal match between Brown City and Marlette had been concluded. Marlette High School won in a match that ended about 6:25 p.m. Tournament director A1 Martus determined that the finals would not begin early, but would start at 7:00 p.m., in accordance with the schedule that had been published for competitors and fans.

The regional finals between Marlette and Goodrich began about 7:02 p.m. and, following a takedown, the score in the first match was 20. When word came that the court had ruled in favor of Lake Fenton the initial match was halted, and the Lake Fenton wrestlers were weighed. . . .

The regional final between Marlette and Goodrich then resumed and continued to completion, with Goodrich winning the opportunity to advance further in the tournament. Lake Fenton did not participate.

The MHSAA has sought in two principal ways to justify its decision to exclude Lake Fenton. First, it was proposed that the use of the word "may" in the circuit court's handwritten order was permissive, and meant that the MHSAA could decide whether to allow Lake Fenton to participate. Of course, in context, the word "may" meant no such thing.

Second, and more plausibly, the MHSAA took the position that it was no longer possible to comply with the court's order, since the regional semifinals, into which Lake Fenton had been granted admission, were concluded before the court ruled. When the court's order was presented, the finals were already under way.

Following these events, Mr. Kirby and Lake Fenton went back to circuit court, and obtained an order requiring the MHSAA to show cause why it should not be held in contempt. At a hearing on Monday, February 27, 1995, the plaintiffs also sought an order reorganizing the tournament so that Lake Fenton could yet participate. . . .

On March 9, 1995, the circuit court heard testimony from Mr. Martus, who testified that he followed the direction of Mr. Bupp. The court also heard testimony from Kenneth Andrzejewski, the principal of Goodrich High School, and from Mr. Roberts, Executive Director of the MHSAA. Mr. Roberts took personal responsibility for the ruling, saying, "I don't believe my position gives me the authority to insert, impose a semi-final round after the finals had begun."

At the conclusion of the hearing, the circuit court held the MHSAA in contempt. It fined the organization $250, and directed that it pay several thousand dollars to reimburse the plaintiffs for costs and attorney fees incurred in the circuit court proceedings that occurred after February 22, 1995.

The MHSAA separately appealed the injunctive order and the contempt order. The Court of Appeals consolidated the appeals, and affirmed both orders.

The MHSAA has applied to this Court, seeking leave to appeal. . . .

There are several problems with this analysis [by the Court of appeals]. First, we perceive no contradiction between the nonadvancement policy and the cited provision in the MHSAA handbook. Second, the testimony in this case indicates that the MHSAA policy prohibiting a defeated team from advancing in tournament play was not "an unwritten rule." Rather, it was a consistently applied policy, reaffirmation of which had been reported in the written bulletins that the MHSAA circulates to member schools. Third, and most important, the Court of Appeals analysis misapprehends the fundamental nature of the relationship between the MHSAA and its member schools — these schools voluntarily cede to the MHSAA full authority to regulate interscholastic athletics.

Athletic competition takes place under a unique set of circumstances. Competitors seek to win in an artificial environment in which a "win" is defined under inherently arbitrary rules, applied by umpires, referees, and other game officials who are themselves a fundamental part of the athletic environment. Formal athletic competition also is typically governed by an external body that sets rules and governs the competition, subject to the agreement of teams and competitors. The means and objectives of athletic competition do not always "make sense" in any external fashion rather, participants seek to better themselves through the discipline of striving for goals that exist within the specific rules of each sport.

Two high school students who wish to wrestle may do so in the park or in the backyard. They can wrestle for five minutes or for ten. They can wrestle for pride or for the right to advance to a match against the student who lives at the end of the block. They can wrestle by whatever rules, or lack of rules, they prefer.

Or these students can choose to join a high school wrestling team. In this instance, all the students and schools chose participation in the interscholastic wrestling program organized and directed by the Michigan High School Athletic Association. Neither students nor schools were compelled to submit to the governance of the MHSAA, yet all did so. As the record indicates, Lake Fenton and all other MHSAA member schools annually adopt a resolution establishing MHSAA membership, and accepting MHSAA governance of the athletic competitions in which the schools participate. . . .

The plaintiffs wish to finely parse that statement, arguing that the non-advancement policy is not found in the handbook, and its placement in the bulletin is inadequate because it is not a "qualification." Again, this misapprehends the nature of MHSAA governance. Schools agree, for the purpose of having orderly competition, to let the MHSAA set the rules and govern the tournaments.

The plaintiffs' complaint and amended complaint each alleges that the MHSAA rules "clearly do not address the situation" found in this case. On that basis, the plaintiffs believe that the MHSAA cannot rule as it did. However, the schools have agreed that tournaments will be run by the MHSAA. Inevitably, this agreement empowers the MHSAA to deal reasonably with situations outside its rulebook as they arise.

Here, the MHSAA nonadvancement rule has a rational policy — it encourages coaches to point out eligibility problems immediately, rather than to wait until the end of a match when there would be no possibility for a substitution and the school that kept quiet would automatically advance. The MHSAA's handling of this matter also serves to maintain the integrity of the tournament process. Lake Fenton lost in the district semifinals to New Lothrop, which defeated Bentley in the district finals. When this matter came before the circuit court, Lake Fenton sought advancement to the regionals, though it had never competed against Bentley. At the hearing in circuit court, Lake Fenton tendered a letter in which Bentley offered to "lose" a hypothetical match against Lake Fenton, but MHSAA officials certainly have the right to insist that state championships be decided on the wrestling mat, not through correspondence.

Long before this controversy arose, Lake Fenton agreed that it would participate in MHSAA-sponsored wrestling competition, under the governance of the MHSAA. Such an agreement is analogous to the consent given by a party entering arbitration, who agrees in advance to be bound by any ruling that is within the scope of the arbitrator's authority, provided the ruling is not clearly violative of law. Here, the MHSAA exercised its authority in the course of such governance, and made a ruling that has no fundamental flaw. Hence, its decision should be upheld.

For these reasons, we set aside the injunctive order of the circuit court.

IV

The Court of Appeals also upheld the contempt citation against the MHSAA. . . .

Holding the MHSAA in contempt, the circuit court expressed considerable irritation over the manner in which its order was handled by the MHSAA. We understand the court's concern, since the order clearly provided that Lake Fenton could participate. The circuit court exercises the judicial power of the state of Michigan under Const. 1963, art. 6, §1, and has broad jurisdiction under Const. 1963, art. 6, §13. A party must obey an order entered by a court with proper jurisdiction, even if the order is clearly incorrect, or the party must face the risk of, being held in contempt and possibly being ordered to comply with the order at a later date. *In re Hague,* 412 Mich. 532, 544-545, 315 N.W.2d 524 (1982).

Nevertheless, we find in this close case that the MHSAA was not guilty of contempt. The court's order directed that Lake Fenton be permitted to "wrestle in the Regional Tournament at Goodrich High School," but the only rational interpretation of that order was that Lake Fenton be allowed to participate in the semifinal portion of the regional tournament (no one had ever argued that Lake Fenton should be allowed to skip all the way from the district semifinals to the regional finals). However, at the point when MHSAA officials were called upon to make their decision, the regional finals between Marlette and Goodrich had already begun, and there was a 2-0 score in the first match. Making the decision by telephone, Executive Director Roberts concluded correctly that it was not possible to grant participation at the semifinal level in a regional tournament where the finals had already begun.

Thus we also set aside the order holding the MHSAA in contempt.

V

For the reasons stated in this opinion, we reverse the judgment of the Court of Appeals and the orders of the circuit court. . . .

QUESTIONS AND DISCUSSION

1. In Hall v. University of Minnesota, 530 F. Supp. 104, 109 (D. Minn. 1982), Miles Lord intimated that amateur sports may not really be as pure as they once were:

   > The court is not saying that athletes aren't capable of school scholarship, however, they are given little incentive to be scholars and few persons care how the student athlete performs academically, including many of the athletes themselves. The exceptionally talented student-athlete is raised to perceive the basketball, football, and other athletic programs as farm teams and proving grounds for professional sports leagues. It may well be true that a good academic program for the athlete is made virtually impossible by the demands of their sport at the college level. If this situation causes harm to the university, it is because they have fostered it and the institution rather than the individual should suffer the consequences.

   Assuming Judge Lord was correct in 1982, is he still on point in 2004?

2. A classic example of amateurism's duality was the track star Carl Lewis, who although he earned millions per year, still maintained his amateur standing. How could that be?

3. The concept of amateurism began in the 1700s as a leisure outlet for the upper class. It was a pure model — how has this pure paradigm been sullied in the last 300 years?

4. Is the Kansas State High School Activities Association, Inc., in *Robinson* an example of a restricted competition amateur athletic association, which establishes rules for competition and devises means for scheduling competition including delineating the eligibility of participants?

5. Is the Michigan High School Athletic Association in *Kirby* an example of a restricted competition amateur athletic association? Does your answer change if the association also included private schools?

6. Can there be a hybrid model of restricted and unrestricted competition? What would such a model look like?

7. Courts' rule interpretations are not substituted for an athletic association's interpretation as long as the latter is fair and reasonable. *See Kentucky High Sch. Athletic Assn. v. Hopkins County Bd. of Educ.*, 552 S.W.2d 685, 687 (Ky. Ct. App. 1977). What interpretations might be unfair and unreasonable? *See generally* Mathewson, '*Intercollegiate Athletics and the Assignment of Legal Rights*,' 35 St. L. U. L Rev. 39 (1990); Popson, '*A Call for Statutory Regulation of Elite Child Athletes*,' 41 Wayne L. Rev. 1773 (1995); Riggs, '*The Facade of Amateurism: The Inequities of Major-College Athletics*,' 5 Kan. J.L. & Pub. Polly. 137 (1996).

B. SCHOLARSHIPS

Scholarships are tools for universities to use to secure athletes for their schools to play sports. Even though scholarships are a major part of the collegiate sporting universe, they are still somewhat difficult to categorize. Are scholarships contracts or just some sort of informal arrangement that does not place duties, responsibilities, or obligations on each party? Another question is whether a scholarship athlete is an employee of the school.

In *Taylor v. Wake Forest University*, a case where an athlete's scholarship was terminated when he decided not to play football, the court held that the scholarship was a contract and that in consideration of the award, the athlete agreed to maintain athletic eligibility, both physically and scholastically.

TAYLOR V. WAKE FOREST UNIVERSITY

191 S.E.2d 379 (N.E Ct. App. 1972)

This action was instituted for the recovery of educational expenses incurred by George J. Taylor, father, and Gregg F. Taylor, son, after alleged wrongful termination of an athletic scholarship issued to Gregg F. Taylor by Wake Forest University.

As early as December 1965, football coaches at Wake Forest were in communication with Gregg Taylor soliciting his enrollment at Wake Forest. This interest was engendered by the football playing ability of Gregg Taylor. Not only was Wake Forest interested in him, but other colleges and universities were likewise showing an interest. As a result of this interest and negotiations, Gregg Taylor and his father, George Taylor, on 27 February 1967, submitted an application entitled, "Atlantic Coast Conference Application For A Football Grant-In-Aid Or A Scholarship."

This application was accepted by Wake Forest on 24 May 1967. . . .

At the time the contract was entered into, Wake Forest did not have a written Grant-In-Aid policy. This policy was not put in writing until January 1969. One of the written policy provisions was to the effect that financial aid could be terminated for "(r)efusal to attend practice sessions or scheduled work-out that are a part of the athletic program or to act in such a manner as to disrupt these sessions." . . . Gregg Taylor . . . at Wake Forest at the beginning of the Fall Session 1967. He participated in the football program during the Fall of 1967.

At the end of that semester, his grade average was 1.0 out of a possible 4.0. Wake Forest required a 1.35 grade average after freshman year, a 1.65 grade average after sophomore year, and a 1.85 grade average after junior year. . . . Gregg Taylor notified the football coach on 6 February 1968 that he would not participate in regular practice sessions . . . during the Spring of 1968. . . . [His grades improved, but he] decided that he would not further participate in the football program. . . .

After a hearing, the Scholarship Committee notified Gregg Taylor that his scholarship had been terminated as of the end of the 1968-1969 academic year, which was the end of Gregg Taylor's sophomore year.

Gregg Taylor continued to attend Wake Forest during the 1969-1970 academic year, which was his junior year, and likewise, the academic year of 1970-1971, which was his senior year; and he received an undergraduate degree from Wake Forest in June 1971.

As a result of the termination of the scholarship, expenses in the amount of $5500 were incurred during those two academic years. It is for this sum of $5500 that this action was instituted. . . .

CAMPBELL, Judge.

Plaintiffs contend that there was a genuine issue as to a material fact and that a jury should determine whether Gregg Taylor acted reasonably and in good faith in refusing to participate in the football program at Wake Forest when such participation interfered with reasonable academic progress. . . .

We do not agree with the position taken by plaintiffs. The scholarship application filed by Gregg Taylor provided:

> . . . I agree to maintain eligibility for intercollegiate athletics under both Conference and Institutional rules. Training rules for intercollegiate athletics are considered rules of the Institution, and I agree to abide by them.

Both Gregg Taylor and his father knew that the application was for "Football Grant-In-Aid Or A Scholarship," and that the scholarship was "awarded for academic and athletic achievement." It would be a strained construction of the contract that would enable the plaintiffs to determine the "reasonable academic progress" of Gregg Taylor, Gregg Taylor, in consideration of the scholarship award, agreed to maintain his athletic eligibility and this meant both physically and scholastically. As long as his grade average equaled or exceeded the requirements of Wake Forest, he was maintaining his scholastic eligibility for athletics. Participation in and attendance at practice were required to maintain his physical eligibility. When he refused to do so in the absence of any injury or excuse other than to devote more time to studies, he was not complying with his contractual obligations.

The record disclosed that Wake Forest fully complied with its agreement and that Gregg Taylor failed to do so. There was no "genuine issue as to any material fact" and summary judgment was proper. . . .

We find no error.

As in *Taylor*, the court in *Gulf South Conference v. Boyd*, noted that the relationship between a college athlete who accepts a scholarship is contractual in nature. The athlete agrees to participate, and the school in return agrees to give assistance to that athlete.

GULF SOUTH CONFERENCE V. BOYD

369 So. 2d 553 (Ala 1979)

BEATTY, Justice.

This is an appeal from an order declaring that the plaintiff, Julian R. Boyd, is eligible to participate in varsity football at Troy State University. We affirm.

On July 12, 1977 the plaintiff Boyd filed his original complaint for a declaratory judgment against the defendant, Gulf South Conference. . . . asking that the court declare him eligible to participate in varsity football at Troy State University. Boyd's complaint alleged that there is a justiciable controversy between the parties and that Boyd is eligible to participate in varsity football at Troy State University under . . . [GSC] eligibility rules and regulations. . . . Boyd requested the court to declare him eligible for the 1977-1978 football season. . . .

A hearing was held on June 28, 1978. On August 2, 1978 the trial judge found that under the evidence as applied to the rules and regulations of the GSC, Boyd was entitled to the relief requested. The court therefore ordered that Boyd was eligible to participate in varsity football at Troy State University for the 1978-1979 football season provided Boyd was a student in good standing and enrolled at the Troy, Alabama campus of Troy State University for the Fall Term 1978. . . .

The essential facts are undisputed. Boyd entered Livingston University in the Fall of 1975 on a full grant-in-aid football scholarship and played on the Livingston University football team during the Fall of 1975. The full grant-in-aid football scholarship awarded to and accepted by Boyd was only for a one-year period (covering only the 1975-76 football season), and was renewable at Livingston University's discretion, subject to Boyd's acceptance. During the

1975-76 football season both Boyd and Livingston University performed all of their commitments to each other as required by the terms of that one-year scholarship.

At the end of the 1975-76 school year Livingston University Coach Jack Crowe forwarded Boyd a written offer to renew his football scholarship at Livingston University for the 1976-1977 school year. Boyd did not accept the offer. By telephone Coach Crowe urged Boyd to return and play on the Livingston football team. During that telephone conversation, Boyd informed Coach Crowe that he could not play football as a running back because of an asthmatic condition he had developed. Boyd also informed Coach Crowe that he did not want to return to Livingston University because he wanted to live in Enterprise, Alabama and work part-time with his father while attending Enterprise State Junior College. Coach Crowe then told him that he could be a specialist player as a punter on the team if Boyd's asthmatic condition would not permit him to be a running back. However, Boyd still declined the offer of Livingston University to renew his grant-in-aid and finally told Coach Crowe that for personal reasons he chose not to go back to Livingston University.

Boyd later enrolled at Enterprise State Junior College for the 1976-1977 school year and was graduated in the Summer of 1977. Boyd then discussed with Dr. Stewart at Troy State University the possibility of transferring to Troy and playing on Troy's varsity football team as a punter. He was informed that he had been ruled ineligible by the Commissioner of the GSC. Troy State, thereafter, appealed the Commissioner's ruling to the Faculty Appeals Committee of the GSC. That committee affirmed the Commissioner's ruling that Boyd was ineligible to play football at Troy State.

Both Livingston University and Troy State University are members of the GSC, an unincorporated voluntary athletic association organized by nine colleges and universities. The stated purpose of the GSC is to promote fair competition between the schools by developing rules and regulations mutually agreed upon by the member schools. The Conference is governed by a Constitution, Bylaws and Rules. Enforcement is exercised through the Commissioner of the Conference and a Faculty Appeals Committee. The GSC is also affiliated with the National Collegiate Athletic Association and subject to its rules and regulations.

The applicable GSC eligibility rules . . . are . . . :

> A student-athlete who transfers from one GSC to another will not be eligible to participate in any sport at the second school unless (1) THE FIRST ONE DROPS THAT SPORT AND ALL OTHER GSC RULES ARE COMPLIED WITH, OR (2) IF THE STUDENT QUALIFIES UNDER . . .
>
> Section 3. Migrants or Transfers are students who enter a college after having been registered in another college . . .
>
> B. Any student who has attended a GSC school but has not been recruited in any way; has not signed a pre-enrollment application, has received no financial aid, and has not participated would be a Transfer upon attending any other GSC school.
>
> C. When a GSC member does not renew the grant-in-aid of an eligible athlete according to NCAA Constitution 3-4(d), the athlete becomes a free agent and may be signed by any other GSC school as a Transfer . . . [and] . . .

A student-athlete who signs a PRE-ENROLLMENT APPLICATION with one GSC school . . . cannot participate with any other GSC school, except: A prospective student-athlete who does not accept the grant-in-aid at that school nor participate becomes a free agent at the end of the two (2) years and can be signed by any GSC school.

The GSC contends that the lower court's order was erroneous for two reasons; the first being that the lower court was without jurisdiction to intervene in the internal affairs of the GSC. . . .

The contention by the GSC that the lower court did not have jurisdiction basically stems from a body of common law involving private associations. . . . Even though we recognize the existence of this non-interference principle, nevertheless this Court has sanctioned judicial review when the actions of an association are the result of fraud, lack of jurisdiction, collusion, arbitrariness, or are in violation of or contravene any principle of public policy. . . .

We hold that the general non-interference doctrine concerning voluntary associations does not apply to cases involving disputes between college athletes themselves and college athletic associations. There is a cogent reason for this position. In such cases the athlete himself is not even a member of the athletic association; therefore, the basic "freedom of association" principle behind the non-interference rule is not present. The athlete himself has no voice or bargaining power concerning the rules and regulations adopted by the athletic associations because he is not a member, yet he stands to be substantially affected, and even damaged, by an association ruling declaring him to be ineligible to participate in intercollegiate athletics. Thus he may be deprived of the property right eligibility to participate in intercollegiate athletics. While there is a split of authority on the question, cf., e.g., *NCAA v. Gillard*, 352 So. 2d 1072 (Miss. 1977), we agree with the following statement of the Oklahoma Supreme Court:

> It is asserted by the NCAA that judicial scrutiny of the bylaw is inappropriate. Courts are normally reluctant to interfere with the internal affairs of voluntary membership associations, however, in particular situations, where the considerations of policy and justice are sufficiently compelling judicial scrutiny and relief are available. . . . The necessity of court action is apparent where the position of a voluntary association is so dominant in its field that the membership in a practical sense is not voluntary but economically necessary. It was proper for the trial court to examine the validity of the bylaw. (*Board of Regents of the University of Oklahoma v. NCAA*, 561 P.2d 499, 504 (Okl.1977).)

We further find that a declaratory judgment action was proper. All that is required for a declaratory judgment action is a bona fide justiciable controversy. . . . Such a bona fide controversy existed on the issue of Boyd's eligibility under the GSC bylaws. This controversy affected a substantial property right. . . .

The defendant GSC also contends that the lower court's order was erroneous because it was contrary to the terms of the GSC transfer rule under the undisputed facts of this case. That contention is untenable. The evidence introduced in the lower court tends to show that Boyd was, in fact, eligible under two of the bylaws. GSC Bylaws, Article V, Section 3(C) states in effect that an athlete becomes a free agent and may be signed by any other GSC school if a GSC member school does not renew the grant-in-aid of that athlete. Here Boyd's one-year scholarship was not renewed because, although Livingston offered to renew it, Boyd became a free agent and was free to sign with whatever school he chose. Livingston University was not obligated to renew or offer to renew Boyd's scholarship, and Boyd was not obligated to accept Livingston's offer. Both parties had performed their obligations to each other and neither party owed any further obligation to the other at the close of the 1975-1976 football season.

Boyd was also eligible under GSC Bylaw, Article VIII, Section 3, which states in pertinent part that "A prospective student-athlete who does not accept the grant-in-aid at that school nor participate becomes a free agent at the end of two (2) years and can be signed by any GSC school." Since Boyd's original scholarship with Livingston was effective only for the 1975-1976 football season, Boyd became a prospective student-athlete for Livingston at the end of his one-year scholarship. Because he did not accept Livingston's offer, did not attend school at Livingston, and did not play football for two years, he became a free agent. The lower court was therefore correct in ruling that Boyd was eligible to play football at Troy State University for the 1978-1979 football season since the 1978 football season occurred at the end of two years after Boyd's refusal to accept the second grant-in-aid offered by Livingston University.

It should be noted that the relationship between a college athlete who accepts an athletic scholarship and the college which awards such an athletic scholarship is contractual in nature. The college athlete agrees to participate in a sport at the college, and the college in return agrees to give assistance to the athlete. The athlete also agrees to be bound by the rules and regulations adopted by the college concerning the financial assistance. Most of these rules and regulations are promulgated by athletic associations whose membership is composed of the individual colleges. The individual athlete has no voice or participation in the formulation or interpretation of these rules and regulations governing his scholarship, even though these materially control his conduct on and off the field. Thus in some circumstances the college athlete may be placed in an unequal bargaining position. The GSC's interpretation of the bylaws in question was that a student football athlete who transfers from one GSC school to another will not be eligible to participate in football at the second school unless the first school drops football or unless the first school does not (merely) offer to renew the grant-in-aid scholarship of the student-athlete. The lower court rejected this interpretation and, as we have shown, that decision was correct. Accordingly, let the judgment be affirmed.

In *Rensing v. Indiana State University Board of Trustees*, where a court was called on to determine whether an injured scholarship athlete was eligible for workers' compensation, the court held that there was no intent to enter into an employee-employer relationship at the time the parties entered into the agreement.

The courts held in both *Boyd* and *Rensing* that scholarship recipients, whether academic or athletic, receive benefits based on their demonstrated ability, which will enable them to pursue higher education, as well as to progress further in their own endeavors.

RENSING V. INDIANA STATE UNIV. BOARD OF TRUSTEES

437 N.E.2d 78 (Ind. Ct. App. 1982)

MILLER, Presiding Judge.

Plaintiff-appellant, Fred W. Rensing, appeals the decision of the full Industrial Board of Indiana (Industrial Board) rejecting his claim for workmen's compensation from the defendant-appellee, the Indiana State University Board of Trustees (Trustees). Rensing, a varsity football player at Indiana State University–Terre Haute (University), was rendered a quadriplegic as a result of an injury occurring on April 24, 1976 during the team's spring football practice. At the time he was injured Rensing was receiving financial aid through a football scholarship awarded by the Trustees. On August 22, 1977 Rensing filed his claim seeking recovery for permanent total disability as well as medical and hospital expenses incurred due to the injury. Rensing's claim was rejected by the Industrial Board's Hearing Member on May 24, 1979, after which Rensing appealed to this Court challenging the Industrial Board's conclusion of law that an employer-employee relationship did not exist between Rensing and the Trustees and, therefore, he was not entitled to benefits under Indiana's Workmen's Compensation Act. . . .

For the reasons stated below, we reverse the Industrial Board's decision and remand this cause to it for further proceedings consistent with this opinion.

Facts

The . . . Trustees, through their agent Thomas Harp (the University's Head Football Coach), on February 4, 1974 offered Rensing a scholarship or "educational grant" to play football at the University. In essence, the financial aid agreement, which was renewable each year for a total of four years provided that in return for Rensing's active participation in football competition he would receive free tuition, room, board, laboratory fees, a book allowance, tutoring and a limited number of football tickets per game for family and friends. The "agreement" provided, *inter alia*, the aid would continue even if Rensing suffered an injury during supervised play which would make it inadvisable, in the opinion of the doctor-director of the student health service, "to continue to participate," although in that event the University would require other assistance to the extent of his ability. . . .

The trustees extended this scholarship to Rensing for the 1974-75 academic year in the form of a "Tender of Financial Assistance." Rensing accepted the Trustees' first tender and signed it (as did his parents) on April 29, 1974. At the end of Rensing's first academic year the Trustees' extended a second "Tender of Financial Assistance" for the 1975-76 academic year, which tender was substantially the same as the first and provided the same financial assistance to Rensing for his continued participation in the

University's football program. Rensing and his father signed this second tender on June 24, 1975. It is not contested the monetary value of this assistance to Rensing for the 1975-76 academic year was $2,374, and that the "scholarship" was in effect when Rensing's injuries occurred. . . .

According to Dr. Richard G. Landini, President of the University, it offered various grants to prospective students based on their respective athletic or scholastic talents. The basis for awarding an athletic scholarship was a recommendation by the University's Athletic Director . . . made to Dr. Landini. In turn Dr. Landini forwarded the recommendations to the Trustees who then officially acted upon the recommendation. Dr. Landini emphasized that ultimate responsibility for awarding any scholarship rested with the Trustees. Significantly, Dr. Landini acknowledged that the University's increase in its student enrollment was attributable (to some degree) to the success of its athletic programs and that one justification for an athletic scholarship program was that such a program benefitted the whole University.

Rensing testified he suffered a knee injury during his first year (1974-75) of competition which prevented him from actively participating in the football program, during which time he continued to receive his scholarship as well as free treatment for his knee injury. The only requirement imposed by the Trustees (through Coach Harp) upon Rensing was attendance at his classes and reporting daily to the football stadium for free whirlpool and ultrasonic treatments for his injured knee. Although the Trustees (through Coach Harp) did not require Rensing to assist the coaching staff in conducting the football program in order to fulfill his obligations under the financial assistance agreement (either after his knee injury or the accident causing his quadriplegia), the uncontradicted evidence demonstrated Coach Harp *could have* required Rensing to assist the football coaches. As noted above, the financial aid agreement provided that in the event of an injury of such severity that it prevented continued athletic participation, "Indiana State University will ask you to assist in the conduct of the athletic program within the limits of your physical capabilities" in order to continue receiving aid. The sole assistance actually asked of Rensing was to entertain prospective football recruits when they visited the University's Terre Haute campus.

During the 1975 football season Rensing participated on the University's football team. In the spring of 1976 he partook in the team's annual three week spring practice when, on April 24, he was injured while he tackled a teammate during a punting drill. Coach Harp described the accident as follows:

> We were working on punt coverage and Fred was covering a punt. . . . The ball was caught right at the time Fred arrived at that point, and in attempting to make the tackle, hit with his head the shoulder pad of the receiver, . . . and went under and sustained the injury.

Harp further described this particular play as a "severe tackle, it was one that you heard very seldom, it was heard all over the [football] stadium and [was] observed by the entire squad as a very hard tackle, [a] very hard hit."

The specific injury suffered by Rensing was a fractured dislocation of the cervical spine at the level of 4-5 vertebrae. Rensing's initial treatment consisted of traction and eventually a spinal fusion. During this period he developed pneumonia for which he had to have a tracheotomy. Eventually, Rensing was transferred to the Rehabilitation Department of the Barnes Hospital complex in St. Louis. According to Rensing's doctor . . . [his] paralysis was caused by the April 24, 1976 football injury leaving him 95-100% disabled. The undisputed testimony revealed Rensing's expenses for medical care and treatment totaled $120,449.26, some of which amount was paid by the University's insurer. . . .

Rensing appealed to the full industrial Board which on June 6, 1980 adopted in full the Hearing Member's above findings and award.

Discussion and Decision

The Trustees concede some manner of contract existed between them and Rensing. However, the Trustees argue, and the Industrial Board concluded, there was no contract for hire or employment within the meaning of the Workmen's Compensation Act. Conversely, Rensing appeals from this conclusion, arguing that his agreement to play football (or, if he were injured, to otherwise help the football program in return for financial assistance) was a contract within the Act. We agree with Rensing. . . .

Our determination that the requisite employer-employee relationship existed between Rensing and the Trustees, initially focuses on the definitions of "employer" and "employee" . . . in the Workmen's Compensation Act. . . .

Thus, in the instant case the central question is not whether our Legislature has specifically excluded college sports participants from the coverage of the Act, since it is apparent the Legislature has not expressed such an intention, but rather whether there was a "written or implied" employment contract within the meaning of the Act which obligated Rensing to play football in return for the scholarship he received.

. . . [T]he conclusion is inescapable [that] the Trustees did contract with Rensing to play football, regardless of whether one views the various documents submitted to Rensing and signed by him as constituting an *express* contract, or merely as evidence of the parties' understanding in support of an *implied* contractual relationship. . . . The parties' financial aid "agreement" clearly anticipated not only that Rensing would play football in return for his scholarship, but also provided that in the event Rensing suffered an injury during supervised play that would make him "unable to continue to participate" in the opinion of the *University* doctor, the Trustees would ask him to assist in other tasks to the extent of his ability. The benefits would continue so long as Rensing was "otherwise eligible to compete." [Therefore,] we . . . find no merit in the Trustees' suggestion [that] Rensing's benefits were only a gift or "grant" intended to further the young man's education. . . .

Additionally, the Trustees also retained their right to terminate their agreement for Rensing's services under certain . . . conditions, a factor tending to distinguish his grant from an outright gift and which [is] . . . a significant indicia of an employer-employee or master-servant relationship . . .

In this regard, we find especially significant the fact that Rensing's scholarship could be terminated if he misrepresented his intention to enroll (and by implication, play football) at the University. A football "letter of intent" signed by Rensing on March 6, 1974 required him to certify his intention to enroll at the University and further specified that if he elected to attend various other participating institutions, his athletic eligibility at the institution of his choice could be restricted.

From these facts, the conclusion is compelling that Rensing and the Trustees bargained for an exchange in the manner of employer and employee of Rensing's football talent for certain scholarship benefits. Admittedly, the issue . . . is novel to Indiana. . . .

The uncontradicted evidence revealed that for the team members football is a daily routine for 16 weeks each year. Additionally, during the "off-season" the "student-athlete" must daily work out to maintain his physical skills and attributes, thereby enhancing his eligibility for the team which is the basis for his scholarship. The University fields a major college football team and participates in a major college conference, The Missouri Valley Conference. In addition, the Trustees employ a large athletic department to administer the University's intercollegiate athletic program (in addition to physical education classes) and a sizable football coaching staff whose primary responsibility is to produce the best possible team so as to generate the largest possible income and whose teaching responsibilities to the general student body are, at best, of secondary importance. With regard to Rensing specifically, Coach Harp actively recruited him — his appearance at the University was not happenstance, liable to chance or an accident. In light of these facts Rensing's employment by the University was not "casual."

The second element of the exception stated at IC 22-3-6-1(b) which the Trustees were also required to prove was that Rensing's employment was *not* in the usual course of the Trustee's business, trade, occupation or profession. This has been defined as meaning "employment on any work in connection with and reasonably necessary to the employer's business" . . .

[M]aintaining a football team is an important aspect of the University's overall business . . . of educating students, even if it may not be said such athletic endeavors themselves are the University's "principal" occupation. Suffice it to say, it was uncontroverted that Football specifically and athletes generally play a beneficial role in creating the desired educational environment at the University, as evidenced by increased enrollments over the last few years as the University has prospered athletically through nationally-recognized intercollegiate athletic teams. [Therefore,] we . . . believe football competition must properly be viewed as an aspect of the University's overall occupation. . . .

[Although] . . . entitled to . . . compensation benefits . . . we must remand . . . for further proceedings to establish the benefits Rensing will receive. Reversed and remanded.

QUESTIONS AND DISCUSSION

1. By signing a scholarship to play sports, the athlete enters into a relationship with the school so that she agrees to maintain certain grade levels and to perform as an athlete; in return, she receives tuition, books, and certain other educational activities. In the big collegiate sports

programs, should the athlete be paid as an employee? Are these athletes more akin to entertainers than students? *See generally* Brown, '*Compensation for the Student-Athlete Preservation of Amateurism,*' 5 Kan. J.L. & Pub. Poly. 147 (1996); Davis, '*The Courts and Athletic Scholarships,*' 67 N.D. L. Rev. 163 (1991); Goplerud, '*Pay for Play for College Athletes: Now, More Than Ever,*' 38 S. Tex. L. Rev. 1081 (1997); Goplerud, '*Stipends for Collegiate Athletics: A Philosophical Spin on a Controversial Proposal,*' 5 Kan. J.L. & Pub. Poly. 125 (1996); Hoeflich, '*The Taxation of Athletic Scholarships: A Problem of Consistency,*' 1991 U. IL. L. Rev. 581; Nestal, '*Athletic Scholarships: An Imbalance of Power Between the University and the Student-Athlete,*' 53 Ohio St. L.J. 1401 (1992); Schott, '*Give Them What They Deserve: Compensating the Student-Athlete for Participation in Intercollegiate Athletics,*' 3 Sports Law. J. 25 (1996). Sobocinski, '*College Athletes: What Is Fair Compensation?*' 7 Marq. Sports L.J. 257 (1996);

2. In *Taylor v. Wake Forest University*, the university terminated a scholarship when an athlete refused to continue in football practice. The court decided that contractually the student was obligated to participate as an agreed-on exchange for his scholarship. It appeared that Taylor needed to concentrate on his studies; should that be a sufficient reason for his refusal to practice?

3. In *Begley v. Corporation of Mercer University*, 367 F. Supp. 908 (E.D. Tenn. 1973), the school sought to terminate a scholarship agreement when it discovered that the entering student did not have the required grade point average. The court held that since the student did not meet one of the conditions of the agreement, he could not expect the school to perform its part of the contract by allowing him to keep the scholarship. *See* Mairo, '*The College Athletic Scholarship: A Contract That Creates a Property Interest in Eligibility,*' 3 Seton Hall J. Sport L. 149 (1993).

4. In *University of Denver v. Nemeth*, 257 P.2d 423 (Colo. 1953), an injured scholarship athlete was allowed to recover workers' compensation on the basis that his agreement called for him to work in and about the tennis courts on campus. Although he was injured during spring football practice, it was held that the injury arose out of and in the course of his employment.

5. Although there are numerous cases that hold that a scholarship athlete is eligible as an employee for workers' compensation purposes, *Rensing* denied benefits and held that an individual on scholarship is not an employee of that particular school. *Rensing* is an Indiana case applying Indiana Worker's Compensation law; should the outcome be different in other states?

6. Pre-*Rensing* cases have decided that scholarship athletes are indeed school employees. See *Begley, Nemeth, Taylor,* and *Van Horn v. Industrial Accident Comm.*, 33 Cal. Rptr. 169 (Cal. Ct. App. 1963). Is *Rensing* just an unwanted abberation that should apply only to Indiana?

7. Scholarship status as discussed in the context of taxation, workers' compensation, and contracts relates to the question of whether the athlete is an employee. Should this unsettled question be answered by federal statute?

C. ELIGIBILITY

Eligibility rules cover all of the possible permutations that might control a potential athlete, including age, years of participation, academic standing, grade point average, length of hair, transfer rules, red-shirting rules, the number of semesters enrolled, and martial status. All of these elements have been used as a way to restrict an athlete's eligibility to participate.

1. Participation as Right or Privilege

A student-athlete usually has only the privilege to participate in sports. However, if there is a right, then the relationship between the athlete and the governing body is on a much different legal status. If the interest in question is a right, then the participant is entitled to due process if the constitutionally guaranteed right involved is either a liberty or property interest.

Hall v. University of Minnesota is the rare case that found a limited property right for a collegiate athlete to continue his athletic eligibility for another year on the basis that the extra year would determine his status as regards his potential as a drafted player in professional basketball.

HALL v. UNIVERSITY OF MINNESOTA

530 F. Supp. 104 (D. Minn. 1982)

This Court is presented with a serious and troubling question concerning the academic standing and athletic eligibility of a University of Minnesota varsity basketball player. The plaintiff in this action is a 21 year old black senior at the defendant University of Minnesota. He is also a formidable basketball player who, up to this season, played for the defendant University of Minnesota men's intercollegiate varsity basketball team. He is before the Court seeking an injunction ordering the University to admit him to a degree program, a prerequisite to the athletic eligibility he lost. . . .

The plaintiff was enrolled in a non-baccalaureate degree program at the defendant University's General College. His program terminated upon the accumulation of approximately 90 credits. Once his program terminated, the plaintiff attempted to enroll in a "degree program" at the University Without Walls (hereafter UWW), a college within the defendant University, and at the General College. The plaintiff was denied admission twice at UWW and once at the General College. By failing to enroll in a "degree program," the plaintiff lost his eligibility to play on the defendant University's basketball team according to Charles Liesenfelt, Director of Registration, Records & Scheduling. Liesenfelt contends that in order for the plaintiff to remain eligible to participate on the basketball team, he must be a "candidate for a degree" under Rule 1, § 1, A. Part Two, of the "Big Ten Handbook."

The plaintiff does meet the Big Ten eligibility standards with respect to grade point average and credit accumulation, but unless he is enrolled as a "candidate for a degree," he is ineligible to practice or play on the defendant University's basketball team. According to the coach of the University basketball team, the plaintiff is the only player he has known who has met the grade and credit criteria of the Big Ten but has been refused admission into a degree program. . . .

According to the evidence, if the plaintiff is accorded the opportunity to represent the University of Minnesota in intercollegiate varsity basketball competition during winter quarter of 1982, his senior year, he will have a significant opportunity to be a second round choice in the National Basketball Association draft this year, thereby acquiring a probable guarantee of his first year's compensation as a player in the National Basketball Association. If the plaintiff is denied the opportunity to participate in inter-collegiate basketball competition on behalf of the University of Minnesota during winter quarter 1982, his chances for a professional career in basketball will be impaired; and it will be extremely unlikely that his compensation as a first year player in the National Basketball Association will be guaranteed. The evidence indicates that without an opportunity to play during the winter quarter of 1982, the plaintiff would likely be a sixth round choice in the National Basketball Association draft.

This Court has no hesitation in stating that the underlying reason for the plaintiff's desire to be enrolled in a degree program at the defendant University is the enhancement of his chances of becoming a professional basketball player. The plaintiff will probably never attain a degree should he be admitted to a degree program since the National Basketball Association draft occurs in April of 1982, well before the plaintiff could accumulate suffi-cient credits for a degree. The plaintiff was a highly recruited basketball player out of high school who was recruited to come to the University of Minnesota to be a basketball player and not a scholar. His academic record reflects that he has lived up to those expectations, as do the academic records of many of the athletes presented to this Court.

The plaintiff applied for admission to the UWW twice, once in August of 1981 and once in October of 1981. In each case, the UWW admissions committee determined, based on the plaintiff's application, that he should be admitted to the UWW introductory program. In each case, the directors of the program (further up in the hierarchy of the UWW) intervened in the admissions process and effectively directed the admissions committee to reject plaintiff's application. This interference by the directors never occurred in any other case as to any other student.

Prior to the intervention of the directors, one of the UWW directors contacted Dean Lupton of the General College concerning the plaintiff. The director summarized the information conveyed by Dean Lupton in a confidential memorandum regarding the plaintiff. . . .

This memorandum was passed on to a successor director who, after the plaintiff reapplied and was again accepted by the admissions committee, effectively vetoed the decision of the admissions committee. . . .

Opposed to the procedure set forth above used in processing the plaintiff's two applications to the UWW, the UWW distributed a pamphlet explaining the policies and procedures of admission. . . .

It seems apparent that the plaintiff was not judged solely on the basis of his applications and the information therein. Each time the admissions committee reviewed the plaintiff's application, they recommended that he be admitted. After the intervention of the directors and the communication of the information outlined in the above-mentioned memorandum, the plaintiff was denied admission. However, in both of the rejection letters sent to the plaintiff, none of the allegations noted in the memorandum were listed as reasons for the plaintiff's failure to gain admission to the UWW.

The plaintiff asserts that he has been denied his right to due process of law arising under the Fourteenth Amendment. Due process protects life, liberty and property. Protected property interests are usually created and defined by sources such as state laws. . . . A student's interest in attending a university is a property right protected by due process. . . . And in any event, even though the plaintiff was denied admission, the circumstances of this case make it more like an expulsion case than a non-admission case. The plaintiff lost existing scholarship rights; he cannot enroll in another college without sitting out one year of competition under athletic rules; and although he has attended the defendant University for several years, he may no longer register for day classes at the defendant University.

But to say that due process applies in the area of a student's interest in attending a university does not finish the analysis. One must [now] answer the question of what process is due. . . . Factors balanced to determine what process is due are: 1) the private interest affected by the action; 2) the risk of an erroneous deprivation of such interest through the procedures used and the value of additional procedural safeguards; and 3) the government's interest involved, including fiscal and administrative burdens. . . .

The private interest at stake here, although ostensibly academic, is the plaintiff's ability to obtain a "no cut" contract with the National Basketball Association. The bachelor of arts, while a mark of achievement and distinction, does not in and of itself assure the applicant a means of earning a living. This applicant seems to recognize this and has opted to use his college career as a means of entry into professional sports as do many college athletes. His basketball career will be little affected by the absence or presence of a bachelor of arts degree. This plaintiff has put all of his "eggs" into the "basket" of professional basketball. The plaintiff would suffer a substantial loss if his career objectives were impaired.

The government's interest, i.e., the defendant University's interest, is the administrative burden of requiring a hearing or other due process safeguards for every rejection of every student who applies to the University. This burden would be tremendous and this Court would not require the defendant University to shoulder it. . . .

In this case, the plaintiff's applications to the UWW were treated very differently than all other applications. The directors intervened in the process and provided the admissions committee with allegations concerning the plaintiff's conduct, a facet of the proceedings that taints this "academic" process and turns it into something much like a disciplinary proceeding. Given this aspect of the proceedings, it would appear that the plaintiff should have at least been notified that allegations had been made regarding his conduct so that he could have presented evidence in his own behalf. Without this safeguard, there exists a chance that the plaintiff may have been wrongfully accused of actions which then form the basis for his rejection. . . .

It appears from the record that there is a "tug of war" going on over this plaintiff. The academicians are pulling toward higher standards of achievement for all students while the athletic department must tug in the direction of fielding teams who contribute to paying a substantial share of the university's budget. In this tug of war the academic department will suffer substantially no ill effects if it loses. On the other hand, the athletic department, directors, coaches and personnel under this system are charged with the responsibility of at least maintaining and fielding teams which are capable of competing with the best in their conference or in the nation. This Court is not called upon to determine any long term solution to the dilemma posed. It is called upon to determine if the rights of an individual caught up in the struggle have been violated.

The only perceivable harm to the defendant University would result from the fact that the National Collegiate Athletic Association (NCAA), of which the defendant University is a member, has rules which permit certain sanctions to be leveled upon the defendant University should a player be declared eligible under a court order which is later vacated, stayed, reversed, etc. This rule defines sanctions including the vacation of the athlete's records for the period for which the athlete played, the forfeiture of games by the team, the declaration of ineligibility of the team for post-season tournaments, to the return of television receipts for games that the athlete played in. However, in this regard, the defendant University's destiny is in its own hands. The University does not have to appeal this Order if it is fearful of the sanctions which might be imposed by the NCAA. And the defendant University's lawyer is of the opinion that the NCAA could not force an appeal. Therefore, an appeal with all of the usual uncertainties accompanying it is not mandated. It would be the defendant University's choice whether it wants to risk these sanctions at this time. . . .

During the summer of 1981, the plaintiff enrolled in 30 credits of classes at the defendant University and successfully completed 26. The plaintiff received three "A's" four "B's" and one "C," and one "satisfactory." Dean Lupton and the defendants' other witnesses were unable to satisfactorily explain to this Court why the plaintiff's most recent academic endeavor would not be good evidence in assessing his capabilities and present attitudes or why they did not evidence "progress in his academic career." Although these courses were not the most esoteric in their nature, they were offered for credit by the defendant University. . . .

This Court is of the opinion that the plaintiff has shown a substantial probability of success on at least his claim regarding the UWW. It is conceivable that the UWW may have had reason to deny the plaintiff admission to its degree program. However, the manner in which the UWW processed the plaintiff's application strongly suggests that he has been treated disparately and in a manner violative of due process. The plaintiff was given no notice nor any opportunity to answer the allegations leveled against him by the Dean of the General College. It is equally conceivable that the plaintiff would have had a "good answer" to these charges had he been given an opportunity to respond.

Balancing all of the above factors, this Court concludes that an injunction should issue requiring the defendant University to admit the plaintiff into a degree program on January 4, 1982 and to declare him eligible to compete in intercollegiate varsity basketball competition. . . .

2. Red-Shirting

The term "red-shirting" refers to the process of holding back students academically so they can mature physically. Many rules in high schools (and colleges) are designed to minimize the effect of red-shirting. These rules, as a group, are known as "anti-red-shirting rules." Also, some athletic associations have devised eligibility rules to prevent red-shirting. These rules are broadly classified as four-year-rules, eight-semester-rules, or age rules. These regulations have in common the goal of restricting eligibility to a certain time period, thus thwarting attempts by the schools to red-shirt athletes with potential.

Many other eligibility rules exist in both high schools and colleges that restrict athletic eligibility on the basis of other considerations that regulatory board administrators deem to be anticompetitive or believe might tend to negatively affect an athlete's amateur standing.

3. No Transfer

The "no-transfer rule" was created to stop the negative effect of recruiting athletes from one school district to another with the intent of creating "super" teams. A rule of this type usually is viewed as rationally related to a legitimate state purpose of preventing school-shopping by athletes and preventing athletes' recruitment by coaches. The courts usually view this type of regulation as not violative of equal protection.

However, in *Sullivan v. University Interscholastic League* a variant of a no-transfer rule did not pass constitutional muster. The rule in question provided that a student who had represented a high school other than his present school in either football or basketball was ineligible for one calendar year after moving to another district to participate in the same sport.

SULLIVAN V. UNIVERSITY INTERSCHOLASTIC LEAGUE

616 S.W.2d 170 (Tex. 1981)

SPEARS, Justice.

Petitioner, John Sullivan, through his father and next friend, Joe Sullivan, brought suit individually and as representative of a class action against the University Interscholastic League, two U.I.L officials, the Austin Independent School District, and four named school officials. Sullivan challenged the constitutional validity of the U.I.L.'s student transfer rule contained in Section 14 Article VIII of the Constitution and Contest Rules of the University Interscholastic League. Sullivan sought declaratory and injunctive relief and individually sought damages under 24 U.S.C § 1983. . . .

The four named school officials filed a motion presenting two grounds for summary judgment: (1) that the rule is constitutional, and (2) there is no genuine issue as to any material fact necessary to establish their affirmative defense of immunity to the damage claim. . . . The trial court granted both motions for summary judgment on all points before it.

. . . The court of civil appeals affirmed the judgment of the trial court. We affirm in part and reverse and remand in part the judgment of the court of civil appeals.

The U.I.L. is a voluntary non-profit association of public schools which is a part of the Division of Continuing Education of The University of Texas. All public schools are eligible for membership in the U.I.L., and its conduct has been held to constitute state action. . . . The U.I.L. promulgated the original transfer rule in 1933, to discourage recruitment of promising athletes. Essentially this rule provides that a student who has represented a high school (other than his present school) in either football or basketball is ineligible, for one calendar year after moving to another district, to participate in the same sport in the school to which he changes. . . .

In March 1977, John Sullivan moved with his family from Vermont to Austin because his father's employment was transferred. John played high school basketball in Vermont but it is undisputed that he was not recruited to play in the Austin schools. When John enrolled in school, he was told that he was ineligible to play U.I.L. sponsored varsity basketball because of the one-year transfer rule.

We granted Sullivan's application for writ of error on three points which are interrelated. First, the transfer rule is not rationally related to the purpose of deterring recruitment of high school athletes. In other words, the enforcement of the transfer rule deprives Sullivan of his Fourteenth Amendment right of equal protection. Second, the rule infringes upon Sullivan's fundamental right of familial privacy. Third, the transfer rule infringes on his fundamental right to interstate travel. We find it unnecessary to discuss the right to familial privacy and travel since we hold that the transfer rule is not rationally related to the purpose of deterring recruitment and therefore the rule violates the equal protection clause of the Fourteenth Amendment. . . .

The transfer rule creates two classes of students: those who do not transfer from one school to another, as compared to those who transfer. The rule treats these two classes of students differently by permitting members of the first group to compete in interscholastic activities without any delay while imposing a one-year period of ineligibility on the second group. The purpose of the transfer rule was to discourage recruitment of high school athletes. This is a legitimate state purpose. However, equal protection analysis still requires us to "reach and determine the question whether the classifications drawn in a statute are reasonable in light of its purpose." . . .

In practical effect, the challenged classification simply does not operate rationally to deter recruitment. The U.I.L. rule is overbroad and over-inclusive. The rule burdens many high school athletes who were not recruited and were forced to move when their family moved for employment or other reasons. The fact that there is no means of rebutting the presumption that all transferring athletes have been recruited illustrates the capriciousness of the rule. The inclusion of athletes who have legitimately transferred with recruited athletes does not further the purpose of the transfer rule. Under strict equal protection analysis the classification must include all those similarly situated with respect to purpose. . . . It is clear that the transfer rule broadly affects athletes who are not similarly situated. . . .

We hold that the transfer rule violates the equal protection clause of the Constitution, and Sullivan and his class are entitled to the injunctive and declaratory relief sought.

Because we hold that the transfer rule is unconstitutional, we find it unnecessary to pass on Sullivan's other points attacking the constitutionality of the rule.

4. Summer Camp Rule

Literally hundreds of rules have been developed to limit eligibility. Many of these rules are designed to stop coaches, schools, and school districts from developing "super" teams. One such attempt is the rule that disallows athletes from attending same-sport summer camps.

In the case of *Kite v. Marshall* the court held that a Texas variant of this rule was constitutional. This rule allowed for a one-year suspension of an athlete's high school eligibility if the student attended certain same-sport summer training camps.

KITE V. MARSHALL

661 F.2d 1027 (5th Cir. 1981)

POLITZ, Circuit Judge:

These consolidated actions challenge the validity of Section 21 of Article VIII of the Constitution and Contest Rules of the University Interscholastic League (UIL) of Texas. The challenged section suspends for one year the varsity athletics eligibility of any high school student who attends certain training camps. The district court enjoined the enforcement of section 21 and subsequently declared the rule unconstitutional as applied. We reverse.

UIL is a voluntary, non-profit association of public schools below collegiate rank in the State of Texas. It functions as an integral part of the Division of Continuing Education of the University of Texas at Austin. . . .

We must determine whether section 21 violates either the due process or equal protection clause of that amendment. . . .

The instant case presents a similar inquiry. Reduced to essentials, the legal questions posed are: (1) whether parents possess a fundamental right to send their children to summer athletic camps; and (2) whether the children have a constitutional right to attend such activities. As is frequently the case in the very postulation of the questions the answer lies. A negative response to both questions is mandated. This case implicates no fundamental constitutional right.

The determination that no fundamental right to participate in summer athletic camp exists establishes the level of scrutiny to which we must subject section 21. The regulation will pass constitutional muster if it is found to have a rational basis.

Due Process

The UIL contends that its rules are designed to make competition among its 1,142 member schools as fair and equitable as possible. The UIL program, including the athletics component, is only a part of the overall educational process. Several reasons are advanced in support of section 21, including the need to control over-zealous coaches, parents and communities, the achieving of a competitive balance between those who can afford to attend summer camp and those who cannot, the avoidance of various excessive pressures on students, and the abrogation of the use of camps as recruiting mechanisms. . . .

Equal Protection

Traditionally, the equal protection analysis has been performed against the backdrop of the standards of strict scrutiny and minimum rationality. To withstand strict scrutiny, a statute must necessarily relate to a compelling state interest. The rational basis test requires only that the legislation or regulation under challenge rationally promote a legitimate governmental objective.

A state action viewed under the rational basis banner is presumed to be valid. In such a situation, "the burden is not upon the state to establish the rationality of its restriction, but is upon the challenger to show that the restriction is wholly arbitrary." Accordingly, only when a demonstration is made that the classification contained in the regulation is wholly arbitrary or does not teleologically relate to a permissible governmental objective is the equal protection clause violated. When "the classification created by the regulatory scheme neither trammels fundamental rights or interests nor burdens an inherently suspect class, equal protection analysis requires that the classification be rationally related to a legitimate state interest."

In view of the Supreme Court's prevailing opinions . . . , we believe that the minimum rationality test provides the guide for our equal protection evaluation.

Admittedly section 21 operates to treat student-athletes who attend summer athletic camps differently from those students who do not. The former lose eligibility in all varsity sports for the next year. But the categorization is not premised on impermissible, suspect grounds. Nor does the classification impinge upon the exercise of fundamental rights. The rule seeks to achieve a balance in interscholastic athletics. It is not unconstitutional.

The judgment of the district court, in these consolidated cases, is reversed.

5. Anti-marriage

Eligibility rules that usually do not pass constitutional standards are those that infringe on a fundamental right. The classic example is the no-marriage rule that prohibits married high school students from participating in high school sports.

In *Bell v. Lone Oak Independent School District*, a regulation that prohibited married high school students from participating in extracurricular activities was found to violate the Equal Protection Clause.

BELL V. LONE OAK INDEPENDENT SCHOOL DISTRICT

507 S.W.2d 636 (Tex. Ct. Civ. App. 1979)

RAY, Justice.

This is a suit to enjoin the enforcement of a school regulation that prohibits married students from participating in extra-curricular activities. Edward Ray Bell, appellant (petitioner), brought suit against the Lone Oak Independent School District and the Board of Trustees of Lone Oak Independent School District, appellees (respondents), seeking a temporary restraining order and injunction against the school and its Board of Trustees to prevent the enforcement of the "married-student rule" so that Bell could play on the local football team. A hearing was held by the trial court and it denied the temporary injunction. Appellant filed his appeal to this court and also filed his application here for a temporary restraining order and temporary injunction to prevent his cause from becoming moot and to preserve the jurisdiction of this court. We granted the temporary restraining order and, after hearing, granted the temporary injunction pending the final disposition of the case.

. . . Appellant contends that the temporary injunction should have been granted by the trial court because the school regulation concerning married students sets up an arbitrary and unreasonable classification that is invalid under 42 U.S.C.A. Sec. 1983, and the Fourteenth Amendment to the U.S. Constitution; that the school regulation was applied in an arbitrary manner; that the regulation infringes upon the right to marry; that the trial court should have applied federal statutes and decisions in making its decision, rather than applying state statutes and decisions; that appellant was denied the right to participate in school activities paid for out of school funds provided under Art. 2902, Tex. Rev. Civ. Statutes. . . .

Basically, we feel that local school officials are in the best position to manage the affairs of the local school district and the local schools. "The quicker judges get out of the business of running schools the better." . . .

The quoted rule of the Lone Oak Independent School District Sets up a classification of individuals to be treated differently from the remainder of the school students without being designed to promote a compelling state interest. As such, the rule violate 42 U.S.C.A., Sec. 1983, and the Fourteenth Amendment to the United States Constitution. There can be no doubt in anyone's mind that if the same rule provided that a particular race or color of person would be ineligible to play football, the state courts and federal courts would promptly strike the rule down as being discriminatory towards a class of individuals. The same logic applies to married students' participation in extra-curricular activities. Appellees have not shown a clear and present danger to the other students' physical or emotional safety and well-being, or any other danger to the students, faculty, or school property, nor any substantial or material danger to the operation of the public schools by allowing married students to participate in athletics. The burden of proof is upon the school district to show that its rule should be upheld as a necessary restraint to promote a compelling state interest.

It is the public policy of this state to encourage marriage rather than living together unmarried. . . .

It may be that an education is not a guaranteed right under our Federal Constitution. It may further be that a school cannot constitutionally be required to provide a student with an athletic program, but if the state and the local school provide free public education and an athletic program, it must do so in a manner not calculated to discriminate against a class of individuals who will be treated differently from the remainder of the students, unless the school district can show that such rule is a necessary restraint to promote a compelling state interest. In the present case, the evidence is legally insufficient to establish that the rule in question is a necessary restraint to promote a compelling state interest, that is, the prevention of drop-outs from secondary schools.

Right to marry is fundamental

. . . This court has concluded that the injunctive relief sought by appellant Bell should have been granted by the trial court because the appellees did not establish that the rule against married students participating in extracurricular activities was a necessary restraint to promote a compelling state interest. We hold as a matter of law that as to married students the questioned rule is on its face discriminatory and in violation of 42 U.S.C.A. § 1983 and the Fourteenth Amendment of the United States Constitution.

The trial court erred in failing to issue the temporary injunction sought by appellant. The judgement of the trial court is reversed and remanded with instructions to issue a temporary injunction enjoining the Lone Oak Independent School District and its Board of Trustees from enforcing the rule prohibiting Edward Ray Bell from participating in football activities of the Lone Oak Independent School District and from excluding him from membership on the school football team because of his marital status. . . .

QUESTIONS AND DISCUSSION

1. *See Boyd v. Board of Directors of the McGehee Sch. Dist. No. 17*, 612 F. Supp. 86 (E.D. Ark. 1985) (football player was suspended by coach for remainder of season; coach was liable for depriving his players of their First Amendment rights when they were suspended after they walked out of pep rally and refused to participate in a scheduled game due to their reasonable belief that the coach purposely manipulated election so as to deprive school of its first black homecoming queen); *Tiffany v. Arizona Interscholastic League, Inc.*, 726 P.2d 231 (Ariz. Ct. App. 1986) (student did not have constitutional right, which was violated, when he was not granted hardship waiver from 19-year-old eligibility rule; but, it was also held that the executive board of the interscholastic athletic association had acted unreasonably, capriciously, and arbitrarily when it failed to exercise its discretion in considering the athlete's request for a hardship waiver on the basis that he was held back in the first grade due to a learning disability).

2. The opportunity to participate in extracurricular activities is not by itself a property interest; however, under certain circumstances, high school student-athletes can establish an entitlement to due process in connection with their suspension and exclusion from sports. See *Tiffany* and *Boyd*.

3. Eligibility questions run the gamut of possible restrictions and include transfer students, marriage, age, grade point average, hair length, hair adornments, and alcohol, drug, and cigarette usage. *Menora v. Illinois High Sch. Assn.* 683 F.2d 1030 (7th Cir. 1982) (ban on basketball players wearing hats included yarmulkes); *Long v. Zopp*, 476 F.2d 180 (4th Cir. 1973) (hair length limitation reasonable but only during season and only for health and safety reasons); *Fusato v. Washington Interscholastic Activities Assn.*, 970 P.2d 774 (Wash App. 1999) (narrow construction against foreign exchange student of hardship exception on transfer eligibility violates equal protection); *See, e.g., Robbins v. Indiana High Sch. Athletic Assn.*, 941 F. Supp. 786 (S.D. Ind. 1996) (transfer rule does not violate Constitution even when the transfer was motivated by religious conversion); *Moran v. School Dist. #7, Yellowstone County*, 350 F. Supp. 1180 (D. Mont. 1972) (prohibition on married students disallowed); *Indiana High Sch. Athletic Assn. v. Carlberg*, 694 N.E.2d 222 (Ind. 1998) (transfer rule advances legitimate association interest); *Bunger v. Iowa High Sch. Athletic Assn.*, 197 N.W.2d 555 (Iowa. 1972) (drinking outside school year not within high school athletic association's scope).

4. Regarding the distinction between participation as a right and participation as a privilege, *Boyd* discussed the different ways in which intercollegiate and high school sports are viewed.

> There is a vast difference between high school football and college football. A high school athlete receives no present economic benefit from playing high school football, his only economic benefit being the possibility of receiving an offer of a college scholarship. The *Scott* case . . . has that such a possibility was too speculative to recognize as a property right [in the context of a high school situation]. In contrast a college athlete receives a scholarship of substantial pecuniary value to engage in college sports. Such scholarships often cover the complete cost of attending a college or university; therefore, the right to be eligible to participate in college athletics cannot be viewed as a mere speculative interest, but is a property right of present economic value. *Gulf South Conference v. Boyd*, 369 So. 2d 553, 556 (Ala. 1979).

What could be added to high school sports to make it more than a mere speculative interest? Did LeBron James, the next Michael Jordan, have more than a mere speculative interest in the continuance of his last few weeks in his high school career?

D. STATE ACTORS

The importance of determining if a regulating entity is a state actor is because the protections of the Fourteenth Amendment Due Process and Equal Protection Clauses do not extend to private conduct that abridges only individual rights. As regards the actions of the National Collegiate Athletic Association (NCAA), after *Tarkanian* the NCAA's interactions regarding student eligibility will probably no longer be viewed as state action. However, all actions by a state high school activities association will usually be construed as state action for constitutional purposes.

In *NCAA v. Tarkanian*, the Supreme Court held that a university's implementation of disciplinary sanctions against its basketball coach in compliance with NCAA rules and recommendations did not turn the NCAA's otherwise private conduct into state action.

NATIONAL COLLEGIATE ATHLETIC ASSOCIATION V. TARKANIAN

488 U.S. 179 (1988)

Justice STEVENS delivered the opinion of the Court.

When he became head basketball coach at the University of Nevada, Las Vegas (UNLV), in 1973, Jerry Tarkanian inherited a team with a mediocre 14-14 record. Four years later the team won 29 out of 32 games and placed third in the championship tournament sponsored by the National Collegiate Athletic Association (NCAA), to which UNLV belongs.

Yet in September 1977 UNLV informed Tarkanian that it was going to suspend him. No dissatisfaction with Tarkanian, once described as "the 'winningest' active basketball coach," motivated his suspension. Rather, the impetus was a report by the NCAA detailing 38 violations of NCAA rules by UNLV personnel, including 10 involving Tarkanian. The NCAA had placed the university's basketball team on probation for two years and ordered UNLV to show cause why the NCAA should not impose further penalties unless UNLV severed all ties during the probation between its intercollegiate athletic program and Tarkanian.

Facing demotion and a drastic cut in pay, Tarkanian brought suit in Nevada state court, alleging that he had been deprived of his Fourteenth Amendment due process rights in violation of 42 U.S.C. § 1983. Ultimately Tarkanian obtained injunctive relief and an award of attorney's fees against both UNLV and the NCAA. NCAA's liability may be upheld only if its participation in the events that led to Tarkanian's suspension constituted "state action" prohibited by the Fourteenth Amendment and was performed "under color of" state law within the meaning of § 1983. We granted certiorari to review the Nevada Supreme Court's holding that the NCAA engaged in state action when it conducted its investigation and recommended that Tarkanian be disciplined. We now reverse.

I

In order to understand the four separate proceedings that gave rise to the question we must decide, it is useful to begin with a description of the relationship among the three parties—Tarkanian, UNLV, and the NCAA.

Tarkanian initially was employed on a year-to-year basis but became a tenured professor in 1977. He receives an annual salary with valuable fringe benefits, and his status as a highly successful coach enables him to earn substantial additional income from sports-related activities such as broadcasting and the sponsorship of products.

UNLV is a branch of the University of Nevada, a state-funded institution. The university is organized and operated pursuant to provisions of Nevada's State Constitution, statutes, and regulations. In performing their official functions, the executives of UNLV unquestionably act under color of state law.

The NCAA is an unincorporated association of approximately 960 members, including virtually all public and private universities and 4-year colleges conducting major athletic programs in the United States. Basic policies of the NCAA are determined by the members at annual conventions. Between conventions, the Association is governed by its Council, which appoints various committees to implement specific programs.

One of the NCAA's fundamental policies "is to maintain intercollegiate athletics as an integral part of the educational program and the athlete as an integral part of the student body, and by so doing, retain a clear line of demarcation between college athletics and professional sports." It has there-fore adopted rules, which it calls "legislation," governing the conduct of the intercollegiate athletic programs of its members. This NCAA legislation applies to a variety of issues, such as academic standards for eligibility, admis-sions, financial aid, and the recruiting of student athletes. By joining the NCAA, each member agrees to abide by and to enforce such rules.

The NCAA's bylaws provide that its enforcement program shall be administered by a Committee on Infractions. The Committee supervises an investigative staff, makes factual determinations concerning alleged rule violations, and is expressly authorized to "impose appropriate penalties on a member found to be in violation, or recommend to the Council suspension or termination of membership." In particular, the Committee may order a member institution to show cause why that member should not suffer further penalties unless it imposes a prescribed discipline on an employee; it is not authorized, however, to sanction a member institution's employees directly. The bylaws also provide that representatives of member institutions "are expected to cooperate fully" with the administration of the enforcement program. The bylaws do not purport to confer any subpoena power on the Committee or its investigators. . . .

The NCAA Investigation of UNLV

On November 28, 1972, the Committee on Infractions notified UNLV's president that it was initiating a preliminary inquiry into alleged violations of NCAA requirements by UNLV. . . .

With the assistance of the Attorney General of Nevada and private counsel, UNLV conducted a thorough investigation of the charges. . . .

The Committee proposed a series of sanctions against UNLV, including a 2-year period of probation during which its basketball team could not participate in postseason games or appear on television. . . .

UNLV's Discipline of Tarkanian

Promptly after receiving the NCAA report, the president of UNLV directed the University's vice president to schedule a hearing to determine whether the Committee's recommended sanctions should be applied. . . .

Pursuant to the vice president's recommendation, the president accepted the second option and notified Tarkanian that he was to "be completely severed of any and all relations, formal or informal, with the University's Intercollegiate athletic program during the period of the University's NCAA probation."

Tarkanian's Lawsuit Against UNLV

The day before his suspension was to become effective, Tarkanian filed an action in Nevada state court for declaratory and injunctive relief against UNLV and a number of its officers. He alleged that these defendants had, in violation of 42 U.S.C. § 1983, deprived him of property and liberty without the due process of law guaranteed by the Fourteenth Amendment to the United States Constitution. Based on a stipulation of facts and the testimony offered by Tarkanian, the trial court enjoined UNLV from suspending Tarkanian on the ground that he had been denied procedural and substantive due process of law. UNLV appealed. . . .

The Lawsuit Against NCAA

Tarkanian consequently filed a second amended complaint adding the NCAA. The defendants promptly removed the suit to Federal District Court on the ground that joinder of the NCAA substantially had altered the nature of the litigation. The District Court held, however, that the original defendants had waived their right to remove the suit when it was first filed, and therefore granted Tarkanian's motion to remand the case to the state court. After a 4-year delay, the trial judge conducted a 2-week bench trial and resolved the issues in Tarkanian's favor. The court concluded that NCAA's conduct constituted state action for jurisdictional and constitutional purposes, and that its decision was arbitrary and capricious. It reaffirmed its earlier injunction barring UNLV from disciplining Tarkanian or otherwise enforcing the Confidential Report. . . .

The Nevada Supreme Court agreed that Tarkanian had been deprived of both property and liberty protected by the Constitution and that he was not afforded due process before suspension. It thus affirmed the trial court's injunction insofar as it pertained to Tarkanian, but narrowed its scope "only to prohibit enforcement of the penalties imposed upon Tarkanian in Confidential Report No. 123(47) and UNLV's adoption of those penalties." The court also reduced the award of attorney's fees.

As a predicate for its disposition, the State Supreme Court held that the NCAA had engaged in state action. . . .

II

Embedded in our Fourteenth Amendment jurisprudence is a dichotomy between state action, which is subject to scrutiny under the Amendment's Due Process Clause, and private conduct, against which the Amendment affords no shield, no matter how unfair that conduct may be. As a general matter the protections of the Fourteenth Amendment do not extend to "private conduct abridging individual rights." . . .

When Congress enacted § 1983 as the statutory remedy for violations of the Constitution, it specified that the conduct at issue must have occurred "under color of" state law; thus, liability attaches only to those wrongdoers "who carry a badge of authority of a State and represent it in some capacity, whether they act in accordance with their authority or misuse it." . . .

In this case Tarkanian argues that the NCAA was a state actor because it misused power that it possessed by virtue of state law. He claims specifically that UNLV delegated its own functions to the NCAA, clothing the Association with authority both to adopt rules governing UNLV's athletic programs and to enforce those rules on behalf of UNLV. Similarly, the Nevada Supreme Court held that UNLV had delegated its authority over personnel decisions to the NCAA. Therefore, the court reasoned, the two entities acted jointly to deprive Tarkanian of liberty and property interests, making the NCAA as well as UNLV a state actor.

These contentions fundamentally misconstrue the facts of this case. In the typical case raising a state-action issue, a private party has taken the decisive step that caused the harm to the plaintiff, and the question is whether the State was sufficiently involved to treat that decisive conduct as state action. This may occur if the State creates the legal framework governing the conduct, if it delegates its authority to the private actor, or sometimes if it knowingly accepts the benefits derived from unconstitutional behavior. Thus, in the usual case we ask whether the State provided a mantle of authority that enhanced the power of the harm-causing individual actor.

This case uniquely mirrors the traditional state-action case. Here the final act challenged by Tarkanian—his suspension—was committed by UNLV. A state university without question is a state actor. When it decides to impose a serious disciplinary sanction upon one of its tenured employees, it must comply with the terms of the Due Process Clause of the Fourteenth Amendment to the Federal Constitution. *Thus when UNLV notified Tarkanian that he was being separated from all relations with the university's basketball program, it acted under color of state law within the meaning of 42 U.S.C. § 1983*

The mirror image presented in this case requires us to step through an analytical looking glass to resolve the case. Clearly UNLV's conduct was influenced by the rules and recommendations of the NCAA, the private party. But it was UNLV, the state entity, that actually suspended Tarkanian. Thus the question is not whether UNLV participated to a critical extent in the NCAA's activities, but whether UNLV's actions in compliance with the NCAA rules and recommendations turned the NCAA's conduct into state action. [The Court ruled that the rules and conduct of the NCAA did not constitute state action.] . . .

Finally, Tarkanian argues that the power of the NCAA is so great that the UNLV had no practical alternative to compliance with its demands. We are not at all sure this is true, but even if we assume that a private monopolist can impose its will on a state agency by a threatened refusal to deal with it, it does not follow that such a private party is therefore acting under color of state law.

In final analysis the question is whether "the conduct allegedly causing the deprivation of a federal right [can] be fairly attributable to the State." It would be ironic indeed to conclude that the NCAA's imposition of sanctions against UNLV—sanctions that UNLV and its counsel, including the Attorney General of Nevada, steadfastly opposed during protracted adversary proceedings—is fairly attributable to the State of Nevada. It would be more appropriate to conclude that UNLV has conducted its athletic program under color of the policies adopted by the NCAA, rather than that those policies were developed and enforced under color of Nevada law.

The judgment of the Nevada Supreme Court is reversed, and the case is remanded to that court for further proceedings not inconsistent with this opinion.

It is so ordered.

Justice WHITE, with whom Justice BRENNAN, Justice MARSHALL, and Justice O'CONNOR join, dissenting.

All agree that UNLV, a public university, is a state actor, and that the suspension of Jerry Tarkanian, a public employee, was state action. The question here is whether the NCAA acted jointly with UNLV in suspending Tarkanian and thereby also became a state actor. I would hold that it did. . . .

In short, it was the NCAA's findings that Tarkanian had violated NCAA rules, made at NCAA-conducted hearings, all of which were agreed to by UNLV in its membership agreement with the NCAA, that resulted in Tarkanian's suspension by UNLV. On these facts, the NCAA was "jointly engaged with [UNLV] officials in the challenged action." and therefore was a state actor. . . .

I respectfully dissent.

The case of *NCAA v. Miller* is a follow-up to *NCAA v. Tarkanian.* In *Miller,* the NCAA sought a declaratory judgment to the effect that Nevada's statutes that required any national collegiate athlete association to provide additional procedural due process protections in enforcement proceedings against Nevada colleges and universities violated the Commerce Clause of the U.S. Constitution.

NATIONAL COLLEGIATE ATHLETIC ASSOCIATION V. MILLER

10 F.3d 633 (9th Cir. 1993)

FERNANDEZ, Circuit Judge:

Jerry Tarkanian, Tim Grgurich, Ronald Ganulin, and Shelley Fischer appeal the district court's order declaring that the provisions of Nevada Revised Statutes §§398.155-398.255 ("the Statute"), which impose certain requirements on interstate national collegiate athletic associations, violate Article I, Section 8, Clause 3 (the Commerce Clause) and Article I, Section 10 (the Contract Clause) of the United States Constitution. The district court granted the declaratory judgement and enjoined appellants from taking any action to seek protection under the Statute. We affirm.

Background

The National Collegiate Athletic Association ("NCAA") is a voluntary, unincorporated association of 1,056 members, including four-year colleges and universities, conferences, associations, and other educational institutions. Members of the NCAA are located in each of the United States.

Among the purposes of the NCAA are these: 1) "to initiate, stimulate and improve intercollegiate athletics programs for student-athletes"; 2) "to uphold the principle of institutional control of, and responsibility for, all intercollegiate sports in conformity with the constitution and bylaws of this Association"; 3) "to encourage its members to adopt eligibility rules to comply with satisfactory standards of scholarship, sportsmanship and amateurism"; 4) "to formulate . . . and publish rules of play governing intercollegiate athletics"; 5) "to supervise the conduct of, and to establish eligibility standards for, regional and national athletics events"; 6) "to legislate, through bylaws or by resolutions of a Convention, upon any subject of general concern to the members related to the administration of intercollegiate athletics[;]" and 7) "to maintain intercollegiate athletics as an integral part of the educational program and the athlete as an integral part of the student body and, by so doing, retain a clear line of demarcation between intercollegiate athletics and professional sports." NCAA Const. §§1.2 and 1.3.1. The Association is also entrusted with the responsibility of promoting the opportunity for competitive equity among its member institutions.

At the annual convention, the member institutions of the NCAA enact legislation dealing with athlete recruiting, eligibility, financial aid, admissions, and other matters. All NCAA legislation must be adopted by a vote of the active members. NCAA legislation consists of both substantive rules and a procedural enforcement program. As a condition of membership, each institution is obligated to apply and enforce all NCAA legislation related to its own athletic programs. The NCAA Manual also specifically provides that: "the enforcement procedures of the Association shall be applied to an institution when it fails to fulfill this obligation."

Whenever an alleged rules violation is reported to the NCAA, the matter is handled pursuant to the enforcement program. The enforcement program is administered by the Committee on Infractions, which establishes investigation procedures that must later be approved by the NCAA Council and the full membership of the NCAA. The Manual details the procedures that must be followed in processing an infractions case. NCAA Bylaws 19, 32.

The first step in the process is for the enforcement staff to notify the institution in question that the NCAA is making a preliminary inquiry into the institution's athletics policies and practices. NCAA Bylaw 32.2.2.4. If the enforcement staff determines that a possible rule violation has occurred, it sends an official inquiry letter to the chief executive officer of the institution. The official inquiry must include a statement of the NCAA rule alleged to have been violated and the details of each separate allegation. The enforcement staff must also provide the institution and other involved individuals with the names of the principals involved and the names, addresses and telephone numbers of any people contacted during the NCAA investigation. The institution is required to notify past or present staff members or prospective, past, or present student-athletes who may be affected by the charges that they have the opportunity to submit any information they desire to the Committee and that they and their personal legal counsel may appear before the Committee. The institution is also required to investigate the charges and to indicate whether it feels that the allegations are substantially correct. It may also submit written evidence to support its response to the official inquiry. *See* NCAA Bylaw 32.5.

After the institution has submitted its written response to the official inquiry in a case involving a major violation, the enforcement staff must "prepare a summary statement of the case that indicates the status of each allegation and identifies the individuals upon whom and the information upon which the staff will rely in presenting the case." The summary is presented to the Committee, the institution, and all other affected individuals before the Committee hearing. NCAA Bylaw 32.5.10(a). The institution and affected individuals and their legal counsel are permitted to review any memoranda or documents upon which the enforcement staff will rely in the presentation of its case, but only at the NCAA national office. NCAA Bylaw 32.5.10(b).

Prior to the Committee on Infractions hearing, prehearing conferences are held with the NCAA staff, the institution and all affected individuals and their legal counsel. At those meetings, the NCAA staff is required to provide all of the information upon which it intends to rely at the hearing. All involved parties review the relevant documents. Areas of factual dispute are identified. Unsupported allegations may be withdrawn and the institution and affected individuals can determine whether they need to conduct any further interviews in order to supplement their responses to the official inquiry. NCAA Bylaw 32.5.10(c).

The Committee on Infractions hearing consists of a detailed presentation of the case by the enforcement staff followed by a response from the institution and any affected individuals (or their legal representatives) who desire to respond. NCAA Bylaw 32.6.5. After the hearing, the Committee members privately make their determinations of fact, determine appropriate corrective action, if any, and prepare their written report. NCAA Bylaws 32.6.6, 32.7. The institution is entitled to appeal the Committee's findings of fact and any corrective action taken against it to the NCAA Council. NCAA Bylaw 32.9.

In 1991, the Nevada legislature enacted the Statute. Essentially, the Statute requires any national collegiate athletic association to provide a Nevada institution, employee, student-athlete, or booster who is accused of a rules infraction with certain procedural due process protections during an enforcement proceeding in which sanctions may be imposed. Many of the procedures required by the Statute are not included in the NCAA enforcement program. For example, the NCAA does not provide the accused with the right to confront all witnesses, the right to have all written statements signed under oath and notarized, the right to have an official record kept of all proceedings, or the right to judicial review of a Committee decision.

The Statute provides that a state district court may enjoin any NCAA proceeding that violates the statutory provisions. Furthermore an aggrieved institution which raises a successful challenge under the Statute is entitled to costs, reasonable attorney's fees, and compensatory damages equal to "100 percent of the monetary loss per year or portion of a year which is suffered . . . as a result of a penalty imposed in violation of [the Statute]." Nev. Rev. Stat. § 398.245. Finally, the Statute prohibits an association from impairing the rights or privileges of membership of any institution as a consequence of any rights granted by sections 398.155-398.255. *Id.* § 398.235(3). Thus, the NCAA can not avoid complying with the Statute by simply expelling its Nevada members.

This action arose when appellants, who were charged with NCAA rules violations in a pending investigation of the University of Nevada, Las Vegas

("UNLV"), asserted their right to have the proceedings against them comply with the Statute. The NCAA filed a complaint for declaratory judgment and injunctive relief in which it sought a declaration that the Statute was unconstitutional because it violated the Commerce Clause and the Contract Clause. The NCAA also sought an order enjoining the application of the Statute to the infractions proceeding. The district court found that the Statute violates both the Commerce Clause and the Contracts Clause and enjoined its application to the NCAA's proceeding against the appellants. This appeal ensued.

Discussion

If either of the district court's determinations was correct, the Statute must fall. As we will demonstrate, the Statute cannot withstand Commerce Clause scrutiny. That being so, we need not and do not address the Contract Clause issue. . . .

B. The Statute Violates the Commerce Clause Per Se

The district court held that the Statute does not violate the Commerce Clause per se because it does not directly discriminate against interstate commerce or favor in-state economic interests over out-of-state interests. That holding was error because discrimination and economic protectionism are not the sole tests. The court should also have considered whether the Statute directly regulates interstate commerce. . . .

The Statute would have a profound effect on the way the NCAA enforces its rules and regulates the integrity of its product. The district court found that in order for the NCAA to accomplish its goals, the "enforcement procedures must be applied even-handedly and uniformly on a national basis." That finding is not only correct, but is also consistent with the Supreme Court's statement that the integrity of the NCAA's product cannot be preserved "except by mutual agreement; if an institution adopted [its own athlete eligibility regulations] unilaterally, its effectiveness as a competitor on the playing field might soon be destroyed."

In order to avoid liability under the Statute, the NCAA would be forced to adopt Nevada's procedural rules for Nevada schools. Therefore, if the NCAA wished to have the uniform enforcement procedures that it needs to accomplish its fundamental goals and to simultaneously avoid liability under the Statute, it would have to apply Nevada's procedures to enforcement proceedings throughout the country.

The practical requirement that the NCAA would have to use the Statute in enforcement proceedings in every state in the union runs afoul of the Commerce Clause in two ways. First, "a statute that directly controls commerce occurring wholly outside the boundaries of a State exceeds the inherent limits of the enacting State's authority and is invalid regardless of whether the statute's extraterritorial reach was intended by the legislature. The critical inquiry is whether the practical effect of the regulation is to control conduct beyond the boundaries of the State."

The Statute would force the NCAA to regulate the integrity of its product in every state according to Nevada's procedural rules. Thus, if a university in state X ("U of X") engaged in illicit practices while recruiting a high school quarterback from state Y, the NCAA would have to conduct its enforcement proceeding according to Nevada law in order to maintain uniformity in its rules. Nevada procedures do not allow the Committee on Infractions to consider some types of evidence, like hearsay and unsworn affidavits, that it can consider under the NCAA Bylaws. As a result, if its case against the U of X were based on unsworn affidavits from unavailable witnesses, the NCAA might not have enough admissible evidence to prove that there was a violation of the recruiting rules. The NCAA could be forced to allow the U of X to use an illegally recruited quarterback from state Y because it could not prove a rules violation under the strictures of Nevada law. In this way, the Statute could control the regulation of the integrity of a product in interstate commerce that occurs wholly outside Nevada's borders. That sort of extraterritorial effect is forbidden by the Commerce Clause. . . .

Nevada is not the only state that has enacted or could enact legislation that establishes procedural rules for NCAA enforcement proceedings. Florida, Illinois, and Nebraska have also adopted due process statutes and similar legislation has been introduced in five other states. Those statutes could easily subject the NCAA to conflicting requirements. For example, suppose that state X required proof of an infraction beyond a reasonable doubt, while state Y only required clear and convincing evidence, and state Z required infractions to be proven by a preponderance of the evidence. Given that the NCAA must have uniform enforcement procedures in order to accomplish its fundamental goals, its operation would be disrupted because it could not possibly comply with all three statutes. Nor would it do to say that it need only comply with the most stringent burden of persuasion (beyond a reasonable doubt), for a state with a less stringent standard might well consider its standard a maximum as well as a minimum. The serious risk of inconsistent obligations wrought by the extraterritorial effect of the Statute demonstrates why it constitutes a per se violation of the Commerce Clause. . . .

The Statute directly regulates interstate commerce and runs afoul of the Commerce Clause both because it regulates a product in interstate commerce beyond Nevada's state boundaries, and because it puts the NCAA, and whatever other national collegiate athletic associations may exist, in jeopardy of being subjected to inconsistent legislation arising from the injection of Nevada's regulatory scheme into the jurisdiction of other states. Because the Statute violates the Commerce Clause per se, we need not balance the burden on interstate commerce against the local benefit derived from the Statute.

C. The Entire Statute Must Fall . . .

Conclusion

We appreciate Nevada's interest in assuring that its citizens and institutions will be treated fairly. However, the authority it seeks here goes to the heart of the NCAA and threatens to tear that heart out. Consistency among members must exist if an organization of this type is to thrive, or even exist. Procedural changes at the border of every state would as surely disrupt the NCAA as changes in train length at each state's border would disrupt a railroad. It takes no extended lucubration to discover that. If the procedures of the NCAA are "to be regulated at all, national uniformity in the regulation adopted, such as only Congress can prescribe, is practically indispensable. . . ." In short, when weighed against the Constitution, the Statute must be found wanting. It violates the Commerce Clause.

Affirmed

In *Brentwood Academy v. Tennessee Secondary School Athletic Assn.*, the Supreme Court held that a high school interscholastic athletic association's rule that prohibited the use of undue influence in the recruitment of student-athletes was state action for purposes of the Fourteenth Amendment.

BRENTWOOD ACADEMY V. TENNESSEE SECONDARY SCHOOL ATHLETIC ASSOCIATION

531 U.S. 288 (2001)

Justice SOUTER delivered the opinion of the Court.

The issue is whether a statewide association incorporated to regulate interscholastic athletic competition among public and private secondary schools may be regarded as engaging in state action when it enforces a rule against a member school. The association in question here includes most public schools located within the State, acts through their representatives, draws its officers from them, is largely funded by their dues and income received in their stead, and has historically been seen to regulate in lieu of the State Board of Education's exercise of its own authority. We hold that the association's regulatory activity may and should be treated as state action owing to the pervasive entwinement of state school officials in the structure of the association, there being no offsetting reason to see the association's acts in any other way.

I

Respondent Tennessee Secondary School Athletic Association (Association) is a not-for-profit membership corporation organized to regulate interscholastic sport among the public and private high schools in Tennessee that belong to it. No school is forced to join, but without any other authority actually regulating interscholastic athletics, it enjoys the memberships of almost all the State's public high schools (some 290 of them or 84% of the Association's voting membership), far outnumbering the 55 private schools that belong. A member school's team may play or scrimmage only against the team of another member, absent a dispensation.

The Association's rulemaking arm is its legislative council, while its board of control tends to administration. The voting membership of each of these nine-person committees is limited under the Association's bylaws to high school principals, assistant principals, and superintendents elected by the member schools, and the public school administrators who so serve typically attend meetings during regular school hours. Although the Association's staff members are not paid by the State, they are eligible to join the State's public retirement system for its employees. Member schools pay dues to the Association, though the bulk of its revenue is gate receipts at member teams' football and basketball tournaments, many of them held in public arenas rented by the Association.

The constitution, bylaws, and rules of the Association set standards of school membership and the eligibility of students to play in interscholastic games. Each school, for example, is regulated in awarding financial aid, most coaches must have a Tennessee state teaching license, and players must meet minimum academic standards and hew to limits on student employment. Under the bylaws, "in all matters pertaining to the athletic relations of his school," the principal is responsible to the Association, which has the power "to suspend, to fine, or otherwise penalize any member school for the violation of any of the rules of the Association or for other just cause."

Ever since the Association was incorporated in 1925, Tennessee's State Board of Education (State Board) has (to use its own words) acknowledged the corporation's functions "in providing standards, rules and regulations for interscholastic competition in the public schools of Tennessee." More recently, the State Board cited its statutory authority, Tenn. Code Ann. § 49-1-302 (1996), when it adopted language expressing the relationship between the Association and the State Board. Specifically, in 1972, it went so far as to adopt a rule expressly "designat [ing]" the Association as "the organization to supervise and regulate the athletic activities in which the public junior and senior high schools in Tennessee participate on an interscholastic basis." Tennessee State Board of Education, Administrative Rules and Regulations, Rule 0520-1-2-26 (1972) (later moved to Rule 0520-1-2-08). The Rule provided that "the authority granted herein shall remain in effect until revoked" and instructed the State Board's chairman to "designate a person or persons to serve in an ex- officio capacity on the [Association's governing bodies]." That same year, the State Board specifically approved the Association's rules and regulations, while reserving the right to review future changes. Thus, on several occasions over the next 20 years, the State Board reviewed, approved, or reaffirmed its approval of the recruiting Rule at issue in this case. In 1996, however, the State Board dropped the original Rule 0520-1-2-08 expressly designating the Association as regulator; it substituted a statement "recogniz[ing] the value of participation in interscholastic athletics and the role of [the Association] in coordinating interscholastic athletic competition," while "authoriz[ing] the public schools of the state to voluntarily maintain membership in [the Association]."

The action before us responds to a 1997 regulatory enforcement proceeding brought against petitioner, Brentwood Academy, a private parochial high school member of the Association. The Association's board of control found that Brentwood violated a rule prohibiting "undue influence" in recruiting athletes, when it wrote to incoming students and their parents about spring football practice. The Association accordingly placed Brentwood's athletic program on probation for four years, declared its football and boys' basketball teams ineligible to compete in playoffs for two years, and imposed a $3,000 fine. When these penalties were imposed, all the voting members of the board of control and legislative council were public school administrators.

Brentwood sued the Association and its executive director in federal court under Rev. Stat. § 1979, 42 U.S.C. § 1983, claiming that enforcement of the Rule was state action and a violation of the First and Fourteenth Amendments. The District Court entered summary judgment for Brentwood and enjoined the Association from enforcing the Rule. *Brentwood Academy v. Tennessee Secondary Schools Athletic Association,* 13 F. Supp. 2d 670 (M.D. Tenn. 1998). In holding the Association to be a state actor under §1983 and the Fourteenth Amendment, the District Court found that the State had delegated authority over high school athletics to the Association, characterized the relationship between the Association and its public school members as symbiotic, and emphasized the predominantly public character of the Association's membership and leadership. The court relied on language in *National Collegiate Athletic Assn. v. Tarkanian,* 488 U.S. 179, 193 (1988), suggesting that statewide interscholastic athletic associations are state actors, and on other federal cases in which such organizations had uniformly been held to be acting under color of state law.

The United States Court of Appeals for the Sixth Circuit reversed. 180 F.3d 758 (1999). . . .

We granted certiorari, 528 U.S. 1153 (2000), to resolve the conflict and now reverse.

B

Just as we foresaw in *Tarkanian,* the "necessarily fact-bound inquiry" *Lugar,* 457 U.S., at 939, leads to the conclusion of state action here. The nominally private character of the Association is overborne by the pervasive entwinement of public institutions and public officials in its composition and workings, and there is no substantial reason to claim unfairness in applying constitutional standards to it. . . .

In sum, to the extent of 84% of its membership, the Association is an organization of public schools represented by their officials acting in their official capacity to provide an integral element of secondary public schooling. There would be no recognizable Association, legal or tangible, without the public school officials, who do not merely control but overwhelmingly perform all but the purely ministerial acts by which the Association exists and functions in practical terms. Only the 16% minority of private school memberships prevents this entwinement of the Association and the public school system from being total and their identities totally indistinguishable. . . .

D

This is not to say that all of the Association's arguments are rendered beside the point by the public officials' involvement in the Association, for after application of the entwinement criterion, or any other, there is a further potential issue, and the Association raises it. Even facts that suffice to show public action (or, standing alone, would require such a finding) may be outweighed in the name of some value at odds with finding public accountability in the circumstances. . . . The state-action doctrine does not convert opponents into virtual agents.

The assertion of such a countervailing value is the nub of each of the Association's two remaining arguments neither of which, however, persuades us. The Association suggests, first, that reversing the judgment here will somehow trigger an epidemic of unprecedented federal litigation. Even if that might be counted as a good reason for . . . decision to call the Association's action private, the record raises no reason for alarm here. Save for the Sixth Circuit, every Court of Appeals to consider a statewide athletic association like the one here has found it a state actor. This majority view began taking shape even before *Tarkanian,* which cited two such decisions approvingly (and this was six years after . . . *Lugar,* on which the Sixth Circuit relied here). No one, however, has pointed to any explosion of § 1983 cases against interscholastic athletic associations in the affected jurisdictions. Not to put too fine a point on it, two District Courts in Tennessee have previously held the Association itself to be a state actor, see *Graham,* 1995 WL 115890, at *5; *Crocker v. Tennessee Secondary School Athletic Assn.,* 735 F. Supp. 753 (M.D. Tenn. 1990), affirmance order, 908 F.2d 972, 973, 1990 WL 104036 (C.A.6 1990), but there is no evident wave of litigation working its way across the State. A reversal of the judgment here portends nothing more than the harmony of an outlying Circuit with precedent otherwise uniform.

Nor do we think there is anything to be said for the Association's contention that there is no need to treat it as a state actor since any public school applying the Association's rules is itself subject to suit under § 1983 or Title IX of the Education Amendments of 1972, 86 Stat. 373, 20 U.S.C. §§1681-1688. . . .

The judgment of the Court of Appeals for the Sixth Circuit is reversed, and the case is remanded for further proceedings consistent with this opinion.

It is so ordered.

Justice THOMAS, with whom THE CHIEF JUSTICE, Justice SCALIA, and Justice KENNEDY join, dissenting.

We have never found state action based upon mere "entwinement." Until today, we have found a private organization's acts to constitute state action only when the organization performed a public function; was created, coerced, or encouraged by the government; or acted in a symbiotic relationship with the government. The majority's holding—that the Tennessee Secondary School Athletic Association's (TSSAA) enforcement of its recruiting rule is state action—not only extends state-action doctrine beyond its permissible limits but also encroaches upon the realm of individual freedom that the doctrine was meant to protect. I respectfully dissent. . . .

QUESTIONS AND DISCUSSION

1. As regards *Tarkanian,* it is a narrowly drawn opinion that establishes only that the NCAA, in that case, did not assume the role of the state when it directed UNLV, a state university, to initiate certain particular actions against one of its employees (Jerry "Tark the Shark" Tarkanian).
2. But *Tarkanian* does not definitely settle the question of whether the NCAA can ever be classified as a state actor. The *Tarkanian* court observed that removing a coach from a state institution *is* state action; however, here, the NCAA did not play a part (per se) in that particular action.

3. Even after 1988, when the U.S. Supreme Court ruled on *Tarkanian*, state action still might lie if a state university by embracing the NCAA's rules is able to transform them into state rules and thereby (arguably) transforming the NCAA into a state actor. An example could be that some states have passed legislation that provides for liability for violation of an NCAA rule. Legislation of this sort might arguably change NCAA regulations into action that could be deemed to represent state action. The most essential aspect of all law is the so-called 'Duck Theory' — if it looks, waddles, and quacks like a duck, it usually is. The Supreme Court's version of *Tarkanian* violated the sacred principle by finding, on rather technical grounds, that the NCAA's action — which all but forced the state to suspend the Shark — was not state action, or even action in the color of state action. Is this a fair analysis? Did UNLV have any reasonable alternatives? Was the NCAA punishing UNLV solely as a ruse so that it could punish an individual employee, Coach Tarkanian, whom the NCAA considered to be a rogue coach?

4. All state high school athletic associations are usually viewed to be state actors. See *Griffin High Sch. v. Illinois High Sch. Assn.*, 822 F.2d 671 (7th Cir. 1987) (a purely voluntary state athletic association that was 85 percent comprised of public high schools was sufficiently public to confer state action status to the association's activities); Florida High Sch. Activities Assn., Inc. v. Bradshaw, 369 So. 2d 398 (Fla. Ct. App. 1979) (the action of an association in declaring that a high school forfeit football games when an ineligible player suited up was construed to be state action).

5. Prior to *Tarkanian*, the NCAA was viewed as a 'state actor' for a number of years. *See, e.g., Howard University v. NCAA*, 510 F.2d 213 (D.C. Cir. 1975); *Parish v. NCAA*, 506 F.2d 1028 (5th Cir. 1975); *Buckton v. NCAA*, 366 F. Supp. 1152 (D. Mass. 1973). *But see Arlosoroff v. NCAA*, 746 F.2d 1019 (4th Cir. 1984); *Hawkins v. NCAA*, 652 F. Supp. 602 (C.D. Ill. 1987).

6. In *Brentwood Academy*, a private high school sued a state interscholastic association under §1983, seeking to prevent enforcement of a rule prohibiting use of undue influence in recruitment of student-athletes. The U.S. Supreme Court held that the association's regulatory enforcement action was "state action" for purposes of Fourteenth Amendment. Similarily, see *Poret v. Louisiana High Sch. Athletic Assn.*, 1996 U.S. Dist. LEXIS 4595 (E.D. La. 1996); *Graham v. Tennessee Secondary Sch. Athletic Assn.*, 1995 U.S. Dist. LEXIS 3211 (E.D. Tenn. 1995). *But see Burrows v. Ohio High Sch. Athletic Assn.*, 891 F.2d 122 (6th Cir. 1989) (association not a state actor). After *Brentwood*, the question appears to be settled. Could *Brentwood* be excepted on a different set of facts?

E. NO PASS, NO PLAY

Although Texas was the first to initiate a no pass program, other states have followed its example. There are some differences: West Virginia, for example, leaves the responsibility of initiating the no pass procedures to each county board of education. The intent of each no pass regulation is to provide a strong incentive for students wishing to participate in extracurricular activities to maintain minimum levels of performance in all of their classes. In Texas, no pass applies to all extracurricular activities, from football to the 4-H Club; in West Virginia, the no pass statute applies only to "nonacademic" extracurriculars, such as interscholastic athletics and cheerleading.

The Supreme Court of Texas in *Spring Branch Independent School District v. Stamos* held that Texas's no pass, no play statute was constitutional on the basis that the rule was rationally related to a legitimate state interest and that participation in extracurricular activities is a privilege, not a right.

Spring Branch Independent School District v. Stamos

695 S.W.2d 556 (Tex. 1985)

Ray, Justice.

This is a direct appeal brought by the Attorney General, representing the Texas Education Agency, and others, seeking immediate appellate review of an order of the trial court which held unconstitutional, and enjoined enforcement of, a provision of the Texas Education Code. . . . We hold that the statutory provision is not unconstitutional and reverse the judgment of the trial court.

Chris Stamos and others brought this suit on behalf of Nicky Stamos and others, seeking a permanent injunction against enforcement of the Texas "no pass, no play" rule by the Spring Branch and Alief Independent School Districts. The Texas Education Agency and the University Interscholastic League intervened. The district court issued a temporary restraining order and later, after a hearing, a temporary injunction enjoining all parties from enforcing the rule. This court issued an order staying the district court's order and setting the cause for expedited review.

The "No Pass, No Play" Rule

The Second Called Session of the 68th Legislature adopted a package of educational reforms known as "H.B. 72." Act of July 13, 1984, Chapter 28, 1984 Tex. Gen. Laws, 2nd Called Session 269. A major provision of these educational reforms was the so-called "no pass, no play" rule, which generally requires that students maintain a "70" average in all classes to be eligible for participation in extracurricular activities. *See* Tex. Educ. Code Ann. § 21.920(b) (Vernon Supp. 1985). . . .

Issues Raised

The sole issue before this court is the constitutionality of the no pass, no play rule. The district court held the rule unconstitutional on the grounds that it violated equal protection and due process guarantees. The burden is on the party attacking the constitutionality of an act of the legislature. There is a presumption in favor of the constitutionality of an act of the legislature.

This court has long recognized the important role education plays in the maintenance of our democratic society. Article VII of the Texas Constitution "discloses a well-considered purpose on the part of those who framed it to bring about the establishment and maintenance of a comprehensive system of public education, consisting of a general public free school system and a system of higher education." Section 1 of article VII of the Constitution establishes a mandatory duty upon the legislature to make suitable provision for the support and maintenance of public free schools. The Constitution leaves to the legislature alone the determination of which methods, restrictions, and regulations are necessary and appropriate to carry out this duty, so long as that determination is not so arbitrary as to violate the constitutional rights of Texas' citizens.

Equal Protection

Stamos challenges the constitutionality of the "no pass, no play" rule on the ground that it violates the equal protection clause of the Texas Constitution. The first determination this court must make in the context of equal protection analysis is the appropriate standard of review. When the classification created by a state regulatory scheme neither infringes upon fundamental rights or interests nor burdens an inherently suspect class, equal protection analysis requires that the classification be rationally related to a legitimate state interest. *Sullivan v. University Interscholastic League*, 616 S.W.2d 170, 172 (Tex. 1981). Therefore, we must first determine whether the rule burdens an inherently suspect class or infringes upon fundamental rights or interests.

The no pass, no play rule classifies students based upon their achievement levels in their academic courses. We hold that those students who fail to maintain a minimum level of proficiency in all of their courses do not constitute the type of discrete, insular minority necessary to constitute a "suspect" class. *See United States v. Carolene Products Co.*, 304 U.S. 144, 152 n. 4 (1938). Thus, the rule does not burden an inherently "suspect" class.

Stamos urges that the rule discriminates against another suspect class, i.e., students with learning disabilities. However, this claim is made on behalf of a person who was not a party to the lawsuit at the time the trial judge signed her order or even at the time this court stayed the injunction and set the cause for argument. Furthermore, the claim is made against a new defendant who was not a party before the district court. By adding new parties, appellees are now attempting to vary their theory of the case. "Parties are restricted in the appellate court to the theory on which the case was tried in the lower court." Therefore, the issue concerning students with learning disabilities is not properly before this court.

Stamos also argues that the rule is subject to strict scrutiny under equal protection analysis because it impinges upon a fundamental right, i.e., the right to participate in extracurricular activities. We note that the overwhelming majority of jurisdictions have held that a student's right to participation in extracurricular activities does *not* constitute a fundamental right. . . .

Fundamental rights have their genesis in the express and implied protections of personal liberty recognized in federal and state constitutions. A student's "right" to participate in extracurricular activities does not rise to the same level as the right to free speech or free exercise of religion, both of which have long been recognized as fundamental rights under our state and federal constitutions. We adopt the majority rule and hold that a student's right to participate in extracurricular activities *per se* does *not* rise to the level of a fundamental right under our constitution.

Because the no pass, no play rule neither infringes upon fundamental rights nor burdens an inherently suspect class, we hold that it is *not* subject to "strict" or heightened equal protection scrutiny. Rather, the rule must be judged by the standard set forth in *Sullivan v. UIL*. In *Sullivan*, this court struck down on equal protection grounds the U.I.L.'s non-transfer rule, which declared all non-seniors ineligible for varsity football and basketball competition for one year following their transfer to a new school. This court emphasized (1) the over-inclusiveness of the rule in light of its intended purpose of discouraging "recruitment" of student-athletes, and (2) the irrebuttable presumption created by the rule. *Sullivan*, 616 S.W.2d at 172-73. In view of these two factors, this court declared that the rule was *not* rationally related to its intended purpose. *Id.*

The no pass, no play rule distinguishes students based upon whether they maintain a satisfactory minimum level of performance in each of their classes. Students who fail to maintain a minimum proficiency in all of their classes are ineligible for participation in school-sponsored extracurricular activities for the following six-week period, with no carry over from one school year to the next. The rule provides a strong incentive for students wishing to participate in extracurricular activities to maintain minimum levels of performance in all of their classes. In view of the rule's objective to promote improved classroom performance by students, we find the rule rationally related to the legitimate state interest in providing a quality education to Texas' public school students. The rule does not suffer from either of the vices found determinative in *Sullivan v. UIL*.

The distinctions recognized in the rule for mentally retarded students and students enrolled in honors or advanced courses likewise do not render the rule violative of the equal protection guarantees of the Texas Constitution. While the statute itself does not deprive students of their right to equal protection of the law, we recognize that the discretion given to school principals in the rule's provision dealing with honors or advanced courses may well give rise to arbitrary or discriminatory application violative of equal protection principles. We are faced with no allegations of discriminatory application of the rule's honors exception in the present case.

Procedural Due Process

We begin our analysis of the due process arguments in this cause by recognizing that the strictures of due process apply only to the threatened deprivation of liberty and property interests deserving the protection of the federal and state constitutions. . . .

Substantive Due Process . . .

In the present case, appellees liken the school principals' unfettered discretion in determining both which classes shall constitute "advanced" or "honors" courses and whether students failing such classes may participate in extracurricular activities to the building inspectors' unfettered discretion over approving commercial building plans. *Spann [v. City of Dallas*, 235

S.W. 513 (1921)] is distinguishable for the obvious reason that a recognized property interest was affected by the Dallas ordinance. As stated previously, students have no constitutionally protected interest in participation in extracurricular activities. Because no constitutionally protected interest is implicated by this delegation of authority to school principals, no violation of due process, substantive or procedural, results therefrom.

We do not agree with Stamos' argument that a school principal's exercise of discretion pursuant to the "honors" exception to the rule is shielded from all review. Arbitrary, capricious, or discriminatory exercise of a school principal's discretion pursuant to subsection 21.920(b) of the Texas Education Code may well give rise to claims based upon equal protection grounds. . . .

Accordingly, we reverse the district court's judgment with regard to the constitutionality of section 21.920 of the Texas Education Code and dissolve the temporary injunction ordered by the district court.

In *Bailey v. Truby*, 321 S.E.2d 302 (W. Va. 1984), the West Virginia Supreme Court held that a county board's no pass, no play rule was constitutional. *Bailey's* analysis is comparable to that of the Texas Supreme Court in *Stamos*. What is interesting in *Bailey* is Justice Harshbarger's dissent:

> The State Board's extracurricular eligibility policy essentially regulates, as the majority recognizes, all extracurricular activities. If any student in grades seven though twelve fails to achieve or maintain a 2.0 grade point average, the student cannot participate in any extracurricular activities. . . . It is a pity that Meredith Wilson's Professor Harold Hill and the townspeople of River City could not have an opportunity to persuade my brethren: "Trouble! Oh we've got trouble. Right here in River City! Right here in River City!. With a capital T and that rhymes with P and that stands for Pool. That stands for Pool! We've surely got trouble! We've surely got trouble Right here in River City! Right here in River City! Gotta figger out a way t'keep the young ones moral after Schooooool." (M. Wilson, *The Music Man*, pp. 38, 39 (1958), at 319, 320.)

As in both *Stamos* and *Bailey*, the Supreme Court of Montana in *State ex rel. Bartmess v. Board of Trustees of Sch. Dist. No. 1*, 726 P.2d 801 (Mont. 1986), found that the version of no pass, no play as promulgated in Lewis and Clark County, Montana, was also constitutional. This particular rule operated on a nine-week grading period. In *Bartmess*, there's another good dissent from Justice Sheehy:

> We have never had before us a scheme of government so patently discriminatory. This Court has followed convoluted equal protection analyses ad absurdum to a silly result. Now a Helena High School girl with a 1.98 grade average and a good soprano voice is excluded from singing with the Helena Starlights. A Gary Cooper or a Myrna Loy, both Helena products, may now be excluded from the Helena drama classes. A student can sign up for Spanish, but that student cannot belong to the Spanish Club, even with a passing grade in Spanish, if his or her overall grade is less than "C." In any test of fair dealing, those results should instantly be held irrational, but this Court does not want

to apply rationality standards. It wants to talk about strict scrutiny and middle term reviews to deny these students perhaps the only time in their lives to use their God-given skills to run in track, to twirl batons, to play in bands.

QUESTIONS AND DISCUSSION

1. *See Thompson v. Fayette County Pub. Schs.*, 786 S.W.2d 879 (Ky. Ct. App. 1990), in which a state court of appeals upheld the constitutionality of their state's version of 'no pass, no play', as was similarly done in *Stamos, Bailey* and *Bartmess. See generally* Sawyer, *'The New Academic Requirements for Amateur Sports: No Pass, No Play,'* 16 Loy. L.A. Ent. L.J. 105 (1995).
2. Since providing a quality education to a state public school student is a legitimate state interest, the no pass rule must only be rationally related to that interest.
3. In Texas, in 1995, the six-week suspension was reduced to three weeks. Does that defeat the purpose of the original legislation? *See generally* Champion, *'The Texas "No Pass, No Play Controversy,"* 14 T. Marshall L. Rev. 27 (1988-1989).
4. Generally, when a state's regulatory scheme neither infringes fundamental rights nor burdens an inherently suspect class, the equal protection analysis requires only that the classification be rationally related to a legitimate state interest. The plaintiff in *Stamos*, however, was obligated to contend that a student does have a fundamental right to participate in extracurricular activities.
5. In *Bell v. Lone Oak Indep. Sch. Dist.*, 507 S.W.2d 636 (Tex. Ct. Civ. App. 1974), it was held that a regulation prohibiting married high school students from participating in extracurricular activities was a violation of the Equal Protection Clause. The *Bell* court found no logical basis for the so-called married student rule. The right to marry, of course, is a basic and fundamental right. Why is *Bell* different from *Stamos*?
6. In *Kite v. Marshall*, 661 F.2d 1027 (5th Cir. 1981), a 'summer camp rule' was found to be unconstitutional. The rule did not allow students to participate in interscholastic sports if they attended a same-sport summer camp. The only possible compelling state interest was the control over the activities of coaches during the summer months. This interest was disproportionately insufficient to outweigh a parent's freedom of choice in family matters. The rule was broader in scope and effect than needed to further this interest and was therefore unconstitutional. This decision emphasized the rights of parents to make developmental decisions for their families, for example, attending summer camp, playing sports, and so on. The strongest argument against no pass is similar; namely, no pass is unconstitutional because it is "anti-family." Why will this approach not work with no pass?

F. THE CHALLENGED ATHLETE

An athlete may be declared ineligible to participate in sports based on his alleged disability, whether physical or emotional. There are rules that restrict an athlete's eligibility to participate based on paternalism and a misguided or illegal view of the disabled's ability to participate. Also, § 504 of the Rehabilitation Act of 1973 and, more lately, the Americans with Disabilities Act (ADA) have established a right for disabled students to participate in interscholastic sports if they are otherwise qualified.

Under the ADA, a disabled individual is one who has a physical or mental impairment that substantially limits one or more of that individual's major life activities. The act, in pertinent part, follows.

AMERICANS WITH DISABILITIES ACT OF 1990

42 U.S.C. §§12101 *et seq.*

Section 2 (42 U.S.C. § 12102). Findings and Purposes

The Congress finds that: . . .

(5) individuals with disabilities continually encounter various forms of discrimination, including outright intentional exclusion, the discriminatory effects of architectural, transportation, and communication barriers, overprotective rules and policies, failure to make modification to existing facilities and practices, exclusionary qualification standards and criteria, segregation, and relegation to lesser services, programs, activities, benefits, jobs, or other opportunities.

Section 3 (42 U.S.C. § 12103). Definitions

As used in this Act: . . .

(2) Disability. The term "disability" means with respect to an individual—

(A) a physical or mental impairment that substantially limits one or more of the major life activities of such individual;
(B) a record of such an impairment; or
(C) being regarded as having such an impairment

Title I. Employment

Section 101 (42 U.S.C. § 12111). Definitions . . .

Section 102 (42 U.S.C. § 12112). Discrimination

(a) General Rule. No covered entity shall discriminate against a qualified individual with a disability because of the disability of such individual in regard to job application procedures, the hiring, advancement, or discharge of employees, employee compensation, job training, and other terms, conditions, and privileges of employment. . . .

Section 103 (42 U.S.C. § 12113). Defenses

(a) In general. It may be a defense to a charge of discrimination under this Act that an alleged application of qualification standards, tests, or selection criteria that screen out or tend to screen out or otherwise deny a job or benefit to an individual with a disability has been shown to be job related and consistent with business necessity, and such performance cannot be accomplished by reasonable accommodation, as required under this Title. . . .

Section 104 (42 U.S.C. § 12114). Illegal Use of Drugs and Alcohol

(a) Qualified individual with a disability. For purposes of this Title, the term "qualified individual with a disability" shall not include any employee or applicant who is currently engaging in the illegal use of drugs, when the covered entity acts on the basis of such use.

(b) Rules of construction. Nothing in subsection (a) of this section shall be construed to exclude as a qualified individual with a disability an individual who —

> (1) has successfully completed a supervised drug rehabilitation program . . .

(c) Authority of covered entity. A covered entity —

> (1) may prohibit the illegal use of drugs and the use of alcohol at the workplace by all employees. . . .

(d) Drug testing.

> (1) In general. [A] test to determine the illegal use of drugs shall not be considered a medical examination [prohibited by § 102(d)].
>
> (2) Construction. Nothing in this Title shall be construed to encourage, prohibit, or authorize the conducting of drug testing for the illegal use of drugs by job applicants or employees or making employment decisions based on such test results. . . .

In *Grube v. Bethlehem School District*, the court upheld an injunction allowing a high school student to play football even though he had only one kidney. Plaintiff showed a likelihood of success on the merits of his claim that he was discriminated against in violation of § 504 of the Rehabilitation Act.

GRUBE V. BETHLEHEM SCHOOL DISTRICT

550 F. Supp. 418 (E.D. Pa. 1982)

HUYETT, District Judge.

1. The plaintiffs are Richard William Grube (Richard), a minor, and his father Richard Wallace Grube (Mr. Grube), and his stepmother, Linda Grube.
2. The student is enrolled in his senior year at Freedom High School in the Bethlehem Area School District. . . .
3. The defendant Bethlehem Area School District is the recipient of federal funds, and meets the definition of recipient as defined under 29 U.S.C. § 794 also known as § 504 of the Rehabilitation Act of 1973.

4. Richard is a vigorous, athletically inclined high school student whose only physical problem is the absence of his right kidney which was removed when he was 2 years of age as a result of a congenital malformation.

5. The kidney which was removed was a non-functioning unit and had been so since birth.

6. Richard's remaining kidney is healthy and fully compensates for the one he lost.

7. Richard has participated in football since the age of eight. He has also engaged in other athletics such as skiing, tennis, baseball and wrestling.

8. Richard has played football as a member of his school's team in ninth, tenth, and eleventh grandes.

9. Richard has also been a member of his school's wrestling team.

10. Richard was selected to be a member of his school's varsity football team for this year. He was awarded first string positions with the offensive and defensive squads.

11. Richard prepared this summer to participate in the team. He attended team workouts. He joined in pre-season team exercises which included physical contact.

12. A few days before the first scrimmage, Richard was informed that he had been declared ineligible from the team by the Superintendent of Schools because he lacks one kidney.

13. Richard is qualified by virtue of athletic ability to play on his school's varsity football team.

14. Richard was barred from the football team solely as a result of his lack of one kidney.

15. In order for Richard to play football, there is no affirmative action required on behalf of the defendant school district regarding any modification of the rules and regulations of the game or the need for the defendant school district to purchase any special equipment for Richard.

16. No substantial adjustments will be necessitated to the existing football program by the defendant school district should Richard play football.

17. Richard's participation as a member of the team will not lower the standards of the team as a whole in relationship to the other schools against whom they play.

18. Richard's handicap would not impede other players' participation in football.

19. Richard's prior participation in interscholastic football while a student at Freedom High School did not necessitate any adjustment to the game of football or of the training of the participating students.

20. Richard and Mr. Grube have agreed to sign a written release accepting all legal and financial responsibility in the event of a football injury.

21. In the second to last or third to last game of the 1981 season, Richard experienced a minor injury to his kidney.

22. The injury occurred when Richard rolled over the helmet of another player. He was unaware of the injury until after the game when blood appeared in his urine.

23. Richard was admitted to the hospital overnight for observation only. The condition remedied itself without medical intervention.

24. During his hospitalization, Richard was attended by a Dr. Lennart, a specialist in urology. Dr. Lennart did not advise Richard to give up football. He stated that it was up to Richard to decide.

25. Since it was Richard's decision to continue to participate in football, Dr. Lennart referred him to Lehigh University to secure appropriate protective equipment.

26. Working with members of the athletic department at Lehigh University and a manufacturer of protective equipment in Texas, Richard obtained a protective "flack jacket" specially designed to protect the ribs and kidneys during football at a cost of $400.

27. Richard has worn this protective device each time he has practiced with the team during the summer training of the 1982 football season.

28. After the injury in the 1981 season, Richard sat out the few remaining games. This was the result of a decision of the coaches, and not a medical decision.

29. Dr. Delp is an osteopathic physician. For 12 years he has held the part-time position of school physician at Freedom High School in addition to his regular practice. In his capacity as school physician, he is the physician for the school's athletic teams.

30. Each year, Dr. Delp conducts a medical examination of team members. He sees approximately 100 students in a one or two day period during which he checks heart, lungs, ears, and nose. This year, during this cursory examination, Dr. Delp decided that Richard should be asked for a note from his "kidney physician" permitting him to play football.

31. Dr. Delp is not a specialist in urology or sports medicine.

32. Richard is not under regular care by a "kidney physician." He contacted Dr. Lennart who attended him during his hospitalization the year before to obtain the note required by Dr. Delp.

33. Dr. Lennart wrote three letters relating to Richard. Each is addressed "To Whom It May Concern." The letters are consistent in concluding that the student is in good general health, that the injury quickly corrected itself, and that his remaining kidney is healthy.

34. The first letter dated July 15, 1982 states that it is not Dr. Lennart's recommendation that Richard continue to engage in "physical activities which may jeopardize his physical condition." The letter goes on to say that if the student intends to continue contact sports, protective equipment has been recommended for him.

35. The second letter dated August 16, 1982 contains the following language: "Mr. Grube and his son have made a personal decision regarding his participation in athletics. This is not a medical opinion. Richard is free to lead a normal existence of his choice." The second letter makes no reference to risk or hazard from physical activity.

36. The third letter is dated August 23, 1982. It contains the following language: "Richard and his father have been advised that participation in contact sports was deemed hazardous and not recommended under these circumstances." There is no further discussion of risk or hazard.

37. Based upon the language in Dr. Lennart's last letter, a telephone conversation with Dr. Lennart, a consultation with another school physician in the school district, Dr. Delp recommended that Richard be barred from playing football.

38. The other school physician contacted, Dr. Hemmerlie, is not a specialist in urology or sports medicine.

39. Dr. Delp conducted no medical research relating to the alleged risk to Richard of playing football.

40. Dr. Delp's relevant clinical experience is as follows: in 12 years as a school and team physician he knows of no case where a football injury resulted in permanent kidney injury or excision of a kidney. Dr. Hemmerlie's experience was comparable. There was no evidence that Dr. Lennart informed them of such case histories.

41. Dr. Delp is not familiar with the protective equipment used by the student.

42. Without any research or clinical foundation, Dr. Delp concluded it was "highly risky" for Richard to participate in football. The risk was not specifically identified to Richard or his father. Dr. Delp now maintains that there is a risk of deceleration injury.

43. Dr. Moyer is a medical doctor who is board certified in orthopedic surgery. He is the director of the well-respected Sports Medicine Clinic at Temple University.

44. Dr. Moyer examined Richard in preparation for his testimony at the preliminary injunction hearing. He concluded that Richard is in good general health and that his remaining kidney is healthy.

45. Dr. Moyer is familiar with the protective equipment used by Richard. In his opinion, this equipment used virtually eliminates any danger of injury from a direct blow to the kidney. Further, in his opinion, there is no injury likely to result to the kidney from deceleration.

46. Dr. Moyer has treated other individuals who lack a kidney and play football. Dr. Moyer treats members of all area professional teams. His associates at the Sports Medicine Clinic whom he consulted with regard to Richard have 20 years of experience in treating members of all area football teams. Dr. Moyer knows of no football injury that has caused significant, permanent damage to a kidney or resulted in excision of a kidney.

47. Dr. Moyer researched the instances of kidney damage from football. He discovered no patients with significant kidney damage from football. There are none who had to have a kidney removed.

48. In Dr. Moyer's professional opinion, Richard can safely play football. The risk of catastrophic injury to his remaining kidney is minute, almost nil.

49. In the extremely unlikely event of a catastrophic injury, Richard's options would be dialysis or kidney transplant.

50. In Dr. Moyer's opinion, Dr. Lennart's statement in his last letter relating to an alleged hazard to Richard and Dr. Delp's and Dr. Hemmerlie's recommendations based thereon, are emotional and not medical judgments.

51. Richard has demonstrated diligence and responsibility in his pursuit of athletic achievement by training on his own as well as part of the team. . . .

56. Richard knows that in the event that the loses the use of his remaining kidney, he would have to depend on dialysis. . . . He understands the catastrophic consequences of the loss of his remaining kidney.

57. Richard is a mature individual. . . . He is capable of making a rational judgment with respect to whether to play football.

58. In playing football, there are other serious life threatening injuries which may equally befall Richard or any other member of the team.

59. There are less than seven games remaining in the team's schedule for this season.

60. Richard is a collegiate caliber athlete.

61. Mr. Grube supports himself, four children and his wife on a salary of less than $400 per week. . . .

Discussion . . .

The plaintiffs' complaint presents two legal theories. First, they assert that Richard has been discriminated against in violation of the Rehabilitation Act of 1973 (Act) § 504, 29 U.S.C. § 706(7) (Supp. 1981). Secondly, they assert that he has been deprived of his fourteenth amendment right to equal protection giving rise to an action under 42 U.S.C. § 1983. . . .

Section 504 of the Act as amended provides: "No otherwise qualified handicapped individual in the United States . . . shall, solely by reason of his handicap, be excluded from the participation in, be denied the benefits of, or be subjected to discrimination under any program or activity receiving Federal financial assistance. . . ." 29 U.S.C. § 794 (Supp. 1981). In interpreting this section, the Supreme Court has held that an "otherwise qualified" person "is one who is able to meet all of a program's requirements in spite of his handicap. . . ."

Turning to the present case, . . . I am bound to uphold an act of Congress which is specifically designed to protect Richard and the right he is asserting.

The school district has advanced two reasons as "substantial justification" for its action. First, according to Dr. LaFrankin was his concern for the liability that might be imposed upon the school district if Richard loses the use of his kidney. This concerned may be answered by the releases which the parents and son have offered to execute. However, the real issue is whether the risk of injury is significant enough to make this concern any justification for the district's decision. . . . The district's second justification for precluding Richard from participating in football is concern for his health, safety, and welfare. This concern is based on a risk perceived by the district that Richard could lose his one functioning kidney.

This case began when Dr. Delp decided that it would be helpful to get an opinion from Richard's kidney physician with regard to his ability to play. From this I. conclude that Dr. Delp did not consider himself qualified to make that determination. At least, he did not hold an opinion concerning Richard's playing. The letters that were produced from Dr. Lennart were equivocal. His letter of August 16, 1982 is the most enlightening. He recognized in that letter that the decision whether or not Richard should play is not properly the subject of a *medical* opinion. The evidence is clear that neither Dr. Lennart, Dr. Delp, nor Dr. Hemmerlie had any facts which would permit them to make a rational medical evaluation of the existence of a risk. In an understandable abundance of caution, all three eventually concluded that the safest course was to say that Richard could not play. I conclude that the opinion of these three doctors cannot serve as substantial justification for the district's actions where their decision lacks a medical basis.

Even if the letter signed by Dr. Delp and Dr. Hemmerlie could be construed as substantial justification at the time it was received, it is not justification for the continued refusal of the district to permit Richard to play in light of Dr. Moyer's opinion. Dr. Moyer has the clinical experience and has performed the research required to come to a medical evaluation of the risk to Richard. His conclusion was that the risk of injury to the kidney is so slim that there is no medical reason why Richard cannot play football. . . .

Richard's selection for the team established that he is otherwise qualified to play football. . . . [T]he defendant's decision to preclude him from playing lacks substantial justification. Accordingly, I conclude that the plaintiffs have made a strong showing of likelihood of success on the merits. . . .

Finally, I conclude that no injury is likely to result to the defendant or the public interest by granting this relief. The plaintiffs are willing to take responsibility for the decision that they have reached. The only credible medical opinion, Dr. Moyer's, shows that the likelihood of the type of injury that concerns the defendant is almost nil. Finally, the public interest is served when plaintiffs such as these vindicate important federal rights. . . .

Conclusions of Law

1. Richard is a handicapped individual within the meaning of the Act. *See* 29 U.S.C. § 706(7).
2. As a recipient of federal funds, the defendant is subject to the requirements of § 504. See 29 U.S.C. § 794.
3. Richard is "otherwise qualified" as that language is used in the Act.
4. The defendant's refusal to permit him to participate on the football team lacks substantial justification.
5. The plaintiffs have made a strong showing of likelihood of success on the merits.
6. The plaintiffs have demonstrated irreparable harm.
7. No substantial harm is likely to result to the defendant.
8. The public interest will not be harmed be granting the relief. . . .

Order

Now, October 6, 1982, upon consideration of the plaintiffs' motion for preliminary injunction, memoranda and proposed findings and conclusions submitted by the parties, following a hearing held in open court, and for the reasons stated in the accompanying memorandum, it is ordered that

1. The motion is Granted.
2. The defendant is preliminarily enjoined from Precluding the plaintiff Richard William Grube from participating as a member of the Freedom

High School football team on the same terms and conditions as apply to all other members of the teams.

3. The plaintiffs shall give security in the sum of $1,000.00.

In *Martin v. PGA, Tour, Inc.*, the Supreme Court held that the PGA's "no cart" rule violated the ADA as regards the rights of a challenged golfer.

MARTIN V..PGA TOUR, INC.

532 U.S. 661 (2001)

Justice STEVENS delivered the opinion of the Court.

This case raises two questions concerning the application of the Americans with Disabilities Act of 1990, 104 Stat. 328, 42 U.S.C. § 12101 *et seq.*, to a gifted athlete: first, whether the Act protects access to professional golf tournaments by a qualified entrant with a disability; and second, whether a disabled contestant may be denied the use of a golf cart because it would "fundamentally alter the nature" of the tournaments, § 12181(b)(2)(A)(ii), to allow him to ride when all other contestants must walk.

Petitioner PGA Tour Inc., a nonprofit entity formed in 1968, sponsors and cosponsors professional golf tournaments conducted on three annual tours. About 200 golfers participate in the PGA Tour; about 170 in the Nike Tour; and about 100 in the Senior PGA Tour. PGA Tour and Nike Tour tournaments typically are 4-day events, played on courses leased and operated by petitioner. The entire field usually competes in two 18-hole rounds played on Thursday and Friday; those who survive the "cut" play on Saturday and Sunday and receive prize money in amounts determined by their aggregate scores for all four rounds. The revenues generated by television, admissions, concessions, and contributions from cosponsors amount to about $300 million a year, much of which is distributed in prize money.

There are various ways of gaining entry into particular tours. For example, a player who wins three Nike Tour events in the same year, or is among the top-15 money winners on that tour, earns the right to play in the PGA Tour. Additionally, a golfer may obtain a spot in an official tournament through successfully competing in "open" qualifying rounds, which are conducted the week before each tournament. Most participants, however, earn playing privileges in the PGA Tour or Nike Tour by way of a three-stage qualifying tournament known as the "Q-School."

Any member of the public may enter the Q-School by paying a $3,000 entry fee and submitting two letters of reference from, among others, PGA Tour or Nike Tour members. The $3,000 entry fee covers the players' greens fees and the cost of golf carts, which are permitted during the first two stages, but which have been prohibited during the third stage since 1997. Each year, over a thousand contestants compete in the first stage, which consists of four 18-hole rounds at different locations. Approximately half of them make it to the second stage, which also includes 72 holes. Around 168 players survive the second stage and advance to the final one, where they compete over 108 holes. Of those finalists, about a fourth qualify for membership in the PGA Tour, and the rest gain membership in the Nike Tour. The significance of making it into either tour is illuminated by the fact that there are about 25 million golfers in the country. . . .

Three sets of rules govern competition in tour events. First, the "rules of Golf," jointly written by the United States Golf Association (USGA) and the Royal and Ancient Golf Club of Scotland, apply to the game as it is played. . . . Those rules do not prohibit the use of golf carts at any time. . . .

Second, the "Conditions of Competition and Local Rules," often described as the "hard card," apply specifically to petitioner's professional tours. The hard cards for the PGA Tour and Nike Tour require players to walk the golf course during tournaments, but not during open qualifying rounds. . . .

Third, "Notices to Competitors" are issued for particular tournaments and cover conditions for that specific event. . . .

II

Casey Martin is a talented golfer. As an amateur, he won 17 Oregon Golf Association junior events before he was 15, and won the state championship as a high school senior. He played on the Stanford University golf team that won the 1994 National Collegiate Athletic Association (NCAA) championship. As a professional, Martin qualified for the Nike Tour in 1998 and 1999, and based on his 1999 performance, qualified for the PGA Tour in 2000. In the 1999 season, he entered 24 events, made the cut 13 times, and had 6 top-10 finishes, coming in second twice and third once.

Martin is also an individual with a disability as defined in the Americans with Disabilities Act of 1990 (ADA or Act). Since birth he has been afflicted with Klippel-Trenaunay-Weber Syndrome, a degenerative circulatory disorder that obstructs the flow of blood from his right leg back to his heart. The disease is progressive; it causes severe pain and has atrophied his right leg. During the latter part of his college career, because of the progress of the disease, Martin could no longer walk an 18-hole golf course. Walking not only caused him pain, fatigue, and anxiety, but also created a significant risk of hemorrhaging, developing blood clots, and fracturing his tibia so badly that an amputation might be required. For these reasons, Stanford made written requests to the Pacific 10 Conference and the NCAA to waive for Martin their rules requiring players to walk and carry their own clubs. The requests were granted.

When Martin turned pro and entered petitioner's Q-School, the hard card permitted him to use a cart during his successful progress through the first two stages. He made a request supported by detailed medical records, for permission to use a golf cart during the third stage. Martin therefore filed this action. A preliminary injunction entered by the District Court made it possible for him to use a cart in the final stage of the Q-School and as a competitor in the Nike Tour and PGA Tour. Although not bound by the injunction, and despite its support for petitioner's position in this litigation, the USGA voluntarily granted Martin a similar waiver in events that it sponsors, including the U.S. Open.

III . . .

. . . [P]etitioner asserted that the condition of walking is a substantive rule of competition, and that waiving it as to any individual for any reason would fundamentally alter the nature of the competition. . . . Their testimony [golf legends] makes it clear that, in their view, permission to use a cart might well give some players a competitive advantage over other players who must walk. . . .

On the merits, because there was no serious dispute about the fact that permitting Martin to use a golf cart was both a reasonable and a necessary solution to the problem of providing him access to the tournaments, the Court of Appeals regarded the central dispute as whether such permission would "fundamentally alter" the nature of the PGA Tour or Nike Tour. Like the District Court, the Court of Appeals viewed the issue not as "whether use of carts generally would fundamentally alter the competition, but whether the use of a cart by Martin would do so." That issue turned on "an intensively fact-based inquiry," and, the court concluded, had been correctly resolved by the trial judge. In its words, "[a]ll that the cart does is permit Martin access to a type of competition in which he otherwise could not engage because of his disability."

The day after the Ninth Circuit ruled in Martin's favor, the Seventh Circuit came to a contrary conclusion in a case brought against the USGA by a disabled golfer who failed to qualify for "America's greatest—and most democratic—golf tournament, the United States Open." *Olinger v. United States Golf Assn.*, 205 F.3d 1001 (7th Cir. 2000).

IV

Congress enacted the ADA in 1990 to remedy widespread discrimination against disabled individuals. In studying the need for such legislation, Congress found that "historically, society has tended to isolate and segregate individuals with disabilities, and, despite some improvements, such forms of discrimination against individuals with disabilities continue to be a serious and pervasive social problem." . . .

In the ADA, Congress provided that broad mandate. See 42 U.S.C. § 12101(b). . . . To effectuate its sweeping purpose, the ADA forbids discrimination against disabled individuals in major areas of public life, among them employment (Title I of the Act), public services (Title II), and public accommodations (Title III). At issue now, as a threshold matter, is the applicability of Title III to petitioner's golf tours and qualifying rounds, in particular to petitioner's treatment of a qualified disabled golfer weighing to compete in those events. . . .

It seems apparent, from both the general rule and the comprehensive definition of "public accommodation," that petitioner's golf tours and their qualifying rounds fit comfortably withing the coverage of Title III, and Martin within its protection. The events occur on "golf course[s]," a type of place specifically identified by the Act as a public accommodation. § 12181(7)(L). . . . It would therefore appear that Title III of the ADA, by its plain terms, prohibits petitioner from denying Martin equal access to its tours on the basis of his disability. . . .

According to petitioner, Title III is concerned with discrimination against "clients and customers" seeking to obtain "goods and services" at places of public accommodation, whereas it is Title I that protects persons who work at such places. . . .

We need not decide whether petitioner's construction of the statue is correct, because petitioner's argument falters even on its own terms. . . .

In this case, however, the narrow dispute is whether allowing Martin to use a golf cart, despite the walking requirement that applies to the PGA Tour, the Nike Tour, and the third stage of the Q-School, is a modification that would "fundamentally alter the nature" of those events. . . .

As an initial matter, we observe that the use of carts is not itself inconsistent with the fundamental character of the game of golf. From early on, the essence of the game has been shot-making—using clubs to cause a ball to progress from the teeing ground to a hole some distance away with as few strokes as possible. . . . The walking rule that is contained in petitioner's hard cards, based on an optional condition buried in an appendix to the Rules of Golf, is not an essential attribute of the game itself. . . .

Indeed, the walking rule is not an indispensable feature of tournament golf either. . . .

Petitioner, however, distinguishes the game of golf as it is generally played from the game that is sponsors in the PGA Tour, Nike Tour, and (at least recently) the last stage of the Q-School—golf at the "highest level." . . . The walking rule is one such rule, petitioner submits, because its purpose is "to inject the element of fatigue into the skill of shot-making," and thus its effect may be the critical loss of a stroke. As a consequence, the reasonable modification Martin seeks would fundamentally alter the nature of petitioner's highest level tournaments even if he were the only person in the world who has both the talent to compete in those elite events and a disability sufficiently serious that the cannot do so without using a cart.

The force of petitioner's argument is, first of all, mitigated by the fact that golf is a game in which it is impossible to guarantee that all competitors will play under exactly the same conditions or that an individual's ability will be the sole determinant of the outcome. . . .

Further, the factual basis of petitioner's argument is undermined by the District Court's finding that the fatigue from walking during one of petitioner's 4-day tournaments cannot be deemed significant. . . .

Moreover, when given the option of using a cart, the majority of golfers in petitioner's tournaments have chosen to walk, often to relieve stress or for other strategic reasons. . . .

Under the ADA's basic requirement that the need of a disabled person be evaluated on an individual basis, we have no doubt that allowing Martin to use a golf cart would not fundamentally alter the nature of petitioner's tournaments. . . . [T]he purpose of the walking rule is to subject players to fatigue, which in turn may influence the outcome of tournaments. Even if the rule does serve that purpose, it is an uncontested finding of the District Court that Martin "easily endures greater fatigue even with a cart than his able-bodied competitors do by walking" . . . The purpose of the walking rule is therefore not compromised in the slightest by allowing Martin to use a cart. A modification that provides an exception to a peripheral tournament rule without impairing its purpose cannot be said to "fundamentally alter" the tournament. What it can be said to do, on the other hand, is to allow Martin the chance to qualify for and compete in the athletic events petitioner offers to those members of the public who have the skill and desire to enter. That is exactly what the ADA requires. As a result, Martin's request for a waiver of the walking rule should have been granted. . . .

The judgment of the Court of Appeals is affirmed.

It is so ordered.

QUESTIONS AND DISCUSSION

1. There has been a strong case history of disabled athletes using the courts in an attempt to enforce eligibility. *Kampmeier v. Nyquist*, 553 F.2d 296 (2d Cir. 1977) (junior high school athletes with one eye); *see also* Comment, Lewis, *'Athletic Eligibility—Too High a Hurdle for the Learning Disabled,'* 15 T.M. Cooley L. Rev. 75 (1998); *Wright v. Columbia Univ.*, 520 F. Supp. 789 (E.D. Pa. 1981) (college football player with one eye); *Poole v. South Plainfield Bd. of Educ.*, 409 F. Supp. 948 (D.N.J. 1980) (wrestler with one kidney); *See Doe v. Marshall*, 459 F. Supp. 1190 (S.D. Tex. 1978), *vacated and remanded*, 622 F.2d 118 (5th Cir. 1980) (emotionally disabled high school football player and no-transfer rule).
2. Public accommodations must allow the disabled to participate in an equal way; reasonable architectural barriers must be removed when doing so is readily achievable.
3. *Martin v. PGA Tour, Inc.*, of course, allows a disabled professional golfer the right to use a golf cart on the professional golf tour. One wonders why the PGA made such a big deal about the integrity of walking the greens for professional golfers. Casey Martin is one of a kind—there are very few truly disabled golfers who are also sufficiently "otherwise qualified" to pass Q-School.
4. Casey Martin, the challenged golfer, objected to the PGA's "no cart" rule that precludes players from using golf carts during the third stage of the PGA qualifying tour and during the PGA. By not providing a cart, the PGA failed to make these tournaments accessible to challenged individuals, in violation of the ADA. *See* Galewski, *'The Casey Martin and Ford Olinger Cases; The Supreme Court Takes a Swing at ADA Uncertainty,'* 21 Pace L. Rev. 411 (2000); Holzbarr, 'Driving into the Rough: Conflicting Decisions on the Rights of Disabled Golfers in Martin v. PGA Tour, Inc. and Olinger v. USGA, '46 Vill. L. Rev. 171 (2000); Pascarelli, 'Casey Martin v. PGA Tour, Inc.: *A New Significance to a Golfer's Handicap,'* 8 DePaul-LCA J. Art & Ent. L. & Poly. 303 (1998); Walsh, *'Civil Rights—the ADA—the PGA Is Subject to the ADA Because It Is Not a Private Club and Its Tournaments Are Places of Public Accommodation—*Martin v. PGA Tour. Inc., 9 Seton Hall J. Sport L. 599 (1999). *See Olinger v. USGA*, 55 F. Supp. 2d 926 (N.D. Ind. 1999), *aff'd*, 205 F.3d 1001 (7th Cir. 2000), *vacated & remanded for further consideration in*

light of PGA Tour, Inc. v. Martin, 532 U.S. 661 (2001) (ADA does not require the USGA to provide a golf cart for disabled golfer, Ford Olinger, during U.S. Open qualifying competition; the court held *contra* to *Martin* that the use of a cart gave some competitive advantage so that nature of U.S. Open would be fundamentally altered; granting use of cart was not reasonable accommodation under ADA).

5. A female high school basketball player, deaf since birth, won the right to require her school to provide a sign interpreter. A school must provide to its disabled population an equal opportunity to participate in extracurricular activities. *See State ex rel. Lambert v. West Virginia State Bd. of Educ.*, 447 S.E.2d 901 (W. Va. 1994).

6. Athlete with hearing disorder and cerebral palsy runs cross country but ran afoul of age rule; court allowed him to compete and athletic association is enjoined from sanctioning school district. See *Kling v. Mentor Public Sch. Dist.*, 136 F. Supp. 2d 744 (N.D. Ohio 2001).

7. Plaintiff wheelchair racquetball player sued to be allowed to play in defendant athletic club's "A" racquetball league; the issue was whether modifications to allow the player to compete with footed players would fundamentally alter the nature of the competition. Relying on *Martin v. PGA Tour, Inc.*, the court ruled that the essence of racquetball is to hit a moving ball before the second bounce and allowing a player two bounces would fundamentally change the nature of the game. *See Kuketz v. MDC Fitness Corp.*, 13 Mass. L. Rptr. 511 (Mass. Super. Ct. 2001). Do you understand the difference with *Martin* that the Massachusetts court relied on? The accommodation in *Kuketz* fundamentally altered the nature of the competition, while in *Martin* it did not. Why?

CHAPTER 9

DISCIPLINE

The most important power of an amateur sports association is **the Power to Discipline and Penalize** teams and individual athletes for infractions of its rules and regulations. This ability is an integral part in determining a player's eligibility to participate.

In **Professional Sports,** the player-employer relationship is based on consent and defined by agreement as detailed in the standard player's contract and the collective bargaining agreement. Those who punish are the clubs and the league commissioners; the athletes are the ones who are the recipients of the discipline.

An important part of discipline is the ability to punish based on **Drug Testing.** After the Supreme Court's decision in *Vernonia Sch. Dist. 47J v. Acton,* the expectation of privacy is deemed to be diminished based on "locker room mentality." Another key way to discipline is by **Terminating Employment.**

A. THE POWER TO DISCIPLINE AND PENALIZE

All sports organizations, both amateur and professional, function smoothly only because of the threat that the organization will use its power to discipline and penalize its members. This power encourages the players to behave in a professional manner both on and off the field. It is also an important aspect in determining a particular athlete's eligibility status.

Athletic organizations enforce their rules through investigations, prosecutions, and adjudications. When a potential problem arises, the organization investigates the institution and, if applicable, the individual player. However, the rule enforcement of a particular athletic regulatory group usually is provided through fair, reasonable, and constitutional procedures. Enforcement must adhere to procedural due process. If the occurrence triggers due process, then the appropriate type of due process must be determined.

1. Due Process Considerations

The enforcement of discipline and penalties must adhere to a procedural due process, which is determined by a judicial evaluation of each particular circumstance. The requirement for due process arises when the act is state action that infringes on a property right. The plaintiff must show a legitimate claim of entitlement to the protected benefit. Next, it must be determined what type of process is due. The courts balance the interest of parties, including the importance of the interest, the type of proceeding in which the interest is reviewed, the appropriateness of the procedure required to prevent any deprivation of the protected interest, and the procedure's cost. Another consideration is the seriousness of the possible sanction. Due process usually requires that before an action is taken, the person must have a fair hearing, which includes notice.

In *Kelly v. Metropolitan County Board of Education,* the court held that due process was denied when a school board suspended the interscholastic sports program of an all-black high school for one year, without a formal charge or hearing.

KELLY V. METROPOLITAN COUNTY BOARD OF EDUCATION

293 F. Supp 485 (M.D. Tenn. 1968)

William E. MILLER, Chief Judge.

This is a motion for additional relief filed in these consolidated civil actions in which, by prior orders the counterparts of the defendant, Metropolitan County Board of Education of Nashville and Davidson County, Tennessee, (School Board), were required to adopt an acceptable plan for the desegregation of their local public schools. Plaintiffs in their motion for additional relief requested the addition as party plaintiffs of a number of students at Cameron High School together with their parents as next friends. This motion was allowed. By supplemental process the Tennessee Secondary School Athletic Association, (TSSAA), of which Cameron High School is a member, was added as a party defendant. The plaintiffs by their motion seek an injunctive order (1) enjoining the action of the School Board and the TSSAA suspending the interscholastic athletic program of Cameron High School for a period of one year, (2) directing the transfer of certain additional plaintiffs and other Negro students to white high schools outside the zone of their residence, and (3) requiring the School Board to file with the Court a plan for full desegregation of its school system, and forcing the TSSAA to integrate its practices and staff. . . .

The present motion was precipitated by the suspension of Cameron High School, an all Negro school, from interscholastic athletic competition for one year from April 4, 1968. The temporary suspension was imposed separately by the School Board and by TSSAA following investigations by them of alleged charges that students and other supporters of Cameron High School had engaged in misconduct at the Region V Basketball Tournament in Nashville, Tennessee, on March 8, 1968. . . .

There is evidence that at the end of the game various groups of spectators departed from tournament standards of conduct; that a group from the

Stratford cheering section violated the tournament rules by rushing onto the playing floor to congratulate their team; and that on the other side of the floor, large numbers of Cameron fans attempted to exit improperly, creating further confusion and causing the next scheduled game to be delayed. . . .

There is also evidence that cheerleaders and fans from the Cameron student section struck and verbally abused the referees; that the spectators refused to return to their seats upon request and it was necessary temporarily to discontinue the following basketball game until order was restored; and that because of the numerous problems and injuries reported to them, the tournament director and the policeman in charge called police headquarters for assistance from on-duty policemen. . . .

The Committee [found:] . . .

1. Certain unidentified Cameron Cheerleaders were actively involved in abusive conduct toward Cameron-Stratford game officials immediately following the game. . . .

4. The administrative staff of Cameron High failed to provide adequate supervision during and following the game. . . .

TSSAA formally suspended Cameron from interscholastic athletic competition on June 17, 1968, effective April 4, 1968 for a period of one year. . . .

The present motion for further relief was filed on September 19, 1968.

Jurisdiction

42 U.S.C.A. §1983 gives plaintiffs the right to bring this action for injunctive relief against defendants (School Board and TSSAA), who, plaintiffs claim, acting under color of state law, deprived them of federally protected rights in suspending plaintiffs' high school from interscholastic athletic competition. Such state action, plaintiffs maintain, violates their rights guaranteed by the Fourteenth Amendment to the Constitution of the United States. . . .

Standing . . .

Unquestionably, it is the Cameron students comprising its athletic teams, and also its band members, its cheerleaders, and the majority of Cameron athletic supporters who are substantially affected by the suspension of Cameron High School from interscholastic athletic competition. . . .

State Action . . .

[T]here is abundant evidence here to support the conclusion that the association is an instrumentality of the state for purposes of the Fourteenth Amendment. . . .

In the Court's view the functions of the TSSAA are so closely identified with state activities that the association is subject to the constitutional limitations placed upon state action by the Fourteenth Amendment.

Due Process
The School Board Suspension

Whenever a governmental body acts to injure an individual, the Constitution requires that the act be consonant with due process of law.

Clearly the action of the School Board in suspending Cameron High School from all athletic competition for the period of one year personally affected the students of Cameron High School in an adverse manner.

Defendants argue that the interests student plaintiffs have in engaging in athletics is a mere privilege and not a constitutional right. . . .

It is undeniable that as stated in the defendant TSSAA's Handbook, "Interscholastic athletics are an integral part of the total educational process."

It is sufficient for purposes of this case to conclude that the right or interest that the Cameron students were deprived of by virtue of the one year suspension, i.e., the right to engage in secondary school athletics, is of such significance and worth as to require that the proceedings which resulted in the one year suspension conform to the standards of due process.

The minimum procedural requirements necessary to satisfy due process of law depend upon the circumstances and interests involved in the particular case. . . .

[T]he School Board had the authority to establish and supervise athletic programs for the schools in its system. In the exercise of its discretion the Board undoubtedly could have discontinued interscholastic sports in the metropolitan school system altogether if for some reason it saw fit to do so. . . .

Authorities recognize that the governmental power with respect to matters of student discipline in public schools is not unlimited. While the private interest involved in those cases is not the exact equivalent of the interest here, the difference is more superficial than real. We are confronted here with the denial of interscholastic athletic activities to an entire school in all sports for a period of one year, a penalty affecting the guilty and the innocent alike. This form of discipline has been correctly characterized in the record as group punishment. Although the right to pursue an academic education is not directly affected, the penalty infringes upon a facet of public school education which has come to be generally recognized as a fundamental ingredient of the educational process. It would appear obvious that before such a valuable interest is denied, the rudiments of fair play would dictate the right to notice and a hearing. . . .

The disciplinary group suspension for misconduct must be particularly distressing and, indeed, frustrating to the members of the Cameron basketball team in light of the Investigating Committee's finding that "the coaches and team members are commended for their conduct immediately following the game," and to participants in other sports, such as football, who had no connection with the events at the tournament in question.

The Court does not hold that group punishment is a constitutionally forbidden form of punishment. What it does hold is that the severity and harshness inherent in this form of punishment are significant factors dictating a closer adherence to the procedural standards of due process than might otherwise be the case.

Plaintiffs admit, as they must, that the defendant Board has a legitimate stake in maintaining public order at athletic events and engendering sportsmanlike attitudes and behavior on the part of the students enrolled in the various schools in its system.

However, plaintiffs strongly contend that the manner in which the Board suspended Cameron violated due process of law, in that Cameron was not notified of the charges against it, nor afforded an opportunity to defend against those charges. . . .

This Court is of the opinion that under the circumstances of this case individual notice and a hearing for each student was not required by due process of law. In cases of possible group misconduct on the part of students due process is satisfied if the notice and opportunity to defend are afforded to a responsible person whose position requires him to represent and speak for the entire group. A school principal occupies such a position.

The TSSAA Suspension

The by-laws of TSSAA provide that member schools, through their principals, shall be responsible for the conduct of the fans and students at every athletic contest; and that "all games shall be properly supervised and policed to insure sportsmanlike contests." . . .

While the association's Constitution and By-Laws do not undertake to particularize the types of unsportsmanlike conduct which shall justify disciplinary action, when the nature and character of athletic contests are considered, the Court is not prepared to hold that the TSSAA regulations fail to meet due process standards because of vagueness or lack of specificity. Unsportsmanlike conduct would necessarily cover such a wide variety of conditions and circumstances that it would be unrealistic to require that all possible types of misconduct should be spelled out or defined with exactitude. . . .

[The TSSAA] provisions are fully sufficient to notify member schools, as well as their students and fans, that unsportsmanlike conduct or misbehavior at athletic contests or games may result in the entire school losing its athletic privileges. With such rules and regulations in effect, neither the school principal nor individual students or fans are in position to contend or claim that they were without notice of the severe consequences which could result from group misconduct at athletic games. The Court is satisfied that due process of law required nothing further in the context of this case insofar as pre-existing standards are concerned. . . .

Under these facts, which appear in the record without substantial dispute, the Court cannot conclude that the association denied Cameron High School due process of law in failing to make a specific charge of misconduct, or in failing to accord a hearing. . . .

Nevertheless, while the Court concludes that the TSSAA has not infringed upon the constitutional rights of Cameron High School, it is of the opinion that since the School Board's suspension has been nullified and hence the principal reason for foregoing an association hearing has now been removed, Cameron should not be held to the consequences of a waiver of the right of an association hearing in accordance with the Constitution, By-Laws and rules and regulations of the association. It is true that the association did offer to reconsider the case upon receiving new evidence from Cameron, but such a limited proffer would not fully comply with the kind of hearing which is required by due process of law and provided for by the association's own Constitution.

Alleged Racial Discrimination

. . . The Court has carefully examined this contention and is wholly unable to find any support for it in the record. . . .

No comment in this opinion relative to the alleged misconduct of Cameron students or fans on the occasion in question should be taken as in any way binding upon the Cameron High School or upon TSSAA or any of its agencies in conducting the hearing.

The judgment shall provide that the Court retains jurisdiction of the actions for the purpose of effectuating the Court's rulings and disposing of all reserved issues.

In *Kelly*, due process protection was initiated as a result of the suspension of all interscholastic sports for a period of one year at a particular high school. In *Neal v. Fulton County Board of Education*, an individual student athlete claimed that his due process rights were violated when his coach allegedly used excessive corporal punishment against him.

NEAL V. FULTON COUNTY BOARD OF EDUCATION

229 F.3d 1069 (11th Cir. 2000)

MARCUS, Circuit Judge:

Plaintiff Durante Neal, a high school freshman and member of the varsity football team, appeals from the district courts dismissal of his complaint alleging that Tommy Ector, a high school teacher and football coach, violated his right under the Due Process Clause to be free from excessive corporal punishment. Ector allegedly struck Plaintiff with a metal weight lock, blinding him in one eye, as a form of punishment for Plaintiff's involvement in a fight with another student. . . . [S]ubstantive due process principles protect a student from corporal punishment that is intentional, obviously excessive, and creates a foreseeable risk of serious injury. . . . [Here] Plaintiff has stated a claim. . . . Plaintiff was a 14-year-old freshman at Tri-Cities High School and was a member of the varsity football team. During football practice, Royonte Griffin, another player, slapped Plaintiff in the face. Plaintiff reported this incident to Coach Ector, who told Plaintiff "you need to learn how to handle your own business." Plaintiff then picked up a weight lock and put it in his gym bag. After practice was over, Griffin again approached Plaintiff. Plaintiff pulled the weight lock out of his bag, hit Griffin in the head with it, and then placed it back in his bag. The two students then began to fight.

While the two were fighting, Coach Ector and Principal Herschel Robinson were in the immediate area. Neither of them stopped the fight.

Ector came over and began dumping the contents of Plaintiff's bag on the ground, shouting repeatedly "what did you hit him with; if you hit him with it, I am going to hit you with it." Ector then, in the presence of Robinson, took the weight lock and struck Plaintiff in the left eye. As a result of the blow, Plaintiff's eye "was knocked completely out of its socket," leaving it "destroyed and dismembered." According to Plaintiff, even after this blow, Plaintiff's eye "was hanging out of his head, and as he was in severe pain," neither Coach Ector nor Principal Robinson stopped the fight.

Based on these alleged facts, Plaintiff sued Ector, Robinson, Superintendent Stephen Dolinger, and the Fulton County School Board under 42 U.S.C. §1983. Plaintiff claimed that Ector's use of corporal punishment was so excessive as to shock the conscience and violate his Fourteenth Amendment substantive due process rights. Plaintiff also claimed that the School Board, Superintendent, and Principal were liable for failing to train, instruct properly, and supervise Ector, and that this failure established a custom within the school district which resulted in the violation of Plaintiff's rights. . . .

Ector's conduct [here] . . . amount[s] to corporal punishment. Ector was spurred to act by Plaintiff's misconduct on school premises. Ector's intent to discipline Plaintiff for that act is evidenced by his statement to Plaintiff that "If you hit him with it, I'll hit you with it." And Ector ultimately did use physical force against Plaintiff. This case is not one where a teacher used reasonable force to restore order in the face of a school disturbance and merely shoved or grabbed fighting students to separate them. On the contrary, Ector never attempted to break up the fight . . . the force allegedly used by Ector was related to Plaintiff's misconduct at school and was for the purpose of discipline. As such, it constitutes corporal punishment. . . .

The case is significantly different [from *Ingraham v. Wright*]. In this case, no one argues that the blow struck by Ector was pursuant to a school corporal punishment policy. Ector did not confer with school administrators before punishing Plaintiff, and Ector was not expressly authorized by school officials to administer the corporal punishment he allegedly inflicted upon Plaintiff. Instead, Ector (a teacher) summarily and arbitrarily punished Plaintiff (a student) by striking Plaintiff in the eye with a metal weight. . . .

The substantive component of the Due Process Clause "protects individual liberty against 'certain government actions regardless of the fairness of the procedures used to implement them'" . . . [A]lmost all of the Courts of Appeals to address the issue squarely have said that a plaintiff alleging excessive corporal punishment may in certain circumstances state a claim under the substantive Due Process Clause. We agree, and join the vast majority of Circuits in confirming that excessive corporal punishment, at least where not administered in conformity with a valid school policy authorizing corporal punishment as in *Ingraham,* may be actionable under the Due Process Clause when it is tantamount to arbitrary, egregious, and conscience-shocking behavior. . . .

In determining whether the amount of force used is obviously excessive, we consider the totality of the circumstances. In particular, we examine: (1)

the need for the application of corporal punishment, (2) the relationship between the need and amount of punishment administered, and (3) the extent of the injury inflicted.

We need not decide today how "serious" an injury must be to support a claim. The injury alleged by Plaintiff here — the utter destruction of an eye — clearly was serious. . . .

On the facts of this case, and consistent with the logic of almost all courts considering the subject, we conclude that Plaintiff has stated a claim. Even assuming that it would not have been improper per se for Ector to have administered some amount of corporal punishment to Plaintiff due to Plaintiff's misconduct, Ector allegedly went much further, intentionally using an obviously excessive amount of force that presented a reasonably foreseeable risk of serious bodily injury. Ector hit Plaintiff in the eye with a metal weight, causing severe injury (indeed, Plaintiff permanently lost the use of his eye). Ector did not strike Plaintiff while trying to break up the fight, nor did he simply punish him by slapping him or administering some other amount of force that arguably might be reasonable. Instead, Ector came upon the scene of the fight, searched Plaintiff's bag while repeatedly shouting, "If you hit him with it, I'm going to hit you with it," found the weapon that Plaintiff had used, and then intentionally struck Plaintiff in the head with it and knocked out Plaintiff's eye.

Because Plaintiff has adequately alleged a violation of his right under the Fourteenth Amendment to be free from excessive corporal punishment, we vacate the district court's judgment dismissing the case, and remand for further proceedings consistent with this opinion.

Vacated and remanded.

2. High School and Intercollegiate Sports

The most prevalent forms of penalties and discipline occur when there is a denial of eligibility to participate in a particular sport or when a team is forced to forfeit victories for competing with ineligible players. Courts usually do not interfere with determinations of eligibility that are made by voluntary state high school athletic associations. The association most often is permitted to enforce its rules without judicial interference unless there is fraud or unless it has acted in an unreasonable manner. Courts usually do not substitute their interpretations of association bylaws for the association's interpretations, as long as the association's interpretation is fair and reasonable. If these associations do not act arbitrarily in applying a law that punishes, disciplines, or permits eligibility, there is no improper influence.

Similar to high school athletic associations, are voluntary associations that control collegiate athletics. The most notable is the National Collegiate Athletic Association (NCAA), although there are others. The NCAA is the preeminent regulatory forum in collegiate athletics. Its primary function is to penalize and discipline athletes and schools that violate its rules and regulations.

QUESTIONS AND DISCUSSION

1. See Mayes, *'Tonya Harding's Case: Contractual Due Process, the Amateur Athlete, and the American Ideal of Fair Play,'* 3 UCLA Ent. L. Rev. 109 (1995). Tonya Harding, former ice skater, was, of course a key player in the allegations behind the assault on her rival, Nancy Kerrigan, in January 1994. The United States Figure Skating Association (USFSA) found "reasonable grounds" to discipline Harding. The question is what process is due to an amateur athlete under the Amateur Sports Act of 1978, the United States Olympic Committee's (USOC) articles of incorporation, and the charter of the USFSA. See Harding v. USFSA, 851 F. Supp. 1476 (D. Or. 1994).

2. *See* Webb, *'Home-Schools and Interscholastic Sports: Denying Participation Violates United States Constitutional Due Process and Equal Protection Rights,'* 26 J.L. & Educ. 123 (1997). Some students who are home-schooled are now allowed to participate in high school interscholastic sports. The question is whether the home-schooled student has a sufficiently important interest in participation so as to receive due process.

3. *Kelley* held that a school board that suspended the interscholastic athletic program of an all-black high school for a period of one year denied the school the protection of procedural due process. What type of process is due?

4. In *Neal,* what would be the result if the coach's action was not meant to discipline?

5. In *Palmer v. Merluzzi,* 868 F.2d 90 (3d Cir. 1989), a high school student-athlete was hit with a 60-day athletic suspension and a 10-day academic suspension for smoking marijuana and drinking beer at a radio station. These penalties were constitutional since the student received all the process that was due and the schools's disciplinary action was rationally related to a valid state interest. Should it make a difference that the infraction did not occur on school property?

B. PROFESSIONAL SPORTS

The athlete-employer relationship in professional sports is based on consent and is defined by agreements such as the standard player's contract (SPK) and the collective bargaining agreement (CBA). These agreements define the boundaries that must be adhered to when athletes are disciplined or penalized for various infractions including gambling, referee arguments, brawls, and drug use. The power to discipline by the club and the league comes from the consent of the player. Within this broad power to discipline is the authority of the league commissioner.

The basic power to discipline and penalize comes from the SPK, which is an agreement between the employer and the athlete. Penalties can be in the form of fines, suspensions, expulsions, or contract terminations. The SPK also establishes the athlete's procedural rights, usually in the form of notice and review. The contract usually establishes that the commissioner has independent disciplinary authority. The question is whether the athlete has consented to be bound by the particular disciplinary rules. The answer depends on an interpretation of the contract's penalty clause and the league's discretion in defining and punishing inappropriate behavior. The SPK is now generally made a part of the CBA.

1. Authority of League Commissioner

The power of the league commissioner to discipline comes from the CBA and the league's constitution and bylaws. The constitution and bylaws, like the SPK, is generally a part of the CBA. Most leagues broadly authorize the commissioner to intervene in disciplinary matters that involve players, clubs, and owners.

All league commissioners or presidents possess broad governing authority, which includes the power to discipline. This is certainly not limited to baseball, even though the baseball commissioner's use of the "best interest" clause is the most publicized. In football, for example, Commissioner Peter Rozelle imposed the 'Rozelle Rule', which delegated to himself the ability to establish the reimbursement value for signing free agents.

In *Atlanta National League Baseball Club v. Kuhn*, the commissioner's decision to suspend the owner of the Atlanta Braves, Ted Turner, was determined to be in the best interests of the game and not an abuse of the commissioner's authority.

ATLANTA NATIONAL LEAGUE BASEBALL CLUB, INC. v. KUHN

432 F. Supp. 1213 (N.D. Ga. 1977)

EDENFIELD, District Judge.

Plaintiffs brought this diversity action pursuant to 28 U.S.C. §1331 seeking to enjoin defendant from imposing certain sanctions against plaintiffs. . . .

Factual Background

Plaintiff Turner is Chief Executive Officer of plaintiff Atlanta National League Baseball Club ("Atlanta Club"). The Atlanta Club, together with 25 other teams, is a signatory to an agreement known as the Major League Agreement. That agreement, the latest version of which was executed on January 1, 1975, constitutes a contract between the two baseball league associations, the American League of Professional Baseball Clubs and the National League of Professional Baseball Clubs, of which the Atlanta Club is a member. The Agreement establishes the office of the defendant, the Commissioner of Baseball, and defines his authority, powers and responsibilities.

The origin of the instant controversy can be traced to the changes that were made in baseball's reserve system in 1976. . . . This system . . . essentially bound a player to a team perpetually unless traded or released. . . . In 1975, the Players Association filed grievances on behalf of two players . . . challenging this system. An arbitration panel . . . concluded that players who had completed their last year of a contract with a particular club would be obligated, at the option of the club, to play only one additional year for that club. . . . The decision of the arbitration panel was upheld by the Court of

Appeals for the Eighth Circuit in *Kansas City Royals Baseball Corp. v. Major League Baseball Players Ass'n,* 532 F.2d 615 (8th Cir. 1976).

In an effort to implement the Kansas City Royals decision, the representatives of the Players Association and the club owners met to hammer out a new collective bargaining agreement. . . .

[In an effort to stop tampering, on] August 27, 1976 the Commissioner issued the first in a series of warnings in the form of a teletyped notice to each major league club. The directive concerned the fact that press reports were circulating which speculated on the amount potential free agents would be paid to sign. Where club personnel were the source of such reports, the conduct was cautioned as constituting tampering, which would no longer be tolerated. . . .

On October 20, 1976 Turner attended a cocktail party in New York City sponsored by the New York Yankees Club, and there engaged in a conversation with Robert Lurie, co-owner of the San Francisco club. In the presence of several media representatives, Turner told Lurie that he would do anything to get Gary Matthews and that he would go as high as he had to. Turner's comments were reported by a few San Francisco newspapers. On October 25, 1976, Lurie filed a complaint concerning these statements with the Commissioner. . . .

The draft was conducted on November 4, and twelve teams drafted negotiation rights with Matthews by the fifth round. The same day a formal hearing was held in which Turner admitted making the above comments, claiming that they were made in jest, but denied that there had been any direct or indirect negotiations of contract terms with Matthews or his agent. . . .

On December 30, the Commissioner announced . . . that Turner's statements were in clear violation of the prohibitions of the directives. . . . In considering appropriate sanctions, the Commissioner decided not to disapprove Matthews' contract with the Atlanta Club which had been signed on November 17. . . . Instead, the Commissioner decided to suspend Turner from baseball for one year, reasoning that (1) Turner had suggested that such a sanction would be appropriate, (2) this was the second Atlanta tampering violation, and (3) the Commissioner had warned in one of his directives that suspensions might be imposed.

As a further sanction, the Commissioner decided that the Atlanta Club would not be entitled to exercise its first round draft choice in the June, 1977 amateur free agent draft. . . .

On March 8, 1977, Turner and the Atlanta Club filed this action, challenging the Commissioner's authority to (1) issue the six directives, (2) conclude that plaintiffs had violated those directives, (3) enforce the collective bargaining agreement, and (4) impose the sanctions described above. Plaintiffs also alleged that the sanctions imposed constituted a tortious interference with the business relations of the plaintiffs. . . .

Although the Commissioner is designated as an arbitrator in Article VII, §1, his task in that capacity is to resolve "(a)ll disputes and controversies related in any way to professional baseball between clubs (including their officers, directors, employees and players)." Plaintiffs argue that this section is inapplicable to the instant situation because this was not a dispute between parties as referred to in §1. . . .

That the Commissioner did not act as an arbitrator herein is supported by the sanctions imposed. Typically in an arbitration dispute the arbitrator adjudicates the rights as between two parties and accords relief to one of them. Here, the Commissioner was not deciding Lurie's rights vis a vis Turner, and granting relief to Lurie; rather, a punishment was imposed which would primarily affect only Turner and the Atlanta Club.

The court is inclined to view the Commissioner's authority as deriving not from the arbitration clause of the Major League Agreement, but from Article I, §2, where he is given the power to "*investigate,* either upon complaint or upon his own initiative, any act . . . alleged or suspected to be not in the best interests of the national game of Baseball," and "*to determine,* after investigation, what . . . punitive action is appropriate. . . . " (Emphasis in original.) Under Article VII, §2, the parties to the Agreement agreed to be bound by the discipline imposed by the Commissioner pursuant to his authority thereunder and to waive appeals to the court. . . .

The Commissioner's Authority . . .

To the extent this case involves a violation of the Major League Agreement, the court has no hesitation in saying that the defendant Commissioner had ample authority to punish plaintiffs in this case, for acts considered not in the best interests of baseball. . . .

Obviously this new agreement modified the Major League Agreement at least as to such subject matter as is covered by the later agreement. The two agreements must now be read together as forming the framework for the government of Major League baseball. The powers of the Commissioner under the Major League Agreement are therefore modified only so as to avoid infringing upon the rights secured by the parties to the collective bargaining agreement. . . .

Since the Commissioner has the authority to sanction that conduct that he concludes is detrimental to baseball, he must also have the authority to issue advance notice as to what acts will constitute forbidden conduct. Essentially the directives served to warn that conduct inconsistent with the directives would be considered not in the best interests of baseball and would be severely dealt with. Accordingly, they were "preventive" measures, and the Commissioner had express authority to issue them. . . .

Authority to Decide the Case . . .

The Commissioner's authority to investigate and decide the case against Turner came not from the Bargaining Agreement, but from Article I, §2, of the Major League Agreement, where he is given the power to determine what conduct is not in the best interests of baseball. There is nothing in the Bargaining Agreement to prevent him from concluding that conduct which he views as violating the Collective Bargaining Agreement is also not in the best interests of baseball. . . .

The Sanctions

Viewing the evidence concerning punishment here, a casual, nonlegalistic observer might say that this case represents a comedy of strange tactical errors on both sides. Both at the hearing before the Commissioner and afterward, but before decision, Turner asked for "suspension" as his punishment in lieu of cancellation of the Matthews contract, which he feared. The Commissioner also did some inexplicable things: He approved Atlanta's signing of Matthews, apparently the only tangible mischief resulting from Turner's remarks, but having approved the act of signing he then punished Turner for publicly suggesting in advance he intended to do it. He also forbade Turner the right to manage his business or to even go on his own property except as a paying customer. . . .

The denial of the June draft choice, however, stands on a somewhat different legal footing. Under the best interests of baseball clause, Article I, §2, the Commissioner is given the authority to "determine, after investigation, what preventive, remedial or punitive action is appropriate in the premises." Those punitive measures which the Commissioner may take are explicitly enumerated in Article I, §3. . . .

[However, denial] of a draft choice is simply not among the penalties authorized for this offense. . . . sanctions in §3 does not preclude the Commissioner from imposing other sanctions that he deems appropriate. He says that *Milwaukee American Ass'n v. Landis,* [49 F.2d 298 (N.D. Ill. 1931)], so holds. The court does not perceive *Landis* as going that far. In *Landis,* the Commissioner had found that the owner of the St. Louis Club, in his handling of a player under contract to that club, had engaged in conduct claimed to be not in the best interests of baseball. As a sanction, the Commissioner declared the player to be a free agent. The St. Louis Club argued that the Commissioner lacked authority to impose the sanction since it was not specifically listed in Article I, §3. Although the court affirmed the action of the Commissioner and in doing so noted his wide range of powers, the question raised by the St. Louis Club in *Landis* and by the plaintiffs herein was left unanswered. . . .

Since the Commissioner had the explicit authority to accomplish the same result by simply refusing to approve the contract, thereby automatically making Bennett a free agent (now under Rule 12(a) of the Major League Rules), there was no need to expand the sanctions listed in §3 to include this measure.

The recent case of *Finley & Co. v. Kuhn,* 76C-2358 (N.D. Ill. 1977), also did not decide the question of whether the sanctions listed in §3 are exclusive, although defendant would suggest otherwise. The issue in *Finley* was again the Commissioner's authority to disapprove certain assignments as not being in the best interests of baseball. Although the court noted that the power to set aside assignments of players was not explicitly listed in the Commissioner's powers under §3, it stated that

> Section 3 does not say that the Commissioner shall have only the power to act
> in the enumerated ways, though that could have been said if it was intended.
> The section says that the Commissioner may act in one of the enumerated
> ways, without expressly so limiting him. . . .

The implication of this [enforcement] provision is that the sum total of punitive sanctions available to the Commissioner are those specifically itemized in the Major League Agreement, Article I, §3, or under the Major League Rules such as Rule 50. . . .

If the Commissioner is to have the unlimited punitive authority as he says is needed to deal with new and changing situations, the agreement should be changed to expressly grant the Commissioner that power. The deprivation of a draft choice was first and foremost a punitive sanction, and a sanction that is not specifically enumerated under §3. Accordingly, the court concludes that the Commissioner was without the authority to impose that sanction, and its imposition is therefore void. . . .

Summary

In summary, the Commissioner's decision to deprive plaintiffs of their first round draft choice in the June, 1977 amateur draft is hereby held to be ultra vires and therefore void. With respect to the balance of plaintiffs' claims, the court concludes that the Commissioner acted within the scope of his authority and hereby awards judgment in favor of defendant. Each party is to bear its own costs in this action.

In *Charles O. Finley & Co. v. Kuhn*, 569 F.2d 527 (7th Cir. 1978), "The two important questions raised by this appeal are whether the Commissioner of baseball is contractually authorized to disapprove player assignments which he finds to be 'not in the best interests of baseball' where neither moral turpitude nor violation of a Major League Rule is involved, and whether the provision in the Major League Agreement whereby the parties agree to waive recourse to the courts is valid and enforceable."

CHARLES O. FINLEY & CO. V. KUHN

569 F.2d 527 (7th Cir. 1978)

SPRECHER, Circuit Judge.

The two important questions raised by this appeal are whether the Commissioner of baseball is contractually authorized to disapprove player assignments which he finds to be "not in the best interests of baseball" where neither moral turpitude nor violation of a Major League Rule is involved, and whether the provision in the Major League Agreement whereby the parties agree to waive recourse to the courts is valid and enforceable.

I

The plaintiff, Charles O. Finley & Co., Inc., an Illinois corporation, is the owner of the Oakland Athletics baseball club, a member of the American League of Professional Baseball Clubs (Oakland). Joe Rudi, Rollie Fingers and Vida Blue were members of the active playing roster of the Oakland baseball club and were contractually bound to play for Oakland through the end of the 1976 baseball season. On or about June 15, 1976, Oakland and Blue entered a contract whereby Blue would play for Oakland through the 1979 season, but Rudi and Fingers had not at that time signed contracts for the period beyond the 1976 season.

If Rudi and Fingers had not signed contracts to play with Oakland by the conclusion of the 1976 season, they would at that time have become free agents eligible thereafter to negotiate with any major league club, subject to certain limitations on their right to do so that were then being negotiated by the major league clubs with the Players Association.

On June 14 and 15, 1976, Oakland negotiated tentative agreements to sell the club's contract rights for the services of Rudi and Fingers to the Boston Red Sox for $2 million and for the services of Blue to the New York Yankees for $1.5 million. The agreements were negotiated shortly before the expiration of baseball's trading deadline at midnight on June 15, after which time Oakland could not have sold the contracts of these players to other clubs without first offering the players to all other American League teams, in inverse order of their standing, at the stipulated waiver price of $20,000.

The defendant Bowie K. Kuhn is the Commissioner of baseball (Commissioner), having held that position since 1969. On June 18, 1976, the Commissioner disapproved the assignments of the contracts of Rudi, Fingers and Blue to the Red Sox and Yankees "as inconsistent with the best interests of baseball, the integrity of the game and the maintenance of public confidence in it." The Commissioner expressed his concern for (1) the debilitation of the Oakland club, (2) the lessening of the competitive balance of professional baseball through the buying of success by the more affluent clubs, and (3) "the present unsettled circumstances of baseball's reserve system."

Thereafter on June 25, 1976, Oakland instituted this suit principally challenging, as beyond the scope of the Commissioner's authority and, in any event, as arbitrary and capricious, the Commissioner's disapproval of the Rudi, Fingers and Blue assignments. The complaint set forth seven causes of action: (I) that the Commissioner breached his employment contract with Oakland by acting arbitrarily, discriminatorily and unreasonably; (II) that the Commissioner, acting in concert with others, conspired to eliminate Oakland from baseball in violation of federal antitrust laws; (III) that Oakland's constitutional rights of due process and equal protection were violated; (IV) that Oakland's constitutional rights were violated by the first disapproval of a player assignment where no major league rule was violated; (V) that the defendants (the Commissioner, the National and American Leagues and the Major League Executive Council) induced the breach of Oakland's contracts with Boston and New York; (VI) that the Commissioner did not have the authority to disapprove Oakland's assignments "in the best interests of baseball"; and (VII) that Oakland have specific performance of its contracts of assignment with Boston and New York.

On September 7, 1976, the district court granted the Commissioner's motion for summary judgment as to Counts II, III and IV. Count II was dismissed on the ground that the business of baseball is not subject to the federal antitrust laws. Counts III and IV were dismissed on the ground that Oakland did not allege sufficient nexus between the state and the complained of activity to constitute state action.

A bench trial took place as a result of which judgment on the remaining four counts of the complaint was entered in favor of the Commissioner on March 17, 1977.

On August 29, 1977, the district court granted the Commissioner's counterclaim for a declaratory judgment that the covenant not to sue in the Major League Agreement is valid and enforceable. The court had not relied on that covenant in reaching its two earlier decisions.

Oakland appealed from the judgments of September 7, 1976, March 17, 1977, and August 29, 1977, arguing (1) that the court's failure to issue a finding on the question of procedural fairness constituted error; (2) that the exclusion of evidence of the Commissioner's malice toward the Oakland club constituted error; (3) that other errors were committed during trial; (4) that the antitrust count was not barred by baseball's exemption from federal antitrust law; and (5) that baseball's blanket waiver of recourse to the courts is not enforceable.

II

Basic to the underlying suit brought by Oakland and to this appeal is whether the Commissioner of baseball is vested by contract with the authority to disapprove player assignments which he finds to be "not in the best interests of baseball." In assessing the measure and extent of the Commissioner's power and authority, consideration must be given to the circumstances attending the creation of the office of Commissioner, the language employed by the parties in drafting their contractual understanding, changes and amendments adopted from time to time, and the interpretation given by the parties to their contractual language throughout the period of its existence.

Prior to 1921, professional baseball was governed by a three-man National Commission formed in 1903 which consisted of the presidents of the National and American Leagues and a third member, usually one of the club owners, selected by the presidents of the two leagues. Between 1915 and 1921, a series of events and controversies contributed to a growing dissatisfaction with the National Commission on the part of players, owners and the public, and a demand developed for the establishment of a single, independent Commissioner of baseball.

On September 28, 1920, an indictment issued charging that an effort had been made to "fix" the 1919 World Series by several Chicago White Sox players. Popularly known as the "Black Sox Scandal," this event rocked the game of professional baseball and proved the catalyst that brought about the establishment of a single, neutral Commissioner of baseball.

In November, 1920, the major league club owners unanimously elected federal Judge Kenesaw Mountain Landis as the sole Commissioner of baseball and appointed a committee of owners to draft a charter setting forth the Commissioner's authority. In one of the drafting sessions an attempt was made to place limitations on the Commissioner's authority. Judge Landis responded by refusing to accept the office of Commissioner.

On January 12, 1921, Landis told a meeting of club owners that he had agreed to accept the position upon the clear understanding that the owners had sought "an authority . . . outside of your own business, and that a part of that authority would be a control over whatever and whoever had to do with baseball." Thereupon, the owners voted unanimously to reject the proposed limitation upon the Commissioner's authority, they all signed what they called the Major League Agreement, and Judge Landis assumed the position of Commissioner. Oakland has been a signatory to the Major League Agreement continuously since 1960. The agreement, a contract between the constituent clubs of the National and American Leagues, is the basic charter under which major league baseball operates. . . .

The Major Leagues and their constituent clubs severally agreed to be bound by the decisions of the Commissioner and by the discipline imposed by him. They further agreed to "waive such right of recourse to the courts as would otherwise have existed in their favor." Major League Agreement, Art. VII, Sec. 2.

Upon Judge Landis' death in 1944, the Major League Agreement was amended in two respects to limit the Commissioner's authority. First, the parties deleted the provision by which they had agreed to waive their right of recourse to the courts to challenge actions of the Commissioner. Second, the parties added the following language to Article I, Section 3:

> No Major League Rule or other joint action of the two Major Leagues, and no action or procedure taken in compliance with any such Major League Rule or joint action of the two Major Leagues shall be considered or construed to be detrimental to Baseball.

The district court found that this addition had the effect of precluding the Commissioner from finding an act that complied with the Major League Rules to be detrimental to the best interests of baseball.

The two 1944 amendments to the Major League Agreement remained in effect during the terms of the next two Commissioners, A. B. "Happy" Chandler and Ford Frick. Upon Frick's retirement in 1964 and in accordance with his recommendation, the parties adopted three amendments to the Major League Agreement: (1) the language added in 1944 preventing the Commissioner from finding any act or practice "taken in compliance" with a Major League Rule to be "detrimental to baseball" was removed; (2) the provision deleted in 1944 waiving any rights of recourse to the courts to challenge a Commissioner's decision was restored; and (3) in places where the language "detrimental to the best interests of the national game of baseball" or "detrimental to baseball" appeared those words were changed to "not in the best interests of the national game of Baseball" or "not in the best interests of Baseball." . . .

The Commissioner has been given broad power in unambiguous language to investigate any act, transaction or practice not in the best interests of baseball, to determine what preventive, remedial or punitive action is appropriate in the premises, and to take that action. He has also been given the express power to approve or disapprove the assignments of players. In regard to nonparties to the agreement, he may take such other steps as he deems necessary and proper in the interests of the morale of the players and the honor of the game. Further, indicative of the nature of the Commissioner's authority is the provision whereby the parties agree to be bound by his decisions and discipline imposed and to waive recourse to the courts. . . .

In view of the broad authority expressly given by the Major League Agreement to the Commissioner, particularly in Section 2 of Article I, we agree with the district court that Section 3 does not purport to limit that authority.

III

Despite the Commissioner's broad authority to prevent any act, transaction or practice not in the best interests of baseball, Oakland has attacked the Commissioner's disapproval of the Rudi-Fingers-Blue transactions on a variety of theories which seem to express a similar thrust in differing language. . . .

We conclude that the evidence fully supports, and we agree with, the district court's finding that "(t)he history of the adoption of the Major League Agreement in 1921 and the operation of baseball for more than 50 years under it, including: the circumstances preceding and precipitating the adoption of the Agreement; the numerous exercises of broad authority under the best interests clause by Judge Landis and . . . Commissioner Kuhn; the amendments to the Agreement in 1964 restoring and broadening the authority of the Commissioner; . . . and most important the express language of the Agreement itself are all to the effect that the Commissioner has the authority to determine whether any act, transaction or practice is 'not in the best interests of baseball,' and upon such determination, to take whatever preventive or remedial action he deems appropriate, whether or not the act, transaction or practice complies with the Major League Rules or involves moral turpitude." Any other conclusion would involve the courts in not only interpreting often complex rules of baseball to determine if they were violated but also, as noted in the Landis case, the "intent of the (baseball) code," an even more complicated and subjective task.

The Rudi-Fingers-Blue transactions had been negotiated on June 14 and 15, 1976. On June 16, the Commissioner sent a teletype to the Oakland, Boston and New York clubs and to the Players' Association expressing his "concern for possible consequences to the integrity of baseball and public confidence in the game" and setting a hearing for June 17. Present at the hearing were 17 persons representing those notified. At the outset of the hearing the commissioner stated that he was concerned that the assignments would be harmful to the competitive capacity of Oakland; that they reflected an effort by Boston and New York to purchase star players and "bypass the usual methods of player development and acquisition which have been traditionally used in professional baseball"; and that the question to be resolved was whether the transactions "are consistent with the best interests of baseball's integrity and maintenance of public confidence in the game." He warned that it was possible that he might determine that the assignments not be approved. Mr. Finely and representatives of the Red Sox and Yankees made statements on the record.

No one at the hearing, including Mr. Finley, claimed that the Commissioner lacked the authority to disapprove the assignments, or objected to the holding of the hearing, or to any of the procedures followed at the hearing.

On June 18, the Commissioner concluded that the attempted assignments should be disapproved as not in the best interests of baseball. In his written decision, the Commissioner stated his reasons which we have summarized in Part I. The decision was sent to all parties by teletype.

The Commissioner recognized "that there have been cash sales of player contracts in the past," but concluded that "these transactions were unparalleled in the history of the game" because there was "never anything on this scale or falling at this time of the year, or which threatened so seriously to unbalance the competitive balance of baseball." The district court concluded that the attempted assignments of Rudi, Fingers and Blue "were at a time and under circumstances making them unique in the history of baseball."

We conclude that the evidence fully supports, and we agree with, the district court's finding and conclusion that the Commissioner "acted in good faith, after investigation, consultation and deliberation, in a manner which he determined to be in the best interests of baseball" and that "(w)hether he was right or wrong is beyond the competence and the jurisdiction of this court to decide."

We must then conclude that anyone becoming a signatory to the Major League Agreement was put on ample notice that the action ultimately taken by the Commissioner was not only possible but probable. The action was neither an "abrupt departure" nor a "change of policy" in view of the contemporaneous developments taking place in the reserve system, over which the Commissioner had little or no control, and in any event the broad authority given to the Commissioner by the Major League Agreement placed any party to it on notice that such authority could be used. . . .

We affirm the district court's judgments of September 7, 1976, March 17, 1977 and August 20, 1977. Affirmed.

Charles O. Finley & Co. v. Kuhn underscores the proposition that the commissioner of baseball is vested by contract to disapprove player assignments that he finds to be "not in the best interests of baseball."

Another famous baseball controversy that concerned the best interests clause involved Pete Rose. This conflict was hotly litigated. See, for example, *Rose v. Giamatti*, 721 F. Supp. 906 (S.D. Ohio 1989). This particular version concerned the jurisdiction of a U.S. district court when a case is removed from state court based on diversity of citizenship of the parties to the controversy; the ability of the commissioner to move with great dispatch when he finds that the actions of a manager are "not in the best interests of baseball" are once again emphasized. Here, of course, the plaintiff is "a baseball figure of national reputation closely identified with the Cincinnati Reds and the City of Cincinnati."

2. Collective Bargaining Agreements

Penalties and discipline in professional sports are controlled by both individual contracts and the CBA;, therefore, the authority to discipline in professional sports is not as broad as in amateur sports. For example, the league's commissioner cannot use his disciplinary power solely to enhance the league's economic position or solely because of a desire to restrict the competitive opportunities of a player.

The following sections from the National Football League's CBA cover both club discipline and commissioner discipline.

NATIONAL FOOTBALL LEAGUE COLLECTIVE BARGAINING AGREEMENT

1993-2003

Article VIII. Club Discipline

Section 1. Maximum Discipline

(a)   For the 1993 League Year, the following maximum discipline schedule will be applicable:

Overweight—maximum fine of $50 per lb./per day.

Unexcused late reporting for mandatory off-season training camp, team meeting, practice, transportation, curfew, scheduled appointment with Club physician or trainer, or scheduled promotional activity—maximum fine of $200.

Failure to promptly report injury to Club physician or trainer—maximum fine of $200.

Losing, damaging or altering Club-provided equipment—maximum fine of $200 and replacement cost, if any.

Throwing football into stands—maximum fine of $200.

Unexcused late reporting for or absence from pre-season training camp by a player under contract except those signed as an Unrestricted Free Agent pursuant to Article XIX (Veteran Free Agency)—maximum fine of $4,000 per day for the 1993-95 League Years and $5,000 per day for the 1996-99 League Years.

Unexcused late reporting for or absence from pre-season training camp by a player under contract signed as an Unrestricted Free Agent pursuant to Article XIX (Veteran Free Agency)—maximum fine of $4,000 per day for the 1993-95 League Years and $5,000 per day for the 1996-99 League Years, plus one week's regular season salary for each pre-season game missed.

Unexcused missed mandatory off-season training camp, team meeting, practice, curfew, bed check, scheduled appointment with Club physician or trainer, material failure to follow Club rehabilitation directions, or scheduled promotional activity—maximum fine of $1,000.

Material failure to follow rehabilitation program prescribed by Club physician or trainer—maximum fine of $1,000.

Unexcused missed team transportation—maximum fine of $1,000 and transportation expense, if any.

Loss of all or part of playbook, scouting report or game plan—maximum fine of $1,000.

Ejection from game—maximum fine of $2,000.

Conduct detrimental to Club—maximum fine of an amount equal to one week's salary and/or suspension without pay for a period not to exceed four (4) weeks.

The Club will promptly notify the player of any discipline; notice of any Club fine in the $4,000/$5,000 maximum category and of any "conduct detrimental" fine or suspension will be sent to the NFLPA. . . .

Section 3. Uniformity

Discipline will be imposed uniformly within a Club on all players for the same offense; however, the Club may specify the events which create an escalation of the discipline, provided the formula for escalation is uniform in its application. Any disciplinary action imposed upon a player by the Commissioner pursuant to Article XI . . . will preclude or supersede disciplinary action by the Club for the same act or conduct.

Section 4. Disputes

Any dispute involved in Club discipline may be made the subject of a non-injury grievance under Article IX. . . .

Article XI. Commissioner Discipline

Section 1. League Discipline

Notwithstanding anything stated in Article IX (Non-Injury Grievance):

(a)   All disputes involving a fine or suspension imposed upon a player for conduct on the playing field . . . or involving action taken against a player by the Commissioner for conduct detrimental to the integrity of, or public confidence in, the game of professional football, will be processed exclusively as follows: the Commissioner will promptly send written notice of his action to the player, with a copy to the NFLPA. Within twenty (20) days following such written notification, the player affected thereby, or the NFLPA with the player's approval, may appeal in writing to the Commissioner.

(b)   Fines or suspensions imposed upon players for unnecessary roughness or unsportsmanlike conduct on the playing field with respect to an opposing player or players shall be determined initially by a person appointed by the Commissioner after consultation concerning the person being appointed with the Executive Director of the NFLPA, as promptly as possible after the event(s) in question. . . .

(c)   On receipt of a notice of appeal under subsection (a) or (b) above, the Commissioner will designate a time and place for a hearing to be commenced within ten (10) days thereafter, at which he or his designee (other than the person appointed in (b) above) will preside. The hearing may be by telephone conference call, if the player so requests. . . .

Section 3. Representation

In any hearing provided for in this Article, a player may be accompanied by counsel of his choice. A representative of the NFLPA may also participate in such hearing and represent the player. In any such hearing, a Club representative may be accompanied by counsel of his choice. . . .

Section 4. Costs

Unless the Commissioner determines otherwise, each party will bear the cost of its own witnesses, counsel and the like.

Section 5. One Penalty

The Commissioner and a Club will not discipline a player for the same act or conduct. The Commissioner's disciplinary action will preclude or supersede disciplinary action by any Club for the same act or conduct.

Section 6. Fine Money

Any fine money collected pursuant to this Article will be contributed to the Brian Piccolo Cancer Fund [and other organizations]. . . .

In *Sprewell*, both the team and the league punished the player for inappropriate behavior.

SPREWELL V. GOLDEN STATE WARRIORS

231 F.3d 520 (9th Cir. 2000)

TROTT, Circuit Judge:
Latrell F. Sprewell challenges the district court's dismissal of his claims against the National Basketball Association and the Golden State Warriors.
. . .
Sprewell raises numerous state and federal claims challenging the validity of the punishments meted out by the NBA and the Warriors in response to Sprewell's physical attack on the head coach of the Warriors in 1997. The district court dismissed Sprewell's federal claims as frivolous, and found Sprewell's state claims to be preempted by section 301 of the Labor Management Relations Act ("section 301"). We have jurisdiction over this matter pursuant to 28 U.S.C. §1291, and affirm the district court.

I. Background

Sprewell joined the NBA in 1992 as a guard for the Golden State Warriors. During Sprewell's tenure with the Warriors, he played under four different head coaches, the last of whom was P.J. Carlesimo. Sprewell's star-crossed relationship with Carlesimo, while initially amicable upon its inception in June of 1997, quickly deteriorated over the ensuing six months to the point that both Sprewell and the Warriors openly entertained the possibility of trading Sprewell to another team.

Tensions between Sprewell and Carlesimo climaxed during a closed-door practice on December 1, 1997, during which Carlesimo told Sprewell to pass the ball to a teammate for a quick shot. Despite Sprewell's contention that he passed the ball "admirably, as one would expect of an All-Star," Carlesimo rebuked Sprewell for not putting more speed on his pass. When Carlesimo subsequently repeated his criticism, Sprewell slammed the ball down and directed several expletives at Carlesimo. Carlesimo responded with a similar showing of sophistication. Sprewell immediately either walked or lunged at Carlesimo and wrapped his hands around Carlesimo's neck. With his arms fully extended, Sprewell moved Carlesimo backwards, saying "I will kill you."

Carlesimo offered no resistance. Sprewell grasped Carlesimo's neck for approximately seven to ten seconds—the time it took for other players and coaches to restrain Sprewell. Sprewell then left the practice floor, saying "trade me, get me out of here, I will kill you," to which Carlesimo countered, "I am here."

After showering and changing, Sprewell returned to the practice facility to again confront Carlesimo. Despite the efforts of two assistant coaches to restrain him, Sprewell was able to approach Carlesimo and throw an overhand punch that grazed Carlesimo's right cheek. Sprewell landed a subsequent blow to Carlesimo's shoulder, but it is uncertain whether it was intentional or the product of Sprewell's attempt to free himself from those restraining him. As Sprewell left the facility, he again told Carlesimo, "I will kill you."

That evening the Warriors suspended Sprewell for a minimum of ten games and expressly reserved its right to terminate Sprewell's contract. Two days later, the Warriors exercised that right and ended Sprewell's reign as a Warrior. The NBA subsequently issued its own one-year suspension of Sprewell after conducting an independent investigation of the matter.

On December 4, 1997, Sprewell invoked the arbitration provisions of his collective bargaining agreement ("CBA") by filing a grievance challenging both his suspension by the NBA and the Warriors' termination of his contract. . . . The arbitrator found that the dual punishments issued by the NBA and the Warriors were permissible under the CBA, but found that: (1) the Warriors' termination of Sprewell's contract was not supported by just cause because after the Warriors' initial suspension of Sprewell, any residual interest of the Warriors was absorbed by the NBA's investigation of the matter; and (2) the NBA's suspension should be limited to the 1997-98 season.

On May 20, 1998, Sprewell filed the instant suit. . . .

II. Analysis . . .

A. Count 1: Vacating the Arbitration Award

Sprewell seeks to vacate the arbitration award pursuant to section 301 of the Labor Management Relations Act, 29 U.S.C. §185 *et seq.* ("section 301"). Section 301 empowers this court to review an arbitration conducted under the terms of a collective bargaining agreement. . . .

Judicial scrutiny of an arbitrator's decision in a labor dispute "is extremely limited." . . .

1. The Arbitration Award Draws its Essence from the CBA

Sprewell contends that the arbitrator's approval of Sprewell's "multiple punishments"—the disciplinary actions taken by *both* the NBA *and* the Warriors in response to Sprewell's misconduct—did not draw its essence from the CBA. The thrust of Sprewell's argument is that the arbitrator improperly ascribed a conjunctive meaning to the word "or" in the CBA provision that subjects players "to disciplinary action for just cause by his Team or by the Commissioner." Sprewell alleges that by failing to read the word "or" in the disjunctive, the arbitrator not only discarded the "plain and unambiguous" language of the CBA, but actually rewrote it. Sprewell additionally argues that the arbitrator's award does not draw its essence from the CBA because "the Arbitrator relied upon the [National Football League's] collective bargaining agreement, which uses different language, i.e., the word 'and' instead of 'or'." Sprewell's claims are legally untenable.

[T]he arbitrator found that: (1) the CBA provision upon which Sprewell relies was not intended to deal with the issue of multiple disciplines, but rather was designed to emphasize "the imperative of just cause in reviewing the matters of discipline"—thus illustrating that the word "or" was likely chosen without careful consideration of its implications; (2) the CBA does not include the word "either," which would have supported the conclusion that the penalties were intended to be mutually exclusive; and (3) as demonstrated by the NFL's CBA, "[h]ad the parties here intended by contract to limit discipline with respect to the same matter to a team or the Commissioner, but not both, one would have expected some expression in the CBA as to which has primacy." Regardless of whether we would reach the same conclusion advanced by the arbitrator, we must defer to the arbitrator's decision on the grounds that he was, at the very least, "arguably construing or applying the contract."

> 2. The Arbitrator Did Not Exceed the Scope of His Authority . . .
>
> 3. The Award Does Not Run Counter to Public Policy . . .
>
> 4. The Arbitration Award Was Not Procured by Fraud . . .

B. Sprewell Fails to Plead Facts Sufficient to Sustain His Federal Claims for Racial Discrimination . . .

C. Preemption Claims

The NBA and the Warriors correctly argue that Sprewell's state law claims for intentional interference with contract and business relations, common law right to fair procedure, civil conspiracy, and unfair business practices are preempted by section 301 of the Labor Management Relations Act. Sprewell argues that the foregoing claims do not necessitate an interpretation of the CBA and therefore fall outside the preemptive ambit of section 301. Sprewell is mistaken. . . .

D. Sanctions

The district court did not abuse its discretion in imposing sanctions against Sprewell's attorneys. Orders imposing Rule 11 sanctions are reviewed for an abuse of discretion. . . .

IV. CONCLUSION

For the reasons outlined above, we affirm the district court's dismissal of Sprewell's claims against the NBA and the Warriors, and affirm the district court's imposition of sanctions.

Affirmed.

Sprewell v. Golden State Warriors involves the ability of both the team and the league to punish a player for physically attacking his coach.

3. Gambling

Gambling is the most serious possible infraction in professional sports. Gambling has always been viewed as contrary to the goal of maintaining competitiveness and credibility in the sport. Fans will no longer believe that the game is honest if gambling, in any form, is tolerated. If a player gambles on a game's outcome, then there will be no guarantee that any athletic contest is one of pure athletic skills and not influenced by the athlete's desire to have his team perform in a manner that would coincide with the views of the oddmakers for sports betting.

Molinas v. Podoloff is the seminal case that allows the president of a basketball association to permanently enjoin a player from continued involvement with the league when the player admits to gambling.

MOLINAS V. PODOLOFF

133 N.Y.S.2d 743 (App. Div. 1954)

JOSEPH, Justice.

Plaintiff brings this action for a permanent injunction to set aside his suspension as a player in the National Basketball Association, to maintain his rights to be a player member in the association and for other relief. The defendant, an unincorporated association, conducts and supervises a professional basketball league consisting of teams owned by nine clubs. The owners of the said clubs comprising the membership of the National Basketball Association (hereinafter designated as N.B.A.) employed professional basketball players known as player members of the association.

A duly-adopted constitution and bylaws regulated the rights, privileges and duties of the members and player members.

The Zollner Machine Works, Inc., of Fort Wayne, Indiana, was the owner of the club known as Fort Wayne Zollner Pistons, a member of the N.B.A.; it entered into a written contract on the form prescribed by the N.B.A. with the plaintiff to play professional basketball in the said league for its club, whereby the club and the plaintiff became bound by the terms of the said agreement, and the constitution and by laws of the N.B.A.

It is undisputed that on January 9, 1954, the police of Fort Wayne, Indiana, conducted an inquiry as to the Zollner Piston Basketball Team, and the plaintiff, by reason of such investigation, in the late evening of that day, or in the early morning of January 10, 1954, signed a written statement of his having wagered on his team. Specifically the plaintiff admitted: "I have been a member of the Zollner Piston Basketball Team since October 1953. After being on the team for approximately a month I called a man in New York by the name of Mr. X, knowing this man for a long period of time I called him on the telephone and asked him if he could place a bet for me. He said that he could and he would tell me the odds on the game either for or against the Pistons. After hearing the odds or points on the game I either placed a bet on the Pistons or else told him that the odds were too great and I did not want to place the bet. Several times I talked to him over the phone and odds or points were not mentioned and I told him that I thought on some occasions that we could win a particular game and I placed a bet. I did this about ten times. At no time was there a pay off to throw any games made to me by Mr. X. Nor was there any mention of the fact; however, the only reimbursement I received was for my phone calls which I made to him. Also I received approximately $400 for the total times that I have been betting with him. This included the phone bill also."

The plaintiff has admitted, and so testified at the trial, that the statement was a voluntary, free and truthful statement of fact.

Maurice Podoloff, President of the N.B.A., and Mr. Zollner, President of the Fort Wayne Zollner Pistons, arrived at the police station about midnight, and subsequent to being shown plaintiff's statement Mr. Podoloff sent for him. In the conversation that ensued, relating to the wagering situation, and the plaintiff's participation therein, Mr. Podoloff informed the plaintiff that he was "through" as a player, and Mr. Podoloff indefinitely suspended the plaintiff.

The plaintiff predicates his action upon two contentions: (1) that no notice of hearing and charges were given the plaintiff as provided by the contract and the constitution; (2) there was no authority to indefinitely suspend the plaintiff. The defendant contends: (1) that there was due notice and hearing; (2) plaintiff's and admissions of wagering constituted a waiver of his rights; (3) plaintiff comes into equity with unclean hands. . . .

After the plaintiff made his statement to the police, he was peremptorily sent for by Mr. Podoloff and Mr. Zollner. Assuming, but not conceding, that there was no due notice and hearing, as provided by the contract and the constitution of the N.B.A., this court finds that elaboration on plaintiff's contentions is rendered unnecessary because of the conclusions reached by this court in the determination of this matter.

Certain amateur and professional sports, and the athletes participating in such sports, have recently occupied the spotlight of unfavorable public attention. The radio and television have been contributing causes for creating industries out of certain sports. America is sport-minded; we admire the accomplishment of our athletes; we are pleased with the success of our favorite teams and we spend a considerable part of our time rooting, but relaxing nevertheless, with our favorite sports. We inherit from the Greeks and Romans a love for stadia and sport competition.

When the breath of scandal hits one sport, it casts suspicion on all other sports. It does irreparable injury to the great majority of the players, destroys the confidence of the public in athletic competition, and lets down the morale of our youth. When the standards of fair play, good sportsmanship and honesty are abandoned, sporting events become the property of the gamblers and racketeers.

Much has happened in basketball to displease the public. Bribing, fixing and wagering, especially when associated with gamblers and racketeers, are matters of serious nature. This court need not review the sordid details. It is necessary to recall them to realize the importance of the situations existing in this case.

Courts take cognizance of public interests and public problems; they reflect the spirit of the times and the sentiment and thoughts of the citizens.

Laws are promulgated and contracts are made to protect the public and are abreast with the demands, interest and protection of the people. The wagering by player members of N.B.A. and the contract calling for expulsion is an aftermath of the abuses with which we are concerned. To maintain basketball competition in the N.B.A., to have open competitive sport, the public confidence and attendance, every effort had to be made to eliminate the slightest suspicion that competition was not on an honest, competitive basis.

The player that wagers on games does much to destroy the sport. Unfortunately, in wagering on a basketball game, it is not merely the bet that the team wins, but it is a wager on points, and the wager on the point spread in the manner which this plaintiff made such wages is censurable. In the light of his knowledge of the basketball scandals, the express prohibitions in wagering and the manner of his betting, I am constrained to say plaintiff's conduct was reprehensible. . . .

The position of the plaintiff, in reality, seems to be one of asserting that he wagered on games, he breached his contract, he violated the constitution of the N.B.A. and was morally dishonest. Nevertheless, he now requests this court to order the defendant to cross all its t's and dot all its i's, and award damages for defendant's suspension without due notice and hearing. . . .

[T]he decision of the court [here] is made against a background of public interest which is based on public morality. That morality is one which concerns the public desire of honest sport and clean sportsmanship. It necessarily follows, as the day follows the night, that one who has offended against this concept of good morals, and who admits such offense in open court, does not by that very fact, satisfy the equitable maxim, that he who comes into equity must come with clean hands. . . .

The maxim of "clean hands" . . . applies to unconscientious acts or inequitable conduct. . . .

In the application of this doctrine, whenever a party seeks to set the judicial machinery in motion to obtain some remedy, and has violated conscience or good faith, or other equitable principle in his prior conduct, then the doors of the court will be shut against him; the court will refuse to interfere on his behalf, to acknowledge his right or to award him any remedy. . . .

Accordingly, the complaint is dismissed on the merits and judgment is directed in favor of the defendant. The above constitutes the decision of the court as required by the applicable provisions of the Civil Practice Act. Settle judgment accordingly.

The case is unusual in that it is very rare for an athlete to admit to gambling and then to seek equitable relief.

QUESTIONS AND DISCUSSION

1. In 1930, Judge Landis, the Commissioner of Baseball, using the "best interests" power, refused to allow the St. Louis Club to assign a player to the minor league. The court upheld the commissioner's use of the "best

interests" power in disapproving the assignment. The commissioner had "all attributes of a benevolent but absolute despot and all the disciplinary powers of the proverbial pater familias." The commissioner had an "almost unlimited discretion in the determination of whether or not a certain state of facts creates a situation detrimental to the national game of baseball." *Milwaukee Am. Ass'n. v. Landis*, 49 F.2d 298, 299, 303 (N.D. Ill. 1931), *app. dismissed*, 61 F.2d 1036 (7th Cir. 1931). *See generally* Reinsdorf, *The Powers of the Commissioner in Baseball*, 7 Marq. Sports L.J. 211 (1996). But, "the Commissioner's authority to investigate, 'Acts,' 'transactions' and 'practices' and to determine and take 'preventative, remedial or punitive actions' does not encompass restructuring the divisions of the National League. There has been no conduct [or misconduct] for the Commissioner to investigate punish or remedy under Article I." *Chicago Natl. League Ball Club, Inc. v. Vincent*, No. 92 C4398 (N.D. Ill. 1992).

The scope of the "best interests" clause is broad on its face and the nonexistence of any limiting clauses in the Major League Agreement suggests that the commissioner had broad powers under the clause. A literal interpretation of the Major League Agreement indicates that there should be a broad reading of the commissioner's powers, absent any express limiting language. Reinsdorf at 245. Can you imagine any action of coach, manager, player, team owner, or scout that is not covered by the "best interests" clause?

2. John Rocker was penalized for his verbal xenophobia on the basis that his comments violated the best interests of baseball clause in his contract, which allowed the league and team to discipline him. *See* Abrams, *Symposium: John Rocker Off His Rocker: Sports Discipline and Labor Arbitration*, 11 Marq. Sports L.J. 167 (2001); Kurlantzick, *Symposium: John Rocker and Employee Discipline for Speech*, 11 Marq. Sports L.J. 185 (2001).

3. For more on the *Sprewell* case, see Javier, *You Cannot Choke Your Boss and Hold Your Job Unless You Play in the NBA: The Latrell Sprewell Incident Underminies Disciplinary Authority in the NBA*, 7 Vill. Sports & Ent. L. F. 209 (2000).

4. Pete Rose sought to prevent the baseball commissioner from conducting disciplinary hearings concerning allegations that, while manager of the Cincinnati Reds, he wagered on major league baseball games. *See generally* Arcella, *Major League Baseball's Disempowered Commissioner: Judical Ramifications of the 1994 Restructuring*, 97 Colum. L. Rev. 2420 (1997); Darney, *Fair or Foul? The Commissioner and Major League Baseball's Disciplinary Process*, 41 Emory L.J. 581 (1992); Dowd Report, Report to the Commissioner, 68 Miss. L.J. 915 (1999) (the Dowd Report was created by authority of the Office of the Commissioner of Baseball to investigate Pete Rose); Feliu, *Foreword: Discipline in Professional Sports*, 17 Hofstra Lab. & Emp. L.J. 129 (1999); Jefferson, *The NFL and Domestic Violence: The Commissioner's Power to Punish Domestic Abusers*, 7 Seton Hall J. Sport L. 353 (1997); Klein, *Rose Is in Red, Black Sox Are Blue: A Comparison of* Rose v. Giamatti, *and the 1921 Black Sox Trial*, 13 Hastings Comm. & Ent. L.J. 551 (1991); Lentze, *The Legal Concept of Professional Sports Leagues: The*

Commissioner and an Alternative Approach from a Corporate Perspective, 6 Marq. Sports L.J. 65 (1995); Pachman, *Limits on the Discretionary Powers of Professional Sports Commissioners: A Historical and Legal Analysis of Issues Raised by the Pete Rose Controversy*, 76 Va. L. Rev. 1409 (1990); Pollack, *Take My Arbitrator, Please: Commissioner "Best Interests" Disciplinary Authority in Professional sports*, 67 Fordham L. Rev. 1645 (1999).

> Why gambling is bad:
> Betting on baseball by a participant of the game is corrupt because it erodes and destroys the integrity of the game of baseball. Betting also exposes the game to the influence of forces who seek to control the game to their own ends. Betting on one's own team give rise to the ultimate conflict of interest in which the individual player/bettor places his personal financial interest above the interests of the team.
> Dowd Report at 916. The Dowd Report determined that Pete Rose did indeed bet on games of the Cincinnati Reds Baseball Club in the 1985, 1986, and 1987 seasons *Id.* at 917.

5. In *Atlanta Natl. League Baseball Club, Inc. v. Kuhn*, the commissioner's decision to suspend the chief executive of a baseball club was not an abuse of discretion but was within commissioner's authority under contract. However, the commissioner's order depriving the baseball club of its first round draft choice in the 1977 amateur draft was ultra vires and void. The commissioner had ample authority to punish the team and owner for acts considered not in the best interests of baseball. Is there any limit to what could or could not be argued to be in the best interests of baseball?

6. The decision in *Charles O. Finley & Co. Inc. v. Kuhn* gives the commissioner a great deal of flexibility to respond to behavior that he deems to be against the best interests of baseball. Does the commissioner have the relevant authority to respond to a Pete Rose or a John Rocker? How far can the commissioner interfere with the private lives of baseball players?

7. In *Rose v. Giamatti*, 721 F. Supp. 906 (S.D. Ohio 1989), *(which see)*, the commissioner of baseball when conducting disciplinary proceedings is not acting as an agent for Major League Baseball so as to render MLB liable for a violation of duty owed by commissioner to person disciplined, to follow the commissioner's procedural rules. The MLB clubs have made the commissioner totally independent of their control, so that his status with respect to disciplinary matters is analogous to that of an independent contractor. Is there a logical inconsistency of the commissioner being both CEO *and* independent contractor?

C. DRUG TESTING

Another form of discipline in sports is the penalties associated with the misuse of drugs. In the various sports, there are many different policies that restrict drug usage. These policies cover the entire range of policing activities from statutory requirements for mandatory drug testing to voluntary programs. The more dangerous sports (for example, boxing and horse racing) have had drug testing and drug requirements as a part of their sports for many years. Although there are numerous policies and programs that detect and punish drug usage in sports, there are limits to the possible range and breadth of these various drug-testing programs. These limits are established by the Constitution.

1. Professional Sports

Every professional sport has a plan to evaluate and monitor drug usage. These programs (usually developed through collective bargaining) typically punish drug usage in a step-by-step program according to the number of offenses. In these programs, elements of review and due process are made a part of the procedures.

Dimeo v. Griffin involves the already heavily regulated sport of horse racing. However, in *Dimeo,* the court held that the provision that called for random drugtesting of all racing personnel, including outriders, parade marshals, starters, assistant starters, drivers, and jockeys, was an unconstitutional invasion of privacy.

DIMEO V. GRIFFIN

924 F.2d 664 (7th Cir. 1991)

HARLINGTON WOOD, Jr., Circuit Judge.

It has long been labeled the sport of kings, but in this country some have come to regard it as the king of sports. Horse racing is now big business in which the state takes considerable interest. Not all involved are in it because of a love of horses. There have been problems generated because of the large sums of money involved in horse race gambling. Cheating and fixing followed gambling. It was not until in the 1960s that a drug problem began to come into prominence. In 1968 the winner of the Kentucky Derby was disqualified after a postrace urine test of the horse, not the jockey, revealed the illegal use of a drug. Now the Illinois Racing Board ("Board"), which closely regulates horse racing on nine tracks, has perceived a new problem, the possible use and abuse of certain substances by the people directly involved in racing licensed as jockeys, drivers, outriders, parade marshals, starters, and assistant starters. The Board believes that drug use risks the safety of the people involved, impairs the state's financial interest in gambling proceeds, and causes the public to doubt the integrity of racing. Several members of the Jockeys' Guild ("Guild") in 1984 asked for Board assistance with the potential drug problem. Representatives of the Illinois Harness Horseman's Association were also consulted by the Board. The Board subsequently developed its own war on drugs by adopting a comprehensive drug rule which is now at issue.

The Board's antidrug program offended plaintiffs, Board-approved licensees, who brought this class action in behalf of themselves and other similar licensees, claiming that the urine-testing rule of the Board violated the fourth amendment's prohibition against unreasonable searches and seizures. Judge Shadur agreed and preliminarily enjoined the Board from enforcing its random urine testing. Judge Shadur also preliminarily enjoined the Board from conducting mandatory urine tests of the plaintiff class without specific articulable facts that meet an objective standard of reasonable cause for believing such individual is under the influence of or has used a controlled substance on the grounds of a race track. This latter injunctive requirement largely tracked the regulations to ensure that the standards would be followed and not based on mere "hunch" as plaintiffs feared. Further defendants were enjoined from initially conditioning licensing upon submission to the urine tests prohibited in the preliminary injunction. As laudable as the motivation and intentions of the Board may be in the war on drugs, they are not enough to make up for the constitutional shortcomings of the Board rule. We agree with Judge Shadur, 721 F. Supp. 958, and affirm.

I. Horse Racing

Horse racing is one of the most ancient of sports. It is believed that chariots drawn by a four-horse team raced in the Olympic games of 700-40 B.C. Riders on single mounts also competed. The chariot drivers were the forerunners of today's harness drivers who now compete in lightweight sulkies drawn by standardbred horses. The Olympic bareback riders were the forerunners of today's jockeys now mounted on the backs of thoroughbreds competing at the run, a faster speed than the harness horse attains at a pace or a trot. In the reign of Richard the Lion-Hearted in England between 1189 and 1199, the first racing purse was offered. The first horseracing trophy on this side of the Atlantic, however, was not awarded until 1665 in the colony of New York.

Although horse racing probably came to North America when Cortez invaded Mexico in 1519, the advent of harness racing in this country came later. Beginning with neighbors racing four-wheel buggies on local roads, harness racing developed in the 1800s into the use of the light, two-wheeled sulkies on race tracks. The origin of this type of harness racing with the use of the distinct standardbred horse is an American creation. Although related, the thoroughbred and the standardbred horses are recognized as distinct breeds.

Plaintiffs' contributions to modern horse racing under their respective licenses must be understood. Jockeys riding thoroughbreds and drivers in sulkies behind standardbred harness horses are recognized, but the duties of the other licensees are less understood.

The outrider in thoroughbred racing is mounted and leads the horses from the paddock area, past the reviewing stands, and into the starting gate area for each race. The outrider makes sure the horses are led out in an orderly fashion without incident. If a horse throws its rider, as sometimes happens, and is running loose, the outrider is responsible for retrieving the horse. The term starting gate does not give an adequate picture of the structure used for starting a thoroughbred race. It is not one large gate stretching across the track. It is more like a series of connected, narrow short stalls, not much bigger than the horse which is led into it. When the horses are all in the gate and ready the electronically controlled door on each individual stall at the command of the starter opens simultaneously, and the race is on.

The parade marshal in harness racing performs much the same duties as the outrider in leading the horses to the starting positions, but the start of a harness race obviously cannot be done by the use of the stationary thoroughbred starting gate. A harness race is begun by the use of a moving pace car with retractable bars extending sideways from the back of the car. The starter rides elevated in the rear of the pace car facing backwards where he can observe the moving horses. The harness horses stride into place side-by-side behind the moving pace car and its extended bars. When moving at the proper gait and under control, the pace car barriers are retracted along the side of the car by the starter and the pace car speeds out of the way to permit the horses to move out in competition.

In a thoroughbred race there are a starter and assistant starters with coordinating but different duties. The starter is located just outside the infield rail and elevated where he can observe the horses in the starting gate. He is responsible for ensuring that the horses are properly loaded into their respective sections of the starting gate. He observes their behavior to determine when a fair start is possible. When the horses are all in proper position he releases the starting gate. The assistant starters, however, are afoot on the track with the responsibility of leading the individual horses into their respective gate sections and to help the jockeys maintain control. An assistant starter may enter into the gate and stand on a small side ledge where he can help make sure the horse is under control with head up and facing down the track. When the gate is opened the assistant starter lets go of the horse turning it loose to run, raising his own arms in the air. This shows there was no delay in a starter's release of a horse possibly causing an unfair start.

[The] . . . revenue from wagers on horse racing total[s] above one billion dollars per year in Illinois. . . . [The] Illinois Horse Racing Act of 1975 ("Act") [was passed] to regulate and control horse racing.

II. The Board Rule

The Act gives the Board discretion to issue occupational licenses to persons working on Illinois race track grounds privately owned by race track organizations. . . .

The attendant power is given to the Board to promulgate reasonable rules and regulations for the purpose of administering the Act and to prescribe reasonable rules and regulations under which Illinois horse race meetings are conducted. . . .

A. Random Testing

The Board determines the volume and frequency of random testing at each race meet, as well as which selected racing programs are subject to testing. The names of all licensees who appear as participants on the official program are placed in a locked container secured by the race stewards, the stewards being the onsite state supervisors of the racing meet. A steward then may draw up to five names of licensees from the container, with a representative of the Guild, the Illinois Horseman's Benevolent and Protective Association, or the Illinois Harness Horseman's Association having been invited to witness the selection process. Following the drawing the stewards locate and notify the licensees selected for random testing. Each licensee drawn must report to the designated sample collection area and provide a urine sample to the stewards or their designee before the last race on that day's racing program. . . .

No licensee is required to provide a sample more than three times in a race meet. . . .

B. Individualized-Suspicion Testing

Any particular licensee who is suspected to be in violation of the Rule will receive written notice from the stewards stating that he or she will be tested and giving the reason justifying the testing. Individualized-suspicion testing must be based on a finding that the licensee is under the influence of drugs as explained in the Guidelines. . . .

C. Urine Collection and Testing Procedures

Any licensee selected for urine testing, either at random or because of individualized suspicion, must present himself or herself at the designated collection site. . . .

If the initial screening reflects any positive reading, a Gas Chromatography/Mass Spectrometry ("GCMS") test is used to confirm the results. GCMS isolates an individual drug or metabolite and identifies it by a characteristic fragmentation pattern similar to a fingerprint. If the GCMS test confirms the sample as positive, both the resealed laboratory sample and the unsealed referee sample are retained by the laboratory in long-term frozen storage for at least one year. . . .

III. Issues

What is being reviewed is the appropriate exercise of discretion by Judge Shadur in the grant of the preliminary injunction prohibiting random urine testing under the Rule or conditioning a license upon submission to the enjoined urine tests. The Board's program as to reasonable suspicion testing was also enjoined by Judge Shadur's order but only to insure that the testing be based on specific articulable facts that meet an objective standard of reasonable cause for believing that the person is under the influence, or has used a controlled substance, on the race track grounds. . . .

IV. Discussion

It is necessarily conceded that urine testing of individuals is a fourth amendment "search" and therefore must meet the constitutional standard of reasonableness. The Board recognizes that an individual has a reasonable expectation of privacy in the ordinarily private act of urination and also in what a chemical analysis of a urine specimen may reveal. However, in an effort to avoid the necessity for a search warrant the Board attempts to bring its rule within a "special government needs" exception in circumstances going beyond the ordinary needs of law enforcement. If the Board drug effort comes within that exception then it may conduct urine testing without a warrant, without meeting a probable cause standard, without individualized suspicion, and without having to show that the group to be tested has or is likely to suffer any incidence of drug abuse. . . .

The integrity of the race affects, among other things, not only who receives the winning purse but also the market reputation of the particular horse involved. The Board's integrity concerns are very important but the Board fails to explain why the criminal remedies for bribery, blackmail, race fixing, and other illegal activity are inadequate. Those ordinary criminal remedies not only punish, but also may deter the conduct purportedly affected by the Rule. Moreover, the sweep of the Rule is overly broad. The integrity risk is greatest with jockeys and drivers who can in various ways directly affect the race outcome. As to the other licensees, the starter might start the race before a particular horse was ready. The assistant starter might hold the horse slightly too long in the starting gate or do something else to distract the horse. The starts, however, are videotaped and the district court found little realistic opportunity for the starter or assistant starters to throw the race at that stage. In any event, that much of the government interest, though important, does not weigh enough when on the scale with the fourth amendment. . . .

There is physical danger in horse racing to the horses and the participants. . . . The accidents are not shown to have any particular relationship to drug use by participants. Jockeys and drivers are at the greatest risk, but they are at risk in racing regardless of drug use. Drug use no doubt would increase that risk as alert, unimpaired, and physically fit participants are critical for the safety of themselves, others, and the horses. . . .

Urine testing, as the district court found, has limited use for these purposes as it does not measure the licensees' present impairment, but only reveals that drugs were previously ingested and were in the person's system. . . .

The other licensees are at less physical risk, outriders, parade marshals, starters, and assistant starters. . . .

V. Conclusion

. . . There are good and valid reasons to strive to keep drugs out of horse racing, but, as important as that is, that cannot be accomplished by disregarding the Constitution. The Board along with all well-intentioned licensees, assuming the drug threat is as serious as the Board believes it to be, should be able to find a constitutional way to accomplish an effective drug program. If not, horse racing may not long survive as the king of sports as it is viewed by some. It may even deteriorate into no sport at all.

Affirmed.

POSNER, Circuit Judge, dissenting.

The majority opinion makes so strong a case *against* its own result that I have little more to do here than to express my perplexity at that result. . . .

2. Amateur Sports

The NCAA requires that all athletes annually sign a consent to a drug testing as part of their three-part statement and consent form on eligibility, recruitment, financial aid, amateur status, and involvement in organized gambling. Those who fail to adhere to this three-part statement and consent form are declared ineligible to participate. In high schools, students are often compelled to sign a consent form for urinalysis before they are eligible to participate. Drug testing is also an integral part of the disciplinary procedures of the United States Olympic Committee.

The Supreme Court of Colorado in *University of Colorado v. Derdeyn* found that the university's random, suspicionless urinalysis drug testing of student-athletes was an unconstitutional search.

UNIVERSITY OF COLORADO V. DERDEYN

863 P.2d 929 (Colo. 1993)

Justice LOHR delivered the Opinion of the Court.

We granted certiorari in order to determine whether random, suspicionless urinalysis-drug-testing of intercollegiate student athletes by the University of Colorado, Boulder (CU), violates the Fourth Amendment to the United States Constitution or Article II, Section 7, of the Colorado Constitution. Following a bench trial conducted in August of 1989 in which a class of current and prospective CU athletes challenged the constitutionality of CU's drug-testing program, the Boulder County District Court permanently enjoined CU from continuing its program. The trial court found that CU had not obtained voluntary consent from its athletes for such testing, and it declared such testing unconstitutional under both the federal and state constitutions. The Colorado Court of Appeals generally affirmed. *See Derdeyn v. University of Colorado*, 832 P.2d 1031 (Colo. App. 1991). We agree with the court of appeals, *see id.* at 1034-35, that in the absence of voluntary consents, CU's random, suspicionless urinalysis-drug-testing of student athletes violates the Fourth Amendment to the United States Constitution and Article II, Section 7, of the Colorado Constitution. We further agree, *see id.* at 1035, that the record supports the finding of the trial court that CU failed to show that consents to such testing given by CU's athletes are voluntary for the purposes of those same constitutional provisions. Accordingly, we affirm the judgment of the court of appeals. . . .

Colorado University argued that there were many instances in the lives of collegiate athletes that would lessen their expectations of privacy. This is the "locker room mentality" argument. The Supreme Court of Colorado concluded differently and reiterated the position of the trial court that Colorado University's random, suspicionless urinalysis drug testing of athletes is an intrusion that is "clearly significant."

In *Todd v. Rush County Schools*, 133 F.3d 984 (7th Cir. 1998), four parents as next friends for their four children filed suit against a school board program that prohibited students from participating in any high school extracurricular activity or driving to and from school unless the student and parent consented to a test for drugs, alcohol, or tobacco in random, unannounced urinalysis examinations. Unlike *Derdeyn*, the court held that Rush County Schools' drug testing program was consistent with the Fourth Amendment.

TODD V. RUSH COUNTY SCHOOLS

133 F.3d 984 (7th Cir. 1998)

CUMMINGS, Circuit Judge.

This suit was filed by four parents and as next friends for their four children, all students at Rushville Consolidated High School in Rushville, Indiana. In August 1996, the Rush County School Board approved a program prohibiting a high school student from participating in any extracurricular activities or driving to and from school unless the student and parent or guardian consented to a test for drugs, alcohol or tobacco in random, unannounced urinalysis examinations. Extracurricular activities include athletic teams, Student Council, Foreign Language Clubs, Fellowship of Christian Athletes, Future Farmers of America Officers and the Library Club. When consent for testing is given, participation in the extracurricular organizations or driving to and from school are permitted. The testing is conducted by Midwest Toxicology Services, which collects the samples, and the Witham Hospital Laboratory Services, which performs the analyses. The $30 test is paid for by a grant.

If a test result is positive, the student and family are informed and permitted to explain the result by showing, for example, that the student is taking a medication that would influence the result. Without a satisfactory explanation, the student is barred from extracurricular activities or driving to and from school until passing a retest. However, a positive test result is not to be used in school discipline proceedings. If a student tests positive, the student and his or her parents will be given the names of agencies that might assist the student's recovery. Also if a student tests positive, he or she may request a new urine test. Otherwise the student may be retested after an appropriate interval but will continue to be barred from extracurricular activities and driving to and from school until testing negative.

This program concerns random suspicionless testing. The high school does reserve the right to test any student if it has reasonable suspicion of drug use. If a student tests positive twice, the school is deemed to have reasonable suspicion justifying further retests even though the student will no longer be permitted to engage in any extracurricular activities due to the prior positive results. Tests based on reasonable suspicion, unlike the suspicionless tests, do subject the student to school discipline.

This case was initiated by the students' and parents' complaint and activated by their motion for summary judgment which was denied. In turn, the defendants Rush County Schools and its superintendent filed a motion for summary judgment, which was subsequently granted.

When the summary judgment motions were filed in the trial court, random tests had been performed on five or six occasions involving 20 to 30 students each time. Five to eight students tested positive, three or four for marijuana and the rest for nicotine. From 1992 to 1997 there were no alcohol related expulsions, zero to one tobacco-related expulsion per year, and one to four drug-related expulsions. Expulsions are not involved in the rule being challenged here. As to suspensions, there were two to nine for alcohol, 21 to 44 for tobacco, and one to nine for drugs.

A 1994 survey of Rush County high school students was conducted by the Indiana Prevention Resource Center and disclosed that cigarette use for Rush County 10th graders was higher than the Indiana average and that alcohol use for 11th and 12th graders was also higher than the state average. Marijuana usage was lower for 9th and 12th graders than the state average. Two witnesses stated that drug use has been increasing at the high school, causing the drowning of a senior and an automobile crash where the students were inhaling the contents of aerosol cans.

As the opinion below reveals, there were 950 students in the Rush County High School for the 1996–1997 school year. Seven hundred twenty-eight agreed to sign with the drug testing program. Of those, 170 did not participate in extracurricular activities (including athletics) or drive to and from school. Plaintiff William Todd's parents refused to sign a consent form for the drug testing program, resulting in his being barred from videotaping the football team. Likewise, the parents of the three plaintiff Hammons children refused to sign the consent form and the children are therefore barred from participating in any extracurricular activities. One of the Hammons children had been a member of the Library Club and another a member of the Future Farmers of America.

The issue before this Court is whether Rush County Schools' drug testing program under which all students who wish to participate in extracurricular activities must consent to random and suspicionless urine testing for alcohol, unlawful drug, and cigarette usage violates the Fourth Amendment rights of those students. For the following reasons, we hold that Rush County Schools' drug testing program is consistent with the Fourth Amendment.

The outcome of this case is governed by *Vernonia School District 47J v. Acton,* 515 U.S. 646, and *Schaill v. Tippecanoe County School Corp.,* 864 F.2d 1309 (7th Cir. 1988). Those cases upheld random urinalysis requirements for students who participate in interscholastic athletics. As in those cases, the testing policy was undertaken in furtherance of the school districts' "responsibilities, under a public school system, as guardian and tutor of children entrusted to its care." 515 U.S. at 665. Noting that "Fourth Amendment rights . . . are different in public schools than elsewhere," *id.* at 656, the Supreme Court in *Vernonia* determined that deterring drug use by students was a compelling interest, finding that "[s]chool years are the time when the physical, psychological, and addictive effects of drugs are most severe." *Id.* at 661.

As defendants explained, similar to the program in *Vernonia,* their program was designed to deter drug use and not to catch and punish users. The difference between the cited cases and the present one is that here the testing is also required of those engaging in other extracurricular activities. However, we find that the reasoning compelling drug testing of athletes also applies to testing of students involved in extracurricular activities. Certainly successful extracurricular activities require healthy students. While the testing in the present case includes alcohol and nicotine, that is insufficient to condemn it because those substances may also affect students' mental and physical condition.

Additionally, while recognizing that extracurricular activities "are considered valuable to the school experience, and [that] participation may assist a student in getting into college," the district judge noted that extracurricular activities, like athletics, "are a privilege at the High School." In *Schaill*, this Court found significant "the fact that [the] plaintiffs are required to submit to random drug testing only as a condition of participation in an extracurricular activity," in that case athletics. *Schaill*, 864 F.2d at 1319. Similar to *Schaill* and *Vernonia*, the Rush County Schools' drug testing program applies only to students who have voluntarily chosen to participate in an activity. As the district court also noted, students in other extracurricular activities, like athletes, "can take leadership roles in the school community and serve as an example to others." As this Court has reasoned, "[p]articipation in interscholastic athletics is a benefit carrying with it enhanced prestige and status in the student community" and thus "[i]t is not unreasonable to couple these benefits with an obligation to undergo drug testing." *Schaill*, 864 F.2d at 1320. Therefore it is appropriate to include students who participate in extracurricular activities in the drug testing.

The linchpin of this drug testing program is to protect the health of the students involved. As we have stated, "[t]he plague of illicit drug use which currently threatens our nation's schools adds a major dimension to the difficulties the schools face in fulfilling their purpose — the education of our children. If the schools are to survive and prosper, school administrators must have reasonable means at their disposal to deter conduct which substantially disrupts the school environment." *Schaill*, 864 F.2d at 1324. We conclude that Rush County Schools' drug testing program is sufficiently similar to the programs in *Vernonia* and *Schaill* to pass muster under the Fourth and Fourteenth Amendments.

Judgment Affirmed.

3. Right of Privacy and Reasonableness of Search

As regards drug testing, the question is whether an athlete has a right to privacy vis-à-vis urinalysis. An expectation of privacy must be one that society is prepared to recognize as legitimate. The legality of urinalysis also depends on the reasonableness of the search under the circumstances. The question of reasonableness is determined by whether it is justified at the beginning of the search and whether the search as conducted is reasonably related in scope to the circumstances that justified the search.

In *Hill v. NCAA*, the trial court found the NCAA's program to be an invasion of plaintiff's right to privacy, and the superior court permanently enjoined its enforcement against plaintiffs and other Stanford athletes. The court of appeal upheld the injunction. However, the Supreme Court of

California reversed, finding that the NCAA's drug testing program did not violate the athletes' right to privacy.

HILL v. NATIONAL COLLEGIATE ATHLETIC ASSOCIATION

865 P.2d 633 (Cal. 1994)

LUCAS, Chief Justice.

The National Collegiate Athletic Association (NCAA) sponsors and regulates intercollegiate athletic competition throughout the United States. Under the NCAA's drug testing program, randomly selected college student athletes competing in postseason championships and football bowl games are required to provide samples of their urine under closely monitored conditions. Urine samples are chemically analyzed for proscribed substances. Athletes testing "positive" are subject to disqualification.

Plaintiffs, who were student athletes attending Stanford University (Stanford) at the time of trial, sued the NCAA, contending its drug testing program violated their right to privacy secured by article I, section 1 of the California Constitution. Stanford intervened in the suit and adopted plaintiffs' position. Finding the NCAA's program to be an invasion of plaintiffs' right to privacy, the superior court permanently enjoined its enforcement against plaintiffs and other Stanford athletes. The Court of Appeal upheld the injunction.

By its nature, sports competition demands highly disciplined physical activity conducted in accordance with a special set of social norms. Unlike the general population, student athletes undergo frequent physical examinations, reveal their bodily and medical conditions to coaches and trainers, and often dress and undress in same-sex locker rooms. In so doing, they normally and reasonably forgo a measure of their privacy in exchange for the personal and professional benefits of extracurricular athletics.

A student athlete's already diminished expectation of privacy is outweighed by the NCAA's legitimate regulatory objectives in conducting testing for proscribed drugs. As a sponsor and regulator of sporting events, the NCAA has self-evident interests in ensuring fair and vigorous competition, as well as protecting the health and safety of student athletes. These interests justify a set of drug testing rules reasonably calculated to achieve drug-free athletic competition. The NCAA's rules contain elements designed to accomplish this purpose, including: (1) advance notice to athletes of testing procedures and written consent to testing; (2) random selection of athletes actually engaged in competition; (3) monitored collection of a sample of a selected athlete's urine in order to avoid substitution or contamination; and (4) chain of custody, limited disclosure, and other procedures designed to safeguard the confidentiality of the testing process and its outcome. As formulated, the NCAA's regulations do not offend the legitimate privacy interests of student athletes.

For these reasons, as more fully discussed below, the NCAA's drug testing program does not violate plaintiffs' state constitutional right to privacy. We will therefore reverse the judgment of the Court of Appeal and direct entry of final judgment in favor of the NCAA.

Statement of Facts and Proceedings Below

Plaintiffs' action for injunctive relief was tried to the court. We summarize the facts as revealed by the uncontradicted evidence in the record and the findings of the trial court.

The NCAA, a private association of more than 1,000 colleges and universities, was created to foster and regulate intercollegiate athletic competition. NCAA rules are made by member institutions, acting collectively and democratically at national conventions. Member institutions and college athletes are required to abide by NCAA rules as a condition to participation in NCAA-sponsored events.

1. Events Leading to the NCAA's Adoption of Drug Testing

In 1973, the NCAA enacted a rule prohibiting student athlete drug use. Ten years later, at the Pan American Games in Caracas, Venezuela, several college student athletes tested positive for prohibited drugs. Others withdrew from competition when faced with the prospect of testing. In response to the incident, the United States Olympic Committee (USOC) developed a drug testing program modeled after the program of the International Olympic Committee, which had been established in the early 1970's. Following the lead of the USOC, the NCAA began to study drug use among student athletes.

The NCAA commissioned Michigan State University to conduct a nationwide survey of college athlete drug use. The results revealed substantial use of a variety of drugs — 8 percent of the athletes surveyed reported using amphetamines, 36 percent marijuana or hashish, 17 percent cocaine, and 4 percent steroids. Nine percent of football players reported using steroids at some time; six percent reported using steroids within the preceding twelve months.

In January 1984, the members of the NCAA's Pacific 10 Conference, including Stanford, introduced a resolution calling on the NCAA to adopt a mandatory drug testing program. The resolution recited that "the use of controlled substances and allegedly performance-enhancing drugs represents a danger to the health of students and a threat to the integrity of amateur sport."

Acting on the Pacific 10 Conference resolution, the NCAA created a special committee to study drug use and testing. The committee recommended a comprehensive drug testing program based on the Olympic model, concluding in part: "The NCAA has a legitimate interest in maintaining the integrity of intercollegiate athletics, including insuring fair competition and protecting the health and safety of all participating student athletes. The use of 'performance-enhancing' drugs by individual student-athletes is a violation of the ethic of fair competition, [and] poses a potential health and safety hazard to those utilizing such drugs and a potential safety hazard to those competing with such individuals. The most effective method of ensuring that student-athletes are not utilizing 'performance enhancing' drugs is through a consistent, national drug testing program."

At the NCAA's 1985 convention, the drug use and testing committee's proposal was referred back for further study and refinement. At the 1986 convention, the committee's revised proposal was adopted by an overwhelming vote of the member institutions. The NCAA's drug testing program has continued, with certain amendments, through the time of this appeal.

2. The NCAA Drug Testing Program

The NCAA prohibits student athlete use of chemical substances in several categories, including: (1) psychomotor and nervous system stimulants; (2) anabolic steroids; (3) alcohol and beta blockers (in rifle events only); (4) diuretics; and (5) street drugs. At the time of trial, sympathomimetic amines (a class of substances included in many medications) were also included in the NCAA's list of banned drugs. The NCAA has amended its rules to delete sympathomimetic amines from its list of proscribed substances.

Student athletes seeking to participate in NCAA-sponsored competition are required to sign a three-part statement and consent form. New forms must be executed at the beginning of each year of competition. The first part of the form affirms that the signator meets NCAA eligibility regulations and that he or she has duly reported any known violations of those regulations.

The second part of the form, entitled Buckley Amendment Consent, authorizes limited disclosure of the form, the results of NCAA drug tests, academic transcripts, financial aid records, and other information pertaining to NCAA eligibility, to authorized representatives of the athlete's institution and conference, as well as to the NCAA. The items of information to be disclosed are identified in the statement as "education records" pursuant to the federal Family Educational Rights and Privacy Act of 1974. (20 U.S.C. §1232g.)

The final part of the form is a "Drug-Testing Consent" including the following provisions:

> By signing this part of the form, you certify that you agree to be tested for drugs.
>
> You agree to allow the NCAA, during this academic year, before, during or after you participate in any NCAA championship or in any postseason football game certified by the NCAA, to test you for the banned drugs listed in Executive Regulation 1-7(b) in the NCAA Manual.
>
> You reviewed the procedures for NCAA drug testing that are described in the NCAA Drug-Testing Program brochure.
>
> You understand that if you test positive (the NCAA finds traces of any of the banned drugs in your body), you will be ineligible to participate in postseason competition for at least 90 days.
>
> If you test positive and lose eligibility for 90 days, and then test positive again after your eligibility is restored, you will lose postseason eligibility in all sports for the current and next academic year.
>
> You understand that this consent and the results of your drug tests, if any, will only be disclosed in accordance with the Buckley Amendment consent.

The Drug Testing Consent contains dated signature spaces for the student athlete and, if the student athlete is a minor, a parent. Failure to sign the three-part form, including the Drug Testing Consent, renders the student athlete ineligible to participate in NCAA-sponsored competition.

Drug testing is conducted at NCAA athletic events by urinalysis. All student athletes in championship events or postseason bowl games are potentially subject to testing. Particular athletes are chosen for testing according to plans that may include random selection or other selection criteria such as playing time, team position, place of finish, or suspicion of drug use.

Upon written notice following his or her participation in an athletic event, the selected athlete must report promptly to a collection station. The athlete may choose to be accompanied by a witness-observer. At the collection station, the athlete picks a plastic-sealed beaker with a personal code number. In the presence of an NCAA official monitor of the same sex as the athlete, the athlete supplies a urine specimen of 100-200 milliliters. The specimen is identified, documented, and divided into two samples labeled A and B. Both samples are delivered to one of three certified testing laboratories. Chain of custody procedures provide for signed receipts and acknowledgments at each transfer point.

At the laboratory, a portion of sample A is tested by gas chromatography/mass spectometry—the most scientifically accurate method of analysis available. Positive findings, signifying use of proscribed drugs, are confirmed by testing another portion of sample A, and then reviewed by the laboratory director and reported to the NCAA by code number. The NCAA decodes the reports and relays positive findings to the athletic director of the college or university involved by telephone and overnight letter marked "confidential." The institution is required to notify the athlete of the positive finding. Within 24 hours of notice of a positive finding, sample B of the athlete's urine is tested. A positive finding may be appealed to a designated NCAA committee.

A positive test finding results in loss of postseason eligibility. Refusal by a student athlete to follow NCAA-mandated drug testing procedures yields the same consequence—the offending athlete is barred from competition.

3. Effects of the Drug Testing Program

In considering whether the NCAA's drug testing program violated plaintiffs' state constitutional right to privacy, the trial court and the Court of Appeal required the NCAA to demonstrate that its drug testing program advanced a "compelling state interest" by proving each of the following: (1) the program furthered its stated purposes, i.e., to safeguard the integrity of athletic competition and to protect the health and safety of student athletes; (2) the utility of the program manifestly outweighed any resulting impairment of the privacy right; and (3) there were no alternatives to drug testing less offensive to privacy interests.

Much of the trial was devoted to a debate among scientists, physicians, and sports professionals regarding the merits of the NCAA's list of proscribed drugs and the general efficacy of its drug testing program. There were sharp differences in professional opinions on a wide range of subjects, including what substances should be banned, as well as the attitudes and behaviors of athletes and coaches toward certain drugs (e.g., steroids) that some may regard as enhancing athletic performance. The trial court's findings, sustained by the Court of Appeal, heavily favored plaintiffs' side of the professional debate.

The trial court found in part that the NCAA drug testing program invades the privacy interests of student athletes by requiring them: (1) to disclose medications they may be using and other information about their physical and medical conditions; (2) to urinate in the presence of a monitor; and (3) to provide a urine sample that reveals chemical and other substances in their bodies.

The court further found that college athletes do not use drugs any more frequently than college students as a general class. It observed that in 1986-1987, the first year of the NCAA's drug testing program, 34 of the 3,511 athletes tested for drugs were declared ineligible because of proscribed drug use. Of the 34 athletes declared ineligible, 31 were engaged in football, 1 was in track and field, and 2 were in basketball. Of the football players, 25 had tested positive for use of steroids. The track and field athlete tested positive for steroids, the two basketball players for cocaine.

From its findings, the court concluded there was no "compelling need" for drug testing to protect the health of college athletes or the integrity of athletic competition. According to the court, the NCAA program was "overbroad" because it banned "useful" over-the-counter medications and prescription drugs "designed to improve the health of the athlete." The court observed the NCAA had not been completely consistent in its professed concern for the health of athletes as shown by its failure to require measles vaccinations of athletes despite previous measles outbreaks at postseason competition or to provide counselling or rehabilitation services for drugusing athletes. The court added that Stanford "believes it is wrong to single out athletes for drug testing" and "favors drug education for its students."

The trial court also found the NCAA had failed to produce evidence that certain banned substances, e.g., amphetamines, diuretics, marijuana, and heroin, actually enhance athletic performance. It did find, however, that marijuana clearly impairs athletic performance and that cocaine may do so. Addressing the alleged perception that use of certain drugs may enhance performance, the court found that drugs are generally not perceived by college athletes and coaches to enhance performance or to be "a major problem." With respect to steroid use, the "perception," according to the court, is that steroids "might only help certain types of positions in football."

On the issue of public perception of drug use, the court offered its general view that "the NCAA drug testing program is probably doing more harm than good" and further determined the NCAA had failed to show that drug education and testing based on reasonable suspicion were inadequate to the task of controlling drug use by athletes.

From its conclusions, the trial court determined that the NCAA's drug testing program violated the state constitutional privacy rights of Stanford University student athletes. It permanently enjoined any testing of those athletes wherever it might be conducted, whether inside or outside of California.

On appeal, the Court of Appeal upheld the trial court's factual findings and sustained its legal determinations regarding the NCAA's drug testing program, including its holding that the NCAA had failed to establish a "compelling state interest" in support of the program. The trial court's judgment, including the permanent injunction, was affirmed. We granted review.

Discussion ...

To resolve the dispute between the parties, we address three questions of first impression in this court: (1) Does the Privacy Initiative govern the conduct of private, nongovernmental entities such as the NCAA; and (2) if it does, what legal standard is to be applied in assessing alleged invasions of privacy; and (3) under that standard, is the NCAA's drug testing program a violation of the state constitutional privacy right?

1. Application of the California Constitutional Right to Privacy to Nongovernmental Entities

Neither plaintiffs nor Stanford assert that the NCAA is an agency or instrumentality of government or a vehicle for state action. Case law generally confirms the status of the NCAA as a private organization, comprised of American colleges and universities, and democratically governed by its own membership. . . .

Although none of our decisions has squarely addressed the question whether our state constitutional right to privacy may be enforced against private parties . . . the Courts of Appeal have consistently answered in the affirmative. . . .

In its day-to-day operations, the NCAA is in a position to generate, retain, and use personal information about student athletes and others. In this respect, it is no different from a credit card purveyor, an insurance company, or a private employer (the private entity examples used in the ballot arguments) in its capacity to affect the privacy interests of those with whom it deals. . . .

2. Standards for Determining Invasion of Privacy Under Article I, Section 1

In evaluating the NCAA's drug testing program, the trial court and the Court of Appeal assumed that private entities were subject to the same legal standards as government agencies with respect to claims of invasion of privacy. Borrowing from a few of our cases involving the conduct of government in its dealings with individual citizens, the lower courts imposed on the NCAA the burden of proving both: (1) a "compelling state interest" in support of drug testing; and (2) the absence of any alternative means of accomplishing that interest. . . .

The privacy tort seeks to vindicate multiple and different interests that range from freedom to act without observation in a home, hospital room, or other private place to the ability to control the commercial exploitation of a name or picture. . . .

Each of the four categories of common law invasion of privacy identifies a distinct interest associated with an individual's control of the process or products of his or her personal life. To the extent there is a common denominator among them, it appears to be improper interference (usually by means of observation or communication) with aspects of life consigned to the realm of the "personal and confidential" by strong and widely shared social norms.

Moreover, the plaintiff in an invasion of privacy case must have conducted himself or herself in a manner consistent with an actual expectation of privacy, i.e., he or she must not have manifested by his or her conduct a voluntary consent to the invasive actions of defendant. If voluntary consent is present, a defendant's conduct will rarely be deemed "highly offensive to a reasonable person" so as to justify tort liability. . . .

In determining the " 'offensiveness' " of an invasion of a privacy interest, common law courts consider, among other things: "the degree of the intrusion, the context, conduct and circumstances surrounding the intrusion as well as the intruder's motives and objectives, the setting into which he intrudes, and the expectations of those whose privacy is invaded."

Thus, the common law right of privacy is neither absolute nor globally vague, but is carefully confined to specific sets of interests that must inevitably be weighed in the balance against competing interests before the right is judicially recognized. A plaintiff's expectation of privacy in a specific context must be objectively reasonable under the circumstances, especially in light of the competing social interests involved. . . .

b. Elements of a Cause of Action for Invasion of the State Constitutional Right of Privacy

Our cases do not contain a clear statement of the elements of a cause of action for invasion of the state constitutional right to privacy. Plaintiffs and Stanford succeeded in convincing the lower courts that the NCAA was required to justify any conceivable impact on plaintiffs' privacy interests by a "compelling interest" and to establish that its drug testing program was the "least restrictive" alternative furthering the NCAA's interests. The NCAA assails the "compelling interest/least restrictive alternative" test; plaintiffs and Stanford naturally come to its defense. We consider the positions of the parties in light of the history of the Privacy Initiative. . . .

For the reasons stated above, we decline to hold that every assertion of a privacy interest under article I, section 1 must be overcome by a "compelling interest." Neither the language nor history of the Privacy Initiative unambiguously supports such a standard. In view of the far-reaching and multifaceted character of the right to privacy, such a standard imports an impermissible inflexibility into the process of constitutional adjudication.

There remains, however, the question of the correct legal standard to be applied in assessing plaintiffs' claims for invasion of privacy. Based on our review of the history of the Privacy Initiative, we will describe in the remainder of this part the elements of the cause of action for violation of the state constitutional right to privacy and the defenses that might be asserted against such a cause of action.

(1) A legally protected privacy interest. The first essential element of a state constitutional cause of action for invasion of privacy is the identification of a specific, legally protected privacy interest. . . .

(2) Reasonable Expectation of Privacy. The second essential element of a state constitutional cause of action for invasion of privacy is a reasonable expectation of privacy on plaintiff's part. . . .

(3) Serious invasion of privacy interest. No community could function if every intrusion into the realm of private action, no matter how slight or trivial, gave rise to a cause of action for invasion of privacy. . . . Actionable invasions of privacy must be sufficiently serious in their nature, scope, and actual or potential impact to constitute an egregious breach of the social norms underlying the privacy right. Thus, the extent and gravity of the invasion is an indispensable consideration in assessing an alleged invasion of privacy.

c. Defenses to a State Constitutional Privacy Cause of Action

Privacy concerns are not absolute; they must be balanced against other important interests. . . .

The NCAA is a private organization, not a government agency. Judicial assessment of the relative strength and importance of privacy norms and countervailing interests may differ in cases of private, as opposed to government, action. . . .

Summary of Elements and Defenses

Based on our review of the Privacy Initiative, we hold that a plaintiff alleging an invasion of privacy in violation of the state constitutional right to privacy must establish each of the following: (1) a legally protected privacy interest; (2) a reasonable expectation of privacy in the circumstances; and (3) conduct by defendant constituting a serious invasion of privacy.

Whether a legally recognized privacy interest is present in a given case is a question of law to be decided by the court. Whether plaintiff has a reasonable expectation of privacy in the circumstances and whether defendant's conduct constitutes a serious invasion of privacy are mixed questions of law and fact. If the undisputed material facts show no reasonable expectation of privacy or an insubstantial impact on privacy interests, the question of invasion may be adjudicated as a matter of law. . . .

3. Application of the Elements of Invasion of Privacy to This Case

The NCAA challenges the decision of the Court of Appeal upholding a permanent injunction against its drug testing program as a violation of the state constitutional right to privacy. We will therefore review the record, including the findings made by the trial court, in light of the elements of a cause of action for invasion of privacy as we have just discussed them.

Plaintiffs correctly assert that the NCAA's drug testing program impacts legally protected privacy interests. First, by monitoring an athlete's urination, the NCAA's program intrudes on a human bodily function that by law and social custom is generally performed in private and without observers. . . . Second, by collecting and testing an athlete's urine and inquiring about his or her ingestion of medications and other substances, the NCAA obtains information about the internal medical state of an athlete's body that is regarded as personal and confidential. . . .

a. Freedom from Observation During Urination

(1) Reasonable expectations of privacy. The observation of urination—a human excretory function—obviously implicates privacy interests. But the

reasonable expectations of privacy of plaintiffs (and other student athletes) in private urination must be viewed within the context of intercollegiate athletic activity and the normal conditions under which it is undertaken.

By its nature, participation in intercollegiate athletics, particularly in highly competitive postseason championship events, involves close regulation and scrutiny of the physical fitness and bodily condition of student athletes. Required physical examinations (including urinalysis), and special regulation of sleep habits, diet, fitness, and other activities that intrude significantly on privacy interests are routine aspects of a college athlete's life not shared by other students or the population at large. Athletes frequently disrobe in the presence of one another and their athletic mentors and assistants in locker room settings where private bodily parts are readily observable by others of the same sex. They also exchange information about their physical condition and medical treatment with coaches, trainers, and others who have a "need to know."

As a result of its unique set of demands, athletic participation carries with it social norms that effectively diminish the athlete's reasonable expectation of personal privacy in his or her bodily condition, both internal and external. In recognition of this practical reality, drug testing programs involving athletic competition have routinely survived Fourth Amendment "privacy" challenges. Drug testing has become a highly visible, pervasive, and well accepted part of athletic competition, particularly on intercollegiate and professional levels. (*Schaill, supra,* 864 F.2d at p. 1319.) It is a reasonably expected part of the life of an athlete, especially one engaged in advanced levels of competition, where the stakes and corresponding temptations are high.

The student athlete's reasonable expectation of privacy is further diminished by two elements of the NCAA's drug testing program- advance notice and the opportunity to consent to testing. A drug test does not come as a unwelcome surprise at the end of a postseason match. Full disclosure of the NCAA's banned substances rules and testing procedures is made at the beginning of the athletic season, long before the postseason competition during which drug testing may take place. Following disclosure, the informed written consent of each student athlete is obtained. Thus, athletes have complete information regarding the NCAA's drug testing program and are afforded the opportunity to consent or refuse before they may be selected for testing.

To be sure, an athlete who refuses consent to drug testing is disqualified from NCAA competition. But this consequence does not render the athlete's consent to testing involuntary in any meaningful legal sense. Athletic participation is not a government benefit or an economic necessity that society has decreed must be open to all. . . .

Plaintiffs and Stanford have no legal right to participate in intercollegiate athletic competition. . . . Their ability to do so necessarily depends upon their willingness to arrive at and adhere to common understandings with their competitors regarding their mutual sporting endeavor. The NCAA is democratically governed by its member institutions, including Stanford. Acting collectively, those institutions, including Stanford, make the rules, including those regarding drug use and testing. If, knowing the rules, plaintiffs and Stanford choose to play the game, they have, by social convention and legal act, fully and voluntarily acquiesced in the application of those rules. To view the matter otherwise would impair the privacy and associational rights of *all* NCAA institutions and athletes.

(2) Seriousness of invasion. Although diminished by the athletic setting and the exercise of informed consent, plaintiff's privacy interests are not thereby rendered de minimis. Direct observation of urination by a monitor, an intrusive act, appears to be unique to the NCAA's program. . . .

(3) Competing interests. To justify its intrusion on student athletes' diminished expectations of privacy, the NCAA asserts two countervailing interests: (1) safeguarding the integrity of intercollegiate athletic competition; and (2) protecting the health and safety of student athletes. The central purpose of the NCAA is to promote competitive athletic events conducted pursuant to "rules of the game" enacted by its own membership. In this way, the NCAA creates and preserves the "level playing field" necessary to promote vigorous, high-level, and nationwide competition in intercollegiate sports. . . .

The NCAA began to study drug testing in response to a specific incident of probable drug ingestion by athletes at the Pan American Games. . . .

But whatever the provable incidence of drug use, perception may be more potent than reality. If particular substances are *perceived* to enhance athletic performance, student athletes may feel pressure (whether internal or external, subtle or overt) to use them. A drug testing program serves to minimize that pressure by providing at least some assurance that drug use will be detected and the user disqualified. As a result, it provides significant and direct benefits to the student athletes themselves, allowing them to concentrate on the merits of their athletic task without undue concern about loss of a competitive edge. These benefits offset the limited impact on privacy imposed by the prospect of testing.

There was ample evidence in the record that certain kinds of drugs — such as anabolic steroids and amphetamines — are perceived by some athletes to enhance athletic performance. . . .

Finally, the practical realities of NCAA sponsored athletic competition cannot be ignored. Intercollegiate sports is, at least in part, a business founded upon offering for public entertainment athletic contests conducted under a rule of fair and rigorous competition. Scandals involving drug use, like those involving improper financial incentives or other forms of corruption, impair the NCAA's reputation in the eyes of the sports-viewing public. A well announced and vigorously pursued drug testing program serves to: (1) provide a significant deterrent to would-be violators, thereby reducing the probability of damaging public disclosure of athlete drug use; and (2) assure student athletes, their schools, and the public that fair competition remains the overriding principle in athletic events. Of course, these outcomes also serve the NCAA's overall interest in safeguarding the integrity of intercollegiate athletic competition. . . .

The NCAA also has an interest in protecting the health and safety of student athletes who are involved in NCAA-regulated competition. Contrary to plaintiffs' characterization, this interest is more than a mere "naked assertion of paternalism." The NCAA sponsors and regulates intercollegiate athletic events, which by their nature may involve risks of physical injury to athletes, spectators, and others. In this way, the NCAA effectively creates occasions for potential injury resulting from the use of drugs. As a result, it may concern itself with the task of protecting the safety of those involved in intercollegiate athletic competition. This NCAA interest exists for the benefit of all persons involved in sporting events (including not only drug ingesting athletes but also innocent athletes or others who might be injured by a drug user), as well as the sport itself. . . .

b. Interest in the Privacy of Medical Treatment and Information

(1) Reasonable expectation. As discussed above, plaintiffs' interest in the privacy of medical treatment and medical information is also a protectable interest under the Privacy Initiative. However, the student athlete's reasonable expectation of privacy is similarly diminished because of the nature of competitive athletic activity and the norms under which it is conducted. Organized and supervised athletic competition presupposes a continuing exchange of otherwise confidential information about the physical (and medical) condition of athletes. Coaches, trainers, and team physicians necessarily learn intimate details of student athletes' bodily condition, including illnesses, medical problems, and medications prescribed or taken. Plaintiffs do not demonstrate that sharing similar information with the NCAA, in its capacity as a regulator of athletic competition in which plaintiffs have voluntarily elected to participate, presents any greater risk to privacy. . . .

(2) Seriousness of invasion. Directed and specific inquiries about personal medications (including questions about birth control pills) in the potentially stressful circumstances of a random drug test are undoubtedly significant from a privacy standpoint. Without a correspondingly important "reason to know," the NCAA would have no right to demand answers to these kinds of questions, Again, however, the extent of the intrusion on plaintiffs privacy presented by the question must be considered in light of both the diminished expectations of privacy of athletes in such questions, which are routinely asked and answered in the athletic context.

(3) Competing interests. Drug testing for multiple substances is a complex process. Although both parties acknowledge the NCAA has used and continues to use the best available methods of laboratory analysis, mistakes are possible and "false positives" can occur. The NCAA's inquiries to athletes about medications and drugs are designed to ensure accuracy in testing. The NCAA maintains that complete and accurate disclosure of these matters by athletes will, in certain instances and with respect to specified substances, serve to explain findings and prevent the embarrassment and distress occasioned by further proceedings. The record supports the NCAA's contentions. These kinds of disclosures are reasonably necessary to further the threshold purpose of the drug testing program — to protect the integrity of competition through the medium of accurate testing of athletes engaged in competition. The NCAA's interests in this regard adequately justify its inquiries about medications and other substances ingested by tested athletes. . . .

In sum, plaintiffs and Stanford did not prove that the NCAA is "collecting and stockpiling unnecessary information about [student athletes] [or] misusing information gathered for one purpose in order to serve other purposes or to embarrass [student athletes]." The NCAA's information-gathering procedure (i.e., drug testing through urinalysis) is a method reasonably calculated to further its interests in enforcing a ban on the ingestion of specified substances in order to secure fair competition and the health and safety of athletes participating in its programs. . . .

Disposition

The NCAA's drug testing program does not violate the state constitutional right to privacy. Therefore, the NCAA is entitled to judgement in its favor. As a result of our disposition, we do not decide whether the recognition of a state constitutional right to privacy in these circumstances would violate the commerce clause of the federal Constitution.

The judgment of the Court of Appeal affirming the permanent injunction against the NCAA's drug testing program is reversed. This case is remanded with instructions to direct entry of a final judgment in favor of the NCAA. The NCAA shall recover its costs. . . .

The Supreme Court of the United States in *Veronia School District 47J. v. Acton* continued the reasoning of the California Supreme Court in *Hill* and the Seventh Circuit Court of Appeals in *Schaill* by holding that a public high school's student-athlete drug testing policy did not violate the student's right to be free from unreasonable searches.

VERNONIA SCHOOL DISTRICT 47J v. ACTON

515 U.S. 646 (1995)

Justice SCALIA delivered the opinion of the Court.

The Student Athlete Drug Policy adopted by School District 47J in the town of Vernonia, Oregon, authorizes random urinalysis drug testing of students who participate in the District's school athletics programs. We granted certiorari to decide whether this violates the Fourth and Fourteenth Amendments to the United States Constitution. . . .

The Policy applies to all students participating in interscholastic athletics. Students wishing to play sports must sign a form consenting to the testing and must obtain the written consent of their parents. Athletes are tested at the beginning of the season for their sport. In addition, once each week of the season the names of the athletes are placed in a "pool" from which a student, with the supervision of two adults, blindly draws the names of 10% of the athletes for random testing. Those selected are notified and tested that same day, if possible. . . .

Fourth Amendment rights, no less than First and Fourteenth Amendment rights, are different in public schools than elsewhere; the "reasonableness" inquiry cannot disregard the schools' custodial and tutelary responsibility for children. For their own good and that of their classmates, public school children are routinely required to submit to various physical examinations, and to be vaccinated against various diseases. . . .

Legitimate privacy expectations are even less with regard to student athletes. School sports are not for the bashful. They require "suiting up" before each practice or event, and showering and changing afterwards. Public school locker rooms, the usual sites for these activities, are not notable for the privacy they afford. The locker rooms in Vernonia are typical: No individual dressing rooms are provided; shower heads are lined up along a wall, unseparated by any sort of partition or curtain; not even all the toilet stalls have doors. . . .

Taking into account all the factors we have considered above—the decreased expectation of privacy, the relative unobtrusiveness of the search, and the severity of the need met by the search—we conclude Vernonia's Policy is reasonable and hence constitutional. . . .

The Ninth Circuit held that Vernonia's Policy not only violated the Fourth Amendment, but also, by reason of that violation, contravened Article I, §9, of the Oregon Constitution. Our conclusion that the former holding was in error means that the latter holding rested on a flawed premise. We therefore vacate the judgment, and remand the case to the Court of Appeals for further proceedings consistent with this opinion.

It is so ordered.

Justice GINSBURG, concur[s]. . . .

Justice O'CONNOR, with whom Justice STEVENS and Justice SOUTER join, [dissents]. . . .

Like the majority in *Acton,* the court in *Brennan* held that the student-athlete's expectation of privacy was diminished because of the locker room environment.

BRENNAN V. BOARD OF TRUSTEES FOR UNIVERSITY OF LOUISIANA SYSTEMS

691 So. 2d 324 (La Ct. App. 1997)

LOTTINGER, Chief Judge.

Plaintiff, John Patout Brennan (Brennan), a student-athlete at the University of Southwestern Louisiana (USL), tested positive for drug use in the second of three random drug tests administered by the National Collegiate Athletic Association (NCAA). Brennan requested and received two administrative appeals in which he contended that the positive test results were "false" due to a combination of factors, including heavy drinking and sexual activity the night before the test, and his use of nutritional supplements. Following the unsuccessful appeals, USL complied with the NCAA regulations and suspended Brennan from intercollegiate athletic competition for one year. Brennan brought this action against USL's governing body, the Board of Trustees for University of Louisiana Systems (Board of Trustees), seeking to enjoin enforcement by USL of the suspension.

In his petition, Brennan alleged that, by requiring him to submit to the NCAA's drug testing program, USL violated his right of privacy and deprived him of a liberty and property interest without due process in contravention of Article I, Sections 2 and 5 of the Louisiana Constitution. The NCAA moved to intervene on the grounds that the drug testing policies and procedures that Brennan placed at issue were developed, administered, conducted and enforced by the NCAA. The intervention was granted.

Following a two day trial, the trial judge entered oral reasons for judgment. Initially, the trial judge stated that he would "pretermit any consideration of the several constitutional issues ... since those issues are mooted by the court's decision." The trial judge then concluded that Brennan was entitled to the preliminary injunction because "the subject test results on the plaintiff based on the one blood sample taken from him was flawed, and therefore that sample should not have been the basis of ... disciplinary action against the plaintiff. . . .

The Board of Trustees and the NCAA appealed and assigned the following error: Having declined to address the only causes of action asserted by Brennan, and having failed to find that Brennan was likely to succeed on the merits of any other cognizable cause of action, it was improper for the district court to issue a preliminary injunction in favor of Brennan.

Validity of the Drug Test

Prior to discussing the assignment of error, it is necessary to review the trial judge's finding that the drug test results were flawed. . . .

After reviewing the record in this case in its entirety, we conclude that the trial judge committed manifest error in finding that the drug test results were flawed. . . .

Upon close review, we find that the record does not contain a reasonable factual basis for the trial judge's conclusion that the test results were flawed. . . . Considering the evidence contained in the record, we conclude that the trial judge was clearly wrong in finding that the test results were flawed.

Preliminary Injunction

Having concluded that the trial judge erred in finding that the test results were flawed, we now consider whether it was proper to issue a preliminary injunction in favor of Brennan. . . .

A. Brennan's Constitutional Claims

Brennan claims that his constitutional rights to privacy and due process were violated. The Louisiana Constitution's protection of privacy provisions contained in Article 1, §5 does not extend so far as to protect private citizens against the actions of private parties. . . . Thus, in order to prevail on the merits of either constitutional claim, Brennan must first show that USL was a state actor when it enforced the NCAA's rules and recommendations.

1. State Action . . .

In the present case Brennan asserts that USL, not the NCAA, violated his constitutional rights to privacy and due process. Without question, USL is a state actor even when acting in compliance with NCAA rules and recommendations. While we conclude that there is state action in this case, the preliminary injunction could only be issued on the constitutional claims if Brennan made a prima facie showing that he had a privacy interest which was invaded or that he had a property or liberty interest which was entitled to due process protection.

2. Brennan's Privacy Interest

In determining whether USL violated Brennan's right of privacy, we are guided by the California Supreme Court's recent decision in *Hill v. National Collegiate Athletic Association,* 7 Cal. 4th 1, 26 Cal. Rptr. 2d 834, 865 P.2d 633 (Cal. 1994). Therein several student-athletes filed suit against the NCAA challenging its drug testing program as an invasion of the right of privacy. *Id.* 26 Cal. Rptr. 2d at 838-39, 865 P.2d at 637. While the court recognized that the drug testing program impacts privacy interests, it reasoned that there was no constitutional violation when the student-athletes' lower expectations of privacy were balanced against the NCAA's countervailing interests. *Id.* . . .

Although Brennan filed suit against USL, the state actor, rather than the NCAA, we conclude, as did the court in *Hill,* that there was no violation of a privacy interest. Brennan, like the student-athletes in *Hill,* has a diminished expectation of privacy. Additionally, we note that USL shares the NCAA's interests in ensuring fair competition in intercollegiate sports as well as in protecting the health and safety of student-athletes. While a urine test may be an invasion of privacy, in this case, it is reasonable considering the diminished expectation of privacy in the context of intercollegiate sports and there being a significant interest by USL and the NCAA that outweighs the relatively small compromise of privacy under the circumstances.

Because Brennan could not make a prima facie showing that he had a privacy interest which was unjustly violated, he could not prevail on the merits of the right of privacy claim.

3. Brennan's Property or Liberty Interest . . .

In sum, Brennan could not make a prima facie showing that he would prevail on the merits of either constitutional claim; therefore, these claims could not be the basis for the issuance of the preliminary injunction.

B. Brennan's Tort Claim

Although Brennan could not prevail on the constitutional claims, he contends that the factual allegations in his petition are sufficient to support a cause of action in tort. . . .

Assuming, for purposes of discussion only, that USL had a duty to warn Brennan, the record establishes that Brennan received adequate information and warnings to protect his eligibility. . . .

In the present case, Brennan affirmed that he was aware of the NCAA's drug testing policy. He was told verbally and in writing to inquire about the program if he had any questions. Brennan was told that if he was taking anything at all, prescription or nonprescription, to check with the USL athletic department. Although Brennan had ample opportunity to inquire about ingesting nutritional supplements, he choose to ingest the supplements without seeking advice from anyone.

Conclusion

For the foregoing reasons, the judgment of the trial court issuing the preliminary injunction is reversed. Costs of this appeal are assessed against the appellee.

Reversed. . . .

Unlike in *Todd, Acton,* and *Brennan,* the Colorado Supreme Court in *Trinidad School District No. 1 v. Lopez* found that suspicionless urinalysis was unconstitutional when applied to band members.

Trinidad School District No. 1 v. Lopez

963 P.2d 1095 (Colo. 1998)

Justice MULLARKEY delivered the Opinion of the Court.

We granted certiorari to review a drug testing policy promulgated by the Trinidad School District No. 1 Board of Education (Board) in July 1996. The policy mandated suspicionless urinalysis drug testing of all sixth through twelfth grade students participating in extracurricular activities. At the beginning of the 1996-1997 school year, the Trinidad School District No. 1 (School District) began regular testing of all students who wanted to take part in extracurricular activities. Carlos Lopez, a senior high school student who was enrolled in two for-credit band classes and participated in the school's marching band, refused to consent to the mandatory drug testing. Consequently, the District superintendent suspended Lopez from the band classes and the marching band.

Lopez, by and through his parents, filed a complaint for permanent injunctive and declaratory relief on September 6, 1996 in the Las Animas County District Court (trial court). Lopez alleged among other things that the Policy violated his right to be free from unreasonable searches and seizures, as guaranteed by the Fourth Amendment to the United States Constitution. Additionally, Lopez alleged that the Policy violated article II, section 7, of the Colorado Constitution. Lopez requested that the trial court enjoin the implementation of the Policy and that he be reinstated to the band classes and marching band.

After entering a temporary restraining order that required the District to reinstate Lopez to the band classes and the marching band, the trial court conducted a two day trial on Lopez's underlying complaint. In an order dated December 19, 1996, the trial court entered its findings of facts, conclusions of law, and judgment. The trial court held that the Policy was not unconstitutionally vague and that the Policy did not violate either the

Fourth Amendment to the United States Constitution or article II, section 7, of the Colorado Constitution.

Lopez appealed from the trial court's order to the court of appeals. Pursuant to C.A.R. 50, both parties then sought expedited certiorari review in this court, which we granted. We now reverse. We hold that, under the facts of this case, the Policy is unconstitutional with respect to the marching band.

The Policy, entitled "Drug Testing Student Athletes/Cheerleaders/Extra Curricular," mandates drug testing for all students in grades six through twelve who want to participate in an extracurricular activity. Under the Policy, the school principal is required to ensure that a student successfully completes an annual drug test prior to participating in the student's chosen first extracurricular activity of the year. In addition to the mandated testing, the Policy allows school officials to test any student participating in an extra-curricular activity based on a reasonable suspicion that the student is under the influence of illicit drugs and/or alcohol. The Policy also requires that a student and the student's parent sign a written form acknowledging the student's consent to be tested. Any student who has been or is currently taking a prescription medication must disclose the use of that medication to school officials before taking the test.

The Policy establishes more severe consequences for successive violations. When a student's drug test indicates a positive result, the laboratory conducting the test performs a second test to confirm the results. If the second test is positive, the student's parent or guardian will be notified and the principal will conduct a due process hearing with the student and his or her parent or guardian. The student then must participate in a drug assistance program and undergo weekly drug tests over a six-week period. If the student refuses, the student will be suspended from participating in extracurricular activities for the current and subsequent seasons and must be tested again prior to the next season for which the student is eligible. If the student commits a second offense, the student's parent or guardian is notified, a due process hearing is held, and the student is suspended from participation in extracurricular activities for the current and subsequent seasons. Thus, when a student commits a second offense, the student does not have the option of enrolling in a drug assistance program in order to participate in the extracurricular activity. Finally, if a student commits a third offense, the student's parents are notified, a due process hearing is held, and the student is suspended from extracurricular activities for the current and next two seasons. . . .

Lopez, who at the time he brought the action was a seventeen-year-old senior at Trinidad High School, was enrolled in two band classes for which he received both credit and grades and participated in the Trinidad High School marching band. As the trial court found, Lopez had been a member of the marching band since 1993 and was a gifted musician who played the baritone trombone, the piano, and the guitar. Lopez testified at the trial that he planned to pursue a music major in college and wanted to be a composer or enter into education.

After Lopez received the consent form in the beginning of the 1997 school year, he consulted with his parents and decided not to sign the form. Lopez testified that by not signing the form, he recognized that he "could be losing scholarship money, or experience that [he] need[ed]." However, he indicated that he was willing to take that risk "because it's what this country was founded on, our rights" and that in his view, the drug testing program was "constitutionally wrong."

II

Lopez . . . challenges the *suspicionless* testing allowed under the Policy. . . .

[The Supreme Court of Colorado, which disallowed testing for college students in *Derdeyn*, prohibits suspiciousless drug testing for high school band members here on the grounds that it violates the Fourth Amendment, primarily on the basis that musicians have higher expectations of privacy than student-athletes. In short, there is not the locker room mentality that the U.S. Supreme Court found controlling in *Vernonia Sch. Dist. 47J. v. Acton.*

The court finds the testing to be a "search" under the Fourth Amendment and that the case is not moot even though the plaintiff is no longer a student. The court finds that there is no relevant information about drug usage among students who participate in extracurricular activities; and that there is no evidence of diminished expectations of privacy in the student body at large based on participation in physical education courses.

"Although band members wear uniforms, they do not undergo the type of public undressing and communal showers required of student atheletes." The court here finds this fact significant. Furthermore, the court holds that "the type of voluntariness to which the *Vernonia* Court referred does not apply to students who want to enroll in a for-credit class that is part of the school's curriculum."]

VII

Based on our analysis of all of these factors, we conclude that the Policy is not reasonable and thus cannot stand under the United States Constitution. First, the nature of the privacy interest invaded was different from that of the student athletes described by the *Vernonia* Court. The absence in this case of both true voluntariness and the type of communal undressing that occurred among the student athletes in *Vernonia* is significant. Second, while the District established that it has a drug abuse problem, the means chosen to deal with that problem were too broad. The Policy's actual scope extended vastly beyond the policy upheld in *Vernonia*. The Policy swept within its reach students participating in an extracurricular activity who were not demonstrated to play a role in promoting drugs and for whom there was no demonstrated risk of physical injury. The Policy also effectively included students enrolled in a for-credit class offered by the District. Even accepting the trial court's reasoning that the invasion of the students' privacy interests was negligible, we find these other distinctions between this case and *Vernonia* to be dispositive. Accordingly, having considered together the three factors announced by the *Vernonia* Court, we hold that the Policy is unconstitutional. We therefore reverse the trial court's order and remand the case to the trial court for further proceedings consistent with this opinion. . . .

4. Due Process and Equal Protection

Drug testing programs trigger questions of the athlete's privacy, due process, and equal protection rights. However, Fourteenth Amendment due process and equal protection rights do not extend to private contracts that abridge only individual rights.

Only state actions can be challenged under the Fourteenth Amendment. The question is whether the particular action is state action or comes under the color of state action.

In *Schaill v. Tippecanoe County School Corp.,* the Seventh Circuit Court of Appeals predated *Vernonia School District 47J v. Acton* by similarly finding that random urinalysis of high school athletes is reasonable under the Fourth Amendment and that the school board's procedures for challenging positive test results satisfied due process.

SCHAILL V. TIPPECANOE COUNTY SCHOOL CORP.

864 F.2d 1309 (7th Cir. 1988)

CUDAHY, Circuit Judge.

In this action brought under 42 U.S.C. section 1983, plaintiffs-appellants Darcy Schaill and Shelley Johnson challenge a random urinalysis program instituted by the defendant-appellee Tippecanoe County School Corporation ("TSC"). Appellants allege that the TSC urinalysis program violates their rights under the fourth amendment and the due process clause of the fourteenth amendment. After conducting a trial on the merits of appellants' claims, the district court ruled that the TSC program was constitutional. We affirm. . . .

Under the program, all students desiring to participate in interscholastic athletics and their parent or guardian are required to sign a consent form agreeing to submit to urinalysis if chosen on a random basis. Each student selected for an athletic team is assigned a number. The athletic director and head coach of each athletic team are authorized to institute random urine tests during the athletic season. In order to select individuals to be tested, the number assigned to each athlete is placed in a box, and a single number is drawn. . . .

II

As a threshold matter, we must consider whether TSC's random urine testing program involves a "search" as that term is employed in the fourth amendment. The Supreme Court has held that "[a] 'search' occurs when an expectation of privacy that society is prepared to consider reasonable is infringed."

There can be little doubt that a person engaging in the act of urination possesses a reasonable expectation of privacy as to that act, and as to the urine which is excreted. In our society, it is expected that urination be performed in private, that urine be disposed of in private and that the act, if mentioned at all, be described in euphemistic terms. . . .

III

Having determined that urine testing constitutes a "search" in the constitutional sense, we must consider what level of suspicion is required to authorize urinalysis of any particular student. . . .

Determining the level of suspicion required before the government may conduct a search requires "balanc[ing] the nature and quality of the intrusion on the individual's Fourth Amendment interests against the importance of the governmental interests alleged to justify the intrusion."

Unfortunately for appellants, we believe that the Supreme Court has already struck the appropriate balance in the context of school searches, and has determined that the probable cause and warrant requirements do not apply. . . .

IV

Since the probable cause and warrant requirements are not applicable to the searches involved in this case, we must consider the TSC urinalysis program under the general fourth amendment standard of reasonableness. . . .

In the present case, TSC plans to conduct a search not only without probable cause or a warrant, but in the absence of any individualized suspicion of drug use by the students to be tested. In these circumstances, TSC bears a heavier burden to justify its contemplated actions. In a criminal law enforcement context, the Supreme Court has been extremely hesitant to condone searches performed without any articulable basis for suspecting the particular individual of unlawful conduct. However, in several carefully defined situations, the Court has recognized that searches may be conducted in the absence of any grounds to believe that the individual searched has violated the law. . . .

A

In general, there is a substantial expectation of privacy in connection with the act of urination. However, the privacy considerations are somewhat mitigated on the facts before us because the provider of the urine sample enters a closed lavatory stall and the person monitoring the urination stands outside listening for the sounds appropriate to what is taking place. The invasion of privacy is therefore not nearly as severe as would be the case if the monitor were required to observe the subject in the act of urination.

We also find great significance in the fact that the drug testing program in this case is being implemented solely with regard to participants in an interscholastic athletic program. In the first place, in athletic programs in general there is a much diminished expectation of privacy and, in particular, privacy with respect to urinalysis. There is an element of "communal undress" inherent in athletic participation, which suggests reduced expectations of privacy. In addition, physical examinations are integral to almost all athletic programs. In fact, athletes and cheerleaders desiring to participate in the TSC athletic program have long been required to produce a urine sample as part of a mandatory medical examination. This sample is not produced under monitored conditions, is only tested for the presence of sugar in the urine and is given to the athlete's physician of choice rather than a school official; however, the fact that such samples are required suggests that legitimate expectations of privacy in this context are diminished.

Further, in the case before us, we are dealing with *interscholastic* athletics. In these programs the Indiana High School Athletic Association has extensive requirements which it imposes upon schools and individuals participating in interscholastic athletics. These include minimum grade, residency and eligibility requirements. In addition to IHSAA regulations, participants in interscholastic athletics are also subject to training rules, including prohibitions on smoking, drinking and drug use both on and off school premises. . . .

V

Appellant's final contention is that the procedures provided in the TSC program for a student to challenge a positive urinalysis test are insufficient under the due process clause of the fourteenth amendment. . . .

Since TSC's drug testing program provides for confirmatory testing at no cost to the student, and provides the student with notice of the results of the test and an opportunity to rebut a positive result, we cannot find that TSC's drug testing program violates the due process clause. . . .

In this case, we believe that the Tippecanoe County School Corporation has chosen a reasonable and limited response to a serious evil. In formulating its urinalysis program, the school district has been sensitive to the privacy rights of its students, and has sought to emphasize rehabilitation over punishment. We cannot conclude that this approach is inconsistent with the mandates of the Constitution. The judgment of the district court is therefore

Affirmed.

QUESTIONS AND DISCUSSION

1. *Dimeo v. Griffin* and *Shoemaker v. Handel*, 795 F.2d 1136 (3d Cir. 1986), involved the so-called seriously regulated industries, such as, in these two cases, horse racing. In *Shoemaker*, the court upheld regulations that directed the jockeys to submit to drug testing. However, *Dimeo*, with similar facts, disallowed similar regulations. Why was that? What is different in *Dimeo*? *Dimeo* enjoined a state racing board from random drug testing and probable cause testing for all racing licensees (outriders, starters, jockeys, and so on). While balancing the interests, the court held that the racing board's interest in safety and integrity were insufficient to outweigh the invasion of privacy through an otherwise unconstitutional random urinalysis. Page, *Drug Testing in the Work Place: Random Testing of Professional Athletes*, 33 Wm. & Mary L. Rev. 144 (1991); Rose & Girard, *Drug Testing in Professional and College Sports*, 36 Kan. L. Rev. 787 (1988); *See* Weinberg, Dimeo v. Griffin: *Another Random Drug Test or the Latest Infringement on the Fourth Amendment Rights of American Workers?* 87 Nw. U. L. Rev. 1087 (1992). *See generally* Marrarzzo, *Athletes and Drug Testing: Why Do We Care if Athletes Inhale?* 8 Marq. Sports L. J. 75 (1997).

2. In *Hill v. NCAA*, 273 Cal. Rptr. 402 (Cal. Ct. App. 1990), *rev'd*, 865 P.2d 633 (Cal. 1994), the Supreme Court of California sided with the NCAA and reversed a California Court of Appeals decision that had granted a permanent injunction against NCAA drug testing on the basis that it violated the right to privacy under the California Constitution. The appeals court held that the NCAA did not show a compelling interest to justify this violation. The California Supreme Court, however, held that the NCAA's drug testing program is not an unreasonable infringement on a student-athlete's expectation to privacy. *See O'Halloran v. University of Wash.*, 679 F. Supp. 997 (W.D Wash. 1988); Champion, *The NCAA's Drug Testing Policies: Walking a Constitutional Tightrope?* 67 N.D. L. Rev. 269 (1991). *See generally* Ludd, *Athletics, Drug Testing and the Right to Privacy: A Question of Privacy*, 34 How L.J. 599 (1991). The court of appeals in *Hill* did not see an interest so compelling to justify the invasion of privacy in that female athletes must reveal medical history that would indicate the use of birth control pills. Does the California Supreme Court in *Hill* and the U.S. Supreme Court in *Acton* scare you? Does it remind you of Big Brother hovering over your shoulder? Can you think of less intrusive methods?

3. *Vernonia Sch. Dist. 47J v. Acton* held that high school student-athletes can be subject to random suspicionless drug tests. The court held that athletes labor under a lessened expectation of privacy due to the "locker room mentality" and that athletes are role models and must be held to a higher standard than most other students. The majority reasoned that urinating as part of a drug test is merely an extension or variation of public showering, which is a component of a typical locker room environment. *See* Champion, *A Critical Look at the So-Called Locker Room Mentality as a Means to Rationalize the Drug Testing of Student Athletes*, 4 Vill. Sports & Ent. L.J. 283 (1997).

   Before *Acton*, the standard for the drug testing of high school athletes was established by the Seventh Circuit Court of Appeals in *Schaill v. Tippecanoe County Sch. Corp.* In *Schaill*, as in *Acton*, the school's program was predicated on the consent of the individual athlete. In both cases, the plaintiff-athlete refused to sign a consent form granting the school the authority to conduct mandatory urinalysis. Student-athletes lose some of their constitutional rights in high school, and provided that the testing procedures are not egregiously bizarre, courts allow urinalysis with consent.

   In a rousing dissent to *Acton*, Justice O'Connor was livid:

   > [B]y the reasoning of today's decision, the millions of these students who participate in interscholastic sports, an overwhelming majority of whom have given school officials no reason whatsoever to suspect they use drugs at school, are open to an intrusive bodily search.

   Analyzing urine is an intrusive bodily search, but the majority in *Acton* now allows suspicionless blanket searches of a closed-set community. Is that the end of the debate? Is the locker room mentality argument inherently weak? Do you see any other way to defeat or thwart a school district's ability to conduct random, suspicionless drug tests?

4. After reading *Brennan v. Board of Trustees for Univ. of La. Sys.*, should there be a different standard with steroids, as opposed to "street drugs"? Steroids have been shown to enhance performance, which could increase the risk of injury to opposing players. Does plaintiff's argument about failure to warn have any validity? The Brennan court opined that the university was not negligent. If plaintiff was a scholarship athlete, would a contract argument fare better?

D. TERMINATING EMPLOYMENT

The power to discipline and punish also includes the power to terminate an employment contract. In *Dambrot v. Central Michigan University*, a basketball coach who was allegedly fired because of offensive racist language was not able to establish that his locker room speech was entitled to First Amendment protection.

DAMBROT V. CENTRAL MICHIGAN UNIVERSITY

55 F.3d 1177 (6th Cir. 1995)

KEITH, Circuit Judge.

There are two sets of plaintiffs in this case (collectively the "Plaintiffs"). The first is Keith Dambrot, ("Dambrot") former head coach of Central Michigan University's men's basketball program. The second includes five students — Leonard Bush, Deshanti Foreman, Keith Gilmore, Tyrone Hicks, and Amere May (collectively the "Student Plaintiffs") — who were members of the 1992-93 Central Michigan University ("CMU") men's basketball team coached by Dambrot. Defendants are CMU and Leonard E. Plachta ("Plachta"), Russ Herron ("Herron"), and Dave Keilitz ("Keilitz") officially and in their private capacities (collectively "Defendants" or "CMU"). Dambrot appears before the court appealing the grant of summary judgment in favor of Defendant CMU regarding his wrongful termination claim. Defendants cross-appeal the district court's grant of summary judgment in favor of Plaintiffs regarding the unconstitutionality of CMU's discriminatory harassment policy. Defendants also cross-appeal the district court's award of attorney's fees to the Student Plaintiffs. The Student Plaintiffs come before the court as cross-appellees. For the reasons stated below, we affirm the district court's grant of summary judgment in favor of Plaintiffs finding the CMU discriminatory harassment policy violates the First Amendment. We also affirm the district court's grant of summary judgment in favor of Defendants finding CMU's termination of Coach Dambrot's employment does not violate the First Amendment. Finally, we affirm the district court's award of attorney's fees.

I. Statement of the Case

On May 12, 1991, Dambrot became the head coach of the Central Michigan University men's basketball team. His responsibilities as head coach included, among other things, offering and renewing player scholarships, deciding which players could remain on the team, determining the amount of playing time for each player and selecting assistant coaches. This lawsuit arises from events which occurred during the 1992-93 men's basketball season.

The 1992 CMU men's basketball team was made up of eleven African Americans and three Caucasians. The team's full-time coaching staff included two assistant coaches, Derrick McDowell (an African American) and Barry Markwart (a Caucasian). The part-time coaching staff included one voluntary graduate assistant, Chip Wilde (a Caucasian), three managers (all Caucasian), and a professional trainer (a Caucasian).

In January of 1993, Dambrot used the word "nigger" during a locker room session with his players and coaching staff either during the halftime or at the end of a basketball game in which the team lost to Miami University of Ohio. According to Dambrot's testimony, Dambrot told the players they hadn't been playing very hard and then said "Do you mind if I use the N word?" After one or some of the players apparently indicated it was okay, Dambrot said "you know we need to have more niggers on our team. . . . Coach McDowell is a nigger, . . . Sand[er] Scott who's an academic All-American, a Caucasian, I said Sand[er] Scott is a nigger. He's hard nose, [sic] he's tough, et cetera." He testified he intended to use the term in a "positive and reinforcing" manner. The players often referred to each other using the N-word during games and around campus and in the locker room. Dambrot stated he used the word in the same manner in which the players used the term amongst themselves, "to connote a person who is fearless, mentally strong and tough."

Prior to the January incident, the record shows Dambrot had used the N-word on at least one other occasion. In November, Dambrot apparently addressed the team after a practice and said he wanted the players to "play like niggers on the court" and wished he had more niggers on the basketball court. He then said he did not want the team to act like niggers in the classroom. . . .

The news Dambrot had used the N-word in the locker room incident became known to persons outside the basketball team. In February 1993, Keilitz interviewed members of the men's basketball team at Dambrot's request. Keilitz reported all the African American players he interviewed said they were not offended by the coach's use of the term. At some point after those interviews, a former member of the men's basketball team, Shannon Norris, complained to the university's affirmative action officer, Angela Haddad, regarding Dambrot's use of the N-word during the November incident. The affirmative action officer confronted Dambrot who admitted using the word but stated he used it in a positive manner. The officer viewed Dambrot's use of the word as a violation of the university's discriminatory harassment policy and recommended Dambrot be disciplined. Dambrot accepted the proposed disciplinary action in lieu of a more formal investigation and was suspended without pay for five days.

News of the locker room incident spread through the campus after Dambrot was suspended. An article in the student newspaper was printed in which Dambrot told his side of the story. The statement was characterized by the district court as "considerably more explanatory and defensive than apologetic in tone." Students staged a demonstration and local, regional and national news media reported accounts of the incident at CMU.

On April 12, 1993, Keilitz, the athletic director, informed Dambrot he would not be retained as head coach for the 1993-94 season. The university stated that it believed Dambrot was no longer capable of effectively leading the men's basketball program.

Dambrot instituted a lawsuit on April 19, 1993, alleging, *inter alia*, he was fired because he used the term "nigger," and the termination violated his First Amendment rights to free speech and academic freedom. Several members of the basketball team joined the lawsuit alleging the university's discriminatory harassment policy was overbroad and vague and violated their First Amendment rights. . . .

II. Discussion

Defendants appeal the district court's grant of summary judgment holding the CMU discriminatory harassment policy overbroad and void for vagueness violating the First Amendment. Plaintiffs appeal the district court's grant of summary judgment holding CMU's termination of Dambrot did not violate the First Amendment. Defendants also appeal the district court's award of attorney's fees to Plaintiffs. For the following reasons we affirm the district court on each issue.

A. The District Court Did Not Err in Granting Summary Judgment for Plaintiffs Finding the CMU Discriminatory Harassment Policy Unconstitutional

1. Standard of Review . . .

2. The Discriminatory Harassment Policy Is Unconstitutional on Its Face

The overbreadth doctrine provides an exception to the traditional rules of standing and allows parties not yet affected by a statute to bring actions under the First Amendment based on a belief that a certain statute is so broad as to "chill" the exercise of free speech and expression. A statute is unconstitutional on its face on overbreadth grounds if there is "a realistic danger that the statute itself will significantly compromise recognized First Amendment protections of parties not before the court. . . . "

The CMU policy, located in the Plan for Affirmative Action at Central Michigan University, states discriminatory harassment will not be condoned. Racial and ethnic harassment is defined in the policy as

> any intentional, unintentional, physical, verbal, or nonverbal behavior that subjects an individual to an intimidating, hostile or offensive educational, employment or living environment by . . . (c) demeaning or slurring individuals through . . . written literature because of their racial or ethnic affiliation; or (d) using symbols, [epithets] or slogans that infer negative connotations about the individual's racial or ethnic affiliation. . . .

CMU argues the policy does not present a "realistic danger" of compromising First Amendment rights because 1) there is no enforcement mechanism and 2) the university enforces the policy with respect for First Amendment rights. Defendants' first argument is not persuasive. Although there are no formal mechanisms of enforcement, it is clear from the sanctions imposed on Dambrot that the university can pursue violations to the policy.

Secondly, CMU argues any concerns the policy will reach constitutionally protected speech have been abated by language in the policy which states:

> The University will not extend its application of discriminatory harassment so far as to interfere impermissibly with individuals rights to free speech. . . .

Similarly, this court declines to accept the representations of CMU. . . .

In the instant case, there is nothing to ensure the University will not violate First Amendment rights even if that is not their intention. It is clear from the text of the policy that language or writing, intentional or unintentional, regardless of political value, can be prohibited upon the initiative of the university. The broad scope of the policy's language presents a "realistic danger" the University could compromise the protection afforded by the First Amendment. . . .

On its face, the CMU discriminatory harassment policy "sweeps within its ambit both constitutionally protected activity . . . and unprotected conduct, making it subject to an overbreadth challenge."

The next step in analyzing an overbreadth claim is to determine whether the policy is "substantially overbroad and constitutionally invalid under the void for vagueness doctrine." . . .

The facts of this case demonstrate the necessity of subjective reference in identifying prohibited speech under the policy. Several players testified they were not offended by Dambrot's use of the N-word while student Norris and affirmative action officer Haddad were extremely offended. The CMU policy, as written, does not provide fair notice of what speech will violate the policy. Defining what is offensive is, in fact, wholly delegated to university officials. This "unrestricted delegation of power" gives rise to the second type of vagueness. For these reasons, the CMU policy is also void for vagueness.

3. Even if the N-word Constitutes a "Fighting Word," the Discriminatory Harassment Policy Remains Unconstitutional . . .

Because the CMU discriminatory harassment policy is overbroad and void for vagueness and because it is not a valid prohibition against fighting words, the CMU discriminatory harassment policy violates the First Amendment of the United States Constitution. The district court's grant of summary judgment in favor of Plaintiffs on this issue is therefore affirmed.

B. The District Court Did Not Err in Finding Dambrot Was Permissibly Terminated

Dambrot seeks relief from an alleged wrongful termination for the following reasons stated in his amended complaint:

> 20. Plaintiff's communication with his players is speech protected by the First Amendment.
> 21. Plaintiff Dambrot's use of the term "nigger" in the sense set forth above in the instructional context is fully protected by the First Amendment.

22. The Defendants, acting under color of state law, terminated Plaintiff's employment, solely because of his exercise of expression fully protected by the First Amendment.

The district court described Dambrot's argument, as stated in the briefs and oral argument, this way: (1) CMU's policy is unconstitutional because it suppresses speech that is protected by the First Amendment; (2) Plaintiff Dambrot was sanctioned pursuant to the policy and eventually terminated from employment as a result of such sanctioning; (3) therefore, plaintiff's termination was violative of the First Amendment. The district court correctly noted while Dambrot's argument has a seductive logic, Dambrot can only demonstrate harm resulted from the application of the invalid policy if his speech was in fact protected. Without a finding that Dambrot's speech is protected under the First Amendment, the application of the policy does not injure Dambrot. Without the demonstration of some harm, Dambrot cannot recover.

The other argument intimated by Dambrot in # 21 of his complaint is that he is protected under the concept of academic freedom. From either perspective, the central issue is whether Dambrot's speech is protected by the First Amendment. We find it is not.

1. CMU's Termination of Dambrot was Permissible Because Dambrot's
Speech Does Not Touch a Matter of Public Concern . . .
2. Dambrot's Speech Does Not Enter the Marketplace of Ideas or the
Realm of Academic Freedom . . .

Dambrot's use of the N-word, . . . was not the essence of his communicative act. . . .

Dambrot's use of the N-word is even further away from the marketplace of ideas and the concept of academic freedom because his position as coach is somewhat different from that of the average classroom teacher. Unlike the classroom teacher whose primary role is to guide students through the discussion and debate of various viewpoints in a particular discipline, Dambrot's role as a coach is to train his student athletes how to win on the court. The plays and strategies are seldom up for debate. Execution of the coach's will is paramount. Moreover, the coach controls who plays and for how long, placing a disincentive on any debate with the coach's ideas which might have taken place.

While Dambrot argues and we accept as true that he intended to use the term in a positive and reinforcing manner, Dambrot's total message to the players is disturbing. . . .

What the First Amendment does not do, however, is require the government as employer or the university as educator to accept this view as a valid means of motivating players. An instructor's choice of teaching methods does not rise to the level of protected expression. . . . In the instant case, the University has a right to terminate Dambrot for recklessly telling these young men to be athletically ardent but academically apathetic in his attempt to boost athletic performance. The University has a right to terminate Dambrot for telling his players that success on the basketball court is not premised on the same principles of discipline, focus and drive that bring success in the classroom. The University has a right to disapprove of the use of the word "nigger" as a motivational tool. . . . Finally, the University has a right to hold Coach Dambrot to a higher standard of conduct than that of his players. Dambrot's resort to the First Amendment for protection is not well taken.

For the foregoing reasons, Dambrot's speech cannot be fairly characterized as touching a matter of public concern. . . . Moreover, there is no need to reach the question of whether the speech was the primary reason for the termination or whether CMU had other reasons for terminating Dambrot. Neither does Dambrot's speech raise any academic freedom concerns. Accordingly, the district court's grant of summary judgment for CMU on this issue is affirmed.

C. The District Court Did Not Err in Its Decision to Grant Attorney's Fees . . .

1. The District Court Did Not Err in Finding Plaintiffs Are Prevailing Parties . . .
2. The District Court Did Not Abuse Its Discretion by Declining to Reduce the Fee Award to Reflect Nonmeritorious or Unsuccessful Claims or Duplicated Efforts . . .

III. Conclusion

For the foregoing reasons, we affirm the grant of summary judgment in favor of Plaintiffs finding the CMU discriminatory harassment policy violates the First Amendment, we affirm the grant of summary judgment in favor of Defendants finding CMU's termination of Coach Dambrot's employment does not violate the First Amendment, and we affirm the award of attorney's fees by the Honorable Robert H. Cleland of the United States District Court for the Eastern District of Michigan, Northern Division.

In *Lee v. Wise County School Board*, a terminated high school basketball coach unsuccessfully argued that the school board's failure to rehire him was based on religious discrimination rather than consistent poor performance as a coach.

LEE v. WISE COUNTY SCHOOL BOARD

133 F.3d 95 (4th Cir 1998)

PER CURIAM.

David Edward Lee, Jr., appeals the district court's grant of summary judgment in favor of the Wise County School Board on his claim of religious discrimination in violation of Title VII. Lee maintains that the school board declined to rehire him as a basketball coach on account of his religion. The district court held that Lee failed to establish a prima facie case of religious discrimination and that Lee's poor performance as a coach provided a legitimate nondiscriminatory reason for its decision not to rehire him. We hold that the school board has provided an adequate reason for its failure to rehire and that Lee has failed to create a triable dispute over whether that reason is pretextual. Accordingly, we affirm the district court.

I

Lee was head coach of the men's basketball team since 1979 at Powell Valley High School, located in Big Stone Gap, Virginia. He also taught English and coached tennis at Powell Valley. Lee attended a Methodist church and had been actively involved in religious affairs such as the Fellowship of Christian Athletes.

From the 1990-91 school year through the 1994-95 school year, the men's basketball team never posted a winning season. During 1994 and 1995, parents and members of the community voiced complaints to Bruce Robinette, a member of the Wise County School Board, and David Dowdy, principal at Powell Valley, about Lee's inadequate job performance as head basketball coach. According to Robinette, the criticisms increased over the course of the 1994-95 school year, and he eventually advised the parents to bring their concerns to the attention of the full school board.

During a school board meeting held on June 28, 1995, a delegation of parents appeared to register their complaints about Lee. To allow the parents to air their concerns privately, the board went into executive session. The parents complained that Lee was not devoting enough time or attention to the basketball program due to other pursuits such as work for a company named Amway and his own painting business. The parents also observed that the basketball team was unable to attend a camp in North Carolina because Lee had failed to submit a timely application. Every school board member stated that the board did not discuss Lee's religious affiliation, convictions, or activities at this meeting. . . .

During the next board meeting, held on July 13, 1995, the board again considered the renewal of Lee's contract as a basketball coach. The board discussed the complaints about Lee's neglect of the basketball program. Although the board never formally voted on Lee's contract, it reached a general consensus that Lee would not be rehired as a basketball coach. The board members did not discuss Lee's religious affiliation, convictions, practices, or activities at this meeting.

After the July meeting, Dr. Graham met with principal Dowdy and advised him of the board's consensus. In Wise County, to renew coaching contracts, a principal submits a slate of coaches to the division superintendent who reviews these recommendations and forwards a list to the school board. For the 1995-96 school year, Dowdy did not recommend Lee as the men's basketball coach. Instead, he recommended Jimmy Mitchell, another Powell Valley employee, who eventually was hired as the interim head coach for that year.

Lee filed a charge with the Equal Employment Opportunity Commission and later brought this complaint. In his complaint, Lee alleged, inter alia, that the school board discriminated against him on the basis of his religion by failing to rehire him as the head basketball coach. The district court granted the school board's motion for summary judgment. Lee now appeals.

II

Title VII prohibits employment discrimination on the basis of religion. 42 U.S.C. §2000e-2(a). Absent direct evidence of discrimination, a plaintiff must first demonstrate a prima facie case of discrimination. Once a party has made a prima facie case, the employer must provide a legitimate nondiscriminatory justification for its action. If the employer advances such a justification, the plaintiff then must prove that this justification is a mere pretext for an actual discriminatory motive.

Lee challenges the district court's holding that he did not establish a prima facie case of religious discrimination. To uphold summary judgment in this case, we need not resolve that question. Assuming that Lee has demonstrated a prima facie case, the school board advanced a legitimate nondiscriminatory justification for its decision not to rehire him — Lee was spending too much time on outside activities and was not sufficiently dedicated to the Powell Valley basketball program. Lee has failed to create a genuine issue over whether this justification was pretextual. The school board, therefore, is entitled to summary judgment. . . .

III

The school board provided ample evidence that Lee was diverted by other pursuits and had not devoted sufficient attention to his coaching duties. Lee's contentions that religion motivated the high school's coaching change are nothing more than speculations. Accordingly, we affirm the judgment of the district court.

Affirmed.

QUESTIONS AND DISCUSSION

1. The coach in *Dambrot* was fired for violating the University Discrimination Harassment Policy. He successfully argued that his words were protected by the First Amendment. *See also Holthaus v. Board of Educ.*, Cincinnati Public Schs., 986 F.2d 1044 (6th Cir. 1993) (high school football coach discharged for attempting to "motivate" with use of "N-word" — however, breach of contract by public employer cannot give rise to a §1983 claim of substantive due process).

2. In *Lee*, the coach claimed that he was not rehired due to religious discrimination. Title VII prohibits employment discrimination based on religion (42 U.S.C. §2000e-2(a)), but in *Lee*, the couut held that the school board provided sufficient evidence to show that Lee was diverted by other pursuits, namely, selling Amway products and running a painting business not to mention that he amassed five consecutive losing seasons). Would

the reaction of the school board have been the same if he had five winning seasons?

3. Coaches' contracts are sometimes terminated due to allegations that they have fraternized with their players, thus compromising a morality code. In two cases, two high school coaching positions were terminated as a result of illicit affairs with female athletes. In one case, a girls' basketball coach married a former player. *Finnegan v. Board of Educ. of Enlarged City Sch. Dist. of Troy*, 30 F.3d 273 (2d Cir. 1994). In the other, it was alleged that a coach took indecent liberties with several students. *Padilla v. South Harrison R-II Sch. Dist.*, 1995 U.S. Dist. LEXIS 5547 (W.D. Mo. 1995). In both cases, defendants were granted summary judgment. In the case of *Finnegan*, should the court have decided it differently on the basis that the coach married the student? We'll assume that the former student did not initiate (or condone) either the complaint or the termination.

4. The power to discipline can also include the decision to not renew an athlete's scholarship. The scholarship relationship would be in the nature of a quasi-contract. *See* Conard v. University of Wash., 814 P.2d 1242 (Wash. Ct. App. 1991), *aff'd in part and rev'd in part*, 834 P.2d 17 (Wash. 1992).

CHAPTER 10

THE NCAA

The National Collegiate Athletic Association (NCAA) is the preeminent governing body controlling intercollegiate athletic competition in the United States. The NCAA is a voluntary, unincorporated association of colleges and universities; its general policies are formally promulgated at annual conventions. The **Administration** of the NCAA in between the annual conventions is controlled by a council, its executive committee, and paid staff. **Eligibility** to participate is based on an extensive body of rules, regulations, and precedents that are interpreted, enforced, and reviewed by NCAA legislative assistants and enforcement personnel. Attorneys are involved when and if litigation occurs. The NCAA has the power to **Discipline** its member schools and the athletes therein.

A. ADMINISTRATION

As regards college sports, the NCAA is the most important governing body in sports of any type at any level. Critics point out its alleged parternalism, particularly regarding propositions that limit academic eligibility based on standardized test scores and high school grade point averages in core courses.

The NCAA is a vestige of the Theodore Roosevelt years. It has historically offered championships in a variety of sports. However, NCAA football television contracts greatly increased its financial and regulatory powers. It is a voluntary, unincorporated association of colleges of which approximately 50 percent are state supported. It is composed of more than 1200 member schools. All schools that are accredited by a recognized academic accrediting agency automatically meet NCAA standards and may become a member. The NCAA sponsors national championships and also makes and enforces rules and regulations. It formulates policy and regulations that govern almost all aspects of intercollegiate athletic participation.

The NCAA is governed by a large and detailed manual of rules and regulations, which contains its constitution and bylaws. It also contains interpretations and executive actions. As noted above, in between annual conventions, the NCAA is controlled by a council, its executive committee, and a paid staff; rule interpretations and enforcement are administered by legislative assistants and enforcement personnel; and attorneys are involved when and if litigations occurs.

General policies are formally approved at the annual convention. Between conventions policy is established, controlled, and directed by the NCAA council, which is elected by the entire membership at the annual meeting.

The following section from the NCAA manual outlines the basic organizational structure.

NCAA CONSTITUTION, ARTICLE 4, ORGANIZATION

4.01 General Principles

4.01.1 Structure. The Association's administrative structure shall include an Executive Committee comprised of institutional chief executive officers (CEOs) that oversees Association-wide issues and shall ensure that each division operates consistent with the basic purposes, fundamental policies and general principles of the Association (see Constitution 1 and 2). In addition, the administrative structure of each division shall empower a body of institutional chief executive officers (CEOs) to set forth the policies, rules and regulations for operating the division. Further, the administrative structure of each division shall empower a body of athletics administrators and faculty athletics representatives to make recommendations to the division's body of institutional CEOs and to handle responsibilities delegated to it. *(Adopted: 1/9/96 effective 8/1/97)*

4.01.2 Guarantees. The Association's overall governance structure guarantees its members the following: *(Adopted: 1/9/96 effective 8/1/97)*

4.01.2.1 Budget Allocations. Members are guaranteed revenue through allocations made to each division from the Association's general operating revenue. *(Adopted: 1/9/96 effective 8/1/97)*

4.01.2.1.1 General Operating Revenue. General operating revenue, as used in this section, shall include at least all sources of revenue existing as of January 9, 1996, including revenue from contracts for these existing sources and revenue from any modified, extended or successor contract for such sources. *(Adopted: 1/9/96 effective 8/1/97)*

4.01.2.2 Revenue Guarantee. All members shall receive revenue from all gross revenue sources received by the Association, unless specifically excluded, through the division's revenue distribution formulas. *(Adopted: 1/9/96 effective 8/1/97)*

4.01.2.2.1 Revenue from New Subdivision Championship. . . .

4.01.2.2.2 Revenue Distribution Formula. As used in this section, the components of the division's revenue distribution formulas as they existed at the time of the adoption of this legislation include the Academic Enhancement, Basketball, Conference Grant, Grant-in-Aid, Special Assistance, and

Sports Sponsorship funds, and the supplemental and reserve funds intended for distribution to the membership. *(Adopted: 1/9/96 effective 8/1/97)*

4.01.2.2.2.1 Proportion of Revenue. The revenue distributed through these funds shall be allocated among the funds in the same proportion as will exist in the fiscal year 2001-02. *(Adopted: 1/9/96 effective 8/1/97, Revised: 1/14/97)*

4.01.2.2.2.2 Formula for Allocation. The formula for allocating each such fund among the members shall be as it existed at the time of the adoption of this legislation. *(Adopted: 1/9/96 effective 8/1/97)*

4.01.2.2.2.3 Waiver of Proportionality Requirement. The Board of Directors may waive the proportionality requirements of the revenue guarantee to permit uniform increases to all programs in the Academic Enhancement, Conference Grant and Special Assistance funds. *(Adopted: 1/14/97 effective 8/1/97)*

4.01.2.2.3 Joint Ventures. All marketing joint ventures, involving sports (other than I-A football) in which the NCAA sponsored a championship as of January 15, 1997, between the Association (or the Association's representative or agent) and a member conference or member institution (or the representative or agent of a member institution or conference) shall be reviewed by the Management Council. *(Adopted: 1/14/97 effective 8/1/97)*

4.01.2.2.3.1 Definition. A marketing joint venture is any marketing program that uses the Association's marks or logos in conjunction with those of a conference or member institution. *(Adopted: 1/14/97 effective 8/1/97)*

4.01.2.2.3.2 Approval Process. The principles and overall program of any joint venture defined in Constitution 4.01.2.2.3.1 shall require the approval of the Management Council and Board of Directors to be enacted as an Association business operation. *(Adopted: 1/14/97 effective 8/1/97)*

4.01.2.3 Championships. Members are guaranteed access to national championships. *(Adopted: 1/9/96 effective 8/1/97)*

4.01.2.3.1 Divisions I-AA and I-AAA—Championships Access. . . .

4.01.2.3.2 Championships—Sports Other Than Football. With the exception of football, not more than one national championship shall be conducted in each men's and women's sport. *(Adopted: 1/14/97 effective 8/1/97)*

4.01.2.4 Membership Services. Members are guaranteed services provided through the Association's national office at least at the level provided as of January 9, 1996 (e.g., membership services, statistics, research). *(Adopted: 1/9/96 effective 8/1/97)*

4.01.2.5 Special Programs. Members are guaranteed the continuation of Association programs operating at the time of the adoption of this legislation (e.g., the catastrophic-injury insurance program, the drug-testing program, the Division I athletics-certification program). In addition, members are guaranteed the continuation of Association programs that were considered by the NCAA Council or Presidents Commission by the spring of 1995 and began operating after the adoption of this legislation. *(Adopted: 1/9/96 effective 8/1/97)*

Courts usually allow suits against the NCAA only if its action violates its own bylaws and constitution. The case of *California State University, Hayward v. NCAA* is that rare example where the NCAA's decision to indefinitely suspend a school's entire athletic program from postseason competition was contrary to the bylaws and constitution and was void as against public policy.

CALIFORNIA STATE UNIVERSITY, HAYWARD v. NATIONAL COLLEGIATE ATHLETIC ASSOCIATION

121 Cal. Rptr. 85 (Cal. Ct. App. 1975)

BRAY, Associate Justice.

Defendant National Collegiate Athletic Association appeals from the order of the Alameda County Superior Court granting a preliminary injunction.

Issues Presented

1. The trial court had jurisdiction to intervene in the dispute between California State University, Hayward (hereinafter "CSUH") and the National Collegiate Athletic Association (hereinafter "NCAA").
2. There was no abuse of discretion in the issuance of the preliminary injunction.
3. Verification of the complaint was not required.

Record

California State University at Hayward and Ellis McCune, in his official capacity as President of CSUH, filed a complaint in the Alameda County Superior Court against the NCAA. The complaint sought injunctive relief enjoining the NCAA from enforcing its decision that the entire intercollegiate athletic program at CSUH was indefinitely ineligible for post-season play.

The court issued a temporary restraining order against enforcement of the NCAA decision, and an order to show cause why a preliminary injunction should not be issued. Prior to the hearing on the order to show cause the NCAA filed a demurrer to the complaint. Following the hearing and an examination of the complaint, affidavits in support of and opposing the preliminary injunction, and the memoranda of points and authorities, the court granted a preliminary injunction enjoining the NCAA from enforcing its order declaring CSUH indefinitely ineligible from participating in NCAA championship athletic events, pending trial of the matter.

Facts

CSUH is a campus of the California State Colleges and University System. The NCAA is an unincorporated association organized to supervise and coordinate intercollegiate athletic programs and events among public and private colleges and universities. It is the largest voluntary association of intercollegiate athletics in the country.

An "active" member of the NCAA is a four-year college or university. CSUH became an active member in 1962. An "allied" member is an athletic conference or association composed of active members. The Far Western Conference (hereinafter "FWC") is an unincorporated California association organized to sponsor and coordinate intercollegiate athletics on a regional basis. The FWC is an allied member of the NCAA. CSUH is also a member of the FWC.

Upon becoming an active member of the NCAA, CSUH agreed to comply with all the requirements of the NCAA constitution and bylaws. Upon becoming an allied member the FWC agreed to abide by and enforce the NCAA constitution and bylaws. And, under article 3, section 2, of the NCAA constitution, the FWC was charged with the responsibility and control of intercollegiate athletics in the conference.

In 1966 the NCAA adopted bylaw 4-6(b)(1), also known as the "1.6 rule" as follows: "(b) A member institution shall not be eligible to enter a team or individual competitors in an NCAA-sponsored meet, unless the institution in the conduct of all its intercollegiate athletic programs: (1) Limits its scholarship or grant-in-aid awards (for which the recipient's athletic ability is considered in any degree), and eligibility for participation in athletics or in organized athletic practice sessions during the first year in residence to student-athletes who have a predicted minimum grade point average of at least 1.600 (based on a maximum of 4.000) as determined by the Association's national prediction tables or Association-approved conference or institutional tables, . . ." The rule caused confusion among NCAA members, and between 1966 and 1973 the NCAA issued several official interpretations in order to clarify the rule. In 1973 the rule was abolished but it was in effect during the period under consideration here. The FWC was responsible for interpreting the NCAA constitution and bylaws for conference members. It interpreted the 1.6 rule as follows in its constitution, article VI, section 3(e): ". . . Entering freshman students who upon graduation from high school predict less than 1.600 grade point average at a member institution according to NCAA procedures, shall not be eligible to compete in intercollegiate athletics until after they have earned at least a 2.0(c) average for at least 10 units for any term."

On or about October 30, 1969, Arthur J. Bergstrom, acting in his official capacity as Assistant Executive Director of the NCAA, sent a letter to the FWC explaining the difference between in-season conference and post-season championship eligibility requirements. This distinction would permit a conference to apply its own eligibility rules for in-season conference activity as long as athletes who were not in strict compliance with NCAA eligibility requirements were not eligible for post-conference championship competition. CSUH knew of this letter and relied on the interpretation the NCAA requirements stated therein as approval of the FWC eligibility requirements set forth in article VI, section 3(e), of the FWC constitution.

In the fall of 1969 one Ronald McFadden was admitted to CSUH under a special admittance program, the Equal Opportunity Program. In the fall of 1970 one Melvin Yearby was admitted under the same program. At the time of admission neither predicted a 1.6 grade point average according to NCAA procedures, and neither participated in intercollegiate athletics his first term at CSUH. At the end of their respective first terms, each had earned better than a 2.0 grade point average for more than 10 units of college work. Each was thereafter permitted to participate in intercollegiate athletics but was not considered by CSUH to be eligible for post-season competition in the freshman year. Article VI, section 3(e) of the FWC constitution was in effect at the time of the admission of McFadden and Yearby to CSUH.

On or about November 27, 1972, the NCAA informed CSUH that McFadden and Yearby had been ineligible to compete in their freshman years because they had failed to comply with the 1.6 rule. The NCAA ordered CSUH to declare the two ineligible to participate in any intercollegiate athletics for a one-year period, 1972-1973. At that time McFadden was a senior and Yearby was a junior. CSUH did not declare the two ineligible and appealed the decision to the NCAA. The NCAA declared the entire intercollegiate program at CSUH to be indefinitely ineligible for post-season play. The CSUH appeal to the NCAA to reverse its decision was refused.

1. Jurisdiction

Defendant NCAA contends that the trial court erred in failing to follow the doctrine of judicial abstention from interference in the affairs of a private voluntary association. However, courts will intervene in the internal affairs of associations where the action by the association is in violation of its own bylaws or constitution. "It is true that courts will not interfere with the disciplining or expelling of members of such associations where the action is taken in good faith and in accordance with its adopted laws and rules. But if the decision of the tribunal is contrary to its laws or rules, it is not authorized by the by-laws of the association, a court may review the ruling of the board and direct the reinstatement of the member. . . .

In the instant case plaintiffs' complaint alleges that the NCAA decision, that the entire intercollegiate program at CSUH is indefinitely ineligible for post-season competition, is contrary to the NCAA constitution and bylaws, and that the decision is void as against public policy because it would force CSUH to violate constitutional rights of its students guaranteed by the Fourteenth Amendment. The trial court has not yet finally adjudicated these claims but plaintiffs are entitled to have the matter determined.

Defendant NCAA asserts that as a matter of law no interest of any member of the NCAA is sufficiently substantial to justify judicial intervention because the interest affected by the sanction in question is the school's potential participation in NCAA championship events, an interest which is a mere expectancy as it is contingent upon performance during the season. The NCAA claims that California courts have only intervened when a vital interest was affected, such as where a member was expelled from a union, where a professional or trade organization's actions threatened disastrous economic consequences to a member, where substantial property interests were threatened by expulsion from an association, or where someone was totally excluded from becoming a member of a group. . . .

As to the claim that CSUH's interest is not sufficiently substantial to justify judicial intervention due to a mere expectancy of participation in championship events, it has already been discussed that a violation by an association of its own bylaws and constitution or of the laws of the land justifies judicial intervention. Further, that CSUH had, and has, more than a mere expectancy that some of its athletes would earn the opportunity to participate in NCAA championship events but for the suspension is evidenced by the fact that at the time of both the hearing on the temporary restraining order and the hearing on the preliminary injunction, there were upcoming NCAA championship events in which CSUH students, without the imposed suspension, were eligible to compete. Additionally, the decision of the NCAA necessarily affects more than just the possibility of being precluded from championship events. The sanction of indefinite probation affects the reputation of CSUH and its entire athletic program, and thereby also affects the reputation of CSUH and its entire athletic program, and thereby also affects CSUH's ability to recruit athletes. Judicial notice may be taken that state schools such as CSUH are deeply involved in fielding and promoting athletic teams with concurrent expenditures of time, energy and resources. The school provides and pays for the coaches, supplies and equipment. It finances, equips, trains and fields the teams. And, its funds pay the NCAA membership dues. The contention that CSUH has no substantial interest to justify judicial intervention lacks merit.

In a case concerning students suspended from the University of Minnesota basketball team by that school, the court commented on whether those students had a substantial interest: "Likewise, the Big Ten has not disputed that the plaintiffs' interest—an opportunity to participate in intercollegiate athletic competition at one of its member institutions—is substantial. Indeed, it would be hard to so dispute in light of analogous cases which indicate the direction in which this area of the law is evolving. While 'big time' college athletics may not be a 'total part of the educational process,' as are athletics in high school, nonetheless the opportunity to participate in intercollegiate athletics is of substantial economic value to many students. In these days when juniors in college are able to suspend their formal educational training in exchange for multimillion dollar contracts to turn professional, this Court takes judicial notice of the fact that, to many, the chance to display their athletic prowess in college stadiums and arenas throughout the country is worth more in economic terms than the chance to get a college education. . . . It has also been held that high school students' interests in participation in athletics are so substantial that they cannot be impaired without proceedings which comply with minimum standards of due process. Surely, the interests of college athletes in participating in activities which have the potential to bring them great economic rewards are no less substantial." (Behagen v. Intercollegiate Conference of Faculty Rep. (Minn. 1972) 346 F. Supp. 602, 604.) While that case differs from the instant case in that it concerned students directly, and their suspension from all competition, the language offers guidance here.

The NCAA also claims that plaintiffs do not contend that the procedural process followed by the NCAA in imposing sanctions on CSUH was not full and fair, and asserts: "While insisting that voluntary non-profit associations follow their own procedures in disciplining their members, courts have refused to disturb the association's decision when there was no procedural unfairness and the proceedings conformed to the requirements established by the group."

As already discussed the courts will intervene where the action by the association is in violation of its own bylaws and constitution. That this rule applies to substantive as well as procedural questions is supported by cases which appellant itself cites. . . .

NCAA also asserts that judicial intervention in this type of case is undesirable and raises a number of policy arguments to that effect. Because it is clear that courts will intervene if an association violates its own rules or the laws of the land, these arguments have no wright.

Plaintiffs have raised sufficient questions as to whether the NCAA has violated its own rules or the laws of the land by its action to justify intervention by the trial court to determine these questions.

2. The Trial Court Did Not Abuse Its Discretion in Issuing the Preliminary Injunction

The NCAA contends that the trial court abused its discretion in issuing the preliminary injunction because plaintiffs failed to show irreparable injury and there is no likelihood that plaintiffs will succeed in any of their claims. . . .

The NCAA produced no affidavits or other evidence at the hearing on the preliminary injunction to show that it would suffer injury were the preliminary injunction granted. CSUH on the other hand in its complaint alleged that unless the preliminary injunction issued its athletes would be precluded from participating in all post-season events, that CSUH would suffer a loss of revenue thereby, and that the recruitment of potential athletes would be impaired. This was supported by the affidavit of the athletic director of CSUH to the effect that six CSUH athletes would be precluded from participation in a swimming and diving championship competition under the NCAA sanction. At the time of the hearing the date of the swimming and diving championship had passed, but the clear implication was that other such events would occur during the pendency of the suit which would cause the same kind of harm. Additionally, at the hearing the trial judge said, "I think without any evidence being presented, I can take as common knowledge or take judicial notice that there is a great deal of potential harm to, at least the institution who would be affected if their institution is wrongfully suspended or ousted permanently."

As to whether plaintiffs have a reasonable probability of ultimately succeeding in the suit, they have raised issues of sufficient seriousness for the trial court to decide.

"Discretion is abused in the legal sense 'whenever it may be fairly said that in its exercise the court in a given case exceeded the bounds of reason or contravened the uncontradicted evidence.'"

The NCAA has failed to show an abuse of discretion in this instance.

Both the NCAA and CSUH also raise in great detail arguments as to the merits of their respective positions in the question of whether a permanent injunction should issue. These questions will be determined by the trial court and are not suitably addressed to this court on this appeal from the granting of a preliminary injunction. . . .

3. Verification of Complaint Not Required

Lastly, NCAA contends that plaintiffs failed to establish sufficient grounds for any preliminary relief because the complaint was not verified, and therefore under Code of Civil Procedure section 446 the court could not consider the allegations in the complaint in issuing the preliminary injunction. NCAA further contends that the declarations filed by plaintiffs, when subjected to the same evidentiary rules as oral testimony which they must be, were alone not a sufficient basis for preliminary relief.

NCAA's contentions are not well founded. It is true that Code of Civil Procedure section 527 reads in pertinent part: "An injunction may be granted at any time before judgment upon a verified complaint, or upon affidavits if the complaint in the one case, or the affidavits in the other, show satisfactorily that sufficient grounds exist therefore. . . ." However, section 446 of the Code of Civil Procedure "relieves an officer of the state acting in his official capacity from the necessity of verifying a pleading . . ." (*Paul v. Wadler* (1962) 209 Cal. App.2d 615, 624, 26 Cal.Rptr. 341, 347.) In *Paul v. Wadler*, the court upheld the issuance of a temporary restraining order and preliminary injunction although the state had not verified the complaint or filed affidavits. When he signed the declaration accompanying the application for preliminary injunction Ellis McCune was acting in his official capacity as President of CSUH as plaintiff, and the complaint herein was signed by a deputy attorney general, a state officer. Therefore under Code of Civil Procedure section 446 the complaint need not be verified.

As earlier discussed, the complaint and affidavits are sufficient to support the issuance of the preliminary injunction. This is without resort to any potentially inadmissible evidence; therefore, the NCAA's contention as to the declarations need not be considered further.

Judgment affirmed.

QUESTIONS AND DISCUSSION

1. See NCAA Operating By-Laws, Art. 12.02, Professional Athlete: "A Professional Athlete is one who receives any kind of payment, directly or

indirectly for athletic participation except as permitted by the governing legislation of the Association." How realistic is this approach when many collegiate athletics are mere "professionals in-the-waiting"? Also, is it possible to excel in sports, train and prepare for sports, and matriculate through your course work (somehow), without some spending money? Does the definition of "professional athlete" mesh with the no-agent rule?

2. Courts do not interfere when the NCAA disciplines or expels its members when those actions are taken in good faith and in accordance with its own adopted laws and rules. What are examples of actions that are not taken in good faith?

3. But courts do intervene in the internal affairs of the NCAA when its actions violate their own bylaws or constitution. If the NCAA action is contrary to its own laws and bylaws, a court may review the ruling and direct reinstatement of the member. In *California State University, Hayward,* the NCAA ruled that the entire intercollegiate athletic program at the university was indefinitely ineligible for postseason play. What NCAA rule is this decision contrary to?

4. The NCAA's decision in *California State University, Hayward* was also found to be void against public policy. Why?

5. The doctrine of judicial abstention was superseded in *California State University, Hayward,* which held that the court had the jurisdiction to intervene when teams in certain sports at the university would have been eligible to compete in postseason competition except for the NCAA's decision. For public policy reasons, should the doctrine of judicial abstention be upheld regardless?

B. ELIGIBILITY

The NCAA rules delineate the eligibility of athletes in member schools based on rules and regulations such as the no-agent rule, first-year eligibility, failed drug tests, and grade point average.

1. No-Agent Rule

The NCAA has a rule that an individual shall be ineligible for participation in an intercollegiate sport if she has ever agreed to be represented by an agent before the end of the athlete's eligibility. A key element of the NCAA's philosophy is to protect amateur collegiate athletes from the temptations and negative side effects of professional sports.

The following rule broadly prohibits representation by agents before the expiration of intercollegiate eligibility.

12.3 Use of Agents

12.3.1 General Rule. An individual shall be ineligible for participation in an intercollegiate sport if he or she ever has agreed (orally or in writing) to be represented by an agent for the purpose of marketing his or her athletics ability or reputation in that sport. Further, an agency contract not specifically limited in writing to a sport or particular sports shall be deemed applicable to all sports, and the individual shall be ineligible to participate in any sport.

12.3.1.1 Representation for Future Negotiations. An individual shall be ineligible per Bylaw 12.3.1 if he or she enters into a verbal or written agreement with an agent for representation in future professional sports negotiations that are to take place after the individual has completed his or her eligibility in that sport.

12.3.1.2 Benefits from Prospective Agents. An individual shall be ineligible per Bylaw 12.3.1 if he or she (or his or her relatives or friends) accepts transportation or other benefits from: *(Revised: 1/14/97)*

(a) Any person who represents any individual in the marketing of his or her athletics ability. The receipt of such expenses constitutes compensation based on athletics skill and is an extra benefit not available to the student body in general; or

(b) An agent, even if the agent has indicated that he or she has no interest in representing the student-athlete in the marketing of his or her athletics ability or reputation and does not represent individuals in the student-athlete's sport. *(Adopted: 1/14/97)*

12.3.2 Legal Counsel. Securing advice from a lawyer concerning a proposed professional sports contract shall not be considered contracting for representation by an agent under this rule, unless the lawyer also represents the individual in negotiations for such a contract.

12.3.2.1 Presence of a Lawyer at Negotiations. A lawyer may not be present during discussions of a contract offer with a professional organization or have any direct contact (i.e., in person, by telephone or by mail) with a professional sports organization on behalf of the individual. A lawyer's presence during such discussions is considered representation by an agent.

12.3.3 Athletics Scholarship Agent. Any individual, agency or organization that represents a prospective student-athlete for compensation in placing the prospect in a collegiate institution as a recipient of institutional financial aid shall be considered an agent or organization marketing the individual's athletics ability or reputation.

12.3.3.1 Talent Evaluation Services and Agents. A prospect may allow a scouting service or agent to distribute personal information (e.g., high-school academic and athletics records, physical statistics) to member institutions without jeopardizing his or her eligibility, provided the fee paid to such an agent is not based on placing the prospect in a collegiate institution as a recipient of institutional financial aid.

12.3.4 Professional Sports Counseling Panel. It is permissible for an authorized institutional professional sports counseling panel to . . . [a]dvise, [etc.].

The similar cases of *Gaines v. NCAA* and *Banks v. NCAA*, 977 F.2d 1081 (7th Cir. 1992), continue to allow the NCAA to restrict eligibility based on the no-agent rule.

GAINES V. NATIONAL COLLEGIATE ATHLETIC ASSOCIATION

746 F. Supp. 738 (M.D. Tenn. 1990)

WISEMAN, Chief Judge.

This cause of action came before the Court on August 31, 1990, on Gaines' Application for Temporary Restraining Order and Preliminary Injunction. This Court denied the Motion for a Temporary Restraining Order on that date. In the September 13 hearing on Gaines' Motion for a Preliminary Injunction, Gaines urged this Court to enjoin the Defendants from enforcing certain rules ("Rules") promulgated by the National Collegiate Athletic Association ("NCAA") which deem Gaines ineligible to compete in the 1990-91 college football season for Vanderbilt University ("Vanderbilt"). This Court denied the preliminary injunction from the bench and now issues this Opinion setting forth the reasons for the denial.

I

The facts leading to this lawsuit are not in dispute. Bradford L. Gaines was a football player for Vanderbilt during the 1986-89 football seasons. He is currently enrolled at Vanderbilt to complete the thirteen additional semester hours he needs to graduate. Gaines has attended Vanderbilt on a full athletic scholarship.

In late March of 1990, Gaines submitted a Petition For Special Eligibility and Renunciation of College Eligibility to the National Football League ("NFL") declaring himself eligible for the NFL draft to be conducted on April 22-23, 1990. . . .

On April 7-8, 1990, Gaines attended a scouting combine in Indianapolis, Indiana. The combine gave Gaines and other college football players a chance to try out before the scouts for various pro football teams. Gaines had no other contact with any NFL team prior to the draft, and he was not selected by any team during any round of the draft.

Shortly after the draft, Gaines was contacted by a representative of one NFL team regarding a possible free agency contract with that team. Mr. Tim Greer, who serves as the agent for Gaines' older brother, a football player in the Canadian Football League ("CFL"), briefly discussed this possible free agency contract with the NFL team. However, the next day the team let Gaines know that they were no longer interested in signing him to a free agency contract. Subsequently, Mr. Greer phoned numerous teams in the NFL and the CFL on Gaines' behalf, but Gaines has never entered into any contract with any professional team. Nor has Greer received any compensation of any kind from Gaines. Additionally, Greer has never compensated Gaines in any way.

As a result of NCAA Rules 12.1.1(f), 12.2.4.2, and 12.3.1, Gaines is now ineligible to complete his fourth year of eligibility as a football player at Vanderbilt. Rule 12.1.1(f) provides that an athlete loses his amateur status when he enters a professional draft or enters into an agreement with an agent to negotiate a professional contract. Rule 12.2.4.2, commonly known as the "no-draft" rule makes a player ineligible for participation in a particular intercollegiate sport when he or she asks to be placed on the draft list or supplemental draft list of a professional league in that sport. Rule 12.3.1, commonly known as the "no-agent" rule, makes any player ineligible for participation in any future intercollegiate sport in which the player agrees, orally or in writing, to be represented by an agent for the purposes of marketing the player's abilities in the sport. This Rule applies even if the player receives no money or financial benefit of any kind from the agent, even if the agent is a family member or a close family friend, and even if the agent has not charged and agrees not to charge the player any fee. . . .

Despite the compelling situation which has befallen Mr. Gaines, he has failed to show a substantial likelihood of success on the merits of his 2 claim. From the outset he shouldered a heavier burden because of the mandatory nature of the relief sought. However, this Court is convinced that Gaines has not carried even the lighter burden of establishing any fair ground for litigation of his claim. There is substantial support in the caselaw for this Court's conclusion that the NCAA eligibility Rules are not subject to antitrust scrutiny. Nonetheless, upon such scrutiny, it is clear to this Court that the NCAA has demonstrated strong business justifications for enforcing the current eligibility Rules, leading to the conclusion that the Rules cannot be deemed unreasonably anticompetitive or exclusionary.

For the foregoing reasons Gaines' Application For a Preliminary Injunction is denied.

Gaines and *Banks*, 977 F.2d 1081 (7th Cir. 1992), are similar in that both attempted to use antitrust analysis to challenge the NCAA's no-draft and no-agent rules. Both were unsuccessful. *Gaines* was a district court case, while *Banks* was from the Seventh Circuit Court of Appeals. The issue appears to be settled.

2. First-Year Eligibility

The current rule that determines first-year eligibility for scholarship athletes is called Proposition 16 (Prop 16). In short, Prop 16 requires a grade point average (GPA) in 13 core courses with a corresponding minimum score on one of the standardized tests.

The relevant rule, Article 14.3, Freshman Academic Requirements, follows.

NCAA CONSTITUTION, ARTICLE 14.3, FRESHMAN ACADEMIC REQUIREMENTS

14.3 Freshman Academic Requirements

14.3.1 Eligibility for Financial Aid, Practice and Competition. A student-athlete who enrolls in a member institution as an entering freshman with no previous full-time college attendance shall meet the following academic requirements, as certified by an initial-eligibility clearinghouse approved by the Executive Committee, and any applicable institutional and conference regulations, to be considered a qualifier and thus be eligible for financial aid, practice and competition during the first academic year in residence. *(Revised: 1/16/93 effective 8/1/94, 1/9/96 effective 8/1/97 for those student-athletes first entering a collegiate institution on or after 8/1/97)*

14.3.1.1 Qualifier. A qualifier is defined as one who is a high-school graduate and who presented the following academic qualifications: *(Revised: 1/10/92 effective 8/1/95)*

The following Bylaw 14.3.1.1-(a) was revised at the November 1, 2001, NCAA Division Board of Directors meeting, effective August 1, 2005, for those student-athletes first entering a collegiate institution on or after August 1, 2005.

(a) A minimum cumulative grade-point average as specified in Bylaw 14.3.1.1.1 (based on a maximum 4.000) in a successfully completed core curriculum of at least 13 academic courses per Bylaw 14.3.1.2, including the following:

English *(Revised: 1/16/93 effective 8/1/96)*	4 years
Mathematics (two years of mathematics courses at the level of Algebra I or higher) . . .	2 years
Natural or physical science (including at least one laboratory course if offered by the high school)	2 years
Additional courses in English, mathematics, or natural or physical science *(Revised: 1/16/93 effective 8/1/96)*	1 year
Social science	2 years
Additional academic courses [in any of the above areas or foreign language, computer science, philosophy or nondoctrinal religion (e.g., comparative religion) courses]	2 years

The record of the above courses and course grades must be certified by the initial-eligibility clearinghouse using an official high-school transcript or official correspondence forwarded directly from the high school or upon a high-school transcript forwarded by an institution's admissions office, and *(Revised: 2/9/95)*. . . .

(b) A minimum combined score on the SAT verbal and math sections or a minimum sum score on the ACT as specified in Bylaw 14.3.1.1.1. The required SAT or ACT score must be achieved under national testing conditions on a national testing date [i.e., no residual (campus) testing or regional testing dates]. *(Revised: 1/10/90, 1/10/92, 1/16/93)*

14.3.1.1.1 Inltial-Eligibility Index. Freshmen may establish eligibility using the following eligibility index: *(Adopted: 1/10/92 effective 8/1/95, Revised: 1/10/95 effective 8/1/96, Revised: 1/9/96 effective 8/1/96 for those student-athletes first entering a collegiate institution on or after 8/1/96).* [e.g., if your core GPA is 2.425, then your SAT must be 860, or your sum ACT 70.] . . .

14.3.1.2 Core-Curriculum Requirements. For purposes of meeting the core-curriculum requirement to establish eligibility at a member institution, a "core course" must meet all the following criteria: *(Revised: 1/11/00 effective 8/1/00 for those student-athletes first entering a collegiate institution on or after 8/1/00)*

The following Bylaw 14.3.1.2-(a) was revised at the November 1, 2001, NCAA Division I Board of Directors meeting, effective August 1, 2005, for those student-athletes first entering a collegiate institution on or after August 1, 2005.

(a) A course must be a recognized academic course and qualify for high-school graduation credit in one or a combination of the following areas: English, mathematics, natural/physical science, social science, foreign language, computer science or nondoctrinal religion/philosophy;

(a) A course must be a recognized academic course and qualify for high-school graduation credit in one or a combination of the following areas: English, mathematics, natural/physical science, social science, foreign language or nondoctrinal religion/philosophy; *(Revised: 11/1/01 effective 8/1/05 for those students first entering a collegiate institution on or after8/1/05)*

(b) A course must be considered college preparatory by the high school; . . .

(c) A mathematics course must be at the level of Algebra I or a higher level mathematics course;

(d) A course must be taught by a qualified instructor; . . .

(e) A course must be taught at or above the high school's regular academic level. . . . However, the prohibition against the use of remedial or compensatory courses is not applicable to courses designed for student's with learning disabilities (see Bylaw 14.3.1.2.1.1).

14.3.1.2.1 Core-Curriculum Time Limitation. Generally, only courses completed in grades nine through 12 may be considered core courses, unless a student repeats a regular term or academic year of secondary studies following completion of the requirements necessary for high-school graduation. . . .

14.3.1.2.1.1 Students with Learning Disabilities. . . .

14.3.1.2.1.2 International Students. . . .

14.3.2 Eligibility for Financial Aid, Practice and Competition— Partial Qualifier and Nonqualifier

14.3.2.1 Partial Qualifier. A partial qualifier is a student who does not meet the requirements for a qualifier but who, at the time of graduation from high school, presents the following core-curriculum grade-point average and the corresponding ACT or SAT score: *(Revised: 1/10/91 effective 8/1/91, 1/10/92 effective 8/1/95, 1/10/95 effective 8/1/96, 1/9/96)* . . .

14.3.2.2 Nonqualifier. A nonqualifier is a student who has not graduated from high school or who, at the time specified in the regulation (see Bylaw 14.3), presented neither the core-curriculum grade-point average and SAT/ACT score required for a qualifier. . . .

14.3.3 Seasons of Competition—Partial Qualifier and Nonqualifier. Partial qualifiers and nonqualifiers, recruited or nonrecruited, shall not engage in more than three seasons of competition in any one sport. A student who transfers to a Division I member institution from another collegiate institution shall not engage in more than four seasons of competition with not more than three of those seasons in Division I. . . .

14.3.4 Residence Requirement—Partial Qualifier or Nonqualifier. . . .

14.3.5 Determination of Freshman Eligibility

14.3.5.1 Participation Prior to Certification

14.3.5.1.1 Recruited Student-Athlete. If a recruited student-athlete reports for athletics participation before the high-school core-curriculum grade-point average and test score have been certified, the student may practice, but not compete, for a maximum of two weeks, provided the student is enrolled full time or has been accepted for enrollment as a regular full-time student. After this two-week period, the student shall have established minimum requirements as a qualifier (as certified by the NCAA Initial-Eligibility Clearinghouse) to continue practicing or to compete, or the minimum requirements as a partial qualifier to continue practicing. *(Revised: 1/11/89)*

14.3.5.1.2 Nonrecruited Student-Athlete. If a nonrecruited student-athlete reports for athletics participation before the high-school core-curriculum grade-point average and test score have been certified, the student may practice, but not compete, for a maximum of 45 days, provided the student is enrolled full time or has been accepted for enrollment as a regular full-time student. After this 45-day period, the student shall have established minimum requirements as a qualifier (as certified by the NCAA Initial-Eligibility Clearinghouse) to continue practicing or to compete, or the minimum requirements as a partial qualifier to continue practicing. . . .

Before entering a school on an athletic scholarship, one must first be certified by the NCAA's initial-eligibility clearinghouse. Article 14.3 establishes the requirements for the various levels of qualification. In *Hall v. NCAA*, the court refused to grant a preliminary injunction so as to allow a student to receive an athletic scholarship for his freshman year.

HALL v. NATIONAL COLLEGIATE ATHLETIC ASSOCIATION

985 F. Supp. 782 (N.D. Ill. 1997)

KEYS, United States Magistrate Judge.

Before the Court is Plaintiffs' application for a preliminary injunction, pursuant to Federal Rule of Civil Procedure 65. For the reasons set forth below, the Court denies Plaintiffs' application for a preliminary injunction.

Procedural History

Plaintiffs filed the underlying nine count Verified Complaint for Injunctive Relief and Damages ("Complaint"), on October 17, 1997, and at the same time moved for a temporary restraining order ("TRO"), preliminary injunction, and expedited discovery. . . .

Findings of Fact

I. The Parties

Reginale Hall ("Reggie") is a 6'7" tall, eighteen year old African-American who excels at basketball, and aspires to play professionally some day. Reggie graduated from Providence St. Mel High School ("St. Mel" on June 1, 1997. St. Mel is a private, Catholic high school with a student body comprised entirely of African-Americans. Reggie was highly recruited nationally by a number of colleges and universities, including Bradley University ("Bradley") in Peoria. He is currently a freshman at Bradley.

Annette Hall is Reggie's mother. The National Collegiate Athletic Association ("NCAA") is an unincorporated association made up of approximately 1,200 member institutions—typically public and private colleges and universities located throughout the United States. NCAA members establish general policies at annual conventions, and then various cabinets and committees are responsible for implementing those policies throughout the year. The NCAA, according to its constitution and bylaws, has several purposes, including improving intercollegiate athletic programs and encouraging members to adopt eligibility rules that comply with satisfactory standards of scholarship, sportsmanship, and amateurism. Bradley is a member of the NCAA, Division I.

II. The Dispute

The matter at bar involves, for the most part, a dispute over four courses that Reggie took while enrolled at St. Mel. The inclusion or exclusion of the four courses—Microsoft Office, Microsoft Works, Scripture, and Ethics/Morality—is critical to the Court's analysis of the propriety of the NCAA's ultimate determination that Reggie is ineligible to play Division I basketball this year.

III. NCAA Eligibility Requirements

Pursuant to the bylaws, the NCAA has established minimum academic eligibility requirements that a new college student must fulfill in order to attain the status of "qualifier." As a "qualifier" a student is eligible to practice with intercollegiate teams, compete in intercollegiate events, and receive financial aid or scholarships. NCAA members are prohibited from permitting "nonqualified" students—those who fail to attain either aforementioned status—to practice with the intercollegiate teams, to compete in intercollegiate events, or to receive financial aid (other than purely need based).

To be a "qualifier," NCAA eligibility requirements for Division I competition mandate that the student have taken at least thirteen high school "core courses" and that the student have achieved a specified minimum grade point average ("GPA") in those "core courses," as well as a specified minimum score on either the Scholastic Aptitude Test ("SAT") or American College Testing Program ("ACT"). Those specified GPA and standardized test minimums are determined on a sliding scale basis; the higher the test score, the lower the required core GPA. If a student has more than thirteen "core courses," the core GPA is computed from the thirteen highest grades.

IV. "Core Courses"

The NCAA must approve of any class claimed by a high school to be a "core course." The NCAA generally defines "core courses" as recognized academic courses (as opposed to vocational or personal-service courses) offering fundamental instructional components in specified areas of study. At least 75% of the instructional content of such a course must be in one or more of the required areas of study, set forth in the NCAA bylaws, like English, mathematics, natural science, and social science. In addition to these areas of study, a student must also take "additional core courses" in at least one of the following subjects: foreign language, computer science, philosophy, or comparative religion.

In order to qualify as core courses, religion classes must be non-doctrinal. . . . Reggie's guidance counselor at St. Mel, Art Murnan, had serious doubts about whether the Scripture class "would get through or not." . . .

As to the two Microsoft computer courses at issue, it was Mr. Murnan's understanding that, as long as a computer class went beyond keyboarding and word processing, it qualified as a core course. However, the NCAA Initial-Eligibility Clearinghouse ("Clearinghouse"), which is an independent contractor with the NCAA (Tr. at 221), and not a party to this lawsuit, stated that, for a computer science course to count as an "additional core course," "at least 75 percent of the instruction in the course must go beyond keyboarding and word processing *and* must be in areas such as the development and implementation of electronic spreadsheets, electronics networking, database management and computer programming."

According to the Microsoft Office course syllabus, one of the goals of the class was "to develop enough keyboarding skill to be able to do useful work in a timely manner." . . .

Given the foregoing, the Court finds that the Clearinghouse, and ultimately the NCAA, was correct in determining that these four courses did not fulfil the requirements of core courses, and that such determination was not made arbitrarily or in bad faith. Furthermore, the Halls have not proven that either the Clearinghouse, or NCAA, applied the core course criteria differently to applicants of different races.

V. Guidance Reggie Received While at St. Mel and the Attempt to Qualify the Four Disputed Courses as Core . . .

VI. NCAA Appeals Process

On July 30, 1997, Bradley applied to the NCAA for a waiver of initial academic eligibility requirements. . . .

The Halls base their argument, for recalculation with a different grade scale, on a recent case reported in the June 2, 1997 "NCAA Register." In that case, the NCAA approved the appeal of a student athlete who failed to achieve the GPA that corresponded with his ACT score. The high school, in that case, offered four levels of courses: level one courses (honors and advanced placement) which received 20% above GPA; level two courses (accelerated/advanced courses) which received 10% above GPA; level three courses (accelerated/advanced courses) which received 5% above GPA; and level four courses (basic curriculum) which received nothing above GPA. The Clearinghouse had only given the student credit for level one courses, so his GPA fell short. Once the weighting system was properly verified by the high school, the NCAA recalculated the student's GPA—which then rose above the required minimum.

The situation in that case is distinct from Reggie's because it concerned the correct *weighing* of classes, instead of use of a particular grading scale. Moreover, NCAA bylaw 14.3.1.3.5, allows for high schools that weigh honors classes differently. . . .

In sum, the Halls have not shown that the Clearinghouse or NCAA applied different standards with regard to grading scales or waivers to applicants of different races, or that the denial of a waiver in Reggie's case was done in bad faith. . . .

VII. Financial Issues . . .

Conclusions of Law
I. Preliminary Injunction Standard . . .
II. Application
A. Likelihood of Success on the Merits . . .

1. *Count I—Breach of Contract.* In Count I of their Complaint, the Halls allege that the NCAA, through the Clearinghouse, entered into a contract with Reggie when Ms. Hall sent in a Clearinghouse Student Release Form (referred to in the Complaint as an initial eligibility application) to the Clearinghouse with a check for approximately $18. . . .

a. Good Faith and Fair Dealing. . . . Similarly, because of the apparent contract between Reggie and the Clearinghouse, the Clearinghouse (and ultimately the NCAA) could not arbitrarily, capriciously, or in bad faith refuse to find Reggie eligible if he indeed clearly met the NCAA's initial eligibility requirements. However, as this Court has already discussed in its Findings of Fact, Reggie did not meet those requirements. Thus, the determination that Reggie was ineligible was not arbitrary, capricious, or otherwise made in bad faith.

b. Core Course Requirements. The Halls contend that the NCAA acted in bad faith by failing to include certain of Reggie's courses in the calculation of the core course GPA. Specifically, they argue that Microsoft Office, Microsoft Works, Scripture, and Ethics/Morality were excluded arbitrarily, capriciously and/or otherwise in bad faith. However, this Court has already found that those classes did not fulfill the NCAA's requirements for core courses. . . .

Likewise, since 1993, the NCAA has had a standard for determining whether computer classes are core. . . .

Thus, the Halls' claims relating to the four courses—Microsoft Works, Microsoft Office, Scripture, and Ethics/Morality do not have a reasonable, or even negligible chance of success.

c. Non-Standard Grading Scales. The Halls contend that the Clearinghouse and NCAA acted in bad faith by failing to take into account St. Mel's "non-standard" grading system. . . .

This Court has found, based on the evidence presented, that the grading scale used to calculate Reggie's core GPA was standard. Thus, neither of the Halls' claims of unfair grade scale application have a better than negligible chance of success.

2. Count II—Negligent Misrepresentation. In Count II of their Complaint, the Halls allege that the NCAA made negligent misrepresentations. . . .

Initially, the Halls have not identified the false material facts that the NCAA allegedly provided to them. Instead they only make the vague and conclusory allegation that "NCAA and the Clearinghouse negligently supplied false and misleading information for the guidance of Reginale in his efforts to become eligible to receive his scholarship. . . . " In the absence of a false statement of material fact by the NCAA, the Halls cannot succeed on this claim. Thus, the Halls' negligent misrepresentation claim has no better than a negligible chance of success.

3. Count III—Promissory Estoppel. The Halls next seek relief under a promissory estoppel theory. Promissory estoppel requires: (1) an unambiguous promise by the NCAA to the Halls; (2) reliance on that promise by the Halls; (3) that the Halls' reliance was expected and foreseeable to the NCAA; and (4) that the Halls actually relied on the promise to their detriment. . . .

Finally, even if, *arguendo*, the Clearinghouse or NCAA had provided information to the Halls indicating that the courses in question would be accepted as core courses, the Halls did not rely to their detriment on any such promise. To the contrary, the attempt to get the two Microsoft computer and two religion classes counted as core courses was a scheme developed by Bradley in late 1996, *after* it became apparent that Reggie would not achieve the GPA/ACT targets required under the original plan. Thus, there was no reliance on

any information provided by the NCAA with respect to core course requirements, and the Halls' promissory estoppel claim has no greater than a
negligible chance of success.

4. *Count IV—Third-Party Beneficiary.* The Halls' third-party beneficiary
claim alleges that Reggie was injured as a result of the bilateral breach of a
contract between the NCAA and Bradley. . . .

5. *Count V—Tortious Interference with Advantageous Contractual
Relationship.* . . .

6. *Count VI—Breach of Implied Covenant of Good Faith and Fair Dealing.* . . .

7. *Count VII—Violation of Civil Rights Act of 1866.* The Halls raise a number
of rather confusing racial discrimination claims; the first is that the NCAA
violated the Civil Rights Act of 1866. 42 U.S.C. §§1981-82 (1994). . . .

The Halls have failed to allege intentional discrimination of the type that
would support a §1981 or §1982 claim, and have provided no evidence of such
discrimination. Therefore, the Halls have no more than a negligible chance of
success with respect to these.

8. *Count VIII—42 U.S.C. §1983.* In Count VIII, the Halls allege that Reggie's
constitutional right to equal protection was denied because the NCAA failed
to adequately respond to its studies showing that, in some situations, African-
Americans graduate at higher rates than whites with identical SAT scores. A
statutory remedy for equal protection violations is provided by 42 U.S.C.
§1983. . . .

Therefore, although the Halls may feel a need or a desire for Reggie to play
basketball at Bradley under an athletic scholarship, their interest does not rise
to the level of a constitutionally protected right. Furthermore, since the Halls
are unable to show that the NCAA is even a state actor, and cannot demonstrate a constitutionally protected property interest, their §1983 claim has no
more than a negligible chance of success.

9. *Count IX—42 U.S.C. §2000a.* Finally, the Halls allege that the NCAA
violated Title II of the Civil Rights Act of 1964. 42 U.S.C. §2000a (1994).
Title II prohibits discrimination in the provision of places of public accommodation. *Id.* However, federal subject matter jurisdiction depends on the
plaintiff's compliance with the notice provisions of Title II. . . .

10. *Conclusion as to the Likelihood of Success.* In sum, Plaintiffs have no more
than a negligible chance of success on the merits with regard to *any* of the nine
counts in their Complaint. Thus, the preliminary injunction must be denied.
Further, even if, *arguendo*, the Halls were assumed to have a somewhat greater
than negligible chance of success on one or more of their claims, the injunction must still be denied because of their failure to meet the other
requirements for the granting of such relief.

B. Lack of an Adequate Remedy at Law, and Irreparable Harm . . .
C. Balance of Harms . . .
D. Public Interest

The public and non-party interests in the outcome of this matter weigh in
favor of denying the injunction. First, strict and definite enforcement of the
NCAA's initial eligibility requirements protects vulnerable high school athletes. In the highly competitive world of high school basketball, the high

school player faces subtle, and sometimes overt, pressure to sacrifice studies in favor of more court time. However, if student athletes, and their high school teachers, counselors, and coaches, know that college athletic participation depends on adequate scholastic achievement, fewer student athletes will miss out on attaining a decent high school education.

The other college student athletes who played by the rules and achieved the core GPA required for eligibility would lose out if the injunction were granted. Certainly, the last person cut from the Bradley basketball team in order to ensure a spot for Reggie has no hope of an injunction to allow him onto the team because his basketball skills were just slightly under Bradley's minimum requirements. By fostering amateurism and competition within a framework of rules which include academic standards, the NCAA's eligibility requirements provide student athletes with a college experience which goes beyond merely being on a "farm team for the pros." If the concept of a "student athlete" is not to be an oxymoron, the NCAA's initial eligibility requirements must be more than an afterthought or an administrative inconvenience for students, teachers, coaches, and counselors.

Conclusion

While it is clear that Reggie is an above average athlete, it is equally evident that he was a below average high school student. Thus, if anyone dropped the ball here, it was Reggie himself (by not doing better academically) and the staff at St. Mel.

Accordingly, Plaintiffs' application for preliminary injunction is denied.

The case of *Cureton v. NCAA*, at least at the trial level, appeared to raise serious constitutional doubts about the continued viability of the NCAA's first-year eligibility requirements. However, in the opinion that follows, the Third Circuit Court of Appeals held that the alleged disparate impact on African American student-athletes was inapplicable to the freshman eligibility rules.

CURETON v. NATIONAL COLLEGIATE ATHLETIC ASSOCIATION

198 F.3d 107 (3d Cir. 1999)

GREENBERG, Circuit Judge.

I. Introduction

This matter comes on before this court on appeal from an order for summary judgment in this action challenging certain academic requirements for participation in varsity athletics promulgated by the National Collegiate Athletic Association ("NCAA"). *See Cureton v. NCAA*, 37 F. Supp. 2d 687 (E.D. Pa. 1999). In particular, the plaintiffs challenge the minimum Scholastic Aptitude Test ("SAT") score requirement for freshman-year varsity intercollegiate athletic participation. While the NCAA also has adopted minimum grade point average ("GPA") requirements, the plaintiffs do not challenge them directly on this appeal. We set forth the background of the case at some length.

A. The Parties

Plaintiff Tai Kwan Cureton is an African-American who graduated from Simon Gratz High School in Philadelphia in June 1996 ranking 27th in a class of 305 students. Cureton was a member of the track team and earned both academic and athletic honors as a high school student. Cureton exceeded the NCAA GPA requirements but did not achieve the NCAA required SAT score. Cureton alleged that several NCAA Division I schools recruited him before he obtained his non-qualifying score on the SAT, but that after he took the SAT a lesser number of Division I schools recruited him and such institutions denied him admission and/or athletic financial aid. Cureton, who alleged he lost an opportunity to compete as a freshman in Division I varsity intercollegiate athletics because of NCAA regulations, enrolled in a Division III school.

Plaintiff Leatrice Shaw is an African-American who also graduated from Simon Gratz High School and was ranked 5th in a class of 305 students. Shaw was a member of the track team and earned both academic and athletic honors and was selected for membership in the National Honor Society. Shaw exceeded the NCAA minimum GPA requirement for freshman-year athletic participation, but failed to achieve the minimum required score on the SAT. The Division I school that Shaw entered did offer her athletic financial aid, but she was unable to compete on the track team during her freshman year because of the NCAA regulations at issue here. . . .

The National Youth Sports Program (the "NYSP"), which is not a defendant but nevertheless is implicated in this case, is a youth enrichment program that provides summer education and sports instruction on NCAA member and non-member institution campuses. The Department of Health and Human Services provides the NYSP with Federal financial assistance. . . . The Fund is regarded as an NCAA "affiliate." . . .

Division I modified these rules in 1992 when it adopted Proposition 16, which is at issue here. Proposition 16 increased the number of core courses to 13 and utilized an index to determine eligibility based on a formula combining the student's GPA and SAT scores. Using this index, the minimum score for a student with a GPA of 2.0 is 1010 on the SAT. Similarly, a student who scored an 820 on the SAT would need at least a 2.5 GPA to meet the eligibility requirements. As the district court pointed out, this modification resulted "in a heavier weighting of the standardized test" because the minimum GPA requirement was two standard deviations from the mean, whereas the minimum test score requirement was only one standard deviation from the mean. *Cureton*, 37 F.Supp.2d at 691.

B. The Action

Cureton and Shaw filed the complaint in this case on January 8, 1997. They alleged the minimum standardized test score component of Proposition 16 had an unjustified disparate impact on African-American student-athletes in violation of regulations promulgated pursuant to Title VI of the Civil Rights Act of 1964, 42 U.S.C. §2000d *et seq.*, which precludes exclusion from participation in, denial of the benefits of, and discrimination under any program or activity receiving Federal financial assistance on account of race, color, or national origin. The NCAA moved to dismiss the complaint, or alternatively for summary judgment, on the following grounds: (1) there is no private right of action for unintentional discrimination under Title VI or its accompanying regulations; (2) the NCAA is not a "program or activity" subject to Title VI; and (3) the NCAA does not receive Federal funds necessary to subject it to Title VI. The plaintiffs moved for partial summary judgment on the grounds that, as a matter of law, the NCAA was a covered program or activity subject to a Title VI action for unintentional discrimination and was a recipient of Federal financial assistance for purposes of Title VI.

On October 9, 1997, the district court issued an opinion and order denying the NCAA's motion but granting in part and denying in part the plaintiffs' motion for partial summary judgment. *See Cureton v. NCAA*, No. 97-131, 1997 WL 634376 (E.D. Pa. Oct. 9, 1997). In that opinion, the court determined that there was a private cause of action under Title VI and its accompanying regulations to remedy cases of disparate impact and that the NCAA was a program or activity covered by Title VI. *Id.* at *2. The court, however, held that it could not conclude on the record before it that the NCAA was a recipient of Federal funds as a result of its relationship with the NYSP.

Thereafter, following discovery, the plaintiffs and the NCAA again filed cross-motions for summary judgment. By an opinion and order dated March 8, 1999, the district court denied the NCAA's motion but granted the plaintiffs' motion. *See Cureton*, 37 F. Supp. 2d at 715. The district court held that Proposition 16's disparate impact on African-Americans violates Title VI and the regulations issued under it.

The court adopted two distinct theories to support its finding that the NCAA is subject to the prohibitions of Title VI. *See id.* at 696. First, the court found that the NCAA is an "indirect recipient of federal financial assistance" because it exercises effective control over a block grant given by the United States Department of Health and Human Services to the NYSP. *See id.* at 694. Second, the court held that Title VI covers the NCAA because member schools, which indisputably receive federal funds, have vested the NCAA with controlling authority over federally funded athletic programs. *See id.*

The court then turned to the plaintiffs' argument that the SAT component of Proposition 16 violates Title VI because of its alleged discriminatory disparate impact on African-American student athletes. *See id.* at 696-712. It found that the plaintiffs provided statistical evidence sufficient to show that the use of the SAT minimum standard "plainly evince[d] that African-Americans are being selected by Proposition 16 at a rate disproportionately lower than whites sufficient to infer causation." Consequently, the plaintiffs raised a prima facie case of disparate impact discrimination. *See id.* at 699-701. . . .

In view of its conclusions, the district court granted summary judgment to the plaintiffs, and permanently enjoined the NCAA from continued operation and implementation of Proposition 16. *See id.* at 714-15. Although regarding the matter as ripe for appeal, the court retained jurisdiction. *See id.* at 715. By order dated March 16, 1999, the district court modified the March 8, 1999 opinion and order so that the NCAA was permanently enjoined from denying student athletes freshmen-year eligibility on the basis of the minimum standardized test score cutoffs in Proposition 16, but nevertheless could use minimum GPA cutoffs. *See id.* at 716.

Subsequently, the NCAA appealed and unsuccessfully sought a stay in the district court. The NCAA then sought a stay from this court, which we granted on March 30, 1999. . . .

III. Discussion

Plaintiffs brought this action pursuant to section 601 of Title VI. . . .

We do not find it necessary to determine whether, by reason of the NCAA's relationship with the NYSP or the Fund, we should regard the NCAA as receiving Federal financial assistance. Rather, we will assume without deciding that these relationships are sufficient to establish that Federal financial assistance to the Fund is assistance to the NCAA itself. But section 601, as originally written, did not preclude recipients of Federal financial assistance from discriminating with respect to a program not receiving such assistance. . . .

We recognize that the dissent suggests that the NCAA constitution requires NCAA members to cede authority over their athletic programs to the NCAA, but the NCAA constitution expressly provides for the retention of institutional control over individual athletic programs. While the constitution requires conformity with the NCAA's rules and regulations, the ultimate decisions whether to conform are made by individual members. Therefore, the constitution is completely consistent with our result. Furthermore, we cannot understand how the fact that the NCAA promulgates rules and regulations with respect to intercollegiate athletics somehow means that the NCAA has controlling authority over its members' programs or activities receiving Federal financial assistance. After all, the institutions decide what applicants to admit, what employees to hire, and what facilities to acquire.

IV. Conclusion

In view of the foregoing determinations, it is unnecessary for us to reach the other issues raised on this appeal. Moreover, inasmuch as the parties agree that there are no disputes of material fact with respect to the question of whether the NCAA is subject to Title VI (and we are aware of none), and we have concluded that the NCAA is entitled to a judgment as a matter of law, there is no reason why this litigation should continue. Consequently, we will reverse the order of the district court of March 8, 1999, and will remand the case to the district court to enter summary judgment for the NCAA. . . .

3. Drug Testing

The NCAA requires all athletes to sign a consent to drug testing form. It also has a random, mandatory drug-testing program in connection with postseason intercollegiate athletic activities. Testing positive negatively impacts the athlete's eligibility to participate in intercollegiate sports. The NCAA manual is specific as to the types of drugs that are banned and the procedures used in determining positive test results.

NCAA CONSTITUTION, ARTICLE 31.2.3, INELIGIBILITY
FOR USE OF BANNED DRUGS

31.2.3 Ineligibility for Use of Banned Drugs. Bylaw 18.4.1.5 provides that a student-athlete who is found to have utilized a substance on the list of banned drugs shall be declared ineligible for further participation in postseason and regular-season competition during the time period ending one calendar year after the student-athlete's positive drug test. The student-athlete shall be charged with the loss of a minimum of one season of competition in all sports if the season of competition has not yet begun or a minimum of the equivalent of one full season of competition in all sports if the student-athlete tests positive during his or her season of competition (i.e., the remainder of contests in the current season and contests in the subsequent season up to the period of time in which the student-athlete was declared ineligible during the previous year). The student-athlete shall remain ineligible until the student-athlete retests negative (in accordance with the testing methods authorized by the Executive Committee) and the student-athlete's eligibility is restored by the Committee on Student-Athlete Reinstatement. If the student-athlete tests positive a second time for the use of any drug, other than a "street drug" as defined below, he or she shall lose all remaining regular-season and postseason eligibility in all sports. If the student-athlete tests positive for the use of a "street drug" after being restored to eligibility, he or she shall lose a minimum of one additional season of competition in all sports and also shall remain ineligible for regular-season and postseason competition at least through the next calendar year. Bylaw 18.4.1.5.2 also provides that the Executive Committee shall adopt a list of banned drugs and authorize methods for drug testing of student-athletes on a year-round basis. In addition, as stated in Bylaw 18.4.1.5.1, a student-athlete who previously tested positive for performance-enhancing drugs as a result of tests administered by any other athletics organization and subsequently tests positive (in accordance with the testing methods authorized by the Executive Committee) shall be subject to these ineligibility provisions. The list per Bylaw 31.2.3.1 is subject to change and the institution and student-athlete shall be held accountable for all banned drug classes on the current list. The list is located on the NCAA Web site (www.ncaa.org) or may be obtained from the NCAA national office. *(Revised: 1/16/93, 1/9/96 effective 8/1/96, 1/14/97 effective 8/1/97)*

31.2.3.1 Banned Drugs. The following is the list of banned-drugs classes with examples of substances under each class: *(Revised: 8/15/89, 7/10/90, 12/3/90, 5/4/92, 5/6/93, 10/29/97, 4/26/01)* [List includes stimulants, anabolic agents, substances banned for specific sports, diuretics, street drugs, and peptite hormones and analogues.]

31.2.3.1.1 Drugs and Procedures Subject to Restrictions. The use of the following drugs and/or procedures is subject to certain restrictions and may or may not be permissible, depending on limitations expressed in these guidelines and/or quantities or these substances used: *(Revised: 8/15/89)*

(a) Blood Doping. The practice of blood doping (the intravenous injection of whole blood, packed red blood cells or blood substitutes) is prohibited, and any evidence confirming use will be cause of action consistent with that taken for a positive drug test. *(Revised: 8/15/89, 5/4/92)* . . .

(c) Manipulation of Urine Sample. The Executive Committee bans the use of substances and methods that alter the integrity and/or validity of urine samples provided during NCAA drug testing. Example of banned methods are catheterization, urine substitution and/or tampering or modification of renal excretion by the use of diuretics, probenecid, bromantan or related compounds, and epitestosterone administration. *(Revised: 8/15/89, 6/17/92, 7/22/97)* . . .

31.2.3.1.2 Positive Drug Test—Non NCAA Athletics Organization. A student-athlete who has disclosed (i.e., in the student-athlete statement) a previous positive drug test for performance enhancing drugs administered by any other athletics organization (e.g., U.S. Olympics Committee) shall be required to submit to a drug test administered by the NCAA and found to have utilized a substance on the NCAA's list of banned drugs shall be declared ineligible for further participation in postseason and regular-season competition in accordance with the ineligibility provisions in Bylaws 31.2.3 and 18.4.1.5 *(Adopted: 1/14/97 effective 8/1/97* . . .

31.2.3.3 Methods for Drug Testing. The methods and any subsequent modifications authorized by the Executive Committee for drug testing of student-athletes shall be summarized in The NCAA News. Copies of the modifications shall be available to member institutions.

31.2.3.4 Events Identified for Drug Tests. The Executive Committee shall determine the regular-season and postseason competition for which drug tests shall be made and the procedures to be followed in disclosing its determinations.

31.2.3.5 Individual Eligibility-Team Sanctions. Executive regulations pertaining to team-eligibility sanctions for positive tests resulting from the NCAA drug-testing program shall apply only in the following situation: If a student-athlete is declared ineligible prior to an NCAA team championship or a certified postseason football game and the institution knowingly allows him or her to participate, all team-ineligibility sanctions shall apply (i.e., the team shall be required to forfeit its awards and any revenue distribution it may have earned, and the team's and student-athlete's performances shall be deleted from NCAA records). In the case of certified postseason football contests, the team's and student-athlete's performances shall be deleted from NCAA records. *(Revised: 1/10/90)*

The case of *O'Halloran v. University of Washington* held that the NCAA's use of monitored urine testing to enforce its drug testing program did not unreasonably infringe on a student-athlete's expectation of privacy.

O'HALLORAN v. UNIVERSITY OF WASHINGTON

679 E. Supp. 997 (W.D. Wash. 1988)

McGOVERN, District Judge.

I. Procedural and Factual Background

The constitutionality of the University of Washington's (University) drug-testing program was challenged in King County Superior Court when that Court ordered that the University join the National Collegiate Athletic Association (NCAA) as a third-party defendant, the NCAA removed the action to federal court. Plaintiff's Motion to Remand was denied.

The University moved for an order enjoining the NCAA from sanctioning it for failure to administer the NCAA program. The motion was denied as premature, this Court noting that the NCAA had not yet had the opportunity of being heard with respect to the constitutionality of its program.

Plaintiff moved this Court to adopt the rulings of the Superior Court and this Court declined. Plaintiff joined the NCAA as a party defendant as required after the third-party action of the University against the NCAA was dismissed.

The parties agreed to a Stipulation and Order of Partial Dismissal, entered by the Court, that the portion of the action concerning the University's drug-testing program had been compromised and settled. Plaintiff's claim against the University's drug-testing program was dismissed with prejudice. The plaintiff's claim against the NCAA's drug-testing program and the University's participation therein remains.

The NCAA's drug-testing program requires student athletes annually, prior to participation in intercollegiate competition during the academic year in question, to sign a statement in which he/she [consents to drug testing]. . . .

Plaintiff O'Halloran now moves for a preliminary injunction against the University and the NCAA, forbidding them from barring her from competition during the pendency of this action.

II. Showing Necessary for Preliminary Iinjunction

The Ninth Circuit standard for the grant of a preliminary injunction may be described as "a continuum in which the required showing of harm varies inversely with the required showing of meritoriousness."

A. Balance of Hardships

Plaintiff argues that since she is currently being denied the opportunity to participate on the University's indoor track team, that without the injunction she will likely lose her entire sophomore year of eligibility during the pendency of this case, that these lost months cannot be restored, and that this loss of opportunity to compete constitutes irreparable harm warranting injunctive relief.

The University argues that Plaintiff does not speak for the other 698 athletes competing for the University, but requests protection from NCAA sanctions should the Court order that Plaintiff be allowed to compete without signing the consent form.

The NCAA argues that NCAA rules do not prevent Plaintiff from participating in University sporting activities; the rules only prevent Plaintiff from competing in intercollegiate regular season and NCAA championship competition. Plaintiff may run with the team, train with the coach, and use the University's facilities. Moreover, she would only be screened if she were to qualify for post-season competition. The NCAA, however, would be harmed to a greater degree because its effective regulation of intercollegiate athletics would be impaired. The Court would be substituting its judgment for the NCAA's, competent athletes might use banned drugs in violation of NCAA rules, and the public interest in fair competition without the use of drugs would not be served.

The balance of hardships tips in favor of the University and the NCAA. The possibility that Plaintiff may qualify to compete in intercollegiate meets or post-season competition this year does not outweigh the fairness of equal treatment owed the hundreds of other student-athletes nor the public's interest in a program for fostering drug free sports competitions and drug education. Plaintiff may still participate in her chosen interest in a program for fostering drug free sports competitions and drug education. Plaintiff may still participate in her chosen sport at the University: she may practice and even set records, if she is able, and she is not precluded from pursuing a livelihood in professional track and field. She is only precluded from competing in intercollegiate meets and post-season championships should she qualify for such events.

On the other hand, if Plaintiff were allowed to compete in intercollegiate and post-season events without having to consent to NCAA drug testing, consenting student-athletes would question the fairness of this action, and the public interest in the commendable goal of deterrence of drug abuse of all types would not be served. Compared with these broader interests of other student athletes and the public, Plaintiff's hardship is less compelling. This is particularly true in view of the defendants' greater likelihood of success on the merits, the other element of the Ninth Circuit's standard.

B. The Merits of Plaintiff's Claims

Plaintiff contends that the NCAA's drug-testing program is constitutionally flawed because it interferes significantly with students' privacy rights: the right to live one's life in private, free from governmental interference. Plaintiff contends that this interference occurs because urination is monitored and because private facts about the student-athlete's activities in addition to the use of drugs may be revealed; for example, pregnancy or the use of pills for birth control, treatment of depression, epilepsy, or diabetes. Such interference in the absence of individualized suspicion impermissibly burdens these privacy interests, argues Plaintiff. Plaintiff also argues that overall, the drug-testing program results in an unreasonable search and seizure because the need for the search does not outweigh the invasion of privacy rights.

Defendant NCAA argues that its enforcement of its rule requiring preseason consent to drug screening as a condition of eligibility to participate in member intercollegiate athletics is not prohibited by the Constitutions of the United States and the State of Washington and the NCAA's conduct is not "state action." The NCAA cites numerous Federal appellate court cases, applying Supreme Court standards, concluding that the rule making by the NCAA and enforcement of NCAA rules constitutes private conduct rather than state action.

The NCAA argues that even assuming state action is present, the screening program invades no constitutionally protected right because (1) the privacy interest alleged does not rise to the magnitude of highly personal family matters addressed in Supreme Court privacy right cases, (2) the privilege of participating in intercollegiate athletics is not a constitutionally protected property or liberty interest, and (3) there is no unreasonable search and seizure since the search is compelled neither by the Government nor by the giving up of a privilege (intercollegiate competition) secured by the State or Federal constitution.

1. State Action . . .

Plaintiff has not met the requirement of 42 U.S.C. Section 1983 of demonstrating that the conduct complained of, enforcement of the NCAA's drug-testing program, is commited by persons acting under color of state law: (1) there is no showing that the State of Washington has exercised coercive power or provided significant encouragement, overtly or covertly, such that either the promulgation or enforcement of the drug-screening rule must be deemed to be state action; and (2) neither is there a showing that the regulation of intercollegiate athletics is a traditionally exclusive prerogative of the state.

2. Constitutional Rights

Not only has Plaintiff failed to state the first element of her Section 1983 claim—without which the claim fails—she has failed as well to demonstrate the second element: that the conduct complained of deprived her of a right, privilege, or immunity secured to her by the Constitution or laws of the United States.

Plaintiff argues that the drug-testing procedure constitutes an unconstitutional invasion of her privacy and an unreasonable search and seizure.

a. *The Fourth Amendment.* . . .

b. *Privacy Interests.* Plaintiff's greatest complaint of an invasion of privacy concerns the testing program's requirement of monitored urination. . . .

Conclusion

Plaintiff has not demonstrated that the balance of hardships tips in her favor; indeed, the balance tips in favor of the University and the NCAA. Plaintiff has failed to demonstrate that she is likely to succeed on the merits in that she has failed to demonstrate that the drug testing complained of is the product of "state action." Moreover, Plaintiff has not demonstrated that there has been an invasion of any constitutionally protected right requiring invalidation the drug-testing program. The invasion of her privacy interest by the specimen collection procedures of the drug-testing program are outweighed by the compelling interest of the University and the NCAA in protecting the health of student-athletes, reducing peer pressure and temptations to use drugs, ensuring fair competitions for the student-athletes and the public, and educating about and deterring drug abuse in sports competition.

Accordingly, Plaintiff's Motion for Preliminary Injunction is denied.

QUESTIONS AND DISCUSSION

1. In Article 12.31, Use of Agents-General Rule, "An individual shall be ineligible for participation in an intercollegiate sport if he or she ever has agreed (orally or in writing) to be represented by an agent for the purpose of marketing his or her athletic ability or reputation in that sport." The essence of a standard representation contract is negotiation of the employment contract, not "marketing" the athlete's ability. Does this language miss the point? How about oral agreements having the same effect as a written representation contract. Can this be effectively enforced?

2. Like *Gaines*, Braxton Banks of Notre Dame, in *Banks v. NCAA*, 977 F.2d 1081 (7th Cir. 1992), lost his eligibility as a result of the NCAA's 'no-draft and 'no-agent' rules. Both players lost their eligibility on unsuccessfully entering the NFL draft. Both Bradford Gaines and Braxton Banks were denied injunctive relief since they failed to show a likelihood of success on the merits that the applicable NCAA rules violated the Sherman Act. In *Banks*, it was held that plaintiff failed to allege an anticompetitive impact on a discernable market. *See* Lock, *Unreasonable NCAA Eligibility Rules Send Braxton Banks Truckin*, 20 Capital U.L. Rev. 643 (1991). Is the Sherman Act the wrong approach for the no-agent rule cases? Is there a better approach?

3. In *Hall v. NCAA*, 985 F. Supp. 782 (N.D.Ill.1997), a student and his mother sued a university and the NCAA after he was declared initially ineligible and lost an athletic scholarship for freshman year; student was not entitled to preliminary relief given negligible chance of success on claims, failure to show irreparable harm, and balance of equities in favor of NCAA. The NCAA did not act in "bad faith" by failing to include certain courses as "core" for purposes of ascertaining first-year eligibility. How much room does the NCAA have in these types of determinations? How much room should they have before public policy is violated?

4. The Supreme Court of the United States in the case of *NCAA v. Smith*, 525 U.S. 459 (1999), allowed the continuation of the NCAA rule that prohibits

students from participation while enrolled in graduate programs other than their undergraduate institution. The athlete in question was a female who attempted to continue her eligibility while in law school at an institution different from her undergraduate school. The Court held that the NCAA is not subject to the requirements of Title IX on the grounds that it receives federal financial assistance.

In *Smith v. NCAA*, 266 F.3d 152 (3d Cir. 2001), the Third Circuit Court of Appeals wrote an opinion based on the Supreme court's remand mandate. The court of appeals held that the NCAA did not trigger Title IX analysis since it did not exercise controlling authority over its federally funded member institutions. But, the court remanded on Smith's theory that the NCAA indirectly received federal financial assistance by virtue of its relationship with youth enrichment program and national youth sports program fund. If proven, these allegations would be sufficient to bring the NCAA under Title IX purview: "[W]e will remand to the District Court to allow Smith to amend her complaint to include the NYSP relationship theory. The district Court should conduct discovery and make findings with respect to this allegation." *Smith* involved the NCAA's "post-baccalaureate bylaw," which prohibited students from continuing athletic participation while in graduate school if that school was different from their undergraduate school. Is there any likelihood that the NCAA will not prevail ultimately? *See generally* Ruiz, NCAA v. Smith: *Must the NCAA Play by the Rules?* 26 J.C. & U.L. 119 (1999).

5. In *Hill II*, 865 P.2d 633 (Cal. 1994), the California Supreme Court reversed the court of appeals decision (273 Cal. Rptr. 402 (1990)) and held that the NCAA's mandatory drug testing program did not violate the athletes' privacy right. *See* Champion, *The NCAA's Drug Testing Policies: Walking a Constitutional Tightrope?* 67 N.D. L. Rev. 269 (1991). But in *Derdeyn v. University of Colorado,* 863 P.2d 929 (Colo. 1993), the Colorado Supreme Court found that U.C.'s drug testing program violated the Fourth Amendment. *See also* Blair, Note, *Constitutional Law—Testing the Fourth Amendment Random, Suspicionless Urinalysis Drug—Testing of Student—Athletes Is Unconstitutional Search—*University of Colo. v. Derdeyn,' 28 Suffolk U.L. Rev. 217 (1994); Roshkoff, Univ. of Colo v. Derdeyn: *The Constitutionality of Random, Suspicionless Urinalysis Drug Testing of College Athlete,* 3 Vill. Sports & Ent. L.F. 361 (1996). What case is the prevailing law, *Hill II* or *Derdeyn*? *Hill II* shadows the locker room mentality of the U.S. Supreme Court in *Acton*. Does *Acton* then reinforce *Hill II* so that now *Hill II/Acton* is controlling as regards NCAA drug testing?

C. DISCIPLINE

The NCAA has the power to penalize colleges and individual players for infractions of its rules and regulations. This ability is an integral part of its power to determine the eligibility of a particular athlete. NCAA rule enforcement includes investigatory, prosecutorial, and adjudicatory actions. If a potential problem arises, the NCAA investigates the member school and/or the individual athlete. Any discipline and the enforcement thereof must be conducted in a fair, constitutional, and legal manner.

1. Sanctions and Penalties

The NCAA's ability to sanction and penalize institutions and individuals for violations of its constitution and bylaws is the key to its effective administration of intercollegiate athletics. This ability, though, has received much negative criticism, mostly on the grounds that NCAA enforcement procedures are overly broad and unusually harsh.

Judge Miles Lord in *Hall v. University of Minnesota*, 530 F. Supp. 104, 109 (D. Minn. 1982), looked at the NCAA's power to discipline in this way:

> The only perceivable harm to the defendant university would result in the fact that the National Collegiate Athletic Association (NCAA), in which the defendant university is a member, has rules which permit certain sanctions to be leveled upon the defendant university should the player be declared eligible under court order which is later vacated, stayed, reversed, etc. This rule defines sanctions including the vacation of the athletes records for the period for which the athlete played, the forfeiture of games by the team, the declaration of ineligibility of the team for post-season tournaments, the return of television receipts for games in which the athlete played in. However, in this regard, the defendant university's destiny is in its own hands. The university does not have to appeal this order, if it is fearful of the sanctions which might be imposed by the NCAA. And the defendant university's lawyer is of the opinion that the NCAA cannot force an appeal. Therefore, an appeal with all of the usual uncertainties accompanying it is not mandated. It would be the defendant university's choice whether it wants to risk these sanctions at this time. Presumably, some impartial arbitrator at the defendant university will make this decision on whether the defendant university will risk these potential sanctions.

In an action involving college basketball coach Jerry Tarkanian, one dissenting judge critically characterized the NCAA and its corresponding power to discipline, sanction, and penalize, and its alleged "efficiency" in this manner:

> [B]ut there is someone who can match Mr. Tarkanian, not in glory, but in infamy—none other than the "embodiment of evil," the "Ayatollah" and the "Gestapo" of sportsdom, namely, the "barbaric" National Collegiate Athletic Association.

NCAA v. Tarkanian, 939 P.2d 1049, 1052 (Nev. 1997) (Springer, J., dissenting).

A more measured view may be found in *Colorado Seminary (Univ. of Denver) v. NCAA*, 570 F.2d 320 (10th Cir. 1978), where the court held that the rights of the scholarship hockey players did not arise to the level of constitutionally protected rights invoking due process. Therefore, the NCAA did not unconstitutionally discriminate against the member university by placing it on probabtion for failure to declare several student hockey players ineligible, absent a showing of discrimination based on arbitrary and recognizable classifications, such as race, religion, or national origin.

Although the NCAA has significant power to invoke sanctions, a few states have contemplated adding legislatively approved sanctions to supplement already-imposed NCAA penalties. For example, Texas has enacted legislation that adds liability or monetary damages that result from sanctions. These damages could include ticket or television revenue lost because of NCAA probation or suspension.

The following sections from the NCAA manual detail some of the NCAA's penalty procedures.

NCAA Constitution, Article 19.6, Penalties

19.6 Penalties

19.6.1 Penalties for Secondary Violations. . . . Among the disciplinary measures are: *(Revised: 1/11/94)*

(a) Termination of the recruitment of a prospect by the institution or, if the prospect enrolls (or has enrolled) in the institution, permanent ineligibility to represent the institution in intercollegiate competition (unless eligibility is restored by the Committee on Student-Athlete Reinstatement upon appeal);

(b) Forfeiture of contests in which an ineligible student-athlete participated;

(c) Prohibition of the head coach or other staff members in the involved sport from participating in any off-campus recruiting activities for up to one year; *(Revised: 1/11/94)*

(d) An institutional fine for each violation, with the monetary penalty ranging in total from $500 to $5,000, except when an ineligible student-athlete participates in an NCAA championship or other postseason competition, in which case the $5,000 limit shall not apply; *(Revised: 4/26/01 effective 8/1/01)*

(e) A limited reduction in the number of financial aid awards that may be awarded during a specified period in the sport involved to the maximum extent of 20 percent of the maximum number of awards normally permissible in that sport;

(f) Institutional recertification that its current athletics policies and practices conform to all requirements of NCAA regulations;

(g) Suspension of the head coach or other staff members for one or more competitions; *(Adopted: 1/11/94)*

(h) Public reprimand . . . ; and *(Adopted: 1/11/94)*

(i) Requirement that a member institution that has been found in violation, or that has an athletics department staff member who has been found in violation of the provisions of NCAA legislation while representing another institution, show cause why a penalty or an additional penalty should not be imposed if it does not take appropriate disciplinary or corrective action against the athletics department personnel involved, any other institutional employee if the circumstances warrant or representatives of the institution's athletics interests. *(Adopted: 1/11/94)*

19.6.2 Penalties for Major Violations

    19.6.2.1 Presumptive Penalty. The vice-president for enforcement services, upon approval by the chair or another member of the Committee on Infractions designated by the chair, or the committee may determine that no penalty is warranted in a secondary case, that an institutional- or conference-determined penalty is satisfactory or, if appropriate, impose a penalty. Among the disciplinary measures are: *(Revised: 1/11/94)* [List following shadows 19.6.1 (a)-(i)].

    19.6.2.2 Disciplinary Measures. In addition to those penalties prescribed for secondary violations, among the disciplinary measures, singly or in combination, that may be adopted by the committee (or the appropriate appeals committee per Bylaw 19.3) and imposed against an institution for major violations are: *(Revised: 1/16/93, 1/11/94, 1/10/95)*

(a) Public reprimand and censure; *(Revised: 1/11/94)*
(b) Probation for at least one year;*(Revised: 1/11/94)*
(c) A reduction in the number of financial aid awards (as defined in Bylaw 15.02.4.1) that may be awarded during a specified period;
(d) Prohibition against the recruitment of prospective student-athletes for a sport or sports for a specified period;
(e) One or more of the following penalties: *(Revised: 4/26/01 effective 8/1/01)*

    (1) Individual records and performances shall be vacated or stricken; or *(Revised: 1/11/94)*
    (2) Team records and performances shall be vacated or stricken; or *(Adopted: 1/11/94)*
    (3) Individual or team awards shall be returned to the Association.

(f) A financial penalty; *(Adopted: 4/26/01 effective 8/1/01)*
(g) Ineligibility for any television programs involving coverage of the institution's intercollegiate athletics team or teams in the sport or sports in which the violations occurred; *(Revised: 1/10/92)*
(h) Ineligibility for invitational and postseason meets and tournaments;
(i) Ineligibility for one or more NCAA championship events;
(j) Prohibition against an intercollegiate sports team or teams participating against outside competition for a specified period;
(k) Ineligibility of the member to vote or its personnel to serve on committees of the Association, or both;
(l) Requirement that a member institution that has been found in violation, or that has an athletics department staff member who has been found in violation of the provisions of NCAA legislation while representing another institution, show cause why: [subparagraphs (1)-(5) follow.]

19.6.2.2.1 Opportunity to Appear. In the event the committee considers additional penalties to be imposed upon an institution in accordance with Bylaw 19.6.2.2-(I) above, the involved institution shall be provided the opportunity to appear before the committee; further, the institution shall be provided the opportunity to appeal (per Bylaw 19.7.2) any additional penalty imposed by the committee.

19.6.2.3 Repeat Violators

19.6.2.3.1 Time Period. An institution shall be considered a "repeat" violator if the Committee on Infractions finds that a major violation has occurred within five years of the starting date of a major penalty. For this provision to apply, at least one major violation must have occurred within five years after the starting date of the penalties in the previous case. It shall not be necessary that the Committee on Infractions' hearing be conducted or its report issued within the five-year period. *(Revised: 1/14/97 effective 8/1/97)*

19.6.2.3.2 Repeat-Violator Penalties. In addition to the penalties identified for a major violation, the minimum penalty for a repeat violator, subject to exceptions authorized by the Committee on Infractions on the basis of specifically stated reasons, may include any or all of the following: *(Revised: 1/11/94)*

(a) The prohibition of some or all outside competition in the sport involved in the latest major violation for one or two sports seasons and the prohibition of all coaching staff members in that sport from involvement directly or indirectly in any coaching activities at the institution during that period;

(b) The elimination of all initial grants-in-aid and all recruiting activities in the sport involved in the latest major violation in question for a two-year period;

(c) The requirement that all institutional staff members serving on the Board of Directors, Management Council, Executive Committee or other committees of the Association resign those positions, it being understood that all institutional representatives shall be ineligible to serve on any NCAA committee for a period of four years; and

(d) The requirement that the institution relinquish its voting privilege in the Association for a four-year period.

19.6.2.4 Probationary Periods . . .

19.6.3 Discipline of Affiliated or Corresponding Member . . .

19.6.4 Recommendation to Committee on Athletics Certification. The Committee on Infractions may recommend to the Committee on Athletics Certification that an institution's certification status be reviewed as a result of the institution's completed infractions case. *(Adopted: 1/16/93 effective 1/1/94)*

The case of *Colorado Seminary (University of Denver) v. NCAA* establishes the principle that challenges to NCAA-imposed sanctions do not unconstitutionally discriminate against the allegedly offending institution.

Colorado Seminary (University of Denver) v. National Collegiate Athletic Association

570 F.2d 320 (10th Cir. 1978)

Per Curiam.

This action was brought by the University of Denver and by several of its student athletes to enjoin the National Collegiate Athletic Association from imposing sanctions against the hockey team and other DU athletic teams. The trial court denied the plaintiffs' motion for summary judgment and granted a like motion of the defendants with some exceptions. The plaintiffs have taken this appeal.

The trial court held that the interest of the student athletes in participating in intercollegiate sports was not constitutionally protected, and that no constitutionally protected right of the University had been violated. We agree with these conclusions, and we agree with the Memorandum Opinion of the trial court appearing at 417 F. Supp. 885.

The facts are described in the trial court's Memorandum, and need not be repeated here. It is sufficient to say that the dispute began between the University and the NCAA as to the eligibility of several hockey players, and culminated with the NCAA placing the hockey team on a two-year probation with no post season participation in NCAA events, and also the probation of all other University athletic teams for a one-year period with similar consequences. . . .

It is obvious that the relative importance of the many school "activities" to each other, and to the academic core, depends on where you sit. The "educational process" is indeed a bundle of diverse situations to which the students are subjected by varying degrees of compulsion, both officially and by their peers. This is basically the *Goss v. Lopez*, 419 U.S. 565; assumption. It is then to be applied with the significant conclusion therefrom reached in Albach v. Odle, quoted above, to the effect that if one stick in the bundle is removed, it does not necessarily mean that a constitutionally protected right of a student has thereby been violated. . . .

Thus here also we must hold that there is present no substantial federal question.

The equal protection argument, as the trial court observes, is answered by *San Antonio Independent School Dist. v. Rodriguez*, 411 U.S. 1. There is here no valid argument based on classification. In the final analysis, the NCAA reacted to the position taken by the University as a member and in response to the

NCAA pronouncements. The matter resulting in the probation sanction became removed from the issue of eligibility of the several hockey players.

Affirmed in all respects.

The *Hairston* case is somewhat different from other cases in this chapter in that the defendant is not the NCAA itself but an athletic conference. In *Hairston,* the athletic conference imposed sanctions on a university for rules violations. As a result, former and current football players sued the conference alleging violations of the Sherman Act and breach of contract. The court held that the players failed to show that sanctions constituted unreasonable restraint of trade and that the players were not third-party beneficiaries of a contract between the conference and its university members.

HAIRSTON v. PACIFIC 10 CONFERENCE

101 F.3d 1315 (9th Cir. 1996)

Cynthia Holcomb HALL, Circuit Judge:

Plaintiffs-appellants Russell Hairston, Frank Garcia, Jovan McCoy and Kyle Roberts appeal the district court's order granting summary judgment in favor of defendant-appellee, the Pacific-10 Conference ("Pac-10"). The district court had jurisdiction over this matter pursuant to 15 U.S.C. §§15 and 26, and 28 U.S.C. §1367. We have jurisdiction over this timely appeal pursuant to 28 U.S.C. §1291. We affirm.

I

Appellants are former and current University of Washington ("UW") football players. Appellee, the Pacific-10 Conference ("Pac-10"), is an unincorporated association of ten universities situated in California, Arizona, Oregon and Washington, formed for the purpose of "establishing an athletic program to be participated in by the members."

On November 5, 1992, the *Seattle Times* reported that UW's star quarterback, Billy Joe Hobert, had received three loans totalling $50,000 from an Idaho businessman. After investigating the allegations, UW officials suspended Hobert and declared him permanently ineligible to play amateur football. One month later, the *Los Angeles Times* published a series of articles alleging that UW's football program had violated several NCAA rules. At this time, UW, in conjunction with Pac-10 officials, began investigating these alleged irregularities.

After conducting an eight-month investigation into the allegations of recruiting improprieties, the Pac-10 placed the UW football team on probation for recruiting violations. The levied sanctions included: (1) a two-year bowl ban covering the 1993 and 1994 seasons; (2) a one-year television revenue ban; (3) a limit of 15 football scholarships each for the 1994-95 and the 1995-96 academic years; (4) a reduction in the number of permissible football recruiting visits from 70 to 35 in 1993-94 and to 40 in 1994-95; and (5) a two-year probationary period.

The imposition of penalties on the UW Huskies devastated both the players and their fans. In an effort to have the sanctions rescinded, appellants filed a complaint against the Pac-10. In their complaint, appellants alleged antitrust violations under Section One of the Sherman Act, 15 U.S.C. §1, and breach of contract. They argued that the penalties were "grossly dispropor-tionate to the University's violations" and evidence of a conspiracy engineered by UW's Pac-10 competitors to sideline UW's football program and thereby improve their own records and odds of winning a post-season bowl game berth. Besides injunctive relief appellants also sought damages, which would include the cost of air fare, lodging, meals and expenses related to a trip to play in a post-season bowl game.

The Pac-10 responded by filing a motion to dismiss all claims. In its motion, the Pac-10 contended that the players lacked constitutional and anti-trust standing. The Pac-10's motion was granted in part as to certain plaintiffs not included in this appeal, but denied as to the issue of the players' standing. *Hairston v. Pacific-10 Conference*, 893 F. Supp. 1485 (W.D. Wash. 1994) ("*Hairston I*"). The district court found that because the players had demon-strated direct antitrust injury, they could pursue their antitrust claims. *Id.* at 1491-92. However, the court dismissed the players breach of contract claim because it found that the players were not intended third-party beneficiaries of the contract between and among Pac-10 member schools. *Id.* at 1494.

The Pac-10 then filed a motion for summary judgment alleging that appel-lants had failed to present any evidence of anticompetitive conspiracy among Pac-10 members or between the Pac-10 and the NCAA. The court agreed and granted the Pac-10's motion. *Hairston v. Pacific-10 Conference*, 893 F. Supp. 1495, 1496 (W.D. Wash. 1995)("*Hairston II*").

This appeal then followed.

II

A district court opinion granting summary judgment is reviewed *de novo*.

III

On appeal, the Pac-10 contends that the motion for summary judgment should be affirmed because appellants lack antitrust standing under Section 4 of the Clayton Act, 15 U.S.C. §4. Although we are not persuaded by the reasoning in the district court's opinion, *Hairston I*, 893 F. Supp. at 1490-92, we need not decide whether appellants have met the requirements for antitrust standing, because they have failed to establish any violation of the antitrust laws. . . .

V

Appellants also argue that the district court erred in dismissing their breach of contract claim.

In their complaint, the players alleged that the Pac-10's Constitution, Bylaws and Articles created a contract between the conference and its mem-bers, and that the players were third-party beneficiaries of this contract. The players further contend that the Pac-10 breached this contract when it levied unreasonable sanctions against UW, thereby injuring the players as beneficiaries. . . .

VI

Appellants have failed to show that the penalties the Pac-10 imposed constituted an unreasonable restraint of trade. As a result, no antitrust violation occurred. Appellants also have failed to allege a breach-of-contract claim since no language in the contract shows the Pac-10 and its members intended to assume a direct obligation to the students. For these reasons, we affirm.

In *NCAA v. Jones*, the Supreme Court of Texas reinforced the NCAA's ability to issue retroactive penalties under its "restitution rule."

NATIONAL COLLEGIATE ATHLETIC ASSOCIATION V. JONES

1 S.W.3d 83 (Tex. 1999)

Chief Justice PHILLIPS delivered the opinion of the Court, in which Justice HECHT, Justice ENOCH, Justice OWEN and Justice O'NEILL joined.

We must decide whether the court of appeals erred in dismissing as moot an appeal from a temporary injunction. The trial court granted Joel Casey Jones, then an offensive guard on the Texas Tech University Red Raiders' football team, a temporary injunction enjoining the National Collegiate Athletic Association ("NCAA") and Texas Tech University ("Texas Tech") from enforcing NCAA rules that would have cost him his eligibility for the 1996 football season. Jones also sought and obtained an injunction prohibiting the NCAA from enforcing NCAA Operating By law 19.8 (the "Restitution Rule") against either Texas Tech or Jones. The Restitution Rule authorizes the NCAA to impose retroactive sanctions if an ineligible student-athlete competes under an injunction that is later voluntarily vacated, stayed or reversed, or found by the courts to have been improperly granted. The NCAA appealed, but the court of appeals declined the NCAA's request to expedite the appeal. As a result, Jones played out the season and completed his eligibility before the appeal was resolved. Finding no justiciable controversy, the court of appeals dismissed the appeal as moot and vacated the injunction. 982 S.W.2d 450. Because we conclude that the appeal as a whole is not moot, we reverse the judgment of the court of appeals and remand to that court for consideration of the merits.

The NCAA is a voluntary, unincorporated association of colleges and universities created for the stated purpose of preserving the proper balance between athletics and scholarship in intercollegiate sports. Among other things, the NCAA promulgates rules and regulations to prevent any member institution from gaining an unfair competitive advantage in an athletic program. This case arose when Texas Tech, a member institution of the NCAA, declared Jones ineligible for the 1996 football season, Jones's final year of eligibility.

Pursuant to NCAA rules, Texas Tech reported its action to the NCAA. However, the school also made repeated appeals for a waiver of the eligibility requirements, each of which the NCAA denied. Jones then filed a declaratory action against the NCAA and Texas Tech, seeking injunctive relief, damages, and attorney's fees. Jones did not claim that he was eligible to play under NCAA rules. Instead, he contended that he relied on representations made to him by Texas Tech officials about the appropriate courses in which to enroll to retain his eligibility. According to Jones, Texas Tech was an agent of the NCAA when it made these statements, so that the NCAA became bound by the representations and was required to grant the waiver. The NCAA filed no claims for restitution against either Texas Tech or Jones, and Texas Tech made no claims against the NCAA.

The trial court first issued a temporary restraining order and then a temporary injunction that: (1) enjoined the NCAA and Texas Tech from taking any action to prevent Jones from participating as a member of Texas Tech's football team, and (2) enjoined the NCAA from imposing any penalty on Jones or Texas Tech for complying with the court's order and specifically enjoined the NCAA from enforcing the Restitution Rule, which would permit the NCAA to impose penalties such as forfeiture of individual records, performances and awards, forfeiture of team victories, records, performances and awards, and forfeiture of receipts from any competition in which the ineligible athlete participated. Although Texas Tech had not 6 sought an injunction against the NCAA, the trial court presumably enjoined the NCAA from enforcing the Restitution Rule against the school based on Jones's claim that he would be adversely affected if the NCAA were free to sanction Texas Tech.

The NCAA filed an interlocutory appeal pursuant to section 51.014(4) of the Texas Civil Practice and Remedies Code, arguing that the trial court abused its discretion in issuing the temporary injunction. Texas Tech was not a party to the appeal. The court of appeals dismissed the appeal as moot and vacated the injunction, holding that both portions of the injunction became inoperative when Texas Tech's 1996 football season ended. 982 S.W.2d at 452. With regard to the portion of the injunction prohibiting the NCAA from imposing retroactive sanctions, the court of appeals further added that the injunction became inoperative at that time "because there was no justiciable controversy or pending action between Jones and the NCAA or the NCAA and Tech concerning the validity or enforcement of the restitution rule." 982 S.W.2d at 452. In so holding, the court of appeals rejected the NCAA's claim that its contractual right to impose retroactive sanctions under the Restitution Rule prevents the appeal of the temporary injunction from being moot. 982 S.W.2d at 451. We granted the NCAA's petition for review.

Appellate courts are prohibited from deciding moot controversies. . . .

Applying these well-established principles, the court of appeals concluded that the appeal from the temporary injunction order was moot as to both the portion of the injunction enjoining enforcement of the eligibility rules and the portion enjoining the enforcement of the Restitution Rule. 982 S.W.2d at 452. The NCAA argues, however, that a judicial determination about the validity of the temporary injunction remains important to resolve whether the NCAA may, contrary to the injunction's dictate, take remedial action against Jones and Texas Tech under the Restitution Rule. Relying on several cases from other jurisdictions, the NCAA contends that there is still a live controversy between the parties because it could impose retroactive sanctions against Jones and Texas Tech if the court of appeals concludes that the trial court abused its discretion in prematurely granting Jones relief. According to the NCAA, dismissal of the case as moot would leave the rights of the parties undecided. . . .

The court of appeals erred in concluding that the second part of the temporary injunction—the portion restraining the NCAA from penalizing Texas Tech or Jones—became inoperative merely because the NCAA had no pending action against either Texas Tech or Jones to enforce its restitution rights or to establish the validity of the Restitution Rule. The NCAA could not have instituted such an action because it was enjoined from doing so and, until a higher court determined otherwise, was bound to follow the trial court's order. This portion of the injunction remained in effect after the 1996 football season ended, barring the NCAA from taking any action against Jones or Texas Tech under Rule 19.8 until the injunction was vacated by the court of appeals. This portion of the injunction would be moot, however, if either Jones or the NCAA, the only parties before the court of appeals, ceased to have a legally cognizable interest in the outcome of the appeal. But if dismissal would leave the rights of the parties undecided, the issues involved are not moot and the appeal should have been decided on the merits.

The NCAA clearly has an interest in having the injunction invalidated and set aside; otherwise, it can never impose any penalties under the Restitution Rule. Whether Jones has a tangible interest in the continued validity of the injunction, however, is a closer issue. If dismissal of the appeal as moot and lifting of the injunction would affect Jones's interest in the fruits of his intercollegiate participation during the 1996 football season, the appeal from the temporary injunction is not moot. Thus, the issue is whether the NCAA could now take any action that would have an adverse effect of substantial significance to Jones if the court of appeals were to address the merits of the temporary injunction.

There is no indication in the record or the parties' briefs as to whether Jones set any records or won any awards while participating under the injunction that could be stricken under the Restitution Rule. Likewise, the record does not reveal whether there are any team awards that could be stricken. The only remaining penalties that Jones could conceivably have an interest in avoiding are erasure of his individual performances, however that may be recorded for an offensive guard, and forfeiture of team victories.

There is some authority that the possibility of retroactive penalties does not prevent an appeal from being moot if the only possible penalty is forfeiture of team victories and the school, like Texas Tech in this case, is not a party to the appeal. . . .

Accordingly, we reverse the judgment of the court of appeals and remand the cause to that court for consideration of the merits of the appeal.

The Supreme Court of Kentucky in *NCAA v. Lasege* held the trial court was unable to enjoin the NCAA from imposing restitutionary sanctions against a university and student-athlete on the basis that the university voluntarily agreed to abide by the rules and regulations of the NCAA.

NATIONAL COLLEGIATE ATHLETIC ASSOCIATION V. LASEGE

53 S.W.3d 77 (Ky. 2001)

KELLER, Justice.

I. Introduction

The National Collegiate Athletic Association ("NCAA") moves this Court for interlocutory relief under CR 65.09 and asks us to vacate the Jefferson Circuit Court's temporary injunction which (1) declares Respondent Lasege eligible to participate in NCAA intercollegiate basketball and (2) prohibits the NCAA from imposing future sanctions against Lasege or Respondent University of Louisville ("U of L") pursuant to its NCAA Bylaw 19.8 restitutionary powers. We find that the NCAA has demonstrated "extraordinary cause" justifying CR 65.09 relief and we vacate the temporary injunction in its entirety.

II. Factual and Procedural Background

Lasege, a citizen of Nigeria, a country in West Africa, enrolled at the University of Louisville during the 1999-2000 academic year with the intention of playing for its intercollegiate men's basketball team. In March 2000, U of L declared Lasege ineligible to play intercollegiate basketball because he had previously entered into professional basketball contracts and had received preferential benefits which compromised his amateur status. U of L asked the NCAA to reinstate Lasege's eligibility because of Lasege's ignorance of NCAA regulations and other mitigating factors. The NCAA's Student-Athlete Reinstatement Staff ("Staff") found that Lasege had violated its Bylaws relating to contracts and compensation, the use of agents, and preferential treatment, benefits, or services, and declined U of L's reinstatement request "[b]ased on the case precedent and the subcommittee's December 1999 amateurism guidelines involving contracts and professional teams. Specifically, the Staff focused on [Lasege's] decisions to sign explicit contracts with a sports agent and a professional team." . . .

U of L appealed the Staff's decision to the NCAA's Division I Subcommittee on Student-Athlete Reinstatement. The Subcommittee, which consists of representatives from NCAA Division I member institutions, found that

Lasege's Bylaw violations exhibited a clear intent to professionalize and affirmed the Staff's decision denying reinstatement.

On November 27, 2000, Lasege filed a Motion and Complaint in Jefferson Circuit Court seeking a temporary injunction requiring the NCAA to reverse its decision as to U of L's request and to immediately reinstate his eligibility to play basketball at U of L. After conducting an evidentiary hearing, the trial court found that the complaint presented a substantial question as to whether the NCAA's ruling was arbitrary and capricious. Specifically, the trial court: (1) suggested that the NCAA had ignored what it described as "overwhelming and mitigating circumstances," including economic and cultural disadvantages, a complete ignorance of NCAA regulations, and elements of coercion associated with execution of the contracts; (2) believed the NCAA's determination to conflict with the NCAA's own amateurism guidelines and past eligibility determinations regarding athletes who had engaged in similar violations; (3) expressed its doubts about whether the first contract signed by Lasege was legally enforceable as an agency contract both because of Lasege's minority at the time he executed it and because the trial court disputed that the contract created an agency relationship; and (4) opined that a clear weight of evidence suggested Lasege committed these violations not in order to become a professional athlete, but only to obtain a visa which would allow him to become a student-athlete in the United States.

The trial court found that Lasege would suffer substantial collateral consequences from an erroneous and adverse eligibility determination, balanced the equities in favor of Lasege, and ordered "the NCAA and its members . . . to immediately restore the intercollegiate eligibility of Muhammed Lasege so as to allow him to participate in all NCAA basketball contests." The trial court also addressed U of L's concern that the NCAA could impose sanctions under NCAA Bylaw 19.8 if the injunction was subsequently vacated. NCAA Bylaw 19.8 allows the NCAA to seek restitution from member institutions who permit student-athletes found ineligible by the NCAA to compete for their athletic teams pursuant to court orders which are later vacated. The trial court therefore "declare[d] that NCAA Bylaw 19.8 is invalid because it prevents parties from availing themselves of the protections of the courts" and ordered . . .

While Lasege played, the NCAA sought interlocutory relief under CR 65.07, but the Court of Appeals found the trial court's findings supported by substantial evidence and denied the NCAA's motion. The Court of Appeals did not address the merits of that portion of the temporary injunction which prohibited the NCAA from seeking restitution under NCAA Bylaw 19.8 because "[a]pplication of the bylaw becomes an issue in this case only in the event that the injunction were to be set aside or a permanent injunction were denied in this matter."

The NCAA thus seeks interlocutory relief from this Court.

III. Discussion
III(A)—Standard of Review . . .

In this case, we find that the trial court abused its discretion by: (1) substituting its judgment for that of the NCAA on the question of Lasege's intent to professionalize; (2)finding that the NCAA has no interest in this case which weighs against injunctive relief; and (3) declaring NCAA Bylaw 19.8 invalid. This combination of clearly erroneous conclusions constitutes extraordinary cause warranting CR 65.09 relief.

III(B)—Reinstatement of Lasege's Eligibility

The trial court made a preliminary determination that "the arbitrary nature of the enforcement of its by-laws by the members of the NCAA and its committees raises a substantial issue concerning the merits of their rules." The trial court further found that "Mr. Lasege faces irreparable harm because without reinstatement, he will not be able to continue in classes, and may be deported back to Nigeria." Although we agree with the trial court's assessment of the magnitude of the harm from an erroneous NCAA eligibility decision, we find that Lasege's chances of prevailing on the merits of his claim are too remote to justify injunctive relief. We believe the trial court clearly erred when assessing the merits of Lasege's claim.

In our opinion, the trial court wrongfully substituted its judgment for that of the NCAA after it analyzed the evidence and reached a different conclusion as to Lasege's intent to professionalize. The mere fact that a trial court considering mitigating evidence might disagree with the NCAA's factual conclusions does not render the NCAA's decision arbitrary or capricious. We have held that a ruling is arbitrary and capricious only where it is "clearly erroneous, and by 'clearly erroneous' we mean unsupported by substantial evidence." Here, the NCAA's ruling has strong evidentiary support—Lasege unquestionably signed contracts to play professional basketball and unquestionably accepted benefits. Contrary to the trial court's allegations of disparate treatment, the NCAA submits that no individual has ever had his or her eligibility reinstated after committing a combination of rules violations akin to those compiled by Lasege. The NCAA's eligibility determinations are entitled to a presumption of correctness—particularly when they stem from *conceded* violations of NCAA regulations. Although we recognize that Lasege's mitigation evidence is relevant to review of the NCAA's determination, we believe the trial court simply disagreed with the NCAA as to the weight which should be assigned to this evidence. Accordingly, we believe the trial court abused its discretion when it found that Lasege had a high probability of success on the merits of his claim. . . .

The NCAA unquestionably has an interest in enforcing its regulations and preserving the amateur nature of intercollegiate athletics. As the trial court entered a *temporary* injunction on the basis of its *preliminary* findings, the trial court could eventually determine that the NCAA properly denied the reinstatement request. If that is the case, the trial court's order would have erroneously allowed an ineligible player to participate in intercollegiate athletics. While the NCAA has no identifiable interest in the arbitrary application of its regulations to the detriment of a student-athlete, it certainly has an interest in the proper application of those regulations to ensure competitive equity.

Here, it appears that the trial court considered the equities of only one party—Lasege—and it overvalued that interest with an unrealistic finding as to Lasege's probability of success on the merits. The trial court could not possibly have weighed the NCAA's interests, because it did not believe the NCAA had any interest for it to consider. Nor does it appear that the trial court gave any consideration to the possible injury to those programs and student- athletes who, because of the temporary injunction, would compete against a U of L Men's Basketball team with Lasege on the roster. In fact, as will be discussed in Section III(C), the trial court stripped the NCAA of even the somewhat ham-fisted, post-hoc restitutionary measures it uses to correct competitive inequities created by court orders. We cannot conclude that the trial court's determination was supported by substantial evidence when it so clearly mischaracterized the equities before balancing them. Logically speaking, a conclusion is flawed when it flows from an invalid premise. We believe this flaw in the trial court's conclusion constitutes clear error and warrants CR 65.09 relief.

We find clearly erroneous both the trial court's finding regarding Lasege's probability of success on the merits and its failure to evaluate the opportunity costs to the NCAA and others when balancing the equities. Accordingly, we vacate that portion of the temporary injunction which declares Lasege eligible to participate in NCAA intercollegiate basketball.

III(C)—Prohibition of NCAA Bylaw 19.8 Restitution

We note some disagreement among the parties as to the nature of the trial court's ruling with respect to NCAA Bylaw 19.8. Lasege argues that the trial court prohibited the NCAA from imposing restitutionary sanctions only during the pendency of the temporary injunction. As the bylaw itself allows the NCAA to seek restitution only if the temporary injunction is dissolved, we disagree with this characterization. . . .

In context, therefore, the trial court's order "that the NCAA and its members are hereby ordered to take no action to prevent or interfere with the University of Louisville's ability to abide by this Order by attempting to enforce NCAA Bylaw 19.8" declares an NCAA Bylaw invalid within the Commonwealth of Kentucky and insulates U of L from restitutionary sanctions for allowing Lasege to participate as a member of its intercollegiate men's basketball team. . . .

By becoming a member of the NCAA, a voluntary athletic association, U of L agreed to abide by its rules and regulations. NCAA Bylaw 19.8 is one of those regulations, and it specifically provides that the NCAA can attempt to restore competitive equity by redistributing wins and losses and imposing sanctions upon a member institution which allows an ineligible player to participate under a subsequently-vacated court order, even if that order *requires* the institution to allow the player to participate. . . .

In fact, contrary to the belief of the trial court the concept of "risk-free" injunctive relief is unheard of—CR 65.05 requires the party in whose favor the injunction is granted to post a bond and wrongfully enjoined parties may recover compensatory damages. Here, U of L and the other NCAA members reached an agreement as to how competitive equity should be restored in the event of an erroneous court determination regarding a player's eligibility, and the trial court simply released U of L from that obligation.

The trial court's belief that the NCAA's Restitution Rule "thwarts the judicial power" is simply without foundation. NCAA Bylaw 19.8, like the Restitution Rules enforced by many state high school athletic associations "does not purport to authorize interference with any court order during the time it remains in effect, but only authorizes restitutive penalties when a temporary restraining order is ultimately dissolved and the challenged eligibility rule remains undisturbed in force." The authority of the courts is thus in no way compromised, and NCAA Bylaw 19.8 merely allows for post-hoc equalization when a trial court's erroneously granted temporary injunction upsets competitive balance. If the trial court's preliminary conclusions carry the day, and a student-athlete's eligibility is confirmed by final determination, no restitutionary remedy is warranted or appropriate, and NCAA Bylaw 19.8 provides for none.

The trial court's curt conclusion that NCAA Bylaw 19.8 "prevents parties from availing themselves of the protections of the courts" does not disclose the basis for this opinion. Perhaps the trial court believed that NCAA Bylaw 19.8 would deter aggrieved student-athletes from seeking judicial redress because of fears that their efforts would only hurt their teams in the long-run. Perhaps the trial court believed that the bylaw created a disincentive for NCAA member institutions to allow players whose eligibility has not yet been finally adjudicated to play in games or other athletic events. Neither conclusion would justify the trial court's order. The decision to seek injunctive relief will always involve a calculated risk on the part of the plaintiff, and those with meritorious claims will decide to proceed. Rather than changing the rules in the middle of the game, trial courts should consider the possibility that an erroneous decision could result in restitutionary sanctions against a student-athlete's institution when they balance the equities.

We recognize that the Court of Appeals reached a different conclusion in one paragraph in *Hopkins*—a case in which the parties did not seek discretionary review in this Court. For the reasons explained above, we find this conclusion unsound, and we overrule *Hopkins* to the extent that it holds that injunctive relief prohibiting a voluntary athletic association from seeking agreed-upon restitutionary sanctions is appropriate.

Accordingly, we vacate that portion of the temporary injunction which prohibits the NCAA from potentially pursuing NCAA Bylaw 19.8 restitution. . . .

V. Conclusion

For the reasons outlined above, we find "extraordinary cause" warranting CR 65.09 relief and vacate the trial court's temporary injunction in its entirety.

COOPER, GRAVES and STUMBO, JJ., concur.

JOHNSTONE, J., dissents by separate opinion with LAMBERT, C.J. and WINTERSHEIMER, J., joining that dissent. . . .

Williams v. University of Cincinnati is a case in which the athlete sues the university but alleges that his academic ineligibility was due to a conspiracy between the school and the NCAA on the basis that the NCAA allowed the university an extension of time to complete an investigation into the student's athletic eligibility.

WILLIAMS V. UNIVERSITY OF CINCINNATI

752 N.E.2d 367 (Ohio Ct. Cl. 2001)

Fred J. SHOEMAKER, Judge.

On April 16, 1996, plaintiff, Charles Williams, signed a National Letter of Intent ("NLI") as a prospect to enroll at the University of Cincinnati ("UC") and to play basketball. Prior to signing the NLI, plaintiff had signed a four-page document that specifically stated his rights and responsibilities under the NLI. As required, the NLI was also signed by a parent of plaintiff and by the director of athletics at UC. The express terms of this NLI obligated UC to provide a scholarship to Williams, providing he was academically eligible to enroll as a full-time student at UC. The NLI would become null and void if plaintiff did not graduate from junior college. He was expected to graduate from Chaffey Junior College ("Chaffey") in the summer of 1996.

In the summer of 1996, plaintiff took three courses from other universities in order to obtain additional credits necessary for graduation from Chaffey in August 1996. At Compton Junior College ("Compton") he dropped a math class but passed reading and composition. He also took Introductory Elementary Algebra at Los Angeles Trade Technology Junior College ("L.A. Trade Tech") from May 27, 1996 through August 17, 1996. On or about August 8, 1996, plaintiff became aware that he would receive a grade of "D" in that course, meaning that the credits would not transfer to Chaffey. Obviously, at this point, plaintiff was not academically eligible to play basketball for UC in the 1996-1997 basketball season. Plaintiff previously had dropped out of high school, and subsequently earned a GED. Now plaintiff created more problems for himself and UC by not earning the necessary summer credits at the junior colleges.

Coach George Tarkanian, basketball coach at Compton, and Assistant UC Coach John Loyer, with plaintiff's knowledge and consent, immediately tried to help plaintiff earn credits at UC even though the final summer term had already begun. Plaintiff enrolled in Introduction to Physical Geography, Physical Geography Lab, and Business Computer Applications during the third summer session from August 5 through 27. The Physical Geography Lab met from 9:40 a.m. to 12:30 p.m., while the Business Computer Applications course met from 9:40 a.m. to 11:30 a.m. Monday through Friday. Because the overlapping schedule would result in plaintiff's missing at least one-third of his class time, some basketball staff members took notes and personally contacted the professors of these classes. Furthermore, Coach Loyer requested that the professors accept written reports for extra credit for both classes. The lab professor accepted written reports; however, the business computer professor refused. Plaintiff wanted to qualify for the 1996-1997 basketball season and Coach Loyer tried to help. Coach Tarkanian provided the money for the classes and for airfare from California to Cincinnati. Coach Loyer made arrangements for plaintiff's enrollment.

Despite his academic background and lack of attendance at the physical geography and physical geography lab, plaintiff obtained sufficient grades in these courses to qualify for credit at Chaffey. However, plaintiff received an "F" in the Business Computer Applications course. Therefore, plaintiff again failed to qualify academically to graduate from Chaffey. Again, Coach Tarkanian and Coach Loyer tried to help plaintiff by paying fees and finding a professor who was willing to teach a math course on a "one-to-one" basis. In late August 1996, plaintiff received permission for his late enrollment in Introduction to Algebra, a mathematics course taught by Bill Swisher, a professor based at Clermont College of UC. Swisher authorized plaintiff's enrollment on August 28, even though plaintiff's formal enrollment did not occur until September 5, seven days after the end of the ten-week summer term (June 10 through August 29). To accomplish this arrangement, Swisher enrolled plaintiff just a day before the end of the term and issued plaintiff a grade of "incomplete." Swisher then taught the course to plaintiff daily in one-to-one sessions for approximately thirteen days. Plaintiff received a "B" grade for the course. Therefore, plaintiff graduated from Chaffey and became eligible to play basketball for UC in the fall of 1996.

On January 28, 1997, the National Collegiate Athletic Association ("NCAA") sent a letter of inquiry to the UC athletic director questioning plaintiff's academic eligibility. The letter reads as follows:

> The NCAA enforcement staff is currently reviewing the large quantity of credit hours earned during summer sessions by several prospective and, in some cases, enrolled student-athletes at Compton Community College (Compton, California).
>
> The available information indicates that some student-athletes did not perform appropriate academic work for some courses but received credit for the courses. Based upon the information, it appears that men's basketball student-athlete Charles Williams was enrolled at Compton during the summer of 1996 and earned an undisclosed number of hours. The staff is aware that Williams attended Chaffey Junior College through the spring of 1996 and would like more complete information concerning the young man's academic record while enrolled in junior college."

As a result of the letter, representatives of UC interviewed plaintiff and many other persons. Plaintiff admitted he took two courses at Compton, even though he was formally enrolled at Chaffey, that he enrolled in a math class at Compton, that he dropped the class because it was held too early (8:00 a.m.), and that he passed his reading and composition course at Compton.

UC had a concern that plaintiff may have been academically ineligible to play basketball under NCAA rules. The consequences of playing an academically ineligible player are very serious to UC and to other student-athletes. The NCAA could forfeit games, suspend UC from tournament competition, and cause bad publicity and loss of television revenues. UC, therefore, suspended plaintiff from the last three games of the regular season and from any post-season tournament games.

UC retained the law firm of Bond, Schoeneck and King out of Kansas City, Missouri, to investigate whether there were NCAA rule violations with regard to the UC's men's basketball program. The investigation not only was quite lengthy but it also involved other student-athletes. UC was granted an extension for filing the self-report as required by NCAA rules. The self-report was filed on October 16, 1997. From January 1997 until October 16, 1997, UC provided periodic verbal reports to the NCAA enforcement staff; and, when appropriate, an enforcement staff representative would participate. The October 16 report consisted of sixty-six pages, plus exhibits, and accurately reflected evidence that UC had obtained at that time. UC advised the NCAA of the following corrective measures:

IV. Corrective Measures

The University of Cincinnati recognizes that the foregoing violations are serious matters that require corrective action. In examining these violations, it has been determined that each is related to men's basketball prospective student-athletes arriving and residing in Cincinnati, Ohio, during the summer prior to their initial full-time enrollment at the University. To address the institution's vulnerability to potential violations arising from these situations, the athletics department has developed additional policies to improve internal communication and to enhance its ability to monitor compliance with NCAA rules in this area. . . .

After UC filed its self-report related to violations of NCAA rules, the NCAA responded on May 5, 1998, with multiple inquiries. UC responded to those inquiries on June 29, 1998. Eventually, a formal hearing was held before the NCAA in Seattle, Washington. The NCAA issued a final ruling that virtually mirrored the findings and conclusions of the committee as set forth in the letter of October 29, 1997. In short, plaintiff regained eligibility for the last six games of the 1997-1998 basketball season at UC as well as USA Conference and NCAA championship games.

Even though plaintiff remained on scholarship throughout the NCAA proceedings, plaintiff dropped out of UC in December 1997, before completing his classes for the fall quarter and before his eligibility was restored.

Ultimately, plaintiff enrolled in the University of California at Bakersfield, a Division II school, on a full scholarship. After five games, plaintiff developed problems involving a prior injury. Although he returned to play five more games, he voluntarily quit the team and dropped out of school. Currently he is assisting Coach Tarkanian at Compton.

Breach of Written Contract Claim

The NLI, by its express terms, both commits a student-athlete to attend a particular college or university and commits that college or university to provide the student-athlete with a scholarship for at least one year. UC never rescinded plaintiff's scholarship. The NCAA, not UC, determined that plaintiff would be ineligible for one basketball season. The NCAA is not a party in this case.

The major concern in this case is that plaintiff was obliged to become academically eligible in order to be admitted to the fall quarter of 1996 at UC. Plaintiff was expected to graduate from Chaffey in the summer of 1996, but he failed to meet that obligation. Coach Tarkanian of Compton and members of the UC basketball staff, with plaintiff's consent, tried to remedy the situation by acquiring eligibility for plaintiff for the 1996-1997 basketball season. Plaintiff received unusual financial support from Coach Tarkanian and unusual academic support by Professor Bill Swisher and others. Without such support, plaintiff would not have been academically eligible to participate in the 1996-1997 basketball season. In addition, plaintiff added to his problems by failing courses at junior college and again at UC.

As stated earlier, it was the inquiry from the NCAA that caused the investigation of plaintiff and other student-athletes in the UC basketball program. UC was required to promptly investigate recruiting policies in place at UC in general and recruiting of plaintiff in particular. UC wanted plaintiff's eligibility to be restored for the 1997-1998 basketball season. However, as a member of the NCAA, UC had no authority to reverse the NCAA decision. UC consistently maintained that Swisher did not violate any UC policy by teaching the one-to-one algebra course in early September 1996. The NCAA made the "inquiry" and made the final judgment on the penalty regarding plaintiff.

The basic purpose of the NLI is to formally recognize a student-athlete's intent to attend UC. The primary obligation imposed upon plaintiff was to graduate from a junior college and attend UC for at least one year. The primary obligation imposed upon UC was to provide plaintiff with "an award for athletics financial aid" for one year.

Quite frankly, it was plaintiff who breached the terms of the NLI by his poor academic performance. UC never rescinded his scholarship. . . .

The financial aid agreements between UC and plaintiff constitute valid contracts. UC performed all obligations imposed by the financial aid agreements. UC cannot control the actions taken by the NCAA regarding plaintiff's request for restoration of his eligibility to play basketball for UC. Contrary to UC's position, the NCAA treated the Swisher one-to-one course as an extra benefit. Without this course, plaintiff would not have been eligible for the 1996-1997 season. Therefore, he would not have been entitled to a free college education.

Based on the totality of the evidence, plaintiff has failed to prove his breach-of-contract claim by a preponderance of the evidence.

Defamation Claim . . .

Oral Contract/Promissory Estoppel

Plaintiff argues that UC failed to do everything it could have done in terms of investigating plaintiff's alleged violation of NCAA rules. Plaintiff also contends that the investigation should have been completed sooner. Plaintiff claims that UC had an obligation to thoroughly instruct him in every aspect of the NCAA rules and that he lost his eligibility because he relied to his detriment upon Coach Loyer's advice. . . .

Intentional Infliction of Emotional Distress . . .

Conspiracy . . .

In conclusion, plaintiff has failed to prove any of his claims by a preponderance of the evidence. Therefore judgment will be rendered for defendant.

Judgment for defendant.

2. Death Penalty

Without doubt, the most serious NCAA penalty is the aptly described "death penalty." Even the threat of it transforms the alleged perpetrator.

Southern Methodist University, of course, is the best known case of a university receiving the death penalty. It was disclosed that numerous boosters and high-ranking officials, including members of the university board of trustees, had been implicated in numerous rule violations. In addition, the State of Texas then enacted a statute that made it a civil offense to violate NCAA rules, holding violators liable for damages suffered by the school as a result of NCAA sanctions. Tex. Civ. Prac. & Rem. Code §§131.001 *et seq.*

The 'death penalty' (§7-(d), NCAA Enforcement Procedures) reads as follows:

> An institution shall be considered a repeat violator if major violations are found within the five-year period following the starting date of a major penalty. The minimum penalty for a repeat violator, subject to expectations authorized by the Committee on Infractions in unique cases on the basis of specifically stated reasons, shall include:
>
> 1. the prohibition of some or all outside competition of the sport involved in the latest major violation for one or two sports seasons and the prohibition of all coaching staff members in that sport from involvement, directly and indirectly, in any coaching activates at the institution during a two-year period;
> 2. the elimination of all initial grants-in-aid and all recruiting activities of the sport involved in the latest major violation in question for a two-year period;
> 3. the requirement that all institutional staff members serving on the NCAA President's Commission, Council, Executive Committee, or other committees of the Association resign those positions, it being understood that all institutional representatives shall be ineligible to serve on any NCAA committee for a period of four years, and;
> 4. The requirement that the institution relinquish its voting privilege in the Association for a four-year period.

The severe price can last for more than two years, with the result that the team is disbanded for that period. The death penalty is reserved specifically for repeat offenders. The NCAA's goal is for it to have a chilling effect on potential future offenders and to facilitate self-policing by member schools.

QUESTIONS AND DISCUSSION

1. *See* Smith, *The National Collegiate Athletic Association's Death Penalty: How Educators Punish Themselves and Others*, 62 Ind. L.J. 985 (1986-1987). *See also* Heller, *Preparing for the Storm: The Representation of a University Accused of Violating NCAA Regulations*, 7 Marq. Sports L.J. 295 (1996). Is it realistic for universities to "punish themselves" in an attempt to deflect possible NCAA sanctions?

2. In *Howard University v. NCAA*, 510 F.2d 213 (D.C. Cir. 1975), a soccer player was declared ineligible, and, as a result, the NCAA imposed sanctions on his school; and, as mandated by NCAA rules, the university assessed penalties against the athlete. Three rules were involved, the "five-year rule," the "1.600 rule," and the "foreign-student rule," which penalized foreign student—athletes for summer amateur participation even though American athletes could freely compete; the latter rule created an unconstitutional alienage classification. In *Howard*, the NCAA was viewed as a state actor, but of course *Howard* was decided in 1975 and the U.S. Supreme Court determined in 1988 that the NCAA was not a state actor in *Tarkanian*. The NCAA lost in *Howard*. Why was the "foreign-student rule" deemed to be an unconstitutional classification?

3. The NCAA's rules behind the probation in *Colorado Seminary* were not unconstitutional since the offending hockey player's interest in participation did not rise to the level of a constitutionally protected property or liberty interest based on arbitrary classifications that affect race, religion, or national origin. How could you change the facts to change the result? If this case were Canadian, should the decision be comparable to *Howard Univ. v. NCAA*?

4. *Hairston* held that the players failed to show that the NCAA's sanctions constituted an unreasonable restraint of trade under the Sherman Act and that the players were not third-party beneficiaries of contracts between conference and its university members. Why did these football players choose antitrust and breach of contract as their cause of actions? Are there other possible legal theories that might have proven more successful?

5. Does *Williams v. University of Cincinnati* take the right approach? The university withdrew the scholarship. Should there be any penalties for what in effect was a premature announcement of a relationship between player and school?

6. What is the restitution rule? What are restitutionary sanctions? Was the school's agreement in *NCAA v. Lasege* truly voluntary?

7. The Supreme Court of Texas in *Jones v. NCAA,* 1 S.W.3d 83 (Tex. 1999), held than an appeal from an order granting a temporary injunction was not moot since the NCAA might issue retroactive penalties under the "restitution rule" against the school even though the football season had ended and the student had completed his eligibility. Does this rule violate public policy?

CHAPTER 11

WOMEN AND SPORTS

Discrimination and Harassment against female amateur athletes have been implemented by numerous methods that limit athletic opportunities. These methods range from exclusionary school regulations to rules that are not discriminatory on their face but that discriminate in the method by which they are applied.

Schools and other institutions have failed to provide equal funding, facilities, and opportunities to female athletes, coaches, and managers. **Title IX** of the 1972 Education Amendments was promulgated to solve these problems: It prohibits any federally funded educational program from engaging in discrimination.

The **Equal Protection** Clause of the Fourteenth Amendment also protects female athletes. Claims made under the Equal Protection Clause must involve a state action; after that determination is made, the next step is to decide if the athletic program's provisions or the enforcement of its prohibitions violate equal protection. Equal protection claims can be combined with Title IX suits and also those based on **State ERAs** (Equal Rights Amendments).

Actions based on a particular state's ERA have an important advantage since state courts can determine under state law whether gender classifications are suspect. If they are determined to be suspect, they then warrant strict scrutiny as a standard of review. However, not all states have passed ERAs.

A. DISCRIMINATION AND HARASSMENT

Sex discrimination has occurred in almost every aspect of sports, including different rules in girls sports, less opportunities for girls to participate in amateur sports, and a paternalistic view that girls were too frail to meaningfully participate in sports.

Sex discrimination is most vividly illustrated by the manner in which opportunities have been limited. Opportunities have been curtailed by school regulations ranging from rules that exclude girls from participation in athletic programs to rules that are not per se discriminatory but discriminate in the method by which they are applied. Discrimination is also manifested by the failure to provide equal funding, facilities, or opportunities for female athletes, coaches, and managers. Methods that have been introduced to ameliorate these concerns have coalesced into three basic types: "separate but equal," "mixed competition," and the "component approach."

Many rules, historically different for females, were demeaning and paternalistic. There are many vestiges of the more onerous rules that still remain, for example, 300 meter hurdles for girls in high school as opposed to 400 meter hurdles for boys and the heptathlon (seven sports) for girls in track and field as opposed to the ten-sport decathlon for boys. *Dodson v. Arkansas Activities Assn.,* 468 F. Supp. 394 (E.D. Ark. 1979) involved half-court basketball for high school girls, but full-court for boys. The court struck down this rule and reasoned that paternalistic tradition alone was insufficient justification for the different rules.

Similarly, in *Israel v. West Virginia Secondary Schools Activities Commission,* the court held that a skilled female baseball player had the right to at least try out for the high school team, even though that school did have softball as an alleged option.

ISRAEL V. WEST VIRGINIA SECONDARY SCHOOLS ACTIVITIES COMMISSION

388 S.E.2d 480 (W. Va. 1989)

MILLER, Justice:

Erin Israel, by her next friend, Patricia Israel, appeals from a final order of the Circuit Court of Pleasants County, entered February 11, 1988, denying her request for a declaratory judgment, injunctive relief, and damages on the basis of alleged gender discrimination. On appeal, Ms. Israel asserts that she was discriminated against in violation of the Equal Protection Clause of the Fourteenth Amendment of the United States Constitution and its state counterpart, Article III, Section 17 of the West Virginia Constitution, as well as the Human Rights Act, W. Va. Code, 5-11-1, et seq. (1987). We have reviewed the record and find reversible error; therefore, we reverse the judgment of the Circuit Court of Pleasants County and remand the case for further proceedings consistent with this opinion.

Ms. Israel has a great deal of experience playing baseball. She began playing baseball at the age of six in the local park and recreation league where she learned the basic fundamentals of the game. At the age of nine, Ms. Israel progressed into the Little League system. . . . While playing Little League, Ms. Israel was nominated for every all-star team. At the age of thirteen, she became the first female to ever play on a Pony League team in Pleasants County. When Ms. Israel was a freshman at St. Marys High School, and expressed a desire to play on the all-male baseball team, the high school baseball coach told her he had no objections to her playing for him and promised to give her a fair tryout. In February, 1984, Ms. Israel tried out for the all-male high school baseball team. She was prohibited from playing on the team because of a regulation promulgated by the Secondary Schools Activities Commission (SSAC).

The Board of Education of the County of Pleasants (Board) is a member of the SSAC. The SSAC is a nonprofit organization created by

W. Va. Code, 18-2-25 (1967), which authorizes county boards of education to delegate their supervisory authority over interscholastic athletic events and band activities to the SSAC. . . . In the exercise of its delegated authority, the SSAC adopted Rule No. 3.9, which provides:

> If a school maintains separate teams in the same or related sports (example: baseball or softball) for girls and boys during the school year, regardless of the sports season, girls may not participate on boys' teams and boys may not participate on girls' teams. However, should a school not maintain separate teams in thesame or related sports for boys and girls, then boys and girls may participate on the same team except in contact sports such as football and wrestling.

Shortly after Ms. Israel tried out to play on the baseball team, she was informed by St. Marys' assistant principal that she was ineligible to play on the baseball team because St. Marys had a girls' softball team. The assistant principal explained that if the school allowed Ms. Israel to play baseball, it would be in violation of Rule 3.9 and would be barred from playing in state tournaments. After numerous futile efforts to have the rule changed through the internal mechanisms provided by the SSAC, Ms. Israel filed a complaint with the Human Rights Commission (Commission).

The Commission issued Ms. Israel a right-to-sue letter, and she filed this action against the SSAC and the Board on April 18, 1986, in the Circuit Court of Pleasants County. The circuit court exonerated the Board, finding that it had made a good-faith effort to have the SSAC change the rule and that if the Board had ignored Rule 3.9, it would have been subject to severe sanctions by the SSAC. Ms. Israel does not appeal this ruling. She does appeal the circuit court's decision that the SSAC rule was valid.

II. Equal Protection

Equal protection of the law is implicated when a classification treats similarly situated persons in a disadvantageous manner. The claimed discrimination must be a product of state action as distinguished from a purely private activity.

A. Fourteenth Amendment Equal Protection

In analyzing gender-based discrimination, the United States Supreme Court has been willing to take into account actual differences between the sexes, including physical ones. . . . On the other hand, the court has disapproved classifications that reflect "archaic and overbroad generalizations."

Under the United States Constitution, a genderbased discrimination is subject to a level of scrutiny somewhere between the traditional equal protection analysis and the highest level of scrutiny utilized for suspect classes. . . .

Under the middle-tier analysis for gender-based discrimination claims, courts have recognized that it is constitutionally permissible under certain circumstances for public schools to maintain separate sports teams for males and females so long as they are substantially equivalent. . . .

From the record in this case, we find that the games of baseball and softball are not substantially equivalent. . . . However, when the rules are analyzed, there is a substantial disparity in the equipment used and in the skill level required. The difference begins with the size of the ball and its delivery, and differences continue throughout. The softball is larger and must be thrown underhand, which forecloses the different types of pitching that can be accomplished in the overhand throw of a baseball.

There are ten players on the softball team and nine on a baseball team. The distance between the bases in softball is sixty feet, while in baseball it is ninety feet. The pitcher's mound is elevated in baseball and is not in softball. The distance from the pitcher's mound to home plate is sixty feet in baseball and only forty feet in softball. In baseball, a bat of forty-two inches is permitted, while in softball the maximum length is thirty-four inches.

Moreover, the skill level is much more demanding in baseball because the game is played at a more vigorous pace. There are more intangible rewards available if one can make the baseball team. For a skilled player, such as the record demonstrates Ms. Israel to be, it would be deeply frustrating to be told she could not try out for the baseball team, not because she did not possess the necessary skills, but only because she was female. The entire thrust of the equal protection doctrine is to avoid this type of artificial distinction based solely on gender.

We agree with the SSAC that by providing a softball team for females, it was promoting more athletic opportunities for females. However, this purpose does not satisfy the equal protection mandate requiring substantial equivalency. We do not believe that by permitting females to try out for the boys' baseball team, a mass exodus from the girls' softball team will result. There are obvious practical considerations that will forestall such a result. Gender does not provide an automatic admission to play on a boys' baseball team. The team is selected from those who apply and possess the requisite skill to make the team. What we deal with in this case is an opportunity to have a chance to try out for the team. . . .

We have in Part II(A), *supra*, analyzed and applied equal protection principles and found that the regulation, as it relates to the games of baseball and softball, fails to meet the substantially equivalent standard. Since this same standard applies under our Human Rights Act, we need not repeat the analysis here.

Ms. Israel does, however, claim her right to reasonable attorney's fees pursuant to W. Va. Code, 5-11-13(c), and we accord her such a right. This case is, therefore, remanded to the circuit court for a determination of her reasonable attorney's fees.

Reversed and remanded.

———————

But, in these types of cases, plaintiff must still prove the alleged discriminatory action or inaction was tainted or motivated by gender bias. In *Croteau v. Fair*, a female high school student who was cut from the varsity baseball team was unable to disprove that this decision was made in good faith and for reasons unrelated to gender.

CROTEAU v. FAIR

686 F. Supp. 552 (E.D. Va. 1988)

ELLIS, District Judge.

Plaintiff is a seventeen year old senior at Osbourn Park Senior High School. On February 20, 1988, she "tried out" for the School's varsity baseball team, which has never before had a female participant. She successfully passed the first "cut." On March 4, 1988, however, plaintiff was cut from the team by defendant Rick Fair, the varsity baseball coach, with the advice and concurrence of Posey Howell, the junior varsity baseball coach. Plaintiff asserts that she was qualified to play for the team, but was cut because she is a female. She brought this suit by her parents and next friends, on March 14, 1988, asserting that she was discriminated against because of her sex, in violation of (i) the Fourteenth Amendment, (ii) Title 42 U.S.C. §1983, (iii) Section 11 Art. 1 of the Virginia Constitution, and (iv) Title IX of the Education Amendments of 1972 (20 U.S.C. §1681 et seq.). Plaintiff seeks preliminary and permanent injunctive relief, compensatory damages in the amount of $100,000, and attorneys' fees.

This matter came before the Court initially on plaintiff's motion for a temporary restraining order. By Order dated March 21, 1988, this Court denied plaintiff's motion and, in lieu thereof, scheduled a full hearing on plaintiff's Complaint for Tuesday, March 22, 1988. During this hearing, at the close of plaintiff's evidence, defendants moved for a dismissal of the Complaint pursuant to Rule 41(b), Fed. R. Civ. P., on the ground that upon the facts and the law plaintiff had shown no right to relief. Based on the findings of fact and conclusions of law stated from the bench, it is hereby ordered:

That defendant's motion to dismiss the Complaint is granted.

In sex discrimination cases brought under the Fourteenth Amendment, plaintiff must demonstrate that the discrimination was intentional. Discriminatory intent can be measured by considering the following four factors: (1) the historical background of the decision; (2) the specific sequence of events; (3) the departure from normal procedures; and (4) contemporary statements by the individual(s) making the decision. Plaintiff need only show, however, "that the underlying discriminatory purpose is a motivating factor; in need not be the sole, or even the dominant factor."

Here, plaintiff has failed to prove that the decision to cut her from the varsity baseball team was tainted or motivated, in whole or in part, by gender bias. Rather the Court is convinced that plaintiff received a fair tryout and that the decision to cut her was made in good faith and for reasons unrelated to gender. . . .

Given the Court's finding that no gender discrimination occurred here, all causes of action in plaintiff's Complaint (*i.e.,* Fourteenth Amendment claim,

Title 42 U.S.C. §1983 claim, and Va. Const. Art. 1, §11 claim) should be and are dismissed. The parties shall bear their own costs.

The Clerk is directed to send copies of this Order to all counsel of record.

In *Wynn v. Columbus Municipal Separate School District*, a female physical education teacher sued the school district that denied her application to the position of athletic director. The court held that the defendants discriminated against the teacher on the basis of gender by refusing to appoint her.

WYNN V. COLUMBUS MUNICIPAL SEPARATE SCHOOL DISTRICT

692 F. Supp. 672 (N.D. Miss. 1988)

DAVIDSON, District Judge.

In this action plaintiff Bertha Wynn ("Wynn") sues the Columbus Municipal Separate School District ("Columbus Schools"), Board of Trustees members, . . . Superintendent James V. Carr, Jr. ("Carr"), and Charles V. Newell ("Newell"), Principal of Lee High School, charging that she was unlawfully discriminated against on the basis of her sex in connection with the denial of her application for the position of Athletic Director at Lee High School in Columbus, Mississippi, in violation of Title VII of the Civil Rights Act of 1964, 42 U.S.C. Section 2000e, *et seq.* ("Title VII").

After a trial on the merits on this action, the court now sets forth its findings of fact and conclusions of law pursuant to the requirements of Rule 52(a) of the Federal Rules of Civil Procedure.

I. Findings of Fact

Plaintiff Wynn, a female, is a resident of Columbus, Lowndes County, Mississippi. At trial, Wynn testified that she graduated from Mississippi University for Women in 1963 with a Bachelors degree in Physical Education. Wynn was employed by Columbus Schools as a physical education instructor at Lee High School ("Lee High") commencing in 1963. Wynn later received her Master's degree at Mississippi State University in 1971. Wynn has been employed continuously by Columbus Schools since 1963.

During her tenure at Lee High, Wynn has taught girls' physical education classes and has coached various girls' athletic teams. In the course of her employment as a physical education teacher, Wynn explained, she has initiated several female sports programs which did not exist at Lee High prior to her employment in 1963. These sports include girls' volleyball, basketball, and softball, among others.

At the time of Wynn's initial employment by Columbus Schools in 1963, Billy Brewer was employed as Head Football Coach and Athletic Director at Lee High. Brewer had occupied these roles since 1961 and continued to serve in the dual capacity of Head Football Coach and Athletic Director until his resignation in 1969. As Mr. James V. Carr ("Carr"), retired Superintendent of schools and later the principal of Lee High performed the Athletic Director duties after Brewer's resignation.

Some time in April 1977, however, the Board of Trustees ("Board") called together all coaches in the Columbus Schools to discuss problems with the overall athletic program and to ascertain why the City of Columbus was not supporting the athletic programs of the Columbus Schools. Apparently, as a result of this 1977 meeting, the Board made the decision to return to the earlier practice of a combined position of Head Football Coach and Athletic Director.

In adopting this interim so-called "bifurcated" arrangement (i.e., separation of the Athletic Director duties from the Head Football Coach functions), the Board promulgated a separate job description for the Athletic Director sometime in 1971. When the positions were again combined in 1977, the Board made the proposed dual position a 12-month contract position (as compared to the previous 9-month contract for Athletic Director and Head Football Coach).

In 1981 the Board promulgated a supplemental "Job Description For Athletic Directors And Head Football Coach–Summer Months 1981." As Carr testified, the summer month duties were added when the Athletic Director and Head Football Coach position was extended to a 12-month contract position. No party to this lawsuit has offered a combined job description entitled Athletic Director/Head Football Coach. . . .

As several defense witnesses testified, the Board's decision to combine the Athletic Director and Head Football Coach functions after 1977 was based on the Trustees' perception that football was the "dominant" sport in the Columbus Schools. Since football was both the major revenue producer, as well as the single greatest cost item in the entire athletic program, the Board concluded that it was logical and reasonable to have the Head Football Coach also serve as Athletic Director. . . .

Meanwhile, in May 1984, the Board met at Lee High for their regular annual meeting at the school. At that time Newell inquired of the Board members concerning their plans for filling the Athletic Director's job. Newell explained that he felt the Athletic Director duties were becoming too heavy a load on him and that he desired some relief from the added responsibilities. Newell testified that the Trustees suggested he make a recommendation for Athletic Director and that appropriate action would then be taken.

Newell made his recommendation via letter dated May 9, 1984, recommending Wilkerson as Athletic Director at Lee High School for the 1984-85 school year. At the Board's regular May 1984 meeting, Newell's recommendation was ratified and Wilkerson was elected Athletic Director at Lee High for the 1984-85 school year.

Carr testified that it was his opinion, considering experience and knowledge of the school district and the entire athletic program, that Wynn was more qualified than Wilkerson. . . .

Mr. John East, a Board member at the time Wilkerson was elected as Athletic Director, testified that when the Board elected Wilkerson as Athletic Director on or about May 14, 1984, the Board gave no consideration to Wynn's or Wilkerson's gender in reaching its ultimate decision. Rather, East maintained, the Board's decision was influenced primarily by the fact that Wilkerson was qualified to serve as Head Football Coach while Wynn and Williford were not. . . .

On cross-examination, however, East conceded that the combination of Head Football Coach and Athletic Director effectively excluded women who were not qualified as Head Football Coach. As East put it, he would not say that a woman could never be Athletic Director, but it would be rare. Unless she could meet the requirements for becoming Head Football Coach, a woman could not act as Athletic Director under the combined position arrangement. . . .

After Wilkerson was elected as Athletic Director in May 1984, Wynn filed a timely charge of employment discrimination with the Equal Employment Opportunity Commission ("EEOC"), in which she complained that she had been discriminated against on the basis of her sex when she was not given the position of Athletic Director at Lee High. After the EEOC conducted an investigation, it issued Wynn a Right to Sue Letter sometime in December 1984. Wynn timely filed her complaint in this action on March 19, 1985.

The court finds that nowhere on the face of Plaintiff's Exhibit 5 is there any indication that the Athletic Director position is a combined position. . . .

Perhaps the most probative evidence that the Head Football Coach and Athletic Director positions are not one and the same is the unrefuted testimony of Jackie Culpepper, a female coach at Columbus Caldwell High School, the sister school to Lee High School. Culpepper testified that for the 1987-88 school year, Randy Martin was serving as Head Football Coach while Assistant Principal Sam Fletcher was performing the job of Athletic Director at Caldwell High School.

Culpepper's testimony, which was not objected to nor impeached on cross-examination, persuades the court that the supposedly combined position of Head Football Coach and Athletic Director is only a unified position when the Board chooses to appoint one person to perform both jobs. At the time Wynn applied for the position in February 1984, no decision had yet been made to combine or separate the two jobs. Rather, the Board's first action after plaintiff applied for the position was its decision in March 1984 to elect Bill Wilkerson as Head Football Coach at Lee High. Wilkerson was not elected as Athletic Director until May 1984, some three months after Wynn applied for that job. Thus, the job remained open after Wynn applied.

II. Conclusion of Law

In this sex discrimination case, the court has jurisdiction over the subject matter and the parties pursuant to 42 U.S.C. Section 2000e-5(f)(3). The provisions of Title VII, 42 U.S.C. Section 2000e, *et seq.,* only prohibit employment discrimination on the basis of race, color, religion, sex, or national origin.

The United States Supreme Court has ruled that the burden of proof in a Title VII case is upon the plaintiff to establish a *prima facie* case of discrimination. Once the plaintiff has put on a *prima facie* case, the defendant must introduce evidence of a legitimate, non-discriminatory reason for its actions. The plaintiff then has the opportunity to prove that the legitimate reasons offered by the defendant are in fact a pretext for discrimination. The court addresses each element of this three-pronged approach separately below.

A. Plaintiff's *Prima Facie* Case

To establish a *prima facie* case of sex discrimination, plaintiff must prove: (1) that she applied for an available position for which she was qualified; but, (2) that she was rejected "under circumstances that give rise to an inference of unlawful discrimination."

1. *Disparate Treatment*

Defendants argue initially that Wynn has failed to make out a *prima facie* case of disparate treatment because she did not apply for an "available" position for which she was qualified, having applied only for the Athletic Director "aspect" of the alleged "combined" position of Head Football Coach and Athletic Director. Defendants state that the Athletic Director "duties" never in fact existed as a separate, available position. The court rejects this contention. . . .

Based solely on the testimonial and documentary evidence adduced at trial, the court holds that plaintiff Wynn was qualified for the position of Athletic Director when she applied for same.

The court must next consider whether Wynn was rejected for the position of Athletic Director under circumstances which give rise to an inference of unlawful discrimination. At this juncture, the court must carefully consider that plaintiff, a female, was rejected along with another male applicant, Bob Williford, for the position. The court is of the opinion that this fact does not represent a fatal flaw in plaintiff's attempt to make out a *prima facie* case of sexually-motivated disparate treatment. . . .

The court is of the opinion that the discriminatory animus plaintiff seeks to prove, however, may reasonably be inferred from the basis of the defendants' decision not to elect Wynn as Athletic Director. As the defendants' witnesses testified, Wynn was not selected as Athletic Director primarily because the position required that the successful applicant also be able to serve as Head Football Coach, a position for which Wynn did not apply and admittedly could not perform.

Seen in its simplest terms, the decision not to appoint Wynn as Athletic Director was based on her sex because a female allegedly was not qualified to act as Head Football Coach and therefore was not qualified to become Head Football Coach and Athletic Director. In applying this requirement to Wynn, the defendants excluded her from consideration for the position while appointing a less-qualified male to fill the vacancy. The inference of discriminatory animus in this decision is clear.

Such wholesale exclusion of a class of job applicants based solely on their sex is valid only when the essence of the business would be undermined by not having members of one sex exclusively, or where the employer can establish some "bona fide occupational qualification" ("BFOQ") reasonably necessary to the normal operation of its enterprise.

Insofar as plaintiff, a protected class member under Title VII, applied for an available position for which she was qualified and which was filled by a lesser qualified and non-protected male the court holds that Wynn has made out a *prima facie* case of sexually motivated disparate treatment. Once the plaintiff has satisfied her burden of proving a *prima facie* case the court's inquiry proceeds to the next stage, requiring that the defendants articulate a legitimate, non-discriminatory reason for their actions.

2. *Disparate Impact*

Perhaps perceiving some weakness in her disparate treatment case, Wynn interposes at this juncture a disparate impact argument, contending that the requirement that the Athletic Director also serve as Head Football Coach has a disparate impact on females and unlawfully excludes female coaches from consideration for the position of Athletic Director. . . .

The disparate impact model is one which is often used by plaintiffs in Title VII cases but one which is often misunderstood or misapplied. . . .

In the case *sub judice*, plaintiff characterizes the requirement that Athletic Director also be qualified to act as Head Football Coach as a facially neutral, objective employment criterion which has a disparate impact on females seeking the position of Athletic Director. Although the court agrees that the requirement has a disparate impact on individuals seeking the Athletic Director position who are not qualified to serve as Head Football Coach—including male and female basketball, volleyball, track, and baseball coaches—the court is not convinced that the requirement has a disparate impact on females only. . . .

In view of the fact that Wynn is the only female coach who has ever applied for the position of Athletic Director within the Columbus Schools, the court concludes that she has failed to establish a *prima facie* case of disparate impact inasmuch as she has failed to establish a causal connection between the requirement that Athletic Director also serve as Head Football Coach and any *actual* effect of excluding a disproportionate number of members of a protected class from employment opportunities. Plaintiff has shown no pattern and practice on the part of Columbus Schools of denying all or a significant number of female applicants consideration for the job of Athletic Director. Plaintiff's statistical proof has little probative value and has been disregarded by the court. It is beyond dispute that "Title VII, however, does not demand that an employer give preferential treatment to minorities or women."

The court holds that although Wynn applied for an available position for which she was qualified and for which she was rejected, Wynn has failed to make out a *prima facie* case of sexually-motivated disparate impact. Plaintiff's disparate impact proof fails to show that Columbus Schools practiced any distinguishable pattern of rejecting female applicants for Athletic Director. Plaintiff has made out a *prima facie* case on her alternate theory of recovery, disparate treatment.

B. Defendants' Legitimate, Non-Discriminatory Reason . . .

Defendants do not and could not seriously contend that the position of Athletic Director poses any danger of physical harm to females or that females are physically incapable of performing the duties of the Athletic Director position. . . .

The thrust of the defendants' argument in response to the plaintiff's disparate treatment claim is that because football is the predominant sport at Lee High School in Columbus, Lowndes County, Mississippi the requirement that the athletic director also be the head football coach constitutes a "bona fide occupational qualification" (BFOQ). Yet the proof in the case *sub judice* reveals that from 1969 to 1977 and from March 1984 to June 1984 the positions were separated at Lee High School. Further at Caldwell High School in Columbus the positions are currently separated. Also at the Lowndes County high schools at New Hope and Caledonia the head football coach is not the athletic director. . . .

C. Pretext

The court holds that the defendants have failed to rebut plaintiff's *prima facie* case. . . .

III. Conclusion

As the Supreme Court has stated time after time, the plaintiff always retains the "ultimate burden of persuading the court that she has been a victim of intentional discrimination." The court concludes as a matter of law that plaintiff has met that burden in the case at bar.

Accordingly, plaintiff is entitled to a judgment and is entitled to be made whole. Plaintiff is entitled to appropriate equitable relief, including placement into the Athletic Director's position and an award of back pay for those earnings she was denied as a result of the defendants' actions in violation of Title VII.

A separate order and judgment consistent with this opinion will be entered.

In *Postema v. National League of Professional Baseball Clubs*, former umpire Pam Postema was able to establish that a material issue of fact existed as to whether the American League was involved in her termination by a minor league that precluded summary judgment on her Title VII claim. Additionally, the court held that baseball's antitrust exemption did not allow baseball blanket immunity for anticompetitive behavior in every context in which it operates.

POSTEMA V. NATIONAL LEAGUE OF PROFESSIONAL BASEBALL CLUBS

799 F. Supp. 1475 (S.D.N.Y. 1992)

Robert P. PATTERSON, Jr., District Judge.

This is an action for damages and injunctive relief alleging employment discrimination in violation of: (1) Title VII of the Civil Rights Act of 1964, as amended by the Civil Rights Act of 1991, 42 U.S.C. §2000e-2(a)(1); (2) New York's Human Rights Law, N.Y. Exec. L. §296; and (3) the common law of restraint of trade.

Defendant American League of Professional Baseball Clubs ("American League") moves: (a) pursuant to Rule 56 of the Federal Rules of Civil Procedure for summary judgment on Plaintiff's Title VII claim, or in the alternative, pursuant to Rule 12(b)(6) for dismissal of Plaintiff's request for a jury trial and prayer for compensatory and punitive damages; (b) pursuant to Rule 12(b)(6) of the Federal Rules of Civil Procedure for dismissal of Plaintiff's Human Rights Law claim, or in the alternative, dismissal of Plaintiff's request for a jury trial and prayer for punitive damages; and (c) pursuant to Rules 12(b)(1) and 12(b)(6) of the Federal Rules of Civil Procedure for dismissal of Plaintiff's common law restraint of trade claim.

Defendants National League of Professional Baseball Clubs ("National League"), Triple-A Alliance of Professional Baseball Clubs ("Triple-A"), and the Baseball Office for Umpire Development ("BOUD") join in parts (b) and (c) of the American League's motion.

For the reasons set forth below, the motions are granted in part and denied in part.

Background

For her complaint, Plaintiff alleges the following.

I. The Parties

Plaintiff Pamela Postema, a California resident, is a former professional baseball umpire.

Defendant National League is an unincorporated association of professional baseball clubs that constitute the National League, one of the two major leagues of professional baseball. The National League has its principal place of business and headquarters in New York City.

Defendant American League is an unincorporated association of professional baseball clubs that constitute the American League, the other major league of professional baseball. The American League also has its principal place of business and headquarters in New York City.

Defendant Triple-A is an unincorporated association of minor league professional baseball clubs that constitute and operate the Triple-A Alliance minor league. Triple-A consists of AAA-rated baseball clubs that were formerly members of two separate AAA minor leagues, the American Association and the International League. Triple-A has its principal place of business and headquarters in Grove City, Ohio.

Triple-A and the other minor leagues of professional baseball are members of the National Association of Professional Baseball Leagues (the "National Association"), an unincorporated association of minor leagues in the United States. The National Association, which is not a party to this action, has its principal place of business in New York City. The National League, American League, and the National Association are all subject to the common oversight and direction of the Commissioner of Baseball.

Defendant BOUD is an unincorporated affiliate of the other Defendants and of the National Association. Its principal place of business and headquarters is in St. Petersburg, Florida. BOUD is vested with responsibility for finding, evaluating, overseeing, training, developing, and supervising umpires for professional baseball games played by members of the National Association.

II. Events Underlying This Lawsuit

After graduating from umpiring school with the rank of 17th in a class of 130 students, Plaintiff began work in 1977 as a professional baseball umpire in the Gulf Coast League, a rookie league. At that time, she was the fourth woman ever to umpire a professional baseball game. Plaintiff worked in the Gulf Coast League during 1977 and 1978. In 1979, she was promoted to the Class A Florida State League, where she umpired during the 1979 and 1980 seasons. In 1981, Plaintiff was promoted to the AA Texas League, and she umpired there in 1981 and 1982. She was the first woman to ever umpire a professional baseball game above the Class A level.

In 1983, Plaintiff was promoted to the AAA Pacific Coast League, where she umpired from 1983 to 1986. In 1987, her contract was acquired by Triple-A, and she umpired in that league from 1987 until her discharge in 1989.

Plaintiff alleges that during her employment as a Triple-A umpire, Defendants conferred on her significant duties and responsibilities, including the following:

- In 1987, Plaintiff was the home plate umpire for the Hall of Fame exhibition game between the New York Yankees and the Atlanta Braves.
- In 1988, Plaintiff was selected to umpire the Venezuela All Star game.
- In 1988 and 1989, Plaintiff was the chief of her umpiring crew, with ultimate responsibility for its umpiring calls and performance.
- In 1988 and 1989, Plaintiff was appointed to umpire major league spring training games.
- In 1989, Plaintiff was the home plate umpire for the first Triple-A Minor League All Star Game.
- In 1989, Plaintiff was asked by Triple-A to become a supervisor for umpires in the minor league system.
- From 1987 to 1989, Plaintiff received high praise from qualified and experienced baseball people, including Chuck Tanner, Tom Trebelhorn, Hal Lanier, and Roger Craig, all current or former managers of major league teams.

Notwithstanding these responsibilities and honors, Plaintiff alleges that throughout her career as a minor league umpire she was subjected to continual, repeated, and offensive acts of sexual harassment and gender discrimination. Such acts included the following:

- On numerous occasions, players and managers addressed her with a four-letter word beginning with the letter "c" that refers to female genitalia.
- Players and managers repeatedly told Plaintiff that her proper role was cooking, cleaning, keeping house, or some other form of "women's work," rather than umpiring.
- Bob Knepper, a pitcher with the Houston Astros, told the press that although Plaintiff was a good umpire, to have her as a major league

umpire would be an affront to God and contrary to the teachings of the Bible.

- During arguments with players and managers, Plaintiff was spat upon and was subjected to verbal and physical abuse to a greater degree than male umpires.
- In 1987, the manager of the Nashville Hounds kissed Plaintiff on the lips when he handed her his lineup card.
- At a major league spring training game in 1988, Chuck Tanner, then the manager of the Pittsburgh Pirates, asked Plaintiff if she would like a kiss when he gave her his lineup card.
- Although Plaintiff was well known throughout baseball as an excellent ball and strike umpire, she was directed and required by Ed Vargo, the Supervisor of Umpiring for the National League, to change her stance and technique to resemble those used by him during his career. No such requirement was placed on male umpires.

Plaintiff continually took action against such conduct through warnings, ejections, and reports. Although the existence of such conduct was well known throughout baseball, no one in a position of authority, including Defendants, took action to correct, stop, or prevent such conduct.

Plaintiff alleges that at the time she began her service with Triple-A, she was fully qualified to be a major league umpire, and she had repeatedly made known to Defendants her desire for employment in the major leagues. While she was not promoted to or hired by the National League or American League, male umpires having inferior experience, qualifications, and abilities were repeatedly and frequently promoted and hired by the National and American Leagues.

Plaintiff alleges that in 1988 and 1989, "events came to a head" in her effort to become a major league umpire. . . .

On November 6, 1989, Triple-A discharged and unconditionally released Plaintiff from her employment as an umpire. The reason for Plaintiff's discharge was that the National League and American League were not interested in considering her for employment as a major league umpire. Plaintiff alleges that the sole reason for her discharge, for her inability to obtain a job in the major leagues, and for the Defendants' other discriminatory conduct was Defendants' malicious, wanton, willful, knowing, and intentional discrimination on the basis of gender.

Plaintiff requests the following relief: actual damages, punitive or exemplary damages, interest on all damages, an award of costs and attorney's fees, an order requiring Defendants to employ Plaintiff as an umpire in the major league, and an injunction preventing Defendants from engaging in the unlawful conduct complained of herein.

Discussion
I. Title VII Claims
A. *The American League's Motion for Summary Judgment . . .*

Plaintiff asserts essentially two separate Title VII claims against the American League: a claim for failure to hire or promote, and a claim for wrongful termination.

1. Hiring or Promotion Claim

The American League maintains that it is entitled to summary judgment with respect to Plaintiff's claim for failure to hire or promote because: (1) any claim Plaintiff has arising from the American League's most recent umpire hiring is time-barred, and (2) Plaintiff cannot establish a prima facie case of discrimination in promotion or hiring where no one, either male or female, was hired for or promoted to the position sought. . . .

Accordingly, the American League is also entitled to summary judgment on Plaintiff's hiring and promotion claim arising from events which occurred within 300 days of the filing of her EEOC charge.

2. Termination Claim

The Complaint alleges that the reason for Triple-A's November 6, 1989 termination of Plaintiff was that the American League and National League were not interested in considering her for employment as a major league umpire. . . .

The American League was not Plaintiff's employer at the time of her termination. Nevertheless, if Plaintiff shows such involvement by the American League in her termination by Triple-A, then she will allege a violation of Title VII against the American League. . . . Where a third-party takes discriminatory action that causes an employer to terminate an employee, that third-party may be held liable under Title VII.

Accordingly, Plaintiff will have an opportunity to conduct discovery to determine whether the American League was involved in her termination. The American League's motion for summary judgment on Plaintiff's termination claim is therefore denied without prejudice to its renewal after discovery has been completed.

B. *Motion to Strike Jury Demand and Prayer for Compensatory and Punitive Damages* . . .

II. Claims Under New York Human Rights Law . . .

B. *Motion to Strike Jury Demand and Prayer for Punitive Damages*

Defendants move to strike Plaintiff's demand for trial by jury and prayer for punitive damages with respect to her Human Rights Law claims. . . .

Accordingly, as to Plaintiff's Human Rights Law claims, the motion to strike Plaintiff's jury demand is denied, and the motion to strike the prayer for punitive damages is granted.

III. Restraint of Trade Claims . . .

It is thus clear that although the baseball exemption does immunize baseball from antitrust challenges to its league structure and its reserve system, the exemption does not provide baseball with blanket immunity for anti-competitive behavior in every context in which it operates. The Court must therefore determine whether baseball's employment relations with its umpires are "central enough to baseball to be encompassed in the baseball exemption." . . .

The Court concludes that Defendants have not shown any reason why the baseball exemption should apply to baseball's employment relations with its umpires. Unlike the league structure or the reserve system, baseball's relations with non-players are not a unique characteristic or need of the game. Anticompetitive conduct toward umpires is not an essential part of baseball and in no way enhances its vitality or viability.

Accordingly, because the baseball exemption does not encompass umpire employment relations, application of New York's common law of restraint of trade presents no conflict with the baseball exemption, and Plaintiff's claims are not preempted.

Conclusion

With regard to the Title VII claims: the American League's motion for summary judgment is granted in part and denied in part, and Defendants' motions to strike the jury demand and prayer for compensatory and punitive damages are denied. With regard to the Human Rights Law claims: Boud's motion to dismiss is granted, the other Defendants' motions to dismiss are denied, Defendants' motions to strike the jury demand are denied, and Defendants' motions to strike the prayer for punitive damages are granted. Defendants' motions to dismiss the common law restraint of trade claims are denied.

All counsel are ordered to appear for a pretrial conference in courtroom 302 on July 24, 1992 at 9:00 a.m.

It is so ordered.

1. Separate but Equal

Often, a school fails to equally provide between its men's and women's athletic programs. It is acceptable to provide separate programs for men and women. The real concern is not so much its separateness but the equality of the different programs. One way that equality is determined is by an examination of the revenue-producing capability of each program. Some athletic programs generate revenue and monies produced from an individual sport that affects the financial support of the program. Regardless, these discrepancies must have a basis in fact. A way to determine if a school's action might result in a disparate impact on one sex at the expense of the other is to review the amount of funding that is budgeted for female athletics as compared to the men's budget. One can also compare the money spent on equipment, facilities, and programs. If blatant differences exist, no other evidence is necessary to show that there is disparate treatment between programs. Attempts to ameliorate this particular form of disparate treatment in colleges and universities is popularly known as "gender equity."

2. Contact Sport Exception

A key in interpreting possible sex discrimination cases has been to view cases involving contact sports differently from those that do not. The general rule is that when only one team is available, both sexes must be allowed to try out for and play on that team. Usually, in noncontact sports where no women's team is afforded, the trend is to allow the women to participate on the men's team. But if there is ample opportunity for women to compete on their own, courts appear less apt to allow women to compete with men in contact sports. However, if no team is sponsored for one sex and the excluded sex has had a history of limited opportunities in that sport, the excluded sex must be permitted to try out. Contact sports include boxing, wrestling, rugby, ice hockey, football, basketball, and other sports in which the purpose is body contact. Some jurisdictions have also deemed baseball and soccer as contact sports.

QUESTIONS AND DISCUSSION

1. *Israel*, held that baseball and softball were not substantial equivalents, making the school's rule that Erin Israel play softball instead of baseball a denial of her equal protection rights. The team is selected from those who apply and possess the requisite skill to make the team. Both sports have their particular skills and values. Is softball a lukewarm version of baseball or an entirely different sport? Following the logic of *Israel*, should there be a boys softball team? *See also Adams v. Baker*, 919 F. Supp. 1496 (D. Kan. 1996).

2. In *Croteau v. Fair*, a 17-year-old female high school athlete brought suit alleging a violation of her civil rights; the court found against her on the basis that she failed to prove that the decision to cut her from the team was tainted or motivated by gender bias. These cases are difficult to prove; especially, as in *Croteau*, when the plaintiff is the team's first female participant. What type of evidence would you present to convince the judge that the decision to cut Croteau was motivated by illegal gender bias as opposed to a good-faith decision based on reasons unrelated to gender? *See also Wynn v. Columbus Mun. Separate Sch. Dist.*, 692 F. Supp. 672 (N.D. Miss. 1988) (female physical education teacher alleges she was discriminated in her application for athletic director; teacher prevailed since discriminatory animus was shown by school board's requirement that athletic director must also serve as head football coach); *Balsley by Balsley v. North Hunterdon Regional Sch. Dist. Bd. of Educ.*, 586 A.2d 895 (N.J. 1990) (attorneys' fees for successful unlawful discrimination suit based on barring of public high school student from trying out for school's football team).

3. Department of Health, Education, and Welfare regulations under Title IX permit an athletic department that receives federal funds to maintain separate teams if selection for those teams is based on competitive skill or if the sport involved is a contact sport. 45 C.F.R. §86.41(b).

4. In *Postema v. National League of Professional Baseball Clubs*, a nearly famous female baseball umpire sued for unemployment discrimination in violation of, inter alia, Title VII of the Civil Rights Act. She claimed that her failure to be promoted to the big leagues was the result of sexual discrimination. She cited numerous examples of harassment, including the well-known example of pitcher Bob Knepper, who told the press "that although plaintiff was a good umpire, to have her as a major league umpire would be an affront to God and contrary to the teaching of the Bible." The end result was that she was allowed her day in court. Can you see how useful Bob's rantings are in proving unlawful discrimination? *See generally* Beck, *'Fairness on the Field: Amending Title VII to Foster Greater Female Participation in*

Professional Sports,' 12 Cardozo Arts & Ent. L.J. 241 (1994); Duncan, *Gender Equity in Women's Athletics*, 64 U. Cin. L. Rev. 1027 (1996); Ensor & Wong, *'Sex Discrimination in Athletics: A Review of Two Decades of Accomplishments and Defeats'*, 21 Gonz. L. Rev. 345 (1985); Ivory, *'Changing the Game Plan: Redefining the Standard for Sexual Harassment,'* 1 Vand. J. Ent. L. & Prac. 91 (1999); Mathewson & Rogers,' *Measuring Gender Equity*, 1 Va. J. Sports & L. 130 (1999); Rasnic, *'Illegal Use of Hands in the Locker Room: Charges of Sexual Harassment from Females in the Sports Media,'* 8 Ent. & Sports Law. 3 (1991); Reaves, *'There's No Crying in Baseball: Sports and the Legal and Social Construction of Gender,'* 4 J. Gender Race & Just. 283 (2001); Schoepfer, Title VII: *An Alternative Remedy for Gender Inequity in Intercollegiate Athletics*, 11 Marq. Sports L. Rev. 107 (2000); Schubert et al., *'Gender Discrimination in Athletics,'* 67 N.D. L. Rev. 227 (1991); Thornburg, *Metaphors Matter: How Images of Battle, Sports and Sex Shape the Adversary System*, 10 Wis. Women's L.J. 225 (1995); Weistart, *Can Gender Policy Find a Place in Commercialized College Sports?* 3 Duke J. Gender L. & Poly. 191 (1996); Wolohan, *'Sexual Harassment of Student Athletes and the Law: A Review of the Rights Afforded Students,'* 5 Seton Hall J. Sports L. 339 (1995); Woods, *'Boys Muscling in on Girls' Sports,'* 53 Ohio St. L.J. 891 (1992) Yasser & Schiller, *'Gender Equity in Interscholastic Sport: A Case Study,'* 33 Tulsa L.J. 273 (1997).

B. TITLE IX

Sexual discrimination in academics called for a response in the form of Title IX of the 1972 Education Amendments. Title IX provides that no person "shall, on the basis of sex, be excluded from participation in, be denied the benefits of, or be subjected to discrimination under in any education program" that receives federal financial assistance. 20 U.S.C. §1681(a) *et. seq.* It prohibits any federally funded educational program from discrimination and is intended to curtail discrimination in any program, organization, or agency that receives federal funds. Its goal is to abolish paternalism by giving women an equal opportunity to develop and apply skills.

The regulations issued by the Department of Health, Education, and Welfare (HEW) in 1975 construed the phrase "federal financial assistance" to include funds received indirectly by a school, including grants and loans paid directly to students but that ultimately are received by the school. However, the U.S. Supreme Court in *Grove City College v. Bell*, 465 U.S. 555 (1984), ruled that only those programs within an institution that receives federal direct financial assistance from the federal government should be subject to Title IX. Because this decision did not reflect the statutory intent of its creators, Congress passed the Civil Rights Restoration Act of 1987, which rewrote the definition of "program."

Courts have attempted to revisualize intercollegiate athletics through Title IX as a means to achieve gender equity. Collegiate compliance with Title IX is usually gained through court-agreed settlements that might include proportional scholarships, increased athletic opportunities, and increased budget stipends. *See Haffer v. Temple Univ.* 688 F.2d 14 (3d Cir. 1982).

EDUCATION AMENDMENTS OF 1972 — "TITLE IX"

20 U.S.C §1681. Sex

(a) **Prohibition against discrimination; exceptions** — No person in the United States shall, on the basis of sex, be excluded from participation in, be denied the benefits of, or be subjected to discrimination under any education program or activity receiving Federal financial assistance. . . .

(b) **Preferential or disparate treatment because of imbalance in participation or receipt of Federal benefits; statistical evidence of imbalance** — Nothing contained in subsection (a) of this section shall be interpreted to require any educational institution to grant preferential or disparate treatment to the members of one sex on account of an imbalance which may exist with respect to the total number or percentage of persons of that sex participating in or receiving the benefits of any federally supported program or activity, in comparison with the total number or percentage of persons of that sex in any community, State, section, or other area. . . .

EDUCATION DEPARTMENT REGULATIONS ACCOMPANYING TITLE IX

34 C.F.R. §106.41 Athletics.

(a) **General.** No person shall, on the basis of sex, be excluded from participation in, be denied the benefits of, be treated differently from another person, or otherwise be discriminated against in any interscholastic, intercollegiate, club or intramural athletics offered by a recipient, and no recipient shall provide any such athletics separately on such basis.

(b) **Separate teams.** Notwithstanding the requirements of paragraph (a) of this section, a recipient may operate or sponsor separate teams for members of each sex where selection for such teams is based upon competitive skill or the activity involved is a contact sport. However, where a recipient operates or sponsors a team in a particular sport for members of one sex but operates or sponsors no such team for members of the other sex, and athletic opportunities for members of that sex have previously been limited, members of the excluded sex must be allowed to try out for the team offered unless the sport involved is a contact sport. For the purposes of this part, contact sports include boxing, wrestling, rugby, ice hockey, football, basketball and other sports the purpose or major activity of which involves bodily contact.

(c) **Equal opportunity.** A recipient which operates or sponsors interscholastic, intercollegiate, club or intramural athletics shall provide equal athletic opportunity for members of both sexes. In determining whether equal opportunities are available the Director will consider, among other factors:

(1) Whether the selection of sports and levels of competition effectively accommodate the interests and abilities of both members of both sexes;

(2) The provision of equipment and supplies;

(3) Scheduling of games and practice time;

(4) Travel and per diem allowance;

(5) Opportunity to receive coaching and academic tutoring;

(6) Assignment and compensation of coaches and tutors;

(7) Provision of locker rooms, practice and competitive facilities;

(8) Provision of medical and training facilities and services;

(9) Provision of housing and dining facilities and services;

(10) Publicity — Unequal aggregate expenditures for members of each sex or unequal expenditures for male and female teams if a recipient operates or sponsors separate teams will not constitute non-compliance with this section, but the Assistant Secretary may consider the failure to provide necessary funds for teams for one sex in assessing equality of opportunity for members of each sex.

(d) Adjustment period. A recipient which operates or sponsors inter-scholastic, intercollegiate, club or intramural athletics at the elementary school level shall comply fully with this section as expeditiously as possible but in no event later than one year from the effective date of this regulation. A recipient which operates or sponsors interscholastic, intercollegiate, club or intramural athletics at the secondary or postsecondary school level shall comply fully with this section as expeditiously as possible but in no event later than three years from the effective date of this regulation.

1. Civil Rights Restoration Act of 1987

Arguably, Congress did not anticipate that *Grove City College, v. Bell*, 465 U.S. 555 (1984), would hold that only those programs that received direct financial aid would be subject to Title IX protection. So, Congress "rewrote" *Grove City College* through a federal statute, the Civil Rights Restoration Act of 1987, 29 U.S.C. §1687, which extended the definition of "program" or "activity" (e.g., the college or university).

After the promulgation of this act, the courts became increasingly active in using Title IX to reassess and improve the relative strengths and weaknesses of female athletics to male athletics in the football-dominated world of inter-collegiate sports.

However, in *NCAA v. Smith*, the U.S. Supreme Court held that the NCAA is not subject to the requirements of Title IX on the grounds that it receives dues from its members, which receive federal financial assistance.

NATIONAL COLLEGIATE ATHLETIC ASSOCIATION v. SMITH

525 U.S. 459 (1999)

Justice GINSBURG delivered the opinion of the Court.

This case concerns the amenability of the National Collegiate Athletic Association (NCAA or Association) to a private action under Title IX of the Education Amendments of 1972. The NCAA is an unincorporated association of approximately 1,200 members, including virtually all public and private universities and four-year colleges conducting major athletic programs in the United States; the Association serves to maintain intercollegiate athletics as an integral part of its members' educational programs. Title IX proscribes sex discrimination in "any education program or activity receiving Federal financial assistance." 20 U.S.C. §1681(a).

The complainant in this case, Renee M. Smith, sued the NCAA under Title IX alleging that the Association discriminated against her on the basis of her sex by denying her permission to play intercollegiate volleyball at federally assisted institutions. Reversing the District Court's refusal to allow Smith to amend her *pro se* complaint, the Court of Appeals for the Third Circuit held that the NCAA's receipt of dues from federally funded member institutions would suffice to bring the Association within the scope of Title IX. We reject that determination as inconsistent with the governing statute, regulation, and Court decisions. Dues payments from recipients of federal funds, we hold, do not suffice to render the dues recipient subject to Title IX. We do not address alternative grounds, urged by respondent and the United States as *amicus curiae*, in support of Title IX's application to the NCAA in this litigation, and leave resolution of those grounds to the courts below on remand.

I

Rules adopted by the NCAA govern the intercollegiate athletics programs of its member colleges and universities; "[b]y joining the NCAA, each member agrees to abide by and enforce [the Association's] rules." *National Collegiate Athletic Assn. v. Tarkanian*, 488 U.S. 179 (1988); see 1993-1994 NCAA Manual, NCAA Const., Arts. 1.2(h), 1.3.2, p. 1. Among these rules is the Postbaccalaureate Bylaw, which allows a postgraduate student-athlete to participate in intercollegiate athletics only at the institution that awarded her undergraduate degree. See *id.*, Bylaw 14.1.8.2, at 123.

Respondent Smith enrolled as an undergraduate at St. Bonaventure University, an NCAA member, in 1991. Smith joined the St. Bonaventure intercollegiate volleyball team in the fall of 1991 and remained on the team throughout the 1991-1992 and 1992-1993 athletic seasons. She elected not to play the following year.

Smith graduated from St. Bonaventure in 2 1/2 years. During the 1994-1995 athletic year, she was enrolled in a postgraduate program at Hofstra University; for the 1995-1996 athletic year, she enrolled in a different postgraduate program at the University of Pittsburgh. Smith sought to play intercollegiate volleyball during these athletic years, but the NCAA denied her eligibility on the basis of its postbaccalaureate restrictions. At Smith's request, Hofstra and the University of Pittsburgh petitioned the NCAA to waive the restrictions. Each time, the NCAA refused to grant a waiver.

In August 1996, Smith filed this lawsuit *prose*, alleging, among other things, that the NCAA's refusal to waive the Postbaccalaureate Bylaw excluded her from participating in intercollegiate athletics at Hofstra and the University of Pittsburgh on the basis of her sex, in violation of Title IX of the Education Amendments of 1972, 86 Stat. 373, as amended, 20 U.S.C. §1681 *et seq.* The complaint did not attack the Bylaw on its face, but instead alleged that the NCAA discriminates on the basis of sex by granting more waivers from eligibility restrictions to male than female postgraduate student-athletes.

The NCAA moved to dismiss Smith's Title IX claim on the ground that the complaint failed to allege that the NCAA is a recipient of federal financial assistance. In opposition, Smith argued that the NCAA governs the federally funded intercollegiate athletics programs of its members, that these programs are educational, and that the NCAA benefited economically from its members' receipt of federal funds.

Concluding that the alleged connections between the NCAA and federal financial assistance to member institutions were "too far attenuated" to sustain a Title IX claim, the District Court dismissed the suit. 978 F. Supp. 213, 219, 220 (W.D. Pa. 1997). Smith then moved the District Court for leave to amend her complaint to add Hofstra and the University of Pittsburgh as defendants, and to allege that the NCAA "receives federal financial assistance through another recipient and operates an educational program or activity which receives or benefits from such assistance." The District Court denied the motion "as moot, the court having granted [the NCAA's] motion to dismiss."

The Court of Appeals for the Third Circuit reversed the District Court's refusal to grant leave to amend the complaint. 139 F.3d 180, 190 (1998). The Third Circuit agreed with the District Court that Smith's original complaint failed to state a Title IX claim. *Id.*, at 189. But Smith's proposed amended complaint, the Court of Appeals said, "plainly alleges that the NCAA receives dues from member institutions, which receive federal funds." *Id.*, at 190. That allegation, the Third Circuit held, "would be sufficient to bring the NCAA within the scope of Title IX as a recipient of federal funds and would the survive a motion to dismiss." *Ibid.* Under the Third Circuit's ruling, all Smith would need to prove on remand to proceed is that the NCAA receives members' dues, a fact not in dispute. . . .

III

Smith, joined by the United States as *amicus curiae*, presses two alternative theories for bringing the NCAA under the prescriptions of Title IX. First, she asserts that the NCAA directly and indirectly receives federal financial assistance through the National Youth Sports Program NCAA administers. Second, Smith argues that when a recipient cedes controlling authority over a federally funded program to another entity, the controlling entity is covered by Title IX regardless whether it is itself a recipient. . . .

For the reasons stated, we conclude that the Court of Appeals erroneously held that dues payments from recipients of federal funds suffice to subject the NCAA to suit under Title IX. Accordingly, we vacate the judgment of the Third Circuit and remand the case for further proceedings consistent with this opinion.

It is so ordered.

In *Roberts v. Colorado State Board of Agriculture*, the court determined that the actions of a university in discontinuing women's fast pitch softball were violative of Title IX, and that an equitable remedy was the proper solution.

ROBERTS v. COLORADO STATE BOARD OF AGRICULTURE

United States Court of Appeals, Tenth Circuit.
998 F.2d 824 (10th Cir. 1993)

LOGAN, Circuit Judge.

The Colorado State Board of Agriculture (SBA or defendant) appeals the decision of the district court finding that it violated Title IX of the Education Amendments of 1972, 20 U.S.C. §§1681-1688, and ordering it to reinstate the women's fast pitch softball team at Colorado State University (CSU) with all of the incidental benefits of a varsity team.

Plaintiffs, CSU students and former members of the fast pitch softball team, brought suit in their individual capacities against SBA and CSU in June 1992 after CSU announced that it was discontinuing the varsity fast pitch softball program. In February of this year the district court found that SBA and CSU had violated Title IX, and issued a permanent injunction reinstating the softball program. Approximately three weeks later, the district court held a status conference and, in the face of apparent foot-dragging by defendant, amplified its earlier orders to require defendant to hire a coach promptly, recruit new members for the team, and organize a fall season. This court denied a motion for a stay but expedited the appeal.

Plaintiffs first contest our jurisdiction to hear these appeals. On the merits, defendant contends that the district court erred in finding a Title IX violation. Defendant also maintains that even if the verdict was correct, the district court abused its discretion when it ordered reinstatement of the softball team and required defendant to follow specific directions in effecting that reinstatement rather than affording defendant the opportunity to present a plan that would bring it into compliance with Title IX. . . .

I

We consider first the challenges to our jurisdiction over these appeals. Plaintiffs maintain that because defendant failed to name CSU as a party in its notice of appeal, and because parties seeking appellate review must join all of their co-plaintiffs or codefendants, we must dismiss this appeal. . . .

In that event, however, since the injunction itself is properly before us, we see no difficulty in reviewing the specific requirements—to hire a coach, recruit players, and schedule a fall season—that the district court imposed on defendant.

II

Defendant maintains that, as a matter of law, it did not violate Title IX. . . .

A

This controversy concerns one subpart of the regulations implementing Title IX. 34 C.F.R. §106.41(c) provides:

A recipient which operates or sponsors interscholastic, intercollegiate, club or intramural athletics shall provide equal athletic opportunity for members of both sexes. In determining whether equal opportunities are available the Director [of the Office for Civil Rights] will consider, among other factors:

(1) Whether the selection of sports and levels of competition effectively accommodate the interests and abilities of members of both sexes[.]

Although §106.41(c) goes on to list nine other factors that enter into a determination of equal opportunity in athletics, an institution may violate Title IX simply by failing to accommodate effectively the interests and abilities of student athletes of both sexes. *See Cohen v. Brown Univ.*, 991 F.2d 888, 897-98 (1st Cir. 1993); *Favia v. Indiana Univ. of Penn.*, 812 F.Supp. 578, 584-85 (W.D. Pa. 1993); *see also* 44 Fed.Reg. 71,413, 71,415-17 (1979) (HEW Title IX Intercollegiate Athletics Policy Interpretation, describing the three major areas of regulatory compliance as "Athletic Financial Assistance (Scholarships)," "Equivalence in Other Athletic Benefits and Opportunities," and "Effective Accommodation of Student Interests and Abilities"); Office for Civil Rights, Department of Education, Title IX Athletics Investigator's Manual 7 (1990) [hereinafter Investigator's Manual] ("[a]n investigation may be limited to less than all three of these major areas"). . . .

In effect, "substantial proportionality" between athletic participation and undergraduate enrollment provides a safe harbor for recipients under Title IX. In the absence of such gender balance, the institution must show that it has expanded and is continuing to expand opportunities for athletic participation by the underrepresented gender, or else it must fully and effectively accommodate the interests and abilities among members of the underrepresented gender.

In addition to assessing whether individuals of both sexes have the opportunity to compete in intercollegiate athletics, the OCR also examines whether the quality of competition provided to male and female athletes equally reflects their abilities. This will depend on whether, program wide, the competitive schedules of men's and women's teams "afford proportionally similar numbers of male and female athletes equivalently advanced competitive opportunities," or "[w]hether the institution can demonstrate a history and continuing practice of upgrading the competitive opportunities available to the historically disadvantaged sex as warranted by developing abilities among the athletes of that sex." However, "[i]nstitutions are not required to upgrade teams to intercollegiate status or otherwise develop intercollegiate sports absent a reasonable expectation that intercollegiate competition in that sport will be available within the institution's normal competitive regions."

B

The district court found that plaintiffs met their burden of showing that defendant could not take shelter in the safe harbor of substantial proportionality. The district court reviewed a substantial quantity of statistical data, and made the undisputed finding that following the termination of the varsity softball program, the disparity between enrollment and athletic participation for women at CSU is 10.5%. Defendant maintains that, as a matter of law, a 10.5% disparity is substantially proportionate. . . .

C

The district court also found that defendant could not prove a history and continuing practice of expansion in women's athletics at CSU. Defendant argues that the district court should have given greater weight to its dramatic expansion of women's athletic opportunities during the 1970s. In essence, defendant suggests reading the words "continuing practice" out of this prong of the test. In support of this position, defendant offers anecdotal evidence of enforcement at other institutions, and the OCR's 1983 finding of compliance for CSU, which was contingent upon CSU's fulfilling the provisions of a plan that CSU never met.

Although CSU created a women's sports program out of nothing in the 1970s, adding eleven sports for women during that decade, the district court found that women's participation opportunities declined steadily during the 1980s. Furthermore, although budget cuts in the last twelve years have affected both men and women athletes at CSU, the district court found that women's participation opportunities declined by 34%, whereas men's opportunities declined by only 20%. The facts as found by the district court (and largely undisputed by defendant) can logically support no other conclusion than that, since adding women's golf in 1977, CSU has not maintained a practice of program expansion in women's athletics, and indeed has since dropped three women's sports.

We recognize that in times of economic hardship, few schools will be able to satisfy Title IX's effective accommodation requirement by continuing to expand their women's athletics programs. Nonetheless, the ordinary meaning of the word "expansion" may not be twisted to find compliance under this prong when schools have increased the relative percentages of women participating in athletics by making cuts in both men's and women's sports programs. Financially strapped institutions may still comply with Title IX by cutting athletic programs such that men's and women's athletic participation rates become substantially proportionate to their representation in the undergraduate population. . . .

D

The district court found that defendant could not demonstrate that CSU's athletic program fully and effectively accommodated the interests and abilities of women athletes. Here we hold that the district court improperly placed the burden of proof on defendant. Because a Title IX violation may not be predicated solely on a disparity between the gender composition of an institution's athletic program and the gender composition of its undergraduate enrollment, *see* 20 U.S.C. §1681(b), plaintiff must not only show that the institution fails on the first benchmark of substantial proportionality but also that it does not fully and effectively accommodate the interests and abilities of its women athletes. *See Cohen*, 991 F.2d at 897. Further, an institution would be hard-pressed to establish the full and effective accommodation of the interests and abilities of its women athletes in the abstract. The ultimate burden must lie with the plaintiffs to show that they have been "excluded from participation in, [or] denied the benefits of" an athletic program "on the basis of sex." 20 U.S.C. §1681(a). However, if plaintiffs establish that their interests and abilities are not being accommodated by the university's athletic program, the institution may still decline to upgrade or create an intercollegiate team if there is no reasonable expectation of competition for that team within the . . . region.

E

Finally, defendant argues that the district court erred in holding that plaintiffs were not required to show discriminatory intent. Defendant reasons that because Title IX was modeled on Title VI of the Civil Rights Act of 1964, 42 U.S.C. §§2000d to -4a, and because discriminatory intent is required to prove a violation of Title VI, *see Guardians Ass'n v. Civil Serv. Comm'n,* 463 U.S. 582, 608 n. (1983) (Powell, J., concurring), proof of a Title IX violation must therefore also require intentional discrimination. . . .

III

Defendant makes two broad objections to the relief ordered by the district court. First, it maintains that plaintiffs have an adequate remedy at law and therefore injunctive relief is inappropriate. Second, defendant argues that it should have been afforded the opportunity to present a plan to the court that would have brought it into compliance with Title IX, rather than ordered to reinstate the softball program and required to take other specific actions with respect to its management of the team.

A

Defendant suggests for the first time on appeal that because plaintiffs have settled their damages suit, they have been made whole and injunctive relief is unnecessary. We draw no such conclusion. . . .

B

Defendant's second argument has more substance. Defendant contends that the district court abused its discretion by prescribing the precise manner in which it must comply with Title IX. Defendant objects to the specificity of the district court's order because it believes the district court has ordered it to maintain a softball team in perpetuity, and because it believes it is entitled to devise a plan for its own compliance. . . .

Because this is not a class action, the broad sweep of the remedy exists only in defendant's imagination. The district court's order does not apply to Colorado high schools. It does not reach any other college or university. It does not extend the effective accommodation test to any other department of CSU. It does not even require CSU to institute women's varsity soccer or alpine skiing, as defendant fears. Only the CSU softball players have established that their athletic interests and abilities are not being accommodated effectively under Title IX. Therefore, relief is appropriate only for them. . . .

Further, because the reinstatement of the softball team is predicated upon defendant's Title IX violation, if that violation were remedied in accordance with either of the other two benchmarks of the effective accommodation test defendant would then no longer be obligated to maintain its softball program.

If, for example, defendant chose to cut its athletic programs in such a way as to meet the substantial proportionality benchmark, plaintiffs would have no basis for asserting their right to play softball. . . . If defendant decided to operate CSU's athletic program in compliance with the underlying mandate of the district court's opinion, plaintiffs' entitlement to individual relief would evaporate.

Finally, we turn to the specifics of the district court's order. . . .

The district court did exceed its authority in demanding that the softball team play a fall 1993 exhibition season. The district court's apparent rationale for ordering a fall season, which had not previously been a regular practice at CSU, was to ensure that CSU would be able to field a "competitive" team the following spring. Nothing in Title IX requires an institution to create a "top flight" varsity team, nor is it within the district court's power, once it reinstates the softball program with all the incidental benefits of varsity status, "to make sure they have a good season." Because a fall season is not required to effect the appropriate remedy, we hold that the district court overstepped its authority in ordering it.

The decision of the district court is affirmed in part and reversed in part. The cause is remanded with instructions that the injunction be modified consistent with this opinion.

Favia v. Indiana University of Pennsylvania began when members of the women's gymnastics and field hockey teams alleged Title IX infractions when the university cut those two programs. *Favia* shows the court's continued interest in facilitating gender equality.

FAVIA V. INDIANA UNIVERSITY OF PENNSYLVANIA

7 F.3d 332 (3d Cir. 1993)

HUTCHINSON, Circuit Judge.

Appellants, Indiana University of Pennsylvania ("I.U.P" or the "University"), I.U.P. Director of Athletics Frank Cignetti, and I.U.P. President Lawrence Pettit appeal an order of the United States District Court for the Western District of Pennsylvania denying their motion to modify a preliminary injunction. The injunction requires them to reinstate two varsity women's sports programs, field hockey and gymnastics. It resulted from a class action filed by appellees, Dawn Favia, Wendy Schandelmeier, Kim Dalcamo, and Amy Phaehler, members of the University women's varsity field hockey and gymnastics teams. They claimed that the University's planned elimination of those intercollegiate women's programs violated Title IX of the Education Amendments of 1972, 20 U.S.C.A. §§1681-1688 (West 1990). I.U.P. sought the modification to allow it to replace the women's gymnastics program with a women's soccer program. It claimed the substitution of soccer for gymnastics would bring it closer to compliance with Title IX and therefore the district court erred in denying its motion to modify the preliminary injunction.

The district court held I.U.P. had not shown the circumstances had changed enough to make continued enforcement of the injunction inequitable.

After examining the record and considering the parties' contentions, we hold that the district court did not abuse its discretion in denying modification of the preliminary injunction. We will therefore affirm.

I

I.U.P. is a state-affiliated university located in Indiana, Pennsylvania. It has 6,003 full-time undergraduate female students (55.6% of the population) and 4,790 male students (44.4% of the population). Prior to the institution of this action, I.U.P. fielded nine male and nine female varsity athletic teams in intercollegiate competition. The number of teams was equal, but the male teams were significantly larger. Thus, 313 men but only 190 women, a 62% to 38% ratio, had an opportunity to compete in intercollegiate athletics. There was also a disparity in athletic scholarships. In 1991, I.U.P. awarded only 21% of its athletic scholarship funds to women, and for each $8.00 spent on men's athletics it spent only $2.75 on women's athletics.

In mid-1991, citing budgetary concerns, I.U.P. decided to shrink the size of its athletic department. It announced plans to discontinue four varsity athletic programs, the men's tennis and soccer teams and the women's gymnastics and field hockey teams.

On October 5, 1992, three student gymnasts, Dawn Favia, Wendy Schandelmeier, and Kim Dalcamo, and one member of the women's varsity field hockey team, Amy Phaehler, filed a class action lawsuit in the United States District Court for the Western District of Pennsylvania. They were seeking a decree that would force the University to comply with Title IX and eliminate the disparity between its men's and women's intercollegiate sports programs. They also asked for a preliminary injunction ordering I.U.P. to reinstate the women's gymnastics and field hockey teams. They alleged that the University's failure to provide athletic opportunities for women at a level comparable to those provided for men violated Title IX and adversely affected all female students who might wish to take part in intercollegiate athletics. They described the affected class as all present and future women students at I.U.P. who participate, seek to participate, or are deterred from participating in intercollegiate athletics at the University. . . .

Although I.U.P. eliminated an equal number of men's and women's teams, the evidence presented showed that it actually increased the imbalance between individual opportunities for men and women in percentage terms. In addition, most of the financial savings from the team eliminations were shown to have resulted from elimination of the women's teams. Their demise saved I.U.P. $110,000.00. Cutbacks in the men's teams saved only $35,000.00. . . .

The district court denied the motion to modify the preliminary injunction on January 22, 1993. It reasoned if it were to permit the school to dissolve the gymnastics team it would in effect make "the original plaintiffs [who prevailed in this case losers." The substitution of teams "would really amount to vacating an order and putting in something entirely different." *Id.* Essentially, the district court looked at I.U.P.'s motion as a belated request for reconsideration of a preliminary injunction that had not been timely appealed.

On February 3, 1993, I.U.P. did file a timely notice of appeal from the district court's order denying modification of the preliminary injunction.

II

The district court had subject matter jurisdiction over this case under 28 U.S.C.A. §1331 (West 1966) and 28 U.S.C.A. §1343(a) (West Supp. 1993). Appellees, the named representative plaintiffs and the class they represent, dispute our appellate jurisdiction. They argue that I.U.P.'s "Motion to Modify the Preliminary Injunction" was an untimely motion for reconsideration of the grant of a preliminary injunction whose denial is no longer appealable or subject to appellate review. . . .

The University argues that two circumstances have changed since the hearing on the preliminary injunction and that they warrant its modification. First, it contends that the posture of the case changed on the date of the entry of the injunction when the district court, without the benefit of evidence or argument, certified the class. I.U.P. says that certification of the class changes the entire complexion of the case and requires the district court to reassess the remedial effect of the injunction. Second, it asserts that graduation of the class representatives, the original named plaintiffs who originally wanted to take part in inter-collegiate gymnastics, is a change in circumstances warranting modification. . . .

Since the entry of the injunction, two of the four class representatives, Dawn Favia and Kim Dalcamo, members of the gymnastics team, have completed competition for the year and have graduated. A third class representative, Wendy Schandelmeier, decided not to compete with the gymnastics team once it was reinstated. Therefore, I.U.P. also asserts that the ineligibility of the class representatives for further intercollegiate competition in gymnastics is a "change in circumstances" that permits favorable consideration of its motion to modify the preliminary injunction.

A change in the status of a plaintiff in a Title IX action can have drastic effects on the outcome. In *Cook v. Colgate University*, 992 F.2d 17 (2d Cir. 1993), five members of the Colgate University women's ice hockey team sought elevation to varsity status and funding commensurate with the men's program. The district court granted the relief and the university appealed. *Cook v. Colgate Univ.*, 802 F.Supp. 737 (N.D.N.Y. 1992), *rev'd*, 992 F.2d 17 (2d Cir. 1993). During the pendency of the appeal, the remaining active plaintiffs graduated leaving no plaintiff on the team. The United States Court of Appeals for the Second Circuit vacated the district court's order and dismissed the complaint as moot reasoning that none of the remaining plaintiffs could benefit from the order. *Cook*, 992 F.2d at 20. In *Cook*, the action was not certified as a class action. In holding the case was moot, the court of appeals stated that the circumstances before it were different from those that confronted the United States Court of Appeals for the First Circuit in *Cohen v. Brown University*, 991 F.2d 888 (1st Cir. 1993) where the case had been certified as a class action. *Id.*

In this case, although the district court certified the class, the principles it considered in reaching its decision and fashioning preliminary relief related directly to the fact that the named plaintiffs, or class representatives, were members of the women's gymnastics team. An alleged change in the composition of that squad or the demand for that program, if proven, could amount to a change in circumstances sufficient to receive modification of an injunction.

The change in the eligibility of the class representatives for participation in gymnastics does change the circumstances that caused the district court to fashion its preliminary injunctive relief. The University therefore has alleged one change in circumstances that allows us to consider its motion as a motion for modification of the injunction rather than a motion for reconsideration.

Furthermore, an important independent question is at stake in the present motion to modify the injunction. That issue is whether the class as it is now comprised is in a posture to challenge successfully the University's request to modify the injunction by eliminating women's gymnastics and substituting soccer. The issue before the district court when it held the hearing on the named plaintiffs' motion for a preliminary injunction concerned the University's decision to eliminate two women's sports programs in the face of an apparent violation of Title IX. In its motion to modify, I.U.P. says it wants to restructure its program to bring it closer to the equal opportunity goal that Title IX requires. In that sense, I.U.P.'s motion presents issues that could not have been raised on appeal or through a request for reconsideration of the preliminary injunction itself. . . .

III

Thus, turning to the merits, we consider whether the district court abused its discretion in holding the circumstances that led to the entry of a preliminary injunction against I.U.P. had not changed enough to require its modification. "When modifying a preliminary injunction, a court is charged with the exercise of the same discretion it exercised in granting or denying injunctive relief in the first place." . . .

In directing the University to reinstate the gymnastics program in the preliminary injunction, the district court necessarily decided that the student-athletes were likely to succeed on the merits of their claim that I.U.P. was violating Title IX and that continuing the gymnastics program would help alleviate that violation. The University does not contend that the addition of a soccer program would bring I.U.P. into full compliance with the mandates of Title IX and, indeed, we do not see how it could do so; however, it does seem that the addition of a soccer program would bring it closer to compliance. By substituting soccer for gymnastics, women's participation in athletics would increase from 159 female athletes (38.97% of the student-athlete population) to 188 female athletes (43.02% of the student-athlete population). In addition, there was testimony that I.U.P.'s proposed enhanced recruiting efforts, using funds that would become available from elimination of the gymnastics program, would be expected to raise the number of female athletes within three to five years to a level which would be closely proportional to the percentage of women enrolled at I.U.P.

Nevertheless, two things militate strongly against a conclusion that the district court abused its discretion. First, the district court did not clearly abuse its discretion by seeking to preserve the athletic program that was at the center of the underlying litigation. A preliminary injunction is intended "to preserve the relative positions of the parties until a trial on the merits can be held." . . .

We have already decided I.U.P.'s argument that the district court certification of the plaintiff class as part of its order granting preliminary injunctive relief is not a changed circumstance. On the merits, therefore, we review its second asserted changed circumstance — the class representatives' altered competitive posture because of their graduation or failure to participate in the challenged athletic programs — only to determine whether continuation of the preliminary injunction without the modification it requires will result in significant inequity either to the University or the members of the plaintiff class.

Although the University correctly points out that the named representatives' interests are no longer at issue, women's gymnastics is still part of the athletic opportunities available to the class of plaintiffs who seek redress. In entering the preliminary injunction, the district court originally determined that reinstatement of the gymnastics team addressed, in part, a likely violation of federal law that affected the plaintiffs as a class, though to differing degrees as individuals. The absence of some individual gymnasts does not show that it is inappropriate to continue to try to maintain the *status quo*. There is testimony in the record that women presently attending, or planning to attend, I.U.P. are still interested in participating in a gymnastics program.

Secondly, it is not clear that the University's proposed substitution of soccer for gymnastics will substantially ameliorate what the district court decided was likely to be a violation of Title IX. Although Title IX and its regulations do not "require institutions to expend equal amounts of money on members of each sex[,]" *Cohen v. Brown University*, 809 F. Supp. 978, 994, (D.R.I. 1992), *aff'd*, 991 F.2d 888 (1st Cir. 1993), funding is at least an element in deciding whether the equality of opportunity Title IX requires is present. Regulations the Secretary of Health, Education and Welfare ("HEW") promulgated, now administered by the Department of Education, pursuant to Title IX provide, *inter alia*, that unequal aggregate expenditures for members of male and female teams will not necessarily establish noncompliance, but the failure to provide funds for teams of one sex may be considered in assessing equality of opportunity for members of each sex. 34 O.F.R. §106.41(c) (1992); *see* 44 Fed. Reg. 71,413, 71,415-17 (1979) (HEW Title IX Intercollegiate Athletics Policy Interpretation describing three major areas of regulatory compliance to include athletic financial assistance, equivalence in other benefits and opportunities, accommodation of student interests); *see also Roberts v. Colorado State Bd. of Agric.*, 998 F.2d 824, 828 (10th Cir. 1993); *Brown*, 809 F. Supp. at 994; *Cook*, 802 F. Supp. at 744-45. Under the regulations and the case law, many of the factors used to determine compliance depend on criteria directly related to funding levels, *e.g.*, provision of equipment, travel and per diem allowances, compensation of coaches and provision of facilities.

Although replacement of the gymnastics program with soccer could increase the percentage of female athletes from 38.97% to 43.02%, it would decrease the overall percentage of athletic expenditures I.U.P. provided for women's athletics because a fifteen member gymnastics team requires a $150,000.00 investment while a fifty member soccer team requires only

$50,000.00. Although more slots for female competition might be created, the funding gap would increase and this result could be viewed as moving I.U.P. farther from the goals of Title IX.

Even if the funding issue is put aside, I.U.P. would still appear not to be in Title IX compliance in other aspects because its student body has 6,003 females (56%) and 4,790 males (44%). *See Brown*, 991 F.2d at 899 (in absence of continuing program expansion, schools must either provide athletic opportunities in proportion to gender composition of student body or fully accommodate interested athletes among under-represented sex). I.U.P. did not have a specific overall plan in place to achieve total compliance at any projected future date. The graduation of three members of the certified class along with a proposal to add a women's soccer team does not make the preliminary injunction inequitable, nor eliminate a continuing need for it. . . .

If final injunctive relief becomes appropriate, we think the district court should consider how violations of federal law, if any, it finally determines are present affect the entire class and fashion final relief accordingly.

IV

The order of the district court will be affirmed.

Gonyo v. Drake University can be viewed as an unsuccessful attempt to disallow "reverse discrimination." That is, in *Gonyo,* male wrestlers tried to use Title IX to reinstate the intercollegiate wrestling program. *unsuccessfully*

GONYO V. DRAKE UNIVERSITY

837 F. Supp. 489 (S.D. Iowa 1993)

VIETOR, District Judge.

Plaintiffs, who were full time students and collegiate wrestlers at defendant Drake University from 1989 or 1990 through the 1992-93 academic year, bring this action against Drake University, its President and Athletic Director. The suit arises out of Drake University's decision last March to discontinue its intercollegiate men's wrestling program. Plaintiffs assert that the decision to discontinue wrestling constitutes gender discrimination in violation of Title IX of the Education Amendments of 1972, 20 U.S.C. §1681, *et seq.*, that Title IX is unconstitutional as applied to plaintiffs, that Drake's decision violates the Equal Protection Clause of the Fourteenth Amendment to the United States Constitution and that Drake's decision constitutes a breach of a contract between plaintiffs and Drake. Plaintiffs filed a motion for a preliminary injunction ordering defendants to reinstate the intercollegiate men's wrestling program at Drake University. Hearing on the motion was held September 27, 1993.

Facts

Most of the following facts are stipulated by the parties. Other facts are based on the evidence presented at the hearing. A few of the "background" facts mentioned in the next paragraph are judicially noticed.

I think it is appropriate to provide some background. Wrestling is a one-on- one combative sport that has several variations. In one form or another, it is engaged in throughout the world, and it is no doubt the most ancient of all sports. The ancient Egyptians and Babylonians wrestled thousands of years ago and so did the ancient Greeks and Romans. Indeed, wrestling was a major contest in the Olympian games in ancient Greece. Henry VIII, King of England, challenged Francis I, King of France, to a wrestling match. (The French king won.) The early colonists in America found that wrestling was popular among the Native Americans. Wrestling has long been popular in the United States. The special values of wrestling are that it demands of the participant a high level of self-discipline, dedication and conditioning, and that it is open to all sizes and shapes of people — many of whom, because of their small stature, would be unable to compete safely and effectively in most other sports. In the past decade or so participation in pre-junior high school wrestling programs has increased and so has participation in post-collegiate amateur wrestling programs. The level of wrestling participation at the junior high school and high school levels has remained stable, but since 1980 the number of intercollegiate men's wrestling programs in the United States has steadily declined from 374 to 265. If that rate of decline continues there will be only 181 collegiate wrestling programs left ten years from now. Colleges and universities are dropping wrestling programs for budgetary reasons. Supporters of college wrestling view this trend as disheartening and they predict that the trend will adversely impact on precollegiate wrestling programs and post-collegiate wrestling programs. Elimination of the wrestling program at Drake University is particularly painful to them because Iowa has a long and impressive tradition as the premier wrestling state in the nation. In the earlier part of this century, when professional wrestling was still legitimate, two world champions were Iowans — "Farmer" Burns and Frank Gotch. In modern times, universities in Iowa have consistently fielded excellent wrestling teams, and the winning of national championships by the University of Iowa has recently become almost routine.

Now on to the more specific facts of this case. Drake University is a private educational institution in Des Moines, Iowa, organized and existing as a non-profit corporation under the Iowa Nonprofit Corporation Act (codified at Iowa Code Chapter 504A). Defendant Michael Ferrari is Drake's President. Defendant Lynn King is Director of Athletics for Drake. He is primarily responsible for the day-to-day operations of intercollegiate athletic programs. Plaintiffs attended Drake paying their own way, either completely or partially, until some were able to obtain full or partial scholarships. Plaintiff Blauvelt is still attending Drake. . . .

Drake does receive federal financial assistance for some of its programs, and therefore must comply with the provisions of Title IX.

Drake is a member of, and subject to the rules and regulations of, the National Collegiate Athletic Association (NCAA). The NCAA has established three "divisions" for sports-Divisions I, II and III. A team in Division I is authorized a substantial number of scholarships, a team in Division II is authorized a limited number of scholarships and Division III teams are not authorized any scholarships.

Drake has had NCAA Division I intercollegiate men's wrestling since 1965. In 1986, Drake's Strategic Planning Commission made recommendations regarding the future of the Intercollegiate Athletics Division, including a recommendation that the Division terminate the wrestling program. This recommendation was made known to defendant King three years ago when he was recruited as Athletic Director, but the wrestling coach, Lon Timmerman, was never told of it. Timmerman and his assistant wrestling coaches recruited plaintiffs and other wrestlers. In doing so, they spoke of Drake's "total commitment" to the wrestling program. They never suggested that Drake might drop its wrestling program before the recruits had graduated, although they did not specifically tell the recruits that Drake would not drop its wrestling program. Plaintiffs responded to the recruitment efforts of Timmerman and his staff and enrolled in Drake to get their college education and wrestle in intercollegiate competition.

In the late 1980's and early 1990's, Drake's Board of Governors made a conscious decision to reallocate a greater share of the resources available to Drake to academic priorities and away from other areas such as athletics, and consequently the Board regularly approved budgets which reduced the athletic budget as a percent of the overall university's budget. At present, Drake's athletic budget is about five percent of its total budget, and in the 1992–93 year about five percent of its athletic budget went to its wrestling program. Cutting athletic budgets because of total school budget constraints has been common throughout the United States in recent years.

By January of 1993, defendant King knew that wrestling would have to be eliminated. On March 10, 1993, King told Timmerman that the following day a public announcement would be made that the wrestling program would be terminated at the end of the 1992–93 season. Up until then, Timmerman had no inkling of such developments.

On March 11, 1993, Drake made a public announcement of its decision to discontinue the wrestling program, stating that financial concerns, discontinuation of wrestling programs by other colleges, the Missouri Valley Conference (of which Drake is a member) not sponsoring wrestling as a sport, and lack of support by the students and community for the Drake wrestling program were the reasons. These stated reasons were, in fact, the true reasons for the decision.

Wrestling is not a revenue producing sport, such as football and basketball. In recent years, many other colleges and universities, due to budget constraints, have discontinued their wrestling programs at the Division I level, including Yale, Colgate, Temple, Louisiana State, Notre Dame and Princeton. Presently there are about 96 schools that have Division I level wrestling.

There have been other changes in Drake's athletic program in the past twenty years. Drake added women's sports to its intercollegiate athletics as a separate department in March of 1974. In June of 1974 Drake dropped men's baseball from its intercollegiate athletic program. Drake dropped women's gymnastics from its intercollegiate athletic offerings in September of 1978.

In 1979 Drake merged its men's and women's athletic departments into the current Intercollegiate Athletic Department. In 1985, Drake dropped men's Division I-AA football from its intercollegiate athletic offerings, and in 1986 added men's soccer. In 1986 Drake played an "exhibition" season of football. From 1987 through 1992 it fielded a Division III football team, and this year (1993) it has returned to Division I-AA football.

The undergraduate student body at Drake during the 1992-93 school year was 57.2% female and 42.8% male. During the 1992-93 school year, 75.3% of the athletes competing in either Division I or Division III sports at Drake were men and 24.7% were women. Of the total athletes participating in Division I sports at Drake during the 1992-93 school year, women comprised 39.4% and men comprised 60.6%.

During the 1992-93 school year, Drake spent approximately 53% of its total athletic scholarship budget on women athletes and approximately 47% on men athletes.

During the 1992-93 school year, Drake spent 71% of its overall nonscholarship athletic budget on men's sports at the Division I and Division III level and spent 29% on women's sports at the Division I level.

During the 1992-93 school year, Drake spent 65% of its overall nonscholarship athletic budget on men's sports at the Division I level (excluding football expenditures) and 35% on women's sports.

During the 1992-93 school year, Drake spent 52.9% of its overall athletic budget on men's sports at the Division I level (excluding football expenditures) and 47.1% on women's sports.

During the 1992-93 school year, Drake spent 56% of its overall athletic budget on men's sports at the Division I or Division III level and spent 44% on women's sports at the Division I level.

There were between nineteen and twenty-three members on Drake's wrestling team and the team was allotted 8.57 scholarships to divide among its wrestlers for the 1992-93 season.

After discontinuing the wrestling program, approximately 59.7% of all Division I athletes at Drake will be men, assuming participation levels in all other Division I sports from the 1992-93 school year remain the same.

During the 1992-93 school year, there were seven men's varsity athletic teams (including football) and five women's varsity athletic teams at Drake.

No wrestler currently under scholarship at Drake has been denied continued scholarship availability through their anticipated graduation date, so long as they remain eligible for such scholarships under the university's athletic scholarship guidelines. . . .

Preliminary Injunction Standard

This case is not before the court for a final decision on the merits. Rather, it is before the court for a determination of whether a preliminary injunction should issue compelling Drake to reinstitute its intercollegiate wrestling program until such time as the court tries this case and reaches a final decision on the merits. . . .

Threat of Irreparable Harm

Unless plaintiffs ultimately prevail on the merits in this case and succeed in getting a permanent injunction requiring Drake to restore intercollegiate wrestling (a matter discussed *infra* under the probability of success portion of this memorandum opinion), the harm to plaintiffs in failing to issue a preliminary injunction is not in the nature of harm to their legal rights.

State of Balance

The state of balance between any harm to plaintiffs in not issuing the preliminary injunction and the injury that granting the injunction will inflict on defendants weighs in favor of not issuing the injunction. While it would be possible for Drake to put together an intercollegiate wrestling program for the 1993-94 season, that could be accomplished only at a considerable budgetary and administrative cost to Drake. Furthermore, and perhaps more important-ly, as an institution of higher education Drake is entitled to exercise, as a matter of academic freedom, its own judgment as to how to apportion its resources and what its academic and athletic offerings will be. . . .

Probability of Success

It is unlikely that plaintiffs will prevail on their claim that Drake's decision to abolish its wrestling program violates the Equal Protection Clause of the Fourteenth Amendment to the United States Constitution. . . .

Likewise, it appears unlikely that plaintiffs will prevail on their state law breach of contract claim. . . .

Plaintiffs' claims that the defendants have violated Title IX and that Title IX as applied to plaintiffs is unconstitutional appear to be the main thrust of plaintiffs' suit against the defendants. On these claims, too, it is not likely that the plaintiffs will prevail. . . .

The regulations state that there must be reasonable opportunities for members of each sex to receive athletic scholarships or grant-in-aid propor-tionate to the number of students of each sex participating in interscholastic or intercollegiate athletics. Plaintiffs urge that this requirement is violated because more athletic scholarship dollars go to women than men, although a large majority of Drake's athletes are men. The defendants point out that under an HEW policy interpretation, if any resulting disparity in this re-spect can be explained by adjustments taking into account legitimate, nondiscriminatory factors, then an institution may be found to be in com-pliance with Title IX. Drake contends it has several legitimate, non-discriminatory reasons for any disparity in its athletic scholarship awards for men and women. In any event, because plaintiffs have not lost their scho-larships there is serious question that they have standing to raise the issue. Furthermore, even if it should ultimately be established in this case that Drake is in violation of Title IX because of disparity in athletic scholarship awards, it is not at all clear that plaintiffs will win an injunction requiring Drake to reinstate its wrestling program. . . .

The court, based on the record made at the preliminary injunction hear-ing, can find no merit to plaintiffs' contention that their interests and abilities are not being effectively accommodated by the Drake athletic program.

Although males are a minority of the student body, three-fourths of the students engaged in athletic competition are males and nearly three-fourths of its nonscholarship athletic budget goes to men's sports. There are seven men's varsity athletic teams and only five women's varsity athletic teams. The record fails to show that plaintiffs are, on the basis of their gender, excluded from participation in, or denied the benefits of, or subjected to discrimination in Drake's athletic program. . . .

For all the foregoing reasons, it is my conclusion that plaintiffs are not likely to prevail on the merits of this case.

Public Interest

If the public interest weighs on one side of the scales or the other in this case, I believe it weighs in favor of permitting colleges and universities to chart their own course in providing athletic opportunities without judicial interference or oversight, absent a clear showing that they are in violation of the law.

Ruling

Plaintiffs' motion for preliminary injunction is denied.

In yet another variation, the plaintiff in *Deli v. University of Minnesota*, although a female, is a former head coach of girls' gymnastics who attempts to use Title IX to seek pay scale parity with her male counterparts.

DELI V. UNIVERSITY OF MINNESOTA

863 F. Supp. 958 (D. Minn. 1994)

MAGNUSON, District Judge.

This matter is before the Court upon Defendant University of Minnesota's motion for summary judgment. For the following reasons, the Court grants the motion.

Background

Plaintiff Katalin Deli is the former head coach of the University of Minnesota (University) women's gymnastics team. In June 1992, the University terminated her employment. Ms. Deli challenged this dismissal through the University grievance procedure. After review, the University upheld the termination, finding there existed just cause for her termination.

On October 12, 1993, Deli filed the present action against the University, alleging the University improperly paid her less than head coaches of several men's athletic teams. Deli contends that this pay differential allegedly based on the gender of the athletes she coached, constituted prohibited discrimination on the basis of sex, in violation of Title VII of the Civil Rights Act, 42 U.S.C. §2000e; the Equal Pay Act, 29 U.S.C. §206(d); and Title IX of the Education Amendments of 1972, 20 U.S.C. §§1681-1688.

The University now moves for summary judgment on all three claims. For purposes of this motion, it is important to clearly delineate the parameters of Plaintiff's claims. Plaintiff contends the Defendant discriminated in the compensation it paid her on the basis of the gender of the athletes she coached. Significantly, Plaintiff does not claim that the University discriminated against her on the basis of Plaintiff's gender, i.e. she does not claim that the University's motivation for paying her less money than the coaches of men's sports was the fact that Plaintiff was a woman and the coaches of men's sports were men. Plaintiff also does not challenge in this action the circumstances, justification or legality of her discharge from employment by the University. Additional facts are discussed as they become relevant.

Discussion

Summary judgment is appropriate if there is no genuine issue of material fact and the moving party is entitled to judgment as a matter of law. . . .

I. Title VII Claim . . .

Plaintiff has failed to state a Title VII claim on which relief can be granted and Defendant is entitled to judgment as a matter of law on Count II of the Complaint.

II. Equal Pay Act Claims . . .
III. Title IX Claims
A. Statute of Limitations . . .
B. Merits of Claims

Alternatively, even if her claims were timely filed, Plaintiff's Title IX claims fail on the merits. . . .

Plaintiff does not assert in her Complaint or elsewhere that the athletes she supervised received lesser quality coaching as a result of the difference between Plaintiff's salary and salaries paid to coaches of the men's football, hockey and basketball teams. To the contrary, the record shows Plaintiff contends she provided superior coaching and opportunities for the athletes she coached, as evidenced by her coaching honors and the accomplishments of her athletes. Because Plaintiff does not claim or provide any evidence to suggest that due to her receipt of a lower salary than that received by coaches of some men's athletic teams, Plaintiff's coaching services were inferior in "quality, nature or availability" to those provided to the men's teams, she has failed to make out a prima facie claim for violation of Title IX. The Defendant is entitled to summary judgment on Plaintiff's Title IX claims.

Accordingly, It is hereby ordered that:

—Defendant's motion for summary judgment is granted and this matter is dismissed. plaintiff's

U of Minn

Let judgment be entered Accordingly.

Cohen v. Brown University stands for the proposition that a college must fully and effectively accommodate the interests of women students—in this case, the interest was to reinstate to the level of university-funded varsity status women's gymnastics and volleyball. *Cohen* is the preeminent gender equality case.

COHEN V. BROWN UNIVERSITY

101 F.3d 155 (1st. Cir. 1996)

BOWNES, Senior Circuit Judge.

This is a class action lawsuit charging Brown University, its president, and its athletics director (collectively "Brown") with discrimination against women in the operation of its intercollegiate athletics program, in violation of Title IX of the Education Amendments of 1972, 20 U.S.C. §§1681-1688 ("Title IX"), and its implementing regulations, 34 C.F.R. §§106.1-106.71. The plaintiff class comprises all present, future, and potential Brown University women students who participate, seek to participate, and/or are deterred from participating in intercollegiate athletics funded by Brown.

This suit was initiated in response to the demotion in May 1991 of Brown's women's gymnastics and volleyball teams from university-funded varsity status to donor-funded varsity status. Contemporaneously, Brown demoted two men's teams, water polo and golf, from university-funded to donor-funded varsity status. As a consequence of these demotions, all four teams lost, not only their university funding, but most of the support and privileges that accompany university-funded varsity status at Brown.

Prior to the trial on the merits that gave rise to this appeal, the district court granted plaintiffs' motion for class certification and denied defendants' motion to dismiss. Subsequently, after hearing fourteen days of testimony, the district court granted plaintiffs' motion for a preliminary injunction, ordering, *inter alia*, that the women's gymnastics and volleyball teams be reinstated to university-funded varsity status, and prohibiting Brown from eliminating or reducing the status or funding of any existing women's inter-collegiate varsity team until the case was resolved on the merits. *Cohen v. Brown Univ.*, 809 F. Supp. 978, 1001 (D.R.I. 1992) ("*Cohen I*"). A panel of this court affirmed the district court's decision granting a preliminary injunction to the plaintiffs. *Cohen v. Brown Univ.*, 991 F.2d 888, 907 (1st Cir. 1993) ("*Cohen II*"). In so doing, we upheld the district court's analysis and ruled that an institution violates Title IX if it ineffectively accommodates its students' interests and abilities in athletics under 34 C.F.R. §106.41(c)(1) (1995), regardless of its performance with respect to other Title IX areas. *Id.* at 897.

On remand, the district court determined after a lengthy bench trial that Brown's intercollegiate athletics program violates Title IX and its supporting regulations. *Cohen v. Brown Univ.*, 879 F. Supp. 185, 214 (D.R.I. 1995) ("*Cohen III*"). The district court ordered Brown to submit within 120 days a comprehensive plan for complying with Title IX, but stayed that portion of the order pending appeal. *Id.* The district court subsequently issued a modified order, requiring Brown to submit a compliance plan within 60 days. Modified Order of May 4, 1995. This action was taken to ensure that the Order was "final" for purposes of this court's jurisdiction, and to expedite the appeal process. *Id.* Finding that Brown's proposed compliance plan was not comprehensive and that it failed to comply with the opinion and order of *Cohen III*, the district court rejected the plan and ordered in its place specific relief consistent with Brown's stated objectives in formulating the plan. Order of August 17, 1995 at 11. The court's remedial order required Brown to elevate and maintain at university-funded varsity status the women's gymnastics, fencing, skiing, and water polo teams. *Id.* at 12. The district court's decision to fashion specific relief was made, in part, to avoid protracted litigation over the compliance plan and to expedite the appeal on the issue of liability. *Id.* at 11. The district court entered final judgment on September 1, 1995, and on September 27, 1995, denied Brown's motion for additional findings of fact and to amend the judgment. This appeal followed. . . .

Brown contends that we are free to disregard the prior panel's explication of the law in *Cohen II*. Brown's efforts to circumvent the controlling effect of *Cohen II* are unavailing, however, because, under the law of the case doctrine, we are bound in this appeal, as was the district court on remand, by the prior panel's rulings of law. While we acknowledge that the law of the case doctrine is subject to exceptions, we conclude that none applies here, and that the decision rendered by the prior panel in the first appeal is not, as Brown claims, "legally defective." Accordingly, we decline Brown's invitation to undertake plenary review of issues decided in the previous appeal and treat *Cohen II* as controlling authority, dispositive of the core issues raised here.

We find no error in the district court's factual findings or in its interpretation and application of the law in determining that Brown violated Title IX in the operation of its intercollegiate athletics program. We therefore affirm in all respects the district court's analysis and rulings on the issue of liability. We do, however, find error in the district court's award of specific relief and therefore remand the case to the district court for reconsideration of the remedy in light of this opinion. . . .

[The court allows for the reinstatement of the two sports to university-funded varsity status. The court rejects the university's "relative interests" approach in the allocation of athletic resources between men's and women's programs on the basis that it fails to accommodate fully and effectively interests and abilities of the underrepresented gender (female athletes at Brown University). The court would review constitutionality of district court's order requiring university to comply with Title IX by accommodating fully and effectively athletic interests and abilities of its female students under an intermediate scrutiny test.]

Brown therefore should be afforded the opportunity to submit another plan for compliance with Title IX. The context of the case has changed in two significant respects since Brown presented its original plan. First, the substantive issues have been decided adversely to Brown. Brown is no longer an appellant seeking a favorable result in the Court of Appeals. Second, the district court is not under time constraints to consider a new plan and fashion a remedy so as to expedite appeal. Accordingly, we remand the case to the district court so that Brown can submit a further plan for its consideration. In all other respects the judgment of the district court is affirmed. The preliminary injunction issued by the district court in *Cohen I*, 809 F. Supp. at 1001, will remain in effect pending a final remedial order.

VIII

There can be no doubt that Title IX has changed the face of women's sports as well as our society's interest in and attitude toward women athletes and women's sports. In addition, there is ample evidence that increased athletics participation opportunities for women and young girls, available as a result of Title IX enforcement, have had salutary effects in other areas of societal concern.

One need look no further than the impressive performances of our country's women athletes in the 1996 Olympic Summer Games to see that Title IX has had a dramatic and positive impact on the capabilities of our women athletes, particularly in team sports. These Olympians represent the first full generation of women to grow up under the aegis of Title IX. The unprecedented success of these athletes is due, in no small measure, to Title IX's beneficent effects on women's sports, as the athletes themselves have acknowledged time and again. What stimulated this remarkable change in the quality of women's athletic competition was not a sudden, anomalous upsurge in women's interest in sports, but the enforcement of Title IX's mandate of gender equity in sports.

Affirmed in part, reversed in part, and remanded for further proceedings. No costs on appeal to either party.

TORRUELLA, Chief Judge (dissenting).
Because I am not persuaded that the majority's view represents the state of the law today, I respectfully dissent. . . .

Cohen began the cry of gender equity and the stipulation that universities must comply with Title IX by accommodating fully and effectively female athlete's interests and abilities under an intermediate scrutiny test. In both *Roberts v. Colorado State Bd. of Agric.*, 998 F.2d 824 (10th Cir. 1993), and *Favia v. Indiana University of Pennsylvania*, 812 F. Supp. 578 (W.D. Pa. 1992), *aff'd*, 7 F.3d 332 (3d Cir. 1993), the universities violated Title IX by discontinuing women's sports teams. But in *Gonyo v. Drake University*, 837 F. Supp. 989 (S.D. Iowa 1993), a discontinued male wrestling program could not use Title IX to force reinstatement. In *Deli v. University of Minn.*, 863 F. Supp. 958 (D. Minn. 1994), an allegedly underpaid female coach's salary discrimination suit did not violate Title IX. In *Klemencic v. Ohio State Univ.*, 263 F.3d 504 (6th Cir. 2001), an individual sexual harassment suit by a female athlete against a coach and university who would not allow her to train with the cross-country team after graduation did not rise to the level of a Title IX violation.

Mercer v. Duke University held that the plaintiff/female kicker stated a claim under Title IX on the basis that the university was prohibited from discriminating against the student-athlete on the basis of her sex once it allowed her to try out for its football team.

MERCER V. DUKE UNIVERSITY

190 F.3d 643 (4th Cir. 1999)

LUTTIG, Circuit Judge:

Appellant Heather Sue Mercer challenges the federal district court's holding that Title IX provides a blanket exemption for contact sports and the court's consequent dismissal of her claim that Duke University discriminated against her during her participation in Duke's intercollegiate football program. For the reasons that follow, we hold that where a university has allowed a member of the opposite sex to try out for a single-sex team in a contact sport, the university is, contrary to the holding of the district court, subject to Title IX and therefore prohibited from discriminating against that individual on the basis of his or her sex.

I

Appellee Duke University operates a Division I college football team. During the period relevant to this appeal (1994-98), appellee Fred Goldsmith was head coach of the Duke football team and appellant Heather Sue Mercer was a student at the school.

Before attending Duke, Mercer was an all-state kicker at Yorktown Heights High School in Yorktown Heights, New York. Upon enrolling at Duke in the fall of 1994, Mercer tried out for the Duke football team as a walk-on kicker. Mercer was the first—and to date, only—woman to try out for the team. Mercer did not initially make the team, and instead served as a manager during the 1994 season; however, she regularly attended practices in the fall of 1994 and participated in conditioning drills the following spring.

In April 1995, the seniors on the team selected Mercer to participate in the Blue-White Game, an intrasquad scrimmage played each spring. In that game, Mercer * kicked the winning 28-yard field goal, giving the Blue team a 24-22 victory. The kick was subsequently shown on ESPN, the cable television sports network. Soon after the game, Goldsmith told the news media that Mercer was on the Duke football team, and Fred Chatham, the Duke kicking coach, told Mercer herself that she had made the team. Also, Mike Cragg, the Duke sports information director, asked Mercer to participate in a number of interviews with newspaper, radio, and television reporters, including one with representatives from "The Tonight Show."

Although Mercer did not play in any games during the 1995 season, she again regularly attended practices in the fall and participated in conditioning drills the following spring. Mercer was also officially listed by Duke as a member of the Duke football team on the team roster filed with the NCAA and was pictured in the Duke football yearbook.

During this latter period, Mercer alleges that she was the subject of discriminatory treatment by Duke. Specifically, she claims that Goldsmith did not permit her to attend summer camp, refused to allow her to dress for games or sit on the sidelines during games, and gave her fewer opportunities to participate in practices than other walk-on kickers. In addition, Mercer claims that Goldsmith made a number of offensive comments to her, including asking her why she was interested in football, wondering why she did not prefer to participate in beauty pageants rather than football, and suggesting that she sit in the stands with her boyfriend rather than on the sidelines.

At the beginning of the 1996 season, Goldsmith informed Mercer that he was dropping her from the team. Mercer alleges that Goldsmith's decision to exclude her from the team was on the basis of her sex because Goldsmith allowed other, less qualified walk-on kickers to remain on the team. Mercer attempted to participate in conditioning drills the following spring, but Goldsmith asked her to leave because the drills were only for members of the team. Goldsmith told Mercer, however, that she could try out for the team again in the fall.

On September 16, 1997, rather than try out for the team again, Mercer filed suit against Duke and Goldsmith, alleging sex discrimination in violation of Title IX of the Education Amendments of 1972, 20 U.S.C. §§1681-1688, and negligent misrepresentation and breach of contract in violation of North Carolina law. . . .

From the district court's order dismissing her Title IX claim for failure to state a claim upon which relief can be granted and its order denying the motion to alter judgment, Mercer appeals.

II

Title IX prohibits discrimination on the basis of sex by educational institutions receiving federal funding. . . .

[The Department of Health, Education, and Welfare was assigned the task to promulgate regulations that would apply Title IX to athletic programs. (34 C.F.R. §106.41(a-b)).]

The district court held, and appellees contend on appeal, that, under this regulation, "contact sports, such as football, are specifically excluded from Title IX coverage." We disagree. . . .

We therefore construe the second sentence of subsection (b) as providing that in non-contact sports, but not in contact sports, covered institutions must allow members of an excluded sex to try out for single-sex teams. Once an institution has allowed a member of one sex to try out for a team operated by the institution for the other sex in a contact sport, subsection (b) is simply no longer applicable, and the institution is subject to the general anti-discrimination provision of subsection (a). . . .

Accordingly, because appellant has alleged that Duke allowed her to try out for its football team (and actually made her a member of the team), then discriminated against her and ultimately excluded her from participation in the sport on the basis of her sex, we conclude that she has stated a claim under the applicable regulation, and therefore under Title IX. We take to heart appellees' cautionary observation that, in so holding, we thereby become "the first Court in United States history to recognize such a cause of action." Where, as here, however, the university invites women into what appellees characterize as the "traditionally all-male bastion of collegiate football," we are convinced that this reading of the regulation is the only one permissible under law.

The district court's order granting appellees' motion to dismiss for failure to state a claim is hereby reversed, and the case remanded for further proceedings.

Reversed and remanded

The Fifth Circuit Court of Appeals reinstated Mercer's Title IX suit against school and coach. The court held that the university was prohibited from discriminating against her on the basis of her sex once the coach allowed her to try out for the football team. On remand, a federal jury awarded her $2 million in punitive damages. 'Female Kicker's Lawsuit Is Good,' N.Y. Times, (Oct. 13, 2000), at C21. However, in *Mercer v. Duke University*, 301 F. Supp. 2d 454 (M.D. N.C. 2004), she lost her punitive damages but was still able to keep 80% of the attorney fees.

QUESTIONS AND DISCUSSION

1. In *Haffer v. Temple Univ.*, 688 F.2d 14 (3d Cir. 1982), the court agreed to a settlement that outlined changes in Temple's athletic program. Although it applied to only one school, it has been viewed as the paradigm for collegiate compliance with Title IX. *See* Longo & Thomas, 'Haffer v. Temple Univ.: *A Reawakening of Gender Discrimination in Intercollegiate Athletics*,' 16 J.C. & U.L. 137 (1989). *See also* Villalobos, *The Civil Restoration Act of 1987: Revitalization of Title IX*, 1 Marq. Sports. L.J. 1499 (1990).
2. There were many cases that expressed out-of-court settlements under the banner of gender equity; for example, in *Cohen v. Brown University*, the gymnastics and volleyball teams were successfully reinstated to varsity status. *See* Richardson, Note, '*Sports Law: A Title IX Lesson for Colleges and Universities on Gender Equity* (Cohen v. Brown Univ. . . .),' 28 Ga. L. Rev. 837 (1994). The *Cohen* decision is like a lighthouse for lawsuits that have followed it. Why was it so important?
3. In *Boucher v. Syracuse Univ.* 164 F.3d 113 (2d Cir. 1999), the court held that the class of all present and future female students at Syracuse University who participated in club lacrosse (and wanted varsity status) and received unequal athletic benefits as compared to male club athletes are certified on the condition that plaintiffs proffer further evidence of sufficient numerosity. What type of evidence did the court have in mind?
4. *Roberts v. Colorado State Bd. of Agric.* held that Colorado State University must fully accommodate the interests and abilities of women by reinstating intercollegiate softball. Could the *Israel* argument of substantial equivalency be used here?
5. Indiana University of Pennsylvania's women's gymnastics teams had twice won the NCAA Division II Championships. Some relevant statistics: 56% of IUP's students were women; women athletes received only 21% of scholarship funds; and women athletes received only $2.75 for every $8.00

spent on male athletes. Would these reinstatements alone be sufficient to achieve "gender equity"?

6. The *Mercer* jurors ruled that her sex was the motivating factor in the way she was treated and that Duke officials, once informed of her complaints, failed to act. But $2 million? Do you think that is excessive? Could the point have been made with less money and more apologies? *See* Crouse, '*Equal Athletic Opportunity: An Analysis of* Mercer v. Duke University *and a Proposal to Amend the Contact Sport Exception to Title IX,*' 84 Minn. L. Rev. 1655 (2000).

7. The version of *Mercer* decided by the District Court for the Middle District of North Carolina, 32 F. Supp. 2d 836 (1998), used the contact sport exception to the general prohibition against sex discrimination in intercollegiate athletics to find that the university had no obligation to allow a female placekicker onto its football team. The court of appeals reversed on the grounds that the university was prohibited from discriminating against Heather Sue Mercer on the basis of her sex, once it allowed her to try out for the team. Would the outcome be different if she was not allowed the opportunity to try out, but male kickers of equal skill were?

C. EQUAL PROTECTION

State action must be found for a case to be based on the Equal Protection Clause of the Fourteenth Amendment. The next step is to determine if the athlete program's provisions or the enforcement of its prohibitions violate the clause. The original standard applied to sexually discriminatory sports rules was one of a "rational relationship." However, the current standard of review for sex-based classifications is whether a gender-based classification serves an important governmental objective and is substantially related to achieving that objective.

In *Dodson v. Arkansas Activities Association*, the court held that half-court basketball for girls violated equal protection.

DODSON V. ARKANSAS ACTIVITIES ASSOCIATION

468 F. Supp. 394 (E.D. Ark. 1979)

ARNOLD, District Judge.

Diana Lee Dodson brought this suit on January 25, 1977. At the time she was 14 years old and in the ninth grade in the public schools of Arkadelphia, Arkansas. She was a good basketball player and had played on her junior high girls' team in the eighth grade. There are three defendants: the school district in which Diana Lee's school is located, the superintendent of schools of that district, and the Arkansas Activities Association. The Association is a voluntary group of schools, mostly public, to which the Arkadelphia schools belong, together with most, if not all, other public junior and senior high schools in Arkansas.

This suit challenges the constitutionality of the rules for girls' junior and senior high basketball laid down by the defendant Association. There is no question of state action. The Association, although not itself a governmental body, is supported in large part by dues paid by public school districts, and the authorities in the member districts make a practice of abiding by eligibility standards and other rules on athletic subjects made and announced by the Association. The Association in effect exercises a delegated governmental power. It is, at least for present purposes, subject to the Equal Protection Clause of the Fourteenth Amendment.

The question presented is whether the differences in girls' and boys' junior and senior high basketball rules, as laid down by the Association for play in Arkansas, are so lacking in justification, and so injurious to the girls, as to deprive them of the equal protection of the laws. This Court holds that the rules place girl athletes in Arkansas at a substantial disadvantage as compared to boy athletes, that no sufficient justification is offered to justify this disparity, and that the resulting discrimination is unconstitutional. A decree will be entered requiring defendants to erase the differences between the two sets of rules.

Girls' basketball, as played in Arkansas, is markedly different from boys'. It is variously referred to as "half-court," "six on six," or "three on three," while the boys' game is known as "full-court" or "five on five." Girls' teams have six players, while boys' have five. Three girls are forwards, almost always on offense, and three are guards, almost always on defense. No players may cross the center line in the middle of the court. The three guards must always stay in the half of the court where the other team scores. The forwards must stay in the half of the court where their own team scores. Only a forward can shoot or score points. If a guard is fouled, she does not get a free throw. The ball goes to the other end of the court, and one of the forwards does the shooting. In "full court" or "boys' rules," by contrast, all five players may range the full length of the court. They all play defense when the other team has the ball, and they all play offense when their own team has the ball. Any player may shoot and score points, both field goals and free throws.

There are some other differences between the two games, but the difference just described is a major one. Arkansas girls simply do not get the full benefit and experience of the game of basketball available to Arkansas boys. Although substitution is possible, and a girl may play both guard and forward at various times, such changes appear to be the exception rather than the rule. Most girls are typed as either a guard or a forward and remain so. A five-person, full-court game requires a more comprehensive and more complex strategy. It also provides more intensive physical training and conditioning, because, if for no other reason, players on a five-person team have to run up and down the full length of the court, not just half of it. Players of the full-court game also learn to shoot from farther out, because there are five opponents, not just three, trying to keep them away from the basket....

All this might not matter so much were it not for the effects on the girls after graduation. Those whose ambition it is to play basketball in college, perhaps even on scholarship, are at a marked disadvantage. College basketball is full-court, for women as well as men. For that matter, almost no one plays half-court any more. Most Arkansas private schools play full-court for boys and girls. International competition is full-court. Every state except Arkansas, Iowa, Oklahoma, and Tennessee is full-court in secondary school . . . . If an Arkansas girl wishes to compete for a position on a college team, she must overcome substantial obstacles. Most of her opposition will have played full-court in high school. The lack of training and conditioning, the psychological barrier of the center line, which she has been schooled not to cross, and, in the case of guards, the lack of shooting experience all these factors make the Arkansas girl less able to compete. . . .

In view of these disparities a movement understandably arose among some schools to change the rules to permit girls to play full-court. This kind of decision is made by vote of the membership of the Arkansas Activities Association. . . . [This effort failed.]

The fact that girls in Arkansas secondary schools are treated differently, or less advantageously, than boys, of course, is not at all conclusive of the claim asserted. The Equal Protection Clause does not forbid differences as such. It remains to ask, what justification is offered for the difference? . . . Half-court may in fact be a better game. But if it's better for the girls, it's better for the boys as well. None of the reasons proffered is at all relevant to a gender-based classification. . . .

The real reason for the difference, and in fact the only operative reason, is simply that girls' rules have always been this way in Arkansas. . . .

A permanent injunction will issue as prayed for in the complaint.

It is so ordered this 4th day of April, 1979.

Judgment

This cause having come on for trial to the Court on October 3, 1977; the parties have stipulated that the undersigned might decide the case based upon the briefs and a transcript of the trial; a transcript having been ordered, prepared, and, on February 1, 1979, filed with the Court; and the Court having filed its Opinion containing findings of fact and conclusions of law;

It is by the Court this 4th day of April, 1979, considered, ordered, adjudged, and decreed, that the defendants, and each of them, their agents, servants, and employees, and all persons acting in concert with them, be, and they are hereby, permanently enjoined and restrained from enforcing as to girls playing junior and senior high school basketball in Arkansas, any rules different from those enforced as to boys.

And that plaintiff do have and recover of and from the defendants, jointly and severally, judgment for her costs expended herein, together with interest at the rate of ten per centum per annum, for which let execution issue at the time and in the manner provided by law.

QUESTIONS AND DISCUSSION

1. In *Dodson,* the difference in the rules deprived the girls of their equal protection rights. How about softball? Is softball the same game as baseball? Is softball a better game? Note that the *Dodson* court did not

speculate whether half-court basketball was a better game than full-court basketball. Do you think they should have?

2. The only rationale behind the different rules in *Dodson* was heritage and tradition. But heritage, tradition and folklore alone, without some supporting substantive gender-based reason, is insufficient to justify the rule changes in light of the fact that those rules placed Arkansas girl athletes at a substantial disadvantage in comparison to their male counterparts.

3. Under equal protection the ultimate test becomes one's ability without regard to sex. Equal protection claims can be combined with a Title IX action and also a state ERA claim. *See Adams v. Baker,* 919 F. Supp. 1496 (D. Kan. 1996) (female high school student allowed to participate in wrestling).

4. Courts apply an intermediate standard of review in their evaluation of the constitutionality of sex-based classifications. Sex-based classifications are allowed only if they are substantially related to an important governmental objective. This test is somewhat subjective, and, as a result, each court's analysis can produce different or mixed results.

5. In *Brenden v. Independent Sch. Dist. 742,* 342 F. Supp. 1224 (D. Minn. 1972), *aff'd,* 477 F.2d 1292 (8th Cir. 1973), female students wanted to compete in male-only sports (tennis, cross-country, skiing, and running). Since they were qualified to compete, the application of the rule prohibiting females from participating was arbitrary, unreasonable, and violative of Fourteenth Amendment equal protection.

D. STATE ERAs

Another way to attack sex discrimination is through a state equal rights amendment (ERA); however, not all states have passed such legislation. Cases that have decided in the complainant's favor on the basis of a state ERA have overcome discriminatory rules and practices that exclude or deny women the opportunities to participate in sports.

In *Blair v. Washington State University,* female athletes and coaches of female athletes brought a sexual discrimination action under the state ERA. Although the court allowed individual sports programs to use generated revenue for their exclusive use, it also held that football was to be included in the gender calculation for sports participation and scholarships.

BLAIR V. WASHINGTON STATE UNIVERSITY

740 P.2d 1379 (Wash. 1987)

DOLLIVER, Justice.

This is a sex discrimination action brought under the state Equal Rights Amendment, Const. Art. 31, §1 (Amend. 61), and the Law Against Discrimination, RCW 49.60. Appellants are female athletes and coaches of female athletes at Washington State University. Respondents are Washington State University, its President, Executive Vice President, and Board of Regents.

The trial court concluded the University had discriminated against the plaintiffs on the basis of sex and awarded damages, injunctive relief, attorney fees, and costs. The plaintiffs now appeal (1) the exclusion of football from the court's calculations for sports participation and scholarships; (2) the trial court's decision to allow each sport to benefit from the revenue it generates; (3) the reduction of the attorney fee award; and (4) the trial court ruling requiring them to file a claim under the tort claims act, RCW 4.92.110, as a condition precedent to bringing this suit. The University in its cross appeal challenges portions of the trial court's award of attorney fees and costs. Subject to the discussion below, we reverse the trial court on issues (1) and (3), affirm on issues (2) and (4), and affirm on the issues raised by the University's cross appeal.

The comprehensive findings of fact of the trial court demonstrate that, despite marked improvements since the early 1970's, the women's athletic programs have continued to receive inferior treatment in funding, fundraising efforts, publicity and promotions, scholarships, facilities, equipment, coaching, uniforms, practice clothing, awards, and administrative staff and support. During the 1980-81 school year, the year before the trial, the total funding available to the men's athletic programs was $3,017,692, and for the women's programs was $689,757, roughly 23 percent of the men's. The funds for the men's programs were derived largely from revenues, both gate admissions ($958,503) and media rights, conference revenues, and guaranties ($943,629). Most of these revenues were derived from football ($1,430,554). Of the funding available to the women's programs, most was derived from legislative appropriations ($451,082). Very little came from gate admissions ($10,535). Although the number of participation opportunities for men increased by 115 positions from 1973-74 to 1980-81, the opportunities made available for women decreased 9 positions during the same period. The budget for men's scholarships increased from $380,056 to $478,052 during that period; the budget for women's scholarships in 1980-81 was $150,000. The trial court observed in its memorandum opinion:

> The non-emphasis on the women's athletic program was demonstrated in many ways, some subtle, some not so subtle. . . . The message came through loud and clear, women's teams were low priority. . . . [T]he net result was an entirely different sort of participation opportunity for the athletes.

On the basis of numerous findings of fact detailing the inferior treatment of the women's athletic program, the trial court concluded the University had "acted, or failed to act, in the operation of the University's intercollegiate athletics program in a manner that resulted in discriminatory treatment of females . . . " The athletes had "suffered unlawful sex discrimination violative of RCW 49.60 and the State Equal Rights Amendment."

The court entered a detailed injunction to remedy the violations. With respect to funding, the court ordered the women's program must receive 37.5 percent of the University's financial support given to intercollegiate athletics during the year 1982-83. The required minimum percentage for women increased each year by 2 percent until it corresponded to the percentage of women undergraduates at the University, 44 percent at the time of the injunction. The trial court provided, however, the level of support for women's athletics was not required to exceed by more than 3 percent the actual participation rate of women in intercollegiate athletics at the University, excluding football participation from the comparison. The injunction prohibited the total budget for women's athletics ever to be less than the base budget of $841,145 for 1981-82, unless the expenditures for men's athletics were correspondingly reduced.

The injunction also specified:

> In determining the level of University financial support of intercollegiate athletics for purposes of the above calculation, the term "University financial support" shall not include revenue generated by or attributable to any specific sport or program. Such excluded sources of revenue shall specifically include gate receipts, conference revenues, guarantees, sale of media rights, concession and novelty sales at games, coach and athlete work projects, and donations attributable to a sport or program.

The injunction apportioned the funding for athletic scholarships in a similar manner. The women received 37.5 percent of all money expended for scholarships, excluding funds expended for football scholarships. The percentage increased yearly until it equaled the percentage of women undergraduates. The allocation could not fall below $236,300, the amount allocated for 1982-83, unless matched by a reduction in male scholarships.

The court also ordered the University to allow for increased participation opportunities until female participation, again excluding football participation from the comparison, reached a level commensurate with the proportion of female undergraduate students. The court noted female participation had increased in recent years and stated in its memorandum opinion, "[t]he change in the last ten years is dramatic, and it seems possible that parity will soon arrive."

The court further required the University to take affirmative steps to make opportunities to generate revenue equally available to men's and women's programs, stating:

> Because past sex discrimination has afforded women's teams and coaches less opportunity to generate revenue, the University should take affirmative action in providing additional personnel with such knowledge and experience. . . .

The trial court required the University to appoint a committee to monitor the application of the funding formulas and other elements of the injunction. The sex equity committee, comprised of students, coaches, and administrators, was also given the mandate to develop recommendations for policies concerning matters affecting sex equity in athletics and recommendations for the promotion of women's athletics. After approval by the Provost, the committee's recommendations are to be implemented and administered in an equitable and timely manner.

In addition to the injunction, the court awarded the plaintiffs monetary damages for certain tangible losses caused by the University's discriminatory policies. The plaintiffs contest *the trial court's* reduction of the damages award. . . .

Finally, the court awarded the plaintiffs approximately $170,000 in attorney fees, expert witness fees, and costs. The court in calculating the attorney fee award concluded the plaintiffs had prevailed but reduced the award after finding the attorneys had duplicated some efforts and expended an excessive amount of time on some issues. The court also noted the plaintiffs' attorneys worked for a nonprofit legal organization.

Appeal was made directly to this court. The University directed its notice of appeal from the award of costs and witness fees to the Court of Appeals, which sent the notice to this court. Attorneys for the American Civil Liberties Union and other amici field an amicus brief in support of the plaintiffs' position.

I

The plaintiffs ask us to review two elements of the trial court's injunction. . . .

A. Football Exclusion

The first issue raised by the plaintiffs is whether the trial court abused its discretion in creating an injunctive remedy which excluded football from its calculations for participation opportunities, scholarships, and distribution of nonrevenue funds. We conclude the trial court did abuse its discretion and reverse on this issue. The Equal Rights Amendment and the Law Against Discrimination prohibit such an exclusion. . . .

The recognized purpose of the Equal Rights Amendment is to end special treatment for or discrimination against either sex. This absolute mandate of equality does not, however, bar affirmative governmental efforts to create equality in fact; governmental actions favoring one sex which are intended solely to ameliorate the effects of past discrimination do not implicate the Equal Rights Amendment.

Neither party disputes the intercollegiate athletics program at Washington State University is subject to the Equal Rights Amendment and the Law Against Discrimination. The trial court found the operation of the program resulted in discriminatory treatment of women and the women's athletic program in violation of these laws. Football is a large and essential part of intercollegiate athletics at the University. To exclude football, an all male program, from the scope of the Equal Rights Amendment would only serve to perpetuate the discriminatory policies and diminished opportunities for women.

The trial court attempted to explain the exclusion of football by stating football was a sport "unique in many respects, the combination of which distinguished it from all other collegiate sports . . . " The court identified such distinguishing characteristics as the number of participants, scholarships, and coaches, amount of equipment and facilities, income generated, media interest, spectator attendance, and publicity generated for the University as a whole. . . .

We do not believe, however, these or any other characteristics of football justify its exclusion from the scope of the injunction remedying violations of the Equal Rights Amendment. It is stating the obvious to observe the Equal Rights Amendment contains no exception for football. The exclusion of football would prevent sex equity from ever being achieved since men would always be guaranteed many more participation opportunities than women, despite any efforts by the teams, the sex equity committee, or the program to promote women's athletics under the injunction.

B. Revenue Retention

The plaintiffs also challenge the portion of the injunction excluding from the division of university financial support the revenue generated by any specific sport or program. The injunction allows each sport to reap the benefit of the revenues it generates. We hold the trial court did not abuse its discretion. Exclusion of sports-generated revenue from the calculations of university financial support is not prohibited under applicable state law and can be supported by several policy considerations. We affirm this portion of the trial court's injunction. . . .

The plaintiffs contend this statute indicates a legislative intent to pool sports-generated revenues to make them available for athletic scholarships.

The legislative history does not support reading such intent into this provision. . . .

The legislative history supports the contention sports-generated revenues are in fact state funds. We believe it does not, however, support the plaintiffs' assertion this statute should be used to prohibit the trial court's decision, nor is plaintiffs' assertion a necessary inference from the language of the statute. The trial court chose an injunctive remedy neither required nor prohibited by applicable law and acted within its discretion in choosing to create a funding plan allowing each sport to benefit from the revenues it generates.

The trial court's funding plan provides incentive for all sports to develop revenue-generating capability of their own. . . .

The funding plan encourages the sports to fund their expenses through their own efforts, rather than depend upon direct legislative appropriations.

The injunction specifically requires the sex equity committee to recommend ways to encourage and promote women's sports to increase their own revenues; the funding plan would further promote such a goal. The plan thus requires the University to create equal opportunity to raise revenue for men's and women's sports.

The funding plan allows disproportionate expenses of any particular sports program to be derived from the program itself. The plan is also gender neutral. It provides a solution which does not violate the Equal Rights Amendment and encourages revenue development for all sports while accommodating the needs of the sports programs incurring the greatest expenses at this time.

Our decision upholding the trial court's conclusion regarding sports-generated revenues does not in any way modify the University's obligation to achieve sex equity under the Equal Rights Amendment. The trial court's minimum requirements for participation opportunities and scholarships, already discussed, must be achieved; the court's guidelines for distribution of nonrevenue funds must be followed, and the remaining portions of the injunction, including promotion and development of women's sports, must be observed.

In addition, our conclusion allowing each sport to use the revenues it generates does not, of course, require the sport to do so. The record reflects the football program was transferring $150,000 or more per year from its revenues to the women's program before the injunction was entered. We encourage such practices to continue, along with other efforts to foster cooperation within the department.

We therefore reverse the trial court's exclusion of football from its calculations for participation opportunities and scholarships and affirm the trial court's decision to exclude sports-generated revenues from its distribution of financial support. We emphasize the portion of the injunction requiring additional promotion of women's sports and development of their revenue-generating capability and encourage continued cooperation and efforts to bring the University's intercollegiate athletic program into compliance with the Equal Rights Amendment. . . .

The trial court abused its discretion in even considering the plaintiffs' public interest representation. Although the court has discretion to reduce the award to the extent the amount sought is due to inefficiency or duplicative efforts, any reduction based simply on the public interest representation of the athletes was error. We reverse the trial court on this issue and remand the case with instructions to ignore the nonprofit status of plaintiffs' counsel in determining a reasonable fee award.

The University, in its cross appeal, argues the attorney fee award for the plaintiffs should be reduced by the percentage of the University's success. The trial court found the plaintiffs were the prevailing parties and awarded them attorney fees, although the University prevailed on a number of issues. The trial court considered the extent to which the plaintiffs prevailed but found the issues and evidence so interrelated as to make a division based on successful and unsuccessful claims impossible without being arbitrary. . . .

The trial court did not abuse its discretion in determining the plaintiffs were the prevailing parties and entitled to all fees awarded. . . .

V

The trial court ruled discrimination is a tort and that RCW 4.92.110 required the plaintiffs to file a tort claim with the State before bringing suit. The plaintiffs originally filed suit October 26, 1979; they filed a tort claim about September 11, 1980. The parties stipulated that if RCW 4.92.110 controls, the complaint would be considered filed as of September 12, 1980. The trial court ruling therefore eliminated about 1 year's worth of damages. The plaintiffs contend the trial court erred in holding RCW 4.92.110 required them to file a tort claim as a condition precedent to bringing suit under RCW 49.60. . . .

To summarize, the injunctive relief provided it by the trial court is affirmed as modified in this opinion. The football program may not be excluded from the calculations of participation opportunities, scholarships, or distribution of nonrevenue funds. The reduction of attorney fees is reversed, while the trial court ruling that plaintiffs must file a claim under RCW 4.92.110 as a condition precedent to bring this suit is affirmed. Pursuant to RAP 18.1, the plaintiff's request for attorney fees and expenses on appeal is granted for an amount to be determined on remand. The issues raised by the University in its cross appeal are affirmed. The entire matter is remanded to the Superior Court to be under its continuing jurisdiction with instructions to take whatever further action is necessary consistent with this opinion.

PEARSON, C.J., and UTTER, BRACHTENBACH, ANDERSEN, DURHAM, CALLOW and GOODLOE, JJ., concur.

QUESTIONS AND DISCUSSION

1. There is no federal constitutional amendment that prohibits sex discrimination (no federal ERA); therefore, ERAs have impacted athletes at the state, but not the federal level.

2. An important advantage of the ERA approach is that state courts can now determine under state law whether gender classifications are suspect and thus warrant strict scrutiny as a standard of review. School rules pass this standard if the gender classification is deemed necessary to achieve a compelling state interest. Strict scrutiny enhances the female athletes' opportunities for success since the school must prove that the classification has a direct relationship to the purpose of the regulation and that the purpose cannot be achieved by less restrictive means.

3. State ERAs have proven instrumental in overcoming discriminatory rules and practices, which in effect exclude or deny women the opportunity of participating in sports.

4. *Blair* held that the trial court was required to include the football program in calculations for participation opportunities, scholarships, and distribution of nonrevenue funds in fashioning an injunction to remedy university's discriminatory practices. This, of course, is the bane of gender equity. How can there be equality if the majority of resources are tied to football? Of course, without football in the calculations, the push for equity would be a farce. Washington has a state ERA; should this holding be used by analogy in those states that are non-ERA?

6. The *Blair* court also held that individual sports programs could use revenue generated by the particular program for their exclusive benefit. Is this a contradiction to their holding that football must be added into the calculations?

12

INTERNATIONAL LAW

The **Olympics** or Olympic Movement consists of annual and semi-annual international sports competition. This generally involves open competition among amateur and professional athletes. The United States Olympic Committee governs American participation in the Olympic and Pan American games.

The **Amateur Sports Act of 1978** coordinates amateur athletics including providing for dispute resolution involving national governing bodies. The act amends the statutory provisions as it relates to the USOC.

A key aspect of international sports is **Drug Testing**. To enforce the ban on certain drugs, the International Olympic Committee requires that each competition site provide adequate testing facilities and that each competitor agree to submit to possible medical examinations or risk exclusion. Many disputes that concern drug testing are resolved in the **International Court of Arbitration for Sport** (CAS), which is a specialized tribunal that adjudicates sport-related disputes that transcend national boundaries.

A. OLYMPICS

The Olympic Charter at 9(1) describes Olympic Games as: "competitions between athletes in individual or team events and not between countries. They bring together the athletes designated for such purpose by their respective NOCs [National Olympic Committees], whose entries have been accepted by the IOC [International Olympic Committee], and who compete under the technical direction of the IFs [International Federations] concerned." Sir Roger Bannister, the great British runner who broke the four-minute mile barrier, described the Olympics as "one of the great leavening forces for good in the 20th century."[1]

---

[1] Nafziger, *International Sports Law* 130 (1988), *as quoted in* Atkin, *Olympic Voices for Reform,* Christian Sci. Monitor, Feb. 12, 1980, at 18, col. 4.

1. United States Olympic Committee

Athletic competition among different nationalities usually involves open competition among amateur and professional athletes. The United States Olympic Committee (USOC) governs American participation in the Olympic and Pan American games and has operated under a federal charter since 1950. 64 Stat. 902, 36 U.S.C. §§371-383. USOC is the sole organization in the United States that is recognized by the international Olympic board, the International Olympics Committee (IOC). There are more than 200 amateur groups in the USOC; but voting is controlled by those groups recognized by the international sports federation for Olympic sports. The USOC has a constitution and bylaws that govern its administrative functions; for example, pursuant to the Amateur Sports Act of 1978, 36 U.S.C. §391, the Athletic Congress (TAC), was designated as the national governing body for track and field.

2. International Olympic Committee

The IOC is registered under Swiss laws as a nonprofit, private society with legal status under tax and labor laws because of its international character. Under the IOC charter, it has legal status under international law and perpetual succession. The Olympic Charter forms the basis of international sports law.

IOC CHARTER

Chapter I—The Olympic Movement

1. Supreme Authority

1—The IOC is the supreme authority of the Olympic Movement.

2—Any person or organization belonging in any capacity whatsoever to the Olympic Movement is bound by the provisions of the Olympic Charter and shall abide by the decisions of the IOC.

3. Belonging to the Olympic Movement

1—In addition to the IOC, the Olympic Movement includes the International Federations (IFs), the National Olympic Committees (NOCs), the Organizing Committees of the Olympic Games (OCOGs), the national associations, clubs and persons belonging to them, particularly the athletes. Furthermore, the Olympic Movement includes other organizations and institutions as recognized by the IOC. . . .

Chapter II—The International Olympic Committee

19. Legal Status

1—The IOC is an international non-governmental non-profit organization, of unlimited duration, in the form of an association with the status of a legal person, recognized by decree of the Swiss Federal Council of September 17, 1981. . . .

4—The decisions of the IOC, taken on the basis of the provisions of the Olympic Charter, are final. Any dispute relating to their application or interpretation may be resolved solely by the IOC Executive Board and, in certain cases, by arbitration before the Court of Arbitration for Sport (CAS).

20. Members

1 — Recruitment

1.1   The IOC chooses and elects its members from among such persons as it considers qualified. They must be nationals of a country in which they have their domicile or their main center of interests and in which there is an NOC recognized by the IOC. Furthermore, such persons must speak at least one of the languages used at the IOC Sessions. . . .

Chapter III — The International Federations

30. Role

1 — The role of the IFs is to:

1.1   establish and enforce the rules concerning the practice of their respective sports and to ensure their application;

1.2   ensure the development of their sports throughout the world;

1.3   contribute to the achievement of the goals set out in the Olympic Charter;

1.4   establish their criteria of eligibility to enter the competitions of the Olympic Games in conformity with the Olympic Charter, and to submit these to the IOC for approval . . .

Chapter IV — The National Olympic Committees

31. Mission and Role of the NOCs

1 — The mission of the NOCs is to develop and protect the Olympic Movement in their respective countries, in accordance with the Olympic Charter.

2 — The NOCs:

2.1   propagate the fundamental principles of Olympism at [the] national level within the framework of sports activity and otherwise contribute, among other things, to the diffusion of Olympism in the teaching programs of physical education and sport in schools and university establishments. . . .

3. Boycotts

Unfortunately, Olympic boycotts occur from time to time when countries attempt to make political gains through not participating. For example, the United States boycotted the 1980 Moscow Olympics as a protest to the U.S.S.R's activities in Afghanistan. The Soviet Union then boycotted the 1984 games in Los Angeles.

Boycotts are illegal when they induce conflict or coercion that would violate the U.N. charter; they are also illegal if they violate international rules by conforming diplomatic nonrecognition.

Sometimes, boycotts fall within the protected range of retaliatory sanctions. To be within this range the boycott must not violate provisions of the

UN Charter or other binding instruments and must conform to state practice and not violate general legal principles. Also, illegal boycotts may be acceptable if they are a reprisal to illegal acts to another state.

In *DeFrantz v. USOC*, the court held that the USOC had the authority to boycott the 1980 Olympics.

DEFRANTZ V. UNITED STATES OLYMPIC COMMITTEE

492 F. Supp. 1181 (D.D.C. 1980)

JOHN H. PRATT, District Judge.

Memorandum Opinion

Plaintiffs, 25 athletes and one member of the Executive Board of defendant United States Olympic Committee (USOC), have moved for an injunction barring defendant USOC from carrying out a resolution, adopted by the USOC House of Delegates on April 12, 1980, not to send an American team to participate in the Games of the XXIInd Olympiad to be held in Moscow in the summer of 1980. Plaintiffs allege that in preventing American athletes from competing in the Summer Olympics, defendant has exceeded its statutory powers and has abridged plaintiffs' constitutional rights.

For the reasons discussed below, we find that plaintiffs have failed to state a claim upon which relief can be granted. Accordingly, we deny plaintiffs' claim for injunctive and declaratory relief and dismiss the action.

The Facts

In essence, the action before us involves a dispute between athletes who wish to compete in the Olympic Games to be held in Moscow this summer, and the United States Olympic Committee, which has denied them that opportunity in the wake of the invasion and continued occupation of Afghanistan by Soviet military forces. Because this dispute confronts us with questions concerning the statutory authority of the USOC, its place and appropriate role in the international Olympic movement, and its relationship to the United States Government and with certain United States officials, we begin with a brief discussion of the organizational structure of the Olympic Games and the facts which have brought this action before us. These facts are not in dispute.

According to its Rules and By-laws, the International Olympic Committee (IOC) governs the Olympic movement and owns the rights of the Olympic games. IOC Rules provide that National Olympic Committees (NOC) may be established "as the sole authorities responsible for the representation of the respective countries at the Olympic Games," so long as the NOC's rules and regulations are approved by the IOC. The USOC is one such National Olympic Committee.

The USOC is a corporation created and granted a federal charter by Congress in 1950. Pub L. No. 81-805, 64 Stat. 899. This charter was revised by the Amateur Sports Act of 1978, Pub. L. No. 95-606, 92 Stat. 3045, 36 U.S.C. §§371 et seq. Under this statute, defendant USOC has "exclusive jurisdiction" and authority over participation and representation of the United States in the Olympic Games.

The routine procedure initiating the participation of a national team in Olympic competition is the acceptance by the NOC of an invitation from the Olympic Organizing Committee for the particular games. In accordance with this routine procedure under IOC Rules, the Moscow Olympic Organizing Committee extended an invitation to the USOC to participate in the summer games. Recent international and domestic events, however, have made acceptance of this invitation, which must come on or before May 24, 1980, anything but routine.

On December 27, 1979, the Soviet Union launched an invasion of its neighbor, Afghanistan. That country's ruler was deposed and killed and a new government was installed. Fighting has been at times intense, casualties have been high, and hundreds of thousands of Afghan citizens have fled their homeland. At present, and estimated 100,000 Soviet troops remain in Afghanistan, and fighting continues.

President Carter termed the invasion a threat to the security of the Persian Gulf area as well as a threat to world peace and stability and he moved to take direct sanctions against the Soviet Union. . . .

With these concerns in mind, the Administration strenuously urged a boycott of the Moscow games. On January 20, 1980, President Carter wrote the President of the United States Olympic Committee to urge that the USOC propose to the IOC that the 1980 summer games be transferred from Moscow, postponed, or cancelled if the Soviet forces were not withdrawn within a month. . . .

Following these statements, the United States House of Representatives passed, by a vote of 386 to 12, a Concurrent Resolution opposing participation by United States athletes in the Moscow Games unless Soviet troops were withdrawn from Afghanistan by February 20th. The Senate passed a similar resolution by a vote of 88 to 4.

As this was unfolding, the USOC's 86 member Executive Board held a meeting in Colorado Springs on January 26, 1980, inviting White House counsel Lloyd Cutler to address them "because no officer or any member of the Board was knowledgeable about the far-reaching implications of the Soviet invasion." . . .

On March 21, 1980, President Carter told members of the Athletes Advisory Council, an official body of the USOC, that American athletes will not participate in the Moscow summer games. On April 8, 1980, the President sent a telegram to the president and officers of the USOC and to its House of Delegates, urging the USOC vote against sending an American team to Moscow. [USOC voted 12-1 in favor of not sending a team.] . . .

Plaintiffs state three causes of action in their complaint. The first, a statutory claim, is that defendant violated the Amateur Sports Act of 1978, supra, in the following respects:

a. Defendant exercised a power it does not have to decide that no United States amateur athletes shall participate in the 1980 Games. . . .

    d. Defendant yielded its exclusive jurisdiction over Olympic matters to the political leaders of the nation.

    e. Defendant acted in a political manner. . . .

Plaintiffs' second cause of action, a constitutional claim, alleges that defendant's action constituted "governmental action" which abridged plaintiffs' rights of liberty, self-expression, personal autonomy and privacy guaranteed by the First, Fifth and Ninth Amendments to the United States Constitution.

Plaintiffs' third cause of action is that the USOC has violated its Constitution, By-laws and governing statute, injuring the USOC and violating the rights of plaintiff Shaw, a member of the USOC's Executive Board, and that defendant is subject to an action to compel compliance with its Constitution, By-laws and governing statute.

Plaintiffs allege that unredressed, these violations will result in great and irreparable injury to the athletes. . . .

In summary, plaintiffs ask this court to declare the April 12, 1980 resolution of the USOC House of Delegates null and void because it violated statutory authority and constitutional provisions and to permanently enjoin the USOC from carrying out that resolution. . . .

Analysis

This action presents us with several issues for decision, falling into two distinct categories; one is statutory and the other is constitutional. We turn first to the statutory issues.

1. The Amateur Sports Act of 1978

Plaintiffs allege in their complaint that by its decision not to send an American team to compete in the summer Olympic Games in Moscow, defendant USOC has violated the Amateur Sports Act of 1978, supra, (The Act). . . .

    (a) The USOC's Authority Not to Send a Team to Moscow . . .

Nothing in the IOC Charter, Rules or By-laws requires a NOC, such as the USOC, to accept an invitation to participate in any particular Olympic contest and the President of the IOC has said that participation in the Olympic games is entirely voluntary. . . .

Because defendant USOC clearly has the power under IOC Rules to decide not to enter an American team in Olympic competition, the question then becomes whether the Amateur Sports Act of 1978, which rewrote the USOC's charter, denies the USOC that power. Plaintiffs emphatically argue that it does, and defendant and the Government just as emphatically argue that it does not.

Defendant and the Government respond that the Act gives the USOC broad powers, including the authority to decide not to accept an invitation to send an American team to the Olympics. [The court agrees with Defendant's argument.] . . .

We therefore conclude that the USOC not only had the authority to decide not to send an American team to the summer Olympics, but also that it could do so for reasons not directly related to sports considerations.

(b) Athletes Statutory Right to Compete in the Olympics . . .

Plaintiffs argue that the Report of the President's Commission on Olympic Sports, which was the starting point for the legislation proposed, and the legislative history supports their argument that the statute confers an enforceable right on plaintiffs to compete in Olympic competition. Again, we are compelled to disagree with plaintiffs. . . .

(c) Statutory Cause of Action

Plaintiffs argue that they have a private cause of action under the Amateur Sports Act of 1978 to maintain an action to enforce their rights under that Act. This argument assumes (1) the existence of a right and (2) the capability of enforcing that right by a private cause of action. As the foregoing discussion establishes, we have found that the statute does not guarantee plaintiffs a right to compete in the Olympics if the USOC decides not to send an American team to the Olympic Games and we have found that defendant has violated no provision of the Act. Thus, the "right" the plaintiffs seek to enforce under the Act simply does not exist. . . .

Under these circumstances, we cannot find that plaintiffs have an implied private right of action under the Amateur Sports Act to enforce a right which does not exist. . . .

Because we conclude that the rights plaintiffs seek to enforce do not exist in the Act, and because the legislative history of the Act nowhere allows the implication of a private right of action, we find that plaintiffs have no implied private right of action under the Amateur Sports Act of 1978 to maintain this suit.

2. Constitutional Claims

Plaintiffs have alleged that the decision of the USOC not to enter an American team in the summer Olympics has violated certain rights guaranteed to plaintiffs under the First, Fifth and Ninth Amendments to the United States Constitution. This presents us with two questions: (1) whether the USOC's decision was "governmental action"(state action), and, assuming state action is found, (2) whether the USOC's decision abridged any constitutionally protected rights. . . .

We accordingly find that the decision of the USOC not to send an American team to the summer Olympics was not state action, and therefore, does not give rise to an actionable claim for the infringements of the constitutional rights alleged.

(b) Constitutionally Protected Rights

Assuming arguendo that the vote of the USOC constituted state action, we turn briefly to plaintiffs' contention that by this action they have been deprived of their constitutional rights to liberty, to self-expression, to travel, and to pursue their chosen occupation of athletic endeavor. Were we to find state action in this case, we would conclude that defendant USOC has violated no constitutionally protected right of plaintiffs. . . .

At this point, we find it appropriate to note that we have respect and admiration for the discipline, sacrifice, and perseverance which earns young men and women the opportunity to compete in the Olympic

Games. Ordinarily, talent alone has determined whether an American would have the privilege of participating in the Olympics. This year, unexpectedly, things are different. We express no view on the merits of the decision made. We do express our understanding of the deep disappointment and frustrations felt by thousands of American athletes. In doing so, we also recognize that the responsibilities of citizenship often fall more heavily on some than on others. Some are called to military duty. Others never serve. Some return from military service unscathed. Others never return. These are the simple, although harsh, facts of life, and they are immutable.

QUESTIONS AND DISCUSSION

1. We're lucky to have an excellent treatise on international sports law to guide us through some rocky terrain on the legality of boycotts. Nafziger, *International Sports Law*, esp. ch. VII (1998). "Since 1948, boycotts and embargoes have plagued the Olympics." *Id.* at 101. Prof. Nafziger explains his terminology this way:

   A state may impose measures to prohibit either participation by its nationals in foreign competition (loosely, a "boycott") or access by foreign athletes to competition on its territory (loosely, an "embargo"). Whether a prohibition attaches to the outflow or the inflow of athletes does, not, however, usually determine its legitimacy under international sports law. The threshold question, is the *purpose, not the nature*, of a particular measure. For convenience, therefore, the term "boycott" will be used to refer to either of the two means of restricting athletes or competition.

2. Should the boycott's legality be based on its motive, for example, boycotting racist countries? Should there be a distinction if the arguably racist countries field an integrated team?

3. Prof. Nafziger poses an important question: "When are boycotts of international sports competition legal?" The answer in part is: "They are clearly illegal when their purpose is to induce conflict or to engage in measures of coercion in violation of the United Nations Charter. They are also illegal when their purpose is to confirm diplomatic nonrecognition in violation of governing international rules." Can you think of any situations when boycotts would be clearly legal?

4. Under the Olympic Charter, the IOC "is the supreme authority of the Olympic movement." Should it be? Are there any potential conflicts with the Amateur Sports Act of 1978?

5. The legal status of the IOC is described as an "international non-governmental non-profit organization, of unlimited duration, in the form of an association with the status of a legal person, recognized by decree of the Swiss Federal Council of September 17, 1981." Would it make more sense if it was based in the United States? Should the major sports countries control the IOC?

6. The mission of the National Olympic Committees (NOCs) "is to develop and protect the Olympic Movement in their respective countries, in accordance with the Olympic Charter." Among other things, a NOC

typically provides for internal dispute resolution procedures and arbitration options. Is this goal of an NOC in conflict with the responsibilities and jurisdiction of the CAS?

7. *DeFrantz* was an athlete's attempt to enjoin the USOC from boycotting the 1980 Moscow Olympics. The court held that under IOC rules and the Amateur Sports Act of 1978, if so desired, not only could the USOC refrain from sending a U.S. team to the Olympics, but it could do so for reasons not directly related to sports considerations (that is, geopolitical concerns). Is that a direct violation of not only the letter but the spirit of the Olympic Movement?

8. USOC, although federally chartered, is a private organization. The Due Process Clause of the Fifth Amendment applies only to actions by the federal government; plaintiffs must show that the USOC vote is state action. The *DeFrantz* court held that the USOC's decision to defer sending a team was not state action and failed to create an actionable due process infringement claim. Is this legally sound or merely politically correct?

B. AMATEUR SPORTS ACT OF 1978

[handwritten margin note: not good legislation, gave the idiots who were screwing up Olympic competition (USOC) more power instead of fixing the problem & confusion]

The Amateur Sports Act of 1978, 36 U.S.C. §§371-396, was created as a response to the report of the President's Commission on Olympic Sports. The purpose of the act is to coordinate amateur athletic activity; to recognize certain rights of amateur athletes; and to provide for dispute resolution involving national governing bodies. The act amends the statutory provisions behind the USOC and allows the USOC to recognize as National Governing Bodies (NGB) any amateur sport group that files an application and is eligible for recognition. But, only one NGB can be recognized for each sport. Before recognition, the USOC holds a noticed hearing, which is open to the public. NGBs must be incorporated as a domestic, nonprofit corporation with the purpose of advancing "amateur" athletic competition; submit an application for recognition; agree to binding arbitration; demonstrate autonomy in governance; allow open membership and equal opportunity without discrimination; govern itself by a board of directors that is selected without regard to race, color, religion, national origin, or sex except in sports where there are separate male and female programs; demonstrate that the board includes individuals who are actively engaged in that sport; provide for reasonable direct representation for any amateur sports organization for which recognition is sought; conduct national programs; demonstrate that none of its officers have conflicts of interest with other NGBs; provide procedures for prompt equitable resolution of grievances; demonstrate that it does not have eligibility criteria relating to amateur status that would be more restrictive than those of the appropriate international sports group; and demonstrate that it is prepared to meet the obligations imposed on an NGB. 36 U.S.C. §391(A).

The USOC will then recommend and support an NGB internationally as a representative of the United States for that particular sport.

The Amateur Sports Act of 1978 is detailed in specifying an NGB's duties and establishes a guide for amateur competition. 36 U.S.C. §392(b). The act also provides that any group that is eligible to belong to an NGB may seek to require the NGB to comply with its responsibilities by filing a written complaint with the USOC, but only after exhausting all remedies within the appropriate NGB for correcting the problems. 36 U.S.C. §395(A). The act further provides that amateur sports groups may seek to replace an NGB under certain circumstances. 36 U.S.C. §395 (c). The act is pro-competitive in that it contains provisions that protect the opportunities for amateur athletes to complete. 36 U.S.C. §§374(8), 382(B).

Pertinent parts of the Amateur Sports Act of 1978 follow:

THE AMATEUR SPORTS ACT OF 1978

36 U.S.C. §373. Definitions

As used in this chapter, the term—

(1) "amateur athlete" means any athlete who meets the eligibility standards established by the national governing body for the sport in which the athlete competes;

(2) "amateur athletic competition" means a contest, game, meet, match, tournament, regatta, or other event in which amateur athletes compete;

(3) "amateur sports organization" means a not-for-profit corporation, club, federation, union, association, or other group organized in the United States which sponsors or arranges any amateur athletic competition; . . .

36 U.S.C. §374. Objects and Purposes of Corporation

The objects and purposes of the Corporation shall be to—

(1) establish national goals for amateur athletic activities and encourage the attainment of those goals;

(2) coordinate and develop amateur athletic activity in the United States directly relating to international amateur athletic competition, so as to foster productive working relationships among sports-related organizations;

(3) exercise exclusive jurisdiction, either directly or through its constituent members or committees, over all matters pertaining to the participation of the United States in the Olympic Games and in the Pan-American Games;. . . .

(4) obtain for the United States, either directly or by delegation to the appropriate national governing body, the most competent amateur representation possible in each competition and event of the Olympic Games and of the Pan-American Games;

(5) promote and support amateur athletic activities involving the United States and foreign nations;

(8) provide for the swift resolution of conflicts and disputes involving amateur athletes, national governing bodies, and amateur sports organization. . . .

36 U.S.C. §391. Recognition of Amateur Sports Organizations

(a) National governing body; application; notice and hearing — For any sport which is included on the program of the Olympic Games or the Pan-American Games, the Corporation is authorized to recognize as a national governing body an amateur sports organization which files an application and is eligible for such recognition, in accordance with the provisions of subsection (b) of this section. The Corporation shall recognize only one national governing body for each sport for which application is made and approved. . . .

36 U.S.C. §392. Duties of National Governing Bodies

(a) For the sport which it governs, a national governing body is under a duty to —

(1) develop interest and participation throughout the United States and be responsible to the persons and amateur sports organizations it represents;

(2) minimize, through coordination with other amateur sports organizations, conflicts in the scheduling of all practices and competitions;

(3) keep amateur athletes informed of policy matters and reasonably reflect the views of such athletes in its policy decisions;

(4) promptly review every request submitted by an amateur sports organization or person for a sanction (A) to hold an international amateur athletic competition in the United States or (B) . . . held outside the United States, and determine whether to grant such sanction. . . .

36 U.S.C. §393. Authority of National Governing Bodies

For the sport which it governs, a national governing body is authorized to —

(1) represent the United States in the appropriate international sports federation;

(2) establish national goals and encourage the attainment of those goals;

(3) serve as the coordinating body for amateur athletic activity in the United States;

(4) exercise jurisdiction over international amateur athletic activities . . . ;

(5) conduct amateur athletic competition, including national championships and international amateur athletic competition in the United States, and establish procedures for the determination of eligibility standards for participation in such competitions. . . .

36 U.S.C. §395. Compelling Compliance with Eligibility Requirements and Performance of Duties by National Governing Bodies . . .

(c) Arbitration of Corporation determinations

(1) The right to review by any party aggrieved by a determination of the Corporation shall be to the American Arbitration Association. Such demand for arbitration shall be submitted within 30 days of the determination of the Corporation. . . .

1. Disputes

Disputes under the Amateur Sports Act of 1978 may be arbitrated by the American Arbitration Association or, under rules of international sports federations, by the CAS or other special tribunals. 36 U.S.C. §§374(8), 382(B).

The *Walton-Floyd* court held that the Amateur Sports Act of 1978 did not provide for an implied cause of action allowing the recovery of monetary damages against the USOC.

WALTON-FLOYD V. UNITED STATES OLYMPIC COMMITTEE

965 S.W.2d 35 (Tex. Ct. App. 1998)

ANDELL, Justice.

The appellant appeals a summary judgment granted in favor of the appellee, the United States Olympic Committee (the USOC). We affirm.

Background

The USOC coordinates the United States's participation in international amateur athletic competitions. It resolves disputes among athletes and sports organizations or between competing sports organizations, and provides uniformity in the area of amateur athletics, thereby protecting the rights of amateur athletes to compete. The USOC has the power to sue and be sued. 36 U.S.C.A. §375(a)(1), (5), (6) (West 1988).

The USOC selects the United States's governing bodies for every sport in the Olympics and Pan-American games. 36 U.S.C.A. §375(a)(4) (West 1988). In track and field, the USOC recognizes The Athletic Congress (TAC) as the national governing body. TAC coordinates and conducts track and field competitions to ensure competitions comply with the rules and regulations of the International Amateur Athletic Federation (IAAF). The IAAF rules provide for punishment or suspension of athletes who use certain performance enhancing drugs. The IAAF publishes a list of the banned substances.

The USOC issued the appellant a card listing many of the more common substances on the banned list. The card warns:

> This list is not complete. It is the athlete's responsibility to check the status of all medications. **CALL THE USOC HOTLINE 1-800-233-0393.**

The appellant's husband, who was also her trainer, obtained a box of Sydnocarb. He testified the box appeared to be labeled in Russian, he could not read the writing, and he did not have it translated. The box had no instructions and did not list ingredients.

The appellant's husband testified that he called the USOC hotline to inquire about Sydnocarb's status and that the USOC operator told him Sydnocarb was a carbohydrate supplement not on the banned list. He admitted, however, that the hotline operator did not specifically tell him that Sydnocarb was safe to use, nor did she give any other assurances. The appellant called the hotline, with similar results, then began using Sydnocarb. She and her husband testified they called the hotline on subsequent occasions to inquire about the status of Sydnocarb, and that each time, the USOC's operator told them it was not on the banned list.

After the appellant's semi-final heat at the IAAF World Championships, she provided meet officials with a urine sample, which they divided into two samples. The first sample tested positive for amphetamines, a prohibited substance. IAAF officials told her the test results and invited her to attend a testing of the second sample, which also tested positive for amphetamines. The IAAF relayed the results to TAC, which suspended her from further competition. The appellant eventually discovered that Sydnocarb was the apparent source of the amphetamines.

The appellant alleges [certain] USOC acts and omissions were negligent . . .

Furthermore, she alleges the USOC negligently breached various duties prescribed by the Amateur Sports Act of 1978 (the Act). 36 U.S.C.A. §§371-396, 392(a)(3), (5), (6), (8), (9) (West 1988). . . .

Discussion

We are asked to determine whether the USOC owed the appellant a federal statutory or Texas commonlaw duty. In seven points of error, the appellant asserts: (1) the USOC owed her a federal statutory and Texas common-law duty; (2) there are fact issues whether the USOC had breached those duties; (3) fact issues exist whether damages can be limited; and (4) fact issues exist whether the USOC was grossly negligent.

Private Right of Action Under the Amateur Sports Act . . .

The judiciary's silence in no way produces an inference that plaintiffs injured while competing in events not within exclusive USOC control maintain a private cause of action.

Voluntary Assumption of a Duty Under State Law

The appellant argues the Act imposes a duty upon the USOC or a duty exists through voluntary assumption of the hotline service. Since we have held there is no private cause of action under the Act, we must determine whether the USOC assumed a duty under state tort law. . . .

The interest of maintaining consistent interpretations among jurisdictions requires the Act to pre-empt claims asserted under state tort law. To hold a common law duty exists outside the scope of the Act, thereby enabling an individual athlete to bring suit, threatens to override legislative intent and opens the door to inconsistent interpretations of the Act.

We hold that the USOC did not owe the appellant a duty under any of the theories pleaded. Accordingly, we overrule points of error one, two, three and four, making it unnecessary to address points of error five through seven.

We affirm.

QUESTIONS AND DISCUSSION

1. "In 1975, President Ford appointed a study-group, the President's Commission on Olympic Sports (PCOS), to examine the United States Olympic program, identify the problems, and recommend solutions." Nafziger, *International Sports Law* 167 (1988). In response, Congress passed the Amateur Sports Act of 1978. Would it make more sense to develop a governmental entity — something like the "Ministry for Sports" to coordinate Olympic competition?

2. Professor Nafziger looks at the structure of the act in this manner:

   The Act is essentially divided into six parts. The first provides definitions, the second outlines the objects and purposes of the USOC, and the third delineates the USOC's general corporate powers and obligations, including the important trademark right to protect Olympic symbols, . . . The fourth and fifth parts concern the establishment and functions of a national governing body (NGB) in each Olympic or Pan-American sport. Specifically, the fourth part stipulates the requirements for an amateur sports organization to become an NGB and the responsibilities and authority of the NGBs. The fifth part is particularly important to lawyers. It provides mechanisms for the resolution of complaints and the selection of a recognized NGB from among several competing organizations. The sixth part, the final paragraph in the Act, gives amateur sports organizations exclusive jurisdiction over restricted competition, that is, competition limited to a specific class of amateur athletes. If a sports organization involved in restricted competition wishes to participate internationally, it must obtain a sanction, that is approval. Nafziger at 168-169.

   Does it seem contradictory that an amateur organization would seek to protect its trademark rights?

3. Given the facts in *Walton-Floyd*, was the punishment too severe?

4. *Walton-Floyd* was a Texas Court of Appeals case, and no Texas court had considered this issue, so the court looked to federal courts for guidance. This interpretation of the Amateur Sports Act yielded the conclusion that it did not imply private causes of action against the USOC. *See Martinez v. USOC*, 802 F.2d 1275, 1281 (10th Cir. 1986); *Oldfield v. TAC*, 779 F.2d 505, 506-508 (9th Cir 1985); *Michels v. USOC*, 741 F.2d 155, 157-158 (7th Cir. 1984); *DeFrantz v. USOC*, 492 F. Supp. 1181, 1190-1192 (D.D.C. 1980). How did this case end up in a Texas court? What advantages and disadvantages, of this jurisdiction could be argued by either side?

5. Actions against USOC have proven successful in two scenarios: (1) disputes between organizations and the USOC; *see U.S. Wrestling Fedn. v. Wrestling Div. of the AAU, Inc.*, 545 F. Supp. 1053, 1061 (N.D. Ohio 1982); and Hollis, Note, '*The U.S.O.C. and the Suspension of Athletes: Reforming Grievance*

Procedures Under the Amateur Sports Act of 1978,' 71 Ind. L.J. 183, 188 (1995); and (2) breach of contract allegations; *See Harding v. U.S. Figure Skating Assn.* 851 F. Supp. 1476, 1480 (D. Or. 1994); *Reynolds v. IAAF*, 841 F. Supp. 1444, 1448 (S.D. Ohio 1992). How should Delisa Walton-Floyd, as a member of The Athletic Congress (TAC), have restructured her complaint so as to increase her chance of success?

C. DRUG TESTING

The Olympic Charter and the constitutions and bylaws of international sports federations have made it clear that the use of illegal enhancement drugs contravenes the spirit of fairness in sports. Drug use is forbidden in all Olympic competition, and competitors are subjected to examinations carried out in conformity with IOC medical competitors. Teams that benefit from their members' use of drugs are disqualified and excluded under Olympic rules.

The IOC requires that each competition site have adequate testing facilities and that each competitor agree to submit to a possible examination at the risk of exclusion. If an athlete refuses to submit to an examination or is found to have used a drug, he is excluded from competition. When a team member is involved, the competition in which the infringement occurred is forfeited by the team. There are degrees of variance in the range of penalties that shift according to whether the use was deliberate or accidental or whether the uses constituted a first or second offense. An offense during competition leads minimally to suspension and forfeiture of all medals won.

The following is an excerpt from the International Amateur Athletic Federation (IAAF) Constitution that stipulates the procedures when there are disputes concerning drug testing results.

INTERNATIONAL AMATEUR ATHLETIC FEDERATION CONSTITUTION

Rule 20 — Disputes . . .
Doping Related Disputes

(i) Where testing has indicated the presence of a prohibited substance, or there is evidence of the use of a prohibited technique, and the athlete concerned considers that, despite the findings of the Member's disciplinary tribunal, doping control was carried out in material breach of Rules 55 to 61 and relevant procedural guidelines.

(ii) Where a Member has held a hearing under Rule 59, and the I.A.A.F. believes that in the conduct or conclusions of such hearing the Member has misdirected itself, or otherwise reached an erroneous conclusion.

(iii) Where testing has indicated the presence of a prohibited substance and, contrary to Rule 59.3, the Member refuses to allow the athlete a hearing.

(iv) Where testing by another sporting body has indicated the presence of a prohibited substance, and the athlete considers that the decision of the other sporting body is unsatisfactory and should not be relied upon.

(v) Where an athlete has been found by the I.A.A.F. or a Member to have committed a doping offense (other than those listed in Rule 60.1 (i) and (ii)) and the athlete believes that the I.A.A.F. or the Member concerned have misdirected themselves or otherwise reached an erroneous conclusion.

(vi) Where the athlete has been found by the I.A.A.F. to have admitted taking a prohibited substance, or using a prohibited technique, and the athlete denies having made any such admission. . . .

Rule 55 — Doping

55.1 Doping is strictly forbidden and is an offense under I.A.A.F. Rules.

55.2 The offense of doping takes place when either: (i) a prohibited substance is found to be present within an athlete's body tissue or fluids; or (ii) an athlete uses or takes advantage of a prohibited technique; or (iii) an athlete admits to having used or taken advantage of a prohibited substance or a prohibited technique (See also Rule 56).

55.3 Prohibited substances include those listed in Schedule 1 to the "Procedural Guidelines for Doping Control." . . .

55.4 The expression "prohibited substance" shall include a metabolite of a prohibited substance.

55.5 The expression "prohibited technique" shall include: (a) blood doping; (b) use of substances and of methods which alter the integrity and validity of urine samples used in doping control. . . .

Rule 56 — Ancillary Offenses

56.1 An athlete who fails or refuses to submit to doping control after having been requested to do so by the responsible official will have committed a doping offense and will be subject to sanctions in accordance with Rule 60. . . .

56.2 Any person assisting or inciting others, or admitting having incited or assisted others, to use a prohibited substance, or prohibited techniques, shall have committed a doping offense and will be subject to sanctions in accordance with Rule 60. . . .

Rule 57 — Out of Competition Testing

57.3 No athlete shall be allowed to compete in his National Championships, nor shall a Member grant a permit under Rule 12.3, unless and until such athlete agrees to subject himself to out of competition testing by both the Member and the I.A.A.F. The Council may make guidelines for the conduct of Challenge Testing. Challenge Testing is the right, subject to the above guidelines, of one Member to designate for testing an athlete under the jurisdiction of another Member. . . .

Rule 59—Disciplinary Procedures for Doping Offenses

59.1 Where a doping offense has taken place, disciplinary proceedings may take place in three stages: (i) suspension; (ii) hearing; (iii) ineligibility.

59.2 An athlete shall be suspended from the time that the Doping Commission, in the case of the I.A.A.F., or its equivalent body, in the case of a Member, reports that there is evidence that a doping offense has taken place.

59.3 Every athlete shall have the right to a hearing before the relevant tribunal of his National Federation before any decision on eligibility is reached. . . .

1. Doping Control Agreements and Blood Doping

The IOC regulations against drug usage are generic and complete; however, there are also individual agreements between the various national Olympic committees that are created to ensure drug testing procedures. For example, the USOC and the Olympic Committee of the Soviet Union (SOC) entered into a doping control agreement committing their organizations to work together to eliminate blood doping and the use of performance-enhancing drugs (for example, steroids) in athletes under their jurisdiction.

The practice of blood packing (and blood doping), although not related to drug testing per se, is strikingly similar in the legal response it generates. In this process, an athlete's blood is drawn from her body during training and then returned to her body (packing) just before competition (doping uses someone else's blood). It is a technique that is increasingly used in sports that require endurance, such as cycling or cross-country skiing. Blood doping transfusions are banned by international rules.

2. Disciplines and Penalties

Under the IOC, any competitor who refuses to submit to an examination or is found to be using a drug must be excluded from competition. If the athlete is a member of a team, the team forfeits the competition in which the violation has occurred.

In *Reynolds v. IAAF*, on outstanding athlete was unsuccessful in appealing his suspension from participation because the court did not have personal jurisdiction over the federation.

REYNOLDS V. INTERNATIONAL AMATEUR ATHLETIC FEDERATION

23 F.3d 1110 (6th Cir. 1994)

LIVELY, Senior Circuit Judge.

The International Amateur Athletic Federation (IAAF) appeals the district court's denial of its motion to quash garnishment proceedings and vacate a default judgment and permanent injunction previously entered by the district court. As it did before the district court, the IAAF argues on appeal that the district court had neither subject matter jurisdiction nor personal jurisdiction over the IAAF in the proceedings resulting in the default judgment and permanent injunction.

I

A

Harry "Butch" Reynolds is a world-class sprinter who regularly participates in international track and field meets. Reynolds currently holds the individual world record in the 400 meters, is a member of the world record holding 4 × 400 relay team, and is a gold and silver medalist from the 1988 Olympics.

On August 12, 1990, Reynolds ran in the "Hercules '90" meet in Monte Carlo, Monaco. Immediately after the competition, Reynolds was tested for illegal performance-enhancing drugs as part of a random drug test conducted after all international track meets. Two different samples of Reynolds' urine were sent to Paris for analysis. Each sample contained trace amounts of the steroid Nandrolone, a drug banned by international track regulations created by the IAAF.

The IAAF is an unincorporated association based in London, England, and is made up of track and field organizations representing 205 nations and territories. Its purpose is to coordinate and control track and field athletes and competitions throughout the world. The IAAF has no offices in the United States, and holds no track meets in Ohio, where Reynolds brought this action. One member of the IAAF is The Athletics Congress of the United States, Inc. (TAC), the United States national governing body for track and field.

After Reynolds' positive drug test, the IAAF banned him from all international track events for two years, thereby eliminating his hopes for competing in the 1992 Olympics in Barcelona. . . .

B

Reynolds immediately brought suit in the Southern District of Ohio, arguing that the drug test was given negligently, and provided an erroneous result. The court dismissed one claim and stayed the remainder of the case after finding that Reynolds failed to exhaust administrative remedies provided by the Amateur Sports Act, 36 U.S.C. §§371-396 (1988) and TAC. Reynolds appealed the district court's decision. This court agreed with the exhaustion requirement but vacated the judgment and directed that the entire case be dismissed for lack of subject matter jurisdiction. Reynolds v. TAC, 935 F.2d 270 (6th Cir. 1991)(Table).

In an attempt to exhaust his administrative remedies, Reynolds participated in an independent arbitration before an AAA panel in June of 1991. Reynolds took this action under the Amateur Sports Act and the United States Olympic Committee Constitution. The AAA arbitrator rendered a decision fully exonerating Reynolds; the arbitrator found strong evidence that the urine samples provided to the Paris laboratory were not Reynolds'. However, the IAAF refused to acknowledge the arbitrator's decision because the arbitration was not conducted under IAAF rules. Accordingly, the IAAF refused to lift Reynolds' two year suspension.

Reynolds then appealed his suspension to TAC, as required by IAAF rules. TAC held a hearing on September 13, 1991. After thoroughly examining the evidence and deliberating for two weeks, the TAC Doping Control Review Board completely exonerated Reynolds. . . .

Still not satisfied, the IAAF reopened Reynolds' case pursuant to IAAF Rule 20(3)(ii), which allows the IAAF to conduct an independent arbitration where it appears that one of its member foundations such as TAC has "misdirected itself." The IAAF arbitration was held on May 10 and 11, 1992, in London, England (the London Arbitration). . . . At the conclusion of the hearing, the IAAF arbitral panel found that the drug tests were valid, and that there was "no doubt" as to Reynolds' guilt. As a result, the panel upheld Reynolds' two year suspension.

II

A

Soon after the IAAF made its final decision, Reynolds filed the present action in the Southern District of Ohio alleging four different state law causes of action: breach of contract, breach of contractual due process, defamation, and tortious interference with business relations. Reynolds sought monetary damages, and a temporary restraining order that would allow him to compete in races leading to the U.S. Olympic trials on June 20, 1992. The IAAF refused to appear in the case, stating in a letter to Reynolds' attorney that the district court had no jurisdiction over the IAAF. The district court issued a temporary restraining order that prevented the IAAF from interfering with Reynolds' attempt to make the Olympic tryouts. Despite IAAF threats to both Reynolds and TAC, Reynolds ran in a few races and qualified to compete in the U.S. Olympic trials in New Orleans.

On June 17, 1992, the district court held a preliminary injunction hearing to decide if Reynolds should compete in the June 20 Olympic trials. The IAAF refused to appear, but TAC intervened to oppose Reynolds. On June 19, the district court issued a preliminary injunction after finding that it had personal jurisdiction over the IAAF and that Reynolds was likely to succeed on the merits of his claims. That afternoon, TAC filed a motion with the Sixth Circuit Court of Appeals, asking for an emergency stay of the district court's decision. At 7:00 that evening, Judge Siler granted the stay. Reynolds v. IAAF, 968 F.2d 1216 (6th Cir. 1992)(Table). The next morning, Reynolds filed an emergency motion with Supreme Court Justice John Paul Stevens, asking for an order vacating Judge Siler's emergency stay. Justice Stevens granted Reynolds' request, finding that the District Court's opinion was "persuasive." Reynolds v. IAAF, 505 U.S. 1301 (1992).

Despite these rulings, the IAAF announced that every athlete who competed with Reynolds at the U.S. Olympic trials would be ineligible to compete in the Barcelona Olympics. Reynolds' events were temporarily postponed while TAC filed an application to the full Supreme Court to vacate Justice Stevens' stay. The Court denied TAC's request, and Reynolds was eventually allowed to compete in the Olympic trials, after an agreement was reached between the U.S. Olympic Committee and the IAAF. Reynolds made the Olympic team as an alternate for the 400 meter relay. However, the IAAF refused to let Reynolds compete at the 1992 Olympics, and TAC removed him from the U.S. Olympic team roster. Moreover, the IAAF increased Reynolds' two year suspension by four months as punishment for participating in the U.S. Olympic trials.

B

On September 28, 1992, Reynolds filed a supplemental complaint with the district court, outlining the above events. The IAAF did not respond to Reynolds' complaint and TAC did not appear in the default proceedings. After the IAAF was given full notice, the court entered a default judgment in Reynolds favor. Soon afterward, the district court held a hearing to determine damages. Again, the IAAF was provided notice but refused to appear. On December 3, 1992, the district court issued an opinion awarding Reynolds $27,356,008, including treble punitive damages. The district court found that the IAAF "acted with ill will and a spirit of revenge towards Mr. Reynolds." . . .

The district court found that it had diversity jurisdiction in this case because Reynolds is a citizen of Ohio and the IAAF is a foreign association. The IAAF is an unincorporated association, and the district court reasoned that the IAAF is deemed to be a citizen of all states where its members are domiciled. The court held that diversity jurisdiction was proper because no IAAF members are citizens of Ohio.

The district court also found that it had personal jurisdiction over the IAAF. The court held that the Ohio long-arm statute was satisfied because the IAAF transacted business with Reynolds in Ohio, and the IAAF's public announcement of Reynolds' positive drug test adversely affected Reynolds in Ohio. The court held that the IAAF had the required minimum contacts with Ohio after finding that TAC acted as the IAAF's agent in the United States.

C

On February 17, 1993, Reynolds began garnishment proceedings against four corporations with connections to the IAAF. The IAAF finally appeared at a garnishment hearing before the district court, and later filed a "Motion to Quash Garnishment Proceedings and To Vacate the Default Judgment" pursuant to Fed. R. Civ. P. 60(b)(4). In its motion, the IAAF contended that the court lacked personal and subject matter jurisdiction. Before the motion was decided, the IAAF filed a recusal motion, arguing that previous opinions by the court put the district judge's impartiality into question.

The district court denied all motions on July 13, 1993. . . .

The IAAF appeals from denial of its motions. Because it contends that the district court lacked jurisdiction in the earlier proceedings, the IAAF seeks to reverse the money judgment and injunction as well.

III

Because we have concluded that the district court lacked personal jurisdiction over the IAAF, the sole defendant in this case, it is not necessary to consider the other issues presented and argued by the parties.

A

The district court found that it had personal jurisdiction over the IAAF under Ohio's long-arm statute. . . .

The IAAF contends that holding it amenable to suit in an Ohio court would offend principles of international comity and put international cooperation at risk. Under this theory, the IAAF should not be required to bear the expense of litigating cases around the world when its only contact with a forum is an athlete's residence. Instead, the IAAF argues that only the courts of England, where it is located, have jurisdiction to review its arbitral proceedings. Reynolds counters that his interest in a convenient forum substantially outweighs the inconvenience to the IAAF. Over half of the IAAF's four year $174.5 million budget is received from United States corporations, one of the IAAF's officers resides in the U.S., and its other officers regularly visit the U.S.

2. Tortious Injury . . .

Reynolds claimed that the false IAAF drug report was both defamatory and interfered with his contractual relationships. . . .

Nevertheless, unless TAC had minimum contacts with Ohio in relation to the "contract" between the IAAF and Reynolds, the court erred in premising jurisdiction of TAC's agency. . . .

Without further evidence concerning the purported contract, we are unable to agree that the district court had personal jurisdiction over the IAAF on the contract claims, either based on its own activities or those of TAC. . . .

In short, the IAAF is based in England, owns no property and transacts no business in Ohio, and does not supervise U.S. athletes in Ohio or elsewhere. Its contacts with Reynolds in Ohio are superficial, and are insufficient to create the requisite minimum contacts for personal jurisdiction. . . .

The leading case on this issue is *Calder v. Jones*, 465 U.S. 783 (1984). In *Calder*, a professional entertainer sued the writers and editors of a Florida magazine for libel in a California court. . . . Because the defendants' intentional actions were aimed at California and the brunt of the harm was felt there, the Court concluded that the defendants could reasonably anticipate being haled into court in California.

We find *Calder* distinguishable for several reasons. First, the press release concerned Reynolds' activities in Monaco, not Ohio. Second, the source of the controversial report was the drug sample taken in Monaco and the laboratory testing in France. Third, Reynolds is an international athlete whose professional reputation is not centered in Ohio. Fourth, the defendant itself did not publish or circulate the report in Ohio; Ohio periodicals disseminated the report. Fifth, Ohio was not the "focal point" of the press release. The fact that the IAAF could foresee that the report would be circulated and have an effect in Ohio is not, in itself, enough to create personal jurisdiction. Finally, although Reynolds lost Ohio corporate endorsement contracts and appearance fees in Ohio, there is no evidence that the IAAF knew of the contracts or of their Ohio origin. *Calder* is a much more compelling case for finding personal jurisdiction.

Reynolds argues, however, that his claims arose out of the IAAF's connection with Ohio because the IAAF intentionally defamed him and interfered with his Ohio business relationships. Under this theory, the IAAF knew that the worldwide media would carry the report and that the brunt of the injury would occur in Ohio.

Even accepting that the IAAF could foresee that its report would be disseminated in Ohio, however, the IAAF would not be subject to personal jurisdiction in Ohio. The press release that the IAAF issued in London did not directly accuse Reynolds of using forbidden substances. It recited the fact that the Paris laboratory had reported a positive drug test and that Reynolds had been suspended and offered a hearing. We cannot hold that this act of the IAAF satisfied the requirements of the Ohio statute, or that permitting the IAAF to be sued in Ohio for the press release would comport with due process. . . .

VI

TAC was carrying out its statutory duty under the Amateur Sports Act and was not acting as the IAAF's agent when it intervened. There is no indication that the IAAF authorized or even requested TAC to appear. Indeed, the IAAF had consistently refused to appear and had taken the position that the district court lacked jurisdiction over the entire proceeding. We conclude that TAC appeared solely in its role as the national governing body under the Amateur Sports Act.

Conclusion

In conclusion, we do not believe that holding the IAAF amenable to suit in an Ohio court under the facts of this case comports with "traditional notions of fair play and substantial justice." The IAAF stated in its brief and at oral argument that it will not challenge the jurisdiction of English courts to determine the validity of the London Arbitration award if Reynolds seeks to have it set aside in the courts of that country.

Our decision renders the IAAF's recusal motion moot.

The district court abused its discretion by denying the IAAF's Rule 60(b)(4) motion for relief. The judgment of the district court is reversed. Upon remand the district court will dismiss this action for lack of personal jurisdiction over the IAAF.

QUESTIONS AND DISCUSSION

1. Should equity have forced the court in *Reynolds* to rectify the wrong as opposed to reversing the judgment on technical grounds that the district court did not have personal jurisdiction over the IAAF? *See also* Fastiff,

Note, *The Proposed Hague Convention on the Recognition and Enforcement of Civil and Commercial Judgments: A Solution to Butch Reynold's Jurisdiction and Enforcement Problems*, 28 Cornell Intl. L.J. 469 (1995); Hatch, Note, *On Your Mark, Get Set Stop? Drug-Testing Appeals in the IAAF,'* 10 Loy. L.A. Intll. & Comp. L.J. 537 (1994); Mack, Note, *The Need for an Independent Tribunal in Int'l Athletic Disputes* (Reynolds v. IAAFU), 10 Conn. J. Intl. L. 635 (1995); Nelson, *Butch Reynolds and the American Judicial System v. the International Amateur Athletic Federation—A Comment on the Need for Judicial Reform*, 3 Seton Hall J. Sports L. 173 (1993); Newman, *The Race Does Not Always Go to the Stronger or Faster Man . . . But the One Who Goes to Court: An Examination of* Reynolds v. IAAF, 1 Sports Law. J. 205 (1994).

2. In *Slaney v. IAAF*, 244 F.3d 580 (7th Cir. 2001), *cert. denied*, 534 U.S. 828 (2001), female distance runner Mary Decker Slaney was punished for a urine test that indicated the possibility of blood doping violations. This violation was reaffirmed by the IAAF sanctioning body. She sued the IAAF and the USOC on state law and civil RICO claims. Defendants' motions to dismiss was granted. *See generally* Galluzzi, *The Doping Crisis in International Athletic Competition: Lessons from the Chinese Doping Scandal in Women's Swimming*, 10 Seton Hall J. Sports L. 66 (2000).

3. In *Michels v. USOC*, 741 F.2d 155 (7th Cir. 1984), the court held that an athlete suspended by an IF has no private cause of action to require USOC to initiate a hearing to determine test validity, even if the suspension precludes the athlete from international competitions. *See Nafziger, International Sports Law* 152 (1988).

4. More on blood doping from Prof. Nafziger:

> A problem related to drugs but not involving them is the practice of blood-packing or blood-doping. Blood-packing is a technique aimed at increasing an athlete's red blood cell count and oxygen level by administering transfusions of the athlete's own blood whereas blood-doping involves a transfusion of someone else's blood. Some athletes believe that blood transfusions increase their stamina. Despite the advantages that are attributed, correctly or not, to transfusions, they are banned by international rules. . . . [P]rohibiting blood-packing or blood-doping is however, very difficult to enforce. It is almost impossible to detect the procedure in the absence of a self-confession. . . .

Nafziger at 154. "Blood doctoring" (the generic term) is often met with the strictest of penalties. Is that fair or even legally correct in the case of blood packing where the procedure is strictly natural? Think of it as "blood out, blood back."

5. *Reynolds* is a good example of the difficulty a banned athlete has in challenging a drug suspension rendered by an international or national sporting body. The district court could not initially accept the case until Butch Reynolds exhausted administrative remedies. *See Barnes v. IAAF*, 862 F. Supp. 1537 (S.D. W. Va. 1993).

However, the NGB for Butch's sport, track and field, The Athletic Congress (TAC) (now USA Track & Field), was required to submit to binding arbitration (to the American Arbitration Association (AAA)) any controversy that involves an amateur athlete's eligibility to participate. 36 U.S.C. §391 (b)(3). The AAA exonerated Reynolds. The IAAF disregarded the AAA and TAC and similarly disregarded the U.S. Supreme Court's ruling that Reynolds could compete in the Olympic trials. Instead, Reynolds was required to appear before an IAAF-appointed arbitration panel in London. *See* Nafziger, 'Symposium, *Sports Law in the 21st Century: Globalizing Sports Law*,' 9 Marq. Sports L.J. 225 (1999) (Nafziger questioned why the *Reynolds* courts did not apply international law). Should the CAS have jurisdiction here? The Sixth Circuit Court of Appeals in *Reynolds* did not permit personal jurisdiction over the IAAF, which argued that subjecting it to suit anywhere in the world where an athlete resides would hinder international competition. Is that a sufficient consideration to outweigh Reynolds's due process rights?

6. *See also In the Matter of the Arbitration Between: Jessica K. Foshi and United States Swimming, Inc.*, Case #77 190003696 (April 1, 1996). The international federation banned Foshi for two years for testing positive; she claimed that the results were wrong, either through sabotage with her water bottle or a mistake in labeling her urine. She appealed to United States Swimming (her NGB), which decided that she lacked knowledge as regards how the drug entered her body, but placed her on two-year probation and struck her times from the 1995 Summer Nationals. She then appealed to the AAA, which removed all sanctions. Unlike in *Reynolds*, the international federation did not subsequently intervene. Why was Butch Reynolds treated differently?

D. INTERNATIONAL COURT OF ARBITRATION FOR SPORT

The IOC established a Court of Arbitration for Sport (CAS) in 1983. The CAS, whose "Statute and Regulation" entered into force in 1984, comprises a panel of 60 jurists (an increase in 1986 from 40) selected by the IOC for their knowledge of sport and geographical distribution. The president of the IOC serves in the honorary capacity of president of the CAS, and the panel itself chooses an executive president. Under authority of the president of the CAS, a secretary general manages a registrar's office. The IOC meets the operating costs of the CAS, including the expenses of the registrar's office. The CAS is the court of general jurisdiction for international sports disputes.

CHARTER OF THE INTERNATIONAL COURT
OF ARBITRATION FOR SPORT

... The disputes [in particular, those connected with doping] to which a federation, association or other sports body is party are a matter for arbitration in the sense of this Code, only insofar as the statutes or regulations of the said sports bodies or a specific agreement so provide.

B The International Council of Arbitration for Sport (ICAS)

1 Composition

§4 The ICAS is composed of twenty members, namely high-level jurists appointed in the following manner. . . .

Upon their appointment, the members of the ICAS sign a declaration undertaking to exercise their function in a personal capacity, with total objectivity and independence, in conformity with this Code. . . .

C The Court of Arbitration for Sport (CAS)

1 Mission

§12 The CAS sets in operation Panels which have the task of providing for the resolution by arbitration of disputes arising within the field of sport in conformity with the Procedural Rules. . . .

To this end, the CAS attends to the constitution of Panels and the smooth running of the proceedings. It places at the disposal of the parties the necessary infrastructure.

The responsibility of such Panels, is, inter alia:

> a. to resolve the disputes that are referred to them through ordinary arbitration;
>
> b. to resolve through the appeals arbitration procedure disputes (including doping-related disputes) concerning the decisions of disciplinary tribunals or similar bodies of federations, associations or other sports bodies, insofar as the statutes or regulations of the said sports bodies or a specific agreement so provide;
>
> c. to give non-binding advisory opinions at the request of the IOC, the IFs, the NOCs, the associations recognized by the IOC and the Olympic Games Organizing Committee (OCOGs). . . .

3 Organization of the CAS

§20 The CAS is composed of two divisions, the Ordinary Arbitration Division and the Appeals Arbitration Division.

> a. **The Ordinary Arbitration Division** constitutes Panels, the mission of which is to resolve disputes submitted to the ordinary procedure, and performs, through the intermediary of its President, all other functions in relation to the smooth running of the proceedings conferred upon it by the Procedural Rules. . . .
>
> b. **The Appeals Arbitration Division** constitutes Panels, the mission of which is to resolve disputes (including doping-related disputes) concerning the decisions of disciplinary tribunals or similar bodies of federations, associations or other sports bodies or a specific agreement so provide. It performs, through the intermediary of its President, all other functions in relation to the smooth running of the proceedings conferred upon it by the Procedural Rules. . . .

IN THE ARBITRATION BETWEEN: MR. ROSS REBAGLIATI AND INTERNATIONAL OLYMPIC COMMITTEE (IOC)

Court of Arbitration for Sport (CAS)/Tribunal Arbitral Du Sport (TAS)

Ad hoc Division/Chambre ad hoc

Ref: CAS arbitration NAG 2

Background and Procedure

1. This matter comes before the ad hoc Division of the Court of Arbitration of Sport (CAS) on the application of Ross Rebagliati of Canada. On 8 February 1998 Mr. Rebagliati was awarded the Olympic gold medal in the snowboard giant slalom competition. On 11 February 1998, the IOC Executive Board, upon the recommendation of the IOC Medical Commission, notified Mr. Rebagliati that it had decided to rescind the award of the medal based on the finding of the metabolite of marijuana in the doping control which followed the competition. Mr. Rebagliati now appeals the decision of the IOC Executive Board.

2. The appeal was filed with CAS at 17:15 hours on 11 February. A panel of three arbitrators was appointed by the CAS Co-presidents, pursuant to the CAS Rules for the Resolution of Disputes Arising During the XVIII Olympic Winter Games in Nagano. [The hearing started] at 21:20 hours on 11 February 1998. . . .

Applicable Rules and Jurisdiction

3. The proceedings are governed by the Rules for the Resolution of Disputes Arising During the XVIII Olympic Winter Games in Nagano (the "ad hoc Rules") of CAS enacted by the International Council of Arbitration for Sport (ICAS) on 9 April 1997. They are further governed by Chapter 12 of the Swiss Private International Law Act of 18 December 1987 ("PIL Act"). The PIL Act applies to this arbitration because the seat of the ad hoc Division and of its panels of Arbitrators is established at Lausanne, Switzerland, pursuant to Art. 7 of the ad hoc Rules.

4. Under Article 17 of the ad hoc Rules, the Panel must decide this dispute "pursuant to the Olympic Charter, the applicable regulations, general principles of law and the rules of law, the application of which it deems appropriate."

5. The jurisdiction of the ad hoc Division arises out of Article 74 of the Olympic Charter and out of the arbitration agreement embodied in the entry form for the Games. At the outset of the hearing, the parties confirmed their acceptance of the jurisdiction of the ad hoc Division and that they had no objection against the composition of the Panel.

6. According to Article 16 of the ad hoc Rules, the Panel has "full power to review the facts on which the application is based."

The Merits

7. The Panel wishes to make clear that it shows no particular leniency toward Mr. Rebagliati on account of the fact that he was announced as the

winner of the event; nor does it treat him with greater severity on this account. This panel considers that all athletes, great or small, are equal before the law, and examines Mr. Rebagliati's appeal accordingly.

8. Mr. Rebagliati does not contest the urine sample collection process or the laboratory analysis which found traces of marijuana metabolites (17-25 ng/ml) in his urine.

9. Mr. Rebagliati alleges that he has not actively used marijuana since April 1997. He further states that he attended parties on 20 and 31 January 1998 at which other people smoked marijuana. Therefore, he argues that the presence of marijuana metabolites in his urine must have come from exposure to second hand marijuana smoke on these occasions, prior to his departure for Nagano on 2 February 1998.

10. In support of his allegations, Mr. Rebagliati offered to call Dr. Andrew Pipe, Chairman of the Canadian Center for Ethics in Sport, to testify that the test results reported in Nagano are not inconsistent with Mr. Rebagliati's version of events and that marijuana metabolites present in the system take a long time to purge themselves from urine. (Thus, metabolites could still be present on 8 February 1998 without any further exposure to marijuana after 31 January.)

11. The representatives of the IOC do not challenge Mr. Rebagliat's statement of facts. They also acknowledge that metabolites of marijuana may be present in an athlete's urine for a substantial period of time after exposure.

12. The IOC rather takes the position that its sanction was justified even if the facts alleged by Mr. Rebagliati are correct. It was therefore unnecessary to hear Dr. Pipe. . . .

14. The issue before the Panel is therefore whether the detection of marijuana metabolites in Mr. Rebagliati's urine in and of itself proves an offense under the text invoked by the Executive Committee, which we will refer to below as "Paragraph B." . . .

16. Prince de Merode and Doctor Schamasch of the IOC Medical Commission testified that marijuana is not a prohibited substance under the Code. Explaining the phrase in Paragraph B *"in agreement with the International Sports Federations,"* they stated that the use of marijuana is not banned unless the IOC and a particular international federation have agreed to enforce a ban on marijuana as adopted by that federation. . . .

17. Prince de Merode and Doctor Schamasch also explained that the IOC has tested all samples collected during Olympic Games for marijuana since the Seoul Olympics in 1988. The purpose of this effort was not to impose sanctions on athletes who were found to have marijuana or its metabolites in their urine, but rather to obtain a base of data from which a determination could be made by the IOC whether marijuana use is a sports related problem which would justify adding marijuana to the banned substances list. Neither the athletes who tested positive for marijuana in prior Games nor their federations were notified of the positive test results. Prince de Merode stated, in his own words, that testing for marijuana in this sense is an: "educative measure, not more. It is not doping."

18. In summary, the IOC Medical Code standing alone does not provide a basis for treating marijuana as a banned substance justifying the finding of a doping offense and resulting sanctions.

19. Since the effect of Paragraph B is to require a joint approach by the IOC and FIS to create sanctions for the use of marijuana, the testimony of Mr. Holder was of the first importance.

20. Mr. Holder told the Panel emphatically and repeatedly that with regard to doping offenses, FIS has adopted the IOC Medical Code in its entirety, with no special rules of its own. . . .

21. According to Mr. Hodler, marijuana has also been given special consideration by FIS, but for other reasons. There are two events, namely the downhill and ski jumping, which are particularly risk-filled. As Mr. Holder stated: "there, marijuana can be a help to overcome a natural resistance against excessive risk."

22. Thus, Mr. Holder explained, FIS's concern regarding marijuana use in these events is to protect the health of athletes who might have accidents, if they were affected by marijuana to the point of recklessness.

23. Mr. Holder then turned to the situation with respect to the giant slalom event, with respect to which he stated that no agreement to test, as required under Paragraph B, had ever been entered with FIS. . . .

24. The representatives of the IOC also acknowledged that there had been no agreement between the IOC and FIS to treat marijuana as a banned substance. . . .

25. The cumulative testimony of Mr. Holder and that of the representatives of the IOC resolves the issue in this case. The sole basis for the present sanction is Paragraph B, which treats the use of marijuana as doping only if there is an agreement between the IOC and the relevant international federation to that effect. There is no such agreement in this case. Hence, the decision of the IOC Executive Board sanctioning Mr. Rebagliati for the presence of marijuana metabolites in his urine lacks any basis. . . .

28. In reaching our result, we do not suggest for a moment that the use of marijuana should be condoned, nor do we suggest that sports authorities are not entitled to exclude athletes found to use cannabis. But if sports authorities wish to add their own sanctions to those that are edicted by public authorities, they must do so in an explicit fashion. That has not been done here. . . . The Panel recognizes that from an ethical and medical perspective, cannabis consumption is a matter of serious social concern. CAS is not, however, a criminal court and can neither promulgate nor apply penal laws. We must decide within the context of the law of sports, and cannot invent prohibitions or sanctions where none appear. . . .

29. . . . It is clear that the sanctions against Mr. Rebagliati lack requisite legal foundation.

30. Finally, the Panel is concerned that Mr. Rebagliati should not suffer from any needless embarrassment on account of misunderstandings or distortions of the factual circumstances of this matter. His performance should not be tarnished by any suggestion that he deserved his punishment but is being saved by a technicality. Mr. Rebagliati has affirmed that he has not ingested cannabis since April 1997, and that any exposure he has had to it since then was second hand. The Panel emphasized that these facts have not

been challenged by either the FIS or the IOC. Mr. Rebagliati has not been accused of being a cannabis user, but of having residual traces in his urine. For the reasons given above, this is not a punishable offense under the applicable rules.

Decision

On the basis of the foregoing factual and legal anaylsis, the ad hoc Division of the Court of Arbitration for Sport renders the following decision:

1. The IOC Executive Board's decision of 11 February 1998 is reversed.
2. No costs are awarded.
3. The decision shall be subject to immediate publication.

Nagano, 12 February 1998.

QUESTIONS AND DISCUSSION

1. The CAS is designed to settle nontechnical, private disputes that arise out of the practice of sport. It has all the powers of an international court of arbitration. *See* Nafziger, *International Sports Law* 36 (1988).
2. The CAS can give advisory opinions and decide contentious cases. For example, the CAS decided a dispute between an athletic club and the national federation that had sanctioned it. In another case, the CAS issued an advisory opinion for the benefit of a National Olympic Committee where it upheld their right to impose a lifetime ban on competition for athletes who have been sanctioned by the IOC for drug use. *See* Nafziger, *International Sports Law* 37 (1988).
3. In *Rebagliati*, the CAS acted as a neutral arbitrator, which resulted in a decision that contradicted the IOC's position. How would the CAS have decided *Reynolds*?
4. The CAS Olympic Ad Hoc Division was established to deal immediately with grievances that occur as a result of participation in Olympic competition. Athletes must sign entry forms in which they agree that all disputes will be submitted to the CAS. CAS arbitration is available on site, and decisions are rendered within 24 hours; as *Rebagliati* shows, the system works. Should CAS expand its jurisdiction to cover all sports related disputes? *See* Raber, *Dispute Resolution in Olympic Sport: The Court of Arbitration for Sport*, 8 Seton Hall J. Sport L. 75 (1998).

13
INTELLECTUAL PROPERTY

The law of intellectual property includes such legal topics as patents, trademarks, copyrights, and trade dress, as well as related fields such as publicity rights, misappropriation, false advertising, unfair competition, and trade secrets. Intellectual property attempts to protect the creation of ideas. In sports, the marketing of both athlete and team is formed and controlled by the laws of intellectual property. Sports marketing has become a huge industry. The growth of sports in the last decade has exposed millions of people to sports every day in one form or another. The National Football League's Super Bowl is the essence of sports marketing; corporate sponsors line up for the right to advertise their products.

Patents are governed by the Federal Patent Act. **Copyrights** are protected by the Copyright Act, which protects original works of authorship embodied in a tangible medium of expression. **Trademarks** are a type of symbol used to identify a particular set of goods and to distinguish them from another's goods. **Trade Dress** protection is available for nonfunctional features if they distinguish the good's origin. **Broadcasting and Licensing Rights** are controlled by the various intellectual property protections and are integral to sports dissemination.

A. PATENTS

A patent confers on the owner the right to exclude others from selling or using the process or product. A patent owner may sue those individuals who directly infringe on the patent by using or selling the invention without proper authority to do so. Patent law covers a variety of sports products, including golf balls, football helmets, skates, rackets, trampolines, and lawn darts.

§100 Definitions . . .

(a) The term "invention" means invention or discovery.

(b) The term "process" means process, art or method, and includes a new use of a known process, machine, manufacture, composition of matter, or material. . . .

§101 Inventions Patentable

Whoever invents or discovers any new and useful process, machine, manufacture, or composition of matter, or any new and useful improvement thereof, may obtain a patent. . . . (July 19, 1952, c. 950, 66 Stat. 797.)

§102 Conditions for Patentability; Novelty and Loss of Right to Patent

A person shall be entitled to a patent unless —

(a) the invention was known or used by others in this country, or patented or described in a printed publication in this or a foreign country, before the invention thereof by the applicant for patent, or

(b) the invention was patented or described in a printed publication in this or a foreign country or in public use or on sale in this country, more than one year prior to the date of the application for patent in the United States, or

(c) he has abandoned the invention, or

(d) the invention was first patented or caused to be patented, or was the subject of an inventor's certificate, by the applicant or his legal representatives or assigns in a foreign country prior to the date of the application for patent in this country on an application for patent or inventor's certificate filed more than twelve months before the filing of the application in the United States, or

(e) the invention was described in a patent granted on an application for patent by another filed in the United States before the invention thereof by the applicant for patent or on an international application by another who has fulfilled the requirements of paragraphs (1),(2), and (4) of section 371(c) of this title before the invention thereof by the applicant for patent or

(f) he did not himself invent the subject matter sought to be patented, or

(g) before the applicant's invention thereof the invention was made in this country by another who had not abandoned, suppressed, or concealed it. In determining priority of invention there shall be considered not only the respective dates of conception and reaction to practice of the invention, but also the reasonable diligence of one who was first to conceive and last to reduce to practice, from a time prior to conception by the other.

§103 Conditions for Patentability; Non-Obvious Subject Matter

A patent may not be obtained though the invention is not identically disclosed or described as set forth in section 102 of this title, if the differences between the subject matter sought to be patented and the prior art are such that the subject matter as a whole would have been obvious at the time the invention was made to a person having ordinary skill in the art to which said subject matter pertains.

Patentability shall not be negatived by the manner in which the invention was made. Subject matter developed by another person, which qualifies as prior art only under subsection (f) or (g) of section 102 of this title, shall not preclude patentability under this section where the subject matter and the claimed invention were, at the time the invention was made, owned by the same person or subject to an obligation of assignment to the same person. . . .

Wilson Sporting Goods Co. v. David Geoffrey & Associates, 904 F.2d 1942 (Fed. Cir. 1990)

This case is an action for patent infringement concerning the design of a golf ball. There are about six major competitors in the golf ball business. The competition is fierce and lucrative.

> For more than a century, golfers have been searching for a "longer" ball. As one of the parties put it, "distance sells." Inventors has experimented with numerous aspects of the ball design over the years, but as United States Golf Association (U.S.G.A) rules began to strictly control ball size, weight and other parameters, inventors focuses their efforts on the "dimples" in the ball's surface. Accordingly to one witness, new dimple designs provide the only real opportunity for increasing distance within the confines of U.S.G.A. rules.

So, essentially there is a "dimple science." Dimples make the ball fly higher and farther. Dimples can be numerous or few and can vary as to shape, width, depth, and location.

Plaintiff/Wilson Sporting Goods' "168 patent" has a pattern of dimples arranged by dividing the cover of the spherical golf ball into 80 imaginary spherical triangles and then placing the dimples into strategic locations in the triangles. The placement of the dimples are grouped into an imaginary "icosahedron" which is completely covered by 20 imaginary equilateral triangles five of which cover each pole of the ball, and ten of which surround its equator. Basically,

> All of the claims of the "168 patent" require this basic golf ball having eighty subtriangles and six great circles. Particular claims require variation on the placement of dimples in the triangles, with one common theme — the dimples must be arranged on the surface of the ball so that no dimple intersects any great circle. Equivalently stated, the dimples must be arranged on the surface of the ball so that no dimple intersects the side on any central triangle. When the dimples are arranged in this manner, the ball has six axes of symmetry, compared to prior balls which had only one axis of symmetry.

There are four accused products; the accused balls (the "Dunlop balls") have dimples which are arranged in an icosahedral pattern having six great circles but the six great circles are not dimple free as the claims literally require.

Infringement may be found, if the court finds that the accused product is substantially equivalent to plaintiff's golf ball.

> Infringement *may* be found under the doctrine of equivalents if an accused product "performs substantially the same overall function or work, in substantially the same way, to obtain substantially the same overall result as the claimed invention." Even if this test is met, however, there can be no infringement if the asserted range of equivalency of what is literally claimed would encompass the prior art. This issue—whether an asserted range of equivalents would cover what is already in the public domain—is one of law. . . .

The court found that Wilson's claims were not infringed under the doctrine of equivalents. Basically, the range of equivalents broad enough to cover the accused balls would also have encompassed prior art.

QUESTIONS AND DISCUSSION

1. The Patent Act defines a potential patent as any "new and useful process, machine, manufacture, or composition of matter" that includes mechanical, chemical, and electrical structures and processes. In order for an invention to be patentable, it must meet four requirements. An invention must be (1) in a subject matter category, (2) useful, (3) novel in relation to the prior art, and (4) obvious from the prior art to a person of ordinary skill in the art at the time the invention was made.

2. In *Demarini Sports, Inc. v. Worth, Inc.*, 239 F.3d 1314 (Fed. Cir. 2001), the court granted summary judgment in a case where patent infringement was asserted for a high-performance, double-walled aluminum softball bat. The allegedly offending bat was found to be based on independent bat design concepts substantially different from the plaintiff's original patent.

3. In *Wilson Sporting Goods Co.*, there was an allegation of infringement of a patent claim for certain configuration of dimples on a golf ball cover. The court held that the claims were not infringed under doctrine of equivalents. Infringement may be found under doctrine of equivalents if the accused product performs substantially the same overall as the claimed invention; even if this test is met, however, there can be infringement if asserted scope of equivalency of what is literally claimed would encompass the prior art. Dependent patent claims for golf balls asserting small variation on theme of icosahedral ball having six great circles were not infringed by accused balls under doctrine of equivalents; a range of equivalents broad enough to cover the accused balls would also have encompassed prior art. What was the prior art?

B. COPYRIGHTS

Copyright law protects original work of authorship embodied in a tangible medium of expression. A work must be within the constitutional and statutory definitions of a work of authorship, the work must be in a tangible medium of expression, and it must be original. There are many copyright concerns in the sports and recreation industries, including autobiographies, instructional videos, TV broadcasts, and rebroadcasts.

COPYRIGHT ACT

(1976, as amended) 17 U.S.C. §§101 *et seq.*

17 U.S.C. §101 Definitions . . .

A work is "fixed" in a tangible medium of expression when its embodiment in a copy or phonorecord, by or under the authority of the author, is sufficiently permanent or stable to permit it to be perceived, reproduced, or otherwise communicated for a period of more than transitory duration. A work consisting of sounds, images, or both, that are being transmitted, is "fixed" for purposes of this title if a fixation of the work is being made simultaneously with its transmission.

To "perform" a work means to recite, render, play, dance, or act it, either directly or by means of any device or process or, in the case of a motion picture or other audiovisual work, to show its images in any sequence or to make the sounds accompanying it audible.

"Publication" is the distribution of copies or phonorecords of a work to the public by sale or other transfer of ownership, or by rental, lease, or lending. The offering to distribute copies or phonorecords to a group of persons for purposes of further distribution, public performance, or public display, constitutes publication. A public performance or display of a work does not of itself constitute publication.

A "work made for hire" is —

(1) a work prepared by an employee within the scope of his or her employment . . .

17 U.S.C. §102. Subject Matter of Copyright: In General

(a) Copyright protection subsists, in accordance with this title, in original works of authorship fixed in any tangible medium of expression, now known or later developed, from which they can be perceived, reproduced, or otherwise communicated, either directly or with the aid of a machine or device. . . .

17 U.S.C. §106. Exclusive Rights in Copyrighted Works

Subject to sections 107 through 120, the owner of copyright under this title has the exclusive rights to do and to authorize any of the following:
(1) to reproduce . . . ;
(2) to prepare derivative works . . . ;

(3) to distribute copies . . . ;

(4) . . . to perform the copyrighted work publicly . . . ;

(5) . . . to display the copyrighted work publicly.

17 U.S.C. §107. Limitations on Exclusive Rights: Fair Use

Notwithstanding the provisions of sections 106 and 106A, the fair use of a copyrighted work, including such use by reproduction in copies or phonorecords or by any other means specified by that section, for purposes such as criticism, comment, news reporting, teaching (including multiple copies for classroom use), scholarship, or research, is not an infringement of copyright. . . .

17 U.S.C. §201. Ownership of Copyright

(a) Initial Ownership. — Copyright in a work protected under this title vests initially in the author or authors of the work. The authors of a joint work are coowners of copyright in the work.

(b) Works Made for Hire. — In the case of a work made for hire, the employer or other person for whom the work was prepared is considered the author for purposes of this title, and, unless the parties have expressly agreed otherwise in a written instrument signed by them, owns all of the rights comprised in the copyright. . . .

In NBA v. Motorola, Inc., a professional basketball league brought an action alleging copyright infringement against the manufacturer and promoter of hand-held pagers that provided real-time information on the professional basketball games. The court held that professional basketball games were not "original works of authorship" protected by the Copyright Act.

NATIONAL BASKETBALL ASSOCIATION v. MOTOROLA, INC.

105 F.3d 841 (2d Cir. 1997)

WINTER, Circuit Judge:

Motorola, Inc. and Sports Team Analysis and Tracking Systems ("STATS") appeal from a permanent injunction entered by Judge Preska. The injunction concerns a handheld pager sold by Motorola and marketed under the name "SportsTrax," which displays updated information of professional basketball games in progress. The injunction prohibits appellants, absent authorization from the National Basketball Association and NBA Properties, Inc. (collectively the "NBA"), from transmitting scores or other data about NBA games in progress via the pagers, STATS's site on America On-Line's computer dial-up service, or "any equivalent means."

The crux of the dispute concerns the extent to which a state law "hot-news" misappropriation claim . . . survives preemption by the federal Copyright Act. . . . We hold that a narrow "hot-news" exception does survive preemption. However, we also hold that appellants' transmission of "real-time" NBA game scores and information tabulated from television and radio broadcasts of games in progress does not constitute a misappropriation of "hot news" that is the property of the NBA.

The NBA cross-appeals from the dismissal of its Lanham Act claim. We hold that any misstatements by Motorola in advertising its pager were not material and affirm.

I. Background

The facts are largely undisputed. Motorola manufactures and markets the SportsTrax paging device while STATS supplies the game information that is transmitted to the pagers. The product became available to the public in January 1996, at a retail price of about $200. SportsTrax's pager has an inch-and-a-half by inch-and-a-half screen and operates in four basic modes: "current," "statistics," "final scores" and "demonstration." It is the "current" mode that gives rise to the present dispute. In that mode, SportsTrax displays the following information on NBA games in progress: (i) the teams playing; (ii) score changes: (iii) the team in possession of the ball; (iv) whether the team is in the free-throw bonus; (v) the quarter of the game; and (vi) time remaining in the quarter. The information is updated every two to three minutes, with more frequent updated near the end of the first half and the end of the game. There is a lag of approximately two or three minutes between events in the game itself and when the information appears on the pager screen.

SportsTrax's operation relies on a "data feed" supplied by STATS reporters who watch the games on television or listen to them on the radio. The reporters key into a personal computer changes in the score and other information such as successful and missed shots, fouls, and clock updates. The information is relayed by modern to STATS's host computer, which compiles, analyzes, and formats the data for retransmission. The information is then sent to a common carrier, which then sends it via satellite to various local FM radio networks that in turn emit the signal received by the individual SportsTrax pagers. . . .

II. The State Law Misappropriation Claim

A. *Summary of Ruling*

Because our disposition of the state law misappropriation claim rests in large part on preemption by the Copyright Act, our discussion necessarily goes beyond the elements of a misappropriation claim under New York law, and a summary of our ruling here will perhaps render that discussion—or at least the need for it—more understandable. . . .

We hold that the surviving "hot-news" *INS*-like claim is limited to cases where: (i) a plaintiff generates or gathers information at a cost; (ii) the information is time-sensitive; (iii) a defendant's use of the information constitutes free riding on the plaintiff's efforts; (iv) the defendant is in direct competition with a product or service offered by the plaintiffs; and (v) the ability of other parties to free-ride on the efforts of the plaintiff or others would so reduce the incentive to produce the produce or service that its existence or quality would be substantially threatened. We conclude that SportsTrax does not meet that test.

B. *Copyrights in Events or Broadcasts of Events*

The NBA asserted copyright infringement claims with regard both to the underlying games and to their broadcasts. The district court dismissed these claims, and the NBA does not appeal from their dismissal. . . .

In our view, the underlying basketball games do not fall within the subject matter of federal copyright protection because they do not constitute "original works of authorship" under 17 U.S.C. §102(a). Section 102(a) lists eight categories of "works of authorship" covered by the act, including such categories as "literary works," "musical works," and "dramatic works." The list does not include athletic events, and, although the list is concededly non-exclusive, such events are neither similar nor analogous to any of the listed categories. . . .

2. *Infringement of a Copyright in the Broadcasts of NBA Games*

As noted, recorded broadcasts of NBA games — as opposed to the games themselves — are now entitled to copyright protection. The Copyright Act was amended in 1976 specifically to insure that simultaneously-recorded transmissions of live performances and sporting events would meet the Act's requirement that the original work of authorship be "fixed in any tangible medium of expression." 17 U.S.C. §102(a). . . .

Although the broadcasts are protected under copyright law, the district court correctly held that Motorola and STATS did not infringe NBA's copyright because they reproduced only facts from the broadcasts, not the expression or description of the game that constitutes the broadcast. The "fact/expression dichotomy" is a bedrock principle of copyright law that "limits severely the scope of protection in fact-based works." "'No author may copyright facts or ideas. The copyright is limited to those aspects of the work — termed "expression" — that display the stamp of the author's originality.'"

We agree with the district court that the "[d]efendants provide purely factual information which any patron of an NBA game could acquire from the arena without any involvement from the director, cameramen, or others who contribute to the originality of a broadcast." Because the SportsTrax device and AOL site reproduce only factual information called from the broadcasts and none of the copyrightable expression of the games, appellants did not infringe the copyright of the broadcasts.

C. *The State-Law Misappropriation Claim*

The district court's injunction was based on its conclusion that, under New York law, defendants had unlawfully misappropriated the NBA's property rights in its games. The district court reached this conclusion by holding: (i) that the NBA's misappropriation claim relating to the underlying games was not preempted by Section 301 of the Copyright Act; and (ii) that, under New York common law, defendants had engaged in unlawful misappropriation. We disagree. . . .

Our conclusion, therefore, is that only a narrow "hot-news" misappropriation claim survives preemption for actions concerning material within the realm of copyright. . . .

2. The Legality of SportsTrax

We conclude that Motorola and STATS have not engaged in unlawful misappropriation under the "hot-news" test set out above. . . .

For the foregoing reasons, the NBA has not shown any damage to any of its products based on free-riding by Motorola and STATS, and the NBA's misappropriation claim based on New York law is preempted. . . .

We agree with the district court that the statements in question are not material in the present factual context. The inaccuracy in the statements would not influence consumers at the present time, whose interest in obtaining updated game scores on pagers is served only by SportsTrax. Whether the data is taken from broadcasts instead of being observed first-hand is, therefore simply irrelevant. However, we note that if the NBA were in the future to market a rival pager with a direct datafeed from the arenas — perhaps with quicker updates than SportsTrax and official statistics — then Motorola's statements regarding source might well be materially misleading. On the present facts, however, the complained-of statements are not material and do not misrepresent an inherent quality or characteristic of the product.

IV. Conclusion

We vacate the injunction entered by the district court and order that the NBA's claim for misappropriation be dismissed. We affirm the district court's dismissal of the NBA's claim for false advertising under Section 43(a) of the Lanham Act.

A typical sports-related copyright problem is identified in *NFL v. Rondor, Inc.* In that case, a professional football league and a local team sued the owners of bars and restaurants for copyright infringement of "blacked-out" games.

NATIONAL FOOTBALL LEAGUE v. RONDOR, INC.

840 F. Supp. 1160 (N.D. Ohio 1993)

MATIA, District Judge.

This action came on for trial before the Court from October 12, 1993, to October 15, 1993. The Court has considered all of the testimony of the witnesses, the demeanor and credibility of the witnesses on the stand, and evidence presented at the trial, as well as the entire record in this matter, and being otherwise advised in the premises, herein enters its findings of fact and conclusions of law.

Findings of Fact

A. *The Parties*

1. The plaintiffs are the National Football League ("NFL" or "League") and the Cleveland Browns, Inc. ("Browns").

2. The defendants are Najahs French Creek Tavern, Inc., dba French Creek Tavern ("French Creek"); [etc.] . . .

B. *The NFL's Blackout Rule*

10. The NFL, on behalf of its twenty-eight (28) member clubs, has entered into exclusive broadcasting agreements with the three major television broadcasting networks, ABC, CBS and NBC, as well as with ESPN and TNT. The NBC contract provides that if a home game of a member club is not sold out at least 72 hours in advance of game time, the telecast of that game will not be broadcast by the network in the home territory of the member club except with the consent of both participating clubs. This provision is known as the "blackout rule." . . .

E. *Copyright Ownership and Registration*

18. Plaintiffs are the owners of a copyright of the telecast of the Browns-San Diego Chargers game of November 15, 1992. . . .

G. *"Home System" Defense*

25. Each defendant asserts that its off-air antenna system falls within the "home system" exemption to the Copyright Act. The "home system" exemption provides in relevant part that there is no infringement where reception is made "on a single receiving apparatus of a kind commonly used in private homes." 17 U.S.C. §110(5). . . .

I. *Misuse*

46. Plaintiffs use their copyright to support the League's blackout rule which is designed to increase ticket sales and bring big crowds of lively fans to the stadiums of the member clubs. . . .

Conclusions of Law

A. *Jurisdiction and Venue* . . .

B. *Copyright Infringement*

3. "In order to prove a case of copyright infringement, the Plaintiff must show (1) his ownership of a valid copyright and (2) copying by the Defendants of protectible expression."

4. In addition, "[i]n the case of a work consisting of sounds, images, or both, the first fixation of which is made simultaneously with its transmission," the copyright holder must serve written notice upon the infringer before fixation and register the work with the Copyright Office within three months of its first transmission. 17 U.S.C. §411(b).

5. The NFL, on behalf of its twenty-eight (28) member teams, and the Browns (as to their games) own and control a valid, enforceable copyright in the subject telecast. . . . [infringement proved.]

C. *Affirmative Defenses*

(i) *The "Home System" Exemption*

10. Each defendant has the burden of proving that its antenna system falls within the terms of the §110(5) "home system" exemption.

11. Each defendant must prove that its antenna system constitutes "a single receiving apparatus of a kind commonly used in private homes."

12. The test for determining whether an antenna system is "common" within the meaning of 17 U.S.C. §110(5) is highly localized:

> [H]ow likely [is it that] the average patron who watches a blacked out game at one of the defendant restaurants [has] the ability to watch the same game at home? . . .

[The defendants' antennas are substantially larger.]

16. The Court therefore concludes that none of the defendants has met its burden of proving that its antenna system falls within the terms of the §110(5) "home system" exemption. . . .

(iii) *Copyright Misuse* . . .

30. Plaintiffs, as copyright holders in NFL game telecasts, have elected not to license to the networks the right to telecast games in a club's home territory that are not sold out 72 hours before the game is to begin. Such limited license is clearly permitted by the copyright law.

31. Therefore, if there is an affirmative defense of copyright misuse, the Court holds that defendants have failed to prove its applicability in this case.

D. *Injunctive Relief, Statutory Damages and Costs* . . .
Memorandum of Opinion

The purpose of this Opinion is to explain why the Court ruled as it did on several key points, since this is apparently a case of first impression with respect to the type of equipment used by the defendant establishments.[1] . . .

I

This cause of action arises from a right given to plaintiffs by an act of Congress known as the Copyright Act. The Copyright Act protects "original works of authorship fixed in any tangible medium," including "motion pictures and other audiovisual works," 17 U.S.C. §102(a). A live broadcast (of a football game, for example) is protected if a fixation (*e.g.*, a videotape) is being made simultaneously with the transmission. 17 U.S.C. §110.

However, Section 110(5) of the Copyright Act specifies that no copyright liability can be imposed for "communication of a transmission embodying a performance . . . by the public reception of the transmission on a single receiving apparatus of a kind commonly used in private homes. . . . "

At the heart of the argument in this case is the meaning of this so-called "home use" exemption. Is the receiving apparatus used by the defendants in this case "of a kind commonly used in private homes"? [The court answers in the negative.] . . .

With respect to the issue of damages, the Court does not find that defendants' actions were willful violations of plaintiffs' rights or of the

---

[1] The use of satellite dishes has previously been found *not* to be within the "home use" exemption. *Nat. Football League v. McBee & Bruno's, Inc.*, 792 F.2d 726 (8th Cir. 1986).

Copyright Act. The equipment the defendants were using had not previously been judicially determined to be outside the scope of the home use exemption. Therefore, the Court will impose only the minimum damage award specified by law ($500.00 per violation). Plaintiffs are also entitled to the issuance of a permanent injunction against future violations.

Judgment Entry and Permanent Injunction . . .

[Plaintiffs received statutory damages from each defendant.] . . .

QUESTIONS AND DISCUSSION

1. A typical modern example of a sports copyright problem, in *NFL v. Rondor, Inc.*, is the unauthorized reception or interception of blacked-out cable or TV sports programming by way of satellite dish antennas. *See NFL of New Haven v. Rondor, Inc.*, 840 F. Supp. 1160 (N.D. Ohio 1993); *HBO v. Champs, Inc.*, 837 F. Supp. 480 (D. Conn. 1993). In this type of suit, the copyright holder usually prevails and is granted a permanent injunction.

2. *See also Seal-Flex v. Athletic Track & Court Constr., 870 F. Supp. 753 (E.D. Mich. 1994) (copyright infringement over a rubber running track surface). Score Group, Inc. v. Dad's Kid Corp.*, 33 U.S.P.Q.2d 1940 (C.D. Cal. 1994) (alleged copyright infringement of hologram baseball trading card).

3. In another example, a professional photographer for *Sports Illustrated* took a photograph of a baserunner being tagged out sliding into home plate. He copyrighted it, and, in turn, it was then issued as a commemorative baseball postage stamp. The photographer alleged copyright infringement under the Copyright Act. The copyright was registered by Time, Inc., for *Sports Illustrated*; but Time and *S.I.* preferred not to get involved in a copyright action against the U.S. Postal Service. Therefore, they assigned all their interests in the copyright to the photographer, Andy Hayt, who sued. Summary judgment was granted since Hayt was not the legal owner of the copyright at the time of the alleged infringement, as required under 28 U.S.C. §1498(b), and cannot acquire such status by way of assignment of the legal owner's claim under the Anti-Assignment Act, 31 U.S.C. §3727. *Hayt v. United States*, 27 U.S.P.Q.2d (BNA) 1386 (Cl. Ct. 1993).

4. In *NBA v. Motorola, Inc.*, the court held that professional basketball games were not "original works of authorship" protected by the Copyright Act and that the league's misappropriation claims were preempted by Copyright Act. Copyright did not protect the NBA here; is there any other legal theory that might protect NBA real-time statistics?

5. There are many suits such as *NFL v. Rondor, Inc.*, in which the league and the team sue owners of bars and restaurants seeking copyright violation for broadcast of football games. What is the home system exemption?

6. In *NFL v. Rondor, Inc.*, the infringers' antennas' were more elaborate and powerful than those in general use. This type of antenna is known as a "deep fringe" antenna. Should they be per se illegal?

C. TRADEMARKS

Trademarks are symbols identifying a particular set of goods and distinguishing them from another's goods. Trademarks are an inherent part of the system of logos and emblems that identify sports teams, leagues, and manufacturers. A trademark owner can prevent others from using the same or similar marks that create a likelihood of confusion or deception. An individual can establish one's manufactured goods and services from another's. Trademark law distinguishes between the following: (1) the right to use a mark, (2) the right to exclude others from using a mark, and (3) the right to register the mark.

The Federal Trademark Act of 1946 (Lanham Act) governs the registration and law of trademarks as well as the remedies and enforcement procedures for infringement. A trademark includes "any word, name, symbol, or device or any combination thereof adopted and used by manufacturer or merchant to identify his or her goods and also to distinguish from those manufactured or sold by others."

Plaintiff must meet five requirements in a trademark infringement action: (1) there must have been either a reproduction or counterfeit of the mark; (2) the reproduction must have occurred without the authority of the registrant; (3) the reproduction has been used in the stream of commerce; (4) the use must have been in the sale, distribution, or offering of goods or services; and (5) the use of the reproduction must be likely to cause confusion.

LANHAM ACT (TRADEMARKS) (1946, AS AMENDED)

15 U.S.C. §§1051 *et seq.*

15 U.S.C. §1114. Remedies; Infringement; Innocent Infringement by Printers and Publishers

(1) Any person who shall, without the consent of the registrant—

(a) use in commerce any reproduction, counterfeit, copy, or colorable imitation of a registered mark in connection with the sale, offering for sale, distribution, or advertising of any goods or services on or in connection with which such use is likely to cause confusion, or to cause mistake, or to deceive; or

(b) reproduce, counterfeit, copy, or colorably imitate a registered mark and apply such reproduction, counterfeit, copy, or colorable imitation to labels, signs, prints, packages, wrappers, receptacles or advertisements intended to be used in commerce upon or in connection with the sale, offering for sale, distribution, or advertising of goods or services on or in connection with which such use is likely to cause confusion, or to cause mistake, or to deceive,

shall be liable in a civil action by the registrant for the remedies hereinafter provided. Under subsection (b) hereof, the registrant shall not be entitled to recover profits or damages unless the acts have been committed with knowledge that such imitation is intended to be used to cause confusion, or to cause mistake, or to deceive. . . .

15 U.S.C. §1125. False Designations of Origin, False Descriptions, and Dilution Forbidden

(a) Civil action

(1) Any person who, on or in connection with any goods or services, or any container for goods, uses in commerce any word, term, name, symbol, or device, or any combination thereof, or any false designation of origin, false or misleading description or fact, or false or misleading representation of fact, which —

    (A) is likely to cause confusion, or to cause mistake, or to deceive as to the affiliation, connection, or association of such person with another person, or as to the origin, sponsorship, or approval of his or her goods, services, or commercial activities by another person, or

    (B) in commercial advertising or promotion, misrepresents the nature, characteristics, qualities, or geographic origin of his or her or another person's goods, services, or commercial activities, shall be liable in a civil action by any person who believes that he or she is or is likely to be damaged by such act. . . .

In *Taylor Made Golf Co., Inc. v. Carsten Sports, Ltd.*, a manufacturer of golf clubs brought an action for, inter alia, trademark infringement under the Latham Act. Defendant produced relatively inexpensive "knock-offs" of plaintiff's expensive, boutique, trademarked, and patented golf clubs. The court found for plaintiff and awarded plaintiff $600,000 in damages and attorneys fees.

TAYLOR MADE GOLF CO. v. CARSTEN SPORTS, LTD.

175 F.R.D. 658 (S.D. Cal. 1997)

BREWSTER, District Judge.

I. Case Type and Jurisdiction

Plaintiff Taylor Made Golf Co. moves for judgment by default against defendant Carsten Sports, Ltd., pursuant to Rule 55(b)(2) of the Federal Rules of Civil Procedure. Defendant has never appeared in this action and has not filed an opposition to this motion. This court has jurisdiction based on 28 U.S.C. §§1331, 1338(a), and 1338(b). Venue is proper under 28 U.S.C. §§1391(b) and 1391(d).

II. Background

Plaintiff manufactures golf clubs and golf apparel. Defendant manufactures and sells golf clubs in competition with Plaintiff that Plaintiff believes are "knock-offs" of its trademarked and patented clubs. Plaintiff seeks judgment by default against Carsten Sports, Ltd. for (1) false representation based on trade dress infringement and false advertising pursuant to 15 U.S.C. §1125(a); (2) trademark infringement pursuant to 15 U.S.C. §1114; (3) patent infringement pursuant to 35 U.S.C. §271; (4) unfair competition under the laws of California; and (5) violation of the California Unfair Trade Practices

Act, Cal Bus. & Prof. Code §17000, *et seq.* Plaintiff is a nationally known golf club manufacturer, and has several patents and trademarks registered with the U.S. Patent and Trademark Office including registrations for the "BURNER BUBBLE" line. The drivers associated with this line were created by Plaintiff with the goal of "distinctive design or appearance so that purchasers or the trade could easily identify Plaintiff's clubs." Plaintiff has spent "substantial sums of money, time and effort to develop, advertise and promote its golf clubs identified by . . . [the] Burner Bubble Trade Dress" through professional golfing events, television and print advertising.

Plaintiff alleges that Defendant Carsten Sports, Ltd., is a foreign corporation residing in Taiwan with its principal place of business in Taiwan. Plaintiff also alleges that Defendant has advertised and sold colorable imitations of Plaintiff's Burner Bubble Trade Dress and that Defendant "has deliberately attempted to ride on the coattails of Plaintiff to capitalize on its well-known and distinctive Trademarks and Trade Dress."

Plaintiff filed its first motion for default judgment on April 23, 1997. On June 16, 1997, the Court held that Plaintiff had demonstrated infringement of its trademark and patent and granted its request for injunctive relief. However, the Court denied, without prejudice, Plaintiff's plea for damages. The Court found that Plaintiff had provided no proof of actual damages, and that the alternative "relief from advertising" methodology offered by Plaintiff was too speculative to support an award of monetary damages. The Court also denied, without prejudice, Plaintiff's request for attorneys' fees because Plaintiff provided no documentation to demonstrate the reasonableness of such fees.

III. Discussion

A. Standard of Law . . .

B. Notice . . .

C. Plaintiff's Remedies

1. Monetary Damages . . .

Therefore, the Court grants Plaintiff's motion for default judgment. Pursuant to 15 U.S.C. §1117(a), the Court trebles the $200,000 in estimated profits by the Defendant, and awards a judgment in the amount of $600,000.

2. Attorney Fees

The Lanham Act permits the court to award reasonable attorney fees in exceptional cases. *See* 15 U.S.C. §1117(a). . . .

Because this information satisfies the Court's request, the Court GRANTS Plaintiff's motion for an award of attorney fees in the amount of $7,910.00.

IV. Conclusion

The Court grants Plaintiff's motion for default judgment against Carsten Sports Ltd. and awards $600,000 in monetary damages and $7,910 for attorney fees.

It is so ordered.

In *Lyons Partnership v. Giannoulas*, the court was asked to decide whether the Famous Chicken (baseball mascot) infringed on the trademark and copyright of Barney (the equally famous purple dinosaur) by using a look-alike in his skits.

Lyons Partnership v. Giannoulas

179 F.3d 384 (5th Cir. 1999)

E. Grady Jolly, Circuit Judge.

Lyons Partnership LP ("Lyons"), the owners of the rights to the children's caricature Barney, sued Ted Giannoulas, the creator of a sports mascot — The Famous Chicken ("the Chicken") — because the Chicken had incorporated a Barney look-alike in its act. The district court granted summary judgment to Giannoulas and awarded attorneys fees.

On appeal, Lyons raises six issues, the most important of which is whether the district court erred when it determined that there was insufficient evidence that Giannoulas's use of the Barney trademark caused consumer confusion under the Lanham Act. Because we agree with the approach taken by the district court, we affirm.

I

This case involves a dispute over the use of the likeness of "Barney," a children's character who appears in a number of products marketed to children. Barney, a sixfoot tall purple "tyrannosaurus rex," entertains and educates young children. His awkward and lovable behavior, good-natured disposition, and renditions of songs like "I love you, you love me," have warmed the hearts and captured the imaginations of children across the United States. According to Lyons, the owner of the intellectual property rights for Barney and the plaintiff in the suit below, the defendants — Giannoulas d/b/a The Famous Chicken and TFC, Inc. ("TFC"), the owner of the intellectual property rights to the Chicken — sought to manipulate Barney's wholesome image to accomplish their own nefarious ends.

The Chicken, a sports mascot conceived of and played by Giannoulas, targets a more grown-up audience. While the Chicken does sell marketing merchandise, it is always sold either by direct order or in conjunction with one of the Chicken's appearances. Thus, the Chicken's principal means of income could, perhaps loosely, be referred to as "performance art." Catering to the tastes of adults attending sporting events, most notably baseball games, the Chicken is renowned for his hard hitting satire. Fictional characters, celebrities, ball players, and, yes, even umpires, are all targets for the Chicken's levity. Hardly anything is sacred.

And so, perhaps inevitably, the Chicken's beady glare came to rest on that lovable and carefree icon of childhood, Barney. Lyons argues that the Chicken's motivation was purely mercenary. Seeing the opportunity to hitch his wagon to a star, the Chicken incorporated a Barney look-alike into his acts. The character, a person dressed in a costume (sold with the title "Duffy the Dragon") that had a remarkable likeness to Barney's appearance, would appear next to the Chicken in an extended performance during which the Chicken would flip, slap, tackle, trample, and generally assault the Barney look-alike.

The results, according to Lyons, were profound. Lyons regales us with tales of children observing the performance who honestly believed that the *real* Barney was being assaulted. . . .

Giannoulas offers a slightly different perspective on what happened. True, he argues, Barney, depicted with his large, rounded body, never changing grin, giddy chuckles, and exclamations like "Super-dee-Dooper!," may represent a simplistic ideal of goodness. Giannoulas, however, also considers Barney to be a symbol of what is wrong with our society—an homage, if you will, to all the inane, banal platitudes that we readily accept and thrust unthinkingly upon our children. Apparently, he is not alone in criticizing society's acceptance of a children's icon with such insipid and corny qualities. . . . further notes that he is not the only satirist to take shots at Barney *Saturday Night Live*, Jay Leno, and a movie starring Tom Arnold have all engaged in parodies at the ungainly dinosaur's expense.

Giannoulas claims that, through careful use of parody, he sought to highlight the differences between Barney and the Chicken. Giannoulas was not merely profiting from the spectacle of a Barney look-alike making an appearance in his show. Instead, he was engaged in a sophisticated critique of society's acceptance of this ubiquitous and insipid creature. Furthermore, Giannoulas argues that he performed the sketch only at evening sporting events. . . .

A trademark is a word, name, symbol or device adopted and used by a manufacturer to identify the source of goods. To establish a trademark violation, Lyons must establish that Giannoulas has used in commerce a mark confusingly similar to Lyons's. 15 U.S.C. §1127. The district court held that there was no likelihood of consumer confusion. In reaching this decision, the district court relied on its finding that the Chicken's performance was clearly meant to be a parody. . . .

A

In general, a parody is defined as an "artistic work that imitates the characteristic style of an author or a work for comic effect or ridicule." . . .

We therefore agree with the district court that Giannoulas's use of the caricature clearly qualifies as a parody. We note that Lyons's insistence that the Chicken's act is not a parody is, in our view, a completely meritless argument.

B

In order to understand Giannoulas's second argument, we must first review our own precedent with respect to consumer confusion under the Lanham Act. . . .

We therefore conclude that the district court did not err in considering the other digits of confusion in the light of its finding that the Chicken's performance is a parody. [Although] . . . use as parody was a relevant factor, we did not intend for the nature of the use to be considered separately from the other digits of confusion. The district court ably considered the other digits of confusion in this respect, and we find no error in its conclusion that there is insufficient evidence to support a violation under the Lanham Act.

In this case, Lyons argued that Giannoulas's use of a Barney caricature violated the Copyright Act and the Lanham Act. The district court disagreed and a review of the record indicates that the district court did not err in doing so. On appeal, we address only the argument related to the relevance that parodic conduct has on determining the likelihood of confusion in a trademark infringement case. We note that in this case the conduct was, without doubt, a parody. Having made that finding, the district court did not err in concluding that the nature of Giannoulas's use is relevant when analyzing the other digits of confusion to determine likelihood of confusion. For the foregoing reasons, the ruling of the district court is affirmed.

In *Indianapolis Colts, Inc., v. Metropolitan Baltimore Football Club Limited Partnership*, the Indianapolis Colts and the National Football League brought suit for trademark infringement against the Canadian Football League's Baltimore franchise in their attempt to call itself "Baltimore CFL Colts." The court granted a preliminary injunction against Baltimore football's team use of the name "Colts" or "CFL Colts." Chief Judge Posner of the Seventh Circuit Court of Appeals found for the Indianapolis Colts (formerly the Baltimore Colts), on the basis that the district court did not commit clear error in finding that Baltimore's use of the name "Baltimore CFL Colts," was likely to confuse a substantial number of consumers, thus warranting issuance of a preliminary injunction.

INDIANAPOLIS COLTS, INC. V. METROPOLITAN BALTIMORE FOOTBALL CLUB LIMITED PARTNERSHIP

34 F.3d 410 (7th Cir. 1994)

POSNER, Chief Judge.

The Indianapolis Colts and the National Football League, to which the Colts belong, brought suit for trademark infringement (15 U.S.C. §§1051 *et seq.*) against the Canadian Football League's new team in Baltimore, which wants to call itself the "Baltimore CFL Colts." (Four of the Canadian Football League's teams are American.) The plaintiffs obtained a preliminary injunction against the new team's using the name "Colts," or "Baltimore Colts," or "Baltimore CFL Colts," in connection with the playing of professional football, the broadcast of football games, or the sale of merchandise to football fans and other buyers. The ground for the injunction was that consumers of "Baltimore CFL Colts" merchandise are likely to think, mistakenly, that the new Baltimore team is an NFL team related in some fashion to the Indianapolis Colts, formerly the Baltimore Colts. From the order granting the injunction the new team and its owners appeal to us under 28 U.S.C. §1292(a)(1). Since the injunction was granted, the new team has played its first two games—without a name.

A bit of history is necessary to frame the dispute. In 1952, the National Football League permitted one of its teams, the Dallas Texans, which was bankrupt, to move to Baltimore, where it was renamed the "Baltimore

Colts." Under that name it became one of the most illustrious teams in the history of professional football. In 1984, the team's owner, with the permission of the NFL, moved the team to Indianapolis, and it was renamed the "Indianapolis Colts." The move, sudden and secretive, outraged the citizens of Baltimore. The city instituted litigation in a futile effort to get the team back—even tried, unsuccessfully, to get the team back by condemnation under the city's power of eminent domain—and the Colts brought a countersuit that also failed. *Indianapolis Colts v. Mayor & City Council of Baltimore*, 733 F.2d 484, 741 F.2d 954 (1984), 775 F.2d 177 (7th Cir. 1985).

Nine years later, the Canadian Football League granted a franchise for a Baltimore team. Baltimoreans clamored for naming the new team the "Baltimore Colts." And so it was named—until the NFL got wind of the name and threatened legal action. The name was then changed to "Baltimore CFL Colts" and publicity launched, merchandise licensed, and other steps taken in preparation for the commencement of play this summer. . . .

The Baltimore team wanted to call itself the "Baltimore Colts." To improve its litigating posture (we assume), it has consented to insert "CFL" between "Baltimore" and "Colts." A glance at the merchandise in the record explains why this concession to an outraged NFL has been made so readily. On several of the items "CFL" appears in small or blurred letters. And since the Canadian Football League is not well known in the United States—and "CFL" has none of the instant recognition value of "NFL"—the inclusion of the acronym in the team's name might have little impact on potential buyers even if prominently displayed. Those who know football well know that the new "Baltimore Colts" are a new CFL team wholly unrelated to the old Baltimore Colts; know also that the rules of Canadian football are different from those of American football and that teams don't move from the NFL to the CFL as they might from one conference within the NFL to the other. But those who do *not* know these things—and we shall come shortly to the question whether there are many of these football illiterates—will not be warned of by the letters "CFL." The acronym is a red herring, and the real issue is whether the new Baltimore team can appropriate the name "Baltimore Colts." The entire thrust of the defendants' argument is that it can.

They make a tremendous to-do over the fact that the district judge found that the Indianapolis Colts abandoned the trademark "Baltimore Colts" when they moved to Indianapolis. Well, of course; they were no longer playing football under the name "Baltimore Colts," so could not have used the name as the team's trademark; they could not have used it on merchandise but chose not to, until 1991 (another story—and not one we need tell). When a mark is abandoned, it returns to the public domain, and is appropriable anew—in principle. In practice, because "subsequent use of [an] abandoned mark may well evoke a continuing association with the prior use, those who make subsequent use may be required to take reasonable precautions to prevent confusion." This precept is especially important where, as in this case, the former owner of the abandoned mark continues to market the same product or service under a similar name, though we cannot find any previous cases of this kind. No one questions the validity of "Indianapolis Colts" as the trademark of the NFL team that plays out of Indianapolis and was formerly known as the Baltimore Colts. If "Baltimore CFL Colts" is confusingly similar to "Indianapolis Colts" by virtue of the history of the Indianapolis team and the overlapping product and geographical markets served by it and by the new Baltimore team, the latter's use of the abandoned mark would infringe the Indianapolis Colts' new mark. The Colts abandonment of a mark confusingly similar to their new mark neither broke the continuity of the team in its different locations—it was the same team, merely having a different home base and therefore a different geographical component in its name—nor entitled a third party to pick it up and use it to confuse Colts fans, and other actual or potential consumers of products and services marketed by the Colts or by other National Football League teams, with regard to the identity, sponsorship, or league affiliation of the third party, that is, the new Baltimore team. . . .

A professional sports team is like Heraclitus's river: always changing, yet always the same. When Mr. Irsay transported his team, the Baltimore Colts, from Baltimore to Indianapolis in one night in 1984, the team remained, for a time anyway, completely intact: same players, same coaches, same front-office personnel. With the passage of time, of course, the team changed. Players retired or were traded, and were replaced. Coaches and other nonplaying personnel came and went. But as far as the record discloses there is as much institutional continuity between the Baltimore Colts of 1984 and the Indianapolis Colts of 1994 as there was between the Baltimore Colts of 1974 and the Baltimore Colts of 1984. Johnny Unitas, the Baltimore Colts' most famous player, swears in his affidavit that his old team has no connection with the Indianapolis Colts, and he has even asked the Colts to expunge his name from its record books. He is angry with Irsay for moving the team. He is entitled to his anger, but it has nothing to do with this lawsuit. The Colts were Irsay's team; it was moved intact; there is no evidence it has changed more since the move than it had in the years before. There is, in contrast, no continuity, no links contractual or otherwise, nothing but a geographical site in common, between the Baltimore Colts and the Canadian Football League team that would like to use its name. Any suggestion that there is such continuity is false and potentially misleading.

Potentially; for if everyone *knows* there is no contractual or institutional continuity, no pedigree or line of descent, linking the Baltimore-Indianapolis Colts and the new CFL team that wants to call itself the "Baltimore Colts" (or, grudgingly, the "Baltimore CFL Colts"), then there is no harm, at least no harm for which the Lanham Act provides a remedy, in the new Baltimore team's appropriating the name "Baltimore Colts" to play under and sell merchandise under. If not everyone knows, there is harm. Some people who might otherwise watch the Indianapolis Colts (or some other NFL team, for remember that the NFL, representing all the teams, is a coplaintiff) on television may watch the Baltimore CFL Colts instead, thinking they are the "real" Baltimore Colts, and the NFL will lose revenue. A few (doubtless very few) people who might otherwise buy tickets to an NFL game may buy tickets to a Baltimore CFL Colts game instead. Some people who might otherwise buy merchandise stamped with the name "Indianapolis Colts" or the name of some other NFL team may buy merchandise stamped "Baltimore CFL Colts," thinking it a kin of the NFL's Baltimore Colts in the glory days of Johnny

Unitas rather than a newly formed team that plays Canadian football in a Canadian football league. It would be naive to suppose that no consideration of such possibilities occurred to the owners of the new Baltimore team when they were choosing a name, though there is no evidence that it was the dominant or even a major consideration. . . .

Confusion thus is possible, and may even have been desired; but is it likely? There is great variance in consumer competence, and it would be undesirable to impoverish the lexicon of trade names merely to protect the most gullible fringe of the consuming public. The Lanham Act does not cast the net of protection so wide. . . .

To help judges strike the balance, the parties to trademark disputes frequently as here hire professionals in marketing or applied statistics to conduct surveys of consumers. . . .

Both parties presented studies. . . .

The defendants argue, finally, that, even so, the injunction is overbroad; it should not have forbidden them to use the word "Colts," but rather confined them to using it in conjunction with "Baltimore CFL." We are baffled by the argument. If they want to use "Colts" in conjunction with anything besides a Baltimore football team, there is nothing in this lawsuit to prevent them. The objection is precisely to their use of the word in a setting that will lead many consumers to believe it designates either the old Baltimore Colts (falsely implying that the Indianapolis Colts are not the successor to the Baltimore Colts or that the new Baltimore team is an NFL team or is approved by or affiliated with the NFL) or the Indianapolis Colts.

The defendants make some other arguments but they do not have sufficient merit to warrant discussion. The judgment of the district court granting the preliminary injunction is affirmed.

QUESTIONS AND DISCUSSION

1. Some trademark cases in sports are *Board of Trustees of the Univ. of Ark. v. Professional Therapy Servs.*, 873 F. Supp 1280 (W.D. Ark. 1995) (trademark infringement suit for unauthorized use of the RAZORBACK name and design logo); *Three Blind Mice Designs v. Cyrk, Inc.*, 892 F. Supp. 303 (D. Mass. 1995) (trademark infringement over caricatures of hockey referees in the form of three blind mice); *Fila U.S.A. v. Kim*, 884 F. Supp. 491 (S.D. Fla. 1995) (trademark infringement over athletic shoes); *Sports Auth. v. Prime Hospitality Corp.*, 877 F. Supp. 124 (S.D.N.Y. 1995) (trademark infringement between "The Sports Authority," a warehouse-type sporting good store and "Sports Authority Food, Spirits and Sports"); *Time Warner Sports Merchandising v. Chicago-Land Processing Corp.*, 1995 WL 107145 (N.D. Ill. 1995) (dispute over licensing of trademarks and trade names associated with the 1994 World Cup of Soccer).

5. Some trademark cases even involve Michael Jordan. In *Chattanooga Mfg., Inc. v. Nike, Inc.*, 140 F. Supp. 2d 917 (N.D. Ill. 2001), plaintiff sued Nike and Michael Jordan for trademark infringement; since 1979, it had used the term JORDAN to identify the products of its Jordan Blouse Division. However, it did not apply for trademark registration of JORDAN for use

on women's wearing apparel until 1997. Michael did not even begin to ascend to Air Jordan status until 1982, his freshman year at the University of North Carolina. As usual, Michael wins, mostly because of plaintiff's long delay and the resulting extreme prejudice to defendants.

6. In *Pebble Beach Co. v. Tour 18 I, Ltd.*, 942 F. Supp. 1513 (S.D. Tex. 1996), famous golf course operators sued a course that specifically replicated America's most famous golf holes on the basis of service mark infringement for copying the holes and then promoting them in advertising materials. At the end of the day, only the truly distinctive signature holes (for example, Hilton Head's Harbour Town 18th par 4, complete with its trademark red and white striped lighthouse) merit protection. Since it was the goal of Tour 18 to copy famous holes, shouldn't there be some way for these famous golf courses to protect their designs?

7. *Taylor Made Golf Co. v. Carsten Sports, Ltd.*, discussed the tenacious defense of the design of expensive boutique golf clubs. The point here was to determine the damages based on infringer's profits. How did the court arrive at the amount of $600,000?

8. In *Lyons Partnership v. Giannoulas*, the creator of the children's Barney dinosaur character brought suit against owner of 'the Famous Chicken' (baseball's first mascot) character for copyright and trademark infringement. Barney lost since the use of the Barney 'look-alike' was a parody for purposes of trademark infringement claim. If infringement was found, what damages could Barney claim?

9. The *Indianapolis Colts* case involved trademark infringement against a CFL team trying to call itself the "Baltimore CFL Colts." This was likely to confuse substantial numbers of consumers, warranting preliminary injunction. Should the threshold question be, was it the intent of the "Baltimore CFL Colts" to cause confusion by choosing that particular name?

D. TRADE DRESS

Trade dress protection is available for nonfunctional features if they distinguish the goods' origin. The Lanham Act provides protection against the creation of confusion by the simulation of a product's or service's "trade dress." Trade dress was once confined to a product's packaging, but now it includes the product's configuration and ornamentation.

In *Taylor Made Golf Co. v. Trend Precision Golf, Inc.*, plaintiff brought an infringement suit alleging that defendant's golf clubs infringed on their Burner Bubble trade dress.

TAYLOR MADE GOLF CO. v. TREND PRECISION GOLF, INC.

903 F. Supp. 1506 (M.D. Fla. 1995)

G. KENDALL SHARP, District Judge.

This matter is before the court on Taylor Made Golf Company, Inc.'s (Taylor Made) Motion for Preliminary Injunction. On a motion for preliminary injunction, the court considers (1) the likelihood that plaintiff will ultimately prevail on the merits of the claim; (2) the irreparable nature of the threatened injury; (3) the potential harm that might be caused to the opposing party or others if the order is issued; (4) and the public interest, if any.

This case involves trade dress infringement. Taylor Made asserts that Trend Precision Golf, Inc. (Trend Precision) is infringing on their Burner Bubble trade dress. The Burner Bubble golf club at issue is copper and black with silver plating on the bottom of the head. Taylor Made is seeking to protect the placement of the copper and black colors on the Burner Bubble golf club.

In determining the likelihood that Taylor Made will ultimately prevail on the merits, both Taylor Made and Trend Precision agree that Taylor Made must show that its trade dress is inherently distinctive or that it has acquired a secondary meaning. At this stage of the proceedings, the court cannot find that the placement of the copper and black colors on the Burner Bubble golf club is inherently distinctive. From the evidence presented to the court, it appears that the color combination is a common design. Further, the court notes that in Taylor Made's advertising, Taylor Made has emphasized the shaft portion of the club containing a bubble with the words "BUBBLE SHAFT" next to the copper color. This emphasis of the "BUBBLE SHAFT" diminishes the distinctiveness of the copper and black color combination. Trend Precision's golf club does not have a bubble on this portion of the club. Moreover, Taylor Made presents evidence that it only recently introduced its Burner Bubble golf club at a PGA show in January 1995.

Taylor Made also fails to show that the copper and black color combination has acquired a secondary meaning. Because the Burner Bubble golf club was only recently introduced, it would be unlikely that the copper and black combination acquired a secondary meaning in such a short time. Nevertheless, Taylor Made fails to present evidence that the color combination did in fact acquire such a secondary meaning. Finally, the court finds that Taylor Made fails to show irreparable harm.

Because the court finds that at this stage of the proceedings Taylor Made fails to show that the copper and black color combination is inherently distinctive, that the color combination acquired a secondary meaning, or that Taylor Made will suffer irreparable harm, the court need not address the other issues raised by the parties. Thus, the court Denies Taylor Made's Motion for Preliminary Injunction.

It is so ordered

In *Callaway Golf Co. v. Golf Clean, Inc.*, a golf club manufacturer successfully used trade dress protection to enjoin a knock-off of its Big Bertha irons.

CALLAWAY GOLF CO. V. GOLF CLEAN, INC.

915 F. Supp. 1206 (M.D. Fla. 1995)

BUCKLEW, District Judge.

This Cause is before the Court on Plaintiff's Motion Requesting an Order to Show Cause as to a why preliminary injunction should not be issued against the Defendants (Doc. No. 2, filed June 26, 1995). This motion was referred to United States Magistrate Mark A. Pizzo on June 27, 1995, for a report and recommendation. Judge Pizzo filed his report on July 18, 1995 (Doc. No. 30), recommending that a preliminary injunction be issued. . . .

District Court's Standard of Review

The motion was referred by this Court to Magistrate Judge Pizzo pursuant to 28 U.S.C. §636(b)(1)(B). Accordingly, the applicable standard of review is a *de novo* determination of the portions of the report to which objections were made.

Accordingly, since no objections were filed, the Court adopts United States Magistrate Judge Pizzo's Report and Recommendation. Plaintiff's Motion Requesting an Order to Show Cause as to a why preliminary injunction should not be issued against the Defendants (Doc. No. 2, filed June 26, 1995) is granted. . . .

Done and ordered.

Report and Recommendation

Pizzo, United States Magistrate Judge.

Callaway Golf Company (Callaway), the manufacturer of "Big Bertha" woods and irons, claims that Defendants' golf clubs, "Canterbury Big Bursar Irons" and "Professional Big Brother Tour" irons, infringe upon Callaway's trademarks and trade dress in violation of the Lanham Act (15 U.S.C. §1051 et seq.). Plaintiff asks the district court to preliminary enjoin Defendants from manufacturing, distributing, or selling these goods until the trial of the merits of the case. Based upon pleadings filed by Callaway, United States District Judge Susan C. Bucklew issued a temporary restraining order on June 27, 1995, prohibiting Defendants from marketing or selling its "Canterbury Big Bursar Irons" (doc. # 8). Judge Bucklew, pursuant to her authority under 28 U.S.C. §636(b)(1)(B), referred Callaway's motion for preliminary injunction (doc. # 2) to the undersigned for a report and recommendation (doc. # 8). For the following reasons, I recommend that a preliminary injunction be issued against Defendants.

I. The Rule 65 Hearing and Defendant's "Professional Big Brother" Irons

In accordance with Fed. R. Civ. P. 65(b) and Local Rule 4.06, this court convened a hearing on July 5, 1995, to review the merits of Callaway's request for preliminary injunction. Defendant, without admitting liability, agreed to cease and desist using any Big Bursar medallions in connection with the sale of any its golf equipment. However, this does not end the dispute. Instead, Defendants offered a replacement club called the "Professional Big Brother Tour," which Defendants argue is sufficiently dissimilar to Callaway's product as to not warrant an injunction. Callaway, unaware of the existence of this "new club" until just prior to the hearing, claimed that this product too infringed upon their trade dress. While this new club is not specifically addressed in Callaway's pleadings (all references are to the "Canterbury Big Bursar"), its characteristics and appearance are strikingly similar to its forbearer, the Big Bursar. Because the issues presented by these new clubs are identical to those presented by Defendants' earlier model, this court concludes that this "counter offer" and Callaway's continuing complaint are ripe for review.

II. The Issue: Is Callaway's Big Bertha Iron Entitled to Trade Dress Protection?

Callaway claims that the Canterbury Big Bursar violates its trademarks and trade dress in violation of the Lanham Act. . . . Callaway steadfastly disagrees, and argues that the Professional Big Brother Tour is materially the same as the Big Bursar and its sale should be preliminarily enjoined.

III. Factual Background

Golf Clean, Inc. is a small corporation which manufactures and markets a golf club and ball cleaning device called "Golf Clean". It also manufactures and sells a golf cooler called the "Cooler Caddy." Golf Clean International, Inc., which does business as the Golf Depot, assembles, sells and distributes golf clubs through its two retail outlets as well as through other retailers. One of the products sold by Golf Clean International, Inc. is the Canterbury Big Bursar irons (this club) . . . looks almost identical to Callaway's Big Bertha irons. . . .

Callaway Golf Company manufactures and markets high quality golf clubs. Callaway introduced its original Big Bertha golf club, the Big Bertha driver, in January 1991, and the Big Bertha fairway metal woods in 1992. The Big Bertha clubs have been extremely successful for Callaway; in fact Plaintiffs claim they are the best selling premium priced metal woods in the world. As a complement to its highly successful Big Bertha metal woods, Callaway developed a line of Big Bertha irons. These irons, which Callaway introduced into the market in early 1994, have been phenomenally successful and have generated more than $147 million in sales. In Florida alone, for example, Big Bertha irons sales exceed $14 million.

Callaway's marketing strategy is to design clubs that are "Demonstrably Superior and Pleasingly Different." Accordingly, the company emphasizes in its Big Bertha advertisements the shape and design of the irons, a design which Callaway promotes is in keeping with its successful Big Bertha wood. Callaway's Big Bertha irons possess the following features:

1. A wide top line with a peened finish similar to that on the striking face of the club;
2. A semicircular relief facet on the sole of the club;
3. A large, straight cut rear cavity;
4. The lowermost score lines on the striking face painted white with the bottom score line being shorter than the oters and centered under them;
5. Set in the rear cavity of the club head, the Big Bertha Irons medallion, which itself features:
   (a) a unique and distinctive shape and layout;
   (b) the federally registered Callaway logo appearing in an arched script;

(c) the federally registered Big Bertha logo appearing in a flared rectangular box;

(d) the "IRONS" designation in block writing on a colored background immediately below the Big Bertha logo; and,

(e) a red black and silver color scheme.

The success of Callaway's clubs, both woods and irons, has resulted in a cottage industry of "knock off" clubs, and the company has vigorously attempted to protect her interests. Prior to this lawsuit, Callaway successfully obtained permanent injunctions in California and South Carolina against retailers and distributors of the Canterbury Big Bursar.

Just like Callaway's Big Bertha irons, Defendants' Canterbury Big Bursar irons exhibit nearly identical features:

1. A wide top line with a smooth finish in contrast to the peened finish on the striking face of the club;
2. A semi circular relief facet on the sole of the club;
3. A large, straight cut rear cavity; and,
4. The lowermost score lines on the striking face painted white with the bottom score line being shorter than the others and centered under them.

This similarity is not happenstance. Prior to filing its papers in this case, Callaway telephonically ordered a set of "Canterbury Big Bursar" irons from Golf Depot in Clearwater, Florida. After inspecting these clubs, Callaway dispatched an investigator to visit one of Golf Depot's stores and masquerade as a customer for the Canterbury Big Bursar irons. A Golf Depot salesperson told this investigator that the Big Bursar irons were made "from the same molds used by Callaway." Defendant's effort to copy Callaway's club includes matching the shape, script, color, and size of Callaway's Big Bertha medallion. . . .

IV. Discussion

Before the district court can issue a preliminary injunction, Callaway must show: (1) a substantial likelihood of success on the merits (i.e. that Defendants have infringed on Callaway's trade dress and trademarks); (2) an irreparable injury if the injunction is not granted; (3) that Callaway's threatened injury outweighs the threatened harm the injunction may cause Defendants; and (4) the granting of the injunction will not disserve the public interest. Of these four factors, the final three are demonstrably in favor of Callaway for reasons that are set forth below. Thus, the focus of the analysis is on the first factor, the likelihood of success on the merits of Callaway's claim of trade dress infringement.

A. The Merits of the Case: Proving Trade Dress Infringement

Trade dress infringement is an implied federal cause of action based upon. . . . Lanham Act §43, 15 U.S.C. §1125. The term "trade dress" refers to the total image of a product, and may include features such as size, shape, color combinations, texture, graphics, or even particular sales techniques.

To succeed on the merits of a trade dress infringement claim, Callaway must prove: (1) that its trade dress has a quality of inherent distinctiveness or has otherwise acquired secondary meaning in the marketplace; (2) that the features of the trade dress are primarily non-functional; and (3) that the trade dress of the products is confusingly similar.

1. Callaway's Big Bertha Irons Are Inherently Distinctive and Have Acquired Secondary Meaning . . .

The Callaway Big Bertha Iron's trade dress undeniably incorporates the common, basic shape and design of a golf club. As Defendant correctly points out, the cavity back design, a wide sole, and scoring on the club's face, are common features in golf clubs. However, trade dresses often use common lettering styles, geometric shapes, or colors. While each of these elements alone would not be inherently distinctive, their combination and the total impression that the dress gives to the observer makes the item distinctive. . . .

The various ornamental and colorful designs of the Callaway Big Bertha Irons were deliberately chosen so as to produce a unique total image for the clubs. An image Callaway touts as "demonstrably superior and pleasingly different." Callaway adopted a "chunky" and "aggressive" wide top line for their club that is almost unique in the field (the Ping Zing club has a similar wide top line). The semicircular relief facet on the sole of the club is a distinctive design of this manufacturer. Added to these peculiar characteristics are the club's other features: namely the large, straight cut rear cavity, the distinguishing white lowermost score lines, and the unique Callaway medallion in the cavity's inset. All these components produce a distinctive club. Indeed, when Callaway introduced their Big Bertha irons in 1994 they looked noticeably different than any other club on the market. . . . Callaway's arbitrary combination of features makes their Big Bertha Irons inherently distinctive. . . .

Because Callaway's irons are inherently distinctive, secondary meaning need not be demonstrated. . . .

A court should consider the following factors in assessing secondary meaning: (1) the length of time and manner of its use; (2) the nature and extent of its use; and (3) the efforts made in the direction of promoting a conscious connection, in the public's mind, between the mark and a particular source of origin.

Callaway has bombarded the golfing consumer with the image of its Big Bertha Clubs by spending over $5 million in advertising. Significantly, Callaway's ads and other promotional materials prominently feature the club head, thus emphasizing its unique and distinctive appearance. Callaway has sold over $147 million worth of the clubs, thereby establishing that the clubs are extremely popular amongst golfers. Numerous articles have been written profiling the development and success of the Callaway Big Bertha Irons. These facts, coupled with Defendant's nearly exact duplication of the Big Bertha and its representations that the Canterbury Big Bursar was made from the same molds as the Callaway Big Bertha, establish that the Big Bertha has acquired secondary meaning.

2. Callaway's Trade Dress Is Primarily Nonfunctional

Trade dress is protectable only if it is primarily nonfunctional. *AmBrit*, at 1537. Notwithstanding this requirement, individual elements of the trade dress can still be functional and the entire package still be protected under the Lanham Act. *AmBrit*, 812 F.2d at 1537. Factors to consider are whether a particular design is superior, whether there are alternative trade dress configurations available, and whether a particular design is comparatively simple or cheap.

As discussed earlier, there are numerous clubs on the market that incorporate individual features of Callaway's trade dress. Hence, alternative trade dress configurations that serve the same function are available to competitors. Further, there is no evidence that Callaway's design is superior to that of other clubs, or that it is comparatively simple or cheap. Granting Callaway an exclusive right to use the Big Bertha trade dress will not hinder effective competition by others. Based upon *Isaly's* test, Callaway's trade dress is primarily nonfunctional.

3. Defendant's Clubs Are Likely to Be Confused with the Callaway Big Bertha

The primary factor in determining trade dress infringement under the Lanham Act is the likelihood of confusion resulting from the defendant's adoption of a trade dress similar to the plaintiff's. The elements that must be considered to determine likelihood of confusion are: the strength of the trade dress, the similarity of design, the similarity of the product, the similarity of retail outlets and purchasers, the similarity of advertising media used, the defendant's intent, and actual confusion. The issue does not turn upon one party's position supporting a majority of these factors; instead, the court must evaluate the weight each factor deserves and then make its ultimate decision. The appropriate weight each factor should be given varies with each case.

a. Strength of Trade Dress. As discussed above, Callaway's trade dress is strong; it has spent millions on advertising and placing the image in the golfing public's eye. Accordingly, for the same reasons that this Court determined that the trade dress is inherently distinctive and has acquired secondary meaning, the Callaway Big Bertha has a strong trade dress.

b. The Similarity of Design. The similarity of design test is nothing more than a subjective eyeball test. After eyeballing the clubs (even after a lengthy gaze), the Callaway Big Bertha and the Canterbury Big Bursar look almost exactly alike. The Professional Big Brother's design copies Callaway's club, even with Defendants' change in logo. Hence, this factor weighs heavily in Callaway's favor.

c. Similarity of Retail Outlets and Purchasers. The possibility of confusion is greater when products have similar trade channels and predominant consumers. Callaway clubs are sold at off-course retail golf shops. Defendants sell their clubs at their own retail stores as well as to other off-course golf shops. Defendants' employee admits to having sold customers Big Bertha clubs at defendant's store. Thus, the trade channels must necessarily be similar if both clubs are being sold at Defendant's store.

d. Similarity of Advertising Media . . .

e. Defendants' Intent. If a plaintiff can show that a defendant adopted a mark with the intent of deriving benefit from the reputation of the plaintiff, that fact alone may be sufficient to justify an inference that there is confusing similarity. . . .

f. Actual Confusion . . .

However, because this court finds that Defendant's proposed Professional Big Brother is substantially the same as the Canterbury Big Bursar, it finds Defendant's argument without merit. Callaway's survey, although not dispositive on the issue of actual confusion, suggests that discovery in this case may well reveal more evidence of actual confusion.

g. Callaway has Demonstrated Likelihood of Confusion. In summary, Callaway has adequately demonstrated the factors necessary for a finding of likelihood of confusion. . . .

V. Conclusion

The Callaway Big Bertha arbitrarily combines its features in such a manner that the clubs are inherently distinctive; further, the clubs have acquired secondary meaning. The features claimed by Callaway as its trade dress are primarily nonfunctional. Finally, Defendants' product is confusingly similar to the Callaway Big Bertha and is likely to be confused by the end user as having some connection to Callaway. This court concludes that Callaway has demonstrated it will likely succeed on the merits of its claim. . . .

Accordingly, it is hereby recommended that a preliminary injunction be issued prohibiting Defendants from:

(A) Manufacturing, producing, distributing, circulating, selling, offering for sale, importing, exporting, advertising, promoting, displaying, shipping, marketing, or otherwise disposing of "Canterbury Big Bursar Irons," "Professional Big Brother Tour" irons, Big Bursar Iron heads, or Big Bursar Iron medallions;

(B) Manufacturing, producing, distributing, circulating, selling, offering for sale, importing, exporting, advertising, promoting, displaying, shipping, marketing, or otherwise disposing of any golf club iron head or club that:

1. Has a polished sole plate with a semicircular relief facet; a heavy or wide top line with a peened or pebbled finish; a striking face with a peened finish, having horizontal score lines with the bottommost score line shortened and centered in the middle of the striking face, and the two bottommost score lines painted a contrasting color; and a large, straight cut rear cavity with a finish similar to that on the top line of the club head; substantially similar to the head on Callaway Golf's Big Bertha Irons as shown on Exhibit A; or

2. Has a medallion substantially similar to Callaway Golf's Big Bertha Irons medallion as shown on Exhibit B;

(C) Using a trade dress confusingly similar to that of Callaway Golf's in the overall appearance of its Big Bertha Irons and/or in the appearance and shape of its Big Bertha Iron medallion in connection with the advertising, promotion, offering, marketing, manufacture, sale or other disposal of iron heads or irons;

(D) Using, manufacturing, producing, distributing, circulating, selling, offering for sale, importing, exporting, advertising, promoting, displaying, shipping, marketing, or otherwise disposing of any iron heads, irons or other products or things (not manufactured by Callaway Golf) that bear any simulation, reproduction, counterfeit, copy or colorable imitation of Callaway Golf's Registered Trademarks, including the Callaway and Design Trademark (Registration No. 1,768,763) and the Big Bertha and Big Bertha and Design Trademarks (Nos. 1,649,164 and 1,720,466);

(E) Removing from any premises under their possession, custody or control, any goods or things bearing any simulation or colorable imitation of Callaway Golf's trade dress or Registered Trademarks;

(F) Disposing in any manner of any merchandise or thing in their possession, custody or control bearing any colorable imitation of Callaway Golf's trade dress or Registered Trademarks; and

(G) Disposing in any manner of any documents or other records evidencing the source or wholesale purchasers of the above-mentioned clubs, club heads or medallions.

It is so recommended this 18th day of July, 1995.

QUESTIONS AND DISCUSSION

1. *Pebble Beach Co. v. Tour 18, Ltd.*, 942 F. Supp. 1513 (S.D. Tex. 1996), the so-called "celebrated golf course design trade dress suit" involved Tour 18, a local Houston golf course that purposefully emulated America's most famous golf holes from America's most prestigious golf courses. The owners of three of the copied holes filed a complaint alleging that Tour 18 violated their design proprietary rights, including infringement of their trademarks, trade dress, copyrights, and goodwill. The court found trade dress infringement only with respect to the reproduction of the "lighthouse" hole (#18) at Harbour Town; Tour 18 was enjoined from any use of it in its promotions. Tour 18 must disclaim in all promotions, signage, etc., any association with the replicated holes. In short, only the truly distinctive signature holes (like Harbour Town's 18th) deserved trade dress protection; other than the truly distinctive holes replicant golf courses do not violate trade dress, trademark, or copyright law. Why was trade dress, as a legal theory, substantially unsuccessful here?

2. There's quite a tempest-in-a-teapot in the use of trade dress to protect boutique golf club manufacturers from knock-offs. In *Taylor Made Golf Co. v. Carsten Sports, Ltd.*, plaintiff vigorously asserted its trademark and patented golf clubs against knock-offs of these clubs. Among its protected registration is the trade dress of its "BURNER BUBBLE" Metal Wood. Plaintiff's motion for summary judgment was granted, along with a monetary award based on infringer's profits. See *Taylor Made Golf Co. v.*

Trend Precision Golf, Inc., (trade dress for Callaway Golf's Big Bertha Irons). See also Burleson & Champion, *Trade Dress as the Only Club in the Bag to Protect Golf Club Manufacturers from "Knock-Offs" of Their Prized Boutique Golf Clubs*, 3 Tex. Rev. Enter. & Sports L. 43 (2002).

3. In *Callaway Golf Co. v. Golf Clean, Inc.*, the trade dress of the golf club was inherently distinctive; therefore, secondary meaning need not be demonstrated. Defendant made the court's job easier by being greedy and copying detail by detail so that confusion was likely, intended, expected, anticipated, and hoped for. Would the court have allowed the injunction if defendant was less greedy?

E. BROADCASTING AND LICENSING RIGHTS

The developing technology in sports broadcasting such as satellite networks, Internet copying, and retransmission has raised many questions that have repercussions in the licensing of copyrighted materials.

For example, in *HBO v. Champs of New Haven*, an action was brought under the Communications Act and the Copyright Act, both as amended by the Satellite Home Viewer Act, against a bar owner for unauthorized interception of plaintiff's satellite cable programming.

The Court held that the failure of defendant to defend against this action promptly did not constitute "mistake, inadvertence, surprise, or excusable neglect" warranting the reopening of a default judgment. It further held that the award of $250,000 in statutory damages to plaintiff was excessive under the circumstances, and should be reduced to $10,000.

HOME BOX OFFICE v. CHAMPS, INC.

837 F. Supp. 480 (D. Conn. 1993)

After full briefing, an evidentiary hearing was held on the record on November 10, 1993, at which the court reserved decision.

Discussion

I.

In support of their motion, the defendants argue that they never received a copy of the plaintiff's motions for default and default judgment. They further argue that the factual allegations involved in this case do not warrant the huge sum of the amount awarded upon default. The defendants contend that they have now retained counsel and that they do intend to present their defenses to this case. They claim that they believed that they were receiving authorized HBO signals and that any unauthorized signal was received by accident or by mistake. In addition, the defendants assert that they received HBO signals only for a brief period of time.

The plaintiff vehemently objects to the defendants' motion, arguing that the defendants' claim that they did not receive the plaintiff's motions for default and default judgment is simply not credible. According to the plaintiff, copies of these motions were personally delivered to defendant

Bova and mailed to Mr. Bova's residence in Branford and to Champs Sports Bar in New Haven.

The plaintiff further maintains that it has expended a great deal of time, money and effort in prosecuting this case, and has made every effort to communicate with the defendants and to settle this action out of court. According to the plaintiff, it has properly complied with the court's procedures in obtaining a Default Judgment, and it should not be forced to go through the whole process again simply because the defendants have now decided that they want to defend this 3 action. According to the plaintiff, the defendants should not now be relieved from the Default Judgment merely because they have finally come to appreciate the seriousness and magnitude of the consequences of their actions. . . .

II . . .

With regard to Rule 60(b)(6), the defendants have not suggested, much less persuasively demonstrated, "any other reason" justifying relief. Put simply, the defendants have not convinced the court of any reason why they should be permitted at this late stage to reopen the merits of this litigation.

Accordingly, the defendants' motion must be denied.

III

While the court declines to reopen the Default Judgment, it does find that the maximum amount of statutory damages — $250,000 — is demonstrably excessive under the circumstances presented. The plaintiff alleges merely that investigations conducted on or about October 31, 1992 revealed that the defendants, without authorization, intercepted, received and commercially and publicly exhibited the plaintiff's satellite cable programming. There are no allegations of repeated violations over an extended period of time, of substantial unlawful monetary gains by the defendants, or, conversely, of any significant actual damages to the plaintiff. On this record, the court is hard pressed to find a justification for awarding to the plaintiff a quarter of a million dollars.

Inasmuch as the amount of statutory damages under 47 U.S.C. §§553(c)(3)(B) and 605(e)(3)(C) and 17 U.S.C. §504 is discretionary, the court, in the exercise of its discretion, finds that the appropriate amount of statutory damages under the circumstances presented is $10,000. Accordingly, the Default Judgment is hereby amended and Final Judgment shall enter against the defendants and in favor of the plaintiff in the amount of $10,000. . . .

Inasmuch as the defendants' motion is in fact denied, the court can now consider the plaintiff's application for costs and attorney's fees. Given the history of this case, including defendant Bova's refusal to cooperate with counsel, his failure to comply with a direct court order, and his repeated attempts to spurn this litigation, the court concludes that an award of costs and reasonable attorney's fees is fully warranted under the circumstances presented.

Conclusion

Based on the record, and for the reasons stated above, the defendant's Motion for Relief from Default Judgment (filed June 7, 1993) (doc. # 24) is hereby denied. The Default Judgment in this action is hereby amended so that

Final Judgment shall enter against the defendants and in favor of the plaintiff in the amount of $10,000 plus costs and reasonable attorney's fees.

It is so ordered.

The following case, *M Sports Productions v. Pay-Per-View Network, Inc.*, involves a license to transmit a boxing event to cable and satellite affiliates.

M SPORTS PRODUCTIONS V. PAY-PER-VIEW NETWORK, INC.

United States District Court, S.D. New York.
1998 WL 19998 (S.D.N.Y.)

BAER, J.

Defendant Pay-Per-View Network ("PPV"), defendants DEB Associates LLC and Harbor Vista Associates Ltd. Partnership (collectively the "Harbor Vista Defendants") and defendant Group W Broadcasting, Inc. ("Group W") move to dismiss the Amended Verified Complaint (the "Complaint" or "Compl.") of plaintiff M Sports Productions ("M Sports") and Arthur Menaldi pursuant to Rule 12(b)(6) and Rule 9(b). For the reasons stated below, the motions are granted in part and denied in part.

I. Background

On November 21, 1996, PPV entered into an Event License Agreement (the "Agreement") with a licensor known as M Sports, pursuant to which PPV was granted a license to transmit to its cable and satellite network affiliates a boxing event (the "Event"), scheduled to air live on February 13, 1997. On the day of the telecast, plaintiff delivered his television signal to a satellite transmission facility operated by Group W. However, as a result of technical difficulties, there was a freeze of the telecast for about 70 minutes, and as a result, some of the Event subscribers asked for and received their money back. The Harbor Vista Defendants are the owners, operators and/or managers of the premises from which Group W telecast the Event.

In his amended complaint, plaintiff brings the following eight causes of action: (1) against PPV and Group W, for breach of the Agreement; (2) against PPV and Group W for tortious interference with plaintiffs business relationships with his sponsors for the event and for future events; (3) against PPV and Group W for injury to plaintiffs business reputation; (4) against Group W for tortious interference with the Agreement; (5) against Group W for negligence; (6) against Burns Security for negligence; (7) against the Harbor Vista Defendants for negligence and (8) against PPV and Group W for fraudulent inducement.

The defendants move to dismiss these causes of action under Rule 12(b)(6) and under Rule 9(b). . . .

II. Discussion

A. First Cause of Action — Breach of Contract by PPV & Group W

Plaintiff alleges that PPV and Group W violated the Agreement by failing to telecast the Event. Plaintiff seeks $5 million in damages for the alleged consequences of this failure to transmit the event. PPV argues that this cause of action must be dismissed because this cause of action seeks consequential damages, which are expressly prohibited by the Agreement. The Agreement provides that "under no circumstances shall either party hereto be liable to the other for any loss of revenue, lost profits, lost capital, overhead or any special, indirect, incidental or consequential damages of any type." Under the Agreement, plaintiff was to be compensated by sharing in the gross revenues from the Event; the complaint does not allege that this provision was breached in any way. . . .

With respect to Group W, Group W argues that this claim should be dismissed against it because there is no allegation that it was a party to the Agreement and thus it could not have breached the Agreement. . . . Here, the uplink agreement provides that under no circumstances shall Group W be liable to any third parties for any loss of revenue, claims of service interruption or any other consequential damages. Thus, plaintiff cannot be considered a third-party beneficiary. Accordingly, plaintiffs first cause of action against Group W must be dismissed.

B. Second Cause of Action Against PPV and Group W—Interference with Business Relations

In his second cause of action, plaintiff alleges that PPV and Group W "interfered with plaintiffs business relationships with his sponsor for the Event" as well as sponsors for future events and that as a result, plaintiffs sponsors have or will terminate their business relationships with plaintiff and fewer new ones will appear. . . . Accordingly, this cause of action is dismissed.

C. Third Cause of Action Against PPV and Group W

In Count Three, plaintiff claims that PPV and Group W deliberately failed to transmit the Event, thereby holding plaintiff up to public contempt and injuring plaintiffs personal and professional reputation and seeks $10 million in damages for injury to his reputation and mental distress. . . .

D. Count Four Against Group W—Interference With Contract

Plaintiff alleges that Group W tortiously interfered with the Agreement between PPV and plaintiff and that such conduct was deliberate, malicious and without excuse. . . .

E. Fifth Cause of Action Against Group W—Negligence

Plaintiff alleges that Group W owed plaintiff a duty to exercise reasonable care in uplinking and maintaining the transmission of the Event, but breached that duty by failing to prevent a freeze of the telecast. Group W argues that it is not liable for negligence because it owed no duty of care to the plaintiff. . . . Thus, plaintiff's fifth cause of action is dismissed.

F. Seventh Cause of Action Against the Harbor Vista Defendants

Plaintiff alleges that the Harbor Vista Defendants, the owners, operators and/or managers of the facility from which PPV and Group W telecast their programs, were negligent in failing to properly maintain the premises and/or equipment therein. . . . Plaintiff contends that a duty should be implied because the Harbor Vista Defendants, as owners of the premises, had a common law duty to maintain them in a reasonably safe condition. I find that plaintiff has stated (albeit barely) a cause of action for negligence based on the Harbor Vista Defendants status as owners of the premises.

G. Eighth Cause of Action Against PPV and Group W—Fraud

Plaintiff alleges that PPV fraudulently represented that PPV and Group W would televise five future boxing events in addition to the Event, and that it was a consequence of that overture that the Agreement was consummated. Plaintiff alleges that it was therefore fraudulently induced to enter into the Agreement. . . . I find that the complaint fails to satisfy the requirements of Rule 9(b) as it fails to allege the precise misstatement, and the time, place and speaker, but in an abundance of caution, this cause of action is dismissed without prejudice. Leave to replead is granted and plaintiff may file a Second Amended Complaint within 20 days from the date oral argument was held in this matter.

III. Conclusion

For the foregoing reasons, defendants' motions to dismiss are granted with respect to plaintiff's first, second, fourth and fifth causes of action, and denied with respect to plaintiff's third and seventh causes of action. Defendant's motion to dismiss plaintiffs eighth cause of action is granted, with leave to replead a third time within 20 days from December 16, 1997.

So ordered.

Worldwide Futgol Associates, Inc., v. Event Entertainment, Inc., concerned a breach of contract suit involving the U.S. television broadcasting rights of international soccer matches.

WORLDWIDE FUTGOL ASSOCIATES, INC. V. EVENT ENTERTAINMENT, INC.

983 F. Supp. 173 (E.D.N.Y. 1997)

DEARIE, District Judge.

This is a diversity action based on a contract (the "Agreement") between Worldwide Futgol Associates, Inc. ("WFA"), a licensor and distributor of United States television rights to international soccer matches, and Event Entertainment, Inc. ("Event"), whereby Event purchased the rights to certain soccer matches. Event has moved to dismiss the complaint, pursuant to Federal Rule of Civil Procedure 12(b)(2), on the ground that it is not subject to the personal jurisdiction of the Court. Alternatively, Event moves for a transfer of venue to the Central District of California pursuant to 28 U.S.C. §1404(a). For the reasons stated below, the motion to dismiss is granted and the action is transferred to the Central District of California.

Background

The Agreement is a one-page memorandum executed by Julio Vanegas, WFA's General Manager, and Rick Kulis, Event's President. It provides for Event to pay $360,000 for the United States ("except California") closed circuit television rights to three international soccer matches: an October 16, 1996 match between Mexico and Jamaica; an October 30, 1996 match between Mexico and Honduras (collectively, the "Matches"). The sale price was to be paid in installments of $120,000, due October 12, 1996, and $240,000, due October 17, 1996. Payment of the second installment was conditioned on Mexico winning the October 16, 1996 Match with Jamaica. WFA claims that Event broadcast the first Match but failed to make either payment. Event claims that WFA failed to provide promised customers for the broadcasts, cut off the satellite feed for the October 16 Match, and withheld certain customer proceeds when Event broadcast the Match through an alternate feed.

Event is a California corporation with its principal place of business in California. WFA is a New York corporation with its principal place of business in New York. Event is in the business of providing broadcasts of limited access sporting events. After acquiring the rights to a particular broadcast, Event accepts orders from customers — sports bars, restaurants and hotels — for the broadcast. Upon receiving payment from a customer, Event directs its subcontractor, which is located in Denver, Colorado, to address the satellite signal of the event, in unencrypted form, to the customer's satellite dish. Each satellite dish bears a unique addressable code number which allows Event's subcontractor to provide unencrypted signals to individual customers.

Prior to entering the Agreement, Event, through a joint venture with another entity, purchased the rights to televise the Matches in California. According to affidavits submitted on WFA's behalf, Event telephoned Ricky Schanks, an independent broker in the field of international soccer, shortly before the first Match to express its interest in obtaining broader rights to the Matches. This and subsequent calls were made by Event representatives in California to Schanks' home in New York. Schanks put Event in contact with WFA, which owned the television rights to the Matches. The parties negotiated the Agreement in a series of bicoastal telephone calls. WFA faxed the Agreement to Event in California for signature and return fax. Event then contracted with numerous customers, a number of which may have been in New York, to provide access to the October 16 Mexico-Jamaica Match.

Discussion

The party seeking to invoke the Court's jurisdiction has the burden of establishing personal jurisdiction over a defendant. . . .

New York law governs the issue of personal jurisdiction in this diversity action. . . .

1. *Transacting Business in New York* . . .

WFA implicitly makes the further claim that Event should be amenable to this action because Event (or Schanks, acting on Event's behalf) may have "transacted business" in New York by attempting to sell the broadcasts to

New York subscribers. As stated above, where jurisdiction is based on the transaction of business in New York, the claim must "arise from" the particular New York transaction of business. A claim "arises from" the New York business transaction if there is a "substantial nexus" between the business transacted and the cause of action. WFA has not alleged any specific secondary activities by Event which would constitute the transaction of business in New York; it merely surmises that such activities may have taken place. Unsupported allegations such as these are insufficient to confer personal jurisdiction. Furthermore, even if Event engaged in substantial New York activities to market the Matches here, this action does not arise from those activities. . . .

2. *Contracting to Provide Goods or Services in New York* . . .
3. *"Doing Business" in New York* . . .

WFA has failed to allege the type of "continuous and systematic" conduct in New York necessary to a finding of jurisdiction under this provision. Instead, WFA merely speculates that the instant transaction may be "typical of the way Event does business," so that Event may have regular customers in New York. Unsupported allegations such as these are insufficient to confer personal jurisdiction over an out-of-state defendant. Thus, for the reasons stated above the Court does not have personal jurisdiction over Event with regard to the instant claims.

4. *Venue Transfer* . . .

Although it does not otherwise appear that this forum is inconvenient for purposes of Section 1404(a), the lack of personal jurisdiction over Event justifies the transfer of this action to the Central District of California, where Event concededly is subject to jurisdiction. This case is hereby transferred to the Central District of California.

So ordered.

In *NFL v. Insight Telecommunications Corp.*, a professional sports league brought an infringement action against a retransmitter of its copyrighted television broadcasts.

NATIONAL FOOTBALL LEAGUE v. INSIGHT TELECOMMUNICATIONS CORP.

158 F. Supp. 2d 124 (D. Mass. 2001)

LINDSAY, District Judge.

Before the court is the motion of the defendant, Insight Telecommunications, Inc. ("Insight"), for summary judgment based on the "passive carrier" exemption from copyright liability, codified at 17 U.S.C. §111(a)(3). The motion for summary judgement and accompanying papers were referred to Magistrate Judge Lawrence P. Cohen. On June 14, 2001, Magistrate Judge Cohen issued his report and recommendation, in which he recommended that Insight's motion be allowed. The plaintiff, National Football League (the "NFL"), submitted a timely objection to the report and recommendation, to which Insight responded. Upon consideration of the report and recommendation and the responses thereto, I accept the recommendation of the magistrate judge that Insight's motion for summary judgment be granted.

On a related matter, the NFL maintains that the magistrate judge's refusal to allow additional discovery on the "passive carrier" defense was erroneous and renders summary judgment for Insight inappropriate. The NFL's failure to object in a timely fashion to the magistrate judge's ruling on the NFL's motion for additional discovery precludes the court from reconsideration of that ruling. *See* Fed. R. Civ. P. 72(a).

The motion of Insight for summary judgment is allowed. The clerk shall enter judgment for the defendant.

So ordered.

Report and Recommendation on Motion for Summary Judgment

Lawrence P. COHEN, United States Magistrate Judge.

In this action, by way of its original complaint, plaintiff, National Football League ("NFL") sues defendant Insight Communications Corporation ("Insight"), for violating its copyright in copyrighted materials by transmitting its copyrighted materials in interstate commerce on a number of occasions in 1999. On account of that, plaintiff seeks statutory damages and injunctive relief under the copyright laws. 17 U.S.C. §§502(a) and 504(c)(2). 6 As part of its answer, Insight averred as its Sixth Affirmative Defense that it was, at all relevant times, a passive carrier within the meaning of 17 U.S.C. §111(a)(3), and thus exempt from liability for infringement — directly or indirectly. Insight has now moved for summary judgment on the basis of this affirmative defense, and the motion for summary judgment was referred to this court for report and recommendation.

I. *Procedural History*

The original complaint was filed on October 5, 1999. On November 2, 1999, plaintiff also filed a motion for preliminary injunctive relief (# 08). On November 23, 1999, defendant filed a motion to dismiss (# 26). That motion to dismiss was premised on the ground that any infringement, if at all, occurred in Canada, not the United States. That motion was denied by the district judge to whom this case is assigned on February 4, 2000 (# 31). On the same day, plaintiff's motion for a preliminary injunction was also denied (# 32).

On August 1, 2000, plaintiff filed a motion to amend the complaint. That motion was allowed in part and denied in part. On August 11, 2000, while plaintiff's motion to amend was pending, defendant filed a motion to stay all discovery pending disposition of its motion for summary judgment filed on the same day. To the extent that that motion sought to stay all discovery, the motion was allowed in part and denied in part. . . .

On August 18, 2000, plaintiff moved to extend the time within which to file a response to the motion for summary judgment (# 54). On August 21, 2000, that motion was allowed by the district judge to whom this case is assigned, and plaintiff was ordered to file its response on or before

September 6, 2000. Seven days later, on August 28, 2000, plaintiff filed an "emergency" motion (# 60) to extend the time within which to file a response to the motion for summary judgment. That motion was based exclusively on a position by the plaintiff that it, notwithstanding the previous order of this court staying discovery, wanted to conduct further unspecified discovery. This court denied that motion. . . .

On September 6, 2000, plaintiff filed its response to defendant's motion for summary judgment (# 50). That response did not include a concise statement of the material facts of record as to which it is contended that there exists a genuine issue to be tried as required by Rule 56.1 of the Local Rules of this Court.

After defendant filed a reply to plaintiff's memorandum in opposition to the motion for summary judgment, plaintiff moved to file a sur-reply. . . .

One week later, plaintiff filed yet another motion—this one captioned "Plaintiff's Motion to Renew Rule 56(f) Request, or, in the Alternative, for Relief under Rule 56(f)" (# 77). This court denied that motion on October 18, 2000 (Order # 80). . . .

II. *Undisputed Material Facts*

Based on the Statement of Undisputed Material Facts submitted, as well as those matters not disputed by the defendant for purposes of its motion for summary judgment, this court finds the following material facts to be undisputed:

1. The NFL owns the copyright in all regular season and post-season NFL game telecasts, as confirmed by the League's contracts with the networks.

2. At the time the original complaint was filed, the NFL was in the process of registering with the U.S. Copyright Office copyright in the following NFL game telecasts (each of which was identified in the Advance Notice of Potential Infringement). . . .

3. Plaintiff is the owner of copyright in all the NFL game telecasts identified in Paragraph 2 above.

4. Insight is in the business of retransmitting telecommunications signals and providing other related services for a wide array of customers in the broadcasting and telecommunications industries. . . .

5. By September, 1999, Insight had entered into a Transmission Services Agreement with Bell Canada. . . .

6. Following execution of the Transmission Services Agreement with Bell Canada, Insight entered into a Transmission Services Agreement with Videocom Satellite Associates, Inc. ("Videocom"), a Delaware corporation with its principal place of business at 502 Sprague Street, Dedham, Massachusetts. Under that Agreement, which was not actually signed until the Fall of 1999, Videocom agreed to provide off-air reception of Boston area television signals and interconnection to the designated video compression equipment. . . .

7. At all times relevant to the Complaint (and Amended Complaint), Insight received the television broadcasts of the Boston television stations through antennas, which are specially tuned to the particular television station frequencies to allow for receipt of the particular television signal radio waves with the least amount of interference. In receiving the signals,

the antennas convert the radio waves to an analog electrical signal, which is carried on a wire to a receiver. . . .

8. The receipt and relay of the Signals ultimately to the video compression equipment is simultaneous with their initial broadcast.

9. Insight does not control or alter the content of the Signals provided to the video compression equipment.

10. Other than delivering the signals to the designated video compression equipment, Insight does not control the recipients, if any, of the Signals it receives.

11. During the relevant period referred to in the complaint and amended complaint, Insight, consistent with the steps referred to in Paragraphs 5 through 10 above, received the television signals of six Boston television stations and relayed those signals to video compression equipment provided by Bell Canada. ExpressVu, in turn, allegedly transmitted to locations in Canada the programming of the Boston television stations affiliated with the CBS, Fox, and ABC networks -respectively, WBZ, WFXT, and WCVB (the "Boston affiliates"). These stations showed NFL game telecasts on Sunday afternoons throughout the NFL season. . . .

III. *Contention of the Parties*

Insight contends that it is exempt from plaintiff's copyright claims because of the fact that it is a "passive carrier" within the meaning of 17 U.S.C. §111(a)(3). Plaintiff in turn, contends that the defendant is not a passive carrier under that statute because Insight is neither a "carrier" nor a "passive" carrier. And plaintiff again suggests that summary judgment is inappropriate absent further discovery.

IV. *The Summary Judgment Standard*

"Summary judgment procedure is properly regarded not as a disfavored procedural shortcut, but rather as an integral part of the Federal Rules as a whole, which are designed 'to secure the just, speedy and inexpensive determination of every action.'"

To survive a motion for summary judgment, the opposing party must demonstrate that there is a genuine issue of material fact requiring a trial. . . .

V. *Discussion*

1. *Whether Insight Is a "Carrier" Within the Meaning of 17 U.S.C. §111(a)(3)*

Plaintiff does not gainsay that, if the conduct of Insight in the circumstances of this case fall within the ambit of 17 U.S.C. §111(a)(3), it cannot succeed in its copyright claims against Insight.

Plaintiff first contends that Insight, in the circumstances of this case, is not a "carrier" within the meaning of 17 U.S.C. §111(a)(3).

In this court's view, however, plaintiff's general argument misses the mark, and its reliance on *Infinity Broadcasting Corp. v. Kirkwood*, 63 F. Supp. 2d 420 (S.D.N.Y. 1999), falls short on the facts.

In contending that Insight is not a "carrier" within the meaning of 17 U.S.C. §111(a)(3), plaintiff relies exclusively on the fact, not disputed, that insight did not own the "wires" — the hardware, if one will — over which the signals were transmitted. Nothing in the authorities or legislative history, however, suggest that Congress intended that section be read in such a crabbed fashion.

Congress, in enacting Section 111(a)(3), did not define the term "carrier" in that section. But the current version is now (and was at all relevant times referred to in the complaint and amended complaint) in its third iteration. . . .

Consistent with this expansive language used by Congress, The Federal Communications Commission has opined, *inter alia* (60 F.C.C.2d 261, at ¶ 101):

> Inasmuch as we have decided that resellers will be engaged in interstate communication by wire and radio, we now shall determine whether they are common carriers within the meaning of the Act.

That, in turn, is consistent with the statutory definition of a "telecommunications carrier" as set forth in Title 47, United States Code, Section 153(44). And it is consistent with those cases indicating that a reseller of the services similar to that provided by the defendant in this case is a carrier, not withstanding the fact that the reseller did not own all of the facilities used for the retransmission. . . . Just as the Copyright Act should be construed with an understanding of changing technologies, so should it be construed consistently with the real business world—a world where "outsourcing" is an accepted method of doing business.

Against all of this, plaintiff relies almost exclusively on one district court case in support of its position that Insight is not a carrier within the meaning of Section 111(a)(3)—to wit: *Infinity Broadcasting Corp. v. Kirkwood*, 63 F. Supp. 2d 420 (S.D.N.Y. 1999). But that case is clearly of a different sort. In that case, the defendant, Kirkland was not, as is the case with Insight, in the business of providing transmissions of signals. . . .

Accordingly, based on settled principles of statutory construction and the precedent set forth above, this court finds and concludes that, on the undisputed material facts set forth in the record before this court, Insight has shown that it is a carrier within the meaning of Section 111(a)(3).

2. Whether Insight Is a "Passive" Carrier Within the Meaning of 17 U.S.C. §111(a)(3)

Plaintiff further contends that even if Insight is a carrier within the meaning of Section 111(a)(3), it was not a "passive" carrier as that term is defined. . . .

This court accordingly concludes that the undisputed material facts show that Insight was a "passive" carrier within the meaning of Section 111(a)(3).

3. *The Need for Further Discovery*

Finally, in an almost recurring theme, plaintiff says that summary judgment is inappropriate absent further discovery. . . . Plaintiff's claim that it is entitled to further discovery comes far too late and in a manner which simply ignores the applicable rules of procedure.

V. *Conclusion*

For the reasons set forth above, this court recommends that the district judge to whom this case is assigned allow defendant Insight's Motion for Summary Judgment on Sixth Affirmative Defense (# 50).

QUESTIONS AND DISCUSSION

1. *HBO v. Champs, Inc.*, concerned the unauthorized interception of plaintiff's cable programming. What is the Satellite Home Viewer Act? What are reasonable damages here?

2. In *M Sports Productions v. Pay-Per-View Network, Inc.*, was the failure to properly transmit negligent, intentional or fraudulent? Who should pay for damages? How should these damages be calculated?

3. *Worldwide Futgol Assocs. v. Event Entertainment, Inc.*, involved the minimum contacts with forum state necessary for personal jurisdiction, or alternatively, a transfer of venue. Why is choice of law so important? What is a long arm statute?

4. In *NFL v. Insight Telecommunications Corp.*, what would it take for defendant to be viewed as something more than a "passive carrier"?

5. Because of the technological advances, this field is by definition an emerging legal area; however, there are thoughtful articles that help to formulate the parameters of future discussion. *See* Deutsch, *Sports Broadcasting and Virtual Advertising: Defining the Limits of Copyright Law and the Law of Unfair Competition*, 11 Marq. Sports L. Rev. 41 (2000); Handa, *Retransmission of Television Broadcasts on the Internet*, 8 Sw. J.L. & Trade Am. 39 (2001-2002); McEvilly, *'Virtual Advertising in Sports Venues and the Federal Lanham Act §43(A): Revolutionary Technology Creates Controversial Advertising Medium,'* 8 Seton Hall J. Sport L. 603 (1998); Note, *'Nothing But Internet,'* 110 Harv. L. Rev. 1143 (1997) (*NBA v. Sports Team Analysis & Tracking Sys. Inc.*, 939 F. Supp. 1071 (S.D.N.Y. 1996), *rev'd sub nom. NBA v. Motorola, Inc. (supra)*; this author concludes that "[a]llowing sports leagues to establish roadblocks on the infobahn by using injunctions to slow or to control the dissemination of real-time information threatens to frustrate impermissibly the goal of maintaining a free and informed society that is enshrined in both the Copyright-Patent Clause and the First Amendment."

TABLE OF CASES

INDEX